THE NEW YORK
PUBLIC LIBRARY

ASTOR, LENOX
TILDEN FOUNDATIONS

A History
of the
Goshenhoppen Reformed Charge
Montgomery County, Pennsylvania
(1727=1819)

PART XXIX OF A NARRATIVE AND CRITICAL HISTORY
PREPARED AT THE REQUEST OF
THE PENNSYLVANIA-GERMAN SOCIETY

BY REV. WILLIAM JOHN HINKE, Ph.D., D.D.
Professor of Semitic Languages and Religions in Auburn Theological Seminary,
Auburn, New York

LANCASTER
1920

Copyright, 1920
BY
WILLIAM J. HINKE

Autograph Edition, 230 copies
No. 43

PRESS OF
THE NEW ERA PRINTING COMPANY
LANCASTER, PA.

PREFACE.

Reformed Church History in this country has long been a subject of study It is interesting to note that the first printed history of the Reformed Church in the United States was published not in America but in Germany. In the year 1846, the Rev. Dr. J. G. Buettner, the first professor of the first Theological Seminary in the State of Ohio, published "Die Hochdeutsche Reformirte Kirche in den Vereinigten Staaten von Nord-Amerika," in Schleiz, Germany. But even before that time, the Rev. Dr Lewis Mayer, the first professor of the Reformed Theological Seminary at York, Pa., had been busy gathering materials for the history of the Reformed Church. Unfortunately he died at York, in 1849, before he had fully utilized the documents he had so carefully collected and copied. Only a brief sketch from his pen appeared in I. Daniel Rupp's "History of the Religious Denominations in the United States," Philadelphia, 1844. A few years afterwards the Rev. Dr. John W. Nevin included a sketch of the German Reformed Church in America in his "History and Genius of the Heidelberg Catechism." Chambersburg, 1847. In it he lamented that the Journal of Michael Schlatter was "the only record we have on the general state of the American German Reformed Church in the middle of the last century."

In 1849, the Rev. Dr. Philip Schaff published in his "Kirchenfreund," Vol. II, a series of three articles on the "History of the German Church in America," in which he traced the origin and growth of the Reformed and Lutheran churches through three successive periods.

But the man who may well be called the father of Reformed history in America was the Rev. Dr. Henry Harbaugh. He not only secured the manuscripts and documents of Dr. Mayer for the use of the church and added to them many others which he collected himself, but upon the basis of these documents he wrote two splendid volumes, which told the story of Reformed history in America with such real enthusiasm and beauty of style, that they have always remained sources of inspiration for later students. They were: "Schlatter's Life and Travels," Philadelphia, 1857, and "The Fathers of the Reformed Church," Vol. I, Philadelphia, 1857. In 1872, Dr. Harbaugh added a second volume to the "Fathers" of the church. In these volumes the lives and labors of the most important German Reformed ministers in America were set forth.

It remained for a former president of the Pennsylvania German Society, the late Rev. Dr. Joseph H. Dubbs, to write the first connected history in his "Historic Manual of the Reformed Church in the United States," Lancaster, 1885. Later he corrected and completed the story in his contribution to the "American Church History Series," Vol. VIII, New York, 1895, and especially in his beautifully illustrated and well-written work "The Reformed Church in Pennsylvania," published by our Society in 1902 as part IX of its "Narrative and Critical History."

A new era was ushered in, however, in 1895–1898, when the rich treasures of manuscripts and documents, stored in the archives of the Reformed Church of Holland, were discovered and made accessible to American students. It was in this connection that the writer first became interested in Reformed Church history. In the summer of 1897, his friend and colleague, the Rev. Dr. James I.

Good, asked him to go to Holland, in order to copy and photograph the records which had been found. He carried out this commission in the summers of 1897 and 1898, with the result that, on the basis of the newly found documents, the history of the Reformed Church in the United States could be entirely rewritten. This was done by Dr. Good in his important book "History of the Reformed Church in the United States, 1725-1792," Reading, 1899.

The writer himself had the privilege of translating and editing two volumes of documents, in 1903 the "Minutes and Letters of the Coetus of Pennsylvania," and in 1916 the "Life and Letters of the Rev. John Philip Boehm." They have placed German Reformed Church History in America upon a safe foundation.

But there are other sources of Reformed history which ought to be made accessible to students. By no means the least important of them are the church records of the oldest Reformed congregations. This volume may be regarded as a contribution to that subject. These church records have long been an object of serious study by the writer. Even before the year 1900 he had copied the first volume of the Goshenhoppen records. It was published in 1900 in Mr. Dotterer's "Perkiomen Region," volume III, and later, with notes, in the *American Monthly Magazine* of the Society of the Daughters of the American Revolution, Vol. XLII, 1913. It is now republished, with some corrections, together with the other volumes of church records, which, when combined and correctly interpreted, tell the story of the Goshenhoppen Charge. It is such a complicated story, that the records by themselves were insufficient to unravel the various difficulties and perplexities. They became intelligible only when studied in the light of all the evidence which had become available in

Europe and America. In the history of the Goshenhoppen churches the writer has made use of all the documents which have come to light, with the result that he has been able to piece together a fairly complete and well-authenticated history. The manuscript was prepared in 1914, hence many letters of Boehm are quoted more at length than they would have been if written after the appearance of Boehm's letters in 1916.

There only remains for the writer the pleasant duty to express his deep obligation to the pastors of the churches whose records are published in this volume. They placed most readily and gladly all their records and other historical documents at his disposal. They answered letters and sent photographs, most of which could unfortunately not be utilized, because of the high cost of engraving at the present time. The completeness of the book owes much to their kind coöperation. The writer is under special obligation to his dear friend, the Rev. John B. Stoudt, who first encouraged him to undertake the writing of this history, and then gave his most loyal assistance in every difficulty that arose. To him the book is most fittingly dedicated as a token of the author's indebtedness and appreciation.

WILLIAM J. HINKE.

AUBURN,
    October 15, 1919

TABLE OF CONTENTS.

INTRODUCTION 5–18

The Goshenhoppen Region—Its Extent—Its First Appearance—Forms of the Name—Old and New Goshenhoppen—First Immigration in 1710—The Rev. Paulus Van Vlecq—The Reformed Church at Whitemarsh—Its First Members—First Reformed Settlers in Perkiomen Valley—Immigration about 1720—The Rev John Philip Boehm—His First Churches—Earliest Reformed Settlers in Goshenhoppen—Indian Legend.

CHAPTER I

MINISTRY OF THE REV GEORGE MICHAEL WEISS, 1727–1730 19–70

First Service of Weiss at Goshenhoppen—Peter Miller's Reference to Weiss—Weiss at Heidelberg University—The Weiss Family at Eppingen—Arrival of the Ship William and Sarah—Captain's List of Passengers—Signers of Oath of Allegiance—Weiss the Leader of the Colony—Certificate of Weiss's Ordination—John Philip Boehm in the Perkiomen Valley—Opposition of Weiss to Boehm—Mr Andrews on Weiss—Ordination of Boehm—Weiss at Goshenhoppen—Book against Newborn—Book on Indians—Condition of Reformed people at Philadelphia—Weiss advertising for Pupils—Collecting Tour of Weiss and Reiff to Holland—Its Origin—Its Object—Reiff's Account of Tour—Power of Attorney given to Reiff—Letter of Skippack Church—Weiss and Reiff in Holland—Expenses of Tour—The First Printed Report on Reformed Church of Pennsylvania—Departure of Weiss from Philadelphia

CHAPTER II.

MINISTRY OF THE REV. JOHN PETER MILLER, 1730–1734 71–95

His Matriculation in Heidelberg University—His Life in Germany—His Father—His Arrival in Pennsylvania—His Meeting with Boehm—His Activity at Skippack and Philadelphia—His

Ordination by the Presbyterians—His Pastorate at Goshenhoppen—In the Conestoga Valley—Letter of Conrad Tempelman—Pastor at Muddy Creek, Reyer's, Zeltenreich and Cocalico—His Activity at Tulpehocken—The Three Reformed Churches in the Goshenhoppen Region—His Conversion in May, 1735—Provost Aciehus regarding Miller—Miller and Conrad Weiser—Miller's Own Account of his Conversion—Boehm's Account of Goshenhoppen in 1734—Miller's Death and Tombstone

CHAPTER III.

MINISTRY OF JOHN HENRY GOETSCHY, 1735-1740... 96-130

Arrival in Philadelphia—Rev Maurice Goetschy—Departure of Colony from Zurich—Journey down the Rhine—Their Experiences in Holland—Emigrants in Goetschy's Colony—Letter of John Henry Goetschy—Application to Presbyterians for Ordination—Activity at Old Goshenhoppen and Great Swamp—Boehm regarding New Goshenhoppen—Boehm regarding Goetschy—Goetschy's Missionary Activity—Goetschy Circulating Letter of Wilhelmius—The Goshenhoppen Churches Subscribing for Pastor's Salary—Ordination of Goetschy by Dorsius in 1741—Goetschy's Activity in Dutch Reformed Church—His Death in 1774.

CHAPTER IV.

MINISTRY OF THE REV. PETER HENRY DORSIUS, 1741-1744 131-148

The Dutch Reformed in Bucks County seeking Pastor in 1730—Wilhelmius Secures Dorsius—His Studies in Holland—His Family at Moers—His Journey to America—Boehm and Dorsius—His Activity at Goshenhoppen—His Journey to Holland and Return to Pennsylvania—Boehm's Account of Goshenhoppen in 1744—Declaration of Trust by Elders—Return of Dorsius to Holland

CHAPTER V.

MINISTRY OF FREDERICK CASIMIR MUELLER, 1745-1748 149-157

Schlatter regarding Mueller at Goshenhoppen—Arrival of Mueller in Pennsylvania—Schlatter and Weiss at Goshenhoppen—Letter of Mueller to Schlatter—Departure of Mueller from Goshenhoppen—His Ministry at Berne—At Longswamp—At Muddy Creek—At Coventry—At Hain's Church—At Lebanon and Swatara—Mueller's Doubles

Table of Contents

CHAPTER VI.

MINISTRY OF THE REV. GEORGE MICHAEL WEISS, 1746–1761 158–192

Weiss in New York State—His Return to Pennsylvania—Weiss in the Coetus—Schlatter regarding Weiss—Letter of Weiss to Schlatter—Debt on Old Goshenhoppen Church Paid—Events of the Year 1750 at Goshenhoppen—Church Farm at New Goshenhoppen—Weiss Welcoming Schlatter and Six New Ministers—Schlatter Bibles Distributed—Division in Coetus—Donations from Holland—Congregational Activity—Subscriptions for Church Land at Great Swamp—Disposal of Mr. Weiss's Property—Inventory and Account of His Estate—Will of Mrs Anna Weiss—Letters of David Schultze.

CHAPTER VII

THE PERIOD OF SUPPLIES, 1762–1766. 193–214

Otterbein Called but Declines—(1) Ministry of John Philip Leydich—His Pastorates—His Activity in the Coetus—His Home—His Death—(2) Ministry of Philip Jacob Michael—His Arrival in Pennsylvania—His Pastorates—His Appearance Before Coetus—Chaplain in the War of the Revolution—His Activity After the War—His Will—(3) Ministry of Jacob Riess—His Arrival in Philadelphia—His Pastorates—His Activity at Goshenhoppen—His Death—(4) Ministry of John Rudolph Kittweiler—His Arrival—His Pastorates—His Activity and Death at Great Swamp—Patent for Great Swamp Church Land

CHAPTER VIII.

MINISTRY OF THE REV JOHN THEOBALD FABER, SR, 1766–1779 .   .   .   215–223

His Birth and Training in Germany—His Certificate from Palatinate Consistory—Letter of Alsentz to Faber—His Marriage—His Activity in the Goshenhoppen Churches—Called by Lancaster Church—Faber Preaching at Tohickon—Progress of the Goshenhoppen Churches under his Ministry—Call to Lancaster Church

CHAPTER IX.

MINISTRY OF THE REV. JOHN WILLIAM INGOLD, 1780–1781 224–229

His Life in Germany—His Arrival in America—His Checkered Career—His Activity at Old Goshenhoppen—Supplies at Great Swamp and New Goshenhoppen—His Pastorate at Reading—At Indianfield and Tohickon—Death of His Wife—Leaves Ministry

CHAPTER X.

MINISTRY OF THE REV. FREDERICK DELLIKER, 1782–1784, 230–234

The Delliker Family at Zurich—His Parents—His Ministry in Europe—Arrival in Pennsylvania—Pastorate in New Jersey—His Pastoral Activity at Goshenhoppen—At Falkner Swamp.

CHAPTER XI.

MINISTRY OF THE REV. FREDERICK WILLIAM VAN DER SLOOT, SR., 1784–1786 . 235–237

His Life in Europe—His Ministerial Descent—Arrival in Pennsylvania—Activity at Goshenhoppen—Ministry in Northampton County.

CHAPTER XII.

SECOND MINISTRY OF THE REV. JOHN THEOBALD FABER, SR., 1786–1788 238–240

Pastorate at Indianfield and Tohickon—His Return to Goshenhoppen—His Pastoral Activity—His Sudden Death

CHAPTER XIII.

MINISTRY OF THE REV. NICHOLAS POMP, 1789–1792 . . 241–248

Call of Rev. N. Pomp—Letter of Pomp to Goshenhoppen Churches—Autobiography of Pomp—Pastorate at Goshenhoppen—At Indianfield and Tohickon—At Falkner Swamp—His Book against Universalism

Table of Contents

CHAPTER XIV

Ministry of the Rev. John Theobald Faber, Jr., 1791–1807 249–255

His Youth and Training—Licensure and Ordination—Letter of Delliker to Faber—Pastoral Activity at Goshenhoppen—Schoolmasters at Old Goshenhoppen—Activity at Great Swamp—Letter of Senn to Faber—Call to New Holland.

CHAPTER XV.

Ministry of the Rev. Albert Helffenstein, 1808–1811 . . . . , .256–258

His Birth and Training—Examination and Ordination—Pastoral Activity at Goshenhoppen—Later Pastorates—His Death

CHAPTER XVI.

Ministry of the Rev. Frederick William Van Der Sloot, Jr , 1812–1818 . 259–266

His Life in Germany—Arrival in Pennsylvania—Licensure and Ordination—Pastorate in Northampton County—His Marriage—At Germantown—At Goshenhoppen—His Appearance—Pastorate in Philadelphia—In Virginia—In York and Adams Counties—His Death

CHAPTER XVII

Division of Charge and Second Pastorate of the Rev. John Theobald Faber, Jr , 1819–1833 267–271

Call of Goshenhoppen to Faber—Old Goshenhoppen Separates from Charge—Rev Jacob William Dechant at Old Goshenhoppen—Upper Milford Added to Charge of Faber—Faber's Sudden Death.

SECOND PART. GOSHENHOPPEN CHURCH RECORDS.

NEW GOSHENHOPPEN RECORDS 272–385
  A. Volume I, 1731–1761 272–311
    Lists of Members 272
    1. Baptisms by John Peter Miller 277
    2. Baptisms by John Henry Goetschy 281
    3. Baptisms by Peter Henry Dorsius 284
    4. Baptisms by Frederick Casimir Mueller . 286
    5. Baptisms by George Michael Weiss 288
    6. Marriages by George Michael Weiss . . 301
    7. Catechumens of George Michael Weiss 307
    8 Miscellaneous Entries by John Henry Goetschy 311
  B Volume II, 1762–1832 312–384
    I. Baptismal Records 312–353
      1. Baptisms by Jacob Riess 312
      2. Baptisms by John Theobald Faber, Sr. . 314
      3 Baptisms by Supplies 329
      4. Baptisms by Frederick Delliker 330
      5 Baptisms by Frederick Wm. Van der Sloot, Sr. 334
      6. Baptisms by John Theobald Faber, Sr. . . . 335
      7. Baptisms by Nicholas Pomp 340
      8 Baptisms by John Theobald Faber, Jr.. 341
      9. Baptisms by Albert Helffenstein . . . 345
      10. Baptisms by Frederick Wm. Van der Sloot, Jr. 347
      11. Baptisms by John Theobald Faber, Jr. 348
      12 Baptisms by Later Hands 352
    II Burial Records 353–362
      1. Burials by John Theobald Faber, Sr. . 353
      2. Burials by Frederick Delliker 359
      3. Burials by Frederick Wm. Van der Sloot, Sr. 359

Table of Contents.

  4. Burials by John Theobald Faber, Sr. .   360
  5. Burials by Nicholas Pomp . .   361
  6. Burials by John Theobald Faber, Jr. ...   361
 III. Marriage Records ..   362–369
  1. Marriages by John Theobald Faber, Sr..   362
  2. Marriages by Frederick Delliker   366
  3. Marriages by Frederick Wm. Van der Sloot, Sr.   367
  4. Marriages of John Theobald Faber, Sr.   367
  5. Marriages by John Theobald Faber, Jr..   368
  6. Marriages by Albert Helffenstein .   369
 IV. Catechumens, 1767–1808 370
 V Communicants, 1809–1815 379

OLD GOSHENHOPPEN RECORD, 1764–1833 ..   386–436
 I. Baptismal Records . .   386–417
  1. Baptisms by Jacob Riess ...   385
  2. Baptisms by John Theobald Faber, Sr   386
  3. Baptisms by John William Ingold   399
  4. Baptisms by Frederick Delliker ...   400
  5. Baptisms by Frederick Wm. Van der Sloot, Sr   402
  6 Baptisms by John Theobald Faber, Sr. .   402
  7 Baptisms by Nicholas Pomp   405
  8. Baptisms by John Theobald Faber, Jr.   408
  9 Baptisms by Frederick Wm. Van der Sloot, Jr   409
  10. Baptisms by Jacob W. Dechant 410
 II. Burial Records . . .   418–423
  1. Burials by John Theobald Faber, Sr. ...   418
  2. Burials by Frederick Delliker ...   422
  3. Burials by John Theobald Faber, Sr.   422
  4. Burials by John Theobald Faber, Jr.   . 423
 III. Marriage Records 424–428
  1. Marriages by John Theobald Faber, Sr. ...   424
  2. Marriages by Frederick Delliker 427
  3. Marriages by Frederick Wm. Van der Sloot, Sr. 427
  4. Marriages by John Theobald Faber, Sr.   428

xvi   *Table of Contents.*

    IV. Catechumens, 1767–1794 428
    V. Communicants, 1813–1815 434
GREAT SWAMP RECORD, 1736–1833 437–479
    I. Baptismal Records 437–464
        1. Baptisms by John Henry Goetschy 439
        2. Baptisms by George Michael Weiss . . . 439
        3. Baptisms by John Theobald Faber, Sr. . . 442
        4. Baptisms by Frederick Delliker . . . 450
        5. Baptisms by Frederick Wm. Van der Sloot, Sr. 452
        6. Baptisms by John Theobald Faber, Sr. . 453
        7. Baptisms by Nicholas Pomp 456
        8. Baptisms by John Theobald Faber, Jr. . . . 457
        9. Baptisms by Albert Helffenstein . . . 458
        10. Baptisms by Frederick Wm. Van der Sloot, Jr. 460
        11. Baptisms by John Theobald Faber, Jr . . . 461
    II. Burial Records 464–469
        1. Burials by John Theobald Faber, Sr. . . . 464
        2. Burials by Frederick Delliker 467
        3. Burials by Frederick Wm Van der Sloot, Sr . 467
        4. Burials by Nicholas Pomp 468
        5. Burials by John Theobald Faber, Jr. 468
    III Marriage Records 469–472
        1. Marriages by John Theobald Faber, Sr. . . 469
        2. Marriages by Frederick Delliker 471
        3. Marriages by Frederick Wm. Van der Sloot, Sr. 471
        4. Marriages by John Theobald Faber, Sr. . . . 471
        5. Marriages by John Theobald Faber, Jr . . 472
    IV. Catechumens, 1767–1795 472
    V. Communicants, 1814–1818 477
INDEX 480

Table of Contents. xvii

ILLUSTRATIONS.

AUTOGRAPHS.

	PAGE
John Philip Boehm	40
George Michael Weiss	45
John Philip Boehm	51
John Bartholomew Rieger	78
Peter Miller	92
John Henry Goetschius	118
John Conrad Wueitz	120
Michael Schlatter	161
John Philip Leydich	195

TITLE PAGES.

Book of Weiss against Newborn	42
Circular Letter of Reformed Ministers	167
Pomp's Book against Universalists	248

LIST OF PLATES.

	FACING PAGE
Frontispiece Pennsylvania Documents in Archives at The Hague, Holland	
Title Page of New Goshenhoppen Record, 1736	118
Old Goshenhoppen Church, built 1744	142
Cornerstone of Old Goshenhoppen Church, 1744	144
House of William Dewees, Whitemarsh.	144
The Rev. Michael Schlatter	150
New Goshenhoppen Church, 1770–1857.	220
Organ of New Goshenhoppen Church	222
The Rev. Clement Z. Weiser	270

Historical Introduction

THE region commonly known as Goshenhoppen extends along the Perkiomen Creek, in the upper end of Montgomery County, Pa., and covers also small strips of land in the adjacent counties of Berks, Lehigh and Bucks. According to Dr. C. Z. Weiser[1] it is a tract "perhaps ten miles long and five miles wide" which extends "from Treichlersville [Lehigh County] to Sumneytown [Montgomery County], north and south and from the Bucks County line to the Perkiomen, east and west. It is a region rather than a township."

The name first appears in the public records of the province in the year 1728,[2] when on May 17, 1728, the inhabitants of Colebrookedale addressed a petition to the governor, asking for relief against the Indians. They report that "we have Suffered and is like to sufer By the Ingians, they have fell upon ye Back Inhabitors about falkners

[1] See C. Z. Weiser's *Monograph of the New Goshenhoppen and Great Swamp Charge, 1731–1881*, Reading, 1882, p. 5; also his statement in Dotterer's *Perkiomen Region*, Vol. I, p. 64.

[2] See *Pennsylvania Archives, First Series*, Vol. I, p. 213 f.

Swamp, & near Coshahopin. Therefore, we the humble Petitioners, With our poor Wives & Children Do humbly Beg of your Excellency To Take It into Consideration and Relieve us the Petitioners hereof, Whos Lives Lies at Stake With us and our poor Wives & Children that is more to us than Life. Therefore, We the humble Petitioners hereof, Do Desire An Answer from your Excellency By ye Bearer with Speed, so no more at present from your poor afflicted People Whose names are here Subscribed."

Among the 48 signers to this petition are several, like Christian Neuschwanger, John Mayer, Christopher Schmidt and Peter Bohn, who appear also as members of the Reformed church at Skippack.[3]

The name of the district was variously spelled. In the Journal kept in the Land Office of the Proprietaries[4] it appears as Cowessahopin, Cowessehoppen, Cowissehoppin, and other similar forms. Mr. Boehm uses[5] Goschenhoppen, Goschoppen and even Goschenhakken. Dr. Weiser quotes[6] in addition: Quesohopen, Cosshehoppa, Coshenhoppe, Coshahopin, Cowissahopen, and Coschehoppe. As the second part of the name appears in the names of two Indian chiefs, Enschockhoppa and Shakahoppa, Dr. Weiser concludes that the name is of Indian origin.[7]

The Goshenhoppen region included from early times

[3] See *Journal of the Presbyterian Historical Society*, Vol I, p 122; Vol VII, pp. 48. 60

[4] See *Perkiomen Region*, Vol I, pp 105, 118, 119, 140, 141, 151, etc.

[5] See *Journal of the P H. S.*, Vol. VII, pp. 56, 122, 124.

[6] Weiser, *Monograph*, p 5.

[7] In the *Perkiomen Region*, Vol III, p 145, Mr Dotterer raises the question whether "Goshenhoppen" might not be a German name, by calling attention to the German place name "Goshenhof" But the Dutch form of "Hof," namely "hoeve," shows that the final "f" in High German becomes "v" or "w" in Low German, but not a single or double "p."

two sections, one nearer Philadelphia, known as Old Goshenhoppen, comprising part of Upper Salford township, the other farther north, in Upper Hanover township, known as New Goshenhoppen. Which one of these districts was settled first has not as yet been determined, so much is certain that, as we shall show later, ecclesiastically New Goshenhoppen was the first, for the first traces of a Reformed church organization appear in the New Goshenhoppen section.

As the Goshenhoppen region is a part of the Perkiomen valley and the latter a part of Montgomery County, we shall preface the history of the Goshenhoppen churches with a brief survey of the general field.

In the Journal of the Land Office of the Proprietaries,[8] the Perkiomen valley, called Perqueaming, appears as early as 1717 On March 15, 1718, "Peter Wents" of Skippack paid quitrent for 100 acres for a period of ten years and for 50 acres for a period of 14 years. Hence he must have settled at Skippack as early as 1704. This makes him one of the earliest settlers of the Perkiomen valley. In 1730 his name appears[9] as a member of the Reformed Skippack Church. His son Peter Wentz was one of the founders of Wentz's Church in Worcester Township in 1762.[10]

But the full tide of German immigration into the Perkiomen valley did not begin till the second decade of the eighteenth century. In July, 1728, the elders of the Reformed congregations of Falkner Swamp, Skippack and Whitemarsh wrote to the Classis of Amsterdam:[11]

[8] *Perkiomen Region*, Vol I, p 28
[9] See an article by the writer in Dotterers *Historical Notes*, p 102 f
[10] See "History of the Wentz's Reformed Church" in the *Journal of the P. H. S*, Vol. III, pp. 332–346, especially p. 339
[11] The full letter has been printed repeatedly, first in the *Mercersburg*

The first settlers in this widely extended region of Pensylvania were Christians bearing the name of Quakers. Hither came also men holding all sorts of opinions. About *eighteen years ago* [1710], there began to come in occasionally and to settle here and there, in places widely separated from each other, certain ones of the Reformed church. These came from different parts of Germany and from other places, and a few also from the neighboring provinces of New York and New Jersey, etc. In time these greatly multiplied, but, in order not to fall into the errors of those among whom they dwelt, they provoked one another to good works, by encouraging each other to hold religious meetings on the Lord's Day, etc., according to the doctrine and order of the Reformed Church, as far as it was understood by us.

As the writers of this petition were themselves living in the Perkiomen valley, their statements are most naturally explained as referring primarily to this region.

These statements find a welcome confirmation in the old record book[12] of the Dutch Reformed congregation, now at Churchville, Bucks County, Pa.

In this record it is stated[13] that "on May 20th, in the year of our Lord Jesus Christ 1710, Mr. Paulus Van Vlecq was installed pastor or shepherd and teacher in the Church of Jesus Christ at Neshaminy, Bensalem, Germantown and surrounding villages." On June 4, 1710, the following consistory was installed at Whitemarsh: as elders, Hans Hendricks Meels and Evert ten Heuven, and as

---

Review, Vol XXIII (1876), pp 529-541; also in the *Ecclesiastical Records of the State of New York*, Vol IV, pp 2425-2437, and in the *Journal of the P. H. S.*, Vol VI, pp. 303-316. In 1916, the writer published the whole Boehm Correspondence in *Life and Letters of the Rev. John Philip Boehm*, Philadelphia, Publication Board of the Reformed Church In that book all the letters of Boehm, quoted below, are given in full

[12] This record was published by the writer in full in the *Journal of the P H S*, Vol I, pp 111-134.

[13] See *l. c*, p 118

deacons, Isaac Dilbeck and William de Wees. The members of the Whitemarsh congregation in 1710 were as follows:[14] Hans Hendrick Meels, Evert ten Heuven, Isaac Dilbeck, Willem de Wees, Jan Aweeg, Johannis Yodder, Antonie Geertheus [Yerkes], Johannes Raevenstock, Gertrude Rembergh, Elisabeth Schipbower, wife of E. ten Heuven, Mary Bloemers, wife of I. Dilbeck, Catrina Meels, wife of W. de Wees, Gertrude Aweeg, Anna Baerents, wife of J. Pieterse, Maria Selle, wife of G. ten Heuven. On December 25, 1710, there were received by profession of faith· Sebastian Bartels and his wife Mary Hendricks and Caspar Staels. On March 31, 1711, were received: Elsa Schol, Sebilla Revenstock, wife of Henry Tibben and Margaret Bon, wife of Caspar Staels. In 1711 there were, therefore, 21 regular members of the congregation. The marriage and baptismal records of the congregation add a number of other names of persons, who may be called adherents of this first Reformed congregation of the province. They were: Herman ten Heuven, Peter Bon, Gabriel Schuyler, William Rembergh, Peter ten Heuven and Jacob Op de Graef. These were married by Dominie Van Vlecq, while he baptized the children of the following persons living at Skippack: Jacob Dilbeck, Cornelius De Wees, Gerhart ten Heuven, Arent Hendricks, Dirk Remberg, Hendricks Pannebacker, Jacob Pieterse, Rightijers Gaebel. In addition to the 21 regular members there were, therefore, 14 Reformed adherents at Whitemarsh and Skippack from 1710–1712.

Of these first Reformed settlers in Pennsylvania Isaac Dilbeck came with Pastorius in 1683.[15] In 1690 Gerrit

---

[14] See *l. c*, p. 120

[15] Pennypacker, *Settlement of Germantown*, pp 135, 190–192, 194; also Dotterer, *Historical Notes*, pp 15–16, 23–26.

10 *History of the Goshenhoppen Charge*

Hendricks De Wees, probably the father of Willem De Wees, bought a lot of land in Germantown. In 1699 Evert ten Heuven, with his sons Herman, Gerhard and Peter, was a resident in Germantown, as was also Hendrick Pannebecker. In 1700 Sebastian Bartels appears, in 1701 Hans Hendrik Meels, in 1702 John Rebenstock and Michael Remberg, with his sons Dirck and Willem, also Peter Bon and Henry Tibben, and 1703 Antoni Gerckes. Some of these settlers took up land at Skippack, Hendrick Pannebecker in 1702; Gerhard and Herman In de Heuven, also Dirck and Willem Remberg in 1706; William and Cornelius De Wees in 1708.

On September 29, 1709, the following Reformed settlers were naturalized by a bill passed in the Provincial Assembly and signed by the governor:[16]

Isaac Dilbeck and his son Jacob Dilbeck; Caspar Stalls and Henry Tubben; Johannes Rebenstock, Sebastion Bartells and his son Henry Bartells; Evert in Hoffe and his sons Gerhard, Herman and Peter in Hoffe.

The ministry of Van Vlecq at Whitemarsh and Skippack continued from 1710 to 1713. On April 24, 1713, he entered his last wedding into the church record. On September 21, 1710, Van Vlecq applied to the Presbytery of Philadelphia[17] for admission. A committee was appointed which considered his application and handed in a report, then "after serious debating thereon it was put to the vote, to admit him a member of the Presbytery or not, and it was carried in the affirmative." In 1712 the charge

---

[16] Keyser, Kain, etc., *History of Old Germantown* (1907), Vol. I, p. 96. See also the paper on "Rev. Paulus Van Vlecq," by the writer, in the *Papers read before the Bucks County Hist. Society*, Vol. IV, pp. 688–702.

[17] *Records of the Presbyterian Church in the United States of America*, Vol. I, pp. 17–40, for statements regarding Van Vlecq from 1710 to 1715

of bigamy was lodged against him, which, after thorough investigation, was sustained in 1713. He was, as a result, suspended from the ministry. In 1715 he is reported as having "run out of the country."

A much larger number of German Reformed people came into the province of Pennsylvania in the period be-between 1720 and 1730.

In a petition addressed by some members of the Philadelphia Reformed Church to Governor Patrick Gordon, on November 23, 1732, they state:[18]

That a great number of Protestants born under the Ligeance of the Emperor of Germany did, about *ten years since* [1722], come into this Province, and having settled in divers parts thereof, but especially in the city of Philada., formed themselves into a Religious Society, commonly called by the name of German Reformed Church.

The same statement is repeated and somewhat enlarged in a bill of complaint which the same persons submitted to the Court of Chancery of the Province on January 23, 1732 [–1733], in which they declared.[19]

The said deponents . . . say that for *above the space of ten years* by gone, great numbers of the subjects of the emperor of Germany, professing the Protestant religion or as 't is equally called the Reformed religion and having suffered hardships in their native country upon the score of their religion, came over into the province of Pennsylvania and settled themselves in sundry parts of the s^d. province and especially in Philadelphia.

In harmony with these statements we find in the

[18] This petition is a part of the Reiff papers, printed in the *Reformed Quarterly Review*, 1893, Vol. XL, p 59 f

[19] This bill of complaint belongs also to the Reiff papers, but it has not yet been printed The original is in the Harbaugh collection of manuscripts, now in the possession of Rev. Prof. J I Good

History of the Goshenhoppen Charge

"Resolutions of the States of Holland and West Friesland," that on June 12, 1722, the Raad Pensionaris (Prime Minister) reported to the States the arrival of a large number of families from Germany, which had come to Holland on various ships, with the intention of being transported to England, to be sent to one of the English Colonies, without any preparation having been made for their journey, or any invitation having been extended by the British government. He asked what steps should be taken. The States decided to confer with the authorities of the province nearest to Germany, to prevent the coming of any more emigrants.[19a]

In the year 1725 John Philip Boehm began his ministerial activity in the Perkiomen valley. For the first communion services, held in 1725, he reported[20] the following members:

On October 15, 1725, at Falkner Swamp, 40 members or 24 males;

In November, 1725, at Skippack, 37 members or 20 males;

On December 23, 1725, at Whitemarsh, 24 members or 14 males.

The totals for these three congregations were, therefore, in 1725, 101 members or 58 males. These three congregations of Boehm continued the organization effected by Paulus Van Vlecq in 1710, for of the latter's members we find Gabriel Schuler and Gerhart In de Heven

[19a] Taken from the Rotterdam Archives.

[20] The number of males in 1725 is mentioned in the appeal of Boehm's elders to the Classis of Amsterdam, dated July, 1728, printed in the *Journal of the P. H S*, Vol. VI, p 308 The number of members is found in Boehm's report of 1744, see *Minutes and Letters of the Coetus of Pennsylvania*, p. 18. See also *Life and Letters of Boehm*, pp 160, 409

First Reformed Services

in Boehm's congregation at Skippack,[21] Willem de Wees, John Rebenstock and Isaac Dilbeck in his congregation at Whitemarsh.[22] If we had the complete lists of Boehm's 101 members we would no doubt be able to find other connecting links besides the five mentioned above.

Such was the beginning of Reformed church life in the Perkiomen valley.

The time when the first Reformed settlers arrived in the Goshenhoppen region cannot be determined with the evidence at hand at present. But it was most probably about the year 1720. So much is certain that in 1727 enough Reformed people had arrived in Goshenhoppen, so that a communion service could be held for them.

In 1736 John Henry Goetschy, the boy preacher, entered the names of 45 heads of families into the Reformed record at New Goshenhoppen (see p. 274). Besides these there appear 68 additional names of men in the baptismal entries from 1731 to 1736 inclusive, so that there were at least 113 settlers, together with their families, in the New Goshenhoppen district by the end of the year 1736. With the help of Rupp's Immigrant Lists the exact time of the arrival of many of these settlers can be determined. The following is a list of those whom the writer was able to identify with some degree of probability:[23]

---

[21] See the documents printed in the *Journal of the P H S*, Vol VII, pp 34, 48, also the letter from Skippack of May 10, 1730, quoted in *Historical Notes*, p. 103.

[22] These three men signed the appeal of July, 1728, see *Journal of the P H S*, Vol VI, p. 316; as well as Boehm's letter of January 30, 1730, in *Journal of P H. S*, Vol. VII, p. 34; *Life and Letters of Boehm*, pp 169, 191

[23] In the case of very common names like Jacob Meyer and Jacob Muller the possibility of mistaken identity must of course remain open.

EARLIEST REFORMED SETTLERS IN THE GOSHENHOPPEN VALLEY.

Names of Settlers	Time of Arrival	At Goshenhoppen
Johannes Huth	September 18, 1727	Go. 1731
Johann Friedrich Hilligass	September 18, 1727	Go 1731
Hans Michel Zimmermann	September 18, 1727	Go. 1733
Hans Georg Welcker	September 18, 1727	Go 1731
Ulrich Hetzell [Hertzel]	September 18, 1727	Go. 1733
Benedict Strohm [Strome]	September 18, 1727	Go. 1736
Frantz Stupp	September 30, 1727	Go. 1731
Burckhard Hoffmann	September 30, 1727	Go. 1732
Johann Peter Hess	October 2, 1727	Go. 1733
Michel Eberhart	October 16, 1727	Go. 1732
Johann Philip Ried	October 16, 1727	Go 1736
Wendel Wiant	August 29, 1729	Go. 1736
Johann Peter Moll	August 29, 1729	Go. 1733
Valentin Griesemer	August 29, 1730	Go. 1731
Thomas Hamma[n]	August 29, 1730	Go 1732
Abraham Transu	August 29, 1730	Go. 1731
Lonhart Hochgenug	August 29, 1730	Go. 1732
John Adam Stadtler	September 5, 1730	Go 1733
Johann Philip Emmert	September 5, 1730	Go. 1731
Casper Holtzhausen [r]	August 17, 1731	Go. 1733
Abraham Sahler [Selei]	September 11, 1731	Go 1732
Johann Bartel Gucker [Kucker]	September 11, 1731	Go. 1732
Johann Michel Moll	September 11, 1731	Go 1732
Christopher Moll	September 11, 1731	Go 1733
Hans Adam Echelen [Euchelen]	September 11, 1731	Go. 1731
Leonard Bock	September 21, 1731	Go. 1737
Jacob Meyer	September 21, 1731	Go. 1736
Hans Jerg Steger	August 11, 1732	Go 1737
Adam Hillegas	August 11, 1732	Go 1737
Georg Mertz	September 11, 1732	Go 1736
Georg Palsgraff	September 11, 1732	Go. 1736
Hans Steinmann	September 19, 1732	Go 1733
Jacob Muller	September 19, 1732	Go 1737
Lorentz Hartman	September 19, 1732	Go 1736
Andreas Lohr	September 19, 1732	Go. 1733
Johan Henrich Jung	September 19, 1732	Go 1736
Georg Peter Knecht	September 21, 1732	Go 1737
Hans Leonhart Herzel	September 21, 1732	Go 1737
Peter Matern	September 30, 1732	Go. 1734
Peter Raudenbusch	September 30, 1732	Go 1733

Reformed Settlers in Goshenhoppen

Johannes Geiger	September 30, 1732	Go. 1734
Georg Michel Favian [Fabion]	...October 11, 1732	Go. 1736
Joh. Jost Ohlwein .	. September 18, 1733	Go. 1736

Here are more than forty German Reformed settlers the exact time of whose arrival can be fixed and who, some time between that date and their first appearance in the New Goshenhoppen record, moved into the Goshenhoppen region. The others, whose date of arrival is as yet unknown, did not necessarily come before 1727. They may have come through another harbor, or reached Goshenhoppen by a circuitous route. For it is a significant fact that of the Lutheran settlers at Old Goshenhoppen only three came before the year 1730, Kilian Gauckler, who came to America in 1717, John George Weicker who arrived in 1724, and John Martin Deer in 1728. Of the rest, nearly thirty, only a few appear in the immigrant lists, although they all came, according to the Church Record, between 1732 and 1750. This proves that the absence of a name from the immigrant lists cannot be used as an argument for or against the early arrival of that person. It must also be remembered that the immigrant lists are incomplete and that the names have in many instances been deciphered incorrectly.

Although the time of arrival of the earliest settlers cannot be established definitely, it is certain that the year 1727 is the first fixed point in the history of the Reformed Church in the Goshenhoppen region.

The Indian traditions, which gathered around the origin and meaning of the name Goshenhoppen are beautifully summed up in a poem of the Rev. Dr. C. Z. Weiser, which may fittingly be inserted here.[23a]

[23a] The writer owes this poem to the Rev John B Stoudt, who kindly transmitted it for publication

THE LEGEND OF GOSHENHOPPEN.

BY C. Z. WEISER

Would you hear of Goshenhoppen,
What it means and where it hails from
Do not trust the pale-faced people,
They are but of yesterday.
'Tis with them but speculation,
Guess work oozed from fever'd brainshop,
Like the webs from working spiders.

Now they have it "Que-se-ho-pen,"
Then they say it's "Coss-he-hop-pe,"
"Cos-she-hop-pa," says another,
"Cos-ha-ha-pin," writes a fourth one;
"Cosh-a-hop-pa"—"Gosh-e-hop-pa,"
Or, again, "Co-wis-se-hop-pen,"
Till at last it's "Gosh-en-hop-pen."

Who can tell in such a Babel,
How to utter it correctly,
How to rightly shape its body,—
And divine its primal meaning?
We must trace it as a river,
From its mouth back to its source spring;
Trace and tail it up and backward,
Through the periods and the ages—
Till we find its secret rising.

Long before Great Brother Omas
Came to own his forest domain,
Had the Redman shared the country
Into tracts and into districts,
Measured it by strips of deer-skin;
Marked it out by trees and rivers,
Or by hills and mountain ranges.

Indian Legend

Every tribe then had its domain,
For to smoke and roam and hunt in;
And each tribe its Sak-e-maker,
He whose name stood for the region,
He who owned and bargained for it.

Thus we know the great "Mough-ough-sin"
Owned the land of "Pah-ke-ho-ma,"
Which is known and called Macungie,
That was sold for two big blankets
And four pairs of leather stockings,
And four bottles of sweet cider.

When we read of "Guch-i-o-thon,"
And besides of "En-shok-hup-po,"
And at last of "Shak-a-hop-pa,"
Who were ancient Sak-e-makers,
Great big Injuns-treaty makers.
These three ancient Sak-e-makers
Ruled the vale of Pah-ke-ho-ma,
Ruled the fair Per-ki-o-men valley,
Shak-a-hop-pa stood as chieftain
Over all the Sak-e-makers,
Since he grew a foot beyond them,
And came nearer the Great Father

Shak-a-hop-pa, the tall chieftain,
Of the vale of Pah-ke-ho-ma,
Sold and barter'd off his title
For two hundred feet of wampun;
And for thirty feet of duffels;
For some sixty feet of mattress;
Thirty shirts and thirty kettles;
Shoes twelve pairs and thirty gimlets;
Sixty stockings, thirty scissors;
Thirty combs and thirty axes;
Thirty-one tobacco pouches;

Thirty small tobacco cases;
Seven awls and thirty glasses;
Thirty bars of lead and powder;
Thirty pounds of lead that reddens;
Beads poured into three full papers;
Thirty pairs of bells that rattle;
Drawing knives one half a dozen;
And some eighteen caps with feathers;
And as many hoes and handles.
This was the consideration,
Which Great Brother Omas tendered,
For the vale of Goshenhoppen,
To the ancient Sak-e-maker,
Shak-a-hop-pa, the BIG SMOKE PIPE.

CHAPTER I.

MINISTRY OF REV. GEORGE MICHAEL WEISS, 1727–1730.[24]

IN November, 1730, the Rev. John Philip Boehm wrote as follows to the Reformed Classis of Amsterdam:[25]

He [Mr. Weiss] preached at a branch place called Goschenhoppen, about ten miles from Falckner Schwam; the last time on October 12, 1727, he celebrated the Lord's Supper without knowing the people, admitting among others two men from Falckner Schwam, who ought to have been taken to account because of their vicious lives.

This passage gives us the first recorded date in the history of the congregation. It names its first pastor and enables us to locate the first place of worship. It could not have been at Old Goshenhoppen, near Salford Station, on the Perkiomen Railroad, which is hardly five miles from Falkner Swamp, but it must have been at New Gosh-

---

[24] For earlier accounts of Weiss see Harbaugh, *Fathers of the Reformed Church, Vol. I,* Lancaster, 1857 pp. 265–274; Good, *History of the Reformed Church in the United States, 1725–1792,* Reading, 1899, pp. 113–152; Corwin, *Manual of the Reformed Church in America,* New York, 1902, pp. 896–899; Dubbs, *History of the Reformed Church in Pennsylvania,* Lancaster, 1902, pp. 83–90; Hinke, *Life and Letters of Boehm,* pp. 26–37.

[25] *Journal of P. H. S.,* Vol. VII, p. 56; *Life and Letters of Boehm,* p. 215.

enhoppen, near East Greenville, which is about ten miles from Falkner Swamp. The first Reformed services were, therefore, held at New Goshenhoppen by the Rev. George Michael Weiss, the first pastor. He is such an important personage in the history of the Reformed Church in America, that he deserves a more elaborate biography than has yet been written of him.

John Peter Miller, the later monk of Ephrata, wrote about Mr. Weiss as follows in his *Chronicon Ephratense:*[26]

> About the year 1726, the first High-German Reformed preacher, Weiss by name, arrived in Pennsylvania. He was born at Stebbach, a Palatine place in the Neckar valley, studied at Heidelberg and finished his course at Koschehoppen [Goshenhoppen] in the county of Philadelphia.

This was all that was known about Weiss's birthplace till 1897, when the writer visited Heidelberg and found there, in the matriculation book of the famous University, the following entry:

1718, October 18.
        Georgius Michael Weiss,
          Philosoph. Stud.
            Eppinga, Palatinus.

This entry shows that Mr. Weiss entered the University of Heidelberg on October 18, 1718, as student of philosophy, and that he gave his birthplace as Eppingen, which is about half a German mile southwest of Stebbach.

On August 15, 1897, the writer visited Eppingen and found in the old church records of the town considerable information about the Weiss family. The oldest representative of the family, mentioned in the records,[27] is Nico-

---

[26] *Chronicon Ephratense,* Engl. transl, Lancaster, 1889, p. 70
[27] See article by the writer in the *Reformed Church Messenger* of October 27, 1898, on "A Contribution to the Life of George Michael Weiss"; also in *Christian Intelligencer* of November 16, 1898

laus Weiss, a citizen of Gross Engersheim, in the Kingdom of Würtemberg. His son, John Michael Weiss, a tailor by trade, married on February 26, 1686, Barbara, widow of Jacob Stierle, citizen and tailor at Eppingen. This union was blessed with two children, Maria Appollonia, baptized December 26, 1686, and Barbara, baptized October 7, 1689. But on June 30, 1692, the mother died, aged 44 years.

On September 16, 1692, "Hans Michel Weiss, citizen and tailor," married a second time, namely Maria, daughter of the late Martin Frank, shoemaker in Bretten. This second union was blessed with six children, as follows:

1. Anna Catherine, Dec 11, 1695, died July 9, 1696.
2. Eva Catherine, July 31, 1697
3. Görg Michael, Jan. 23, 1700
4. Maria Elisabeth } twins, March 29, 1703.
5. Christophel
6. Maria Elisabeth, born July 10, bapt July 12, 1705.

In the case of the first five children but one date is given in the record, without any statement as to whether the date of birth or of baptism is intended. But as the names are entered in the baptismal record, it is more probably the date of baptism. The dates of the last child show that baptism took place usually on the third day after birth.

These entries prove that Georg Michael Weiss was not born at Stebbach, but at Eppingen. What is more remarkable is that, according to information received from the pastor of Eppingen, Stebbach never belonged to Eppingen ecclesiastically, but to a neighboring parish.

What became of Mr. Weiss, after he had finished his studies at Heidelberg, is still unknown. We meet him again ten years later, when on September 21, 1727, he with fifty other Palatines appeared before the Provincial

Council of Pennsylvania, in the Court House of Philadelphia and signed the oath of allegiance to the King of England.

As early as September 14, 1727, the Governor, Patrick Gordon, had called the Provincial Board together,

> to inform them that there is lately[28] arrived from Holland, a ship with four hundred Palatines, as 'tis said, and that he has information they will be very soon followed by a much greater number, who design to settle in the back parts of this province; & as they transport themselves without any leave obtained from the Crown of Great Britain, and settle themselves upon the Proprietors untaken up Lands without any application to the Proprietor or his Commissioners of property, or to the Government in general, it would be highly necessary to concert proper measures for the peace and security of the province, which may be endangered by such numbers of Strangers daily poured in, who being ignorant of our Language and Laws, & settling in a body together, make, as it were, a distinct people from his Majesties Subjects.[29]

In answer to this representation of the governor the board ordered,

> that the Masters of the Vessells importing them shall be examined whether they have any Leave granted them by the Court of Britain for the Importation of these Foreigners, and that a List shall be taken of the Names of all these People, their several Occupations, and the Places from whence they come, and shall be further examined, touching their Intentions in coming hither; And further, that

---

[28] This proves that the ship *William and Sarah* did not arrive on September 18, 1727, as has been wrongly inferred from the list published in the *Pennsylvania Archives*, Second Series, Vol. XVII, p 7. This list was drawn up on September 18, but the ship had landed before September 14, " lately " may mean a day or even several days earlier.

[29] See *Colonial Records*, Vol III, p 282 f., for this list and the following extracts

Ship William and Sarah

a Writing be drawn up for them to sign declaring their Allegiance & Subjection to the King of Great Britain & Fidelity to the Proprietary of this Province, & that they will demean themselves peaceably towards all his Majesties Subjects, & strictly observe, and conform to the Laws of England and of this Government.

In consequence of this order a signed list was laid before the board at its meeting on September 21, containing

the names of one hundred & nine Palatines, who with their Families, making in all about Four hundred Persons, were imported into this Province in the Ship William and Sarah, William Hill, Master, from Rotterdam, but last from Dover, as by Clearance from Officers of his Majesties Customs there; And the said Master being asked, if he had any Licence from the Court of Great Britain for transporting those People, & what their Intentions were in coming hither, said that he had no other License or Allowance for their Transportation than the above Clearance, and that he believed they designed to settle in this Province.

This list of 109 Palatines, as submitted to the Provincial Board on September 21, 1727, has been published in Vol XVII, of the second series of the *Pennsylvania Archives*, pp. 7-8, but it is so imperfect and inaccurate, full of typographical and other mistakes, that it seems worth while to submit a corrected list. Such a new publication is all the more justified because the list as submitted to the board, indicates the number of people in each family, which figures, though important, were omitted in the *Pennsylvania Archives*. The list is as follows:[30]

---

[30] The original list is now in the State Library at Harrisburg, Department of Public Records, at present (1914) in charge of Mr. Luther R Kelker, who very kindly allowed the writer to examine and copy the original list, as well as others mentioned later.

History of the Goshenhoppen Charge

A LIST OF YE PALATINE PASSENGERS IMPORTED IN YE SHIP WILLIAM AND SARAH, WILL'M HILL, MAST^R., FROM ROTTERDAM, PHILAD'A YE 18 SEPTEMBER 1727.

[1] Hans Jerrick Swaep . . 6
[2] Hans Martin Levisteyn 2
[3] Benedic Strome. 2
[4] Jan Hend^k Scaub . . 3½
[5] Hans Jerrick Shoomaker. 6½
[6] Abraham Beni . . . 5
[7] Hans Martain Shoomak^r 1
[8] Frederick Heiligas . 4½
[9] Hans Mich. Pagman . 1
[10] Sebastian Creef . . 4
[11] Johan Habaraker . 2½
[12] Alex. Diebenderf. . . 2
[13] Hieronemus Milder 2
[14] Johann Willm Mey . . 2
[15] Henericus Bell . . . 1
[16] Caspar Springler . . 4
[17] Hans Heri^k. Siegler . 3
[18] Michael Peitley . 4½
[19] Hans Mich. Tiell . 3½
[20] Jan. Barn. Levinstey . . 1
[21] Jacob Jost . . . 2
[22] Johannes Hoet. 3½
[23] Daniel Levan 8
[24] Hans Mich^l. Weider . . 2
[25] Andr^w. Simmerman . 8
[26] Leonart Seltenreich 2
[27] Hans Jerrick Wigler . 2
[28] Willm Jurgens... . . . 1
[29] Johan Wester, sick . 1
[30] Willm Heer. 1
[31] Hans Adam Milder . . 2
[32] Anspel Anspag . . 2½
[33] Henrich Meyer . 4
[34] Adam Henrich . 2
[35] Jacob Gons... . . 2
[36] Ulrich Heere . 3
[37] Sebastian Vinck 2
[38] Tonicus Meyer . . 5
126

[39] Jacob Swicker, sick . . 1
[40] Hans Jer. Herzels . 4
[41] Jan Bernard Wolf 6
[42] Steven Frederick . . . 3½
[43] Ann Floren. . . . 1½
[44] Philip Fernser.. . . . 1
[45] Hans Jacob Eckman . . . 2
[46] Hans Fill. Heysinger . 1
[47] Hendrick Witte 1
[48] Hans Jerrick Hoy, sick . 1
[49] Jacob Pause . 2½
[50] Andr^w Saltsgerrer . . 1
[51] Hans Jerrick Wolf 2½
[52] Jacob Milder, dead. . 3½
[53] Hans Jerrick Bowman 1
[54] Johannes Wester*.. . . 1
[55] Johannes Stromf, boy . . 1
[56] Hans Jerig Anspag 2½
[57] Philip Swyger . . 2
[58] Christ Milder, dead . . 2
[59] Elias Meyer . 3½
[60] Peter Springler 1
[61] Martin Prill 3
[62] Joh Tob^s. Serveas . . 1
[63] Peter Seyts 4½
[64] Johannes Eckman . . 4
[65] Johannes Hend^k Gyer, sick . . . 2
[66] Christ^r. Labengyger . 2
[67] Johannes Berret 4
[68] Andrew Holtspan. 4
[69] Jacob Swarts 4
[70] Hans Jerick Schaub . 3
[71] Hans Mich^l Phauts . 5
[72] Christian Snyder . 2
[73] Bastian Smith . . 2
[74] Johannes Barteleme . . 1
92
[75] Tobias Freye . . . 4

The Captain's List

[76] Johannes Tiebenderf	4	[97] Hans Adam Beinder	4½
[77] Jacob Mast, Skipach	4	[98] Christopher Wittmer,	1
[78] Joseph Aelbragt	3½	[99] Hendrick Hartman	3
[79] Nicholas Adams	2	[100] Clement Eirn	2
[80] Jacob Meyer	2	[101] Philip Jacob Reylender	5
[81] Johannes Leyb	4	[102] Johanes Mich¹. Peepell	1
[82] Johanes Balt, Germt	4	[103] Ernst Roede	1
[83] Conrad Miller, sick	5	[104] Philip Seigler	5½
[84] Christopher Walter	4	[105] Philip Roedeull	2
[85] Ulrich Hartsell, Skippach	2	[106] Rudolph Wilkes	3
[86] Hans Adam Stoll	3	[107] Hans Jerig Milder	1
[87] Hans Jerrick Guyger	4½	[108] Abraham Farn	4
[88] Hans Martin Wilder	2½	[109] Uldrich Staffon	3
[89] Hans Jerig Viegle	6½		107
[90] Hans Jerig Ardnold, dead			
[91] Hans Jerig Cramer	3		
[92] Hans Jerig Peter (?)	2½		
[93] Albert Swoap	1		
[94] Hendrick Gouger, sick	3½		
[95] Diederick Roede	1		
[96] Hans Jerig Roedebas, Skipach	2		

This is a true list of Passengers Imported in the ship William & Sarah, Willm. Hill, Mast^r., from Rotterdam among whom are no convicts, given upon oath,

by THO. TOBER

The totals of the three columns are said to be $126 + 92 + 107 = 325$. But in reality the figures in none of the columns have been added correctly. The correct totals, supposing all the figures to be accurate, are: $118 + 91 + 108 = 317$. The whole number of passengers was, therefore, much nearer 300 than 400.

Of these colonists not more than 51 actually appeared on September 21, 1727, in the Court House at Philadelphia to sign the following oath of allegiance:

We Subscribers, Natives and late Inhabitants of the Palatinate upon the Rhine & Places adjacent, having transported ourselves and Families into this Province of Pensilvania, a Colony subject to the Crown of Great Britain, in hopes and Expectation of finding a Retreat & peaceable Settlement therein, Do Solemnly promise & Engage, that We will be faithful & bear true Allegiance to his

* Name erased, see No 29.

present MAJESTY, KING GEORGE THE SECOND and his Successors, Kings of Great Britain, and will be faithfull to the Proprietor of this Province, And that we will demean ourselves peaceably to all His said Majesties Subjects, and strictly observe and conform to the Laws of England and of this Province, to the utmost of our Power and best of our understanding

The names signed to this declaration have been published repeatedly, but so full of inaccuracies, that a new transcript of the original is absolutely necessary. The figures placed before them identify them with the corresponding names in the first list. The signatures to the Declaration of Allegiance are as follows:

PALATINES IMPORTED IN THE SHIP WILL^M & SARAH, WILL^M HILL, COMM FROM ROTTERDAM WHO HEREUNTO SETT THEIR HANDS, THE 21ST OF SEPT 1727, IN PRESENCE OF THE GOV^R & COUNCIL.

G M. Weiss, V D.M [31]
[1] Johann Georg Schwab
[41] Hans Bernhart Wolff
[8] Joh. Friederich Hilligass
    Rudolff Leyb
[19] Hans Michel Diel
[10] Sebastian Graff
[22] Johannes Huth
[101] Filibs Jacob Rheinlender
[104] Filib Zigler, × his mark
[75] Tobias Frey
[56] Hans Jerch Anspacher
[63] Johan Peter Seitz
[78] Joseph Albrecht
[64] Johanes Eckman
[5] Jerich Schuhmacher
[21] Jacob Jost

[18] Michel Bóttle
[106] Rutolff Wellecker
[92?] Jeorg Petter
[88] Hans Mart (W) Weller
[89] Hans Jerg Vogelle
[30] Willem Herr
[67] Johannes Barth
[16] Hans Caspar Spengler
[90] Hans Gorg Cremmer
[61] Hans Martin Mill
[68] Andreas (A) Holsbacher
[49] Jacob Bausel
[31] Hans Adam | Miller
          his mark
[35] Johan Jacob Cuntz
[51] Hans Jerg Wolff

---

[31] The Clerk of the Provincial Council (see minutes in *Colonial Records*, Vol III, p 284) wrote the name "G. M. Wey," but a photograph of the original, kindly furnished by Mr Luther R. Kelker, shows plainly that it is "G M Weis"

[105] Philip Rutschly	[81] Johannes Leib
[103] Hans Ernst Rudi	[99] Joh Henrich Hartman
[59] Elias Meyer	[17] Hans Georg Ziegler
[25?] Hans Michel Zimmerman	[11] Johannes Haberacker
[27] Hans Görg Welcker	[33] Henrich Meyer
[57] Hans Philip Schweikhardt	[80] Jacob Meyer
[12] Alexand. Dubendorffer	[84] Christoph Walter
[2] Hans Martin Liebenstein	Henry (H) Sippen
[95] Johan Diderich Rudi	[71] Hans Michel Pfautz
[40] Hans Jerg Hertzel	

A comparison of these two lists shows how carelessly the captain's list was made. The writer made no attempt to ascertain the correct spelling of the names. He merely wrote down what he supposed he heard when the names were pronounced to him. For Welcker he heard Wigler and in a second case Wilkes. For Mill he put down Prill, for Miller he wrote Milder. Schweikhardt he turned into Swyger, Spengler into Springler, Rutschli apparently into Roedeull. In some cases the scribal monstrosities are so great that no identification is possible. No wonder that it is so difficult to identify immigrants, when the captains' lists are so badly corrupted and the passengers' own signatures are sometimes such awful scrawls that they need a second list as a key to decipher them correctly.

The relation of Mr. Weiss to these immigrants has long been doubtful. The question whether he was merely their fellow passenger or the recognized leader of a colony could not be determined till very recently. There are now three documents at hand which answer this question. The first is the earliest printed report concerning the Reformed Church in Pennsylvania, printed in Holland in 1731. It was submitted in that year to the Synod of South Holland which met from July 3 to 13, 1731, at Dortrecht.

In this report we find the following statement about the

religious conditions in Pennsylvania and the coming of Mr. Weiss to America:[32]

But as the Quakers were not numerous enough to colonize this territory, William Pen, when he projected and built a city, called it Philadelphia, that by a name so friendly he might attract other Europeans thither. Not long after the first settlement many of the oppressed inhabitants of Germany, particularly from the Palatinate and from the districts of Nassau, Waldeck, Wittgenstein and the Wetterau, emigrated to Pennsylvania, with their wives and children and the proceeds of the property which they sold, whether more or less.

Among them are Mennonites, Lutherans and Reformed, but at the present time the Reformed, holding to the old Reformed confession, constitute about half of the whole number, being about 15,000. The German Palatines, migrating from their own country to Pennsylvania, year after year, were unable to provide themselves with ministers. Finding no religious worship, many, attracted by the good morals and blameless conduct of the Quakers, joined themselves to them, preferring their worship to none.[33]

At last four years ago, the Upper Consistory of the Palatinate sent over a minister by the name of Do. [Dominie] Weis, with a number of people migrating from the Palatinate. They formed a consistory at Schibbach, a place about six miles from Philadelphia. A wooden church was erected and he [Dominie Weis] preached for the congregation and administered the ordinances of Baptism and the Lord's Supper. There most of the Palatines live close one to the other.

In this report it is distinctly asserted that the Upper Consistory of the Palatinate sent Mr. Weiss with these

[32] Two copies of the Report of 1731, entitled *Berigt en Onderrigtinge nopens en aan de Colonie en Kerke van Pensylvanien*, 2 pp preface and 18 pp. text, are known to be in existence One is in the possession of Rev. Dr. J. I Good, the other was in the library of late Governor Pennypacker. The writer has used a photographic copy.

[33] This is in agreement with the testimony of Muehlenberg, see *Hallesche Nachrichten,* new ed , Vol. II, p. 195.

emigrants. This statement is supported by another report, which was presented on October 31, 1735, to the Synodical Deputies (an executive committee of the Synods of North and South Holland). In this report, Do. Wilhelmius, then pastor at Rotterdam, the best friend of the Palatines in Holland,[34] gave an extensive account as to how the Synods had come to take up the care of the churches in Pennsylvania. In it he wrote:

> These present Germans in Pennsylvania have immigrated thither from various parts of Germany, not in order to secure liberty of worship, which they enjoyed in their own land, but to realize better means of subsistence. Most of them came from the Palatinate, concerning whom the Great Consistory of the Palatinate, consisting of civil and ecclesiastical persons, addressed itself to the Synod of this country by means of letters, sent some years ago to me, and by me delivered to the Very Reverend Synod, showing that being oppressed as they were, they were not in a condition to furnish any assistance to these people, for the securing of any ministers of the Word, and asked therefore that our Synod would be kind enough to extend a helping hand. This the Synod subsequently accepted as an affair of the utmost importance, these people belonging to the pure Reformed religion and having been accustomed to our Catechism and Confession of Faith. . .
>
> In the next place the condition of the church among them ought to be noted. They consist of several thousand, whose exact number cannot even be guessed at, because they live scattered through the whole country in forests, without any civil or ecclesiastical union, so that those living in Philadelphia know as little about

[34] John Wilhelmius, son of William Wilhelmius, was born December 4, 1671, at Hardwyk He studied at Leyden, where he also took the degree of doctor of philosophy. He was first pastor at Twisk, then professor of theology in the Reformed University at Lingen, and finally pastor at Rotterdam, 1713-1748 He died March 3, 1754 He was a faithful friend of the Reformed Church of Pennsylvania See *Biographish Wordenboek der Nederlanden,* 20ste Deel, Haarlem, 1877

those living at other places, as we in Holland know about our co-religionists in Poland or Hungary . . .

These people have organized themselves in three places into congregations and have built for themselves three churches, of which the first is in Philadelphia, where they now have a small stone church, towards which those of the larger English church have manifested their liberality. The second is at Germantown, a village eight hours[35] distant from it, that being a large barn built upon the land of the notorious [befaamden] Ryff and now enlarged, on which account they are in debt to the amount of 2500 guilders. The third [church] is at Schibbach.

For the ministry of these churches Do. Wys [Weiss] has been in service, who came over with a colony of these Palatines [die met eene Colonie dezer Paltzers is overgekomen] and who now has left his service, having been called to one of the churches of New Netherland [New York] The other is Do. Boom [Boehm], against whom the congregation is greatly embittered, and from whom they have no service. The third is candidate Rieger, who came over with another colony and became minister there, but now has openly turned Quaker and refuses to baptize children and publicly teaches, to the disturbance of these congregations, that one can be saved in every religion.

There are a number of points in this report which deserve special emphasis. We notice first of all that the grossly exaggerated figures of the 1731 report, regarding the Reformed people in Pennsylvania, have been materially reduced. Instead of 15,000 we read only of "several thousand," which is certainly much nearer the truth. We also learn that the Reformed people in Pennsylvania passed under the care of the "Fathers" in Holland in answer to the urgent representations made to them by the

[35] This distance is of course much too great Eight hours represent twenty-four miles. In reality the Reformed churches of Philadelphia and Germantown were only six miles apart See the statement of Boehm in his report of 1734 in *Minutes and Letters of the Coetus of Pennsylvania*, p. 1

Upper Consistory of the Palatinate   The first letter from the Heidelberg Consistory was laid before the South Holland Synod in 1728. Moreover, both Mr. Weiss as well as Mr. Rieger came with Reformed colonies to Pennsylvania. The statements about the three Reformed churches in Pennsylvania in 1735 are inaccurate in almost all particulars. No small stone church, erected by Reformed people, existed in that year in Philadelphia. The religious services of the Reformed people were rather held in an old butcher shop.[36] It stood on Arch Street above Fifth and belonged to Mr. Andrew Hamilton, who had rented it to Reformed and Lutherans for their joint use. The stone church of which the report speaks was rather built in Germantown.   Mr. Boehm is authority for the fact that there was "a well built, pretty large stone church"[37] in Germantown, erected by the Reformed people there in 1733.   Finally it was the Skippack Reformed church

[36] Mr. Boehm, in his report of 1744, refers to it in the following words: "At Philadelphia we had thus far, in common with the Lutherans, an old and dilapidated butcher's shop, at an annual rent of three pounds, finally this was raised to four pounds, which we must pay alone, for the Lurtherans have built a church there 70 by 45 feet" See *Minutes and Letters of the Coetus of Pennsylvania*, p 23   A similar statement is made by Muehlenberg, see *Selbstbiographie*, Allentown, 1881, p. 128   Zinzendorf calls it "an old barn," see *Budingische Sammlungen*, Vol III, p. 579, cf. *Hallesche Nachrichten*, new ed, Vol. I, p 39. It belonged to Andrew Hamilton, Esq, until his death in 1741, when it passed into the hands of his son-in-law, Justice William Allen   See Dotterer, *Rev John Philip Boehm*, p 9   Schlatter entered into the church record at Philadelphia the following statement regarding it: "Thus far [till December, 1747] the congregation has worshipped, every other Sunday, in an old small house, made of boards, from November, 1734, together with the Lutheran congregation. But when the Evangelicals [Lutherans] built a stone church in the year 1744, we had it alone and paid annually to Mr William Allen the sum of four pounds" See also *Life and Letters of Boehm*, p 329, note 213

[37] See his report of 1739, in the *Minutes of Coetus*, p 12

which was built on the land of Mr. Reiff, not the church in Germantown, and that there was a debt of 2500 guilders resting upon it is another remarkable exaggeration in the Dutch records, due no doubt to exaggerated reports that had come from Pennsylvania.

In view of these inaccuracies in the report of Dr. Wilhelmius, his statement about Weiss might also be open to doubt, were it not for the fact that it is fully supported by a Latin testimonial which was given to Mr. Weiss by the Palatinate Consistory on May 1, 1727. The original of this certificate is no longer in existence, but a copy of it was entered by Mr. Weiss himself into the church record of the old Catskill Reformed Church at Catskill, N Y., of which Weiss was pastor from 1732 to 1735. As it is an important historical document which has thus far escaped the notice of historians[38] we offer a translation of the whole certificate:

ORDINATION CERTIFICATE OF REV. GEORGE M. WEISS, MAY 1, 1727.

Greeting to the Kind Reader!

He who once foretold that at evening time it shall be light [Zech. 14: 7], when contrary to the hope and expectation of all, the King of kings and the Lord of lords shall, as it were, suddenly take his stand for His struggling Church, even as He appeared at one time to the Apostles in the night following the resurrection, when, for dread of the Jews, the doors were closed,—whence no one can doubt that in the same manner He will be near His holy Church, when it will be shut in by foes and deserted by its own For thus it has pleased the Divine Wisdom and Goodness that just then

[38] It was mentioned by Dr. Corwin in his *Manual of the Reformed Church of America*, 3d ed, 1879, p. 544 The writer owes his copy to the kindness of the present pastor, Rev. John H. Dykstra, who very readily gave him access to it

when the Omnipotent has seen that the hand of the defenders has failed, the arm of the Lord should put on strength and claim for Himself His own, whereby should become all the more conspicuous that great Salvation, which was promised to the Sardensian circle [Rev. 3: 4], numbering few survivors only, but also to each most beloved Philadelphia, when He shall see it [Philadelphia] drawing near and yearning to unite with Him: Then it will surely come to pass that, after its forces have become very small, it shall grow into large forces, large companies and into an army formidable unto its enemies, to which even the most distant peoples and nations shall be accessible and doors shall be opened, never afterwards to be closed; whereby there shall be gathered to the Savior, the Son of God, a people wholly new, even if it must be sought in another continent.

Wherefore, since the most excellent Sir, distinguished through ability and learning, George Michael Weiss, from Eppingen in the Palatinate, a candidate of Sacred Theology, determined to apply the divinely granted gifts to this most laudable use, that he might labor to the best of his ability for the extension of the Kingdom of God, which is the kingdom of love; hence, after having devoted himself to the fine arts of the humanities and to philosophy, he consecrated himself wholly to the even sublimer studies of theology, in which he made such happy progress in a short time that he was deemed worthy to be permitted to undergo the examination for the ministry. In this he proved his diligence to our Senate in such a manner that we not only hoped but were also confident that he would some day perform a useful work for the Church of Christ.

Wherefore, since he announced of late that he had conceived the plan with some of his fellow-citizens and other friends, well known to him, to undertake a journey to the transatlantic parts of the world, if it should please the Divine Providence to entrust him there with the leadership of a congregational flock, to teach and to guide them there, and since he asked that to that end he be fully inducted into the spiritual office with the laying on of hands,

Therefore, since the purity of his morals, his humility and especially his piety that flows from it, were well known to us, and since our Senate was at the same time well aware of the progress he had made in the knowledge of the theological sciences and in thorough acquaintance with the sacred languages, we hesitated all the less to grant his request since we could cherish the certain hope that the Chief Shepherd of the sheep, to whom his own are well known, though they live in the most distant parts of the world, would not withhold his support from the undertaking of an honest mind.

Hence we have admitted him to the office of the ministry of the divine Word and have ordained him by the imposition of hands and by extending to him the right hand of fellowship in the sacred ministry.

It now remains for us only to implore God, the best and the highest, the ruler of the world and the church, that He may prove himself to be the companion of his journey. May He bless his labors most abundantly and whatever plans he makes, whatever labors he undertakes, may He crown and advance them with the most desired success

Given in Heidelberg on the Calends of
May in the year of our Lord MDCCXXVII.
Director and Councillors of the
Senate of the Palatinate Church.
C. L. MIEG.   PL. PASTOIR.
P. R. FOLAD.

In view of this document there can be no longer any doubt that Mr. Weiss was actually the leader of the colony, at whose head he appeared in signing the declaration of allegiance on September 21, 1727.

Of the colonists who came with Weiss to Pennsylvania, apparently only four remained in Philadelphia, the rest scattered over the province. Those who are found among the Reformed members in Philadelphia are: Hans Michel Diel, Rudolf Wellecker, Hans Georg Kremer and Hans

Henrich Weller.[39] To Goshenhoppen went five, Johann Friedrich Hillegas, Johannes Huth, Hans Michel Zimmerman, Benedict Strohm, and Hans Georg Welcker. Alexander Dubendorffer appears later as a member at Great Swamp. Three settled at Skippack,[40] Hans Georg Bowman, Sebastian Smith and Ulrich Staffon [Stephen], and two in the Conestoga valley, Hans Georg Schwab and probably Leonart Seltenreich. The rest have not yet been found.

When Mr. Weiss appeared in Pennsylvania in 1727, he found the beginnings of religious life among the Reformed people in the province already in existence. In 1725 the beginning had been made by two laymen, by John Philip Boehm in the Perkiomen valley and by Conrad Tempelman in the Conestoga valley No sooner had Weiss heard that Boehm, a layman, was acting as a minister than he tried to stop him in his work. On October 2, 1727, he addressed a letter to Mr. John George Schwab,[41] one if his travelling companions, who had settled in the Conestoga valley, in which he informed him of his readiness to preach for the Reformed people at Conestoga, but also expressed his surprise

that Mr. Boehm allows himself to be used as a minister, indeed that he usurps such privileges and authority as do by no means belong to him, nor have been accorded to him by the clergy, as I have learnt, to my satisfaction from the ministers here, but that he assumes so important an office merely at the instigation of the peo-

---

[39] These names appear among others signed to a call which was given to Mr. Boehm by the Philadelphia congregation on April 20, 1734, see *Journal of P H S*, Vol VII, p 117, *Life and Letters of Boehm*, p. 233

[40] For these names see the letter of the Skippack congregation, dated May 30, 1730, printed below, p 58, and Dotterer, *Historical Notes*, p. 103.

[41] Printed in full in *Journal of P. H. S*, Vol. VII, pp. 51-53; also in *Life and Letters of Boehm*, pp 212-214

ple, while he cannot boast either of an external or of an internal call. . . . Wherefore I cannot conscientiously recognize Mr. Boehm as a Reformed teacher and preacher, until he submits to an examination and is ordained in Apostolic manner, which he will never be able to do.

Weiss followed up this letter with a personal letter addressed to Mr. Boehm[42] on November 28, 1727, in which he challenged his right to the ministry and summoned him to appear in the manse of the Presbyterian minister in Philadelphia for the purpose of being examined as to his qualifications for the ministry. Mr. Boehm, of course, ignored this letter, but his followers called upon Mr. Weiss to produce a proof of his own claims to be considered a regularly ordained minister. Weiss showed them his Latin certificate from Heidelberg, dated May 1, 1727, but none could read it. He was then challenged to produce a German certificate, which ordinary people were able to understand. As a result Mr. Weiss was compelled to write to Heidelberg, on December 3, 1727, and he received from the authorities there the following reply, dated April 26, 1728, of which he has also left a copy in the Catskill record book:[43]

CERTIFICATE OF PALATINATE CONSISTORY, APRIL 26, 1728.

Whereas Mr. George Michael Weiss, born in Eppingen, in the Electoral Palatinate and at present stationed as a High German Reformed minister at Philadelphia in Pennsylvania, under date of December 3rd, of the last year, made his report to the Consistory

[42] This letter of Weiss is translated and printed in *Journal of P. H. S.*, Vol. VII, p. 54 f ; *Life and Letters of Boehm*, p. 211 f

[43] First published by Dr. Weiser in his *Monograph*, p. 28 f, but with a number of minor inaccuracies, as my own transcript made directly from the record shows. My translation differs accordingly from his in a few places.

of the Electoral Palatinate concerning the present condition of religion and of the church affairs there—

And whereas, on this occasion he gave us to understand, that (although he received from this Consistory a Latin certificate of his life and doctrine at the time of his journey thither) he needs also a certificate in German, because of certain circumstances in which he is placed and especially on account of those who do not understand any other language [but German]:—

Therefore, we testify, as we did before, that he is not only orthodox in his doctrine and unblamable in his life, peaceable and sociable in his conduct, but he has also been found edifying in the sermons which he has preached on several occasions, and we have no doubt that, if the Lord grant him life and health, he will be of great usefulness under divine blessing and be a means of edifying many souls.

The infinitely good and merciful God and Father extend to him light and strength in full measure, from the fulness of his grace which is in Christ Jesus, that the work of the Lord now begun may, through his ministry, make great progress, that the wealth of the nations be brought to the Lord and their kings be led unto him.[43a]

Heidelberg, the 26th of April 1728.

(L.S.)   A. VON LULS.   L. C. MIEG.

When Mr Weiss shortly afterwards came in contact with the Presbyterian minister, at Philadelphia, Mr. Jedidiah Andrews, the latter formed an equally good opinion of him, for on October 14, 1730, he wrote a letter to his friend, the Rev. Thomas Prince of Boston, in which he paid Mr. Weiss a fine tribute. He wrote:[44]

There is, besides, in this Province, a vast number of Palatines, and they come in still, every year Those y^t. have come of late years are, mostly, Presbyt'n, or, as they call themselves, Reformed,

[43a] Cf. Isaiah 60: 11.
[44] First printed in *Hazard's Register*, Vol. XV, p. 200

the Palatinate being about three fifths of that sort of people; they did use to come to me, for baptism of their children, and many joined with us, in the other sacram't. They never had a minister, 'till about 9 [read 3][45] years ago, who is a bright young man and a fine scholar. He is at present absent, being gone to Holland, to get money to build a ch'ch, in this city; but they are scattered all over the country; those yt. live in Town, are mostly a kind of Gibeonites, hewers of wood etc. They are diligent, sober, frugal people, rarely charged with any misdemeanors. Many of 'em, yt live in the country and have farms, by their industry and frugal ways of living, grow rich, for they can underlive the Britons, etc. The first comers of 'em, tho' called Palatines, because they come lastly from that country, are mostly Switzers, being drove from the Canton of Bern, for they are Baptists,[46] and won't fight or swear. They don't shave their heads and are many of them wealthy men, having got the best land in the Province. They live 60 or 70 miles off, but come frequently to Town with their waggons, laden with skins, (which belong to the Indian traders), butter, flour etc. There are many Lutherans, and some Reformed, mixed among 'em. In other parts of the country they are, chiefly, Reformed, so that I suppose the Presbyt'n party are as numerous as the Quakers or near it.

The opposition of Weiss to Boehm's ministry instead of driving Boehm out of his office, induced the elders of his three congregations at Skippack, Whitemarsh and Falkner Swamp to appeal to the Classis of Amsterdam through the Dutch Reformed ministers of New York. The petition

[45] This statement has caused a good deal of discussion, see Weiser, *Monograph*, p. 17 f., and Good, *History*, p 117, note The easiest solution of the difficulty is to suppose a misprint of 9 for 3, because the letter as originally printed in *Hazard's Register*, Vol XV, p 200 f, uses the figure 9, not the word "nine," as the later reprints of the letter do.

[46] This statement refers to a colony of German Mennonites, who settled in 1709 and following years along the Pequea Creek in Lancaster County, see Rupp, *History of Lancaster County*, pp 72–114; C. H. Smith, *The Mennonites in America*, Scottdale, 1909, pp 134–181

Ordination of Boehm

of the consistories of Boehm's churches was drawn up in July, 1728. A preliminary answer was given by the Classis on December 1, 1728, and a final decision on June 20, 1729, in which the call, extended to Boehm by the people, was declared valid and the Dutch ministers of New York were asked to ordain Mr. Boehm. This ordination of Mr. Boehm took place in the Dutch Reformed Church in New York on November 23, 1729.[47] On the following day a public reconciliation between Mr. Boehm and Mr. Weiss (who had also been summoned to New York) took place, in which each promised to recognize the ministry of the other and confine himself to his own congregations, Mr. Weiss to Philadelphia and Germantown, Mr. Boehm to Falkner Swamp, Skippack and Whitemarsh. These promises were unfortunately not kept by Mr. Weiss, but he allowed himself to be persuaded by his followers to disregard them.

Of the ministry of Weiss at Goshenhoppen little is known, and all that we know comes from the pen of Mr. Boehm. The first communion service, on October 12, 1727, has already been referred to. In the same letter of Boehm, quoted above, he writes:[48]

> At the above mentioned Goschenhoppen on the same 12th of October and later on the 19th at Schipbach, that is in the very place in which I had been regularly called, and also on the 26th in Philadelphia, in these public assemblies he spoke of me by name and declared me to be an incompetent preacher, whom he did not regard as fit to administer the holy sacraments.

[47] The papers relating to the ordination of Mr. Boehm have been printed repeatedly. See *Mercersburg Review*, Vol XXIII (1876), pp. 528-557, *Ecclesiastical Records of the State of New York*, Vol. IV, pp 2425-2437, 2468-75, 2478-88, *Journal of P. H. S.*, Vol. VI, pp. 303-324; also *Life and Letters of Boehm*, pp 155-183.

[48] *Journal of P H. S.*, Vol VII, p. 56, *Life and Letters of Boehm*, p 216

In his report of 1739, Mr. Boehm writes of Goshenhoppen as follows:[49]

Of this congregation I know little, for it never wanted to be under our Church Order, but desired to be its own master. When Do. Weiss, as stated above, came into the country and created great confusion, they faithfully adhered to him.

It was during his ministry at Goshenhoppen that Mr. Weiss made numerous missionary tours throughout the province. Thus he preached repeatedly to the Reformed settlers in the Conestoga valley. He was also the first Reformed minister who preached at Oley, unless Rev. Samuel Guldin was there before him, of which, however,

we have no contemporaneous evidence. As to his activity at Oley, Mr. Boehm wrote as follows to Holland in November, 1730:[50]

Mr. Weiss celebrated the Lord's Supper, without previous preparation, at a place named Oley, where the sect calling itself the "New Born" (originated) and baptized at the same time several children, among (as is reported) were also Indian children, who as unbelievers, go about like wild animals, without knowledge of God or of his Word. Of which he boasted with his own mouth before Peter Zenger, sexton of the Reformed Church in New York, as the latter himself declared.

[49] *Minutes of Coetus,* p. 9.
[50] *Journal of P. H. S.,* Vol. VII, p. 58; *Life and Letters of Boehm,* p. 217 f.

Book of Weiss on Newborn

The contact of Mr Weiss with the New Born at Oley called forth the first book written by a German Reformed minister in Pennsylvania and printed there in 1729.[51] Its title may be rendered as follows in English:

The Preacher, / traveling about in the American Wilderness / among different nationalities and religions / and frequently attacked, / portrayed and presented / in a conversation with a / Citizen and a New Born. / Treating of different subjects but especially of / the New Birth. / Prepared and / brought to light out of his own experience and / for the advancement of the glory of / Jesus, / by George Michael Weiss, V.D M /
Printed at Philadelphia / by Andrew Bradford, 1729.

The purpose of the book was to show that the doctrines taught by the New Born were neither rational nor scriptural. Their rejection of prayer and of the holy scriptures, their repudiation of the ministry and of religious worship, including the sacraments, together with their claims of perfect sinlessness could not be accepted because they were against reason and Holy Scripture.

The reference to the baptism of Indian children at Oley, sometime between 1727–1730, is decidedly interesting It is by far the earliest Indian baptism in Pennsylvania known to the writer. That Weiss was much interested in the Indians is shown by a book which he wrote later in life at Burnetsfield, New York. The minutes of the Classis of Amsterdam, under date September 3, 1742,

[51] The only known copy of this exceedingly rare book was found by the writer in 1899 in the Congressional Library at Washington, D C. For an account of it see *Reformed Church Messenger* of March 9 and 16, 1899, also Dr. Sachse's *German Sectarians of Pennsylvania*, Vol I, pp. 155–159 It was reprinted and translated in *Penn Germania*, Vol I, pp. 336–361

DER
IN DER AMERICANI-
SCHEN WILDNUSZ
Inter Menschen von verschiedenen
Nationen und Religionen
Hin und wieder herum Wandeles
Und verschiedentlich Angefochtene
PREDIGER,
Abgemahlet und vorgestellet
In einem Gespraech mit Einem
Politico und *Neugebarenen.*
Verschiedene Stuck insonderheit
Die *Neugeburt* betreffende,
Verfertiget, und zu Beforderung der Ehr
JESU
Selbst aus eigener Erfahrung an das
Licht gebracht

Von Georg-Michael *Weiss* V. D. M.

Zu PHILADELPHIA.
Gedruckt bey *Andrew Bradfordt,* 1729.

refer to the receipt of a letter of Weiss, dated May 10, 1741:[52]

THE BOOK OF WEISS ON THE INDIANS, 1741.

This letter was accompanied by a package, in which the Rev. Weiss sends over: (1) A small painting of the wild men of North America, mentioned above in the letter. (2) "A faithful description of the savages in North America, as to their persons, characteristics, tribes, languages, names, houses, dress, ornaments, marriages, food, drink, domestic implements, housekeeping, hunting, fishing, war, superstitions, political government, besides other remarkable matters, composed from personal experience, by George Michael Weiss, V. D. M " Thus reads the title This description covers ninety-six and a half pages, in 8 vo , besides the preface [dedication], which is brief, to the Classis. In this he states the reasons which induced him thereto [viz. to prepare this book] and to communicate the same to the Classis. He doubted not that it would be agreeable to the Classis, and would be looked upon favorably, since he is cognizant of the paternal love which the Rev. Classis bears towards him. It ends with a wish for our prosperity and blessing. The introduction is signed at Albany, N. Y, by Rev. Weiss of Burnetsfield, October 4, 1741. Then follows the description itself.

Unfortunately no copy of this book has been preserved, which is much to be regretted, as his description of Indian manners and customs would no doubt have proved to be very interesting.

When Weiss came to Pennsylvania he found most of

[52] *Ecclesiastical Records of New York*, Vol. IV, p 2778 In a letter to the Classis on July 14, 1741, Weiss informs the Classis " that, inasmuch as he has had excellent opportunities to observe the ways of the wild men (Indians), and inasmuch as these people are very interesting, he has on several occasion spoken to them by means of an interpreter, about Christian doctrines, and has baptized many of them, at their request," *l c*, p. 2760.

the Reformed people there in great poverty, unable to pay their minister a decent salary. A letter of Rev. John B. Rieger and Dr. John Jacob Diemer sets forth the situation very clearly. They write to the Deputies of the Synods, under date March 4, 1733.[53]

For most of the people, who come hither and have no means, are compelled to sell themselves and also their children who generally must serve until their 20th year, as here in Philadelphia some hundreds are in the service of the English people, but have the privilege to attend our services. . . At Philadelphia, which is the capital, and where most of the grain is shipped, in order to convey it to other lands, there are but ten [Reformed] families, which are well-to-do, all the others are in service. Among the townships Schippach is the most thickly settled, where about forty families may be counted, but they are for the most part poor, and it is nearly thirty miles from the city The other localities are at a still greater distance.

When Mr. Weiss faced these conditions for the first time he felt much inclined to give up his work in Pennsylvania and return to Germany. This appears clearly in a statement of Jacob Reiff, which will be presented later in connection with his trip to Holland.[54]

Meanwhile, in order to increase his income, Weiss offered to give instruction in some of the subjects which he had studied in the University of Heidelberg.

Beginning with February 10, 1730, and continuing through eight successive weekly issues of the *American Weekly Mercury;* printed by Andrew Bradford in Phila-

[53] This letter is preserved in the Synodical archives at the Hague, 74, I, 15. The numbers of the documents at the Hague are quoted according to the number given to them in the printed catalogue, entitled *Catalogus van het Oud Synodaal Archief,* bewerkt door H. Q Janssen, 's Gravenhage, 1878

[54] See below, p 46.

delphia, Weiss had the following notice inserted in that paper:

This is to give notice, that the subscriber hereof, being desirous to be as generally useful as he can in this country (wherein he is a stranger) do declare his willingness to teach Logick, Natural Philosophy, Metaphysicks etc. to all such as are willing to learn. The Place of Teaching will be at the widow Sprogel's in the Second Street, Philadelphia, where he will attend, if he has encouragement, Three times a week for that Exercise.

N. B. All persons that come, either as Learners, or Hearers, will be civilly Treated. By G. M. Minister of the Reformed Palatine Church.

In the first insertion he signs himself "G.M.," then twice "G. Michael," then six times, from March 3–April 6, 1730, in full "G. Michael Weiss."

It is very doubtful whether the people of Philadelphia at that time, struggling for the very necessaries of life, cared much about being instructed in the mysteries of philosophy or the abstractions of metaphysics. At any rate, a month after the last advertisement we find Weiss preparing to return to Holland for the purpose of raising there some money for his needy churches.

THE COLLECTING TOUR OF WEISS AND REIFF TO HOLLAND, 1730–31.

It is interesting to trace this new undertaking of Weiss to its origin. When three years later [in 1733], Jacob Reiff was cited into court, to give an account of the moneys collected in Holland, he stated:[55]

He [the defendant] further answereth and saith that the said congregations of Philadelphia and Skippack in conjunction with their minister George Michael Weitzius (alias Weiss) did *prefer a petition to the excellent Classis of Divinity in the United Provinces,* which petition this defendant saith was signed and subscribed by the church wardens or elders of both the said congregations of Philadelphia and Skippack and (as this defendant remembers) it set forth the unhappy and necessitous condition of the said congregations and prayed the charitable donations of the said Classis, and this defendant *delivered the said petition to Dr. Wilhelmus* in the Bill named. This defendant believes a report was spread in Pensilvania that collections of money had thereupon been made, and that *before such news arrived the said George Michael Weitzius (alias Weiss) had prepared to return to Holland or Germany,* and that upon receiving the said news the said congregations or one of them might entreat him to stay, to which the said George Michael Weitzius (alias Weiss) might make such answer as in the complainants said bill of complaint is set forth, and might promise to serve them to the utmost of his power; and this defendant doth acknowledge himself to have been a *member* of the German Reformed Church of Skippack from its first establishment, but not of the German Reformed Church of Philadelphia, as in the bill charged. And this defendant doth deny that he usually traded into Holland or Germany, as in the complainants said bill of complaint is falsely suggested, other than and except that this defendant went over there in the year of our Lord one thousand seven hundred and twenty seven to fetch his relations and laid out his money (as

[55] See papers in Reiff Case, printed in *Reformed Quarterly Review,* Vol XL (1893), p 61.

passengers generally do) in goods fit for sale in this country. And this defendant saith that before or since that time he never carried on any trade to or from Holland or Germany (except as hereinafter mentioned). And this defendant doth admit that he was acquainted with Doctor Wilhelmus in the bill named, and was informed by him that a collection had been made in favor of said congregations of the German Reformed Church of Philadelphia and Skippack to the amount of about two hundred guilders, but knows not of his own knowledge what sum was collected. And this defendant saith that the said Doctor Wilhelmus requested him this defendant to receive the monies so collected for use of the sd. congregations of Philadelphia and Skippack. But this defendant absolutely refused so to do, having been informed by letter from some of his friends in Pensilvania that some of the members of the sd. congregations were jealous or entertained some suspicions of this defendants' honesty, or to that purpose. And this defendant saith that he this defendant returned to [from] Holland from [to] Pennsylvania in August in the year of our Lord 1729.

From this statement a number of important facts can be gathered:

1. The Reformed congregations of Philadelphia and Skippack had drawn up a petition, addressed to the Reformed Classis of Holland, asking for a collection to be taken up in their behalf.

2. This petition was personally delivered by Jacob Reiff to Dr. Wilhelmius, then pastor in Rotterdam. And, as Reiff, according to his own statement, went to Holland only once before his journey in 1730, namely in 1727, when he intended "to fetch his relations," this petition must have been written and was delivered in 1727.

3. Weiss had become so disheartened in Pennsylvania, that even before an answer to this petition was received, he had made up his mind to return to Europe, and it was only when it became apparent that the people of Holland

had acted favorably upon the petition that he promised his congregations in Pennsylvania to serve them to the utmost of his power.

4. That when Reiff returned from Germany to Holland, Dr. Wilhelmius offered to turn the money collected for the Reformed congregations of Philadelphia and Skippack over to him, but Reiff refused to accept it, as he had learnt from letters that his honesty had been questioned in Pennsylvania.

5. Reiff returned to Philadelphia in August, 1729. The lawyer, who wrote Reiff's answer to the bill of complaint, evidently exchanged the prepositions "to" and "from." In 1729 Reiff returned "from" Holland "to" Pennsylvania and not vice versa.[56] This is shown by the immigrant lists, for on August 19, 1729, Reiff landed in Philadelphia on the ship Mortonhouse, from Rotterdam. With him were Johannes Reif, evidently a relative, Wendel Wiant, Jacob Sellser [Selzer], Johann Peter Moll, who settled in Goshenhoppen; Richard Fetter and Hans Michael Fröhlich, who became members of the Reformed congregation at Philadelphia; David Montandon, who is found in Skippack in 1730 and Johan Philip Ranck and Conrad Wörntz, also Reformed people, who settled in the Conestoga valley. It is not impossible that Reiff was really the leader of this whole company.

The petition of 1727, which Weiss and his consistories addressed to the Classes of Holland and which was delivered to Dr. Wilhelmius, found its way to the Synod of

[56] This conclusion is made absolutely certain by a sentence which occurs a little later in the same document. "On the contrary this defendant saith that on his return from Holland to Pensilvania in the year of our Lord as aforesaid . he had no thought or design of going abroad any more"; *l. c., p* 62

Synods of Holland

North Holland. In the minutes of the North Holland Synod, dated July 27–August 5, 1728, we read:[57]

> The corresponding delegates of the South Holland Synod recommended Philadelphia, from which this Christian Synod also received a letter, containing a request to take up a collection for them, for the building of a new church by our fellow believers who have fled thither from the Palatinate.

This is the very first reference in the minutes of the North Holland Synod to the Reformed congregations in Pennsylvania. Weiss's petition of 1727 has, therefore, the distinction of being the first link in the chain which brought the Reformed churches of Holland and Pennsylvania together and was the beginning of a union which lasted 65 years (1727–1792).

But Weiss had written not only to Holland, he had also addressed himself to the consistory of the Palatinate. In the German certificate, which the Upper Consistory of the Palatinate signed for him on April 26, 1728, it is distinctly stated that in asking for this certificate in a letter dated December 3, 1727, he had "made a report to the Consistory of the Electoral Palatinate concerning the present religious and ecclesiastical affairs there."

The effect of this letter can also be traced in the Holland records, for at the meeting of the South Holland Synod at Woerden, from July 6–16, 1728:

> The president read a letter addressed to this Christian Synod by the Great Consistory of Heidelberg, containing a request to receive something for the building of a Church in Pennsylvania by our fellow-believers, who have gone thither from the Palatinate, because they are compelled to conduct divine service under the blue sky. It has been thought, that under the blessing of the Almighty, this affair [undertaking] might result in a large blessing for the

---
[57] *Ecclesiastical Records of New York,* Vol. IV, p 2424

Church and, therefore, it was resolved to recommend it earnestly to the Classes

This letter is also the first one on record, by which the South Holland Synod was made acquainted with the condition of the Reformed people in Pennsylvania. Thus we are brought to the important conclusion that in July, 1728, the attention both of the North and the South Holland Synods was drawn to the Reformed churches of Pennsylvania through the influence of the letters of Weiss, written in 1727. The appeal of Mr. Boehm's congregations, written to the Classis of Amsterdam in July 1728, did not reach Holland till November, 1728. On November 14, 1728, it is first mentioned in the Classical Minutes.[58] Hence it is evident that the letters of Weiss must be given the credit of having first directed the attention of the "Fathers" in Holland to the struggling Reformed churches in Pennsylvania.

When Mr. Weiss heard that, in answer to his letters to Holland and the Palatinate, collections had been taken in Holland for the poor Reformed settlers in Pennsylvania, he determined to return to Holland, in order to take charge of this money personally. Before he left he arranged several farewell services with his adherents at Skippack. On May 17, 1730, John Philip Boehm wrote about them as follows to the Dutch Reformed ministers in New York:[59]

Then he [Weiss] stayed away [from Skippack] for some time until now, on the 30th of April, he returned at the request of the seceders, and held the preparatory service and on May 1st celebrated the Lord's Supper. He likewise preached on the 7th, being Ascension day, and again to-day. They are all called farewell

[58] *Ecclesiastical Records of New York,* Vol IV, p. 2440
[59] *Journal of P. H S.,* Vol VII, p. 47, *Life and Letters of Boehm,* p 208.

services. Moreover, after these sermons and at other occasions he baptized various children and married people. He thus revealed what intention he had in mind during all this time. Through all this our poor congregation, which has been completely split by him, has been kept thus far in such harmful division and strife.

Boehm had also heard about the object of Weiss's journey and was not at all pleased with it. He regarded it only as a means of strengthening still more the opposition to him. Continuing the above quoted letter to New York, he wrote:

Moreover he [Weiss] is now setting further mischief on foot, for he has resolved to cross the ocean with the avowed intention of going to Holland to receive the money which, he claims, has been collected there in answer to his letter. He intends to put this out at interest, so he can live on it. Then he is going to return. Through this the poor seceding members, who have been driven into rebellion through him, will still further be hardened.

When Weiss was ready to leave, his elders associated Jacob Reiff with him, a well-to-do man and member of the Skippack congregation, for they feared that Weiss might be persuaded to stay in Holland or return to Germany. In that case Reiff was to take charge of the collected money and also try to secure them another minister. That this was the reason why Reiff was associated with Weiss is asserted in a letter of Rev. John B. Rieger and Dr. John Jacob Diemer, written on March 4, 1733, to the Synodical Deputies. They write in the course of their letter:[60]

When Dominie Weiss, about three years ago, resolved to go to Holland and Germany to present our need to good-hearted souls eager to advance the honor of God, a doubt arose in the minds of some of us, whether he might not allow himself to be persuaded to remain in Germany, whereby our good efforts would prove fruitless. For this reason we associated with him Jacob Reif, a naturalized citizen of this country and a well-to-do man, who intended to travel to Germany, and we gave him a special power of attorney, by virtue of which he was requested to take charge of the collection, in case Weiss would not return, and act in accordance with the orders of the consistory of Amsterdam and Rotterdam

That a possible change of ministers was contemplated appears also from a statement made by Do. Wilhelmius before the Synod of North Holland, held at Enkhuysen, July 29–August 7, 1732. The minutes of that meeting state:

Do. Wilhelmius has heard that the Society of Merchants has bought a large district in Pennsylvania, but intended to sell this land again, for which purpose J. Ryff has traveled to the Palatinate. The said Mr. Wilhelmius had proposed Mr. Hottinger to J Ryff, with the view of sending him to Pennsylvania, for the purpose of organizing the Church there. About this matter J. Ryff had written to Wilhelmius, that he had spoken to Mr. Hottinger about it and that he was not without hope that Mr. Hottinger could be persuaded to do this

From these two documents we learn incidentally that Jacob Reiff had other reasons for going to Holland and Germany in 1730. He was traveling in behalf of a so-

[60] The original is in the Hague archives, 74, I, 15

ciety of merchants as a land agent, and probably induced a number of those who are later found as his traveling companions on the ship "Mortonhouse" to go with him to Pennsylvania.

Reiff himself hotly denied in his answer to the bill of complaint preferred against him in 1732, that he had any other motive for going to Holland in 1730 except to serve the congregations of Philadelphia and Germantown. He said:[61]

ANSWER OF REIFF TO BILL OF COMPLAINT, SEPTEMBER 4, 1733.

[This defendant] denies that he did acquaint the said congregations, church-wardens or elders, or any person or persons whatsoever, that he intended a voyage to Holland and from thence to Frankfort in Germany, or that he should be glad of the company of the said George Michael Weitzius (alias Weiss) or that he would willingly assist him in doing any service he could to his brethren of the Reformed Church of Philadelphia; or that if he should stand in need of any money for that purpose or for his own private wants that he this defendant would furnish him, or anything to that or the like purpose, as in the said bill of complaint is falsely suggested But on the contrary this defendant saith that on his return from Holland to Pensilvania in the year of our Lord 1729 as aforesaid (or any time afterwards till prevailed on as hereafter mentioned) he had no thought or design of going abroad any more. But several of the church-wardens or elders of the said congregations of Philada and Skippack and the said George Michael Weitzius (alias Weiss) frequently applied to the defendant and earnestly entreated him to go to Holland and Germany once more, to accompany and assist the said George Michael Weitzius (alias Weiss) in collecting and receiving monies collected and to be collected for the use of the said congregations. And the better to prevail on this defendant to comply with their request, they voluntarily and of their own accord faithfully promised that they would

[61] *Reformed Quarterly Review*, Vol XL, p. 61 f.

reimburse and pay to him this defendant all costs and charges and expenses that he should be at in the said voyage, and that they would likewise pay and allow him any reasonable satisfaction for his time and trouble therein. But this defendant often refused to take the said voyage, this defendant being then employed in carrying on certain buildings on his plantation at Skippack, and it was likely to be very prejudicial to this defendants affairs. And this defendant saith that in order to get rid of their importunities he endeavored to get some other person to undertake the said voyage in his stead and accordingly offered £5 out of his own pocket to one Hans William Rohrich who was willing to go But neither of the said congregations thought fit to trust him. And this defendant saith that by the continued importunities of the said members of the said congregations, their elders or church wardens and minister, induced by their fair promises expecting that agreeable thereto he should be reimbursed all the charge and expense he should be at and be also generously rewarded for his trouble, and upon the said elders or church-wardens signing an instrument for that purpose, he the said defendant was at length prevailed upon to undertake the said voyage, tho' hazardous, troublesome and very prejudicial to this defendants affairs and interest, and the great displeasure and uneasiness of his most intimate friends and relations. And this defendant saith that true it is a power was given to this defendant signed by the elders or church wardens of both the said congregations of Philadelphia and Skippack, but denies that the said power is of the purport or contents in the bill set forth or that he was thereby enjoined to observe the directions of the Classis in Holland, as may appear by the said power now in the defendants possession and ready to be produced to this honorable court, a copy whereof is to this defendants answer annexed, which this defendant prays may be taken as part of this his answer.

This power of attorney, written in incoherent German, with several words left out, as well as poorly spelled, was, according to Reiff's copy [presumably correct] as follows:[62]

[62] Reiff's copy of this power of attorney is in the Harbaugh collection of manuscripts; printed in the *Reformed Quarterly Review*, Vol. XL, p. 58.

POWER OF ATTORNEY GIVEN TO REIFF, MAY 19, 1730.

Forasmuch as our pastor, Mr Weiss, has resolved to take a journey, accompanied by Jacob Reiff, to England and Rotterdam, for the purpose of receiving the collection which is said to be lying ready there, [intended] for the erection of a church in this country; authority is herewith given to Jacob Reiff to take entire charge, so that Mr. Weiss may be expedited on his immediate return with the same to Pennsylvania. Therefore we also entrust everything to his good conscience, and give him plenary power in everything. In testimony whereof we subscribe our names Given at Philadelphia, May 19, 1730

We hereby request Jacob Reiff to arrange matters in such a way that, if Pastor Weiss should or would not return to this country,[63] he, Reiff, may at once bring with him a minister from Heidelberg, and provide him with whatever is most necessary, because if monies collected should be no longer on hand, we deem is unnecessary that Mr. Weiss proceed further in his journey, but that, according to his best judgment, Jacob Reiff should deliver the letters at their proper destination and personally ask for a reply thereto.

Signed by all the elders of the two congregations at Philadelphia and Skippack:

[Philadelphia]	[Skippack]
J. DIEMER, D.M.P.	WENDEL KEIBER
PIETER LECOLIE	DEOBALT JUNG
JOHANN WILLEM RORIG	CHRISTOFFEL SCHMITT
HENRICH WELLER	GERHART (G.I.H.) INDE HEVEN
GEORGE PETER HILLENGASS	GEORGE REIF
HANS MICHEL FROLICH	GEORG PHILIP DODDER
MICHEL HILLENGASS.	

It is significant of the state of affairs that Reiff admits in his answer to the bill of complaint "that at the time when the said power was given, the said George Michael

[63] This statement shows that there was still a lurking suspicion in the minds of some of his members that Weiss would not return to Pennsylvania

Weitzius (alias Weiss) was absent and this defendant believes it was given without his knowledge."

When Weiss and Reiff left for Holland they took with them several letters. The consistory of the Dutch Reformed congregation at Neshaminy, Bucks County, sent through Mr. Reiff a letter, dated May 3, 1730, to the Rev. David Knibbe of Leyden and the Rev. John Wilhelmius of Rotterdam,[64] asking them to issue in their name a call to a minister for the Dutch Reformed church in Bucks County at a salary of sixty pounds, and sending at the same time a sum of money to pay his traveling expenses. Two other letters, dated May 10, 1730, almost identical in contents, were sent by the followers of Weiss at Skippack, one to the Classis of Amsterdam, the other to the Classis of Rotterdam. As these letters have not been published before, we offer herewith a translation of the letter to the Classis of Amsterdam, which is the more interesting of the two, because 41 signatures of people living at Skippack in 1730, are affixed to it. It reads as follows :[65]

LETTER OF THE SKIPPACK REFORMED CHURCH TO THE CLASSIS OF AMSTERDAM, MAY 10, 1730.

Very Worthy, Very Learned, our Highly Respected Gentlemen of the far famed Classis of Amsterdam.

A whole congregation ventures, upon the request of the elders and deacons of the Reformed Church and Congregation at Skippack, to submit this present letter to the very Reverend Classis of

[64] This letter, together with the old church records of the congregation, is now in the archives of the Theological Seminary at New Brunswick, N. J It was translated and published by the writer in a paper, read before the Bucks County Hist Society, January 19, 1918, on the *Life and Work of the Rev. Peter H. Dorsius*

[65] The original of this letter is in the archives of the Classis of Amsterdam, " Pennsylvania Portfolio," new letters, No 4

Letter of Skippack Church

Amsterdam with the request to look upon it with favorable eyes. It is indeed a great comfort to us here in this wilderness that a Reverend Classis has taken our affairs somewhat to heart, which favor we are certainly unable to appreciate sufficiently with a thankful spirit, yet it pains us that we are unable to accept and recognize Mr. Boehm as our minister, in whose behalf a letter was addressed to the Reverend Classis, in the name of the congregation at Schibach This is due to the fact, that he did not hesitate, without our knowledge and against our will, to deceive with a false statement your Reverences, for whom we have and shall always maintain the highest respect. For in our name and with the addition of some signatures he asked and petitioned a Reverend Classis about things which we have not even thought of. We recognize that, in answer to Mr. Boehm's supplications, the Reverend Classis had the best interests of the Reformed Congregation in view and acted very wisely, but it was certainly desirable that Mr Boehm should have made the same profession of his intentions here in this country as before a Reverend Classis, so that we would not be compelled to annoy you with complaints.

We, the whole congregation in the neighborhood of Schibach creek, are well satisfied with our minister, Mr. Weiss, who, in answer to a regular call and upon our repeated requests and desires, undertook the service of the ministry among us. We are deeply grieved that he is to be taken from our congregation. It appears to us so hard, because we feel as if we were no longer worthy to hear the Word, which is the only saving means of grace, from a duly ordained minister of God's Word, who insists on a virtuous, loving and God-fearing heart. We can have great confidence in a man, who leads a good life, but little in one who has a restless head and mixes too much in worldly affairs. Rev. Mr. Weiss read on December 7, 1729, after his sermon at Schibach, the decision of the Reverend Classis regarding the ordination of Mr. Boehm which had taken place. But, as we were greatly dismayed about this, we asked Mr Weiss to spare us in this, as we could not possibly accept Mr. Boehm and recognize him as a minister. The letter which Mr. Boehm had written some time ago to the Reverend

Classis, had not been sent with our knowledge and consent. Now the Reverend Classis can easily see what to think of Mr. Boehm's petition and how he deceived us all.

We hope that for this reason the Reverend Classis will not take it amiss, inasmuch as we do not wish to give thereby offence to the whole Reformed Church nor any occasion for slander to the manifold sects in this country.

However, we heartily forgive Mr. Boehm for what he has done in this matter, if only he will give up his purpose. We herewith request the Reverend Classis to favor us with a reply in so important a matter, in order that we may be governed by it and not be hindered in our divine services.

With all dutiful respect all of us remain greatly indebted to the Reverend Classis,

Schibach, May 10, 1730.

The most submissive and obedient servants of the Reverend Classis, Deacons and Elders of the Congregation at Schibach:

WENDEL KEUPPER	GERHART (G I.H.) INDFHEVEN
CHRISTOPHEL SCHMITT	HANS GEORG REIFF
DEWALD JUNG	JACOB KELLER
JOHANNES SCHOLL	MARTE HILTEBEUDEL
JOHANNES LEFEBER	ULRICH STEFFEN
JOHANNES LEMAN	JOHAN JACOB ARNDT
JOST FERER	HANS ADAM (H M) MAUER
FELIX GUTH	JOHANN PHILB RIED
HENRICH H HUWER	PHILLIPS HENRICH SÓLLER
JERG (G) GERNAN	JOHANNES LEBO
VALENTIN (V H A) HANS AMEN	BASTIAN SCHMIT
LORENTZ SCHWEITZER	HANS FILB STEINHEINDIG
JOHANNES (O) WILLHE	JACOB HEIDSCHUH
PETER WENCE	JOST SCHEULER
NICKLAS LÖSCHER	JACOB HANF
CHRISTIAN WEBER	DAVID MONTANDON
PETER BORGER	HANS JERG BAUMAN

CARL LUDWIG KEIPPER
ANDREAS HACK
LUDWIG SCHEIER
WILIHELM SCHMIT

FRIDERICH SCHOLL
JACEL LEIDY
GEORG PHILIB DODDER.

The point made against Boehm in this complaint was of course poorly taken. In order to have a valid petition Boehm did not need to have the signatures and consent of all the members of his congregations. It was enough that he had the signatures of all his elders. The plaint of the seceders at Skippack amounts simply to this, that Boehm did not take them, his enemies, into his confidence. There was no deception in that and no sensible man can blame him for not doing it. It was the part of wisdom to keep his own counsels.

Before Weiss and Reiff reached Holland the Synod of South Holland had been held July 4 to 14, 1730, at Breda,[66] at which its president, Rev. Dr. Wilhelmius of Rotterdam, read a lengthy report. In it he stated among other things that the number of Reformed confessors from the Palatinate then in Pennsylvania was 15,000. They were increasing year by year through new arrivals. Only a few weeks before the meeting of Synod, three ships with 600 emigrants had passed through Rotterdam. The same report was also read before the Synod of North Holland, held July 21 to August 3, 1730. As a result of this report the church of Pennsylvania was earnestly recommended to the benevolence of the Classes.

Weiss and Reiff arrived in Holland shortly after the sessions of these Synods. We first meet them at Haarlem[67]

[66] There is no evidence that Weiss and Reiff were present at the Synod of Breda Their names are *not* mentioned in the minutes of that meeting

[67] These dates are based on the list of contributions printed in the writer's "History of the Reiff Case," in Mr Dotterer's *Historical Notes*, p 153 There are three contemporaneous copies of this list. (1) In the

on August 10, where the Rev. Jacob Geelkerke handed them fl. 390, collected by the Synod of North Holland. A few days later, on August 15 to 16, they were at Rotterdam, where the Rev. Alardus Tiele gave them, by order of the Synod on South Holland, held at Kuilenburg in 1729, fl. 696.12, and the Rev. Barth. Van Velse handed over the contributions of the Synod just held at Breda in 1730, namely fl. 79. At the same time they appeared before the Synodical Deputies, whose minutes of August 15 to 16, 1730, give us the following information

WEISS AND REIFF BEFORE THE SYNODICAL DEPUTIES

1. The Deputies of the Synods have requested the Rev. Classis of Schieland to appoint some of her midst to make further inquiries, in accordance with the resolution of the Rev. Synod of South Holland, held at Breda, regarding the report touching the churches in Pennsylvania, which had been presented to the Synod. They hear with much satisfaction from the mouth of the president, Do. Wilhelmius, that a good opportunity will be afforded to do this, because the Rev George Michael Weitzius, minister at Philadelphia and an elder of that congregation[67a] are at present in Rotterdam.

2. Who having been interviewed at length by the Deputies about the condition of the church and the contents of the memorial, presented before Syond, it was resolved to further discuss the matter with them tomorrow at the house of Do. Wilhelmius.

3. Having met here, the above mentioned Do. Weitzius

(a) presented to the Deputies his certificate of examination and the commission given to him by Upper Consistory at Heidelberg,

Harbaugh manuscripts (see *Ref Quarterly Review*, Vol XL (1893), p. 68 f.); (2) in the Minutes of the Synodical Deputies, under date April 13-16, 1739 (see Dotterer's *Historical Notes*, p 153); (3) in the letter book at the Hague, 74, II, 3. pp. 15. 16.

[67a] Reif was *not* an elder, but only a member of the Skippack Church, see *Life and Letters of Boehm*, p. 237, see also his own statement, above, p 46

dated May 1, 1727, and renewed by the said Consistory on April 26, 1728.

(*b*) He gave an account of the large number of Reformed people in Pennsylvania, who have been served hitherto by him alone and by a certain Philip Beem [Boehm], who has set himself up as a teacher, although being without education and having no proper call, but who through wrong information was examined, it seems, and admitted to the ministry by one of the ministers of New Netherland, upon the order of the Rev. Classis of Amsterdam, about which the congregation at Philadelphia and at Skippack wrote a letter to the Classis of Amsterdam and also to the Classis of Schieland, dated May 30, 1730, signed by forty-four persons, requesting that the above mentioned Beem might not be forced upon them as their minister.

(*c*) He accepted the request to prepare a chart, showing the different colonies of the Palatines, the distance of one from the other, and how many churches ought to be built there for their service and how many shepherds or teachers would be necessary to serve them properly, and he agreed further to give a detailed written account concerning the whole condition of the land and the Palatines living therein.

The minutes of the meeting of September 12 to 14, 1730, add: "This report came after the close of the sessions and was communicated to the Deputies."

It is very unfortunate that this report and chart of Weiss are no longer in existence, for they would have given us no doubt important information regarding the various German settlements in the province and the earliest Reformed congregations.

On September 4, 1730, Weiss and Reiff were in Amsterdam, where they appeared before the famous Classis of that city. The Classical Minutes states that·

Do G. Mich Wijs, minister at Philadelphia, appeared with an elder of Schibach and made known that the congregation at Schibach, from which also a letter had been received, is very much disturbed and in great confusion, because the congregation refuses to recognize Do. Boehm as a properly ordained minister, who has been installed as their pastor, in accordance with the order of this Classis, by the ministers of New York, which can be seen in the Acts of January 11, 1729. His Reverence requested this Classis to take such measures as would restore the peace of the congregation. Whereupon the Deputies for foreign affairs were asked to investigate this matter carefully and present their recommendations to this body.

Further his Reverence requested a contribution to build a church at Philadelphia in Pennsylvania, which congregation is recommended to the charity of all the congregations under the jurisdiction of this Classis.

The two travelers remained in Amsterdam for several months. On October 18, 1730, the burgomasters of the city permitted them to collect fl. 600. A list of contributions spread out upon the minutes of the Synodical Deputies under date April 14, 1739, shows that this sum was actually collected. The permit issued to them has been translated and printed several times, but as it is desirable to have all the documents, bearing on their stay in Holland, put together in one place, we may be pardoned for repeating it in this connection, with a few minor corrections:[68]

PERMIT OF BURGOMASTERS OF AMSTERDAM, OCTOBER 18, 1730

The Burgomasters and Magistrates of the City of Amsterdam, upon the report made to their Honors by George Michael Weiss, minister, and Jacob Reiff, elder, as commissioners of the Reformed congregation at Philadelphia, concerning the miserable condition of the said congregation, consisting in general of poor and needy

[68] A contemporaneous copy of this permit in Dutch, from which the above translation was made, is found at the Hague, Vol 74, II, 3

people, who were compelled by religious persecution or from lack of subsistence to emigrate thither, and after long and expensive journeys had to settle there empty handed; and being without places and opportunities for the exercise of their religion, and for the propagation of the Christian Reformed religion, have resolved, in order to so far come to the aid of these poor banished brethren in the faith, in the attainment of their desires, as to grant and permit to their aforesaid commissioners, being assisted by John Peter Bolthuysen, a resident of this city, that these same, within this city and its jurisdiction, may visit the homes of the good citizens and residents and may solicit of the same most courteously the gifts and donations of their Christian sympathy, such as they may be willing to contribute to them; moreover, that they may accept such gifts and contributions with gratitude to the amount of six hundred guilders and no more.

Done at Amsterdam on the 18th of October 1730.
By ordinance of their Excellencies aforesaid
(L.S)   S. B. ELIAS.

On October 19, 1730, the consistory of the Reformed Church at Amsterdam gave fl. 150, through Rev. John Visscher, pro tem. president of Synod and on the following day the diaconate added fl. 600, through Wm. Coevenhoven, deacon

During October and November private persons in Holland contributed fl 217, so that the total of all the contributions received was fl. 2132 12.

The last reference to the presence of the two delegates in Holland is found in the minutes of the Classis of the Hague, which mentions, under date November 6, 1730, a Latin letter of Do. Weiss, addressed to the Classis, in which he asked for their help and encouragement.

The later movements of Weiss can fortunately be traced by an account which he submitted in May, 1738. At that time he made a trip from German Flats, N. Y., to Skippack, Pa., in order to bring the long standing "Reiff Case" to a final settlement. At a conference held at Skippack, Weiss submitted the following paper to be signed by his former elders. He did not succeed in getting them to sign it, but they made a copy of his statement, which ultimately fell into the hands of John Philip Boehm, who promptly forwarded it to Holland.[69] The statement of Weiss was as follows:

STATEMENT OF WEISS REGARDING MONEY COLLECTED IN HOLLAND.

SCHIPACH, May 8, 1738.

Account, made with J. Reiff, concerning the collected money, which he received in my presence in Holland at Rotterdam, Haarlem and Amsterdam, from the respective donors, of which he made the following disposition, namely:

Receipts, according to the collection book added together in sum total .... fl. 2104.—

Expenditures, being for necessary expenses:

1. For voyage from Philadelphia to London without the provisions taken along ....£18.—
2. For provisions in London during about one month, with the duty for myself and Jacob Reiff . . . .£5.sh.7.d.6.
3. For passage from London to Rotterdam for each 15sh. sterling, 1 chini [guinea] for the bed and 3sh. sterl. for the board.
4. Expenses for half a year's board in Holland and necessary travels, 700 Dutch guilders.
5. At Rotterdam, shortly before my return to London, Jacob Reiff gave me 250 Dutch guilders, with which I paid to passage from Rotterdam to London (when J. Reiff remained in Holland, 15sh one chini [guinea] for the bed, 6sh. for the board.

[69] Boehm's copy is in the Pennsylvania Portfolio of the Classical Archives, No 20

The passage from London to Maryland £8 —without the provisions taken along.

The journey from Maryland to Philadelphia by sea £3,sh.12,d.1. Board in London 16sh.

In addition for my labor and trouble I ask £50 for the year.

N.B   Jac Reiff declares to have paid me for clothes and books 110fl.14 stuivers.

When pounds and shillings are referred to, sterling money is meant.

This statement reveals the fact that Weiss stayed in Holland six months. Since he arrived about August 10, 1730, he must have left it about February 10, 1731. Then he returned to Pennsylvania by way of London and Maryland.

Besides collecting about fl. 2100 for the congregations of Philadelphia and Skippack and rousing much interest for the Reformed people in Pennsylvania, the visit of Weiss in Holland had another important result. It led to the publication of the first printed report regarding the Reformed Church in Pennsylvania, which was laid before the Synod of South Holland, convened at Dortrecht from July 3 to 13, 1731, and was ordered printed by that Synod. The minutes of that meeting state regarding it:

MINUTES OF SOUTH HOLLAND SYNOD ON REFORMED CHURCH IN PENNSYLVANIA, JULY 3-13, 1731.

The Reverend Deputies of the Synod reported, that, in obedience to the resolution of Synod, they had gathered full information, with the assistance of the commissioners of the Reverend Classes of Delft and Delftland as well as of Schieland, from the lips of Do. Georgius Michael Weitzius, minister at Philadelphia and from his elder, who have come over hither [to Holland],[70] as well as from

[70] This statement proves that the "Berigt" of 1731 was based on the reports of Weiss, but it was not actually written by him, as has been stated

thorough reports and letters, regarding the condition of the churches in Pensylvania, which consist of 30,000 baptized members, among whom are about 15,000 [adult] members They were served hitherto by only one minister, namely the aforesaid Do. Weitz, besides by another, Philippus Beem [Boehm], who, however, has had no [preparatory] studies nor a call, but was forced upon the congregation rather than elected by it They are now busy with the building of a stone church with materials from that country. They will need in course of time at different places four other churches, together with a minister and schoolmaster for each. . . .

Furthermore, the Reverend Deputies read before Synod a draught of a church order [constitution], composed at the express request of the Palatine colonists in Pennsylvania, by their Reverences together with the Commissioners of the Classis of Delft and Delftland, as well as those of Schieland, which according to their opinion (subject to correction) can be introduced to a large extent into the distant churches, in harmony with the usages of the Palatinate. . .

The Christian Synod is of the opinion that the Reverend Deputies and Commissioners of the Classes of Delft, Delftland and Schieland ought to be thanked for the trouble and efforts expended in this far-reaching affair and for the draught of a church order which has been read.

This draught should be printed as quickly as possible, so that during the sessions of this Synod[71] their Reverences, the corresponding delegates as well as the members of Synod, may be provided with copies and thus be better able to express their opinion regarding it, that if necessary, the draught may be changed or amended and then be sent as soon as possible to the congregation [in Pennsylvania]. The commisioners for this affair shall put such a title

repeatedly. There is reason to think that the author of the "Berigt" was the Rev John Wilhelmius, see *Life and Letters of Boehm*, p. 306, note 190.

[71] The Synod at which all these events happened was the Synod of Dortrecht (or Dort), held in 1731, and not the Synod of Breda of 1730, as has been stated by Dr Good in his *History of the Reformed Church in the United States*, p. 136, and repeated by Dr Corwin, *Manual of the Reformed Church in America*, 4th ed., p. 897.

or statement upon it as shall make it evident that this draught is only an advice or counsel which the Deputies of this Synod, together with the Commissioners of Delft, Delftland and Schieland, drew up at the request preferred to them, so that no suspicion may be provoked by it. This was done and the copies [of the draught] were handed over to the members present and to each Classis, according to the number they had asked for.

Copies of this printed report have come down to us. One was bought by the writer in Holland for his friend, the Rev. Prof. J. I. Good, D.D. It is entitled:

Berigt, / en / Onderrigtinge, / nopens en aan de Colonie / en Kerke / van /, Pensylvanien. / Opgestelt en Uytgegeven door de Gedeputeerden van / de E. Christelyke Synodus van Zuyd-Holland, / benevens de Gecommitteerden van de / E Classis von Delft en Delfsland, / en Schieland.

Title page, one page of introduction and 18 pages of text, in small quarto.

The title reads in English:

Report and Instructions, concerning and for the Colony and Church of Pennsylvania. Prepared and published by the Deputies of the Rev. Christian Synod of South Holland, together with the Commissioners of the Rev. Classis of Delft, Delftland and Schieland.

As the title indicates the booklet consists of two parts: (1) a report, covering five pages, (2) an instruction for the regulation of the churches there, pp 6–18.

The report gives a brief description of Pennsylvania, its location, climate, nature of soil, products, metals and inhabitants. It then traces its history from the first occupation of the country by the Swedes, to its surrender to the English in 1665 and its acquisition by Penn in 1681 It refers to the establishment of Philadelphia and the efforts of Penn to attract settlers to the colony It states that many inhabitants of Germany were attracted to Pennsylvania, Mennonites, Lutherans and Reformed, but that the last were nearly half of the whole population or about 15,000. This is, of course, a greatly exaggerated figure. Of the Reformed people it is said that, being without religious services, many had gone over to the Quakers. Four years ago [1727] their first minister had arrived, Weiss, under whom they had formed a congregation at Skippack, but that one minister and one church was not sufficient for the widely scattered Reformed settlers. Therefore they needed the help of the Reformd Church of the Netherlands. With their help even the Indians might be reached and converted. The log church at Skippack should be replaced by one of stone and four additional churches should be erected.

The second part of the pamphlet, called instruction, proposes the complete organization of the Church in Pennsylvania, looking forward even to the formation of a Classis, but demanding of its ministers subscription to all the formulas of unity, adopted by the Synod of Dort, including the Heidelberg Catechism, Belgic Confession, Decrees as well as Post-Acta of the Synod of Dort.

Two remarkable facts should be noted with regard to this proposed constitution for the Reformed churches of Pennsylvania. The first is that it exerted absolutely no influence upon the constitutional history of the Reformed Church. Mr. Boehm clung tenaciously to his own constitution, drawn up in 1725, which had been permitted by the Classis of Amsterdam in 1729, and which became the constitution of the Coetus of Pennsylvania in 1748. The other fact is that the opponents of Boehm circulated an interpolated manuscript copy of this constitution, written it was claimed by Do. Wilhelmius in Rotterdam, which declared that the church in Pennsylvania was an altogether independent church and could choose as their ministers whomsoever they pleased Through this letter the opponents of Boehm tried to justify their existence of a separate organization.[72]

When Weiss returned to Pennsylvania, in the summer of 1731, he found the churches of Philadelphia and Germantown under the care of another minister and as the Reformed congregation at Huntersfield, Schoharie County, N. Y., gave him a call, he accepted it and removed to the State of New York.[73]

Before Weiss left Philadelphia, however, he requested and received the following letter of commendation from his elders at Philadelphia. Of this letter, too, he has spread a copy upon the church record at Catskill, from which the writer copied the original German recently. The following is a translation of this certificate:

CERTIFICATE GIVEN TO WEISS BY PHILADELPHIA REFORMED CHURCH.

Copy of the Attestation given to me by my late congregation at Philadelphia in Pennsylvania, after I had received a letter from Schohary, not far from Albany.

Inasmuch as our late pastor, the Rev Mr. G. M. Weiss, has now resolved to leave Philadelphia and go to Albany, to enter there

[72] A copy of this forged letter of Wilhelmius was sent to Amsterdam by Boehm It is in the Pennsylvania Portfolio of letters at Amsterdam, new letters, No 10 It is printed in full in *Life and Letters of Boehm*, pp. 303-311

[73] After a short ministry Weiss left Huntersfield in February, 1732 A testimonial given him at the time of his removal, February 22, 1732, from the Huntersfield congregation, is spread upon the Catskill record Weiss received and accepted a call from the Dutch Reformed Church at Catskill, N Y., dated February 8, 1732. He opened the Catskill record on February 25, 1732 His last baptism there was entered into the record July 6, 1735

upon his calling, according to the divine providence, a credible testimonial is given him herewith by the congregation here, that, according to the obligations of a minister, he discharged the duties of his office piously, faithfully and diligently and led such a Christian life that the whole congregation was well satisfied with him, as we also wish him the blessing of God for his undertaking. In testimony of which and in the interest of truth we, the elders of the Reformed Congregation, have hereunto set our signatures and affixed our seals.

Given in Philadelphia, the 22nd of September 1731.

JOH. DIEMER, (L.S.)   PIETER LECOLIE   (L.S.)
                       JOHANN WILHELM RÖHRIG   (L.S.)
                       HENRICH WELLER   (L.S.)
                       CONRAD REIFF   (L.S.)
                       GERHARDT IN DE HEFFEN   (L.S.)

With this letter Weiss left Philadelphia and went to his new field of labor in the state of New York.

CHAPTER II.

MINISTRY OF REV. JOHN PETER MILLER, 1730–1734.

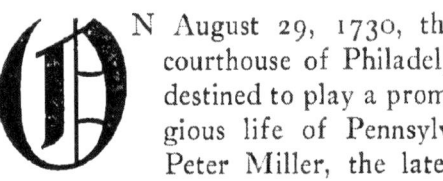N August 29, 1730, there appeared in the courthouse of Philadelphia a man who was destined to play a prominent part in the religious life of Pennsylvania. It was John Peter Miller, the later monk at Ephrata, who came to Pennsylvania as a Reformed candidate of theology.

The life of John Peter Miller has often been sketched,[74] but no one has ever attempted to gather together all the documents bearing on the few years which he spent as minister of the Reformed Church in Pennsylvania. This shall be our aim, to shed as much light as possible upon his short career as a Reformed minister.

On December 29, 1725, there registered in the matriculation book of the University of Heidelberg "Johannes

[74] For earlier accounts of Peter Miller see Harbaugh, *Fathers of the Reformed Church*, Vol. I (1857), pp. 301-311; Dubbs, *Historic Manual of the Reformed Church*, 1885, pp. 175-187; Good, *History of the Reformed Church in the United States*, 1725-1792, Reading, 1899, pp. 160-165; Dubbs, *Reformed Church in Pennsylvania*, 1902, pp. 94-99; Sachse, *German Sectarians of Pennsylvania*, Vol. I, passim; also "John Peter Miller" in *The Pennsylvania German*, Vol. I, No. 2 (April, 1900), pp. 3-17; also *Life and Letters of Boehm*, pp. 44-48.

Petrus Mullerus, Altzbornensis." Alsenborn is a village about two and a half German miles northeast of the city of Kaiserslautern, in the Rhenish Palatinate, now a part of Bavaria.

In the Burial Register of the Ephrata Community for the year 1796, John Peter Miller is recorded as having "died September 25, 1796, aged 86 years, 9 months."[75] Counting back 86 years and 9 months from the day of his death we are brought to December 25, 1709, as the day of his birth

Of his life in Germany nothing is known except a brief allusion which occurs in a letter from Ephrata signed K., a letter that was published in the *Berliner Monatschrift* of 1784, to which the late Prof. Jos. H. Dubbs first called attention.[76] After giving a somewhat discouraging account of the condition of the Ephrata community, the writer makes the following reference to Peter Miller:

Peter Miller, the only educated man (in the society) studied in Heidelberg and was authorized to preach, but not to baptize. With thirty guldens in his pocket he left his father. Afterwards he preached in this country, and at the request of a German country congregation was ordained by the Presbyterian clergy of Philadelphia. After four years he resigned his congregation, was converted, baptized others and was himself baptized; and six months after the organization of this society he joined it. Previously he had lived as a hermit.

A correspondence carried on with the Reformed pastor at Alsenborn, shortly before the Great War, brought to light some facts regarding the family of Peter Miller. His father was the Rev. John Muller, who from 1708–14

---

[75] Sachse, *The German Sectarians of Pennsylvania*, Vol II, p. 516 This statement is corroborated by the inscription on his tombstone, see below, p 95

[76] Dubbs, *The Reformed Church in Pennsylvania*, p 98, note 99

was pastor at Zweikirchen and Wolfstein, near Kaiserslautern. Later, from 1714–26, he was pastor at Alsenborn, and from 1726–41 pastor at Altenkirchen, near Homburg in the Rhine province. He died at Altenkirchen May 11, 1741. His son, John Peter Muller, must have been born at Zweikirchen, during his father's pastorate at that place. Unfortunately neither the church nor the church records of Zweikirchen are now in existence, so that we are unable to supply further details However, we now know that the reference to Alsenborn in the matriculation book at Heidelberg does not mean that John Peter Muller was born there, but that it was his temporary home, because his father was pastor there, when he matriculated in the university.

On August 29, 1730, a list was presented in the courthouse at Philadelphia, containing the names of seventy-five men, who with their families making in all about two hundred and sixty persons, were imported in the ship *Thistle* of Glasgow, Colin Dunlap,[77] master, having come from Rotterdam, but last from Dover, England, as by clearance from that port. They subscribed the "Declaration of Fidelity and Abjuration" Among these names is "Peter Muller," in bold German characters.

With Miller came a number of persons whom we afterwards find as members of the Reformed Church at Goshenhoppen. They are: Valentin Giiesemer, Hans Jacob Diehl, Thomas Hamman, Abraham Transu, Hans Simon Mey. Lonhart Hochgenug, Bernhard Siegmund and Johannes Scherer became members of the Reformed Church at Philadelphia and Christian Leman appears in 1734 at Skippack, while John Henrich Schmidt is enrolled in the same year as a Reformed deacon in Falkner Swamp.

[77] The correction "Calvin Dunlap" in the *Pennsylvania Archives,* 2d Ser, Vol. XVII, p. 20, is entirely unjustified

Soon after his arrival Peter Miller came in contact with John Philip Boehm, who was at that time (1730) the only ordained Reformed minister in the province Miller called on Boehm in his home and had with him a lengthy conversation, of which Boehm sent the following report to Holland, in a letter dated November 12, 1730:[78]

LETTER OF BOEHM REGARDING MILLER, NOVEMBER 12, 1730.

Meanwhile no peace can yet be expected, for there arrived this fall another man, named Miller, whose father is pastor in the Electoral Palatinate, under the inspectorate of Kaiserslautern He likewise avails himself of the liberty of this country, and so far has been preaching to the seceders at Schipbach, as the enclosed letter, marked F, shows He has promised them, as also the people in Philadelphia and Germantown, to take the place of Mr. Weiss until the latter returns In order to carry this out successfully, he betook himself to the Presbyterians in Philadelphia (because he is unordained), that he might be ordained by them. This he told me himself in my house on October 19th, saying that in the preceeding week he had handed to them his confession of faith concerning the points they had asked of him, and expressing the hope that the affair [of his ordination] would be concluded in the following week, which so far as I know has not yet taken place.

I warned him in a friendly way and advised him to go to the reverend ministers of New York and endeavor to have his ordination take place in accordance with the church-order of the Reformed Church, whereby it would stand a better test before the world. To this he replied, that such a course was far too circuitous for him, if he could gain his end by a shorter way, he would take it, as there was no great difference in it. Moreover, he said, he would like to know who had given authority to the Classis of Amsterdam to rule over the Church in this country. He thought the King of England was more important than the Classis of Hol-

---

[78] *Journal of P. H. S.,* Vol VII, pp 36–38; *Life and Letters of Boehm,* p 199 f.

land. Then I answered that it was asking too much who had given her the authority, and that I did not care anything about that, but that I believed, if the Classis had no such authority she would not have taken us under her care and supervision, that I for one was subject to her and would always be glad to act under her direction, etc. Then I received this fine reprimand: "There is such a glorious liberty in this country that the people themselves are free to elect, accept and also dismiss their preachers. It is not right to attempt to deprive them of this liberty and to subject them to a Classis, which can then force upon them such ministers as she desires. Christians have liberty and are in this world under no head, Christ alone is their head in heaven."

He also remarked that the people had called me only temporarily, until they could get another minister. I showed him my call. He said there was nothing in it, that they had called me for life. Then I answered him "The Reverend Classis had recognized it as a lawful call, if he was wiser than the Classis, he would have to take it up with her. I furthermore reminded him, that I also regarded Christ as the head of his church, yet I believed that Christ ruled his church on earth through agents, wherefore I would rather be under supervisors divinely appointed, in order to preserve good order in the Church of Christ, than stand up on my own freedom." On this point he did not agree with me.

It is interesting to see the difference in the character of these two men, thrown into such strong relief in this conversation. Boehm methodical, exact, strong for order and church government, firmly attached to the customs and traditions of the fathers, seeing in them the safeguards of the Church. Miller, easy-going, chafing under restraint, glad to be free from the restrictions of the old world, caring little for traditions and customs, or even for the visible Church. To his sanguine temperament the ideal and spiritual alone appeals. He thinks of the liberty of the children of God and the glory of the invisible Church. This conversation furnishes us therefore the key to his later conversion.

The elders of Skippack, writing with Mr. Boehm to the Reformed ministers of New York, under date November 5, 1730 (in the enclosure, marked F, referred to the above), make the following statement about Miller:[79]

> The harmful division, caused in our congregation by Mr. George Michael Weiss and continued by him until his departure from here, contrary to all order and the solemn covenant made with him, all this has hitherto been kept up by Mr Miller, who came to this country this fall. Coming into this country as an unordained minister and willing to be ordained by the Presbyterians in Philadelphia (as we hear), we have no other prospect before us but a continuous division in our poor congregation. Our hope for a good and God-pleasing harmony, established in brotherly love, which we expected to be able to report with rejoicing, after the departure of Mr. Weiss, has been entirely taken away from us through the above mentioned Mr. Miller.

The same unwillingness which the people of Skippack manifested to submit themselves to the supervision of the Classis of Amsterdam, appeared also in Philadelphia, under the inspiration of Weiss and Miller, for Boehm writes again:[80]

> With respect to the Reformed people of Philadelphia, I have been compelled to hear repeatedly, with a sad heart, from several of them the reply, (when I recommended the good work to them): "We are here in a free country, and the Classis of Holland has no right to give us any orders." This statement, however, has been prompted, as I believe, by the persuasion of Mr. Weis alone, which is now continued by Mr. Miller.

It is rather curious to see how eager these independents

---
[79] *Journal of P. H S.*, Vol VII, p 59, *Life and Letters of Boehm*, p 219
[80] *Journal of P. H. S*, Vol VII, p 44; *Life and Letters of Boehm*, p 205.

Ordination of Miller in Philadelphia.

were to accept the benefactions of the Classis of Amsterdam, but when it came to accept their well meant advice, they drew the line. Consistency, thou art a jewel!

We must now turn to the story of Miller's ordination by the Presbyterians in Philadelphia.

On September 19, 1730, the Presbyterian Synod of Philadelphia passed the following resolution:[81]

> It is agreed by Synod, that Mr John Peter Miller, a Dutch probationer, lately come over, be left to the care of the Presbytery of Philadelphia to settle him in the work of the ministry.

Unfortunately the minutes of the Philadelphia Presbytery from 1717 to 1732 are lost, so that it is impossible to give the exact details. A well known letter of Rev. Jedidiah Andrews, from 1698 to 1747 pastor of the old Buttonwood Presbyterian Church, supplies the omission partially. It was written on October 14, 1730, to his friend, the Rev. Thomas Prince, pastor of the Old South Church of Boston. In it he writes:[82]

> There is lately come over a Palatine candidate of the ministry, who having applied to us at the Synod, for Ordin'n, 't is left to 3 ministers to do it. He is an extraordinary person for sense and learning We gave him a question to discuss about Justification, and he has answered it, in a whole sheet of paper, in a very notable manner. His name is John Peter Miller, and speaks Latin as readily as we do our vernacular tongue, and so does the other, Mr. Weis.

Many years afterwards Peter Miller himself wrote the following account of his ordination to a friend in a letter dated December 5, 1790:[83]

---
[81] *Records of Presbyterian Church,* Vol I, p 99.
[82] *Hazard's Register,* Vol XV, p 201
[83] *Hazard's Register,* Vol XVI, p. 254.

As concerning our transactions during that long term of our residence at Ephrata, I wish I could satisfy thine curiosity. I have published a *Chronicon Ephratense,* of which I could make thee a present, if thou art master of the German language. However I will do something to satisfy thee. In August 1730, I arrived at Philadelphia, and was there at the end of said year upon order of the Scotch Synod, ordained, in the old meeting house by three eminent ministers, Tenant, Andrews and Boyd.

Peter Miller served the congregations, Skippack, Germantown and Philadelphia, according to Boehm's letter of November 12, 1730, till the fall of 1731. On September 21, 1731, the Rev. John Bartholomew Rieger arrived at Philadelphia, who became Miller's successor in these congregations.

On November 22, 1731, the Reformed congregation of Philadelphia wrote to the Rev. Dr. Wilhelmius of Rotterdam:[84]

In order that the minister's chair might not remain vacant, since Mr. Weis has left us, we have, sometime ago, elected and accepted as our teacher the newly arrived Candidate Rieger, to whose planting and watering among us the Lord may grant his blessing from on high.

As a result we find Miller turning to the interior German settlements. He first appears at Goshenhoppen. In

[84] The original is in the Hague archives, 74, I, 10.

his report of 1739, Mr. Boehm locates him definitely at Goshenhoppen:[85]

Of this congregation [Goshenhoppen] I know little, for it never wanted to be under our church-order, but desired to be its own master. When Do Weiss, as stated above, came into the country and caused great confusion, they faithfully adhered to him. When he traveled to Holland in order to obtain the well known moneys collected there, they immediately clung to Miller, who, assisted by another person, continued to serve Goshenhoppen. By their services at Skippack, they kept the congregation there in a state of continued restlessness, which had been begun by Weiss. All my petitions, entreaties and warnings were in vain

In course of time Miller extended his activity. In 1733 we find him ministering to the Reformed people in the Conestoga valley, Lancaster County, and in the Tulpehocken valley, Berks County.

On March 4, 1733, Rev John B Rieger and the Philadelphia physician, Dr. John Jacob Diemer, write in a letter to the Synodical Deputies:[86]

The church at Conestoga and vicinity has a preacher by the name of Joh. Petrus Muller, who was ordained in the Presbyterian church here. He administers divine services there [at Conestoga]. The churches at Schippach, Germantown and Philadelphia have a preacher who came over a year and a half ago, Bartholomeus Rieger, who has taken the place of Do. Wys He preaches one Sunday at Schippach, the second at Germantown and the third at Philadelphia.

We learn still more about the activity of Miller in the Conestoga valley from a very important letter of Conrad Tempelman, who did for the Conestoga valley what Mr. Boehm did for the Perkiomen valley. He began the first

[85] *Minutes of Coetus*, p 9
[86] The original is at the Hague, archives 74, I, 15.

Reformed services in that region. In this letter Tempelman writes to the Synods of North and South Holland under date February 13, 1733:[87]

LETTER OF CONRAD TEMPELMAN REGARDING THE REFORMED CHURCH IN CONESTOGA, FEBRUARY 13, 1733.

The church at Chanastoka took it origin in the year 1725, with a small gathering in houses here and there, with the reading of a sermon and with song and prayer, according to their High German church order, upon all Sundays and Holidays, but, on account of the lack of a minister, without the administration of Baptism and of the Lord's Supper.

Thereafter Dominie Bohm served them, at first [1727] voluntarily at the request of the people, later, after being fully ordained, he administered baptism and communion to them for the space of two years [1730–1731], upon a yearly call, although he lived a distance of 21 hours [about 63 miles] away from them, being satisfied with their small, voluntary gifts. He also subsequently established a church-order [constitution] among them and the congregation chose elders and he himself exercised a strict and careful supervision, so that things went on in good order in this congregation.

Further the writer reports that the congregation, on account of its enlargement and the great distances between the members, has divided itself into six meeting-places in Chanastoka, whereof three places are served by a Reformed minister, Johan Peter Muller, by name, by whom also another strong congregation is served about seven hours [21 miles] distant, called Dalbenhacken [Tulpehocken].

But that they now, by reason of the division of the congregation, cannot any longer be served by Do. Boehm, as also not by the aforesaid Muller, both by reason of the great distance of the localities and because of the manifold occupations and heavy labor wherewith he is overburdened. . . .

[87] Only an abstract of Tempelmann's letter in Dutch has been preserved at the Hague, archives 74, I, 14

Letter of Tempelman

The entire north side, 20 hours [60 miles] distant from Philadelphia, named Chanastoka (which is no town, but a tract of land so named after a certain creek) is settled by Germans and English There are three of the meeting places of the Reformed people, covering an area 7 hours [21 miles] long and 7 hours [21 miles] wide. But they say further, that they can give no report to the Rev Christian Synods of the 3 places, ministered unto by Do Muller. Nevertheless they hope that the said preacher will make known his own needs (inasmuch as he cannot well subsist by the free-will gifts of his people) as well as the condition of his congregation and his elders. . . .

Regarding the three first named meeting places they give further report to the Rev. Christian Synods [Classis] of Amsterdam and Rotterdam, concerning the members and elders belonging to them, with the autograph signatures of the latter.

It is signed

Conrad Tempelman

Reader of the Congregation

(N.B. He seems to be the writer of the letter.)

Members 55, Elders:	Rudolf Heller	(L.S.)
	Michel Albert	(L.S.)
	Andries M .	(L.S.)

At the second meeting place there are the following number of members and elders:

Members 51, Elders:	Hans Georg Swab	(L S.)
	Johannes Gohr	(L S)
	Conrad Werns	(L S.)

At the third meeting place there are the following members and elders:

Members 30, Elders:	Johann Jacob Hook	(L S.)
	Andries Halsbrun	(L.S.)
	Nicolaus	(L.S.)

The fact that Tempelman has given us the names of the elders of these congregations enables us to identify them.

The first of these preaching places is now represented by Heller's church in Upper Leacock township.[88] The second is the Cocalico church near Ephrata, and the third is the Lancaster church. Its elder, John Jacob Hock, was elected the first pastor of the Lancaster church in 1736.

As to the congregations served by Miller, we can only speak with some degree of probability. One was probably Muddy Creek, for in the Lutheran Muddy Creek record two children are recorded as having been baptized by Peter Miller, one on January 20, 1730[31], the other on February 3, 1733.[89] The second congregation seems to have been Reyer's Church (now at Brickerville), Elizabeth township, where Tempelman made entries in an old church record, beginning with the year 1735. The third was most likely Zeltenreich, near New Holland, where a Reformed Church was in existence in 1744, ministered to by Jacob Lischy.

Sometime during this period (1730–1734), probably before the division into six preaching places had occurred, Miller also preached at Cocalico, near Ephrata, for in a list of pastors of that congregation, drawn up in 1766 by the Rev. John George Wittner, the name Peter Miller occurs. As this important list has never been published, it may be well to insert it here in full, with some comments:

[88] A full discussion of the evidence was given by the writer in the *Reformed Church Messenger* of January 4, 1900, also by Prof Jos. H. Dubbs, D D, in the "Earliest Church in Lancaster County," a paper read before the Lancaster County Historical Society, *Proceedings*, Vol V (1900), No. 1 See also *Life and Letters of Boehm*, p. 64

[89] A photographic reproduction of that page is given by Dr Sachse in his *German Sectarians in Pennsylvania*, Vol I, p. 237

LIST OF ALL THE TEACHERS AND PASTORS WHO FROM THE FIRST BEGINNING HAVE OFFICIATED IN THE CONGREGATION AT THE COCALICO, OR THE SO-CALLED KELLER'S CHURCH

[1] Bohm [John Philip].
[2] Bechtold [otherwise unknown].
[3] Hoock [John Jacob, of Lancaster].
[4] Tempelmann [John Conrad].
[5] Wieser [otherwise unknown, unless it be George Michael Weiss]
[6] Rieger, post et Med D. [John B. Rieger, afterwards Doctor of Medicine].
[7] Fock [Lewis Ferdinand Vock].
[8] Peter Miller, in Ephrata Jaibetz.[89a]
[9] Loscher [unknown, unless it be Jacob Lischy, who preached at Cocalico].
[10] Joh Waldschmidt [1752-1762]
[11] Deckert [John Henry Decker, 1762-1763]
[12] Friz Muller [Frederick Casimir Muller; 1763-1765].
[13] Berger from Reading, supplied the congregation for two years.
[14] J G Wittner [1766-1770].
[15] Joh Christoph Gobrecht [1770-1779].
[16] Anthony Hautz [1786-1790, September]

The first part of the list up to the fourteenth minister is in the handwriting of Rev. Mr. Wittner, by whom the record was begun. With regard to the earlier entries (Nos. 1-9) it should be noted that they are *not* in strict chronological order. Hence from the position of Peter Miller after Vock, who was pastor in 1750, it should not be inferred that Peter Miller served the congregation after that time, when he was Prior of the convent at Ephrata. The Reformed people would never have permitted that. The only safe inference to make is that Peter Miller was one of the early pastors of the congregation, while other evidence makes it certain that Mr. Wittner did not insert him in his proper chronological

[89a] In Ephrata Peter Miller adopted the name Jabez, based on I Chronicles 4 9 It is there explained as meaning "Borne with sorrow." It refers no doubt to his remarkable conversion. The words "in Ephrata Jaibetz" were added about 1786 by Anthony Hautz.

place. This applies equally to all the other early ministers from the first to the ninth.

In the light of all the available evidence, I offer the following *chronological* list of the earlier pastorates:

1725—Origin of the German Reformed Church in the Conestoga valley
1725-1727—Religious meetings in private houses conducted by Conrad Tempelman.
1727, October 15—First Reformed Communion service in the Conestoga valley. Brief ministry of Rev. John Philip Boehm
1728-1729.—Ministry of George Michael Weiss.
1730, May 30.—Formal organization of the Conestoga Congregation, now Heller's in Upper Leacock township
1730-1732—Origin of the Reformed congregations at Lancaster and Cocalico, and probably also at Muddy Creek, Reyer's and Seltenreich
1733, February 13—Six Reformed preaching places in existence in the Conestoga valley.

REFORMED MINISTERS AT COCALICO, NOW BETHANY, NEAR EPHRATA [90]

1. Ministry of John Philip Boehm, 1730-1731.
2. Ministry of John Peter Miller, 1731-1734.
   Miller's conversion, 1735, May.
   Visit of Boehm to Conestoga, 1735, May 11
3. Ministry of Bechtold, 1735-1736

The ministry of Peter Miller at Tulpehocken has left its traces in several documents.

Miller himself, in the Ephrata Chronicle (Engl. Ed., p. 70), gives the following account:

At that time the region of Dulpehakin was settled entirely by Protestants. These had agreed among themselves not to suffer among them any who were differently minded; so that many who were of like persuasion came to them. But shrewdly as they contrived it, God yet at last set up his candle on a candlestick in that then dark region, as will soon be narrated These now had called the afore-mentioned P.M. [Peter Miller] to be their teacher,

[90] A history of the Cocalico congregation was given by the writer in the *Reformed Church Messenger*, January 4-18, 1900, and continued in the *Reformed Church Record*, February 15-March 1, 1900.

which office he served among them and in other places during four years.

The Moravian church record of Tulpehocken, now preserved in the archives at Bethlehem, tells the following story of the origin of the Lutheran congregation there and Peter Miller's ministry among them:[91]

In the year 1723 Tulpehocken was first settled and inhabited by people who had dwelt in Schocheri Most of them were brought under conviction and made restless in their hearts while still residing in Schocheri [Schoharie] through Bernhard von Thieren, who was their pastor there, and who had promised these people also to move to Tulpehocken and continue to be their minister. But he made only occasional visits, administered the Lord's Supper at various times, baptized also the children and then went back again to Schocheri. There came also at times a preacher named Henckel from Falkner Swamp to visit us and administered occasionally the Lord's Supper He advised us to build a church, which was done in 1727. Peter Muller a Reformed preacher also came to us and preached sermons for almost two years. Afterward he went among the Seventh Day people [Siebentager].

It was during the ministry of Peter Miller at Goshenhoppen that the three Reformed congregations in the Goshenhoppen district first come into view.

Old Goshenhoppen appears first in the year 1730. On November 12, 1730, Rev. John Philip Boehm wrote to the Classis of Amsterdam.[92]

[91] The claim of the writer, in the *Reformed Church Record* and in the *Reformed Church Messenger*, to have "discovered" this record in the Bethlehem archives has been questioned (*History of the Lutheran Church in Pennsylvania*, p. 447, note 520) The facts in the case are as follows In the summer of 1902 the writer spent five weeks in the archives of the Moravian Church at Bethlehem and found there among other documents this church record It was spoken of as a discovery (in the articles mentioned above), because *it was at that time unknown to Reformed historians.*

[92] *Journal of P H S*, Vol. VII, p 43 f *Life and Letters of Boehm*, p. 204

The same action [namely a request for organization] was taken in another small congregation, of about fifteen families, with the same humble request to the Reverend Classis. It is situated about ten miles from here The place has as yet no definite name, but it is called after the river on which it lies Bergjamen [Perkiomen].

As there is no other Reformed congregation along the Perkiomen Creek, about ten miles from Boehm's home in Whitpain township, than Old Goshenhoppen, we have little hesitation in identifying the two names. This identification is indirectly corroborated by the fact that, according to the Old Goshenhoppen Lutheran record, "in the year 1732 a warrant was taken up jointly by the Lutherans and the Reformed. In the fall of that year a union schoolhouse was built upon this land." In this schoolhouse, the first of its kind in the charge, the religious services of the congregation were no doubt held.

In 1734 the congregation at Great Swamp appears for the first time. On December 12, 1734, Rev. John Martin Boltzius, a Lutheran minister at Ebenezer, Georgia, wrote to Dr. G. A. Francke, head of the Institutions at Halle, Germany:[93]

In the above mentioned Great Swamp there is also a small Reformed congregation, which has its own pastor.

In a preceding reference to Great Swamp the writer remarked:

Not far from Oley is the Great Swamp, where the Evangelical [Lutheran] congregation has a preacher named Kaspar Steber [Stoever], whom the Rev. Schultze had ordained before his departure. This Steber is at present involved in a quarrel with his congregation, because they do not want to give him the salary that was promised to him They are said to promise often something,

[93] Quoted in Muhlenberg's *Selbstbiographie*, Allentown, 1881, p. 213.

but when the minister preaches and applies the truth too strongly, they become rude and refuse to pay the minister's salary.

The Reformed pastor in Great Swamp in 1734 can hardly be any one else than Peter Miller. This is corroborated by a letter of Boehm, who in a report to the Holland Synod, dated October 18, 1734, refers distinctly to Peter Miller's activity in the Goshenhoppen district. He writes.[94]

> Nevertheless one of them is still in this country, namely, Peter Miller When this man could not bring the people over to his opinion, he quitted the ministry altogether and he is now an oil-miller But what he was after, and thought of persuading the people to do, is plainly to be seen from this, overlooking everything else: About two years ago he went with one of his elders, whom he had installed in the congregation at Goshenhoppen into the house of a Seventh Day "Tumpler" [Dunker], and there they allowed themselves to be called brethren and to have their feet washed by him; and this is the truth, whereupon followed his complete apostasy.

The two references of Mr. Boehm to Peter Miller's activity in Goshenhoppen, the one made in 1734 and the other in 1739 (already quoted above), definitely settle the fact that from 1731 to 1734 Peter Miller was the Reformed pastor in Goshenhoppen. This is corroborated by the New Goshenhoppen church record, in which 69 baptisms were entered by one hand from June, 1731, till July, 1734. At one of these baptisms, on April 16, 1732, "Johann Peter Müller" acted as sponsor. This is no doubt the pastor. As these are the only baptisms which Peter Miller most likely entered himself, we reproduce the page bearing his name in facsimile.

Miller's inclination toward the Ephrata Community

---
[94] *Coetus Minutes*, p. 2 f.

began in 1732. Two years later it led to the surrender of his ministerial functions. But it was not till May, 1735, that Miller actually joined the Seventh Day Dunkers by public immersion. This act of Miller threw the Reformed people into consternation, as can be seen clearly from the accounts of Boehm, describing this remarkable and important event. On January 14, 1739, Mr. Boehm wrote as follows to Holland, regarding the Conestoga congregation:[95]

Then Do. Weiss slandered me in this congregation by a very abusive letter, which I have in my possession. He thereby misled them and drew the congregation to himself. But soon afterwards he again left them, whereupon Miller went there to carry on the work of Weiss. At that time Miller drew also Tulpehocken to himself. I warned them frequently against this false spirit, but the misguided and simple-minded people clung to him, until finally the deception, with regard to which I had warned them so faithfully came to light, and this Miller publicly went over to the wicked sect of the Seventh Day "Tumpler" [Dunkers] and was baptized in Dunker fashion at Conestoga in the month of April 1735.[95a] He took with him about ten families, Lutheran and Reformed, from the congregation of Dolpihacken [Tulpehocken] who followed his example

This caused a great alarm among the congregations. Those that were kept by God sent therefore again messengers and letters to me and once more asked for help, which I did not dare to refuse. Hence I again went to them, and there were on May 11, 1735, in the above mentioned first congregation or Hill church, at Conestoga, 92 communicants.

It is interesting to place alongside of these statements

[95] *Coetus Minutes*, p 8

[95a] Miller himself stated repeatedly that this baptism took place in May, 1735. See *Ephrata Chronicle*, Engl Transl, p 73; also Miller's letter of December 5, 1790, quoted below, p 92

Conversion of Miller 89

of John Philip Boehm the well known account of Peter Miller himself in the Ephrata Chronicle:[96]

> The Superintendent [Conrad Beissel] soon after found occasion to make a visit to Tulpehocken with several of his disciples, where he was received by the teacher [Peter Miller] and elders with the consideration due to him as an ambassador of God. While on his return the teacher and C.W. [Conrad Weiser], an elder, accompanied him over the mountains for six miles The result of their visit in Tulpehocken was that the teacher, the elders and several others withdrew from the church; whereupon a venerable Pietist, by the name of Casper Leibbecker, took the teacher's place in the church. Among these seceders was C.W., an elder of the Lutheran faith, a man who had received from God remarkable natural gifts and sound judgment. . . .
>
> Accordingly they were baptized together under the water, after the teaching of Christ; which was done on a Sabbath in May of the year 1735. Thus the teacher, the schoolmaster, three elders, besides various other households, went over from the Protestants to this new awakening.

These same events are briefly reviewed and an excellent description of Peter Miller, as he appeared to his contemporaries, is given by the Rev. Israel Acrelius, Provost of the Swedish Churches in America and Rector of the Old Swedes Church, Wilmington, Deleware. In his well-known "History of New Sweden," he gives a description of his visit to Ephrata, which he made on September 7, 1753, in company with his friend, George Ross. After describing the cloister and the religious life fostered there, he draws the following pen-sketch of Peter Miller himself:[97]

[96] See English edition, pp 71, 73.
[97] Acrelius, *History of New Sweden* (Memoirs of the Hist Society of Pa, Vol XI), Philadelphia, 1876, p. 374.

There was also a brother named Jabez, who, before his rebaptism was called Peter Muller. He had been a German Calvinistic Minister, came into the country, according to their custom, as a candidate for the Ministry of the Reformed Church of the country, was afterwards ordained by the Presbyterian Minister, Mr. Andrew, in Philadelphia, and for a long time preached in the various parts of the country among the Germans before that, eighteen years since [1735], he betook himself to Ephrata. He is a learned man, understands the Oriental languages, speaks Latin, discusses theological controversies as well as other sciences; although, in his present condition he has forgotten much. He is of a good stature, with a friendly face and friendly manners, on which account strangers always get introduced to him, and seek his society. He is open-hearted toward those to whom he takes a liking, and is modest and genial. The brethren have great respect for him, and not without reason, for he is a prudent man, upon whom their order chiefly depends, although he gives himself no higher name than that of a single brother. In their Public Worship he reads the Scriptures and also baptizes when so directed by Father Friedsam.

Another remarkable incident in connection with this conversion of Miller is told by Mr. Boehm in his now extremely rare book, which he published in 1742 against the Moravians. It was the dramatic burning of Reformed and Lutheran devotional books by the new converts. Thus far we had only traditional accounts about this event, which are now superseded by this contemporaneous account of Mr. Boehm.

Criticizing especially the conduct of Conrad Weiser, Boehm writes:[98]

[98] Boehm's *Getreuer Warnungsbrief,* Philadelphia, 1742, p 29. The only known copy of this now exceedingly rare book is in the possession of Rev Dr. J I. Good, who bought it at the sale of late Governor Pennypacker's library.

But whether we can entertain any hope with regard to him, let every Evangelical Christian think what kind of a man he is. Will he help to establish the honor of the gospel of Jesus Christ? For when Peter Miller, the former pretended Reformed minister of Dolpihaken, became a regular disgrace to our Reformed Church by letting himself be baptized in Dunker fashion as a member of the Seventh Day Tumpler [Dunker] sect, together with several others, this Conrad Weiser was one of them. (He was indeed a Lutheran and at that time an elder of the Lutheran congregation at Dolpihacken.)[99] Moreover, when four Seventh Day Tumpler [Dunkers], namely Peter Miller (above mentioned) Michel Miller, Conrad Weiser (above mentioned) and Gottfried Fidler, burnt with fire the Reformed Heidelberg Catechism, the Lutheran Catechism, the Psalms of David, the " Paradeys-Gartlein " and the " Exercise of Piety " [Ubung der Gottseligkeit], in all 36 books in derision and in disparagement, in the house of Gottfried Fidler, he was one of them Nor has it become known that since that time he has turned from them in repentance and has again betaken himself to his former Lutheran religion.

[99] The Lutheran membership of Conrad Weiser has been called in question recently, see Dubbs, *Reformed Church in Pennsylvania*, p. 97, note 96, but without sufficient reason All *contemporary* writers are agreed that he was a Lutheran. This is the testimony of Boehm and Miller, in the extracts from their writings quoted above. Zinzendorf makes the same statement, see Fresenius, *Nachrichten von Herrnhutischen Sachen,* Vol III, p. 710 Weiser took part in a Lutheran communion service, see *Hallesche Nachrichten,* new ed., Vol. I, p. 202. Muehlenberg reports him as a Lutheran, cf. *Hallesche Nachrichten,* new ed , Vol I, p. 362. "At Tulpehocken, many years ago, some Lutherans, among whom was Mr Weiser, had taken up a piece of land " Finally Weiser himself stated, according to Muehlenberg, that "he held the principles of our Evangelical religion," see *Hallesche Nachrichten,* new ed , Vol. I, p 449 The fact that Mr Weiser acted as trustee of the Reformed Church at Reading (see D Miller, *History of the Reformed Church in Reading,* p 17), proves nothing, for he was also a trustee of the Lutheran Church at Reading, see J. Fry, *History of Trinity Lutheran Church,* Reading, 1894, p 18

The account of Peter Miller's activity as a Reformed pastor may fittingly be closed with another account of his conversion, written by himself on December 5, 1790, to a friend:[100]

Your Excellency's

most humble Friend

Peter Miller

MILLER'S ACCOUNT OF HIS CONVERSION.

Having officiated among the Germans several years I quitted the ministry and returned to private life. About that time our small state was in its infancy: I never had an inclination to join it, because of the contempt and reproach which lay on the same; but my inward Conductor, brought me to that critical dilemma, either to be a member of this new institution, or to consent to my own condemnation, when also I was forced to choose the first. In my company had been the schoolmaster, three elderlings (Conrad Weiser one), five families and some single persons, which raised such a fermentation in that church, that a persecution might have followed, had the magistrates consented with the generality. We have been incorporated with said congregation in May, 1735, by holy Baptism; When we were conducted to the water, I did not much differ from a poor criminal under sentence of death. Whoever [!] the Lord our God did strengthen me, when I came into the water and then in a solemn manner renounced my life with all its prerogatives without reservation and I found by experience in subsequent times, that all this was put into the divine records; for

---

[100] First printed in *Hazard's Register,* Vol. XVI, p. 254 f.

God never failed in his promise to assist me in time of need. At that time the solitary brethren and sisters lived dispersed in the wilderness of Canestogues, each for himself, as Heremits, and I following that same way, did set up my Hermitage in Dulpehakin at the foot of a mountain,[101] on a limped spring, the house is still extant there with an old orchard   There did I lay the foundation to solitary life, but the melancholy temptations, which did trouble me every day, did prognosticate to me misery and affliction: Whoever [!] I had not lived there half a year, when a great change happened: for a camp was laid out for all solitary persons at the very spot, where Ephrata stands, and where at that time the President lived with some hermits   And now, when all heremits were called in, I also quitted my solitude and exchanged the same for the monastic life, which was judged to be more inservient [!] to sanctification than the life of a hermit, where many under a pretense of holiness did nothing but nourish their own selfishness

The profound impression which this remarkable conversion made upon the Reformed churches is seen by the fact that in popular story the number of converts gradually increased until it has reached several hundred   On March 1, 1738, the Rev. Peter Henry Dorsius, who had not been in Pennsylvania when the events took place, wrote to the Synodical Deputies as follows:[102]

In this connection [I wish to state that] Do. Muller, having fallen away from our faith, has persuaded no less than three hundred souls to go over with him to the errors of the Dunkers [Dompelaars], whereof very many promise to return to our Christian religion, if only they were deemed worthy, through the providence of God, of being provided with an orthodox minister.

[101] The same fact is told, with some additional detail, in the Ephrata Chronicle: "Soon after the Brethren erected a solitary residence for the teacher at the foot of a hill in Tulpehocken, where, however, he lived no longer than till the next November," *Chronicon Ephratense,* English translation, p 73

[102] The letter of Dorsius was spread upon the Minutes of the Deputies, under date June 16–20, 1738

Mr. Boehm gives as usual the best survey of this period in the history of the congregation. In his report of October, 1734, he gives the number of members at Goshenhoppen (presumably New Goshenhoppen), "according to the statement of some members as about 40." Of the charge as a whole he writes:[103]

BOEHM'S ACCOUNT OF GOSHENHOPPEN IN 1734.

A fourth minister would greatly be needed at Goshenhoppen, about thirty-six miles from Philadelphia.[104] He might conduct services there every three weeks, and use the rest of the time to feed the poor sheep at the end of the wilderness, in the above mentioned Saucon, Macungie, Maxatawny and Great Swamp, who thirst for the hearing of God's word as the dry earth for water. Many people of these regions have already been to see me in great sadness, and complained of the pitiable state of their souls. There were also some, who being able to make the journey, have come at various times to communion in the congregation entrusted to me at Falkner Swamp, a distance certainly of twenty-five to thirty miles, and brought children to baptism, which journey, however, is impossible for old persons and weak women, so that it is not to be wondered at (especially when one remembers that there are children who for lack of a minister cannot be brought to baptism until they are several years of age) that my heart breaks and my eyes are full of tears about this condition. But I cannot accomplish this work alone, for my years are beginning to accumulate, and my poor body is also getting feeble, since I must not only make long

[103] *Minutes of Coetus*, p 2

[104] This statement refers to New Goshenhoppen, as can be seen from a quotation of Thomas F Gordon's *Gazetteer of Pennsylvania*, 1832 (quoted by Mr. Dotterer in his *Perkiomen Region*, Vol. I, p 14) "New Goshenhoppen, a post town and village in Upper Hanover township, Montgomery County, situated in the forks of Perkiomen creek, 37 miles northwest of Philadelphia, and about 21 northwest of Norristown" The same authority states of Upper Hanover township "The central distance from Philadelphia is 35 miles northwest," *l c*, p 12.

journeys and preach, but also, because these poor people are not able to support me, must support my large family with manual labor.

After being for many years the moving spirit in the Ephrata community, Miller died there and was buried in the little cemetery belonging to the cloister. His tomb is next to that of Conrad Beissel, the founder of the society. It bears the following inscription:

>Hier Liegt Begraben
>PETER MILLER
>Gebuertig im Oberamt
>Lautern in Chur Pfalz
>Kam als Reformirter
>Prediger nach America
>Im Jahr 1730. Wurde
>Unter die Gemeine in
>Ephrata getaufet im
>Jahre 1735 und genant
>Bruder Jaebez. Auch ward
>Er nachmals ihr Lehrer
>Bis an sein Ende. Entschlief
>Den 25sten September, 1796.
>Alter 86 Jahr und 9 Monath.

In English it would read: "Here lies buried Peter Miller, born in the Oberamt Lautern in the Electoral Palatinate. He came as a Reformed preacher to America in the year 1730. He was baptized into the congregation at Ephrata in the year 1735 and was called Brother Jabez. Became afterwards their teacher until his end. Fell asleep the 25th of September, 1796. His age 86 years and 9 months."

CHAPTER III.

Ministry of John Henry Goetschy, 1735–1740.

AFTER the departure of Peter Miller, Goshenhoppen remained without a pastor for nearly a year. In the summer of 1735, however, a new minister appeared in the person of young John Henry Goetschy.[105]

On May 29, 1735, the ship *Mercury*, William Wilson, master, from Rotterdam, landed in Philadelphia with 186 passengers. Among them were Esther Goetschy, aged 44 years and her eight children: Henry, 17 years; Rudolph, 12 years; Mauritz, 10 years; Anna, 24 years; Barbara, 18 years; Esther, 16 years; Beat, 8 years; Magdalena, 6 years. With them came also Conrad Wuertz, who had married Anna Goetschy, and like John Henry Goetschy became a minister of the Reformed Church.[106]

These people, who arrived in Philadelphia on May 29, 1735, with the ship *Mercury*, formed a colony from Switzerland, and, as it is one of the few colonies whose his-

---

[105] For earlier accounts of John Henry Goetschy see Harbaugh, *Fathers of the Reformed Church*, Vol. I, pp. 292–296; Good, *History of the Reformed Church in the United States, 1725–1792*, pp. 171–189; Dotterer, "Goetschy's Colony," in *Historical Notes*, pp. 171–173, 179–186; Dubbs, *Reformed Church in Pennsylvania*, pp. 104–110; Corwin, *Manual of the Reformed Church*, 4th ed., pp. 489–492; also *Life and Letters of Boehm*, pp. 51–54.

[106] *Penna. Archives*, 2d Series, Vol. XVII, pp. 113–117.

tory can be told with some detail, it will be interesting to trace them in their journey from Zurich, Switzerland, until they step upon the shores of the New World.

The leader of this colony was the Rev. Maurice Goetschy, whose son, John Henry, became pastor at Goshenhoppen in 1735.

The members of the Goetschy family had been for many generations citizens in Zurich, Switzerland The first person of that name who is mentioned in the genealogical records of the city was Henry Goetschy, who in 1315 A.D., was mayor of the city. Maurice Goetschy was born in 1686 [107] On December 4, 1702, he matriculated in the Latin school at Zurich. On February 24, 1710, he married Esther Werndli, and was in the same year admitted to the ministry. In 1712 he became first deacon at Bernegg in the Rhine valley (Canton of St. Gall), and in 1720 pastor at Salez. In 1733 he was deposed from the ministry. On March 8, 1718 his son John Henry was born. The younger Goetschy matriculated in the Latin school at Zurich on March 23, 1734. But before he had spent half a year at school, his father with his whole family left for Pennsylvania.

On October 7, 1734, the *Nachrichten von Zurich,* a newspaper of the city, published the following account of the departure of the colony of Maurice Goetschy:[108]

Departure of Mr. Maurice Goetschy from Zurich, October 4, 1734.

The past Monday [October 4th], Mr. Maurice Goetschy, together with his wife and children and with a considerable number

---

[107] The statements regarding Maurice Goetschy and his family are taken from the *Lexicon Geographico-Heraldico-Stemmatographicum,* zusammengetragen von Johann Friedr. Meyss, A°. 1740, Vols I–VII, manuscripts in the city library of Zurich (Msc. E 54), Vol. II, Letters D–G, p 806

[108] Printed by Mr. Dotterer in *Historical Notes,* p. 172.

of country people, old and young, took passage on a boat, and started for the so called Carolina island, in the hope of meeting there with better fortune than he had found in his native land. He was urgently dissuaded by our gracious Lords [of the government] and by the local clergy, but he persisted in his resolution, and took his departure. Shortly afterwards another boat followed him with like, we must say, silly people, making a total of 174 persons for that day. Many thousands saw them depart with great pity for them, especially because they were undertaking so thoughtlessly, with wife and child, and but poorly provided for, the dangerous journey of 300 hours in cold, rain and wind, now, when the days are getting shorter. Nevertheless, kindhearted and distinguished persons supplied them with all kinds of articles, such as bread, shawls, caps etc. The following day the third boat started off. These were liberally provided, from the office of charities, with a large amount of bread, flour, stockings and other supplies. Especially the neighborhood of the exchange showed itself deeply sympathetic; nor will they be likely to forget what was given to them at the Salthouse for bodily refreshment In like manner many merchants assisted them. Upon the last boat were 82 persons, who would have been worthy of more consideration if they had been compelled to leave for the honor or the truth of God. They must bear the consequences of their act, be they good or ill At the same time, upwards of 20, induced by the wise representations of worthy gentlemen and citizens, changed their intentions, choosing the better part They remained here and will be very kindly returned to their homes. Meanwhile we should pray God that the great number who have gone on this journey, may either soon return or reach the destination they so much wish for. May He fill their hearts with patience, and, as many sad hours are likely to embitter their voyage, may He comfort them with the thought that, if they remain faithful, a far better life is reserved for them.

The journey of the colonists from Zurich to Basle down the Rhine is told at length in a pamphlet which Ludwig

Weber, one of the emigrants, who returned to Zurich from Holland, wrote and published at Zurich in 1735 as a warning to later venturesome spirits.[109] We shall follow his story in tracing the movements of the party.

The emigrants turned from Zurich northward till they reached the Rhine at Laufenburg. Then taking a boat on the Rhine they came, on October 5, to Rheinfelden, where they had to show their passports. Towards evening of the same day they reached Basle. There they had to wait until a passport could be secured from Comte du Jour, the commanding general of the French army at Strassburg It cost 44 guilders, which some gentlemen at Basle paid for them. After securing this passport they waited two days longer for the ships that were to carry them down the Rhine. Meanwhile several became impatient at the delay A tailor from Lichtensteg advised them to take the road through France, claiming that he knew the way and was able to speak French. Thirty-one persons followed him, but nothing more was heard of them. From forty to fifty others resolved to travel through Lorraine by way of Namur to Rotterdam They were fortunate enough to secure alms at several places along the route and, although they had many quarrels and difficulties, they finally reached Rotterdam eight days after the main party.

At Basle eighty refugees from Piedmont joined them in a separate ship. The main party, consisting of 194 persons, embarked in two ships. They suffered intensely on the ships through rain and cold, against which they were but poorly protected with scanty clothes and provisions.

---

[109] The title page of this pamphlet reads *Der Hinckende Bott von Carolina oder Ludwig Webers von Wallıselen Beschreibung seiner Reise von Zurich gen Rotterdam, mit derjenigen Gesellschaft welch neulich aus dem Schweizerland nach Carolinam zu ziehen gedachte,* Zurich, MDCCXXXV, pp 32. Only known copy in the city library at Zurich

After leaving Basle their first encampment was upon an island, covered with trees and shrubs, in the middle of the Rhine. Such continued to be their night quarters, although the nights were wet and cold. Moreover the ships were crowded so badly that there was hardly enough room to sit, much less to lie down. There was no opportunity for cooking on the ships; and as they were sometimes compelled to stay days and nights on the ships, the cries of the children were pitiful and heart-rending. Whenever they could get ashore they cooked, warmed themselves and dried their clothes. Many would have liked to return home, but as the armies of the French and the Austrians lay on both sides of the river, they did not dare to risk it. Quarrels among men and women were frequent. Mrs. Goetschy, the chronicler tells us, often quarreled with her husband, called him all kinds of names and one morning tore a cane from his hand and belabored his back soundly.

At night they saw the camp fires of the imperial troops on one side and of the French on the other, which terrified them by their ghostly appearance. As they were afraid of an attack from one or both armies almost at any time, they refrained carefully from making the least noise, so as to pass by unnoticed. Nevertheless, they were stopped repeatedly. At Old Breysach, in the Breisgau, all their chests were opened and examined. Goetschy, who called on the commandant of the fort, was advised to leave immediately, as the French on the other side of the river were aiming three field pieces at the boats. Of course they made off with all possible speed. At Ketsch, near Schwetzingen, west of Heidelberg, the dragoons of the imperial army stopped the boats and compelled Mr. Wirtz of Zurich, who acted as self-appointed commissary, to go to Heidelberg and secure a passport for 30 guilders, from the Duke of Wurtemberg, the commanding general of the imperial army. They were also forced to make an extra payment of two ducats for each vessel.

Nine miles below Mayence the dragoons again rode after them and would not have allowed them to pass on, if their leader had not been of the Reformed religion. They took the meat away from Goetschy's plate with their sabers, which they swung about his head, so that he quite lost his appetite. Shortly before reaching Mayence from forty to fifty men had exhausted all their money, so that they did not even have enough to pay their boat fare They were compelled to continue the journey on foot

At Mayence they were delayed four days because they could not agree with the captain of the boats about the passage money to be paid to Rotterdam. Finally they agreed on three guilders for adults and half fare for children.

After leaving Mayence their journey was a little more comfortable, for they had at least a chance to cook on the ships. Their spiritual needs, however, were sadly neglected, for, if we can believe the chronicler of the journey, the pastor, Mr. Goetschy, always had the pipe or the wineglass near his mouth Mornings and evenings, one of the men, Heinrich Scheuchzer from Zurich, read a prayer. When Goetschy actually did preach a sermon, in which he compared some of the leaders of the company to the followers of Korah, Dathan and Abiram, he almost caused a riot.

When they reached Neuwied four couples were married by a Reformed minister:

1. Hans Conrad Wirtz and Anna Goetschy.
2 Conrad Naff, of Walliselen and Anna N.—
3. Jacob Rathgeb and Barbara Haller, both of Walliselen
4 Conrad Geweiller, a gardener

The Count of Wied desired them to remain in his territory, offering to give them houses and land, but as he did not promise as much as they expected to receive in Carolina, they did not accept his offer, but left.

From Neuwied they continued their journey down the Rhine until they reached Collenburg (now Culenborg) in Holland. There they were compelled to stop four days because of a strong contrary wind. Goetschy was invited to preach in the principal church at Culenborg, which he did with much acceptance. As a result a collection was taken up by the congregation for the party, so that each received one guilder. From Culenborg Goetschy sent a party of three men to Rotterdam, where he said two English ships were waiting for them. The party consisted of Abraham Bünninger, a carpenter of Bachenbülach, Jacob Issler, a tailor, and Abraham Weidman, a blacksmith of Luffingen. At Culenborg they also sold their ships, which they must have bought at Basle, for 45 Dutch guilders, apparently a very small sum. Then, contrary to their agreement, they were compelled to take another ship to convey them to Rotterdam. In their hurry to get off several children fell overboard into the water, from which they were rescued with difficulty Early the following morning they reached Rotterdam.

Having reached Rotterdam they heard to their dismay that no ships were waiting for them. Moreover the captain of the ship with which they had come wished to return at once, so they had to unload their goods quickly and, having no other place, they dumped them on the bank of the river on one heap.

Mr. Goetschy received a letter from a certain Mr. Schobinger, a native of St. Gall, who was living at the Hague, asking him to come to the Hague. So he left the

Arrival in Holland

emigrants to their own devices and with his son-in-law hurried off to comply with the request.

In a few days Mr. Wirtz returned and comforted them with the news that several oxen would be sent to them from the Hague, that the States General would send them to England at their own expense and that a large sum of money had been collected for them in England. Unfortunately none of these statements proved to be true. A few days later Goetschy also returned and reported that the States General had offered him a position as a minister of great importance, that he and his family had thus received unexpected help and he advised them to secure similar help for themselves.

In this extremity some indeed tried to help themselves by begging, but in that they were soon stopped by the magistrate with a threat of a fine of 25 guilders. Meantime some became sick from want and hunger, and two of them died. A tailor from Buchs, Sebastian Neracher by name, who was married in Rotterdam, came to see them. Most of them were in an inn outside of the city. He took care of those from Buchs. He brought with him a Mr Schapenhaudt, who interceded for them so successfully that many people took pity on them and distributed food and clothes among them. They also paid for their lodgings at the inn.

Mr. Schapenhaudt presented their sad condition to Rev. Mr. Wilhelmi of Rotterdam, who advised them to go to the Hague and apply there to Mr. von Felss, at the English embassy, to present their needy condition to him. Three men were sent to the Hague. When they reached the Hague, they first hunted up Mr. Goetschy and told him of their intention. He was greatly displeased with their plan and told them he had already spoken with Mr.

Felss, who was sufficiently well informed about their plans and condition. Goetschy entertained the three men at dinner and then offered to send a letter with them to Mr. Wilhelmi at Rotterdam. After waiting an hour for the letter, he sent them word that he had already dispatched it with his boy. Hence they had to return to Rotterdam without having accomplished their purpose.

Meanwhile Goetschy had been very successful in his interview with Mr. Felss, whom he calls an antistes,[110] but who was a prominent statesman, probably the Grand Pensionary himself.

In a letter, dated November 26, 1734, Goetschy gives a glowing account of this interview to Mr. Friess of Zurich,[111] the city treasurer and a near relative of his. After having related their experiences to Mr Felss, he answered him (according to Goetschy's letter) as follows:

> My dear brother, for six years we have been searching for a man through whom the churches of God in Pennsylvania, which consist of more than 60,000 souls, of whom 20,000 have not yet been baptized, could be organized. Divine Providence has sent you to us. Now I shall promote your call as general superintendent of the whole of Pennsylvania, which has more than eight cities and more than 600 boroughs and villages. You shall receive a yearly salary of more than 2000 thalers, until all has been accomplished. I shall see to it that the people get support from the Dutch government. But first you must write to your government for the requisite testimonials and then you will be examined before the General Synod.

Consequently Goetschy implored Mr. Friess to help him in securing the necessary testimonials. His son, John

[110] Antistes is a term used in Switzerland for the chief minister of a town. It was originally a Latin term, used of the chief priest of a temple, literally it is one who stands at the head, *antisto = antesto*.

[111] A copy of this letter is preserved in the city library of Zurich *De Rebus Saeculi XVII*, Vol XXXV.

Henry, supported his father's request in a separate letter, saying that, if the testimonial from Zurich would be favorable to his father, Mr. Felss had promised him to send him to the University of Leiden to study there for the ministry, so that he might become the successor to his father.

Meanwhile Rev. John Wilhelmi [Wilhelmius] of Rotterdam wrote also to Switzerland, to the Rev. John Baptista Ott of Zurich, to learn more of Goetschy's past. On February 5, 1735, Mr. Ott replied to him He sketched Goetschy's life as student in the Zurich Gymnasium, as deacon at Bernegg and as pastor at Salez. He praised him for his scholarly attainments, as an evidence of which he states that it was popularly reported that he conducted family worship with the Bible in the original language before him. He acknowledged that he had been guilty of immorality, but expressed the hope that as the authorities in Zurich had dealt leniently with Goetschy, simply dismissing him as a minister, so the Dutch people would find him worthy to send him out as their missionary [112]

Whether this letter reached Holland before the time of the departure of the emigrants is doubtful, as Ludwig Weber states in his report that after his return to Switzerland he heard that the party had left Holland on February 24, 1735.

When Goetschy had received from Mr. Felss the assurance of his appointment as minister to Pennsylvania, he returned to Rotterdam and acquainted his party of emigrants with his changed plans. Most of them readily accepted his proposal to change their destination from Carolina to Pennsylvania There were, however, some who refused to have anything to do with him Weber reports

---

[112] All these letters referred to above are in the city library at Zurich

88 as taking ship to England, but what became of them is unknown. The rest, 143 persons, signed their names for passage to Philadelphia. They agreed with the owner of a ship [Schiffpatron] to pay six doubloons for an adult and three for a child. If any of them should die, the survivors pledged themselves to pay their passage money.

The names of those who registered to sail for Pennsylvania were, according to Weber's report, as follows:

EMIGRANTS IN GOETSCHY'S COLONY

Home in Switzerland,	Name of Head of Family	Number
Appenzell	Jacob Mettler	1
Bachss	Jacob Bucher, shoemaker	4
Basserstorff	Heinrich Brunner	1
Basserstorff	Heinrich Dubendorffer	5
Basserstorff	Jacob Dubendorffer	2
Basserstorff	Kilian Dubendorffer	5
Basserstorff	Heinrich Hug, wheelwright	1
Bertschicken	Rudolph Walder	3
Buchss	Jacob Schmid	6
Buchss	Jacob Murer (Maurer)	5
Buchss	Heinrich Huber	4
Buchss	Conrad Meyer	3
Diebendorff	Jacob Dentzler	6
Esch	Rudolf Egg	1
Flunteren	Balthasar Bossart	5
Flunteren	Jacob Schellenberg and servant	2
Greiffensee	Johannes Heid	2
Hirsslanden	Caspar Notzli and his children	
Illau	Rudolf Hotz	1
Iloten	Verena Kern	3
Langenhuet	Hans Ott	1
Luffingen	Abraham Weidemann, blacksmith	2
Hennidorff	Hans Ulrich Ammann	1
Mulliberg	Jacob Possart	6
Opffikon	Barbara Eberhardt	1
Riesspach	Heinrich Schreiber, "blatmacher"	4
Rumlang	Rudolf Weidman, tailor	3
Steinmeer, Upper	Hans Meyer	4
Stein	Conrad Geweiler, and second wife	2

Sultzbach	Jacob Frey	5
Wallisellen	Heinrich Merck	6
Wallisellen	Martin Schellenberg	3
Wallisellen	Ludwig Lienhardt	1
Wallisellen	Jacob Wust	1
Wallisellen	Hans Rudolf Aberli	1
Wallisellen	Conrad Keller	3
Wallisellen	Jacob Naff	5
Wallisellen	Conrad Naff	5
Wallisellen	Jacob Naff	2
Wangen	Caspar Guntz	1
Windli	Hans Ulrich Arner	6
Winckel	Jacob Meyer	5
Zummikon	Jacob Bertschinger	1
Zurich	Heinrich Scheuchzer	1
N.—	Hans Muller	4
N—	Jacob Muller and brother	2
N—	Abraham Wackerli	4
N.—	Hans Kubler	4

This company with some others who evidently joined them after Ludwig Weber had started on his return journey to Switzerland, and whose names he could not therefore record, reached Philadelphia on May 29, 1735, in the ship *Mercury*, William Wilson, master. It carried in all 186 passengers, 61 men, 51 women, 37 boys and 34 girls. The above list forms an important supplement to the list in the *Pennsylvania Archives,* as it gives in each case the place in Switzerland from which the several persons came.

The journey itself and some of the later experiences of the Goetschy family are given in a letter which John Henry Goetschy, then a boy of 17 years, wrote on July 21, 1735, to Mr. Werdmüller, deacon at St. Peter's church in Zurich. As this letter has never been published and is quite interesting, we present it in full:[113]

[113] Original in Zurich library, see *Zusatze zum Lexicon Geograph-Herald-Stemmatogr.,* Vol II, F-H, pp 196-199 (Msc E. 62).

LETTER OF JOHN HENRY GOETSCHY TO ZURICH, JULY 21, 1735.
Very Reverend, Very Learned Mr. Deacon!

I, the most submissive servant of my very reverend, highly and very learned Mr. Deacon, cannot forbear to report to your Reverence, how we are getting along. After we had left Holland and surrendered ourselves to the wild, tempestuous ocean, its waves and its changeable winds, we reached, through God's great goodness toward us, with good wind, England within 24 hours After a lapse of two days we came to the island of Wicht [Wight] and there to a little town, called Caus [Cowes], where our captain supplied himself with provisions for the great ocean [trip] and we secured medicines for this wild sea Then we sailed, under God's goodness, with a good east wind away from there. When we had left the harbour and saw this dreaded ocean, we had a favorable wind only for the following day and the following night. Then we had to hear a terrible storm and the awful roaring and raging of the waves when we came into the Spanish and Portuguese ocean For twelve weeks we were subjected to this misery and had to suffer all kinds of bad and dangerous storms and terrors of death, which seemed to be even more bitter than death. With these we were subject to all kinds of bad diseases The food was bad, for we had to eat what they call "galley bread " We had to drink stinking, muddy water, full of worms. We had an evil tyrant and rascal for our captain and first mate, who regarded the sick as nothing else than dogs. If one said: " I have to cook something for a sick man," he replied: ' Get away from here or I'll throw you overboard, what do I care for your sick devil " In short, misfortune is everywhere upon the sea. We alone fared better. This has been the experience of all who have come to this land and even if a king traveled across the sea, it would not change. After having been in this misery sufficiently long, God, the Lord, brought us out and showed us the land, which caused great joy among us. But three days passed, the wind being contrary, before we could enter into the right river. Finally a good south wind came and brought us in one day through the glorious and beautiful

Telewa [Delaware], which is a little larger than the Rhine, but not by far as wild as the latter, because this country has no mountains, to the long expected and wished for city of Philadelphia.

When we reached here our dear father, because of the great and tedious journey and the hardships so unbearable to old people, was very sick and weak. On the last day, when we were before Philadelphia, the elders of the Reformed congregation came to him and showed their great joy over him. They spoke with him as their pastor, who had been appointed to that position by the ruling persons in Holland, as was shown by his testimonials which he had with him. They discussed one or other church affair with him and showed their great joy. He spoke heartily with them, as if he were well. The following day they came and took him to the land. When he reached the land he was so exhausted by his sickness that he could not walk alone, but was carried in a chair to the house assigned to him. When they were there, they wished to talk with him about one or other subject. Of his own people none were with him but mother, the children were yet on the ship on the water. Then he said "It is so dark before my eyes, let me lie down and sleep." As they did not want him to sleep in that room, since people were coming in continually and he would have been unable to sleep, they carried him upstairs to the bed room. In the middle of the stairway he sat down, lifted his hands to his heart and his eyes to heaven, heaved a sigh and died. On the third day a very distinguished funeral took place in the principal English Presbyterian church in Philadelphia, with a large attendance of people. All the members of the consistory of the Reformed church and very many of the congregation were present.

Now we, his wife and eight poor, forsaken orphans, are in a strange land among strange people, who do not know us, poor and without comfort. We, therefore, commend ourselves most submissively to all those in Zurich to whom our misfortune will become known and whose hearts will be touched, in order that they may graciously grant us their assistance. It can easily be sent into this country, if they will only send it through Mr. Wilhelmius at Rotterdam, for which I ask most humbly, for the sake of the merciful Jesus.

Very Reverend Mr. Deacon, when I showed my testimonials, and the people saw that I had been engaged in study, they almost compelled me to preside over the congregations as well as I could. Hence, through the goodness of God, I preach twice every Sunday and teach two catechetical lessons. For this I make use of the books which I have brought with me and through good diligence I am enabled, thank God, to perform this in such a way, that each and every person is well satisfied with me. Now the first Sunday I preach in Philadelphia both in the forenoon and the afternoon and always give with it catechetical instruction. On the second Sunday in Schippach, which is a very large congregation, a sermon and catechetical instruction in the forenoon. In the afternoon at Old Goshenhoppen, two hours [six miles] from Schippach, a sermon and catechetical instruction. It is also a pretty large congregation, as large as any in the canton of Zurich. On the third Sunday I preach in New Goshenhoppen and have catechetical instruction there in the forenoon. In the afternoon at Great Swamp [Grossen Schwam], which is also one of the large congregations All this I can do through the strength given me by God's spirit, to the great satisfaction of the people. I expect to be consecrated next Christmas by the English Presbyterians, in order that I may be able to administer the communion, unite people in marriage and baptize children. With the help of God I intend to do this. I would be able to do this all the better and put forth greater efforts for the souls of abandoned and confused sheep, if I had my library, which is in charge of Mr. Goichen [George] Kromer. I therefore ask your Reverence most humbly, if at all possible, to send it to me very kindly, not only for my sake and the large number of poor orphans left by my sainted father, but also for the sake of the many thousand strayed and shepherdless sheep, who go about in error and in a destitute condition, yea for the sake of the many heathen, who thereby might be led to the Lord Jesus, as has already been done.

   Given on the 21st of July 1735.
     HENRY GOETSCHIUS,
       Philadelphia in Pennsylvania.

The condition of the land is as follows· There are in it Englishmen, Germans and French from all parts of Europe. Most of them are Reformed. The others are people of all kinds of imaginable sects, Atheists, Anabaptists, Quakers, Arians, Enthusiasts, Nestorians, Pietists, Mennonites, Waldensians etc., etc, many hundred kinds, for in this country there is perfect liberty of conscience. The Reformed are scattered through seven congregations and thus there is among many thousand sheep no shepherd.

This letter bears the following inscription·
Letter of Henrich Goetschi, minister at Philadelphia to
Mr. Werdmuller, " Diacon " at St. Peters in Zurich

In order to prepare himself for the next important step in his life, his ordination, Mr. Goetschy wrote on September 26, 1735, to John Lavater, professor of Latin and Greek in the " Collegium Humanitatis " at Zurich, asking him for a certificate of his work and conduct while there. This certificate was written on May 28, 1736,[114] and it testified to the fact that, after having been instructed in the fundamentals of the arts and ancient languages by his father he had entered the Latin school and spent there a year and that he had been " faithful and diligent in his studies, upright in his life and morals, modest and pious in his conduct."

On May 27, 1737, Goetschy applied to the Presbyterian Synod of Philadelphia for ordination. The minutes of that meeting[115] state that,

a letter was brought in from Mr. Henricus Goetschius to Mr. Andrews, signifying his desire and the desire of many people of the German nation, that he might be ordained by order of Synod to the work of the ministry, upon which the said Mr. Goetschius was desired to appear before the Synod, that they might see his credentials and have some discourse with him; which being done, he

[114] Archives of Classis, Pennsylvania Portfolio, new letters, No. 11.
[115] *Records of Presbyterian Church,* Vol I, p 133.

produced testimonials from Germany, which were ample and satisfactory to the Synod respecting his learning and good Christian conversation; whereupon he was recommended to the care of the Presbytery of Philadelphia, to act upon further trials of him, with respect to his ordination, as to them should seem fit.

Formerly it was supposed, without further investigation, as a matter of course, 'that the Presbytery granted his request. But when the writer some years ago examined the unpublished minutes of the Philadelphia Presbytery, he discovered that this supposition was not correct.

On the same day, May 27, 1737, the Presbytery met and took up the case referred to them by Synod. The minutes state:[116]

The affair of Mr. Henry Goetschius his tryale and ordination, being by the Synod recommended to this Presbytery, they took the same under consideration and agreed to meet tomorrow morning at Mr. Andrews' chamber, in order to take his tryale and then conclude upon what is further to be done in his affair as things shall then appear and Mr. Andrews agrees to give him notice that he may be present at the above time and place.
May 28, 1737.
Memorandum that three members of this Presbytery and three other ministers met at Mr. Andrews's chamber as above directed and having read an exegesis composed by Mr. Goetschius on the article of justification and discoursed with him largely in order to discover his qualifications for the ministry, they unanimously came to this conclusion, that tho' he appeared well skilled in the learned languages, yet inasmuch as they found him altogether ignorant in college learning and but poorly read in Divinity, his ordination to the ministry must at present be deferred. And therefore for his

[116] *Minutes of Presbytery of Philadelphia*, Vol. III, 1733-1784, a manuscript preserved by the Presbyterian Historical Society at Philadelphia. The extract given above was printed, from copy furnished by writer, in *Ecclesiastical Records of New York*, Vol. IV, p 2684 f.

better instruction advised him (being willing to encourage him) to put himself under the tuition and care of some minister for some competent time, that he may be better accomplished for the work he is engaged in, and they also agreed, that, considering the necessitous condition of the people, that they desire his labours, he may sometimes preach to them in the meantime, as he has done for some time past.

The presence of Mr. Goetschy in the Goshenhoppen region soon made itself felt in the activity of the people

At Old Goshenhoppen, the Lutheran church record informs us,

in the year 1737, on January the 26th, the church land was surveyed and it was found to contain 38¼ acres of land, with allowance for roads. In the same year, February 7th, [it was] entered in the office for Recording of Deeds for the City and County of Philadelphia, in Patent Book A, Volume VIII. p. 325, by Mr. Brockden. Anno 1738, January 12th, the expenses were paid by Mr. Michael Reiher in behalf of the Lutherans and by Jacob Keller in behalf of the Reformed. They were as follows·

	£	s	D
1 For 38¼ acres of land . .	5	17	9
2. To Surveyor General for warrant and return .	—	9.	0
3 For the patent to the Secretary of the Proprietor	1	5	0
4 For the recording by Brockden . .	—	5	0
5. To Mr. Grashold for his trouble .	—	7	6
Total	£8	4	3

At Great Swamp warrants for land were taken out on May 23, 1738, and

there was surveyed on the twenty-seventh day of September, following unto Michael and Joseph Everhart a certain Tract of Land situate in Upper Milford Township, formerly in the County of Bucks, now Northampton . . . containing one hundred and thirteen Acres and seventy perches and the usual allowance of six Acres per cent for Roads and Highways . . . in Trust for minister,

Elders and Congregation for the time being of the said reformed Calvinist and their successors settled and to be settled from time to time in the said several Townships of Upper and Lower Milford, the said Congregation having now erected [1762] on the said Tract a Church and School House for the use of them and their successors.[117]

At New Goshenhoppen John Henry Sproegel had donated a tract of land consisting of fifty acres. Unfortunately no deed was given and hence the date and the circumstances cannot now be determined. But that it took place at an early time is vouched for by the report of John Philip Boehm, written to the Synods of Holland on April 20, 1744. He writes:[118]

Regarding the congregation at Goshenhoppen, it has also a suitable frame church upon a piece of land consisting of 50 acres, donated by some one, that all religions and sects should have the privilege of building a church thereon, and I lately learned from an old elder of theirs that the church is paid for. Two years ago four of them bought a plot. They intended to hand it over to the congregation for a parsonage if they were reimbursed for their outlay. How much it costs I do not know.

The fact that John Henry Sproegel[118a] was the donor of

[117] Printed by Dr. Weiser in his *Monograph*, pp. 42-46.
[118] *Minutes of Coetus*, p. 26.
[118a] John Henry Sprogell (Sproegel) was born February 12, 1679. His father, John Henry, was an eminent Lutheran minister and head of a Lutheran Seminary at Quedlinburg, Germany His mother was a daughter of the celebrated composer of music, Michael Wagner Godfried Arnold, the church historian, married his sister He came to Pennsylvania with his brother, Ludwig Christian, about 1702 In 1727 he is reported as having lived in the province twenty-five years, see Pennypacker, *Hendrik Pannebecker*, p. 86. In 1705 Pastorius says (see Pennypacker, *History of Germantown*, p. 76) that "about two years ago one John Henry Sprogel arrived in this province" In the beginning of 1705 both brothers were naturalized. John Henry Sproegell purchased about 600 acres in Pottsgrove, on which he settled with his family. The present Sprogel's run

this land is not only traditional but it rests on good documentary evidence. The congregation still owns a draught made by the surveyor, David Schultze, of which we present a facsimile, which is described by the surveyor as "a draught of a tract of land divided into several tracts, situate in Upper Hanover Township in the County of Montgomery and State of Pennsylvania, containing together Fifty acres and 26 Perches of land. Being part of 13,000 acres, in former Times belonging to John Henry Sproegel and afterwards to Thomas Tresse, Senior, deceased."

A curious fate overtook the donation of John Henry Sproegel. He died without giving the congregation a deed. The same happened to the Falkner Swamp Lutheran Church. As a result the New Goshenhoppen congregation was compelled to purchase the land of the heirs of John Henry Sproegel. For David Shultze states on his draught, above referred to, that "in the year 1749 [it] was by the Agents or Trustees of the said deceased Tresse's Family, sold to the settlers thereof, and the above tract *was jointly purchased of them*, by the Calvinists and Mennonists Congregations for the use of Churches, Meeting House, School House and Burying Ground." To an-

---

was called after him and flows through this tract. From a stone in an ancient graveyard east of the borough line we learn that his wife, Dorothea, died August 7, 1718, aged forty years A son, Frederick, died in 1716, one year old (See Buck, *History of Montgomery County,* p 110.) In 1719 John Henry Sprogell gave fifty acres of land to the Lutherans in New Hanover township Hendrick Pannebecker surveyed it and laid it out, the survey being completed April 17, 1719, see Pennypacker, *Hendrick Pannebecker,* p 73 ff

His brother, Lodowick (Ludwig) Christian Sprogell, died at Philadelphia in 1729 His will is No 129 of 1729, Book E, p 114

His sister, known as widow Sprogell, lived on Second Street, Philadelphia, see advertisement in *Weekly Mercury* of February 10, 1730, quoted above, p. 45 She died at Philadelphia December 20, 1760, see *American Ancestry,* Vol IV, p. 5.

ticipate the later history, it may be noted here that in 1749 the congregation was again unable to secure a deed. Not before February 23, 1796, was the deed actually made out and the final transfer of the land to the congregation consummated.

The church at New Goshenhoppen reported by Boehm as standing on the Sproegel tract in 1744, can be traced to a still earlier date. It had been erected before January, 1739, for at that time Mr. Boehm reported to Holland:[119]

> Goshenhoppen. As I have heard from people that live there, they have built a pretty large church at that place, which will be sufficient for them for some time, but it is poorly made of wood.

Of the ministry of John Henry Goetschy at Goshenhoppen we have a somewhat extended description by John Philip Boehm in his report of January, 1739. Goetschy, like Weiss and Miller, soon after his arrival came in conflict with Mr. Boehm, because he entered several of his congregations. Hence Boehm condemned his work severely. Continuing the history of the Goshenhoppen church after the departure of Miller, Boehm writes:[120]

> After these men had failed, they arbitrarily made Henry Goetschi their pretended minister, when he was hardly eighteen years of age and but half a year before had received the Lords Supper for the first time from Do. Rieger at Germantown. Goeschi then undertook to administer the Lord's Supper and to baptize, to install elders and to marry people In short, he did what belongs to the office of a regular minister. Goshenhoppen has him at the present time [1739] as its preacher, and permits him to establish and to carry on all this disorder from Goshenhoppen as a center, not only at Skippack, but at other places also. He has done this, at Oley, where he has misled the congregation,

[119] *L. c.,* p. 12
[120] *L. c.,* p. 10, *Life and Letters of Boehm,* p 277 f

which was established by me in 1736 at their request, and he now also serves this congregation. At Tulpehocken he attempted to do the same thing through three un-called-for visits, but he was refused. Yet he continues such improper actions.

Meanwhile this Goshenhoppen is a congregation or a place where a faithful shepherd and minister is greatly needed, through whose wise administration a flourishing congregation ought soon to be established There are also several places near Goshenhoppen which should be provided for, as Great Swamp and Saucon Creek. These, although they might be served by the minister of Goshenhoppen with the administration of the sacraments and sometimes with a sermon, yet need to be provided with readers, who have the ability to catechise, especially at Saucon Creek, because it is a somewhat out-of-the-way place and many Reformed people live there.

We learn more about the extensive activity of young Goetschy from the title page of the oldest New Goshenhoppen Reformed Record, by which he informs us that he preached at eleven preaching places, namely at Skippack, Old Goshenhoppen and New Goshenhoppen in Montgomery County; Great Swamp and Egypt in Lehigh County; Saucon in Northampton County; Maxatawny, Moselem, Oley, Berne and Tulpehocken in Berks County. In four of these places church records, begun by him, or containing at least entries by his hand, are still in existence.

In New Goshenhoppen he entered 60 baptisms, beginning on April 25, 1736, and ending on September 24, 1740. He also wrote the title page of this record, probably in 1736, when he began his entries. Moreover, we have from his pen the first list of members at New Goshenhoppen, 45 in all, written about 1736, and the first list of elders, elected April 25, 1736, namely John Steinmann, John Bingemann, J. Georg Welcker and Henry Gallman.

At Great Swamp he started a church record on April 24, 1736. On that day he wrote the title page of this record and entered, at the same time, a brief but comprehensive constitution for the congregation and six baptisms into the record. In all he recorded there but fourteen baptisms, the last on February 28, 1738.

On March 22, 1739, he opened the Egypt record with a Greek and Latin sentence. The Greek sentence reads: Οὐδὲν ἁλὲς γράφῃς, which means neither "*Ohne Versuch schmeckt man nichts,*" as Dr. Weiser renders it,[121] nor "nothing without writing," as Mr. Roberts translates it,[122] but "Mayest thou write nothing crowdedly," or rendered freely: "Write everything plainly." These and other doubtful Latin and Greek phrases are of course reminiscences of the Latin school at Zurich, and were evidently used by the young preacher to impress the German farmers of his congregations with his great learning.

22. Martii 1739.

J. Henricus Goetschius, M.
Helvetico — Tigurinus.

Only three baptisms in the Egypt records are in the handwriting of Goetschy. They took place on June 12, June 27 and September 30, 1739, but two other children were also baptized by him on earlier dates. John Traxel, son of Peter Traxel, was baptized "by Rev. Mr. Götschi" on October 26, 1736, and Peter Roth, son of Daniel Roth on July 27, 1737. These two entries were probably made by Peter Traxel, "Vorsteher der Reformirten Gemeinde allhier," who acted as sponsor at the second baptism.

[121] See *Monograph*, p. 15.
[122] *Pennsylvania Archives*, 6th Series, Vol. VI, p. 134.

TITLE PAGE OF NEW GOSHENHOPPEN RECORD, 1736

On March 24, 1739, the Berne church record was opened by Mr. Goetschy. An earlier baptism which had taken place in May, 1738, was also most probably entered in March, 1739. On July 11, 1739, three children were baptized by Mr Goetschy at Berne. At one of the baptisms, that of John Henry Jaeger, son of Philip Carl Jaeger, Goetschy acted as sponsor. Later dates on which baptisms were performed by Mr. Goetschy at Berne were: July 12, September 12 and November 26, 1739. In all there are fifteen baptisms entered by Mr. Goetschy at Berne from April, 1738, till November 26, 1739. Eleven other baptisms, from March 1, 1740, till August 20, 1740, though entered by a different hand, may possibly have been performed by Mr. Goetschy also, as we know from the New Goshenhoppen record that he officiated in the charge till September, 1740.

It was during the ministry of Mr Goetschy that the first schoolmaster appeared in the Goshenhoppen region. It was John Conrad Wirtz, the brother-in-law of Goetschy. The exact time of his stay is uncertain, but the fact of his presence at Goshenhoppen is vouched for by Mr. Boehm. In his last letter to the Classis of Amsterdam, dated December 2, 1748, he writes about Wirtz:

> He was accepted at Old Goshenhoppen to teach school, but they soon got tired of him and sent him away Afterwards the Mennonites at Cannastocka accepted him for the same work, but he was dismissed by them just as quickly.

Later he assumed the ministry in various country congregations. From September, 1742, to December, 1743, we find him at Egypt in Lehigh County When Schlatter came in 1746, he was ministering at Saucon, Springfield and the Forks of the Delaware, now Easton. He was in these churches probably from 1745-1749.

September 27, 1750, he applied to the Presbyterian Synod of New York for admission. He was received as a probationer by the Presbytery of New Brunswick, September 3, 1751, and was ordained by this Presbytery as pastor of Rockaway, N. J., June 5, 1752. He served this church and others in its neighborhood until 1761. He was then dismissed by the Presbytery to become the pastor of the Reformed Church at York, Pa., where he officiated from May, 1762, to September, 1763. He died

at York, September 21, 1763. His numerous descendants have recently presented a beautiful memorial tablet to the Church in York, to commemorate his labors.

Mr. Goetschy came in conflict with Mr. Boehm by circulating everywhere a letter of Rev. Wilhelmius of Rotterdam, which Boehm claimed was forged. This letter gave the Reformed congregations in Pennsylvania the privilege to engage and dismiss their ministers at pleasure.

Finally, in the spring of 1740, the letter fell into the hands of Mr. Boehm, who sent at once a copy of it to the Classis of Amsterdam and wrote the following important letter concerning it, in which he also touches upon his relation to Mr. Goetschy:[123]

LETTER OF BOEHM TO THE CLASSIS OF AMSTERDAM, APRIL 4, 1740

Very Reverend Classis, Reverend and Devout Church Fathers!

I had serious doubts about sending the enclosed copy to the Reverend Classis, believing that on its account I might be regarded with displeasure. Yet I thought it indispensably necessary, in whatever aspect I considered it, to let the Very Reverend and Devout Church Fathers see it, for they, in their exalted wisdom, will know what to do with it, in order that your poor fellow-servant may be guarded against further trouble.

This letter caused constant mischief and was the continual support of the wicked associates of Jacob Reiff, since the time of its arrival in this country. (Do. Weiss brought it along from Holland). The Christian Synods in their letters to his Reverence, Mr. Dorsius, have sufficiently declared their displeasure with the unordained preachers and hirelings

About eight years ago, I was shown this letter (of which the enclosed is a copy) from a distance, with the statement that they did not concern themselves much about me and my church-order, here they had a right church order and they knew what power and liberty they had.

But although I tried hard during all this time, yet I could not obtain the letter, until a few weeks ago. It came by accident out of their hands into mine.

Now I believe firmly that this letter was cunningly forged, for 1st. A long time ago I heard from the lips of Reiff himself that he had received the same from Do. Wilhelmi in the Dutch language and that he had it translated into the German language in Holland. 2nd. The signature is written by the hand of the translator, while the name of the translator is not mentioned. This ought to be entirely different.

[123] The original letter of Boehm is in the Classical Archives at Amsterdam First printed in *Life and Letters of Boehm*, pp 300–303.

3rd. The letter consists of six sheets, which have been sewed together with a blue silk ribbon and sealed. I cannot believe that it is Do. Wilhelmi's seal, for I have his seal on two letters in three forms, none of which is like it.

4th. In these letters Do. Wilhelmi wrote me, after I had notified him that they did such things in the name of his Reverence (which they did as the letter shows) and he assured me, if such was done in his name it was done without his knowledge and approval. His letter was dated June 30, 1736.

5th. The so-called "Report and Instructions concerning Pennsylvania," drawn up by ten commissioners and printed by order of the Christian Synods (probably in 1731) is almost uniform with the regulations of the enclosed letter. But nothing is mentioned [in the Report] about that which is contained in the beginning of the letter, in regard to the power and liberty which the letter grants to the people of this country and to the exercise of which it urges them.[124] The letter likewise does not say to whom money

[124] The letter of Dr Wilhelmius is too long to be given entire. But a few of the more important paragraphs of the first part of the letter may be quoted In the beginning of the letter the writer expresses his pleasure that he was permitted to appeal in behalf of the Pennsylvania churches to the church of Holland, with the result that the latter would take up the cause of the Pennsylvania churches and assist them with counsels and contributions He expresses his regret to hear of their troubles and divisions, caused by the ordination of Mr Boehm He reports that he had transmitted their letters to their destination. The first he had sent to the Classis of Amsterdam, which, however, he informs them, continued to be of the opinion that Dom. Boehm should be supported in his position Hence on November 21 [1730] he had submitted their second letter to the Classis of Rotterdam with the result that a committee of ten persons had been appointed to investigate the whole case But as their report would not be submitted to the Classis before next Easter, and as he did not want Mr Weiss to return empty-handed, he would give them his own personal opinion in the matter.

First of all he advises them to accept the counsel of the Classis of Amsterdam in order to preserve by it peace and harmony among the churches, until after the death of Mr. Boehm a change would take place. By doing this they would be sure of gaining the favor and good will of the Classis, inasmuch as the ordination of Boehm had taken place in answer to a

had been given in Holland The printed pamphlet, however, mentioned that a considerable sum had been placed into the hands of Do. Weis in Holland.

Therefore I cannot believe that Do. Wilhelmi ever wrote such a letter

For this reason no one would be a more fitting person to lead the poor misguided people back upon the right way and to bring about unity, love and a God-pleasing order, by exposing such cunning and fraud, than his Reverence, Do. Wilhelmi, whom God may graciously reward for it. This would certainly be the case because many have passed away without being reconciled, and many have gone over to the sects on account of the trouble and disharmony occasioned by this letter, so that my heart often bled and sighed to God I should be very glad to have a letter regarding it in my hands (for if it gets into the hands of Reiff's adherents, it will be hidden). Then, with the help of God, I would soon gather my sheep and perform my work among my congregations

petition received from them and Mr Boehm could not be removed from his office without much scandal and bitter feeling.

After these sensible admonitions, there follow four paragraphs which are out of harmony with all that precedes and follows and which were no doubt inserted by Reiff and his followers It is inconceivable that Dr. Wilhelmius could have written them They read as follows.

"In case this advice be not acceptable to you and your minds cannot unite with him, nor be edified, improved and comforted by his ministry and your church be exposed to ridicule and contempt, as you write in your letter and I have heard from the two delegates, I give it as my own personal opinion, that, in order to remove the present and future quarrels, you have the divine right, given to you by God in Christ Jesus, which you can and must use, to elect on your own responsibility a minister according to the word of God and the church order

"For your nation, which is living in a free land, is a perfectly free chuich, dependent upon none, which has in herself the right to govern herself, to elect such elders as she may please, if it be only done according to the word of God. Being independent of every church in the world, whichever it may be, you can accept advice and follow it or decline to do so This is entirely different with the churches in New Netherland, which have been organized by the church of Holland

"Inasmuch as this is so, the congregation of Schippach, Schwam and

with a double joy and my bitter sorrow would soon be sweetened.

But as long as this letter has been here my work has been rendered useless among many. The slanderers and liars found it a weapon against me and I had to put up with a small compensation for all my difficult and wearisome toil and labor and thus lose my food for the support of my body. But the most painful result was that I had to see my labor made fruitless with many, because of the letter, and had to behold more harm in all the congregations of the whole country than I could bring about growth.

The Reverend Classis can, therefore, clearly see that it is not my fault that our true church in this country did not grow. For Henry Goetschy has shown this letter everywhere and thereby caused me very much persecution, until he learned differently from his Reverence, Inspector Dorsius. Then he heartily repented and asked my forgiveness in the presence of his Reverence, which I granted him with all my heart. I also wish him success and intercede for him with God and our Reverend Church Fathers. He obediently submitted to the decision of the Reverend Christian Synods and desisted immediately. May God give him blessing and grace that he may become an efficient instrument to edify others.

neighboring places, has the divine right herself to elect a minister whom she may find fit for that position, and it is my opinion that the following procedure should be adopted. The consistory should assemble and investigate the conduct of the men, who in the name of the whole congregation wrote to the Classis of Amsterdam, asking for Boehm and when it shall appear that they did not act truthfully, or that they themselves were deceived, the consistory must bring them to a confession of their guilt, and exclude these men from the table of the Lord and his communion, they being the cause of this disturbance. They should treat Dom. Boehm in the same manner, and if it be found that he deceived these men in their simple-mindedness, by his cunning and artifice, I suggest that these things be properly recorded and sent to the Classis, in order to justify yourselves and to assure the Classis that her resolution was based upon deceptive tales.

"After this has been done, the consistory shall notify all male members to meet at the specified time and vote one by one for the election of a minister, acting according to the church order of the Palatinate, then pro-

I also made this suggestion to his Reverence, Inspector Dorsius, to propose to the Christian Synods, in sending the desired ministers, to ordain each for his particular place. For some places are more acceptable than others and the people also differ. I think that thereby future quarrels could be avoided entirely, and all would have to be content. May God give his gracious blessing upon his work for the salvation of many.

Your obedient servant commends herewith the Very Reverend Classis, your reverend persons, with all your families and holy service to the dear heavenly father and to the word of his grace and himself to your blessed and affectionate care, and he remains,

Very Reverend Classis,
Your most submissive and obedient servant,
JOH. PH BOEHM,
Minister at Falckner Schwam, Schip Bach and Weitmarge.
Witpen Township, Philadelphia County,
Pennsylvania, April 4, 1740.

ceed to the ordination, and, in order that all this be done orderly, the advice and guidance of the nearest regular minister, that can be secured from Staten Island or Bucks County, should be requested, who should be present and preside over the whole transaction"

No arguments are needed to prove that these sections constitute the forgery of which Boehm complained. It is incredible that any minister in his right mind could have written them They are not only inconsistent with Dr Wilhelmius' preceding advice to submit to the counsel of the Classis of Amsterdam, but they are also inherently absurd The ridiculous insistence on a supposed "divine right" of the congregation is enough to discredit them Moreover, why should the writer have taken the great trouble to work out elaborate rules for the guidance of the churches in Pennsylvania (which follow these sections immediately), if in his opinion the Palatinate church order was sufficient for their government? The pity of it all was that the "Fathers" in Holland paid no attention to these just complaints of Boehm, allowing his enemies to go on unrebuked The letter of Wilhelmius is dated December 31, 1730 Boehm's copy of this letter is in the Pennsylvania Portfolio, archives at Amsterdam, new letters, No. 10 It was printed in full in *Life and Letters of Boehm*, pp 303-311

In the spring of 1740, Mr. Boehm visited the Goshenhoppen congregations to secure from them, as he had secured from all the other Reformed congregations in Pennsylvania, a statement as to what they were willing to give towards a pastor's salary

In March, 1740, Boehm reported as follows to the Classis regarding his visit to Goshenhoppen:[125]

Concerning the congregation of Goshenhoppen I know not what to say. I have been there three times, yet I have not been able to do anything, although I entreated them very urgently not to cast aside the grace of God, now so clearly visible. When I went to them the third time, they [namely the elders] held a meeting on the 21st of February, and a part of them promised me at last to come to me on the 26th or 27th in order to sign the paper. I also heard that the people in Great Swamp and those at Saucon Creek were not at fault. However I did not see any of them.

Shortly afterwards, however, they sent in a report through Mr. Goetschy; the New Goshenhoppen congregation promising ten pounds, Great Swamp five pounds and Saucon Creek five pounds. The paper signed by the elders of the three congregations was as follows:[126]

(1). The congregation in New Goshenhoppen promises Ten Pounds.

> Herman Fischer
> George Steinmann
> Caspar Holtzhauser
> Andreas Greber
> } Elders

(2) The congregation in Great Swamp promises Five Pounds.

> Felix Brunner
> Michael Eberhard
> Christian Willauer
> Jacob Wetzel
> } Elders

---

[125] The original of Boehm's report is in the Classical archives. Printed in *Life and Letters of Boehm*, p. 296 f

[126] Also in archives of Classis See *Life and Letters of Boehm*, p. 293

(3) The congregation at Saucon Creek promises Five Pounds.

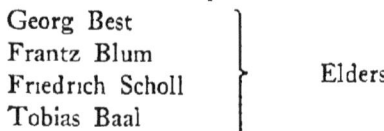

Georg Best
Frantz Blum
Friedrich Scholl
Tobias Baal
} Elders

At the same time when Boehm secured these pledges for pastor's salary, he also proposed to the Classis that the congregations in Pennsylvania be organized into six charges. The last and sixth charge to consist of New Goshenhoppen, Great Swamp and Saucon Creek. It is strange that he passes Old Goshenhoppen by entirely, which was certainly in existence, as is evident from the documents which we have already presented.

In repartitioning the congregations in 1740 (an earlier partitioning into four charges had been proposed by him in 1734), Boehm suggested not only how the congregations might be most advantageously combined into charges, but he also pointed out where the residences of the ministers might be most conveniently located. Thus he wrote of Goshenhoppen:[127]

VI. Goshenhoppen. As in the last two congregations [Oley and Tulpehocken], a place might here also be found for a minister's dwelling which would not be too inconvenient in order to supply Great Swamp and Saucon Creek from it.

The good feeling and spirit of cooperation, which was established between Boehm, Dorsius and Goetschy in 1740 did not last very long. In the winter of 1739-1740, Mr. Boehm had made an extended tour of visitation to all the Reformed congregations, traveling 300 miles on horseback to visit the various congregations, in order to ascertain how much each was willing to pay towards a pastor's salary.

[127] *Minutes of Coetus*, p. 16, also *Life and Letters of Boehm*, p 298.

The result of his visits was embodied by him in an elaborate report, which he placed into the hands of Dorsius, in order that he might transmit it to Holland. Instead of doing so, Dorsius made a summary of it in Dutch and sent that to Holland in his own name, giving there the impression that he himself had secured all the information which had been requested.[128] When Boehm heard of it he became very angry and on July 25, 1741, wrote a long letter of complaint to the Classis. In it he wrote:[129]

It seems to me that my sending over [a copy of] this letter [of Do. Wilhelmius] accounts largely for the ill-will, which his Reverence, Mr. Dorsius, bears me. For after I had secured this letter from Mr. Goetschi, after many efforts, and it became known to Mr. Dorsius, Goetschi came directly to me, brought me greetings and implored me to give him the letter again, under all kinds of pretense. He also said, that the Inspector, Mr. Dorsius, deemed it advisable to return the letter to the people, otherwise trouble might arise. But I thought that they were trying to make the letter disappear. I, therefore, declined in a friendly way and retained the letter. Now, whether his Reverence, Mr. Dorsius, is also of the opinion that every one in this country may do as he pleases, I leave to men, endowed with wisdom, to find out. For his Reverence ordained this young Goetschi, who caused so much harm here through the assistance of disorderly people and by the arbitrary transgression of our Reformed church order and customs. This ordination took place after he left Goshenhoppen, and had lived half a mile from his Reverence and studied under him for one year, on the 7th of April last [1741], with the assistance of Do Freilinghausen, of Randany [Raritan] and of another whose name I have not been able to find out as yet. But as far as I have heard, he is said to be one of the Tennents, who are of the Whitfield fol-

[128] Incorporated into the minutes of the Synodical Deputies, under date March 7–8, 1741.

[129] In Classical Archives, Pennsylvania Portfolio, No 14; see *Life and Letters of Boehm*, p 324 ff

lowers, otherwise called Presbyterians. I shall try to make certain. This Goetschi, as reported in my last submissive letter, had indeed asked for my forgiveness, in the presence of Mr. Dorsius, of the wrong committed against me and promised to live according to all order. This occurred on the 21st of February 1740. But what he did soon afterwards (and it can hardly be thought that he did it without the knowledge of his Reverence, Mr. Dorsius) may be seen from the enclosure, marked C He likewise made two oral offers to my regular congregation in Oley (according to their testimony) whereby this congregation also was separated and divided.

Enclosure C. is a letter from the elders at Tulpehocken,[130] addressed to Mr. Boehm, dated April 20, 1740, informing him that Mr Goetschy had written to them a letter in which he notified them that he and Mr. Dorsius would come to Tulpehocken in May and administer the Lord's Supper there.

In his report of 1744, Mr. Boehm confirms and enlarges upon his previous statements regarding the ordination of Mr. Goetschy and the conditions prevailing at Goshenhoppen. He writes:[131]

This congregation up to this time has claimed the privilege accorded to them in the letter which Reiff had when he returned from his collecting tour, and which purported to have been written by his Reverence, Doctor Wilhelmi of Rotterdam (whereof a copy may be found among the Pennsylvania papers). Hence they will not submit to any church-order. And no matter how much I may admonish them, they remain of the same mind. They had taken young Goetschi to be their pastor, but when Do. Dorsius arrived he withdrew from them, went to him, and studied a year with him, and after this year he was ordained as minister for Long Island in the month of April 1741, by Mr. Dorsius, assisted by Do. Fre-

[130] Classical Archives, Pennsylvania Portfolio, No. 17. Printed in *Life and Letters of Boehm*, p 342
[131] *Minutes of Coetus*, p 26, also *Life and Letters of Boehm*, p 419

linghuysen, of Raritan, and still another (as I learned afterwards) Tennant by name, of whom it was said that he was one of the Whitfielders.

In 1739, the Synods of Holland had notified the Pennsylvania churches (see *Life of Boehm*, p. 284) that they could expect no help from them, unless they would "refuse to hear the unordained ministers and hirelings." As a result Goetschy stopped preaching in 1740 (see p. 124), went to Dorsius, studied with him for a year, and was then ordained by Dorsius, Frelinghuysen and Tennent on April 7, 1741.

In October, 1740, Mr. Goetschy had gone to Long Island where he visited the congregations of Newtown, Jamaica, Hempstead and Oyster Bay, which extended a call to him.[132] This he accepted and moved to Long Island in the following year. Thus he left the German Reformed churches of Pennsylvania and assumed the ministry of the Dutch Reformed churches of Long Island. The validity of his ordination in 1741 was questioned and in order to preserve peace among his congregations and remove all objection he submitted to another examination and ordination in 1748.

In 1743 Goetschy published a sermon on the "Unknown God," which he had preached in Dutch in 1742 at several places. After a long and successful ministry of thirty-four years in the Dutch Reformed Church he died at Schraalenberg, N. J., November 14, 1774.[133]

[132] Corwin, *Manual of the Reformed Church in America*, 4th ed., p. 490 f.
[133] Corwin, *l c*, pp 489–492; Sprague, *Annals of the American Pulpit*, Vol IX, Part 2, pp. 15–17; Taylor, *Annals of the Classis of Bergen*, 1857, p. 185.

CHAPTER IV.

MINISTRY OF REV. PETER HENRY DORSIUS,
1741–1744.

IN Boehm's report of 1744, quoted above, is found the earliest reference to the next pastor at Goshenhoppen. Continuing the history of Goshenhoppen after the departure of Goetschy to Long Island, Mr. Boehm writes:[134]

Meanwhile, since Goetschi is no longer with them, Do. Dorsius has several times administered the Lord's Supper to this people before his journey to Holland.

This passage introduces us to a young minister, who had come to Pennsylvania in 1737.

As early as May 3, 1730, the elders of the Dutch Reformed congregation at Neshaminy, Bucks County, had written a letter to Rev. David Knibbe of Leyden and Rev. John Wilhelmius of Rotterdam, Holland, stating that, although small in number, they were anxious to secure a minister and had for that purpose canvassed the congregation and found that they were able to give 60 pounds, Pennsylvania currency, as salary to a pastor. Hence they asked these two Dutch pastors to secure them as a minister "a suitable young man of about 30 years of age, who has a distinct enunciation, is well grounded in the doctrine of

[134] *Minutes of Coetus*, p. 26.

the truth, able to instruct, admonish and to silence all adversaries, but no less edifying in his life."[135] They also guarantee him a free dwelling, fire wood and a free passage for himself and his baggage to Pennsylvania.

On May 29, 1734, Rev. Wilhelmius notified them that he had found a young candidate by name of Masius, whose father was pastor in the Low-German Reformed congregation at Altona near Hamburg. But when the time of his departure for Pennsylvania had come near, he had withdrawn. But, he informed them, that he had continued his efforts and had, a few weeks before, found "a certain young man suitable and pious, 24 years of age, who still needs one year to complete his studies. He shows great desire and eagerness to preach the Word of God among you. This man, I believe, will, under God's gracious blessing, be a useful and successful preacher among you, and I heartily recommend him to you. But the question is whether you will grant him a year's time to complete his studies, and whether I can advance him for this purpose such an amount of the money which I have received from you, as will be necessary for it and for his examination and ordination in this country." He reports further that the money which Reiff had given him in their name was still in his care and that the reason why he had not written sooner was partly because he had had no earlier opportunity, partly because Reiff had failed to call on him before his departure in order to take a letter along.

On October 30, 1734, nineteen members of the Nesha-

[135] This letter, as well as the later letters exchanged between the Dutch ministers in Holland and the Reformed Church at Neshaminy, Bucks County, are deposited in the archives of the Theological Seminary at New Brunswick, N. J. This letter is printed in full in a paper, submitted by the writer to the Bucks County Hist. Society, January 19, 1918, entitled "Life and Work of the Rev Peter H Dorsius."

miny congregation answered the letter of Dr. Wilhelmius. They expressed their willingness to wait for their pastor and gave Wilhelmius authority to use their money for him, but with the condition that he should see to his examination, ordination and transportation to America. They also reported that they were already busy in buying 40 or 50 acres as glebe land for their pastor's use.

On March 1, 1735, Dr. Wilhelmius sent another letter to the Bucks County people. He expressed his pleasure that they were satisfied with his choice of a pastor. He reported that the young man, just about 26 years old and unmarried, had already made such good progress in the ancient languages, Latin, Greek and Hebrew, that he was instructing others in them. He was also well advanced in theological studies. He was a pious young man and was burning with desire to preach the gospel of Jesus in another part of the world He had made him sign a paper, in which he obligated himself to go to Pennsylvania immediately after completing his studies, or to return the money advanced to him with double interest. Wilhelmius stated that the bearer of his letter was a Reformed minister from Switzerland [Rev Maurice Goetschy], through whom they hoped the churches in Pennsylvania would be well organized.

Another set of letters was exchanged between Wilhelmius and the congregation in 1736, and finally on May 22, 1737, Dr. Wilhelmius reported that Do. Dorsius had been ordained at Groningen and had left for Philadelphia with Captain Stedman.

On April 5, 1734, Dorsius had matriculated at the University of Groningen and on September 17, 1736, at Leyden. The entry in the matriculation book of the latter university is as follows:

Petrus Henricus Dorsius, 1736 Sept. 17.
Meursanus, 25. T.

This means that on the above date Peter Henry Dorsius, a native of Meurs, 25 years old, matriculated as a student of theology. This corrects the statement of Dr. Wilhelmius as to his age. According to his own statement in the matriculation book he was born in 1711.

Fortunately we are now able to present definite information regarding the family and age of Mr. Dorsius from the church records at Meurs (now Moers), which the present pastor, Rev. W. Rotscheidt, very kindly communicated to the writer,[136] for which he deserves the gratitude of the Reformed Church in the United States.

Peter Henry Dorsius was the son of Johann Henrich "Dorschius" of Moers. His father was a widower when he married Peternella Gravers of Altkirch, on September 15, 1708. Their children were as follows:

1 Alethea, baptized November 15, 1709.
2. Peter Hendrich, baptized January 2, 1711.
3 Abraham, baptized August 5, 1712
4. Isaac, baptized December 22, 1713, died soon afterwards.
5 Isaac, baptized March 8, 1715

An older relative of his, who acted as sponsor at his baptism, Samuel Dorsius, entered the Gymnasium Adolphinum at Moers on May 8, 1708. Isaac Dorsius, probably his younger brother, entered the gymnasium on May 5, 1727. His own name does not seem to be registered there. Hence he probably studied somewhere else. In 1734 he entered the university of Groningen, as we have seen, and in 1736 that of Leyden. In the following year he left Holland for Pennsylvania.

He himself has given a description of his journey to

[136] In a letter, dated February 16, 1914.

Dorsius leaves Holland

Pennsylvania and his first experiences there in a letter, which he addressed to the Synodical Deputies in June, 1749. He writes:[137]

It is about twelve years ago, after I had been received, on April 30, 1737, by the Classis of Schieland at Rotterdam among the number of the candidates of theology, and on May 29th of the same year had been ordained by the very learned theological faculty at Groningen to be a minister of the gospel, that, on July 11 [1737], I undertook the great and dangerous journey from Rotterdam to Pennsylvania, when we did not arrive safely at Philadelphia till October 5th; however, with the loss of many persons, who had died at sea and had been buried in the great ocean. Then I inquired immediately after my location. I learnt at once at the beginning that I, as well as others, had been woefully misled, and thus was sadly compelled to preach in the barn of one farmer after another, because there was no house of God; and at the same time take up my lodging with one family after another in the woods [bosch], as they are accustomed to call it in this land. This made me think of returning speedily, but I was kept back by my conscience and the example of early Christians. Through the encouraging and cheering letters of the very learned Rev. Mr. Ernest Engelbert Probsting, p t., scriba of Synod, written to me in the name and by the order of the Reverend Deputies of both Synods, I was much strengthened to continue in the difficult work of the ministry which I had undertaken

Mr. Boehm refers to the arrival of Dorsius in a letter addressed to the Classis of Amsterdam on March 10, 1738, in which he says:[138]

Last fall there came to this country Do. Dorsius, as a regular minister of the Dutch Reformed congregation at Neshaminy, Bucks County, and with him another by the name of Van Basten, who,

[137] Hague Archives, 74, II, 12
[138] Classical Archives, Pennsylvania Portfolio, No 1 See *Life and Letters of Boehm*, p 259 f

although he was not ordained, yet travels here and there through the country and preaches, saying that he had been sent from Holland. But he has given us absolutely no cause for joy.

Turning to the immigrant lists of Rupp, we find that on September 26, 1737, John Herman von Basten,[139] "Candidatus S. Th.," arrived at Philadelphia in the ship *Andrew Galley*, John Stedman, master, from Rotterdam. This must have been the ship on which Mr. Dorsius came. We know from the letter of Dr. Wilhelmius, quoted above, that he came with Captain Stedman, and we know from his own letter of June 1749, that he arrived on October 5, 1737. The latter is the date according to the "new style." It is, however, surprising that the name of Dorsius does not occur in the list as given by Rupp, while in the list given in the *Pennsylvania Archives*, Second Series, Vol. XVII, pp. 138–140, both names are wanting.

The bill for the ship's passage of Mr. Dorsius from Captain Stedman and the receipt of Dorsius given to his consistory on September 28, 1737, are still in existence.[140] They read as follows:

	Myn Heer Dorsius	Dr
	To John Stedman	
to his passage & goods	. . .	.. P. 15 —
to Duty in England		.... P. 1·½
to Citty Dues		. 3/2
to fresh Provision in England		. P. 2 ½
	Total	. P. 19·0

[139] The immigrant list in Rupp's *Thirty Thousand Names*, p 109, give us at last the correct Christian name of Van Basten. In December, 1738, Dorsius reports him as having preached at Amwell, N J, and on Long Island and as being at that time at Fishkill, N. Y, see *Ecclesiastical Records of New York*, Vol IV, p. 2741 In 1739-40 he is reported as preaching at Jamaica, Success, Oyster Bay and Newtown, N. Y But he was addicted to drink, hence his activity as a minister was brief After 1740 he disappears. See Corwin, *Manual*, 4th ed , pp. 807, 1011, 1016

[140] Part of church records at New Brunswick, N. J

Receipt of Rev. P H. Dorsius,

I, the undersigned, acknowledge clearly and distinctly to have received from the Reverend Consistory, elders and deacons, the sum of six and twenty pounds, fifteen shillings and two pence, Pennsylvania currency, for the passage money of person and goods, together with the expenses from Rotterdam to Pennsylvania for Captain John Stedman.

Given in Philadelphia, September 28, 1737.

P. H. DORSIUS, minister in Bucks County, Pennsylvania.

Dorsius and Boehm worked together very harmoniously till the spring of 1740, when Boehm in answer to the request of the Holland Synods, communicated to him through Dorsius, had prepared his elaborate report of 1739, and had handed it to Dorsius with the request to send it to Holland. When Dorsius failed to do this, Boehm became very indignant

On November 30, 1740, the elders of Boehm wrote a defence of their pastor to the Classis, with affidavits regarding the events that had taken place.

In the affidavit it is said:[141]

When Mr. Dorsius, minister at Neshaminy, was at Goshenhoppen on the 24th of September 1740, and baptized children, in his anger against our minister, Mr. Boehm, he burst out without any reserve, in the following expressions among others: "If Boehm says that I have not sent the letters, which he wrote regarding the church, to Holland, he lies like a scoundrel" and this he repeated several times.

Privately to Boehm, Dorsius had admitted that the letter had not been sent off. In support of Boehm his elders wrote.[142]

[141] Classical Archives, Pennsylvania Portfolio, No 15 See *Life and Letters of Boehm*, p. 338

[142] L c, No 16. See *Life and Letters of Boehm*, p. 339

138   History of the Goshenhoppen Charge

His Reverence [Mr. Dorsius] visited the congregations Saucon and New Goshenhoppen on his return home from Minisink. As far as we know he did not visit any other congregations in the back woods. At that time his Reverence had the young Goetschi preach the sermon and read the baptismal formula, while he baptized the children. Afterwards all that is stated above took place. It is impossible for us to let the case rest here because his Reverence has not only treated our beloved and faithful pastor so unkindly, but he also attacked the respect due to the reverend men and devout church fathers, who established our pure divine worship in this country.

During the ministry of Dorsius, in the year 1742, the second schoolmaster appears in Goshenhoppen. On December 21, 1742, the Bethlehem Diary reports a visit at Bethlehem of "John Adam Luckenbach, schoolmaster at Goshenhoppen." He was born in 1713 at Winckelbach, near Hachenburg, in Nassau, Germany. On September 30, 1740, he arrived with two other members of his family at Philadelphia. He served as schoolmaster in various localities, first at Goshenhoppen. In 1743, we find him at Muddy Creek, where he assisted Jacob Lischy. When Lischy moved to York County, in 1745, Luckenbach accompanied him and became schoolmaster in Kreutz creek. In 1754, he was schoolmaster in Allemaengel, Lynn township, Lehigh County. He married Eva Maria Spiess, who bore him one son and two daughters. He died in 1785 at Saucon and was buried in the Moravian cemetery at Bethlehem.[142a]

According to Boehm's report of 1744, already quoted, Dorsius administered the Lord's Supper "several times" before his journey to Holland, which took place in 1743.

[142a] See Reincke, *Register of Moravians*, pp 111, 131, Schultze, *Guide to the Old Moravian Cemetery at Bethlehem* (PROC OF PA. GERM SOC, Vol XXI, p. 14).

In perfect agreement with this statement we find thirteen children baptized at New Goshenhoppen on August 30, 1741, and six children on September 4, 1742. Then there is a break in the baptismal record till May, 1744 In the interval Dorsius undertook a journey to Holland. This was undertaken, as he explained later to the Deputies, because there was no prospect of growth for the Dutch Reformed Church in Pennsylvania, first, because their number was becoming constantly smaller through sickness and death; secondly, because through intermarriage the members were lost to the church, and thirdly, because they had no school-teachers to teach the children the Dutch language. In view of this condition Dorsius desired permission either to accept a call to another church or to remain in Holland. As his letter to the Deputies, written in June, 1749, gives an interesting account of this journey, it may be quoted in part:[143]

I considered all this very carefully, besides, the continual complaints of the consistory (which had to collect the pastor's salary), that they were no longer able to pay the 68 pounds of salary which they had promised, without injuring their own families, as they were not able to secure the promised salary from the congregation, but had been compelled to add each year enough money so as to complete the salary; hence after full deliberation I concluded to return to my fatherland and to undertake the difficult and expensive journey in the strength of the Lord of Lords, also to call the consistory together, submit to them my plans, ask for a certificate, in case it should happen that I would not return. This was done on the 9th of March, o s. My just request was granted and a certificate was given to me, together with a petition to the Rev. Deputies for another faithful shepherd and teacher, at a lower salary, in as much as I might feel inclined to stay in my own country. This certificate and also the letters written to me by the

[143] The same letter of Dorsius quoted before, see note 137.

learned Mr. Probsting, I handed over to the Christian Synod of North Holland in the year 1743, in answer to the request of the Rev. Mr. Cornelius Houthoff, p. t., deputy of the Synods These writings are most likely still in the hands of the reverend gentlemen.

Then I began the great journey on the 26th of May, 1743, o.s., from New York to Amsterdam, where I arrived safely and well on the 14th of July at Texel. Then on the 26th and 27th of July I appeared before the Christian Synod of North Holland held at Hoorn, in order to make known the lamentable and desolate condition of the American Reformed churches, especially of the Dutch people, over whom I had been placed as shepherd and teacher. This, however, did not have the result or effect, which I had desired or expected. I could not stay in Holland because on the one hand it was to be feared that the fire of war might break out between France and England, which would make the Spanish Sea, over which we had to sail, unsafe and dangerous to travelers, as to our grief, it proved to be the case in the spring of the following year. On the other hand, my domestic affairs (of which I do not wish to speak further) could not be arranged so as to make it possible for me to stay longer in Holland. Moreover, a suitable opportunity offered itself so that I could readily bear the expense of the journey and return home again.

Hence on the 19th of October 1743, o.s., I again undertook the great journey across the sea, when after suffering, especially in the neighborhood of Ireland, many hardships and dangers on the ocean, common to the winter season, I did not reach Philadelphia till January 16, 1744, o.s., though in good health. From there I returned to Bucks County, where I tried to discharge the duties of the ministry faithfully.

Shortly after his return from Holland, Dorsius visited Goshenhoppen again. Boehm in his report of 1744 refers at length to this visit:[144]

[144] *Minutes of Coetus*, p. 26 f.; also *Life and Letters of Boehm*, p 419 f.

BOEHM'S ACCOUNT OF GOSHENHOPPEN IN 1744.

As I learned on Tuesday after last Easter at Goshenhoppen from a ruling elder, it is arranged that he [Dorsius] shall again administer the Lord's Supper to them in the next coming month of May. On this Tuesday after Easter, when I happened to come to Goshenhoppen, I found this among them: On Good Friday, they allowed the base deceiver, Jacob Lischy, to preach in their church, who at the same time baptized two children. When I represented to two elders, who were together on this Tuesday after Easter, the impropriety of this act in the presence of several people, in having permitted a Moravian to do such things they answered me that they themselves had held it up to him, but he had protested with an oath and called upon God to forsake him if he were a Moravian. He claimed to be a Reformed preacher from Switzerland. Then I showed them his Moravian hymn book, entitled "Shepherd Songs of Bethlehem, for the use of all who are humble," which before this was his own pocket hymn book, and came to my hands in a wonderful but honorable way, in which he had written his name with his own hand; When they compared the letter he had written to them with it and saw that it was his own handwriting, they realized his wicked conduct, the more so because, when they told him that I had this little book, he denied it was his, saying that he knew nothing of the book, that others could easily write his name in a book; he could not prevent that, and that for this reason he had long regarded me as a treacherous Boehm, of whom he had heard before in Holland, etc. Then they acted as if they were sorry. But one among them, Michael Radner, confessed that it was his fault alone that Lischy had come into the church Whereupon I took my departure. The next day I spoke with another ruling elder, who was not present the day before. This one said to me with a sad heart, almost with tears: "But what shall we do? Mr. Dorsius has told us we should not think that we could get ministers from Holland. We should ourselves see to it, what was to be done." The Hollanders had said: "What do the Pennsylvanians imagine themselves to be? They live in a free country, have nothing to pay to any royal court, yet want to give but ten pounds in such a large congregation to a minister; then we cannot provide them with a minister," etc. Nevertheless I admonished them to remain steadfast in prayer, and without being discouraged to wait upon God's favor. As for me, I felt assured that if our pious church Fathers desired to admonish us or were displeased about anything, they would not thus rudely present it, but speak of it in an amicable and friendly manner, becoming to servants of God. But according to my expectations the affairs of our church would take quite a different turn under the providence of God and his guidance. And thus we separated . . .

Do. Dorsius has also promised the people at New Goshenhoppen to administer the Lord's Supper there on May 6th, and that on the 7th he would be at Old Goshenhoppen, situated about four miles from Skippack, where the Lutheran and Reformed people wish to build a union church (whereby again some members will be drawn away from Skippack, for until now this district had belonged to Skippack) and on May 7th he will there lay the cornerstone. On this occasion the Lutheran preacher, Andres by name, and Do. Dorsius are each to preach a sermon. Do. Dorsius asked said Lutheran pastor to announce this from his pulpit for the benefit of his Lutheran congregation, which he did on April 8th. Afterwards I was told by some of my elders who were present that the Lutheran minister distinctly said: "Rev. Inspector Dorsius will administer the Lord's Supper on May 6th at New Goshenhoppen for the Reformed people, and on the 7th ditto, at the laying of the corner-stone of the union church at Old Goshenhoppen, he as well as myself (the Lutheran pastor) will preach the first sermon (which words a certain man who had heard them told me with astonishment in my house on the 16th of April). . . .

P.S. On May 6th, Do. Dorsius administered the Lord's Supper at New Goshenhoppen, several persons from Falkner Swamp communed there without saying anything.

On May 7th, the corner-stone of the above mentioned union church was to be laid; a considerable number of people were pres-

OLD GOSHENHOPPEN CHURCH, BUILT 1744.

THE NEW YORK
PUBLIC LIBRARY

ASTOR, LENOX
TILDEN FOUNDATIONS

ent, but the day was rainy. Do Dorsius did not come It was postponed till Whit Monday, May 14th, old style. Do Dorsius again did not come. But an elder of New Goshenhoppen was appointed to represent Do. Dorsius, and the work was thus accomplished.

The presence of Do. Dorsius at New Goshenhoppen in May, 1744, is corroborated by the church record, for on May 5, 1744, six children were baptized, and their baptisms entered into the church record by one of the elders. The pastor who officiated was undoubtedly Mr. Dorsius.

The cornerstone laying at the Old Goshenhoppen church is described more fully in the Old Goshenhoppen Lutheran record, which has also preserved the agreement, then drawn up by the Lutheran and Reformed people. It is as follows:

AGREEMENT PLACED IN CORNERSTONE OF OLD GOSHENHOPPEN CHURCH, MAY 14, 1744

Anno 1744, May 14th, through the wonderful providence of the all-wise God and against all expectations, these two congregations, Lutheran and Reformed, began to build a large, beautiful stone church. In this year was laid the cornerstone, in which the following writing was put and deposited:

IN THE NAME OF THE BLESSED TRINITY, AMEN.

Through the all-wise providence of God it has come to pass that both Evangelical congregations, Lutheran and Reformed, concluded to build a new stone-church, for which the corner-stone was laid today in the name of God Inasmuch as under such circumstances, and for the safety of both parties, a written agreement is necessary, showing in what manner each congregation is to conduct itself and what rights each possesses, therefore, the following contract has been made and established by us:

First: We implore unitedly and with burning hearts the almighty and all-gracious God, that he may not allow any discord or dissension to arise among us, but may preserve us in love and unity, that our Christian work, undertaken by us, may have a happy issue.

Secondly: No congregation, neither Lutheran nor Reformed, shall have any preference in the divine service, nor shall any congregation have more rights in the church than the other, but everything shall be done in love, without confusion and disorder, nor shall either congregation disturb the divine services of the other.

Thirdly: We stipulate mainly and earnestly, that no false teacher, suspected of heresy, who adheres to neither the Lutheran nor the Reformed doctrines, shall under any circumstances be permitted or tolerated in our house of God, but in such a case either congregation shall have authority, right and power to close and lock the church against such a false teacher.

To our posterity we wish temperal and eternal blessedness. And, inasmuch as Jesus Christ is the only corner-stone and foundation of our faith, who is made unto us wisdom, righteousness, sanctification and redemption, therefore may he grant that this our faith may be continued and preserved to all times, in order that we all at last, when heaven and earth perish, may be translated from the church militant unto the church triumphant, and then, before the throne of the Lamb, all of us, with one accord, may honor and praise God, through our dear Lord Jesus Christ.

In testimony whereof the elders of both congregations have affixed their own signatures.

Old Goshenhoppen, May 14, 1744.

Reformed:	Lutherans·
CHRISTIAN SCHNEIDER	MICHAEL REIHER + his mark
CHRISTIAN LEHMANN	BALSAR GERLACH
BERNHARD ARND	PHILIP GABEL
JOHANN ZIEWER.	⸜CONRAD SCHNEIDER.

As to the cost of the church nothing certain is at hand, because, in the first place, the two congregations have helped and given much, and in the next place, other friends have also contributed their share.

CORNERSTONE OF OLD GOSHENHOPPER CHURCH, 1744.
(See Page 145.)

HOUSE OF WILLIAM DEWEES, WHITEMARSH.
(REFORMED PEOPLE OF WHITEMARSH MET HERE, 1725-1745.)

The cornerstone of the first church at Old Goshenhoppen is still preserved in the right hand corner of the present building. It bears an interesting Latin inscription:

LIberaLItas pLebIs	i. e. The liberality of the people
LVtheranæ atqVe	Lutheran and also
reforMatæ has æDes	Reformed this house
Vna eXstrVXIt.	unitedly has erected.
I C. ANDREÆ. PAST. LVTH.	J. C. Andreae, Luth pastor.

The inscription is unique because the capital letters when added together give the year 1744. This can be easily demonstrated:

Line 1.	LI.	LI	LI = 153
Line 2	L	V	V = 60
Line 3	M	D	= 1500
Line 4	V.	X.	VXI = 31
			1744

This ingenious method of indicating the date is probably due to the Lutheran pastor, J. C. Andreae, whose name was put into the last line of the inscription.

Shortly before the cornerstone laying of the Old Goshenhoppen church took place, the church wardens or trustees of the two congregations had drawn up a "declaration of trust," which because of its contents and remarkable English deserves to be published in full, spelling and all, verbatim and literatim. It is dated April 16, 1744:

DECLARATION OF TRUST BY OLD GOSHENHOPPEN ELDERS, APRIL 16, 1744

To all Christian People to Whom these Presents Writings Shall Come Know Ye that We Michael Reyer, Churchwardens of the Lutherian Congregation & Jacob Keller, Churchwardens of the Reformirth Congregation of Upper Sollford Township in the

County of Philadelphia are Lawfully Invested by a Warrant of the Hounorable the Propriedais Date the twelfth Day of January anno Domini 1737 there was Surveyed and laid out on the Sixteenth Day of the Said Month unto us the said Michael Reyer and Jacob Keller of the County of Philadelphia a certain Tract of Land Seituate in the s^d Upper Sollford Township in the s^d County BEGINNING at a Post in a Line of other Land of the said Jacob Keller and Extending thence by the Same South East Seventy Perches to a Post thence by other Land of the Said Michael Reyer Southwest ninety three Perches to a Post at a Corner of Adam Mayrers Land thence by the same North west Seventy Perches to a Post thence by Vacant Land North East Neinty three Perches to the place of Beginning Containing thirty Eight acres and a quarter and an allowance Proportional to Six acres Per Cent. for Roads and Highways as in and by the Survey thereof remaining in the Surveyor Generals Office may appear—

Now KNOW YE that we the s^d. Michael Reyer & Jacob Keller, Chosen Churchwardens of both the said Congregations have gathered so moch money as woult pay for s^d tract of Land and Cost and Charges to pay, and was agreed between them two said Congregations that this place shall be for no other use but to built a Shoolhause and in Fouture to come a Chirch to keep a Schoolmaster upon said pleace Either between the both Congragations or Every on for them selfes and also built a Church between both s^d Congregation or Every one for them selfes and we Paid for said Land & patend warrant and Recortern and sum other Costs Eight pounds nine Shillings & Three pence of the money we gathered. Now because the Patend and also the Draught of s^d tract is made upon us and in our names weilst it Could not be Done otherwise, So we Prodest and Declear by and with this presents, that we or our Heirs, Exect^s, Administ^s, or Assigns shall have no claim or Demand of in or to the s^d Land or any part thereof From or after our Decease but to permit and Suffer the s^d two Congregations their Heirs and Assigns and Every of them to have, possess and enjoy to their own use for Ever the said Land and Every part thereof without any Let or disturbance of or by us our Exect^s

Administs or Assigns or of or by any other person or persons or by this or any of their acts means consents or procurements Clearly released acquitted and Discharged of and from all Incumbrances What So Ever by them had, made and Committed or Done or to be had made Committed or Done but the two Congarigations between them shall pay the Quittrend Due and for Ever to come to the Hounorable the Propriedars according as it is mentioned in the patend we have and Shall also have the two Congrigations the Reight and Power given in the patend to us, that we never have any more to Demand than another man of the s^d two congrigations and that also for the true performans We give to Every Congrigations this writings from unter our hands and Seals Dated this 16th Day of Aprill in the year of our Lord one Thousand Seven Hundred and fourty four Annoque Domini 1744.

Sealed & Delivered in the presence of us

CHRISTIAN $\times$ LEHMAN his mark	MICHAEL $\times$ REYER (SEAL) his mark
ADAM $\times$ MEYRER his mark	CHRISTIAN SCHNEYDER in place of JACOB KELLER (SEAL)

Philad^a 12th Jany 1737 Received of Michael Royer and Jacob Keller five pounds Seventeen Shillings & nine Pence in full for thirty eight acres of Land Surveyed to them in Salford Township in the County of Philadelphia. Received for the use of the Proprietaries.

£5 17s. 9d.   JAMES STEELYARD.

After 1744, Dorsius visited Goshenhoppen no more, although he remained pastor of Neshaminy, Bucks County, till 1748, when he returned to Holland. There he died about the year 1757. [145] The last reference to him is in

---

[145] For earlier accounts of Dorsius see Harbaugh, *Fathers of the Reformed Church*, Vol II (1872), p. 375 f ; Good, *History of the Reformed Church*, pp 190–199; Dubbs, *Reformed Church in Pennsylvania*, pp 92–94, Corwin, *Manual of Reformed Church*, 4th ed , pp 429–31. The most

the minutes of the Classis of Amsterdam, under date October 5, 1750.[145a] From 1752 to 1776 his widow received support from the Coetus of Pennsylvania.

extensive account of the "Life and Work of the Rev. Peter H. Dorsius" was given by the writer in a paper submitted to the Bucks County Hist. Society, see above, note 135.

[145a] *Ecclesiastical Records of New York,* Vol. IV, p. 3138.

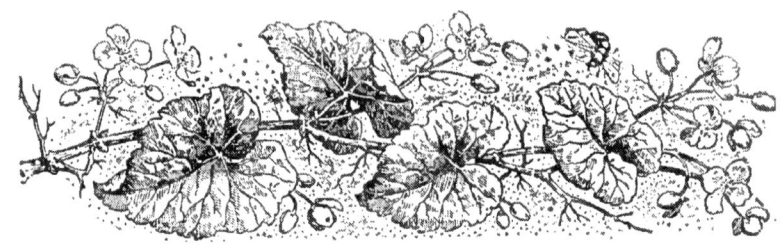

CHAPTER V.

Ministry of Frederick Casimir Mueller, 1745–1748.

ON July 7, 1745, a new handwriting appears in the New Goshenhoppen record. It is that of Frederick Casimir Mueller. On September 27, 1745, he acted as sponsor at the baptism of a son of Johan Adam Mengel. On March 23, 1746, a son of Frederick Casimir Mueller himself was baptized with Johann Hoffmann and Friedrich Helwig as witnesses. The record itself gives no indication that Mueller was actually the pastor of the congregation. All that can be inferred from the record is that between July 7, 1745, and April 28, 1750, he entered thirty-five baptisms into the record. But what is lacking in the record is fully supplied by other evidence.

In Schlatter's private diary we read under date September 20, 1746:[146]

I preached in the new stone church at Old Goshenhoppen, but inasmuch as a considerable part of the New Goshenhoppen congregation adheres to a certain hireling, Frederick Casimir Mueller, who was a school teacher but now wants to be a minister, I was not able to accomplish anything. I concluded to investigate this

[146] Printed in *Journal of P. H. S.*, Vol. III, p. 111 f.

matter at some other time and then fix the salary I shall also endeavor to bring about, with the help of God, unity in the congregation, since Do. Weiss is generally liked. But, whereas some adhere to the above-mentioned Fred. Mueller, it is necessary to use prudence, because he is a bold fellow and was in the congregation before Do. Weiss returned from Rhinebeck.

At a later place in the same diary Schlatter refers at length to Casimir Mueller and sheds considerable light on his activity:[147]

The above mentioned Frederick Casimir Mueller is the only one thus far known to me, who is not willing to submit to any order, but, as he states himself, will create as much dissension and division as possible But I trust to Almighty God, that Mueller alone will not be able to hinder the progress of God's work, which otherwise is blessed everywhere.

He has now 10 or 12 small congregations in and about Oley and in New Goshenhoppen about 18 men, who adhere to him and refuse to side with Do. Weiss, being so to speak bewitched with his bragging and assurance. During the whole week he rides about and tries to make the kind intention of the Reverend Synods obnoxious to his adherents, pretending that if they submit to them they will lose their liberty and accept unbearable fetters.

I asked him to come to see me in Oley on September 23rd. At that time he appeared to me rather favorable, and in view of your Reverences' counsel, I made to him the following proposition in the presence of Do. Weiss: Whether, if he were a true Reformed man, he would from now on abstain from administering the Lord's Supper and from uniting people in marriage, until I had written to the Reverend Fathers and received their answer, whether the Reverend Synods deemed it wise that, like Dom. Boehm in former years, he be ordained by a Coetus and be installed as a regular minister in a regular congregation? To this he heartily agreed, but on the following Sunday, through God's wonderful providence,

[147] L c, p 119

THE PENNSYLVANIA-GERMAN SOCIETY.

Michael Schlatter

he made himself unworthy of the good opinion which I had formed about him. For he baptized children as before and announced the administration of the Lord's Supper in four weeks. Hence I lost all desire to write to you in his behalf

From the Hebron Diary, written by the Moravian pastors at Lebanon, it appears that Frederick was the call name of Frederick Casimir Mueller, for his name always appears there as Frederick Mueller. The same conclusion can be drawn from his own signature, which is usually Friederich C. Müller.

Rupp's *Thirty Thousand Names,* notes the arrival of three Friedrich Muellers from 1727–1744. On September 30, 1743, a Friedrich Miller qualified, whose name was written by the clerk, probably because he himself was unable to write. On September 24, 1742, a Friederich Muller qualified, who came in the same ship as John Jacob Riess, another Reformed pastor at Goshenhoppen. A third Friedrich Muller arrived October 28, 1738. We are inclined to regard the second Mueller identical with our Frederick Casimir Mueller, because he was apt to make his presence felt shortly after his arrival.

In spite of Schlatter's unfavorable opinion, Mueller preached acceptably to numerous Reformed congregations and no doubt did a good work, in his own way. It may serve, therefore, a useful purpose to put together the scattered references to his life and work.

In a letter of Schlatter, dated October 3, 1746, which is lost in the original, but an extract of which has been preserved in the Minutes of the Synodical Deputies of March 21–22, 1747, Schlatter states that Mueller had been a school teacher at a place near Mayence, in the Palatinate. In July, 1745, he appears for the first time in Pennsylvania, as pastor of the New Goshenhoppen congregation.

On October 19, 1746, Schlatter visited New Goshenhoppen again, in order to restore if possible order and harmony in the congregation. His private diary describes his experiences at that time as follows:[148]

On the 19th, I traveled to New Goshenhoppen, 18 miles, together with Dos. Boehm and Weiss, in order to remove if possible the division which had been caused in the congregation by the above mentioned Miller

I preached from II. Chron. 15 · 2-4. After that I tried to gain the adherents of Miller with love and kind words and win them for Do. Weiss, but Miller, who was in the church, controlled his party to such an extent that all my efforts were in vain. He is said to have declared from the pulpit, last Sunday, October 16th, that even if the black and white wigs (meaning the Hollanders and Switzers), would come, they could not drive him away. Finally I wanted to know how strong his adherents were and asked them to raise their right hand, but they refused, saying that they would not swear an oath. Then I asked them that, as a sign of their difference, they should put on their hats, but they refused that also At last I asked that those who held with Do. Weiss should cover their heads, thus I was able to count the others against their will, namely 17 or 18 families. Thereupon I admonished them all to be peaceful and I caused the party of Do Weiss, numbering about 30, to put upon paper their contribution toward his salary, which amounted to about 15 pounds and thirty bushels of wheat.

In Schlatter's diary, as published by Dr. Harbaugh in his "Life of Rev. Michael Schlatter," p. 140, is this additional sentence: "Although we did not, at this time, succeed in accomplishing this object, yet the Lord interposed some time afterwards and restored order."

Almost immediately after the visit of Schlatter, Mueller wrote him a letter on October 29, 1746, which, following the "old style," he dated October 18, 1746. As it is the

[148] *L c*, p 160.

only letter of Mueller in existence and reveals clearly his attitude and spirit, we shall give it in full:[149]

LETTER OF FREDERICK C. MUELLER TO SCHLATTER

Goshenhoppen, October 18, 1746.

I have thought much about you, since I saw and heard you at Goshenhoppen, for the reason that I expect you to organize everything in good order. You ought to know that church questions cannot be treated like secular affairs, which was done nevertheless. At the city hall I saw how people were asked to raise their hands or make a sign with their hat. That is the way it looked at your organization, to the amusement of the sects

I do not wish to make you proud, but simply to write you the thoughts of my heart. I care little or nothing whether you send a petition to Holland or not, nor will I allow you to forbid me anything. If I need a petition, my congregations are willing to draw it up themselves, for they can give the best testimonial regarding me. I am ready to submit to an honorable Church Council, but not to beg for anything, and if my congregations submit a testimonial to the honorable Church Council as to you and take as much interest in it as you, I shall have good help, but they will not drive me away from the congregations which love me heartily You should know that neither money nor anything else will induce me to give up the congregation, even if Mr. Weiss's salary for two years be offered to me. You promised to secure me a place as a schoolteacher. I hope you will stand by your word, but if you are unable, because you can issue no command which the farmers must respect, I shall look for such a place myself

I wish you heartfelt humility from him who can give abundantly. I shall report the outcome of the affair to the Rev. Mr Bruynings in Amsterdam, whom I know and love heartily.

Your ever ready (Servant)
FRID. CASIMIR MULLER.

[149] Hague Archives, 74, I, 51 (9).

154 *History of the Goshenhoppen Charge*

We cannot state definitely when Mueller left Goshenhoppen. It may have been in 1747, for on September 29, 1747, Rev. George Michael Weiss reported New Goshenhoppen as one of his congregations.[150] But inasmuch as Do. Weiss dates the beginnings of his ministry in 1748, it is more likely that Mueller withdrew in that year. Weiss heads his baptismal entries with the statement "from 1748 till the year 1758, the following adult persons were baptized, upon the profession of their faith." Also his catechumens were recorded from the year 1748. Nevertheless, Mueller continued his visits to Goshenhoppen, for in 1749, January to July, he entered five baptisms into the record and one on April 28, 1750. The record book remained in the hands of Mueller's followers till 1757, when it passed into the custody of Weiss. But even as late as 1752 we hear of a Mueller faction in New Goshenhoppen.

In order to realize the importance of Mueller for the Reformed Church, we must review his labors outside of Goshenhoppen. It is at present impossible for us to identify all of the ten or twelve congregations in and about Oley, which Schlatter reports him as serving in 1746 We can, however, trace his activity in a number of congregations.

In 1746, he appears in Berne, Berks Co. An entry in the Berne record by his hand reads: " Register [showing] how many and whose children were entered by me Friedrich Casimir Muller, at this time preacher, 1746." His handwriting stops in November, 1746. Then there is a break till February, 1749, when a new set of entries begins running till April, 1752. Though not written by Miller himself, it is barely possible that the baptisms were performed by him.

[150] *Minutes of Coetus*, p. 33.

Pastorates of Mueller

In 1748, Mueller appears in Long Swamp, Berks County. After stating that the first church there had been begun in September, 1748, Jacob Weimer, the faithful schoolmaster, writes in the Long Swamp record: "After having completed this church to the honor of God and for their own salvation, they called the Rev. Fridrig Casemer Miller to dedicate this house and they accepted him as their preacher, who served them for some time." How long Mueller stayed at Long Swamp is not certainly known, but probably till 1752.

In October, 1752, the Minutes of Coetus report[151] that he was "supported by a part of that congregation" at Muddy Creek, whereby he was causing considerable trouble to the pastor, Rev. John Waldschmidt.

On October 11, 1753, Mueller applied to the factional Coetus, held at that time at Cocalico, to be received as a member. But his request was not granted [152]

In the same year Mueller appears as pastor of Coventry (now Brownback's), in Chester County. On February 18, 1753, he baptized there the first child. His entries extend there till November, 1761.

In 1762 he signed an account at the Heidelberg Church (now Hains' Church), near Wernersville, Berks County. In the same year he appears as pastor of the Reformed Church at Lebanon. On July 18, 1762, he dedicated the newly-built Reformed Church there, as is stated in the Hebron Diary. He opened the church record at Lebanon on November 24, 1764.[153] His entries, eighteen in number, extend till April 5, 1766. On September 28, 1764,

---

[151] *Minutes of Coetus*, p 73

[152] *L. c*, p 108

[153] For the ministry of Frederick Casimir Mueller at Lebanon, see the writer's "History of Tabor Reformed Church, Lebanon, Pa.," in the *Reformed Church Messenger* of August 4 and September 8, 1904

156 *History of the Goshenhoppen Charge*

the Hebron Diary reports the death of Rev. Mueller's wife, who was a daughter of Veronica Leidolt. The Moravian pastors at Lebanon speak of Mueller in a friendly way[154] and exchanged visits with him. But while Mueller's handwriting stops in the Lebanon record in April, 1766, it is continued at Swatara till July 3, 1768. He probably died soon afterwards.

Frederick Casimir Mueller has had the distinction of having had two doubles.

In 1855, Rev. Henry Wagner published a *Kurzgefasste Hundertjahrige Geschichte der Bergkirche in Lebanon County, Pennsylvania*, in which he refers, p. 4, to a Mr. Friederich, a Swiss minister, who followed Tempelman in 1760 He is said to have had a quick temper and soon returned to Europe. His name is perpetuated by Dr. Harbaugh in his *Fathers of the Reformed Church*, Vol. II, p. 384; by Dr. Corwin, *Manual*, 3rd ed., p. 265; and also by Dr Good, *History of German Reformed Church*, p. 649 Later, when the *Hebron Diary* became known, it was found that, beginning with 1762, it men-

[154] What appears at first sight as a very serious charge against Mueller is made in Saur's paper, *Pennsylvanische Berichte*, under date June 16, 1749, where the following notice is inserted " Henry Adam of Maxetani makes known that his wife Maria has left him faithlessly and turned to (hat sich gewendet zu) Friedrich Casimir Muller None may loan or give her anything on his [Adam's] account, as he will not pay it" This statement does not necessarily prove that the woman had eloped with Mueller She may have left her husband and entered Mueller's family as a servant The New Goshenhoppen record proves that Mueller was married in 1745. The Hebron diary at Lebanon shows that Mueller's mother-in-law, Veronica Leidolt, was living with him in 1765. While in between these years he was constantly serving Reformed congregations This would no doubt have been impossible if he had been guilty of adultery. The well-known facts of his life are best reconciled with the notice in Saur's paper by the supposition that Mrs Maria Adam had become Mueller's maid servant in 1749.

Mueller's Doubles

tioned Frederick Miller as the Reformed pastor at Lebanon; see Klopp, *History of Tabor First Reformed Church, Lebanon,* 1892, p. 54. Alongside of these two men, Frederick Casimir Mueller was known as the Reformed pastor at Long Swamp, see Harbaugh, *Fathers,* Vol. II, p. 380. Thus it came to pass that Mr. Frederick, Mr. Frederick Miller and Mr. Frederick Casimir Miller figured as three Reformed pastors in history, see Good, *History,* pp. 517, 649. The truth is that all three are but one man. The Lebanon Reformed church record shows unmistakably the handwriting of Frederick Casimir Mueller. Moreover, of the 18 children whose baptisms Mueller entered, he acted as sponsor in the case of three, signing his name Friederich C. Müller, in his well-known wretched script.

CHAPTER VI.

Ministry of Rev. George Michael Weiss, 1746–1761.

WHEN Michael Schlatter arrived in Pennsylvania in September, 1746, he found a new minister in the Goshenhoppen charge. It was the Rev. George Michael Weiss. We left Weiss in 1732 as pastor of Catskill and Coxsackie, N. Y. There he remained till 1735. His last baptism was entered July 6, 1735. From Catskill he went to Burnetsfield or German Flats, now in Montgomery County, N. Y. There he was pastor from 1736 to 1742. In the latter year he removed to Rhinebeck, Dutchess County, N. Y., where he served as pastor from 1742 to 1746. He then returned to Pennsylvania.

While pastor at Catskill, Mr. Weiss was married by the Rev. Petrus Van Driessen on November 25, 1733, to Anna Broenckh, daughter of John Broenckh, one of his parishioners, in her father's house. Weiss himself entered the record of the marriage into the marriage register at Catskill. The couple had no children.

The time of Mr. Weiss's removal from the State of

New York is fixed as about June, 1746, in a letter of Schlatter to the Synodical Deputies, dated October 3, 1746. The letter itself is no longer in existence, but an elaborate abstract of it was inserted in the Minutes of the Synodical Deputies, from which we take the following statement, regarding Schlatter's visit to Old Goshenhoppen on September 20, 1746. He writes:

On September 20th he [Schlatter] preached in the nearly completed stone church at Old Goshenhoppen from II. Chron. 15: 1, 2 To this place Do. Weiss was called from Albany and has now [September 1746] been pastor there for three or four months. Here he [Schlatter] attempted to restore order, but he could not persuade the congregation at New Goshenhoppen to unite with Great Swamp for this purpose, because they allowed themselves to be served by a hireling, Miller (who had been a schoolmaster at Steticheim[155] near Mayence in the Palatinate), although there was hope for this [union] in the future.

The same time of removal is indicated in the first part of Schlatter's private journal, dated December 15, 1746, and published by the writer in the *Journal of the Presbyterian Historical Society*.[156] There we read:

Do. Weiss returned about six months ago from Esopus in the government of [New] York, for fear of the war about Canada and at the request of the congregation at Goshenhoppen. He is now willing to remain with his wife in Pennsylvania.

To complete the evidence about Weiss's coming to Pennsylvania, we may add the passage from Schlatter's Diary, as printed by Dr. Harbaugh in his "Life of Rev. Michael Schlatter":[157]

---

[155] This name has not been transcribed correctly from the Minutes of the Deputies or from Schlatter's letter, for an inquiry at Mayence brought the answer that there is no such place near Mayence.

[156] *Journal of P H S*, Vol. III, p 108

[157] *Life of Rev. Schlatter*, p. 132 f.

Mr. Weiss, who several months ago, had fled from his church at Rhinebeck near Albany in New York, from fear of war, had come hither on invitation of this and other congregations in this vicinity. He is also beloved by many, yet, on account of the adherents of the one who had irregularly thrust himself into the service of the church, it is necessary still to exercise great prudence.

On October 12, 1746, Weiss met with Schlatter, Boehm and Rieger at Philadelphia for a preliminary conference with a view to perfecting an organization of the Reformed churches and ministers in Pennsylvania. "This was the first assembly in which these Reverend Brethren had all been together, notwithstanding one and another of them had already been laboring about 20 years in this part of the Lord's vineyard."[158]

On October 19, 1746, Schlatter, Boehm and Weiss met at New Goshenhoppen in order to overcome, if possible, the division existing there through the presence of Frederick Casimir Mueller. But although Schlatter succeeded in ascertaining the number of Mueller's and Weiss's adherents, being eighteen and thirty heads of families respectively, and although the latter promised fifteen pounds and thirty bushels of wheat to Do. Weiss's salary, yet Mueller could not be dislodged. It was probably not till 1748, when the baptismal record of Weiss begins at New Goshenhoppen, that Mueller withdrew, although he continued to make occasional visits till April, 1750.

Schlatter's estimate of Weiss was quite favorable in 1746, for in the first part of his private diary, dated December, 1746, he reported to Holland:[159]

Do. George Michael Weiss is now minister at the above mentioned places. He is, as far as I can see, innocent in the affair

[158] *L c*, p. 136
[159] *Journal of P H S*, Vol III, p 117

Weiss at Coetus of 1747

with J. Reif, for the latter always received the money, according to his own confession. Moreover Do. Weiss has asked him a thousand times for God's sake to settle this matter. His Reverence has otherwise a good reputation in this country and Do. Boehm himself told me, that Do. Weiss has always carried himself as a quiet, diligent, sober and orthodox minister. He also took the trouble to travel with me to "Tolpehaken" and "Canastoke."

Mich. Schlatter
Ecc̄lae gs Christo colligatum in America Philadelphia Paston.

At the first meeting of the Coetus of Pennsylvania, held from September 29 to October 2, 1747, at Philadelphia, George Michael Weiss was present with delegates of his three congregations, namely, Christian Schneider and Daniel Hister, of Old Goshenhoppen, John Huth and Philip Ried, of New Goshenhoppen, and John Huber and Nicholas Montbauer of Great Swamp.

From the second meeting of Coetus, held on September 29, 1748, at Philadelphia, Weiss was absent. But shortly afterwards, on December 12, 1748, he sent a letter to Schlatter, excusing his absence because of sickness. In this letter he makes the following report regarding his congregations:[160]

In my congregations nothing of importance has taken place. They are quite harmonious. They only lack money in order to pay for the newly built church at Old Goshenhoppen and to give their minister his salary according to promise. For I have not yet been fully paid for the first year and now am still expecting the salary of almost a year and a half. The conditions with regard to this are very bad. The one pays, the other does not. Many

---
[160] Hague Archives, 74, I, 51 (19).

depend upon the promised help from Holland I stand on a very loose footing If my congregations will not be able to give me my dues, I shall not be able to stay, but must seek my fortune elsewhere.

With regard to the debt resting on the Old Goshenhoppen church, Schlatter states in his private diary that it amounted to about 600 guilders or about 240 dollars.[161]

The Old Goshenhoppen Lutheran record states with regard to this subject:

As to the cost of the church nothing certain is at hand, because in the first place the two congregations have helped and given much, and the next place other friends also have contributed their share.

And again:

As to the interior finishing of the church, on July 12, 1748, a joint contract was made by the two congregations with the carpenter to make and paint the seats and gallery for 15 pounds.

The pulpit was ordered and presented by Gabriel Schuler, Reformed.

The story as to how the church debt was finally paid is given in the Old Goshenhoppen Lutheran record as follows:

In the year 1751 there remained 30 pounds of church debts and, after consultation, we deemed it proper to send out collectors by the Evangelical Lutherans alone, because each congregation had its separate debts. Hence on November 7, 1751, the beginning was made by two collectors appointed for the purpose, who brought home on the 14th of December of this year 13 pounds and 14 shillings, not counting 1/3 of the proceeds which went to the collectors. For this may the rich Lord bless all benevolent givers in body and soul.

Anno 1752, two joint collectors were sent out, one by the Lu-

[161] *Journal of P H S*, Vol. III, p. 170

therans, the other by the Reformed, in order to collect contributions in the State of New York. They returned in this year, as our exclusive third part, 11 pounds, 3 shillings and 9 pence.

At the Coetus meeting held in 1749 at Lancaster, Weiss acted as secretary.

In the year 1750 two important events occurred which stirred the congregations deeply.

On May 1, 1750, the following notice appeared in Saur's Germantown newspaper, called *Pennsylvanische Berichte:*

It is reported from Goshenhoppen that there is a woman who has left two husbands that are still living and wanted to marry the third man. There are in that district three preachers, the one was so white [play on the name Weiss] that he would not marry the pair, but the other [play on the name Andre] who had before married the good woman to another man hesitated indeed, because the second husband lived so near, but the bridegroom, knowing that everything can be obtained from some people for money, heaven and salvation Christ and forgiveness of sin, offered no small remuneration for the marriage. The reverend minister was pleased to accept and married them in the name of God, without proclamation (otherwise there might have been some objection) for 30 shillings. The farmers in his three congregations were startled, not knowing whether all their wives might not be married away to others. They formed a church council and consistory, deposed their minister, for they preferred to be out of danger.

In June, 1750, the Goshenhoppen region was startled by a murder. The wife of one of its most respected citizens, David Schultz[162] (whose tomb is in the New Goshenhoppen Reformed churchyard) was brutally slain by one of her servants.

[162] For a sketch of David Schultz's life, see the PENNSYLVANIA GERMAN, Vol. IX, pp 499–505.

George Schultz, his wife and their son David arrived in Philadelphia with the ship *Pennsylvania Merchant*, John Stedman, captain, on September 18, 1733. They settled in the Perkiomen Region. On October 29, 1745, David Schultz married Anna Rosina, daughter of Abraham Beyer. In May, 1749, he bought 180 acres and 60 perches of land for 72 pounds 3 shillings, lying in Upper Hanover township, what is now East Greenville, Pa.

As he was a surveyor, David Schultz was much away from home. During his absence the management of the farm naturally fell to his wife. In June, 1750, he had a servant, Hans Ulrich Sailer, whom his father-in-law, Abraham Beyer, had brought with him from Holland during the previous summer, on condition that he serve him seven years for the passage money. He was a Swiss boy, of a lazy and surly disposition. David Schultz thought that he could manage him with kindness, hence he took him and his indenture along to his farm. His wife found frequent occasion to urge him to do his work better. Afterwards the young man claimed she even slapped his face, which may not be true. At any rate he took a decided dislike to his mistress and determined to get even with her.

In the night of June 14, 1750, he climbed through a window into her bedroom with a long, pointed knife. But as she turned around in bed, he left the room again. After some time he entered the second time but she turned again. On his third entry he found everything quiet. Then he stabbed her in the neck, cutting the jugular vein. After thus satisfying his revenge, he ran out and hid in a neighbor's haystack. Mrs. Schultz rose from her bed and went downstairs to call for help, but fell at the foot of the stairs upon her face, where she was found dead the next day. The murderer was soon caught and confessed everything. He was taken to Philadelphia, where he was placed on trial and found guilty of murder on October 22 He was executed by hanging on Wednesday, November 13, 1750.[163]

Close to the New Goshenhoppen church is the tomb of Mrs. Schultz, with this inscription:

> Anna Rosina Schultzin
> Murdered June 14, A D. 1750.
> Aged 29 years. Funeral Text:
> Jeremiah 9: 21.

In 1750 and 1751 the people at New Goshenhoppen made the first effort to secure a deed for their minister's farm. The details have fortunately been preserved by David Schultz, who interested himself more than any other in securing the property for the congregation. On February 3, 1776, he sent a letter to Mr. Rundle[164] regarding this land, from which the following statements are taken:

> After all the land had been surveyed to the settlers thereof, agreeable the general agreement this tract was left vacant.
>
> Sometime before the general agreement was made, Edward Scull was ordered to survey the greatest part of his 13,000 acres, but after the general agreement was made and the remaining surveys were to be completed, he not having time to do it himself, ordered me to finish the remainder, under his examination; which was done and [I was] employed with the Mr. Parsons, Ross and Greenway. I accordingly surveyed the tract now in question on the 19th No-

---

[163] The story of Mrs Schultz's murder and of the trial and execution of her murderer is given at length in Saur's *Pennsylvanische Berichte* of July 16, 1750, November 1 and 16, 1750; cf. also *Colonial Records*, Vol V, p 488. The New Goshenhoppen record shows that David Schultz married his second wife, Elizabeth Lar, on June 27, 1758 This union was blessed with four daughters.

[164] This letter was first printed in the *Daily Norristown Register* of March 6, 1883 It was reprinted in the *Penn Germania*, Vol. I, pp. 364-368.

vember 1750, for the said congregation, in the presence of the elders or church wardens thereof, containing 42 acres, with allowance (of six acres per hundred for roads) at their request, with an intention to build a house thereon for their minister to live in, and continually to keep this same for such use forever.

Also with intention, when it should suit them, to agree and pay for the land, with the above named three gentlemen.

They immediately built a dwelling house and stable on it, dug a well and began to clear some land in the spring 1751. Their minister came to live there with his negro family, at his request the congregation allowed him for his better support to clear some more land. He continued from time to time with cleaning, though sometimes forbid by the congregation, till almost all was cleared a few acres excepted.

In August, 1752, Mr. Weiss and other Reformed ministers hastened to Philadelphia to welcome Schlatter and the six young ministers, whom he had brought from Holland. Their arrival was an event of great importance[165] for the Reformed church in Pennsylvania and was fittingly marked by a meeting of all the Reformed ministers in the province at Philadelphia, from August 10 to 13, 1752.

On September 2, 1752, Rev. John Philip Leydich, pastor at Falkner Swamp, sent a letter to Rev. Jacob Lischy,

[165] The importance of this event was duly recognized by a Circular Letter, issued in 1752 by Messrs. Weiss, Leydich and Lischy It was entitled: *Circular Schreiben der Vereinigten Reformirten Prediger in Pennsylvanien, an dasige sammtliche nach Gottes Wort Reformirte Gemeinen: Darin sie kurzlich darlegen, wie der grosse Jehovah die von Sr. Ehrw. Michael Slatter, V D.M., an unsere Hochw. Christl Kirchenvater ubernommene Commission zu ihrer Rettung und Hulfe, in Gnaden gesegnet etc. Zu Allgemeiner Nachricht herausgegeben von Georg Michael Weiss, Joh Phil Leydich, Jacob Lischy* Lancaster, Gedruckt bey H. Muller und S Holland, 1752, 4to, pp 11 The title page was published from a photograph taken by the writer, by Prof Jos H Dubbs, in his *Reformed Church in Pennsylvania*, p. 165 The only known copy of the booklet is in the archives at the Hague, 74, II, 21

pastor at York, in which he refers to the third schoolmaster at Goshenhoppen, whose name has been preserved. He writes:[166]

Let me add a few words, regarding the bearer of this letter,

Circular-Schreiben
der Vereinigten
Reformirten Prediger
in Pennsylvanien,
an dasige, sämtliche nach GOttes Wort
Reformirte Gemeinen:
Darin sie kürzlich darlegen,
Wie der Grosse JEHOVA die von Sr. Ehrw.
MICHAEL SLATTER, *V. D. M.*
an unsere
Hochw. Christl. Kirchenväter
übernommene Commission zu ihrer Rettung und Hülfe, in Gnaden gesegnet:
Und
Wie solches von sothanen Gemeinen solle gebührend erkant, mit Danksagung angenommen, und recht gebraucht, ja, zum Lobe GOttes und dem Heil ihrer unsterblichen Seelen angewandt werden.
Zu
Allgemeiner Nachricht
herausgegeben von
GEORG MICHAEL WEISS.
JOH. PHIL. LEYDICH.
JACOB LISCHY.

LANCASTER, Gedruckt bey H. Müller und S. Holland, 1752.

namely John William Wigand, at present schoolmaster at New Goshenhoppen, a man with excellent testimonials, as their presentation will show you in detail. He cannot subsist in said congre-

[166] Hague Archives, 74, I, 72 (3).

gation because of the division caused by the so-called Fritz-Mueller and Weiss parties He has a special desire to work under the dear Brother [Lischy] and according to his instructions.

In the following year the schoolmaster at Goshenhoppen received £5 s 8 support from the donations sent from Holland.[167]

In 1752 five hundred folio Bibles, sent by the Classis of Amsterdam, were distributed among the Reformed ministers at the meeting of Coetus. It was resolved to place one copy of these Bibles in each pulpit and to distribute the rest among the various ministers.

It was resolved to send Do Weiss 24 copies of the folio Bibles, one half to be sold and one half to be given to the poor, and with the same understanding the others were assigned.[168]

These so-called "Schlatter Bibles" are becoming exceedingly scarce. None seem to have survived in the Goshenhoppen congregations. For their identification the following may be noted. As stated in the minutes of Coetus, it was a large folio Bible, printed at Basel, "im Verlag Johann Ludwig Brandmüllers, im Jahre Christi MDCCXLVII.

When in 1753 serious dissensions arose in the Coetus, Weiss sided with Leydich, Steiner, Rubel, Waldschmidt and Wissler against Schlatter and his friends This separation was due among other causes to the desire, as expressed by Weiss, to "maintain love and peace among their congregations, inasmuch as they were not in favor of subordination to Holland and to our Coetal institutions and directions."[169]

On September 10, 1753, a convention was held by the

[167] *Minutes of Coetus,* p 89
[168] *L. c.,* p 69.
[169] *L. c ,* p 92

Holland Donations

dissatisfied ministers at the house of Mr Weiss at Goshenhoppen and then an attempt was made by them to convene a regular Coetus at Cocalico, in Lancaster County, on October 10 to 12, 1753 At this meeting Mr. Weiss presided. But this attempt to wrest the control of Coetus from Schlatter and his friends failed, as the "Fathers" in Holland refused to recognize Weiss and his followers and threatened to withhold all donations from them This threat was more powerful than all arguments and had the desired effect. At the Coetus, held at Philadelphia in October, 1754, a reconciliation took place and the two parties pledged themselves to forget their differences.

Beginning with the spring of 1753, the ample donations from Holland put ministers and schoolmasters in more comfortable circumstances. The following table shows the total amounts distributed and the share that fell to Mr. Weiss and the Goshenhoppen schoolmaster:

Year	Total Amounts	Weiss's Share	Schoolmaster's
1753	£363 s. 8	£20	£5 s. 8
1754	£289 s 7	£20	- - - -
1755	£418 s 15 d 6	£35 s 15	- - - -
1756	£366 s 12	£27 s 10	- - - -
1757	£357 s 2 d 10	£27 s 10	£1 s 10
1758	£385 s 14	£30	£1 s 10
1759	£339 s 9	£30	£1 s 10
1760–61	£337 s 17 d 10	£30	£2
1762	£321 s 5	£10	- - - -

The last amount in 1762 was given to Mr. Weiss's widow. His salary during this period amounted to 40 pounds annually.

Besides these contributions from Holland, Reformed ministers and schoolmasters shared in the benefactions of an English society, organized to maintain charity schools among the Germans in Pennsylvania. The first payment from this source was made on June 16, 1756, when ten Reformed ministers received 91 pounds.[170] Similar payments followed in the next three years. At each of these occasions Weiss received ten pounds, although no charity school was established in the Goshenhoppen region.

The development of the Goshenhoppen congregations during this time cannot be followed in detail. Only at Old Goshenhoppen has the Lutheran church record preserved some interesting details of congregational activity

During the year 1753, beginning May 3, the churchyard was enlarged at Old Goshenhoppen and it was surrounded by new posts, clap boards and new gates were put up.

In 1754 a new stove was bought for 4 pounds. In 1755 all church debts were completely paid by the Lutherans and let us hope by the Reformed people also. In the same year a new well and spring house were made. In 1757,

the church was improved both inside and outside with carpenter work. Five new windows with glass were inserted, new seats were put in and painted and a new roof was put on the kitchen of the schoolhouse. All was paid and the [Lutheran] congregation has still a balance of 6£ 18s 9d.

In 1757 a long and lingering sickness befell Mr. Weiss, which made it impossible for him to attend the meetings of Coetus any longer. In October, 1759, Coetus met at Goshenhoppen "in the home of the sick Do. Weiss."

Of the year 1759 we have the first statistical report by Mr. Weiss regarding his congregations. It was submitted to the Coetus that met May 28, 1760, at Falkner Swamp, and was as follows:[171]

[170] *L c*, p 144; also p 198.
[171] As the references to the *Minutes of Coetus* can be located in the printed minutes without difficulty, it is not necessary to give in every case

At Old Goshenhoppen Do. Weiss has 30 families, at New Goshenhoppen 45, and at Great Swamp, 33. In 1759 he baptized in the three congregations 60 children, and instructed 33 persons in the confession of Faith and received them as members. About the schools he could give no report.

At the meeting of Coetus on October 21 to 22, 1760, held at Germantown, the congregations of Weiss expressed their willingness "patiently to bear with his age and infirmity."

In 1761 Weiss reported 120 families in his churches. "He baptized, during 1760 and up to the present time, 45 children and received 36 members."

This is the last reference to Weiss. He died in August, 1761. David Schultz, Esq., in a letter to Daniel Rundle, dated February 3, 1776, writes: "Anno 1761 in August, their said minister, Geo. Michael Weiss died."

Shortly before Mr. Weiss died, in May, 1761, the Great Swamp congregation made an effort to pay for its church land. Accordingly a paper was circulated (now much worn and partly torn) on which the members subscribed certain sums to pay this debt. A similar effort seems to have been made in Decmber, 1748, but was probably only partially successful. At that time the following members made subscriptions for this purpose:

SUBSCRIPTIONS FOR CHURCH LAND AT GREAT SWAMP.

Anno 1748 (?), December 26th, an agreement was made by the members of our congregation that we are willing to pay for our church land. Each one gives at his own free will as follows:

	£	s
Michel Kohler	—	10

the exact page reference. The minutes of Coetus were edited by the writer in 1903 under the title *Minutes and Letters of the Coetus of the German Reformed Congregation in Pennsylvania, 1747-1792* Reformed Church Publication Board, Philadelphia, 1903

	£	s.
Johannes Bleyler	—	15
Johannes Huber	—	10
Jacob Wetzel	—	15
Jacob Dubs	—	10
Christian Willauer	—	10
Paul Samsel	—	10
Caspar Erb	—	10
Johannes Griesemer	—	5
Michel Nussbach	—	10
Alexander Diebenderfer	—	15
Peter Walbert	—	10
Ludwig Bitting	1	—
Abraham Ditlo	—	15
Henrich Hitz	—	5
Nickel Mombauer	—	10
Henrich Huber	—	5
Abraham Faust	—	10
Henrich Bach	—	5
Michel Braun	—	5
Peter Scholl	—	5
Nickel Bach	—	3
Philip Heger	—	6
Ruthe Fricki	—	6
Dewalt Brauchler	—	5
Jacob Rite	—	5
Michel Eberhard	—	10
Matheis Bischof	—	10
Abraham Kreither	—	5
Ruthe Huber	—	5
Philip Brunner	—	13
Joseph Eberhard	1	—
David Streib	1	—
Ulrich Riser	—	5
Gorg Lein	—	5
Michel Hornberger	—	5
Conrad Zimmerman	—	10
? Endross	—	5
? ?	—	10
Total	£17	s 13

As the cost of the land was only £17 11s. 7d., it would not have been necessary to start a second subscription list, unless for some reason the first had not been paid, or at least had not been paid in full The latter seems to have been the case. For on the same paper with the above subscription is the note:

Today, April 10, 1749, I, Michel Kohler have paid for the church land eleven pounds ten shillings and for a warrant one shilling and six pence.

JOHANN GEORG BLATT.

On May 30, 1761, twenty members signed £20 2s. 9d on another subscription list. This may have been only tentative, for on June 8, 1761, still another list was signed which read as follows:

SUBSCRIPTIONS FOR CHURCH LAND AT GREAT SWAMP, JUNE 6, 1761.

On June 6, 1761, we have made an agreement to pay for the church land and whatever we promise we shall faithfully keep and pay. Christian Willauer and Valentin Huber are the deputies. The head of each family signs what he will give to the Reformed congregation in Great Swamp:

	£	s.	d.
Ulrich Spinner pays	2	0	0
Peder(?) Bleiler pays	1	0	0
Henrich Huber, the tailor pays	0	15	6
Henrich Huber, the wheelwright pays	1	0	0
Dewalt Brauchler, pays	0	10	0
Peter Samsel pays .	1	0	0
Paul Samsel pays	0	5	0
Nicklaus Mumbauer pays	0	10	0
Henrich Hitz pays	0	7	6
Henrich Crob pays	0	10	0
Rudi Huber pays	0	10	0
Abraham Ditlo pays	0	15	0
Henrich Bleiler pays	1	0	0
Rudi Frick pays .	—	10	0

Jacob Huber, the [. . .] pays	—	10	0
Total	£11	2	6
Nicklaus Faust	—	3	—
Jacob Meier . . .	—	5	—
Adam Willauer	—	7	6

Lutwich Hersch pays 3 sh. for the farmer
Paul Samsel pays one sh for the churchyard
Nicklaus Mumbauer pays one sh for the churchyard.
Peter Weber pays 5 sh. for the churchyard.

Disposal of Rev. Mr Weiss's Property.

WHEN Mr. G. M. Weiss died in August, 1761, he left no will. For some unknown reason his widow, Anna Weiss, delayed asking for letters of administration till October 2, 1764, when they were granted to her and to Christian Schneider, as executors, inventory to be exhibited in the Court at Philadelphia on or before October 2, 1765. Before the inventory was filed, Mrs Anna Weiss herself made a will on May 9, 1765. She died within a month afterwards, on June 2, 1765. On August 20, 1765, her will was probated. By the terms of her will she not only freed, under certain conditions, her negro family, consisting of a man and his wife, together with nine children, but also bequeathed to them all the improvements of the farm, belonging to the congregation, on which she lived By this act she involved the congregation in a long and tedious law-suit, and thus the history of the disposal of Mr Weiss's property becomes part of the history of the congregation. In order to clear up this whole case, which has often been alluded to by historians, but was never fully understood, we present the following documents.

[I. Letters of Administration Granted to Mrs. Weiss.]

Book of Administration, Register of Wills Office, Philadelphia, Vol. G. p. 417.

Memorandum, that Letters of Administration were granted to Anna Weiss and Christian Schneider in the Estate of the late Michael Weiss, dec. Inventory to be exhibited on or before the

2nd day of October 1765   Given under the seal of the Register General's Office, at Philadelphia, the 2nd day of October 1764

WILLIAM PLUMSTED,

Reg. Genl

[II INVENTORY OF THE ESTATE OF GEORGE MICHAEL WEISS. OCTOBER 2, 1764.]

Office of Register of Wills, Philadelphia,
1764, No. 114

Inventory of the Estate chattels, moveables and Household goods of Michael Weiss late of Upper Hanover Township in the County of Philadelphia and Province of Pennsylvania, Minister of the reformed congregation, deceased, as the same being valued and appraised by Adam Hillegas and John Coleman on this 11th day of September Anno 1764.

	£	s	d.
Six books mostly Latin, in quarto	1.	0.	0
To one Book in folio, five dito in octavo, Latin	0	15	0
to six books octavo Latin, Greek & Hebrew	0	12	0.
to fifteen small books, mostly Latin	0	7	6
to the Table	1	0	0
to the round Table	0	3.	0
to two old chairs	0	1	6
to another round table	0	15	0
to an old looking glass and a pair of Pictures	0.	7.	6
to a pair of fire dogs	0	7	6
to five pewter Dishes, two Basons	1	15	0
to one dozen plates and one dozen spoons	0	7	6
to two pewter Tea Pots & a coffee pot	0	7	6
to six delft tea cups & saucers	0.	2	6
to two Cannisters & a funnel	0	1.	6
to Tea Kettles	0.	10	0
to a water pot	0	4	0
to two Iron Pots with Pot-hooks Two Pans	0	12	0
to three Tubs two buckets	0.	3.	6
to his Bed with the Bedstead and appurtenances	2.	10	0
to another Bed with Bedstead	2	0	0
to three Cows, two Calves	9	0	0.
to a side sadle	1.	5.	0.

	£	s	d
to an old Horse . . .	3	0.	0
to one gray Horse .	4	0	0
to an old waggon with the Geers . .	11.	0	0.
to the Plough and Harrow . .	1	0	0
	£43	7	6
The amount of the first page brought over	43	7	6.
to an ax, cropping Howe dung fork, pitch fork	0	10	0
amount to	£43	17	6

appraised by
    Adam Hilligas
    Johannes Gallman

There is fifteen acres of land a 35/ . .	26	5.	—
four Hogs a 10/ .	2.	—	—
five sheep a 6/ . .	1.	10	—
	£29	15	—

[The last four lines are crossed out with the remark "to be left out"]

Besides the above there is a Negro Family belonging to said Minister deceased, viz.

A negro Man named Gideon, aged about 44 years old, but now a cripple, who is not appraised			
His wife Jenny, aged 42 years with a female child about six months old, valued at	£30.	0	0
A negro lad, named Jacob, old 20 years .	50	0	0
A negro wench, named Elizabeth, 18 years old .	40	0	0
A negro lad, named Henry, 16 years old .	40	0	0
A negro wench, named Anne Mary, 14 years old .	30.	0.	0.
A negro girl, named Catherine, 11 years old .	30	0	0
A negro girl, named Margareth, 9 years old .	25.	0	0
A negro girl named Susan, 6 years old .	20	0	0
A negro boy, named John, 4 years old	15.	0	0.
Amounts to	£280	0	0.

appraised by
    ADAM HILLIGAS
    JOHANNES GALLMANN
[Endorsed]
    Inventory of Mich¹. Weiss's Estate
      Exhibited 2. October 1764.

[III. Account of Michael Weiss's Estate July 8, 1766.]

Register of Will's Office, Philadelphia,
1764, No 114

The accompt of Christian Schneider, surviving Administrator of the Estate late of Michael Weiss deced. as well of all and singular the Goods, Chattels, Rights and Credits which were of the said deced. and which came to this Accomptant's Hand and Possession as of the several payments and disbursements made out of the same.

Imprimis 1764.

The said Accomptant charges himself with all and singular the Goods Chattels Rights and Credits which were of the said deced as mentioned in an Inventory remaining in the Reg^r Genl Office at Philad^a. am. to £280		0	0
The said Accomptant charges himself with the further sum of £129-11, being the app^d. value of the goods and what the deceased's goods sold for more than appraised at including ye negroes	129	11	0
The said accomptant charges himself with the following sum reced for work done by the Negroes to the following persons, viz.			
from Adam Hillegas	£ 3	3	10.
from Jacob Derr ..	3.	5	3.
from John Wisler .	—	4	—
from Peter Hilligas	—	17	8
from Andreas Greaver	—	10	—
from George Miller	—	2	3
from Bernard Bispham .	3.	10	—
	£ 11	13	—
Ditto with the sum of 30/ being what a large Bible sold for and not included in ye aforesaid Inventory	1	10	—
	£422	14	—
Item			
The said Accomptant prays Allowance for his several payments and disbursements made out of the same as follows, viz—			
By cash paid for Letters of Adm . ..	—	17	—

paid sundry Expenses on appraising Goods amounting to	£ 1.	2	6
paid David Shultz for services, etc	—	5.	—
paid to Frederick Snyder for eight days services on business of the Estate by order of Wm Plumsted, then Reg^r Genl. ...	4.	—	—
paid John Ross for advice .	1	10	—
paid B Chew Esq for ditto	1.	14.	—
paid Conrad Frank for sundry services in and about the Estate, allowed & approved by Wm Plumsted, Esq.	6	—	—
paid to Advertisements	—	6.	3.
paid Christian Hambach per receipt	1.	14	—
paid at the office for these amounts 17/6 and a Clk for services 7/0	1.	5.	—
	£ 18.	13	9.
By an allowance for reced £422. 14	21	2.	6.
ditto on paying 4. 18. 13 .	—	18.	8
Ballance of £381 19. 1 to be disposed of according to Law as follows:			
To the widow, one half	£190.	19.	6½
To the Heirs of the deceased	£190.	19.	6½
	£381.	19.	1
	£422	14.	—

Philadelphia July 8, 1766.

Error excepted

Examined & pass'd   CHRISTIAN SCHNEIDER

July 8, 1766   The Adm^r. being first thereto sworn by

                                    BENJ. CHEW,
                                         Reg^r Genl

[IV. ADDITIONAL ACCOUNT OF THE ESTATE OF G. M. WEISS. DECEMBER 12, 1771.]

The Additional Acct. of Christian Schneider surviving Administrator of the Estate of Michael Weiss, deceased

The said Accomptant charges himself with the Ballance of the last settlement on the other side of this paper	£381	19	1

The said Accomptant prays Allowance for the several payments and disbursements made out of the same since last settlement, viz

Paid expenses of Arbitration at Daniel Etters p. account	1.	18	0.
Paid James Tilghman, Esquire, for his counsel and assistance in the affair of the Negroes .	6	0	0
paid Expenses of Arbitration at Mr Davenport p account	1	13	—
paid Mr. Lewis Weiss for translating sundry writings from Germany	—	15	—
paid for stating the add' acc^t. 7/6 and for examing & passing etc. 17/6	1	5	—
	£ 11	11	—
By Leonard Thomas Bond for Negroes sold him at Vendue not received	82	—	—
By Andrew Oel for the remainder of his Bond for one Negro sold him	40	5	—
By the sum of 30—being for one negro boy sold George Righter, received by Leonard Melchior	30	—	—
By paying £11 11 at 5 p cent	0	11	0.
	£164.	7.	0
Ballance on this settlement exclusive of the above bonds £130 ..	217.	12	1
	£381.	19	1.

Philadelphia, December 12, 1771.
    Error excepted   CHRISTIAN SCHNEIDER.

[V. FINAL ACCOUNT OF THE ESTATE OF G M WEISS. NOVEMBER 6, 1789]

The final Acc^t. of Leonard Melcher and Christian Schneider as Administrators etc. of George Michael Weiss and Ann his wife both deceased.

To Ballance on their first acc^t settled in Register's Office July 8, 1766 .	£381	19	1
Bal^l in favor of the said Administrators	£272.	0	—½
	£654	9	1½

N. B. Sundry Papers respecting the foregoing account are tied in a Bundle and lodged in the desk of this office

By Am^t. of their disbursements on 2nd Acc^t. rendered in Reg Office Dec 1771	£ 12	2.	—
By Am^t appraism^{t}s & sales of Negroes charged to the said Administrators in their first acc^t. (the said negroes having since obtained their freedom and the Adm^{rs} obliged to refund .	193	5	—
By Amo^t. of Interest costs paid to Michael Bishop over and above first cost of Negro sold him	8	6	9
By Amo^t ditto paid Saml. Heads Adm. over & above first cost of Negro sold him	70	8	8
By Amo^t disbursements etc as per 1st acc^t. settlm^t. of Ann Weiss rendered 8th March 1769	109	10	8
By amo^t ditto on 2nd Acco^t of d^o. rendered Dec 17, 1771	12	—	—
By amo^t monies remitted to the Heirs in Germany	103	13	10½
By Cash paid at Philad^a by Christian Schneider to Geo Mich Weiss & Martin Weiss, Agents & Representatives of the Heirs in Germany	20.	2.	2.
By Amo^t. of Principal of Andrew Ohl & Leonard Thomas two Bonds given for Negroes sold to them—which Bonds the said Schneider assigned & delivered to the said George Mich^l. Weiss & Martin Weiss as Agents & Representatives	122	5	—
By Cash paid Clerk for stating Acco^t	2.	5	—
By d^o paid Reg^r. for examining & passing this acco^t with copy	—	10	—
	£654.	9	1½

Frederick Schneider and Henry Frantz, executors for the Testament and last will of Christian Schneider, dec^d, who was the surviving Administrator of George Michael Weiss afors^d., on their solemn oaths do depose and say that the foregoing account as it stands stated and settled both as to the charge and discharge thereof is true and just to the best of their knowledge and belief. Sworn the 6th day of November 1789

FREDERICK SNIDER
HENRY FRANZ

Before me
    GEO. CAMPBELL, *Reg^r*

[VI. WILL OF MRS. ANNA WEISS, DATED MAY 9, 1765, PROBATED AUGUST 20, 1765.]

Book of Administration, Register of Wills Office,
Philadelphia, Vol. H. p 1

In the Namce of [God] Amen.

Whereas I, Anna Weiss, as Relict Widow of George Michael Weiss late of Upper Hanover Township in the County of Philadelphia, Reformed Calvinist Minister deceased, do find myself in an advanced age and very weak in body but of sound mind and understanding and Memory, thanks be to God, and calling to Mind the Mortality of my body and knowing that it is appointed to all men once to die, so do I on this ninth day of May in the year of our Lord one thousand and seven hundred and sixty five make and oidain this my last Will and Testament.

And first of all, I recommend my soul into the Hands of Almighty God that gave it, and do desire that aftei my death my body be buried in a Christian like and decent manner and as touching to my worldly estate I do hereby dispose of the same in the following manner.

Imprimis, it is my will that all my Just debts contracted by me oi my negroes be duly paid and discharged, and also that my hereunto named Executors shall demand ask and get in all the outstanding debts that aie due to my deceased Husband for his services if they can be got,

And further it is my will and I give and bequeath unto my beloved Cousin Leonard Brunk living in the County of Albany in the government of New York and to his Heirs or Assigns all my fine Clothes and Garments as also six great silver spoons and also my three Golden Rings as in full for his Hereditary Share and Portion of my Estate to be delivered to him on demand by my Executois.

And whereas I have a Negro family consisting at Present of Eleven Persons as the Negroe man named Gideon and the wife named Jenny, the man aged about forty four years and the woman's age about forty two, their children's names are Jacob about Twenty years old and Elizabeth about Eighteen years, and Henry about sixteen years and Anne Mary about fourteen years and Catherina about eleven years, and Margareth about nine years, and Susanna about six years and John about four years and also a young female child about one year old named Eva, which all accordingly have been baptized to the Christian Protestant reformed Religion.

And whereas lately some claim hath been made by a Relation of the s^d. deceased Rev^d. Minister my s^d. Husband in favour of his other Relations in Germany claiming the half of our Estate, as also with an intention to sell said Negroes for slaves contrary to the sentiments and Intentions of my s^d. deceased Husband who died Intestate, so it is my will that the said Negroe children may be bound out to serve from time to time or as long as necessary in order to make up such a sum of money as may be required or ordered to be sent to the Brethren and Relations of my s^d. deceased Husband in Germany for their Hereditary share and Portion, and further it is my will that all my said whole Negroe family shall after the time of my death be free, and I do hereby declare them altogether without distinction or Exception to be an entire free Negroe family, so that they never shall or may be bound out to eternal slavery, but shall hereby fully have and enjoy their liberty, only hereby excepted as above said to get so much money by servitude as necessary on the above said demand, as from year to year or otherwise as it shall seem best to my hereunto named Executors:

And I do hereby further give devise and bequeath unto my said Negro Man Gideon Moor and to his Heirs and assigns as to my said whole Negroe family forever a certain Tract of Land situate in Douglas Township in the County of Philadelphia adjoining the land of Michael Read, Mathias Walther, Andreas Weiler and Philip Leidecker and containing fourteen acres and six Perches of Land which I lately Purchased of Peter Hillegas & obtained a Deed for the same with all Hereditaments and Appurtenances whatsoever. To hold to them my said Negroe family and for their use and behoof forever,

And I further give and bequeath all my Right Claim and demand (if any I have) of in and to any Improvement and Land where I now live unto the said Gideon Moor and for his and their Proper Use and Behoof for ever, saving to others their Right to the same if any they have,

And I do hereby further give devise and bequeath unto my said Negro man Gideon Moor and to his Heirs and Assigns forever all the remainder of my Moveable and personal Estate as my other Clothes, chests, money, furniture and all and every sort of household goods and Tools whatsoever. To hold to him the said Gideon Moor his Heirs and Assigns and to their only proper use and Behoof for ever, Provided hereby that all my debts now due by me be all regularly paid and I devise that all may be done according to the true Intent and meaning hereof,

And I further devise that care may be taken that all the said Negroe Children may be taught & instructed in the Doctrine of the true Christian reformed Religion, in the best manner it can be done, and I do hereby wish that they all may enjoy hereafter endless Felicity.

And I do hereby nominate constitute and appoint my trusty and beloved friends as Jacob Arndt, Esquire, one of his Majestys Justices of the peace for the County of Northampton and Peter Hillegas of Upper Hanover Township in Philadelphia County yeoman to be the sole Executors of this my Last Will and Testament and I do hereby declare this and no other to be my last will & Testament.

In Witness and Confirmation whereof I the above named Anna Weiss have hereunto set my Hand and Seal. Dated the day and year as first above written.

her
ANNA △ WEISS (Seal)
mark

Signed sealed published and declared by the said Anna Weiss as her last Will and Testament in the presence of us the subscribers

JOHANNES WISHLER
DAVID SCHULZ
JOHANNES TAUBST

PHILADELPHIA August 20th 1765,

There personally appeared Johannes Wissler and David Shultze two of the witnesses to the foregoing will and on their solemn affirmation according to Law did declare they saw and heard Anna Weiss the Testatrix therein named sign seal publish and declare the same will for and as her last Will and Testament and that at the doing thereof she was of sound mind memory and understanding to the best of their knowledge.

Coram BENJAMIN CHEW, Esqr. *Reg. General.*

Memorandum that Letter of Administration of the Estate of Anna Weiss dece^d. with the will of the said Anna annexed were granted to Christian Schneider and Leonard Melchior (the Executors in the said will named having first renounced) Inventory to be exhibited on or before the 20th day of September next and an acct. on or before the 21st day of August 1766.

Given under the seal of the Register General's Office at Philadelphia the 20th day of August 1765.

p. BENJAMIN CHEW,
Reg^r. Genl.

[VII. LETTER OF DAVID SCHULTZE, ESQ., TO MR DANIEL RUNDLE, FEBRUARY 3, 1776; PRINTED IN *Daily Norristown Register* OF MARCH 6, 1883]

To MR. DANIEL RUNDLE.

Sir!

Whereas the Reformed Calvinist congregation in these parts have already had a considerable deal of trouble with that negroman called Gideon Moor, who was a slave to their minister, the late Geo. M. Weiss, so that they are engaged in a tedious lawsuit with him and though I never inclined to be very much troublesome to you about this affair, yet as it seems that that congregation might possible lose their cause: if not properly assisted. So I find myself under necessity to give you some information of the matter, as short as possible, as the said congregation also most humbly request your assistance therein, as far as thought necessary. The more especially, since you had a hand in the land affairs from the beginning, and for the present time are looked upon by the parties as the chief of those parties concerned therein. We also hope that you will remember that about five or six years ago some of the members of the said congregation applied to you about the same cause, when you gave them your promise that they should have that land as soon as the affair with your partners was settled.

But the better to explain their cause I shall be obliged to repeat the affair from its beginning.

After all the land had been surveyed to the settlers thereof agreeable the general agreement this tract was left vacant.

Sometime before the general agreement was made, Edward Scull was ordered to survey the greatest part of his 13,000 acres, but after the general agreement was made and the remaining surveys were to be completed, he not having time to do it himself, ordered me to finish the remainder under his examination which was done and employed with by the Mr Parsons, Ross and Greenway, I accordingly surveyed the tract now in question on the 19th November 1750, for the said congregation, in the presence of the elders and churchwardens thereof containing 42 acres with allowance [of six acre per hundred for roads] at their request, with an intention to build a house thereon for their minister to live in and continually to keep this same for such use for ever.

Also with intention, when it should suit them, to agree and pay for the land, with the above named three gentlemen

They immediately built a dwelling house and stable on it, dug a well and began to clear some land in the Spring of 1751. Their minister came to live there with his negro family; at his request the congregation allowed him for his better support to clear some more land, Though who [he] continued from time to time with cleaning Though sometimes forbid by the congregation, till almost all was cleared, a few acres only excepted. The timber required for building, and mostly rails, was carried there by said people from their own lands. Since there was scarce any on the premises. The greatest part thereof was but a barren plain. They applied to Mr. Greenway about the land about 1767 or 1768, he returned for answer, that they should have the land, but since some of the heirs were under age, he would not undertake to make a deed for it. We applied to you about it and received nearly the same answer.

Anno 1761 in August, their said minister, Geo. Mich. Weiss died and though the said congregation got another, yet out of compassion to the deceased's widow, allowed her to live on that land with her negro family and left her the full use thereof, without demanding a penny rent of her for it. They rented another house for their new accepted minister to live in, until in the year 1765, June 2nd, the said, relict widow Anna Weiss died also, having no children, only her said negro family, he died without a will, but she made a will, whereupon she gave all her estate to the said negro family and also her right to the improvements, if any she had

But in my opinion she could claim no further right thereon. She only had the use and produce there during her stay on the premises and that only by permission of the said congregation. Then in about three months afterwards, the said negro family were all sold for slaves by Christian Schneider and Leonard Melchior, who had administered for the estate The said negro man with his wife and two children were sold to Leonard Thomas, an inhabitant of this township. Sometime afterwards the congregation got an inmate to live in the house on the premises.

The said Leonard Thomas, weary of his negroes, allowed the man liberty and time to try for to obtain his freedom, during which interview the said Gideon, by some lawyer's contrivances came and took possession again of the said premises, about the latter end of 1767 or the beginning of 1768. This occasioned new trouble to the congregation.

They soon after applied for the land to you and to John Margotroyd and received yours and his promise in their favor, to get it done as soon as those affairs were settled, but they could have a deed for mortgage, on the 16th of February 1768. Sent with order to that negro-man to go off from the premises with his family and effects within a week, otherwise he would sue him for trespass. Until, as I suppose in April 1769 (some think 1770) the congregation being tired with the like vexations, went there and carried his family and goods to his said master's house, repaired and fitted up the dwelling for their new minister to live in, who resides thereon since. He put the fences in good condition to save the winter grain for the benefit of the said negroes, who got the grain next harvest. But in return said Gideon sued them for trespass, which occasioned the trial in September court 1770, when those of the congregation who done that act were obliged to pay a small fine, with a considerable deal of costs Since this time the said Gideon hath sued them again for damages, that he says, he suffered merely by some trivials on rags, which he left lying before in the weather and muddled before his said master's house. His loss can be but very small, but though it be ever so little, yet it may prove probably possible, that the congregation might be sued again and also obliged to pay a considerable deal of costs too, and thereby be obliged to submit to this hero Lord South, if not timely supported. I have further to add that several witnesses were also sued to give evidence in favor of the said negro but they refused to appear Then before March Court last, I also had a subpoena sent me to attend in favor of the negro, but by reason of my weak state and condition of health, I did not attend nor any other witness, nor did I incline to meddle with it till August last a writ of attachment was served on me and also on the other witnesses, for disobedience or contempt of court, by the high Sheriff himself, so that we have to thank the high Sheriff's generosity and benevolence for it, for not putting us to goal for it, for near a whole month till September court about this affair. A strange instance indeed to observe, that this great Lord South, who was but lately a slave and to whom almost every one of us, at one time or another, out of compassion to him proved to be a benefactor, on his being supported by others, should have obtained so much power as to send six freeholders to gaol at his pleasure God beware, that the mighty Lord South does not obtain power to treat the members of our honorable Congress in the same manner

This affair disturbed my mind terribly at that time, but we appeared in town on the 6th of September last, as the day appointed by the high Sheriff. Wm. Lewis and Fisher are the two lawyers on the negro case. Mr. Lewis examined us, but found my testimony not to be that told him, but told us the case could not be tried now, but was put off.

Andrew Maurer, who had been sued for said damages and thereby obliged to stand foremost on the congregation's part, did not take a lawyer till September court last, when he employed Andrew Allen to act on their behalf. The trial was to be had on the 8th of January, now past, when I was obliged to go to town again, at the request of Mr. Allen, for Mr. Lewis had acquitted me in September court, since I could not give my evidence in favor of the said negro-man's cause before September last. I had not been in town for the space of five years together, chiefly by reason of my weak condition of health. When on calling at Mr. Allen's he informed us that we should have some deed or agreement or writings to show that the owners of the land had either sold or at least promised the same to the congregation, in order to show it as their title to the land at court, without which he could not consent to let the trial go on. This was the reason that we called at your house three times on the same morning, the 8th of January past, in order if possible to obtain such writings. But by reason of your indisposition, we were prevented to speak to you about it, or to inform you of the importance of it, so that Mr. Allen thought it suitable to remove the cause to the Supreme Court, but we find that Mr. Lewis bound over his witnesses to appear again on the 9. March next, as at the next close of the Common Pleas Court. So I have now thought necessary to inform you of the circumstances of this affair, in order that you may observe how troublesome the negroman hath already been to the said congregation who always have been and are yet ready to agree with you about the land and pay for it and have been long soliciting for it. For I conclude from the examination made on me by Mr. Lewis, that they intend yet to lay claim on the improvements, to which I think by no means that the negro can have a right, since whatever he did thereon, while a slave, they had the full use thereof, during their stay thereon, and I don't doubt, if you can spare time as to consider the matter all over again, you will be of the same opinion.

I am sorry to trouble you with this long detail, but I should think it a defect, if I should not do, what is possible in behalf of the congregation

Well what we most humbly desire of you, Sir, to be done is this. That you would be pleased to make an agreement with some of the members of the said congregation and put the same in writing, for the said tract of 42 acres and allowance with . . . per land I have made a new draught for the same to them, or if a deed could be made out now to the congregation, it will be found the better, before the time of the trial comes. Then we suppose all the vexations of the negro fellow and his supporters against the said congregation would terminate and be at an end. We think in these turbulent times we have and yet may expect trouble and calamity enough already.

We shall ever remain, dear Sir, your most affectionate and humble servant.

D. SCHULTZE.

By some boastings dropt by said Gideon, it seems that his lawyers intend to scruple the validity of our title in general to the land at court.

All to Daniel Rundle, the 3rd February 1776, sent Febr. 6th pr. Andrew Maurer

[VIII. LETTER OF DAVID SCHULTZE, ESQ., TO ANDREW ALLEN, ESQ., FEBRUARY 3, 1776. PRINTED IN THE *Daily Norristown Register*, MARCH 6, 1883.]

To ANDREW ALLEN, ESQUIRE!   1776. February 3rd.

Sir!

About the affair of the bearer hereof, Andrew Maurer, I have to inform you at first, since we could not speak to Mr Daniel Rundle, when in town, by reason of his indisposition, who is one of the three parties or owners to the land in question, so I have now wrote a letter to him of the affair very circumstantially, and alleged the necessity to get either a deed for the premises if possible or at least an agreement signed from under their hands

I also wrote another letter to Thomas Pugh, who is executor for the last deceased Thos. Tresse, Junior, another of the said partners to the land.

I spoke to him about it when in town, who promised to do all in his power in favor of the congregation, as to John Margotroyd, as the third partner. We could not learn where he lives now. What Mr. Rundle's answer will be I cannot know. One difficulty may perhaps obstruct the affair, for those three parties have been at variance with each other for many years past, and not yet settled, which hath been the chief reason, that no deed could be got out ever since the dec'd of old James Margotroyd—otherwise this land would have been long ago paid for. If our proposal for a particular agreement should not succeed, we have yet in reserve the general agreement, made with Parsons, Ross and Greenway, in April 1749, which on certain conditions includes the whole tract of 13,000 acres, signed by their own and many of our hands. Though it may not suit so well now, than if a new particular one can be obtained.

We have further to mention, when on our return to town, we met the other three witnesses, that they then informed us, that on that afternoon Mr. Lewis had bound them over by recognizance in Mr. Biddle's offices, to appear and attend again on the 9th of March next, as at the close of the next Court of Common Pleas, as if the cause was then to be tried Though as we understand from you, that the cause was removed to the Supreme Court, which we should like much better, in order to gain more time, for we cannot know what difficulty we may find or what time will be required to obtain what is required.

Now if you could prevail on Mr. Lewis, to send a written order to his three witnesses, Jacob Miller, Jacob Wissler and Ulrich Graber, not to attend on the said 9th of March next Then they will stay at home, otherwise they will certainly attend for fear of falling into the same unwelcome disgrace as in August last.

For what reasons Mr. Lewis hath, that he then acted in this manner we cannot know, if to increase the costs or for some other advantage?

Second Letter of David Schultz 191

So we humbly desire that you would be pleased to rectify this affair

By some boasting words, dropt by that negroman, as I was told of when in town, I suspect that his lawyers intend to dispute the validity of our title in general to these lands, which I think is a matter of no concern at all to them, we had trouble enough in former times already, until the cause was decided by the Supreme Court, anno 1754 in favor of Parsons, Ross and Greenway. I could make out a large description of the whole, but I should now think it unnecessary, see paper No. 2.

It is strange to observe that these gentlemen Fisher and Lewis and their supporters, of whom Mr. Israel Pemberton is looked upon as their chief, under the applauded pretext by assisting the needy and oppressed, by their endeavors are doing a considerable injury to a large number of people, especially at a time, when the utmost necessity requires it for every one to be as cautious as possible to avoid contentions nor to give offence to any.

I observed to you formerly, that I suspect those lawyers will perhaps lay claim again to that improvement, which if they do, it will seem so much the more strange, if they take for their foundation the foolish fancy of that old Irish low Dutch woman I look upon them as gentlemen, who would proceed on good reasonings. They forget themselves so far, while under a laudable pretext, they are putting numbers to loss and unnecessary charges. This small tract of land will cost the people dear enough besides.

The whole affair about the estate of that deceased minister hath to my opinion not been transacted according to law, nor agreeable to his will, nor even (if I dare say) to equity, for agreeable to the law, will and equity, the half of his relict estate should have been transmitted to Germany to his relations, to his brother eldest son, which hath not been done.

There is a strong supposition that the minister had a good purse in ready cash, which was concealed at the appraisement by his widow and afterwards by the negroes, for she paid almost no debts contracted by his negroes during the four years she outlived her husband. Christian Schneider was after his death obliged to pay above a hundred pounds debts and costs, if he has been repaid, I did not inquire. It must be true, since that can be proved by living witnesses, thus running the estate so much in debt in so short a time by his negroes while all the produce of the premises were also left him, it will appear, that he was none of the best economists, by the congregation gratis benevolence.

Did any of his supporters consider the matter with more deliberation, or think if any of their deceased tennants negroes should re-enter their premises and claim a right to their works done for their master, while slaves, how they would behave. I hope they would desist from what they are doing. Their own consciences (if any they have) would probably give them better instructions.

To MR. ALLEN
Febr. 3, 1776.

CHAPTER VII.

The Period of Supplies, 1762–1766.

WHEN Mr. Weiss died, the Goshenhoppen churches lost a faithful and able pastor. They struggled along for a few years with supplies, without being able to find a worthy successor.

At the Coetus of 1762, held on June 30 and following days at New Hanover,

three elders from Old and New Goshenhoppen and Great Swamp were admitted and reported that these three congregations would remain inseparably together. They then urgently asked that a minister of the Coetus be given to them in place of their faithful pastor, Do. Weiss, now deceased. And if they might be permitted to name the minister they would choose Do. Otterbein. The Reverend Coetus took this under consideration and promised them to make known the answer through Do. Leydich. After they were dismissed Do. Otterbein refused their request because of trifling reasons.

As Otterbein declined to serve Goshenhoppen, Leydich took his place. This is evident from the first entry in the second New Goshenhoppen record book, which reads:

Church Record for the Congregation of New Goshenhoppen, from the year in which Rev. Weiss died [1761] [containing the names of] all the children, who from that year to the year 1766 were baptized by me, Jacob Riess, Leyte [Leydich] and Michel and also those of later years.

Taking the statement in the Coetus minutes and this entry in the church record together, the most probable inference is that Mr. Leydich followed Weiss immediately. In view of the willingness of the congregations to apply to the Coetus for a minister, the most natural supposition is that a minister of the Coetus first supplied them after the death of Weiss and that, when he was no longer able to hold them, they drifted into the hands of independent ministers.

1. THE MINISTRY OF REV. JOHN PHILIP LEYDICH, 1762–1763(?).

John Philip Leydich was in 1762 pastor of Falkner Swamp and Providence (now St. Luke's at Trappe), Montgomery County, and of Vincent, Chester County.

John Philip Leydich was born April 28, 1715, and baptized May 5 of the same year, at Girkhausen, near Berleburg, in Westphalia.[172] He was the son of the Rev. Leonhard Leydich, then pastor at Girkhausen. John Philip Leydich studied for the ministry and in course of time became assistant to his father. In July, 1748, he appeared before the Synod of South Holland, then held at Briel, where he was commissioned for service in Pennsylvania. We next meet him in Philadelphia Schlatter in his Journal states:[173] "On the 15th of September, 1748, to my exceeding great joy, came to my house, healthy and

[172] The facts about the birth and parentage of the Rev John Philip Leydich were discovered by Mr Dotterer, see his various articles in his *Historical Notes*, pp. 2, 50, 59 f.
[173] *Life of Rev. Schlatter*, p. 182

happy, John Philip Leydich, with his wife and two children." Immediately after his arrival Leydich became pastor at Falkner Swamp and Providence. This incident is touchingly described by Mr. Boehm in his last letter, written on December 2, 1748,[174] to the Classis of Amsterdam:

> Shortly afterwards came my dear and kind brother, the Rev. John Philip Leydich, who was found to be suitable to take my place. At the Coetus of this year Do. Leydich willingly accepted his call to Falkner Swamp and Providence, as Do. Hochreutner to Lancaster and Do. Bartholomie to Tulpehocken. Coetus commissioned me to install Do. Leydich and Do. Bartholomie in their charges, which commission was carried out on October 16th at Falkner Swamp and on October 23rd at Tulpehocken.

Johann. Philipp Leydich
V. D. M.

Leydich was pastor at Falkner Swamp from 1748 to 1765; at Vincent, Chester County, from 1753 to 1765; at Coventry, now Brownback's, in Chester County, from 1769 to 1784; at Upper Milford and Salzburg, in Lehigh County, from 1766 to 1771, and at Pottstown from 1770 to 1784.

During the first twenty years of his ministry, Mr. Leydich took a prominent part in the work of the Coetus. He preached the opening sermon of the second Coetus, September 28, 1748, but a few weeks after his arrival. The same is true of the third Coetus, which was opened September 27, 1749, at Lancaster, "with a well arranged

---

[174] Classical Archives, Pennsylvania Portfolio, No. 33. See *Life and Letters of Boehm*, p. 449 f.

and edifying sermon by Do. Leydich." He was the president of Coetus in 1757 and 1760, and acted as its secretary in 1753, 1756 and 1768. In 1753 his salary is given as 40 pounds. After the year 1768 he retired to the background. That may have been due to his failing health, for in 1757, 1771, 1772 and 1776 he is reported as absent because of sickness or infirmity of old age.[175]

On October 16, 1749, Mr. Leydich purchased one hundred and five acres of land in Frederick township, on the banks of the Swamp Creek. This became the family homestead.[176]

He died January 14, 1784, leaving three sons and four daughters. He was buried on Leydig's graveyard, a private burial place, in part located on land originally purchased by him. The inscription on his tombstone reads in an English translation:

> John Philip Leydich
> Reformed Minister
> was born 1715
> the 28th of April
> Died January 14, 1784
> Aged 69 Years
> 2 Tim. 2· 3.

How long Leydich supplied Goshenhoppen cannot be made out with entire certainty, but probably a year, for at the Coetus meeting of May 5 to 6, 1763, Goshenhoppen is referred to as vacant.

On May 19, 1763, the Commissioners of the Classis of Amsterdam wrote as follows to the Coetus of Pennsylvania:

[175] For other sketches of Mr. Leydich's life see Harbaugh, *Fathers of Reformed Church*, Vol. II, pp. 24-28; Good, *History*, pp. 493-496.
[176] Dotterer, *Historical Notes*, p. 60

Inasmuch as the congregations of Old and New Goshenhoppen as well as some others desire a minister, we have now a good opportunity to send them a well tried teacher, who has done camp service with much praise in a Swiss regiment in the service of our country. This gentleman, who has a wife and several children, cannot decide to come over to you unless the congregations which desire his services shall have indicated how much they will be able to raise for his yearly salary and how much they are willing to send over for the traveling expenses of himself and his family; to which we expect a speedy answer.

When Coetus informed the Fathers that the sending of traveling expenses to Holland was impossible, the expected minister from Holland did not materialize.

2 THE MINISTRY OF PHILIP JACOB MICHAEL, 1763–1764(?).

In the opening statement of the New Goshenhoppen record, quoted above, Mr. Michael is placed after Mr. Leydich as the next pastor at Goshenhoppen. This is indirectly confirmed by the minutes of the Coetus of May 2 to 3, 1764, which state·

Regarding Goshenhoppen, we mention that it is provisionally supplied with preaching by another minister, until it shall be in a better condition to call a regular pastor

The fact that the name of the minister is not given is rather surprising. Was it because Coetus was employing one who was not one of its members and did not want the Fathers in Holland to know the fact? This question suggests itself naturally and an affirmative answer becomes highly probable, because recently another letter has come to light, in which the same state of affairs is said to have prevailed in another congregation. In January, 1773, Simon Dreisbach, a member of the Indian Creek congregation (now Stone Church in Northampton County) wrote to Rev. John Henry Helffrich about his congregation as follows:

> A minister was promised us, as soon as one should come in [from Holland]. Meanwhile Rev. Mr Leydich and Rev. Michael were to supply us until a minister should come in Each of these congregations gave twelve pounds to the said ministers to come to us on a week day, every three weeks, for one year, which was done and our congregation got its share, until several ministers came in [Stapel in 1761 and Weyberg in 1762].[177]

In view of these facts it is highly probable that the unnamed supply of Goshenhoppen in the Coetus minutes of 1764 was Philip Jacob Michael. It was at this same meeting of Coetus that he asked for admission. Although he was an independent Reformed minister, yet he did a useful work, that is well worthy of recognition.

When Michael appeared before the Coetus in 1764, he is said to have been 48 years of age, hence he was born in 1716. Rev. Wm. A. Helffrich states in his "History of Some Churches of Lehigh and Berks Counties," "that he was a weaver by trade."[178]

A Jacob Michael, and the only person of that name before 1744, qualified in Philadelphia on October 14, 1731, having arrived with the ship *Snow Louther*, Joseph Fisher, master. We are probably justified in identifying this Jacob Michael with the Reformed minister, Philip Jacob Michael. Inasmuch as in Germany the second

---

[177] This letter was first quoted by Ben Trexler in his *Skizzen aus dem Lecha = Thale*, Allentown, 1886, p. 107. More recently it was again brought to light by Rev. John B Stoudt of Northampton, Pa , and published by him in the *Cement News* of Siegfried, Pa , January 30–February 13, 1914; also in the *Reformed Church Review*, April, 1914, pp. 206–218

[178] Wm. A. Helffrich, *Geschichte verschiedener Gemeinden in Lecha und Berks Counties*, etc, Allentown, 1891, pp. 8, 79

Christian name serves as call name, the first is usually omitted.

Mr. Michael first appears as minister in the year 1744. His first field was Heidelberg, Lehigh County. Rev. Wm. A. Hellfrich says of him in his "History" [179]

"In the year 1744 a log church was built [at Heidelberg] and dedicated by Philip J. Michael" On March 28, 1745, he signed a contract drawn up by the Reformed and Lutheran congregations, worshipping in that church.

In 1750 we find him present at the dedication of Ziegel church in Lehigh County. On July 6, 1750, he signed a contract drawn by the Reformed and Lutheran members of that church. At the dedication of the church, July 29, 1750, Michael preached the first sermon and was the first pastor of the congregation

In the same year, 1750, the first church building of Jacobs church, in Jacksonville, Lynn township, was erected. Here again Michael officiated at the dedication of the church and was elected as the first pastor of the congregation.[180]

Two years later we meet him at Longswamp, in Berks County. Of this Jacob Weimer, the schoolmaster of the congregation, reports in the old church record:

After this work [the building of the church] had been completed to the honor of God and for their own salvation, they accepted the honored Mr. Frederick Casimir Miller for the purpose of dedicating this church and accepted him as their preacher, who served them for some time. But when he left them, they looked for another shepherd and accepted the honored Mr. Philip Jacob Michael as their minister During his and the preceding pastor's ministry, Fridrich Holwig has acted as cantor and precentor until the present time when this was written.

[179] L c, p 32.
[180] L. c., p. 52.

200   *History of the Goshenhoppen Charge*

The ministry of Michael at Longswamp extended probably from 1752–1753.

In 1753 Michael appears in Reading, where he baptized a number of Reformed children. Curiously enough the baptisms are entered into the Lutheran record, possibly because the parents became later members of the Lutheran church. The last baptism of Michael at Reading took place on November 10, 1754.[181]

In 1761 Michael dedicated the first church of the Ebenezer congregation, also called "Organ Church," in Lynn township, Lehigh County, and acted as its pastor from 1760 to 1770.

In 1761 Michael began his ministry also in the Weisenberg congregation, in Weisenberg township, Lehigh County. He served that congregation until the middle of the seventies, or about 1775.[182]

During the same time, from about 1759 till 1770, he was pastor at Maxatawny, Berks County, now De Long's Church, at Bowers. In October, 1771, the minutes of Coetus report Maxatawny, "formerly served by Do Michael," as vacant for some time and appealing to Coetus for a minister.

In 1764 Mr. Michael appeared before Coetus. The minutes state:

Philip Jacob Michael appeared with an earnest petition that he might be admitted as a member of Coetus. His credentials, from far and near show that, according to the rules of our Reformed Church, he has been faithful in doctrine, life and conduct for four-

[181] Daniel Miller, *History of the Reformed Church in Reading, Pa*, Reading, 1905, p. 12. A sketch of Michael's life is given there by the writer, pp 13–15.

[182] For Michael's work in these two churches see Helffrich's *Geschichte*, pp. 47, 39–41.

teen years [1750–1764] and constantly served the same congregations in Maxatawny and therefore, he does not deserve the name of an adventurer or Moravian. He showed that twelve years ago [1752] Mr. Schlatter would not recognize or admit him because of unfounded reasons Wherefore he would not apply again, although he labored continually in harmony with us.[183] We can state this all the more readily, because all his congregations are well known to us and we know how he has unweariedly aimed for this end, and even now, in he 48th year of his age, he supplies with the greatest zeal twelve congregations. This earnest request and petition we could not refuse. But since he has not been ordained, according to the order of our church, we herewith request permission, and proper authority from the Reverend Synods to ordain him. And as several of our number have heard him preach, and in his ministrations all is clearly in accordance with the Reformed church-order in doctrine and life, we expect that our request will not be in vain, so that we may thus be strengthened, by bringing under our control the congregations which he is serving, and comply with his reasonable request. We would not put our pen to this were we not convinced that it would be of advantage to us, and of greater profit to his congregations We expect at the earliest opportunity a favorable reply from the Reverend Synods.

In spite of this earnest plea the Holland Fathers refused to consent to his ordination in Pennsylvania, but demanded that he should come to Holland. That was of course impossible. Hence he did not press his request. The minutes of 1765 state:

We shall leave Mr. Michael to himself, and say nothing further about him, because the Reverend Fathers seem much disinclined to grant our request, and he being aged does not press his case, and his congregations are satisfied with him without ordination.

[183] This statement supports our contention, p 198, that Coetus appointed Michael to supply Goshenhoppen in 1764

In 1769 Michael founded the Lowhill congregation, in Lehigh County. On September 3, 1769, the first church was dedicated by him and he served as pastor of this congregation from 1769 to 1772 [184]

In the same year he also founded Michael's Church (named after him) in Upper Berne township, Berks County.

When the War of the Revolution broke out Michael resigned his churches. On May 17, 1777, he was appointed as chaplain of the first battalion of the Berks County militia.[185]

After the war he again entered upon his duties as pastor at Longswamp. There he had served a second pastorate from 1762 to 1774. His last baptism was on October 23, 1774. A third pastorate began there in January, 1781, and ended sometime in 1785. A baptism on December 25, 1785, was probably performed by Heinrich Hertzel, his successor. His will is dated May 6, 1786, and was probated at Reading, June 17, 1786.[186] Between these two dates he must have died. His will shows that he was the owner of 94 acres of land, situated partly in Rockland and partly in Longswamp township. He left to survive him a widow and five children.

The last will and testament of Mr. Michael is an interesting document, which deserves preservation. It reads as follows:

[184] Helffrich, *Geschichte*, p 43.

[185] *Pennsylvania Archives,* 2d Series, Vol. XIV, p 257 The name given there is Jacob Michael, but that is in perfect harmony with German custom, which uses the second Christian name as a call name, dropping the first entirely.

[186] *Pennsylvania German,* Vol VIII, p 191.

LAST WILL AND TESTAMENT OF THE REV. PHILIP JACOB MICHAEL, MAY 6, 1786.

(Register of Wills Office, Reading, Pa.)

In the name of God, Amen I, Philip Jacob Michael, of Rockland township, in the County of Berks and State of Pennsylvania, Minister of the Gospel, Being of an old age and weak and sick in Body, but of a Good and Sound mind, memory and understanding, Thanks be to Almighty God, and Calling in mind the Mortality of my Body, I being willing to make this my Last Will and Testament, In manner and form following:

First of all, I recommend my Immortal Soul into the Hands of Almighty God, through the merits of Jesus Christ, our Precious Lord and Saviour, and my Body to be Buried in a Christian like, decent manner, at the Direction of my Dear Wife Sara

It is my will and I do Order that my said Dear Wife Sara shall hold and Enjoy free and Clear Dwelling abode in my Present Dwelling house, undisturbed and unmolested During her Natural Life, if she remains a Widow, and also such Proper Pieces of Ground and of the Garden as she will Properly want to and for her use near the said dwelling abode And so much of my movable Estate as will be Necessary to and for her use in housekeeping, and so much Income of my Estate that will Properly be sufficient to and for her Livelihood, support and maintenance during her natural life, if she remains a Widow aforesaid, But in case she should Marry again, all aforementioned shall be disallowed unto her and she shall then receive nothing out of my Estate.

It is my will that all my Messuages or Tenements and Lands I hold and possess, situate Partly in Rockland and Part in Longswamp Township, in the County of Berks aforesaid, Consisting in two Parts, Containing in the Whole Ninety-four Acres of Land, or thereabouts, be the same more or less, Shall after my decease within the time of one Year, be appraised by three honest, reputable freeholders at a Reasonable rate and value thereof, and such Proper

Terms as may seem meet, having Regard to such Reservations for my Dear Wife aforesaid, And it is my will That then my oldest son John Michael shall have the first Choice to hold and Enjoy for him, his Heirs and Assigns forever my said Real-Estate, with all and every the appurtenances, at and for said sum, as the same will be appraised aforesaid, And in Case he should not except [!] thereof, then It is my will that my son Moses Michael shall have the next choice for him, his Heirs and assigns forever as aforesaid. And in case he would not except thereof, then it is my Will that it shall come to the choice of my son Philip Michael, to have and to hold the same unto him, his Heirs and Assigns forever as aforesaid, Provided that such of my said three Sons aforenamed, who shall or will hold my said Real Estate as aforesaid, shall out of such appraised valuation Pay all my just Debts and then the Remainder sum It is my will shall be equally divided to and among all my Children, to wit, John Michael, Moses Michael, Philip Michael, William Michael, And Sara Michael, share and share alike.

Item. It is my will that such of my Sons aforesaid as will hold my Real Estate aforesaid, Shall also hold my Wagon, Horses & Mares, with the Geers, Ploughs and Harrows and the Stock of Horned Cattle by the Appraisement, if he Chooses, and It is my will that my said five children shall have due regard for their said Mother, after my decease, and for her Livelihood, Support and Maintenance as herein aforesaid, And I give and Bequeath unto them my said five above named Children (observing my directions aforesaid) Equal shares and Portions, Share and Share alike of my whole Estate, And I do hereby ordain, Constitute and appoint my Trusty Friend Paul Grosscup, Esq. to be the Executor of this my Last Will and Testament, and I do hereby revoke and make void all former wills and testaments by me made, Hereby Ratifying and Confirming this and no other to be my Last Will and Testament.

In Witness Whereof I, the said Philip Jacob Michael, have

hereunto set my Hand and Seal the sixth day of May, In the Year of our Lord One Thousand Seven hundred and Eighty-six.

Signed, sealed pronounced and declared by the said testator as his last will and testament in the presence of us, who at his request have hereunto set our names as witnesses to the same.

PHILIP JACOB MICHAEL (SEAL)

HENRY HOFFMAN
GEORGE BOWER

Register of Wills Office, Reading, Berks County, June 17, 1786.

Personally appeared Henry Hoffman & George Bower witnesses to the above written will and upon their oaths did severally Depose and say that they were present and did see and Hear Philip Jacob Michael, the Testator therein named, sign seal pronounce, Publish and Declare the above Writing to be his Last Will and Testament, and that at the time of Doing thereof, he was of sound mind, memory and understanding, as they verily believe, and further that the names of said Deponents by them respectively subscribed thereunto as Witnesses, are each of his own handwriting, done in the presence of each other at the request and in the presence of the said Testator.

Coram me   HENRY CHRIST, *Register.*

His ministry at Goshenhoppen probably did not last longer than a year. In 1765 a new minister had come into the charge.

3. MINISTRY OF JACOB RIESS, 1765–1766.

The next minister of Goshenhoppen is introduced to us by the Coetus minutes of May 8 to 9, 1765. Here we read

Goshenhoppen, about which your Reverences inquire, has taken an old, ordinary man, a shoemaker [Jacob Riess] for their minister, because we could not provide the members with some one to their satisfaction

Not much is known about Jacob Riess. It is probable that he is identical with Johan Jacob Riess, who on September 24, 1742, qualified at Philadelphia.

We first find Riess as minister at Tohickon. There he opened the first church record in 1749:

Church Record for the Reformed Congregation on the Tohickon in Bedminster township, in which I have recorded those children which I, Jacob Riess, have baptized as Reformed preacher from the year 1749.

The first baptism was entered by him on August 27, 1749, the last on March 28, 1756.

At Indian Field, Bucks County, Jacob Riess opened the first record on June 3, 1753. The first baptism recorded by him took place on July 14, 1754. From that date till August 11, 1766, he entered nearly 250 baptisms into the Indian Field record.

At Springfield, Bucks County, Jacob Riess opened the church record on August 24, 1760. From that date till December 18, 1763, he entered forty-seven baptisms into that record.

At New Goshenhoppen Riess began the second record book, but the exact time cannot be determined. The baptisms are entered by families and he evidently made it a point to enter all the children of the families in which he performed any baptisms. Thus of the Cunius family he probably baptized himself only the last child, born on October 7, 1765. The children born before July, 1761, were baptized by Mr. Weiss. Some of them are actually found in the first volume. His last baptism at New Goshenhoppen was that of two negroes, father and son, brought to baptism by Thomas Mabry on January 26, 1766.

The elders at New Goshenhoppen during the ministry of Mr. Riess were Johann Ehrhart Weiss and Michael Moll, the deacons Ulrich Greber and Peter Hillegas

At Old Goshenhoppen the oldest record book, now in possession of the congregation, was also begun by Mr. Riess. Here again earlier baptisms were entered by him. The first baptism which he himself may have performed is dated June 5, 1764, although the baptism which is actually placed first took place on January 22, 1765.

The elders during his ministry at Old Goshenhoppen were Jacob Hauck and Johannes Goetz, the deacons Isaac Sumne and Andreas Ohl.

It may be that David Schultz had this minister in mind when he wrote, on February 3, 1776, to Daniel Rundle:

Anno 1761 in August, their said minister, Geo. Michael Weiss died, and though the said congregation got another in his stead, yet out of compassion to the deceased's widow, allowed her to live on the land with her negro family, and left her the full use thereof without demanding a penny rent of her for it. They rented another house for their new accepted minister to live in, until the year 1765, June 2nd, the said relict widow Anna Weiss, died also, having no children, only her said negro family, he died without a will, but she made a will, whereupon she gave all her estate to the said negro family and also her right to the improvements, if any she had [187]

The last baptism by Jacob Riess at Old Goshenhoppen took place on March 15, 1766 After that he disappeared. His tomb is in the graveyard adjoining the Tohickon church His tombstone bears the following inscription·

[187] See above, p. 186

208   *History of the Goshenhoppen Charge*

>   Jacob Riess
>   Gewesener Reformirter Prediger
>   Geboren den 10 April 1706.
>   Gestorben den 23. December 1774.

The minutes of the Coetus, held September 3 to 4, 1766, at Reading, inform us that

> Old and New Goshenhoppen, as well as Great Swamp have dismissed their shoemaker, Ries by name. They earnestly request that we provide them with a minister. Resolved that they be taken under the care of Coetus, and that they shall have one of the first new ministers.

At Great Swamp Riess has left no traces, but the above extract shows that he preached there as well as in the two Goshenhoppen churches. But while at Goshenhoppen Riess was preceded by Michael and Leydich, this does not seem to have been the case at Great Swamp. Tradition as well as direct evidence point to another pastor at Great Swamp, filling out the interval between the death of Weiss and the coming of Riess into the field. It was the Rev. John Rudolph Kittweiler.

4. MINISTRY OF JOHN RUDOLPH KITTWEILER AT GREAT SWAMP, 1762–1764.

On September 28, 1749, Hans Rudolph Kittweiler appears as one of 242 immigrants, brought to Philadelphia in the ship *Ann*, John Spurrier, master. The immigrants are described as "foreigners from Basel, Wirtemberg, Zweibrücken and Darmstadt."[188] Kittweiler belonged to the first group, for later he was known in his congregations as the "Schweitzer Pfarrer."

According to recent investigations, carried on at the

[188] Rupp, *Thirty Thousand Names*, p. 214

John Rudolph Kittweiler

request of the writer by Mr. Fritz Hensler, assistant in the University Library of Basel,[189] "Johann Rudolf Kindweiler" (this form or Kindwyler is the one commonly used at Basel) was born (or perhaps baptized, which took place at the latest eight days after birth) on May 26, 1716, at Basel, as son of Hans Jacob Kindweiler and his wife Catherine, née Spörlin. This baptism, together with that of several other children, is entered into the church record of the St Elizabeth congregation in Basel.

There is no evidence that Hans Rudolph Kindweiler studied in the University of Basel or was an ordained minister in Basel, as is stated by Rev. William A. Helffrich.[190]

From documents in the state archives at Basel it appears that in the year 1749 three hundred persons emigrated to Pennsylvania from villages, then belonging to the territory of the city of Basel. The first of such emigrations from Basel had taken place in 1738. When the new movement began in 1749, the government wanted to know what induced the people to leave. They gave poverty as the reason of their desire to leave for Pennsylvania.

The name Kindweiler does not appear in the lists of emigrants at Basel, probably because he was a free citizen of Basel. But when they arrived in Philadelphia, we find him as one of a company of Swiss emigrants.

Mr. Kindweiler (or Kittweiler as he was known in Pennsylvania) appears first as pastor of the Weisenberg congregation, in the northwestern corner of Weisenberg township, Lehigh County, where he organized the congregation and was present at the dedication of the first church

[189] The following facts were communicated to the writer by Mr. Fr Hensler, assistant librarian in the University Library at Basle, in a letter, dated February 10, 1914

[190] Helffrich, *Geschichte,* p 26

in 1754. Rev. Wm. Helffrich gives the following account of these events in his "History":[191]

> The organization of the congregation took place about the year 1747. Divine services were held in private houses as elsewhere. From 1749 that was done by Rev Kitenweiler, who was known as the "Swiss Preacher" and resided within the congregation. John Holben is named as an elder of the congregation at that time. The building of the first church took place in June 1754. The church was, as everywhere else at that time, a log church; but it was built better than others. . . . As the Rev. Daniel Schumacher testifies, the church was dedicated by Rudolph Kitweiler and Jacob Frederick Schertlein, the first pastors of the congregation. . . . Both preachers, Kitweiler and Schertlein, were ordained ministers.

He was pastor of the Weisenberg church till about 1761, when he was succeeded by Philip Jacob Michael.

Kittweiler also appears at Longswamp. The church record there informs us that "when the above mentioned preacher [Michael] had made his farewell, they accepted, about the middle of May, 1754, Mr. Rudolph Kidenweiler, who preached 7½ years to the congregation. When he could not gain his purpose, he left the congregation defiantly." That must have been about the close of the year 1760.

In 1759 Kittweiler was present at the dedication of the Eastern Salisbury Church, also called "Die Morgenland Kirche," Lehigh County. The Rev. Daniel Schumacher, first Lutheran pastor of the congregation, has preserved the following record of it in the old Lutheran church book.[192]

[191] *L. c*, p. 39
[192] *Hallesche Nachrichten*, new ed., Vol. I, p. 593, and "History of the Jerusalem Church Eastern Salisbury," in *Proceedings of the Lehigh County Historical Society*, Vol. II (1910), p. 72

The Christian Evangelical Lutherans and Reformed, both adhering to the Protestant religion, have together erected a church in Salzburg township in Northampton County, in the year of the Lord 1759. This church was built after the Indians had again ceased to burn and kill in this neighborhood, and by poor people only, who were, however, assisted by their brethren with small contributions.

The first preacher on the part of the Reformed congregation, at the dedication of this new church, was the Rev. Rudolph Kidweiler, popularly known as the Swiss preacher.

How long Kittweiler served this congregation is not known.

The time when Kittweiler came to Great Swamp cannot be determined definitely, but it was probably some time after the death of Weiss, that is, about the year 1762. The evidence of his presence at Great Swamp consists of an entry in the Great Swamp account book and of his tombstone in the graveyard near the church. The inscription on the tomb reads as follows:

HIER LIEGT BEGRABEN
DER GEWESENE REFORMIRTE PREDIGER
JOHANN RUDOLPH KITWEILER
SEIN ALTER WAR 47 JAHR 9 MONAT
IST GEBOREN DEN 2 JANUAR 1717
GESTORBEN DEN 2 OCTOBER 1764.

The entry in the account book, made March 31, 1766, states:

Of the above mentioned money of Ulrich Spinner there was paid to the wife [widow] of Rev. Rudolph Gittenweiler £1 0.6.

It is probable that during the pastorate of Kittweiler the Great Swamp Church secured a deed for its land. Although printed before, this document is important enough to be given a place here. It reads as follows:[193]

[193] First printed in Dr. Weiser's *Monograph*, pp. 42-46

PATENT OF GREAT SWAMP CHURCH LAND, DECEMBER 16, 1762.

Thomas Penn and Richard Penn, Esquires, true and absolute Proprietors and Governors in Chief of the Province of Pennsylvania and Counties of Newcastle, Kent and Sussex on Delaware, To all, unto whom these Presents shall come, Greeting: Whereas in pursuance of Warrants under seal of our Land Office, dated the twenty third day of May, one thousand seven hundred and thirty eight, there was surveyed on the twenty seventh day of September, following, unto Michael and Joseph Everhart a certain Tract of Land situate in Upper Milford Township, formerly in the County of Bucks, now Northampton, Beginning at a marked white oak, a corner of the said Michael and Joseph Everhard's Lands, thence by Land of Bartle Hornberier South-West one hundred and thirty perches to a post, Thence by Land of Lawrence Erb North West one hundred and forty eight perches to a post, thence by Land of Felix Brunner North-East one hundred and thirty perches to a stone in a line of the said Joseph Everhard's Land, thence by the same South-East one hundred and forty-eight perches to the place of Beginning, containing one hundred and thirteen acres and seventy perches and the usual allowance of six Acres per cent for Roads and Highways, as in and by the said Warrant and Survey remaining in the Surveyor General's Office and from thence certified into our Secretary's Office more fully appears, And Whereas the said Warrant was granted and the said Tract surveyed thereon at the instance and request and by the direction and at the proper cost and charges of the Minister, Elders and Congregation of the reformed Calvinist Society settled in Upper Milford aforesaid and adjacent Township of Lower Milford, who have now humbly besought us to grant unto the said Michael Everhard and to Joseph Everhard, the son of the said first Joseph Everhard, who is since lately deceased, in Fee the said described Tract of Land in Trust for the Minister, Elders and Congregation for the time being of the said reformed Calvinist and their Successors settled and to be settled from time to time in the said Two several Townships of Upper and Lower Milford the said congregation having now erected on the said Tract a Church and School House for the use of them and their successors And we favoring their request. Now know ye that for and in consideration of the sum of seventeen pounds eleven shillings and seven pence lawful money of Pennsylvania to our use paid being the money of the said congregation by the said Michael Everhard and Joseph Everhard their heirs and assigns, the Receipt whereof we hereby acknowledge and thereof do acquit and forever discharge the Michael Everhard and Joseph Everhard their heirs and assigns by these Presents and of the yearly Quit Rent hereinafter mentioned and reserved WE HAVE given granted released confirmed and by these Presents for us our Heirs and Successors as give grant release and confirm unto the said Michael Everhard and Joseph Everhard their Heirs and Assigns the said one hundred and thirteen acres and seventeen perches of Land as the same as now set forth, bounded and limited as aforesaid. With all Mines Minerals Quarries Meadows Marshes Savannahs Swamps Cripples Woods Underwoods Timber and Trees Ways Waters Water Courses Liberties Profits Commodities Advantages Hereditaments and appurtenances whatsoever thereunto belonging or in any wise appertaining and lying within the bounds and limits aforesaid Three full and clear fifth parts of all Royal Mines free from all deductions and Reprisals for digging and refining the same and also one-fifth part of the ore of all other mines delivered at the pitts-mouth only excepted and hereby reserved and also free leave right and liberty to and for the said Michael Everhard and Joseph Everhard, their Heirs and Assigns to Hawk Hunt Fish and shoot in and upon the hereby granted Land and Premises or upon any part thereof. To have and to hold the said one hundred and thirteen Acres and seventy Perches of Land and Premises hereby granted (except as before excepted) with their appurtenances unto the said Michael Everhard and Joseph Everhard their Heirs and Assigns forever IN TRUST nevertheless and for the use of the Minister Elders and Congregation for the time being of the said reformed Calvinist Society and their Successors settled and to be settled from time to time in the said two several Townships of Upper and Lower Milford and to and for no other use or purpose whatsoever TO BE HOLDEN of us our Heirs and Successors, Proprietaries of Pennsylvania as of our Manor of Tamor in the County of Northampton aforesaid in free and common Socage by Fealty only in lieu of all other services. YIELDING AND PAYING thereof Yearly unto our Heirs and Successors at the Town of Easton in the County aforesaid at or upon the first day of March in every year from the first day of Marsh last one-half Penny sterling for every acre of the same or value thereof in coin current according as the exchange shall then be between our said Province and the City of London to such Person or Persons as shall from time to time be appointed to receive the same and in case of non-payment thereof within ninety days next after the same shall become due then it shall and may be lawful for us our Heirs and Successors our and their receiver or receivers unto and upon hereby granted Land and Premises To-Re-enter and the same to hold Possess until the said quit-rent and all arrears thereof together with the charges accruing by means of such non-payment and Re-entry be fully paid and discharged.

WITNESS James Hamilton Esquire Lieutenant Governor of the said Province, who by virtue of certain powers and authorities to him for this purpose (inter alia) granted by the said Proprietaries hath hereunto set his Hand and caused the Great Seal of the said Province to be hereunto Affixed at Philadelphia this sixteenth day of December in the Year of our Lord one thousand seven hundred and sixty two. The Third Year of the Reign of King George the Third over Great Britain.

CHAPTER VIII.

MINISTRY OF REV. JOHN THEOBALD FABER, SR., 1766–1779.

AFTER four years of supplies, the congregations were again provided with a regular pastor in the fall of 1766. It was the Rev. John Theobald Faber, Sr.

He was born February 13, 1739, at Zozenheim, south of Bingen, at one time in the Palatinate, but now in the archduchy of Hesse. He matriculated at Heidelberg University, February 5, 1760, as student of philosophy and theology.

His examination as candidate for the ministry took place at Heidelberg on April 20, 1763. Three years later he left the Palatinate for Holland. At his departure he requested and secured the following certificate:[194]

Inasmuch as the Consistory of the Electoral Palatinate has learned with special pleasure that the Palatine Candidate for the Ministry, Faber of Zotzenheim, according to the commission given to him, intends to go to America as minister, therefore his petition made to us yesterday, namely that his eventual return to his father-

---

[194] The German text is given, with several misprints, in Dr. Weiser's *Monograph*, p. 63.

land might not be forbidden to him, is hereby not only granted, but on the contrary in such a case special regard shall be given to his advancement. In witness whereof the large seal of the Consistory's Chancery and the usual signatures have been affixed.

Heidelberg, the 28th of April 1766.
    Consistory of the Electorate Palatinate
             J. W. F. HADS, *Antz.*

Seal of the
 {SEAL}
Reformed Consistory of the Palatinate.

On June 27, John Theobald Faber, John George Wittner, another candidate from Bellheim in the Palatinate, and Carolus Lange, a third candidate, from Innsbruck, Tyrol, appeared before the deputies, were examined and received their commissions and 250 fl. each as traveling expenses to America. Their ship left Rotterdam for New York on July 10, 1766. They arrived in Pennsylvania in September, 1766.

Shortly after their arrival, Rev. John George Alsentz of Germantown wrote Mr. Faber the following letter.[195]

LETTER OF ALSENTZ TO FABER, SEPTEMBER 19, 1766.

          GERMANTOWN, the 19th of
            September 1766.

Very Reverend
 and much esteemed Sir!

    My heart is full of thanks to the faithful Father for His gracious guidance of your Reverence and your happy arrival in our vineyard. My heart rejoices and I congratulate myself because of the help that has reached us, which we so much need. I have

[195] This letter is now in the library of the Reformed Theological Seminary at Lancaster. It was placed at the disposal of the writer, together with a number of other letters from the correspondence of Mr Faber, through the courtesy of Prof. Geo W. Richards, D.D.

understood that you preached yesterday in Philadelphia and that you will come up to me next Sunday. I have accordingly informed the Rev. Weyberg that I had announced a communion service and that you might choose a sermon fitting for the occasion If that letter should have been delayed, I ask you herewith to make note of this. In addition I wish to ask you to notify me whether you prefer to preach in the forenoon or afternoon, so that I may be governed by your choice. This I may tell you in advance that in the morning the church will be best filled, because many people live far away. Hence it is the best service for a strange minister to be heard. Besides I ask you to inform me whether you are a Mr. Faber from Zozenheim and what the names of the other gentlemen are,

I remain very respectfully
Your Reverence's
Faithful Brother
Jo. Geo. Alsentz.

P.S. More orally. Please attribute my brevity to my ill health

Faber reached his charge in October, 1766. On October 21, 1766, he performed his first ministerial act, by officiating at a funeral at New Goshenhoppen He made his home at first with Daniel Hiester. On February 29, 1769, £1.12.10, was paid by the Great Swamp congregation as "house rent for the minister to Daniel Hiester."[196] This remained the place of his residence probably till he married on August 7, 1770, Barbara Rose, daughter of Erhardt Rose of Reading. After his marriage he moved into the parsonage, built on the glebe land near the New Goshenhoppen church.[197]

At the Coetus of 1768, held September 8 to 9, 1768, at Easton, Faber reported for the first time the statistics of his congregations. Old Goshenhoppen had then 30 fami-

---

[196] According to an entry in the account book of the congregation.
[197] See letter of Mr Schultz, printed above, pp 184-9, esp p. 187

lies, New Goshenhoppen 90, and Great Swamp also 30 families He had baptized during the preceding year 60 and confirmed 22. These figures increased only slightly during the next four years. Thus in 1771 he reported 40 families at Old Goshenhoppen, 90 at New Goshenhoppen and 40 at Great Swamp, 63 baptized and 25 confirmed. It is, however, remarkable that in his report of 1773 the sum total of his membership jumps from 170 families in 1772 to 260 in 1773, together with 87 baptized and 36 confirmed. In the last year of his pastorate, 1779, the figures were 270 members in the three congregations, 69 baptisms and 48 confirmed. Complete statistics cannot be given from the Coetus Minutes, as the reports for two years (1774 and 1778) are missing.

It may, however, serve a useful purpose to give a summary of his pastoral activity on the basis of the various church records. Into them he entered 764 baptisms, 262 funerals and 127 weddings. The record for the separate congregations stands as follows·

At New Goshenhoppen he entered from January, 1767, till October 6, 1779, 312 baptisms; he officiated from October 21, 1766, till August 5, 1779, at 126 funerals, and married from March 3, 1767, till September 30, 1779, 56 couples His first class of catechumens was confirmed on April 17, 1767, his last on April 2, 1779.

At Old Goshenhoppen he recorded from November, 1766, till September 24, 1779, 282 baptisms; from December 26, 1766, till October 18, 1778, he held 82 funerals; and from January 20, 1767, till October 5, 1779, he officiated at 52 weddings.

At Great Swamp he baptized from November 19, 1766, till October 27, 1779, 170 children; he entered 54 funerals from April 21, 1767, till June 11, 1779, and united in marriage 29 couples from March 5, 1767, till August, 1779.

These entries make it plain that Faber's pastorate extended from October, 1766, till October, 1779.

Faber was honored by the Coetus in being elected its secretary in 1771 and its president in 1772

The ability of Faber as a preacher was recognized by other congregations than his own. When the congregation of Lancaster became vacant in 1769 through the removal of Mr Hendel to Tulpehocken, they called Faber. The minutes of 1770 state: "The congregation made an urgent request for an ordained minister and gave a special call to Do. Faber of Goshenhoppen." But since he had many scruples with regard to leaving his congregations he asked for four weeks' time to consider, which was granted him by the Reverend Coetus, and it was at once resolved that he might accept the call without waiting for a further decision of the Coetus. The Coetal letter of that year, written on December 7, 1770, reports that "Faber has concluded to remain at Goshenhoppen."

In 1775 Lancaster became again vacant through the removal of its pastor, Charles L. Boehm, to Hanover, hence the Lancaster congregation renewed its call to Mr. Faber. At the Coetus held May 10 to 11, 1775, at Lebanon, "two delegates from Lancaster appeared with a written call for Do. J Th. Faber, who, however, could not decide to leave his congregations."

In 1779 the call of the Lancaster congregation was renewed for the third time and was at last accepted by Faber

Before, however, recounting these final events in the ministry of Faber at Goshenhoppen a few other facts ought to be mentioned.

History of the Goshenhoppen Charge

In 1773 the Minutes of Coetus state:

Trumbauer Congregation, in Bucks County, which was at first served by Do. Gobrecht, and afterwards, from time to time by Do. Faber, asked the Reverend Coetus for Do. Gebhard.

Gobrecht was in Bucks County as pastor of the Tohickon charge from 1766 to 1770, hence Faber must have supplied that congregation from 1770 to 1772, when Mr. Wack became the pastor at Tohickon.

A remarkable entry in the Coetus Minutes, connecting Gobrecht with Great Swamp ought to be mentioned. The statistics of 1769 and of 1770 report Gobrecht as serving Tohickon, Indian Field and Great Swamp, while at the same time Faber is reported as the pastor of Great Swamp and, moreover, the Great Swamp church record shows that the baptismal entries of Faber at Great Swamp run without break through 1769 and 1770 as through all the other years from 1766 to 1779. Perhaps the easiest way to get rid of this difficulty is to regard it as a simple mistake of the clerks of Coetus. Such an explanation would seem to be demanded for 1769, where the statistics of Gobrecht and Faber follow each other immediately and where Gobrecht is said to have reported for Great Swamp 30 families, 16 baptisms and 1 catechumen. Incidentally the same figures are reported by Faber for Great Swamp. Surely there must be a confusion in this case. But what caused the confusion in 1770, if there be one, remains unexplained.

The progress of the charge under the care of Mr. Faber is seen in the fact that during his ministry two of the congregations built new churches.

In 1769 the cornerstone was laid and in 1770 a large new stone church was completed at New Goshenhoppen.

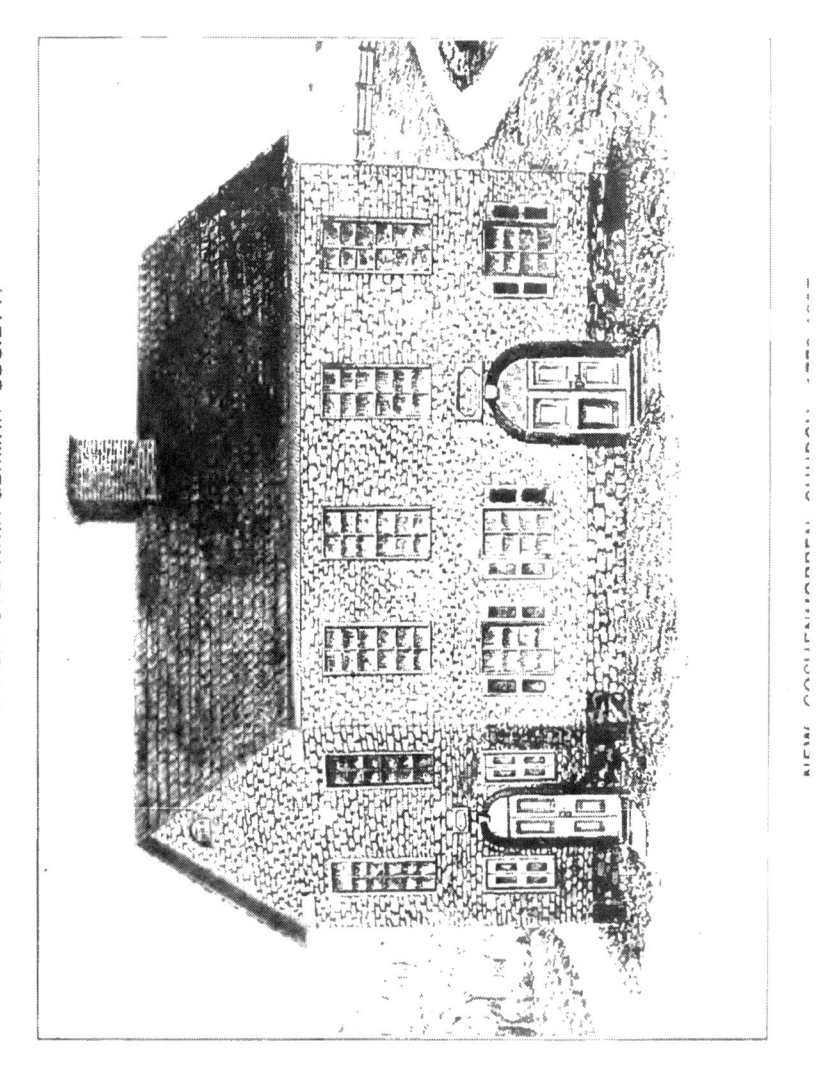

THE PENNSYLVANIA GERMAN SOCIETY.

NEW GOSHENHOPPEN CHURCH, 1744-1916

THE NEW YORK
PUBLIC LIBRARY

ASTOR, LENOX
TILDEN FOUNDATIONS

At Old Goshenhoppen a similar stone church was built in 1772. In the same year a new parsonage seems to have been built at New Goshenhoppen. For in the Old Goshenhoppen account book we find the following entry in 1772:

Two and Twenty Pounds and eleven shillings were paid by Christian Hollebusch for the parsonage at New Goshenhoppen to Adam Hillegas and in addition 3 pounds to Abraham Seckler, as per receipt, dated June 7, 1772. Thirteen shillings 6 pence were paid to me by Ulrich Hertzel on account of the building expenses of the parsonage.

WEYGAND PANNEBECKER

The organist and schoolmaster at Old Goshenhoppen from 1772 to 1778 was Henrich Hemsing, who at first (in 1772) received five, later six pounds as salary for playing the organ.

The organist at New Goshenhoppen during this period is unfortunately not known, but the organ has been preserved and what is more remarkable it is still in use. It is probably the oldest organ in use in the Reformed church. It was put into the second church in 1770 when it was finished. It was built by the well-known organ-builder Tannenhäuser of Lititz, Lancaster Co., Pa.

In August, 1779, the congregation at Lancaster sent the following call to Mr. Faber:[198]

CALL OF LANCASTER CHURCH TO FABER.

LANCASTER, August 30, 1779.

Reverend Sir —It is without doubt already known to your Reverence, that the Rev. Mr Helffenstein has left our congregation for some time past. In order, therefore, to obtain another pastor, the congregation assembled yesterday in the schoolhouse; on which

[198] Weiser, *Monograph*, p 67

occasion your Reverence was unanimously elected. If you will, then, have the goodness to visit us and preach for us we will be very thankful. The Consistory, accordingly resolved, with the consent of the congregation, to send the bearer, William Jacob Schaeffer, to wait upon you, and urge upon you our call. Should you consent to preach a trial sermon, on some day of your own choosing, we will then be fully prepared to extend you the proper call. To this end, Mr. William Jacob Schaeffer is authorized to confer with you in detail.

Meanwhile we remain your Friends. Done in the name of the Consistory of the German Reformed Church, Lancaster,

NICHOLAS JOB
WILLIAM BUSH
LUDWIG SCHELL

But the people at Goshenhoppen were not willing to give up their pastor. Hence they framed and forwarded a protest to the Coetus. In it they stated that his charge "unanimously desires to retain him as their pastor; that he is greatly beloved by all, and that he is very useful." They furthermore promised "to give him £225 lawful money, sixty bushels of wheat and rye, the use of the parsonage, fuel and the hay of a meadow." They expressed the hope that the Reverend Coetus "would grant their desire and allow Mr. Faber to remain with them."

In spite of this protest, however, Faber left Goshenhoppen in October, 1779. The Coetus Minutes of 1781 report: "Mr. Faber has accepted Lancaster. He left Goshenhoppen because they did not give him the necessary support which they were sufficiently able to do." This plain statement stands in glaring contrast to the promises of the congregations. Indeed the salary of Faber as reported for 1770 and 1771 was only £65. In 1785 he reported it at £100, while the highest salary any

ORGAN OF NEW COPENHAGEN CHURCH

THE NEW YORK
PUBLIC LIBRARY

ASTOR, LENOX
TILDEN FOUNDATIONS

minister of the Coetus received in 1785 was £150. We are, therefore, justified in questioning the accuracy of the above translation. If a supposition may be ventured, the writer would suggest it to be a misprint for £75 or perhaps £85. That would be in harmony with general conditions.

CHAPTER IX.

MINISTRY OF REV. JOHN WILLIAM INGOLD, 1780–1781.

SOME time in September, 1780, the following heading was put over a series of baptisms in the Old Goshenhoppen Record:

"The following children were baptized by me, Johann Wilhelm Ingold, pastor loci."

This heading is followed by fifteen baptismal entries, in the handwriting of Ingold, extending from September, 1780, to July 30, 1781. These entries introduce us to a minister of an entirely different type than his predecessors.

On August 4, 1754, "Joh. Wilhelmus Ingoldius" matriculated in the University of Heidelberg, as a student of theology, from Simmern, in the Palatinate, at present in the Rhine province, in the "Regierungsbezirk" Koblenz. He was ordained at Heidelberg May 10, 1762. He appeared before the Deputies June 1, 1774. He produced as his testimonials a letter of recommendation from Hospital, consistorial councillor at Heidelberg, dated May 23, 1773. He also had a letter from the German Reformed Church of London, where he had been pastor for four months, dated February 20, 1774. His credentials were found to be sufficient, and he was appointed by the Synodical Deputies. On June 9, 1774, a letter of introduction to the Coetus of Pennsylvania was given to him and 150 fl.

as traveling expenses. Shortly afterwards he left for Pennsylvania, where he arrived in the fall of that year. He had a very checkered career. From 1775 to 1790 he is mentioned in the Minutes of Coetus, serving in these fifteen years no less than seven different charges. His whole ministry was filled with quarrels. He paid no regard either to the resolutions of the Coetus or the wishes of his congregations. Hence he was constantly in difficulty. The verdict of Coetus on his ministry is expressed in these words: "Rev. Ingold during his stay with us has not conducted himself to the satisfaction of his brethren."[199]

Shortly after his arrival he took Witpen and Worcester in Montgomery County. At Witpen (now Boehm's Church at Blue Bell) his baptismal entries begin November 7, 1774, and end May 25, 1775. At Worcester (now Wentz's Church) a receipt for salary shows that his ministry there began on November 10, 1774. It lasted for one year. At the end of that time the people were unwilling to continue paying him £75 as salary.

At the close of the year the congregations offered a smaller sum, and said if he should not be satisfied with this they would close the church against him. Thereupon Mr. Ingold preached no longer for them, but continued to live in the parsonage until he no longer dared to remain there. He then moved to another house in the neighborhood, where he wholly consumed the gathered crumbs. His brethren were sorry for him, gave him oral and written advice, and helped him to Saucon. But here again he left immediately and went to Easton, hoping to draw the united congregation to him.[199a]

In Easton his baptismal entries begin on July 7, 1776,

[199] *Minutes of Coetus*, p 373.
[199a] *Minutes of Coetus*, p. 373.

and continue from that date uninterruptedly till March 17, 1786. It was thus while pastor at Easton that the Goshenhoppen charge became vacant and was entered by him. The Minutes of 1781 continue the story:

Easton being a small congregation and unable to support him, and he in addition losing the love of the people, and finally even being persecuted, tried to gain the favor of Goshenhoppen. He offered to take only as much salary as their kindness and free-will would give. The result was that two small congregations [Old Goshenhoppen and Great Swamp] allowed him to preach in their churches; but the strongest congregation, New Goshenhoppen, protested against this, and many persons also in the two smaller congregations did not want to have anything to do with him, until he should be accepted by the three united congregations as their minister. Nevertheless, Ingold settled among these congregations on his own account. Hence there arose the greatest confusion among them which a committee of Coetus tried to settle. But Ingold opposed and frustrated the attempt of his brethren. When all these actions of this man were placed before Coetus, the following resolution was adopted:

a. That the three united congregations shall meet for the election of a minister. Mr. Ingold may be a candidate in this election, if the congregations so agree.

b. That this action be recommended, in writing, to the congregations and Mr. Ingold likewise be advised to help in bringing about this election; otherwise the Coetus will be compelled to take extreme steps in his case.

When Coetus met again on May 1, 1782, at Reading, they report:

Mr. Ingold, who was not present at the Reverend Coetus, having left the congregations in Goshenhoppen half a year ago, informed the Reverend Coetus by a letter presented by an elder, that he had begun to serve the congregations Easton, Dryland and Greenwich. The Reverend Coetus was obliged to approve of this action, because for several years it has been thought advisable to allow all vacant congregations to call a minister of the Coetus according to their pleasure; even as a minister is also at liberty to accept such congregations at pleasure.

This entry shows that Ingold left Goshenhoppen about November, 1781, probably because the election was unfavorable to him.

The activity of Ingold in the Goshenhoppen charge can only be traced at Old Goshenhoppen. Besides the baptisms, to which reference has already been made, he entered a class of catechumens (22 boys and 19 girls) into the record on April 21, 1781. Besides, he signed the account of the treasurer on May 18, 1781, with A. M. Ache, the schoolmaster.

At Great Swamp different hands entered eleven baptisms from September 18, 1780, till July 22, 1781. According to the minutes of the Coetus of May, 1781, Caspar Wack,[200] pastor of Tohickon and Indianfield, was supplying the Swamp church. In the minutes of the Coetus of 1782, held May 1, 1782, at Reading, we read:

The congregations Tohickon, Indianfield and Great Swamp, which, by the departure of Mr. Wack, had become vacant, asked, through delegates for another minister. The Reverend Coetus could do nothing but give these congregations liberty to call a minister.

[200] Caspar Wack was the son of John George Wack, who arrived at Philadelphia on September 16, 1748 Caspar Wack was born at Philadelphia August 15, 1752 He was educated by Rev Caspar Weyberg, licensed by Coetus in 1770; catchist at Lancaster, 1770–71, ordained June, 1772 His first pastorate was at Tohickon and Indianfield 1772–1782, to which Nacomixon was added in 1773. He was pastor of German Valley, Foxhill and Rockaway, N J, 1782–1809; of Germantown and Whitemarsh, 1809–1821; of Whitemarsh alone 1821–23 He died at Trappe, Montgomery County, July 19, 1839 See Harbaugh, *Fathers*, Vol. II, pp 173–192, Good, *History*, pp 570–72

228   *History of the Goshenhoppen Charge*

During this period we find at New Goshenhoppen 17 baptisms recorded from June 18, 1780, till March 12, 1781. Most of these entries are in the handwriting of the Rev. John Henry Helffrich,[201] then pastor of Maxatawny, Heidelberg, Lowhill, Upper Milford, and Salzburg, all of which, except the first, are located in Lehigh County. He was one of the strong men of Coetus, who did much to uphold order and religion in his own as well as in neighboring congregations.

After Ingold left Easton in 1786, he went to Reading. His call to that congregation is dated September 14, 1786. After serving that congregation for a year and a half, which was rich in quarrels, he left it in April, 1788. Coetus does not want to put all the blame on him, but remarks that "a repulsive conduct is likely to bring about such consequences." From there he went to Indianfield, Tohickon and Trumbauers. At Indianfield his baptismal entries run from June 19, 1788, till November 1, 1789 While pastor there, he lost his wife. He himself made the following entry in the Indianfield record:

"March 29 [1789], Mrs. Catharine Barbara Ingold, wife of the pastor died, aged 40 years, 6 months, 3 weeks and 4 days." At the meeting of Coetus held in June, 1790, he is reported as having been "rejected by his congregations." After that his name appears only once more in the official records of the church. It was to make his

[201] John Henry Helfrich was born at Mosbach in the Palatinate, October 22, 1739. He matriculated at Heidelberg University, February 2, 1758 He was ordained in September, 1761; became assistant pastor to his father at Sinsheim and Rohrbach; was then vicar at Reyen, Kirchhard and Steinfurth; was commissioned for Pennsylvania July, 1771; arrived at New York January 14, 1772. He was pastor of the Maxatawny charge all his life, 1772-1810, which consisted among others of Lowhill, Heidelberg, Kutztown, etc. He died December 5, 1810. See Helffrich, *Geschichte,* pp. 73-86, Harbaugh, *Fathers,* Vol II, pp. 240-251.

separation from the church complete and final. In 1801 Synod notified him that by his continued absence he had excluded himself from the church. His name was therefore dropped.[202]

[202] For sketches of Ingold's life see Harbaugh, *Fathers,* Vol. II, p. 399 f.; Good, *History,* pp. 561–563; Miller, *History of the Reformed Church in Reading,* pp. 86–90.

CHAPTER X.

MINISTRY OF REV. FREDERICK DELLIKER, 1782-1784.

AT the same meeting of Coetus, at which the departure of Ingold from Goshenhoppen was announced, we also find the announcement of the arrival of a new pastor.

Mr. Daelliker informed Coetus why he had left his former field in New Jersey, including the congregations Rockaway, Valley, Foxhill, and a few months ago, accepted a call from the congregations of Goshenhoppen.

Frederick Delliker (or Dälliker) was descended from an old Zurich family. They became citizens in Zurich, 1376. During the seventeenth century there were at least three ministers in the family. The coat of arms of the family showed a man with two burning candles in his hands. This design was based on the name of the family which was originally "Talliker," meaning the "candle maker" (cf. the German Talg and the English tallow). These facts, taken from the "Lexicon Geographicum-Stemmatographicum"[203] in Zurich, dispose entirely of the old tradition that the name of the family was originally

---

[203] In the city library at Zürich, Msc. E. 54; Vol. II, pp. 5-8; cf. also above, p. 97, note 107.

Frederick Delliker

De la Cour and that he was, therefore, of Huguenot descent. The family was rather an old Swiss family and could not possibly have been Huguenot. What actually happened was that Frederick Delliker adopted for a time, while in French services, a French name.

Hans Rudolph Dalliker, the father of Frederick Dalliker, was a painter and in 1750 became "Oberster Salzhausdiener," which position was probably equivalent to the manager of the saltworks. His mother was Maria von Brunn of Basel, who married his father on March 23, 1732. She died March 23, 1754, while the father died April 23, 1769, at Schaffhausen.

Frederick Delliker was born in 1738, according to the Zurich records. Dr. Harbaugh[204] gives February 2, 1738, as the date of his birth, but that cannot be correct. His tombstone at Falkner Swamp states that he died January 15, 1799, aged 60 years, 10 months and 17 days,[205] hence the date of birth must have been February 27, 1738. According to the genealogical records in Zurich, Frederick Dälliker was ordained in 1757. In the year following (1758), he became German "Diakon," or assistant minister in Geneva. In 1760 he became chaplain of the French regiment "Lochmann." It was while he was a French chaplain that he assumed temporarily the name De la Cour. The French name never appears in his later life. In 1766 he left French services.

In December, 1766, he arrived at Amsterdam, and on April 17, 1767, he appeared before the Classical Commissioners. In May his presence and application for service in Pennsylvania was announced to the Synodical Deputies. He was examined at the Hague, June 25, 1767, signed

[204] Harbaugh, *Fathers,* Vol II, p 382
[205] Roth, *History of the Falkner Swamp Reformed Church,* 1904, p 37

the formula of unity and was given his commission. When he arrived in Pennsylvania in the fall of 1767 (probably October), he was sent to Amwell, New Jersey, now at Ringoes, Hunterdon County, N. J In 1768 Germantown gave him a call but he declined it and announced that he had determined to serve, in addition to Amwell, Alexandria (Mt. Pleasant), Rockaway (Lebanon), Foxhill (Fairmount) and German Valley, four new congregations, which asked "to be taken into the fellowship of Coetus." At Rockaway his entries begin in the church record on November 6, 1768.[206] In 1769 charges were brought against him at Amwell, as a result of which he left Amwell, but continued to serve the other congregations. The statistics of 1769 report him as unmarried, residing at Rockaway, and serving the four congregations mentioned above.

Delliker continued as pastor in New Jersey until the spring of 1782, when, through the departure of Ingold from Goshenhoppen, these congregations had become vacant. In May, 1782, he informed Coetus that he had gone to Goshenhoppen "a few months ago." In entire harmony with this statement we find that his baptismal entries begin at New Goshenhoppen on March 3, 1782, at Great Swamp on March 10, and at Old Goshenhoppen on March 17, 1782. On June 6, 1783, he signed a receipt for salary at Old Goshenhoppen from February 1, 1782, to February 1, 1783. This fixes the beginning of his ministry definitely as February 1, 1782. On May 1, 1782, Delliker made the following report of his congregations: "170 families, 33 baptisms, 35 confirmed and 3 schools." This is the first definite evidence in the Coetus Minutes that each of the three congregations had a parochial school.

[206] Chambers, *Early Germans in New Jersey*, p. 105 f

Delliker at Goshenhoppen 233

At the meeting of Coetus on May 14, 1783, in Philadelphia, Delliker is reported as supplying six congregations in New Jersey, part of them his former charge, Rockaway, Valley and Foxhill, also in part Nolton, Hartwick and Newton. At the same time he made detailed report about the three congregations of which he was the regular pastor. Of New Goshenhoppen he reported 95 families, 37 baptized, 17 confirmed, 2 schools with 48 scholars; of Old Goshenhoppen 45 families, 18 baptized, 8 confirmed, 1 school with 32 scholars; of Great Swamp 37 families, 12 baptized, 26 confirmed, 1 school with 31 scholars. Unfortunately we know nothing more of the two schools at New Goshenhoppen.

The pastoral activity of Delliker in the Goshenhoppen charge can be summed up as follows: 141 baptisms, 21 funerals and 16 weddings. The record for each of the churches is as follows:

At New Goshenhoppen he entered 77 baptisms, beginning on March 3, 1782, and ending March 21, 1784. There were 12 funerals from June 5, 1783, to March 11, 1784, and 7 weddings from March 24, 1782, to March 16, 1784.

At Old Goshenhoppen he officiated at 30 baptisms from March 17, 1782, to January 18, 1784, at 4 funerals from February 12, 1783, to January 15, 1784, and at 5 weddings from August 6, 1782, to May 20, 1783.

At Great Swamp he had 34 baptisms from March 10, 1782, till March 18, 1784, 5 funerals from April 17, 1783, and 4 weddings from April 23, 1782, to April 1, 1783.

From these summaries it is apparent that the pastoral activity of Delliker at Goshenhoppen extended from March, 1782, till March, 1784. During this time he was not, as has been commonly reported, the pastor at Falkner Swamp. The ministry of Rev. Nicholas Pomp came to an end at Falkner Swamp after the meeting of Coetus on May 14, 1783, when he is still reported as pastor of Falkner Swamp and Vincent. He did not leave these congregations till the fall of 1783 for Baltimore. Pomp's first baptismal entry made in the Baltimore records was on September 15, 1783, and he himself states in that record that he preached his installation sermon [Eintrittspredigt] on the first Sunday of September, 1783.

In the spring of 1784, Delliker was called to Falkner Swamp to become Pomp's successor. Delliker's first entry in the Swamp records was made on April 9, 1784. At the Coetus meeting held on May 12, 1784, Delliker is reported as having gone from Goshenhoppen to Falkner Swamp.

He remained pastor of Falkner Swamp and Vincent to the end of his life. He died at Falkner Swamp June 15, 1799, and was buried in the Falkner Swamp graveyard.[206a]

He was a prominent member of Coetus, as is seen from the fact that he was the secretary of Coetus in 1774, 1783, 1786, 1788, 1789, and its president in 1775, 1787 and 1790. In 1789 he had the honor, as secretary of Coetus, to send a congratulatory address to Washington, on having been elected first president of the United States.[207]

An old man who personally remembered him described him to Dr. Jos. H Dubbs as "a little, good-humored, red-faced man, with a shock of white hair."[208]

[206a] While pastor at Falkner Swamp Frederick Delliker married Maria Juvenal, October 12, 1786 The marriage is recorded in the church record of the First Reformed Church at Philadelphia (see *Pennsylvania Archives*, 2d Series, Vol VIII, p. 663) and also in the Falkner Swamp Record, see *Pennsylvania Archives*, l c, p 603

[207] *Minutes of Coetus*, p. 434.

[208] Dubbs, *Reformed Church in Pennsylvania*, p 195

CHAPTER XI.

Ministry of Rev. Frederick William Van Der Sloot, 1784–1786.

AT the meeting of Coetus, held May 12, 1784, in Lancaster, "the congregations of Old and New Goshenhoppen and Great Swamp request Do. Frederick William Van der Sloot for their pastor. This Van der Sloot was born in Anhalt-Zerbst, and, according to his testimonials, has preached frequently, as candidate of theology, in the Cathedral of Berlin. For two and a half years he acted as inspector of the Joachimsthal Gymnasium. As his other circumstances are the same as those of Do. Wynckhaus, mentioned in the previous article (they were not sent by the Fathers in Holland), the same action was taken regarding him; that he shall minister to the said congregations until we have ascertained the opinion of the Reverend Fathers."

The new minister at Goshenhoppen seemed by descent and training well fitted for his position and work.

He was descended from a ministerial family. Both his grandfather as well as his father had been ministers before him. His grandfather, Friederich von der Schloth, was pastor at Barby on the Elbe River, southeast of Magdeburg.[208a] His father, Friedrich Heinrich von der Schlott, was pastor of the Reformed church of Aken, 1725 to 1743, and of St. Nikolai at Zerbst, in the principality of Anhalt-Zerbst, from 1743 to 1751. While pastor of this church he married Sophia Wilhelmine von Boller, August 20, 1743. Their only son was Philip Wilhelm Frederick von der Sloot, born in Zerbst, September 27, 1744. Apparently later in life he changed his Christian name to Frederick William. He studied for the ministry and became pastor of Zornitz, Poetnitz, Scholitz and Nauendorf in the province of Brandenburg. Later he was conrector of the Latin school at Dessau and then for two and a half years Inspector of the Joachimsthal Gymnasium in Berlin. There he married, May 5, 1772, Louisa Henrietta, daughter of the Rev. Prof. Schultz, professor in the same school.

According to his great-grandson,[209] he came to Pennsylvania in 1779 or 1780, leaving his wife and family (one son at least) in Germany. His first charge was in Allen township, Northampton County.

In April, 1784, he came into the Goshenhoppen charge. At Great Swamp he entered the first baptism on April 18, 1784, at New Goshenhoppen on April 25, 1784, and at Old Goshenhoppen on May 2, 1784. At New Goshenhoppen he entered 21 baptisms between April 25, 1784, and November 21, 1784; at Old Goshenhoppen 6 baptisms between May 2, 1784, and October 14, 1784, and at Great Swamp 16 baptisms between April 18, 1784, and May 14, 1786.

The reason for the sudden termination of his work at

[208a] The antecedents and history of Mr. Van der Sloot have been cleared up by one of his descendants, Lewis Vandersloot, who in 1901 published the *History and Genealogy of the Von der Sloot Family,* Harrisburg, 1901, pp. 68, see especially pp 9-17

[209] L c, p. 16

New and Old Goshenhoppen is furnished by the Coetus Minutes of 1785, which read:

> As was stated in Art. VI of last year's minutes, Fred. Wm. Van der Sloot preached at Old and New Goshenhoppen and Great Swamp The former two congregations have now locked the churches against him on account of a very disgraceful and unlawful act; but the latter congregation, namely Great Swamp, still allows him to preach. This was the deed. He had left a wife and child in Germany, but married here a single woman. A short time after his marriage it became known through his own statements that he had another wife, whereupon his father-in-law took his daughter back to his home. Then Van der Sloot was locked out by the two Goshenhoppen churches

In corroboration of this statement we find the following entry in the New Goshenhoppen record, made by Van der Sloot himself:

> June 29, [1784], Rev. Daliker married me, Friedrich Wilhelm Von der Sloot, only son of Friedrich Heinrich Von der Sloot, late minister in Anhalt-Zerbst, Germany to Anna Margaretha Riedt, oldest daughter of Jacob Ried of Hatfield township, Philadelphia County

Judging by the church records, the ministry of Van der Sloot at Great Swamp ended in May, 1786. There was a baptism as late as May 14, and a funeral on April 3, 1786, by Van der Sloot. But it is possible that he was then merely a visitor, for even at the Coetus meeting of April 27 to 28, 1785, Faber reported Tohickon, Indianfield and Great Swamp as the congregations which he was then serving. The actual removal of Faber, however, to the Goshenhoppen field did not take place till the spring of the following year.

Van der Sloot meanwhile returned to Northampton County, where he ministered to congregations in Allen, Moore and Lehigh townships. He died there in 1803.

CHAPTER XII.

SECOND MINISTRY OF JOHN THEOBALD FABER, SR., 1786-1788.

WE left Faber in 1779 as pastor of the Reformed Church in Lancaster. He began his work there in November, 1779, but he stayed hardly three years. The city life evidently contrasted unfavorably to his mind with the quiet country life in the Goshenhoppen valley. He became restless and homesick. One evidence of this is that the consistorial minutes were almost entirely neglected during his ministry. He, therefore, determined to return to the lower counties as soon as possible.

In September, 1781, the Indianfield and Tohickon congregations in Bucks County became vacant through the removal of Rev. Caspar Wack. Hence Faber accepted a call to that field, only fifteen miles from his former charge. His ministry at Indianfield began on July 14, 1782; at least on that day he entered his first baptism into the Indianfield record. From that time till April 27, 1786, he recorded 57 baptisms in the Indianfield record. The latter date must have marked approximately the end of his ministry in that field, for in May, 1786, his entries begin in the New Goshenhoppen record.

John Theobald Faber, Sr   239

On May 17 to 18, 1786, the minutes of Coetus report:

J. Theobald Faber left Indianfield, Tohickon and Trumbauer's Church and accepted his former congregations of Old Goshenhoppen, New Goshenhoppen and Great Swamp.

Apparently he was very happy to get back to his first friends. Dr. Weiser has preserved a tradition[210] that on the day of his return his parishioners had gathered in the parsonage to welcome him.

When nearing the premises, he stood up in a large wagon, and with uncovered head cried out: *"Ihr Goschenhoppener! Ich verlass euch in meinem Leben nicht mehr. Hier will ich leben und sterben."*

The reunion was a happy one and resulted well for pastor and people. In 1787 Faber reported of his three congregations 230 families, 76 baptized, 93 confirmed and 78 scholars in the schools. The whole record for his second pastorate at Goshenhoppen is as follows: 179 baptisms, 67 burials and 28 weddings. Unfortunately his ministry was not of long duration. His death was sudden and unexpected. The Coetal letter of 1789 gives us a contemporaneous record of it.[211]

We have to report that the Lord has taken from us a brother, namely Do. Theobald Faber, late minister in New Goshenhoppen and Great Swamp. His departure was unexpected. On November 2, 1788, a deathly weakness attacked him while in the pulpit. Having finished half of the sermon, he, with difficulty, repeated the Lord's Prayer, He was then carried from the pulpit and an hour and a half later died in the school-house. It was remarkable that his sermon was on death, for he was just preaching on Jairus'

---

[210] Weiser, *Monograph*, p 74

[211] The traditional account given by Dr Weiser, *Monograph*, p. 74 f, varies from this statement in several interesting particulars, cf *Minutes of Coetus*, p. 431.

daughter, Matt. IX being the gospel lesson of that day. How dear he was to his people is proved by the fact that, altogether contrary to the custom of this country, they gave him a burial-place under the altar, also that they desired his oldest son for his successor, if this is at all possible.

The elder Weiser placed a memorial tablet over his remains with this inscription:

TRITT LEISE!
HIER RUHET DER
EHRW JOH. THEOB. FABER,
EHEMALS GEWESENER PREDIGER
DIESER GEMEINDE.
GEBOREN DEN 13TEN FEBR 1739,
STARB DEN 2TEN NOV. 1788.
ALTER 49 JAHR 8 MO. UND 18 T.

His funeral sermon was preached by the Rev. Mr. Blumer, then pastor at Allentown. His text was Hebrews 13: 17.

Mr. Faber left behind him a wife and seven children, whom the congregation permitted to remain in the parsonage for several years. They also aided his oldest son in his studies to become his father's successor.

To Dr. C. Z. Weiser, Mr. Faber was described as "a man of small, portly figure, full of vivacity and jovial."

His widow married again, a Mr. Christian Sheidt of Sumneytown. She outlived even her second husband and died, 82 years old, in the home of her son-in-law, Dr. Tobias Sellers.[212]

[212] Weiser, *Monograph*, p. 75 f

CHAPTER XIII.

Ministry of Rev. Nicholas Pomp, 1789–1792.

AFTER the death of Mr. Faber the congregations of the Goshenhoppen charge were for more than a year without a regular pastor. An entry in the Old Goshenhoppen records throws some light on this period:

After the death of the sainted Mr. Faber, when the congregation was without a minister, the following children were baptized, some by Mr. Roller, some by the ministers who visited this congregation, and, at the request of the parents, their names were entered by Johann Daniel Jung, schoolmaster.

Rev. Conrad Roeller was from 1772 to 1799 the pastor of the Old Goshenhoppen Lutheran congregation. Four baptisms were entered by Mr. Jung from February to November, 1789.

In the New Goshenhoppen record the history is continued by the next pastor:

After the Rev. J. Theobald Faber had died unexpectedly on November 2, 1788, and the congregation had been without a pastor for more than a year, I, N. [Nicholas] Pomp, was called to serve in his place and commenced my ministry here, in the name of God, in these congregations, in the beginning of the month of December 1789.

Dr. Weiser in his "History"[213] has preserved an interesting letter of Mr. Pomp, which reveals his spirit and the conditions under which he entered upon his work in the new field. It reads as follows:

LETTER OF REV N POMP TO THE GOSHENHOPPEN CHURCHES

BALTIMORE, MD, October 2nd, 1789.

To the three united Consistories at Old and New Goshenhoppen and Great Swamp·

Since it has seemed good to the Rev. Ministers, Hendel, Dellicker and Helffrich, that I should supply the three congregations of your charge, now without a pastor, I have concluded to lay before [you] certain conditions, without compliance therewith, I could not under any considerations acquiesce in your wish.

First· The Widow and Family of the late Pastor Faber, still abiding among you, must not be made to suffer any sacrifice by my coming. The sainted Faber and I were bosom friends, and I can, therefore, rejoice the more over the warm and true regard which the charge has manifested toward his bereaved household, from love to his memory.

Secondly· The membership must prove of one mind in the choice of myself as their temporary pastor. I cannot tolerate any dispute to arise, and will not consent to serve, unless the people are a unit.

Thirdly. No definite period of time must be fixed. I shall labor solely for the welfare of the flock, and in the same spirit in which I served at Falconer Swamp. As soon as you determine upon the services of the young Faber, or of any other devoted Pastor, I wish it in my power freely to relinquish the field in his favor.

Fourthly· In regard to Parsonage and Salary I shall say nothing. I will leave all that over to yourselves, and agree to be satisfied with what you consider right and just. My family is small—

[213] *L c*, pp. 77-79

myself and wife. We need no roomy house then. It will not prove a hard task, I think, to find a spot for me to occupy.

Fifthly. My removal will not be attended with much trouble and expense, as my goods can be conveyed by water from Baltimore to Philadelphia, and thence by wagons

The Consistories ought to assemble and deliberate over these several points. The matter is very important, and concerns the welfare of many souls, whose interests suffer in consequence of your want of a regular Minister. Consider well and prayerfully. May you be guided in determining on the wisest course. You can forward the result of your deliberations to Pastor Weyberg, who will report to me

I am affectionately yours,
N. POMP.

According to Dr. Weiser, the joint consistory met at the parsonage on October 24th, concluded to comply with Mr. Pomp's conditions and extended to him a unanimous call, which he promptly accepted. In the beginning of the month of December, 1789, he moved into his new field.

Nicholas Pomp was one of the strong and influential men of the Reformed Church and deserves a more extended notice. About his life in Europe Mr. Pomp himself has left a short, but fragmentary autobiographical sketch, which we reproduce in full in an English translation:[214]

AUTOBIOGRAPHY OF THE REV NICHOLAS POMP.

I, Nicolaus Pomp, have deemed it well to write up an account of my life so that my late descendants may be able to read and see how their ancestor has fared in this world.

I saw the light of day in Manbuchel, then in the Duchy of

[214] It was formerly in possession of Dr. Jos H Dubbs, who published it in part in his *Reformed Church in Pennsylvania*, pp. 190-192. It is now in possession of the writer

Zweibrucken, January 20, 1734. My honored father was Peter Pomp. My dear mother Elisa, his lawful wife. These parents brought me on the fourth day after my birth to holy Baptism. After which only this is to be noted that for three years I lay sick, as my parents told me. Nevertheless I got well again, so that I could go to school and was able to work. In my 14th year I had read the Bible several times and was also able to recite the Heidelberg Catechism. Catechetical instruction, which I received from ministers, was so effective that I became a new man and loved the triune God heartily. With worldly people I did not want to have anything to do Hence I sought solitude, where I could pour out my soul to God and in which my soul took much delight. My only desire for the world was this, that I might become a minister, whereby I could call sinners to repentance. But my father did not want to consent to it, because it would cost him too much to let me study, without which I could not become a minister. He, therefore, urged me against my will to take to tailoring, which trade means constant sitting and which, after a few years, undermined my health completely. Hence my father did not insist that I should continue this trade, but gave me the permission to study, so that in time I might become a minister, if my health and his resources would permit it.

I was now 20 years of age when my studying began with all seriousness. I spent a period of four years in school, where I learnt Latin and Greek as well as Hebrew pretty thoroughly. Then (in the 24th year of my age) I went to Marburg, in Hesse, to study theology in the university.

Here there is a break in the manuscript, the lower part of the page being torn off. The story is continued on the next page:

Although they had before been inclined to disparage me, being unwilling to make me a candidate [of theology], now so were so well disposed towards to me, that without my request they were ready to assist in my ordination and introduction into the ministry. When information came from Holland that the Synod there wished to promote me to the ministry in America, I was ordained in the city of Cassel and sent with an excellent testimonial to Holland The Synods examined me and, because they found me well qualified, they gave me 535 guilders for traveling expenses and a good recommendation to the congregations in America, which I was expected to serve. I was 15 weeks on the ocean from Holland to Philadelphia, where I arrived December 8, 1765

At the same time my ministry in Falkner Swamp and Vincent began. After I had spent seven years with these congregations, I married Elisabeth Dotterer,[215] a widow with six children and no property, but we lived happily together. I was not rich either, but we had as much as we needed day by day One son was born to us in wedlock, who remained our only child and whom I called Thomas.[216] After we had raised him, I myself educated him for the ministry as well as I could. He became indeed a minister and has been a great comfort to myself and his mother.

About my life I would have to say much at this place if I wished to relate everything that happened to me at Falkner Swamp. I

[215] On the same paper on which his autobiography is written, Nicholas Pomp gives also a brief sketch of the life of his wife. Her maiden name was Elizabeth Antes, born January 29 (or February 9, new style), 1734, at Falkner Swamp Rev John Philip Boehm baptized her (see *Perkiomen Region*, I, 51). Her father was Henry Antes and her mother Christina, née Dewees When eight years old she was taken to Bethlehem, where she stayed till her twelfth year. In May, 1754, she married George Philip Dotterer, with whom she had six children, two sons and four daughters. Her husband died August 23, 1771. She married again, April 23, 1772, Rev. Nicholas Pomp, with whom she had one son, Thomas Pomp She died at Easton, May 20, 1812 See also *The Dotterer Family*, by H S Dotterer, p. 65 f

[216] Thomas Pomp was born February 4, 1773 in Skippack township, Montgomery County He studied under his father, was examined and ordained in 1795. In the following year he became pastor of the Easton charge, then consisting of Easton, Plainfield, Dryland and Mt Bethel In place of the last Lower Saucon was substituted after some years. He remained pastor of this charge for fifty-six years, much beloved and highly respected by his people. He died at Easton April 22, 1852 See Heisler, *Fathers of the Reformed Church*, Vol. IV, pp 15-30.

only want to say this, that I remained 18 years in the service of this congregation and then I accepted a call to Baltimore in 1783. My departure from Falkner Swamp caused much bitterness and sadness among the people, for the welfare of whose souls I had cared so long and so earnestly. Hardly a single person wanted to be satisfied with my removal, although they could soon get another and perhaps a better preacher. Yet they were not satisfied with it I also went away with a sad heart, but with the thought that I had done more good among these people than I had believed before.

In Baltimore I could only stand it for six years [1783-1789] and, although I did my best to build up this congregation, I was unable to stay any longer with a quarreling church For the new church which they had to build, caused a division into two parties and I could side with only one party . . . [The rest of the manuscript is torn off.]

At the meeting of the Coetus, held June 7-8, 1790, at Falkner Swamp,

the three united congregations in Goshenhoppen sent their delegates with a call for Do. Pomp, thus far minister in Baltimore. They desired to have him as their regular pastor in place of Do. Faber, deceased But, as the parsonage of the congregation is still occopied by the widow of Do. Faber, whom one would not like to drive out, the congregations are advised to provide a house for Do. Pomp, and to continue the kindness towards the widow, as far as possible.

At the same meeting Pomp reported about his new congregations. There were 200 families, 40 baptized, 52 confirmed, 3 schools with 120 scholars.

But the ministry of Pomp at Goshenhoppen was of short duration. At New Goshenhoppen his baptisms extend from November 26, 1789, to July 25, 1790, and his weddings from December, 1789, to August 10, 1790. At Great Swamp ten baptisms were entered by him from January 3, 1790, to June 18, 1790. Only at Old Goshenhoppen his ministry seems to have been longer. His baptismal entries there extend from January 3, 1790, to May 28, 1792. The annual financial settlement at Old Goshenhoppen, made on July 19, 1791, was written by Mr. Pomp. But one of the items of the account was "£2 5s. for fire wood for Rev. Mr. Faber" At the meeting of Coetus on June 27 to 28, 1791, at Lancaster, Pomp is marked absent "on account of indisposition," but he is already called "minister in Indianfield."

In August, 1790, Mr. Pomp began his ministry at Indianfield (now called Indian Creek) and Tohickon. His entries in the Indian Creek record are headed with this statement:

After I, Nic. Pomp had been called to the service of this congregation in Indian Creek and Tohickon and in the beginning of the month of August entered upon this service, there follow now the names of the baptized children of said congregation

The first baptism following this beginning is dated August 26, 1790. Mr. Pomp remained pastor at Indian Creek till August, 1797 From April, 1794, till August, 1796, Whitpain, now Boehm's church at Blue Bell, was part of his charge. In 1797 he retired to Easton to live with his son, Thomas Pomp, who had become pastor there. He died at Easton, September 1, 1819.

It was while pastor at Falkner Swamp that Mr. Pomp wrote a book, by which he is best known. It was a refutation of the teachings of the Universalists, as contained in the book of Paul Siegvolck, entitled "Das Ewige Evangelium," which had been published in German by Saur, the Germantown printer, in 1768. Pomp's book, while not a profound treatise, was a creditable performance.

Translated into English the title reads: "Brief Examination of the Doctrine of the Eternal Gospel, by which it is clearly shown that the Restoration of all things is vainly

Kurzgefaßte
Prüfungen
der Lehre
des
Ewigen Evangeliums:
Womit

deutlich gezeiget wird,

Daß man die **Wiederbringung** aller Dinge in der heiligen Schrift, vergeblich suchet.

Auf Begehren vieler Freunde zum Druck befördert

von

N. Pomp, V. D. M.

Philadelpia,
Gedruckt bey Henrich Miller,
1774.

sought in Scripture. At the request of many friends published by N. Pomp, V.D.M., Philadelphia, printed by Henry Miller, 1774," 12mo, preface 12 pp., and text 200 pp.

CHAPTER XIV.

Ministry of Rev. John Theobald Faber, Jr., 1791–1807.

IN 1791 the wish of the Goshenhoppen people was gratified to have their former pastor's son with them as the successor of his father.

John Theobald Faber, Jr., was born in the parsonage of New Goshenhoppen, in Upper Hanover township, as the oldest child of his parents. His father himself entered the record of his birth into the New Goshenhoppen book: "On September 24, 1771, a son was born to me, Pastor Faber, named Johannes Theobald. Witness was Daniel Gross, minister at Saucon and Springfield."

As a boy he enjoyed the advantages of the parochial school of the New Goshenhoppen congregation and the additional instruction of his father.

When fifteen years of age he headed a class of 61 catechumens at New Goshenhoppen, who were confirmed by his father on April 9, 1787.

He pursued his classical studies under the Rev. Frederick Valentin Melsheimer, pastor of the Lutheran congregation at Hanover, York County. He studied theology with

Rev. Dr. William Hendel, Sr., from 1782–1794, pastor at Lancaster, Pa. As his course of special study covered only three years it was at most incomplete and hurried.

He was licensed probably sometime in the year 1791, for his baptisms begin in the spring of 1792.

At the meeting of Coetus, held May 6 to 7, 1792, at Philadelphia, "the congregations of Old and New Goshenhoppen presented a call for Mr. John Faber, and asked that he be examined and ordained. The Reverend Coetus resolved that he be examined on the following day by Do. Hendel, Helffrich and Pomp."

On the following day the minutes report:

In accordance with the resolution of the first session, Mr. John Faber was examined by Dos. Hendel, Pomp, Helffrich and Blumer. The committee made a report in reference to the examination of Mr. Faber, and stated that he had not given such satisfactory answers to the dogmatical questions proposed as they had expected from him; still, out of regard to the Goshenhoppen congregations and his widowed mother, the examination was approved and, by a majority of votes, he was recognized as qualified for the ministry, and it was resolved that Dos. Helffrich, Blumer, Pomp and Dellicker ordain him as soon as possible.

The ordination of the young candidate took place at Goshenhoppen on June 23, 1792, as appears from the following letter of Mr. Delliker, addressed to young Faber.[217]

LETTER OF DELLIKER TO FABER, JR., MAY 12, 1792.

My dear Faber·

I congratulate you from the bottom of my heart, on the successful issue of your examination. The Lord sustain you continually. The request, deo volente, I will endeavor to comply with and preach the sermon on the day of your ordination. I have received

[217] Weiser, *Monograph,* p 83.

no letter from Synod, but have at hand one addressed to Pastor Helffrich. We will speak more definitely, when I shall have the pleasure to be with you on the day before the 23rd of June.

I am, Reverend Sir, in sincere friendship,
Our highest regards to you all

Falkner Swamp,   Your humble servant
May 12th, 1792.   FRED. DELLIKER.

Dr. Weiser has preserved a traditional account of his introductory sermon from one who heard it, which may well be repeated:

In his introductory (sermon) he did not fail to call attention to the peculiar solemn position in which he found himself placed. The death of his beloved father occuring, as it were in the very spot on which he was then speaking, his mouldering remains lying under his very feet; his youth and hasty preparation to become his sire's successor; the questionable propriety of becoming a prophet in his own country—on all these points the young pastor delicately touched with much trembling and many tears One who heard it all says: " When he exclaimed ' Who is sufficient for these things?' all became strangly affected, and many wept "

In the spring of 1792 young Mr. Faber began his pastoral work in his three congregations Indeed he seems to have been so eager for his work that he officiated as a minister even before he was ordained, baptizing several children at Old Goshenhoppen in May, 1792. During the first few years he kept the various church records fairly well. Thus at New Goshenhoppen he entered 59 baptisms from the summer of 1792 to September, 1795, at Old Goshenhoppen he entered 24 baptisms from May, 1792, to April, 1795, and at Great Swamp 33 baptisms from the summer of 1792 till September, 1796. But after the latter date his records were entirely neglected, no entries of any sort being made after June 1, 1797. It may of course be that he kept private records in which he recorded his ministerial acts, but judging from the incomplete and careless entries actually made in the records, that is hardly to be expected.

Fortunately the lack of information regarding his pastorate is partly supplied by the account books of the Old Goshenhoppen and Great Swamp congregations, from which the following interesting entries are taken.

In the Old Goshenhoppen account book (opened in 1772) we find that on July 19, 1791, the congregation paid to the schoolmaster, Mr. Jung, 15 shillings. On June 15, 1792, there were paid to Mr. Faber, Jr., 15 shillings; to Mr. Peter Hollebusch for expenses to go to the Coetus 7s. 6d; to the schoolmaster Jung for the year 1791, £2. 5s. On December 5, 1793, Mr. Faber signed his first receipt for salary from the congregation, amounting to £24. 8s 11d. This was probably one third of the whole amount he received from the charge. Later on his salary increased. Beginning with the year 1803, Old Goshenhoppen paid its pastor £33. 6s. 8d. From at least 1804 to 1807 Nicolaus Weinel was the schoolmaster of the congregation, who was paid £6 for playing the organ and leading the singing. The account book makes us acquainted with three of the early schoolmasters of Old Goshenhoppen, Henrich Hemsing, from at least 1772 to 1782. Then there was probably a change. Payments to the schoolmasters are noted from 1785 to 1789, but no name is mentioned. In July, 1791, schoolmaster Jung is mentioned How long he served cannot be made out. From 1804 to at least April 1, 1807, Nicolaus Weinel served in that capacity.

From the Great Swamp account book (begun in 1759,

but poorly kept, with many years, e g., 1770 to 1793, entirely wanting), we have culled some items of interest:

On August 5, 1794, the following payments were entered into the record:

	£	s.	d
Paid to Mr. Hendel	—	1	10½
paid as rent to Mrs. Levy for Mr Pomp	—	15	—
paid to Mr Jost Wiand to fetch Mr Faber from Lancaster	—	12	—
paid to go to Coetus	—	8	—
paid to Mr. Hendel	—	15	—
" " ditto	—	3	9
" " Mrs Levy as rent for Mr. Pomp	—	15	—
" " ride to the Coetus	—	5	—
" " Mr. Philip Eberhard to go to the Coetus in Phila [1792]	—	11	—

On March 19, 1796, we find:

	£	s.	d
Paid to Mr. Faber, minister, on account of his salary	12.	7	6
paid to the administrator of the late Mr. Faber for salary still due him	24	11	4

Received on March 15. 1796, from Philip Eberhard, Jacob Schmid, Johannes Jung and Philip Mumbauer, deacons and elders at this time, the sum of 100 dollars to secure a patent for the pastor's land [glebe] at Goshenhoppen.

DAVID SPINNER.

On November 16, 1797, the following items deserve notice:

	£	s.	d
Paid for 15 bushels of lime for the schoolhouse	—	15.	—
paid for the masons	—	18	—
paid for 12 pounds of nails	—	15.	—
paid for glass	2	16	10
paid for 100 shingles for the parsonage	3.	15.	—
paid for 205 feet of boards for the same	—	17.	—
paid for puddy	—	4.	6.
paid for a ten plated stove	6	—	—
paid to ride to Synod	3	15.	—
paid for glass for use of Mr. Faber	—	10	—

paid for springhouse at parsonage	—	10	—
paid for pump at parsonage	3	0.	7.
On August 9, 1804, £2.14 3. were paid for repairs to the schoolhouse.			
Paid for a bake-oven in the parsonage	1	6.	2.
On May 23, 1805, £6 2 10. were paid for repairs to the parsonage			

From 1797 to 1804 John Jung signed receipts for repairs to the schoolhouse. He is probably identical with the schoolmaster Jung mentioned in 1791 in the Old Goshenhoppen book.

In 1801 the four united congregations of Northampton, Jordan, Union and Egypt extended a call to Mr. Faber to become their pastor, but he declined it.[218]

Faber attended the meetings of Synod faithfully, except in 1803 and 1806. In the former year he was sick. In 1807 he was secretary, in 1808 president of Synod.

A letter of Rev. Jacob Senn, pastor at Tohickon and Indianfield, to Mr. Faber, referring to his sickness, is preserved in the archives of the Reformed Seminary at Lancaster. It is interesting enough to be inserted here:[219]

LETTER OF REV. JACOB SENN TO REV. JOHN T. FABER, JR.

ROCKHILL, February 22, 1803.

Dear Friend and Brother!

I received your letter and heard with pleasure that you are again improving. I entertain the hope, that (God willing) you will soon regain your former health and strength, and thus be able to attend again to your ministry, which is no doubt much to be desired both by yourself and your congregations.

I have also had sickness in my family for a long time. My wife has been unwell for almost two years and sometimes I have had

[218] Minutes of the Synod of 1801, Session I, § 2.

[219] This letter also was placed at the disposal of the writer by Prof Geo. W. Richards, D D, of the Lancaster Seminary

little hope for her recovery, but now (thank God) she is better again.

As regards your request, I am willing and ready to serve you, but I cannot do it at the time set by you. I can never take away a Sunday (as you no doubt know yourself) without first informing the congregation and that cannot be done before three weeks. Three weeks from yesterday I am, therefore, ready to serve you, if that is agreeable to you. You may therefore announce it, if agreeable, that I shall conduct services for you on March 13th.

With a friendly greeting to yourself and wife, I remain,

(Address)   Your Friend and Servant

  Rev. Mr. J. T. Faber,   JACOB SENN.

    New Goshenhoppen.

In 1807 Mr. Faber accepted a call from the New Holland charge, Lancaster County, where he remained pastor till 1819, when he returned to Goshenhoppen.

CHAPTER XV.

MINISTRY OF REV. ALBERT HELFFENSTEIN, 1808–1811.

SCHOOLMASTER Nicolaus Weinel of Old Goshenhoppen introduces us to the next minister. In the Old Goshenhoppen account book he made an entry which fixes the exact time when the new pastorate began:

On June 19, 1808, the young Rev. Mr. Helfenstein delivered his first introductory sermon here in Old Goshenhoppen. On Sunday before he made the beginning at New Goshenhoppen.

Albert Helffenstein was the fifth son of the well-known Reformed preacher of Germantown, John Conrad Albertus Helffenstein, and of his wife, Catharine Kircher, a native of Philadelphia.[220] He was born in Germantown, March 13, 1788. He was baptized and confirmed in his father's church.

He received his theological education from Rev. Dr. Christian Ludwig Becker, from 1795 to 1806 pastor at Lancaster, and from 1807 to 1818 pastor at Baltimore. Dr. Becker was a fine scholar and pulpit orator and well qualified to prepare young men for the ministry. Nine-

---

[220] They were married on February 11, 1773, at Philadelphia. Their marriage is recorded in the old record book of the First Reformed Church at Philadelphia, see *Pennsylvania Archives*, 2d Series, Vol. VIII, p. 678.

teen students received their theological instruction from him during the last sixteen years of his life (1800–1816).[221]

After completing his theological training Helffenstein appeared before Synod, which met at his native place, May 15, 1808 At that time "a call was received from Goshenhoppen and Great Swamp for Mr. Albert Helffenstein."

Similar calls were received at the same time for other candidates. It was then resolved "that the candidates Messrs. Runkel, Jr., Gloninger, Schaffner, Becker and Helffenstein be examined this evening. The committee of examination consists of Messrs. Helffrich, Wack, Hoffmeier and Senn."[222]

On the next day the committee "who were appointed to examine the several candidates last evening, reported, that the young gentlemen sustained a perfectly satisfactory examination. It was resolved, that these young men be ordained this evening. Messrs. Faber, Geistweidt and Hoffmeier were appointed the committee of ordination."

Helffenstein entered upon his work at Goshenhoppen immediately after the meeting of Synod, preaching on June 12, 1808, his installation sermon at New Goshenhoppen, as the record of schoolmaster Weinel, already quoted, proves On June 21 he had his first funeral at New Goshenhoppen. But his ministry was of short duration. On May 11, 1811, he entered his last baptism at New Goshenhoppen.

The record of his pastoral work at Goshenhoppen is not complete. He only entered 70 baptisms, 22 funerals and

[221] Good, *History of the Reformed Church in the United States in the Nineteenth Century*, New York, 1911, p. 13 f

[222] Minutes of the Synod of 1808, Session I, §§ 3, 7; Session III, § 2.

12 weddings into the records. There are no weddings recorded by him at Great Swamp and even the other entries are incomplete, most of them stopping in 1809.

His ministry seems to have extended till October, 1811, for on October 27, 1811, he signed a receipt for salary for four months from the Great Swamp congregation. His salary was apparently one hundred dollars from each congregation. In July, 1809, 1810 and 1811, he signed receipts for $100 each from the Great Swamp congregation.

Dr. Weiser reports[223] that like Mr. Pomp he resided at first with a widow Levy at New Goshenhoppen, later with Mr. Pannebecker, until the new parsonage was completed.

Being a city boy and more accustomed to the English language than the German, he felt ill at ease among the German farmers at Goshenhoppen. He, therefore, accepted in 1811 a call to Carlisle, where he stayed till 1819. Then he was pastor at Baltimore from 1819 to 1835. After that he left the Reformed Church, removed to Ohio and entered the Protestant Episcopal Church. In 1851 he applied to Lebanon Classis to be received back to the church of his fathers. His request was granted with certain conditions which he fulfilled. At the same meeting of Classis he presented a call from the Elizabethtown charge in Lancaster County, which Classis confirmed. He labored in this field till 1853, when he retired from the ministry. In 1859 he removed to Shamokin, where he resided with his nephew, Chas. P. Helffenstein. There he died January 30, 1869.[224]

[223] Weiser, *Monograph*, p. 89.
[224] For a sketch of Albert Helffenstein's life see Heisler, *Fathers*, Vol. IV, pp. 67–70.

CHAPTER XVI.

Ministry of Rev. Frederick William Van der Sloot, Jr., 1812–1818.

AFTER Mr. Helffenstein had left Goshenhoppen in October, 1811, the congregations were without a pastor for more than a year. In November, 1812, they succeeded in securing a new pastor. He himself has left a statement in the New Goshenhoppen record which fixes the time of his arrival. "On November 12, 1812, I entered upon my ministry, but funerals did not occur till 1813." This new pastor was Frederick William Van der Sloot, Jr., son of the former pastor.

Frederick William Van der Sloot, Jr., was born November 15, 1773, at Dessau, in the Duchy of Anhalt, Germany.[225] The following is a translation of the baptismal entry in the church record at Dessau:

To Mr. Philipp Wilhelm Friedrich Van Der Sloot, appointed conrector of the Latin school of this place and to his wife, née Schultz, a young son was born, Friedrich Wilhelm, early at one o'clock, Monday morning, the 15th of November 1773, and was baptized in the house on the same day.

---

[225] For the history of Mr. Von der Sloot, Jr., see *History and Genealogy of the Von der Sloot Family*, pp. 18–23.

He studied in the University of Leipzig, and, after completing his studies, emigrated to America in the year 1801. He landed at Charleston, S. C., whence he continued his journey to Philadelphia. From there he made his way in a "market wagon" to Northampton County, Pa., where he found his father ministering to seven or eight congregations.

In 1802 young Van der Sloot appeared before the Synod of the Reformed Church, which met from May 16 to 18, 1802, at Philadelphia. On Monday, May 17,

a communication was received from the congregations in Allen, Moretown, Lehigh and Hanover townships, asking Synod to hold a tentamen with young Mr. Van der Sloot, and to place him in a position to serve them as their pastor. Resolved, that a committee of five be appointed to hold a tentamen with him. The following persons constituted the committee: Messrs. Hendel, Wagner, Wack, Sen., Runkel and Wack, Jr.

On Tuesday morning, May 18,

the committee consisting of Messrs. Hendel, Wagner, Wack, Sen., and Wack, Jr., reported that they held a *tentamen* with Mr. Van Der Sloot, and found his qualifications such that he can with propriety be licensed as a candidate for the ministry. Resolved that Mr. Van Der Sloot be licensed.[226]

Later on in the same session we read that,

to Mr. Van Der Sloot, in connection with his *tentamen,* was assigned the duty of preparing a sermon on Rom. 8: 1.

At the meeting of Synod, held May 8 to 10, 1803, at Lebanon,

application was made this morning by the congregations of Mr. Van Der Sloot for his ordination. The subject was again taken into consideration this afternoon. It was resolved that Mr. Van

[226] Minutes of the Synod of 1802, Session I, § 5, Session III, §§ 1, 6.

Der Sloot be ordained Messrs. Helffrich, Pomp, and Hoffmeier were appointed a committee to ordain him in his congregations on the second Wednesday after Whitsuntide,[227] (June 8, 1803).

In May, 1811, Mr. Van der Sloot informed Synod that he had left the congregations he had heretofore served, and accepted a call from the congregation at Germantown. The call was confirmed by Synod [228]

Shortly after entering upon his ministry in Northampton County Mr. Van der Sloot had been married, on November 11, 1802, to Catharine Pauli, daughter of the Rev Philip Reinhold Pauli, of Reading, Pa. The marriage ceremony was performed by the Rev. Dr. Wm. Hendel, Jr., then pastor at Tulpehocken.

Mr. Van der Sloot remained only a short time in Germantown. As we have learned from his own entry in the New Goshenhoppen record, he came to Goshenhoppen in November, 1812.

The record of his ministry at Goshenhoppen is very incomplete. Even his baptisms were not fully recorded. At New Goshenhoppen are 21 baptisms by him from January 24, 1813, to August, 1818; at Old Goshenhoppen he recorded 20 baptisms from February 28, 1813, to December, 1817, and at Great Swamp 19 baptisms were entered into the record by him from May 22, 1814, to November 22, 1818. The records of his funerals are entirely wanting, five lonely burials at New Goshenhoppen excepted.

While pastor at Goshenhoppen Mr. Van der Sloot also supplied the Reformed congregation at the Trappe, Montgomery County.

Dr. Weiser draws this interesting picture of him as pastor at Goshenhoppen:

[227] Minutes of the Synod of 1803, Session II, § 9
[228] Minutes of the Synod of 1811, Session III, § 15.

His large, burly form, his stentorian voice, his peculiar power to sing, pray and preach, his natural abilities and pulpit aptitude, his jovial nature, funded with wit and anecdote, his affable and friendly mien—all these bold features of the man are still to be freshly traced in the minds of his old parishioners, and are likely to perpetuate his portrait life-sized to another generation.[229]

As now a full century has passed since the beginning of Mr. Van der Sloot's pastorate at Goshenhoppen, it is hardly probable that the recollection of his jovial personality and short labors is still so vividly retained by the present generation

His ministry at Goshenhoppen came to a close in November, 1818. From entries in the Old Goshenhoppen account it appears that his annual salary from that congregation was $200, the other two congregations contributing probably an equal sum.

In December, 1818, we find him in Philadelphia As nothing has appeared thus far in English regarding his activity in Philadelphia, it may be well to insert here a brief sketch of his labors there, based upon a recent investigation of the writer.

In the summer of 1818, English church services were introduced into the old Reformed church at Philadelphia The German element of the congregation, which had for years fought against their introduction, felt so much aggrieved that they left their church and formed an independent congregation. In July, 1818, they rented the "Old Commissioners Hall" on Third Street below Green and asked a Lutheran minister, Rev. Karl R. Demme, to preach for them. On August 26, 1818, they elected the first consistory, consisting of four elders, four deacons and five trustees. On September 1, 1818, they sent a petition

[229] Weiser, *Monograph,* p 91

to Synod, which met September 8 at Carlisle, asking that their action be confirmed and they be allowed to organize a German congregation. Their petition was readily granted and a committee was appointed to install the consistory.[230] This took place on September 20, 1818. On November 9, 1818, an election for pastor took place, as a result of which Frederick William Van der Sloot was elected. He hesitated at first to accept it, but after his salary had been fixed at 1,200 dollars, he accepted on December 2. On January 1, 1819, he delivered his introductory sermon, in Zion's Lutheran Church to a large audience, preaching from the text Ezekiel 3: 17, "Son of man, I have made thee a watchman unto the house of Israel."

Under the leadership of the new pastor steps were at once taken for the building of a church. On February 15, 1819, the congregation resolved to build a church 50 feet wide and 67 to 70 feet long. On March 27 the congregation was incorporated In April a schoolhouse was bought on Rose Alley, the present Bodine Street.

The cornerstone of the new church was laid with special services on May 9, 1819. At this time the church was named "Salem Church," which is still its name. A special feature of the celebration were a series of hymns which the pastor had written and for which the schoolmaster, Jacob Bibighaus, had composed the music. The church was dedicated October 24, 1819, with a still more elaborate celebration, for which the pastor had again composed the hymns and the schoolmaster had written the music. The following verses may be quoted as a sample of pastor Van der Sloot's German poetry:

[230] Minutes of the Synod of 1818, p 14, §§ 10, 11.

> Ist's wirklich?—Nicht ein susser Traum?
> Dass hier, aus diesem oden Raum—
> Zu Menschen Gluck und Gottes Lob—
> So schnell sich dieses Haus erhob?
>
> *Chorus*
>
> Nein! Nicht ein Traum. Der Gott, der uns're Vater
> In fruh'rer Zeit berieth, der ist auch spater—
> Noch unser Gott. In seinem Arm gestutzet,
> Umschliesst er uns; er ist ihm nicht verkurzet:
> Umschliesst er uns mit himmlischen Erbarmen—
> Beseelet uns mit Muth in Seinen Armen.

Another verse refers to the name of the new church:

> Durch Christum war der Herr euch nah,
> Auf! Singet laut Hallelujah!
> Zieht jubelnd in eu'r Salem ein:
> Der mit euch war, wird mit euch sein.

But although the congregation had now a beautiful property and a new home, their joy was by no means unmixed, for there was also a large debt on the property. But the members did not lose courage Several committees were at once appointed. One to collect among the members of the congregation. Another committee went to Baltimore where they succeeded in raising $208. Then they wrote letters to the different congregations of the Synod, asking them to take up a collection for them. To satisfy the most urgent creditors a mortgage of $5,000 was taken upon the property on July 23, 1821. In November of the following year they asked the legislature of the state for permission to start, in accordance with a then prevailing custom, a lottery to pay off their debt. But their petition was apparently not granted.

As they felt that they could not meet their obligations,

the consistory, in January, 1821, fixed the pastor's salary at $800, but when Van der Sloot expressed his unwillingness to serve for that sum, they allowed him to take up an extra collection for the remaining $400 But such an arrangement could not be continued for any length of time. Evidently Van der Sloot, too, saw that their expenses had to be curtailed, hence he handed in his resignation on December 26, 1823. The four years which Van der Sloot had spent in the congregation had not been without success. In 1819 he reported 304 members, 26 confirmed, 50 baptisms and 19 funerals. In 1820 the number of members had risen to 346. That there was also a healthy internal growth is shown by the fact that in February, 1821, the first society of men was organized, and in April, 1823, the Sunday School. But the finances of the congregation could not be put on a sound basis till, on January 5, 1824, Henry Bibighaus was elected Van der Sloot's successor at a salary of $400, which was better within the reach of the congregation to pay.[231]

From Philadelphia Van der Sloot went to Virginia, where, in March, 1824, he accepted a call of eight, later ten, congregations in Rockingham and neighboring counties. Here he preached for about three years, until, in the spring of 1827, he was called to York and Adams counties, where he served nine congregations—Pigeon Hill, Holtzschwam, Straher's, Rosstown and Franklin in York County, and Bermudian, Oxford, Abbottstown and Berlin in Adams county. These congregations he served up to the time of his death, which took place in Paradise town-

[231] A more extensive history of Salem's Reformed Church at Philadelphia, was read by the writer on October 15, 1899, in that church, and printed in the *Kirchenzeitung*

ship, on December 14, 1831. He was buried in the graveyard of the Holtzschwamm church.[232]

Mr. Van der Sloot was a good linguist and he had also talent and taste for poetry. A number of his poems and hymns have been printed. As a minister he was an untiring worker. In the thirty years of his ministry he is said to have served thirty-three congregations. He was prominent in the counsels of the church. In 1821 he was elected clerk of Synod and in the following year its president. When Philadelphia Classis was organized in 1820, F. W. Van der Sloot became its first president and Jacob W. Dechant its first secretary.

[232] For a sketch of F. W. Von der Sloot's life see Harbaugh, *Fathers*, Vol. III, pp. 118-121.

CHAPTER XVII.

The Division of the Charge in 1819, and Rev. John T. Faber's Second Pastorate, 1819–1833.

HISTORY often repeats itself. This proved to be the case at Goshenhoppen. Just as the elder Faber, after an absence of seven years, was glad to return to the field of his first labors, so the younger Faber followed in the footsteps of his father, when after the departure of F. W. Van der Sloot, Jr., he accepted a call from his first congregations to return to them. The call extended to him is an interesting historical document which deserves preservation. It reads as follows:[233]

Call of the Goshenhoppen Congregation to Mr. Faber, Jr.

Reverend Sir:—

Inasmuch as the Rev. Mr. Von Der Sloot has resigned the office of pastor over us and accepted a call from the new German congregation in Philadelphia, we are compelled to renew our efforts to secure the services of another shepherd. At the suggestion of several members of the consistory of the congregation at Old

---

[233] Weiser, *Monograph*, pp. 98–101.

Goshenhoppen, we resolved to hold an election in the three congregations. As you have been our pastor in former years, as well as your father before, and as we have always cherished a peculiar love and affection for you, it is our heart's desire that you return to us again. This general esteem and confidence which we have ever borne you, manifested itself also, at the time of our election, on which occasion the congregations at New Goshenhoppen and Great Swamp cast a unanimous vote in your favor. To this unanimity Old Goshenhoppen, it is true, forms an exception. There the election was not held on the appointed day; but that congregation will be obliged to submit to the will of the majority—as is but right and proper. After having learned the result, we, the elders and deacons, in the name of the congregations, call the Reverend John Theobald Faber, at present pastor over the New Holland charge, as our minister and pastor over our congregations, to preach the word of God among us, to administer the holy sacraments, and to discharge all those duties becoming a faithful Christian minister of the German Reformed Church. And as he who ministers at the altar shall also live by the altar, we, therefore, promise on our part, and in the name of the congregations, to pay you annually the sum of *four hundred and fifty dollars;* and besides, the possession of the parsonage, and whatsoever else is customary to be given as perquisites on funeral, marriage and confirmation occasions.

We now pray you to accept our call, which we as representatives of our charge extend to you, and to favor us with an answer, in writing, so that we may make arrangements to bring you and your dear family among us. Do not allow yourself to be discouraged by the fact that the election was not held at Old Goshenhoppen at the time appointed, but on a wholly different day—which was irregular—and that on that occasion a majority of votes was cast for the Rev. Mr. Zeller. Our three congregations constitute a pastoral charge—the majority of whose votes were cast in your favor. Though the *two* congregations elected you—unanimously, to say—and a minority of the third even, you will yet be the choice of the large majority of the charge; and you are hereby truly and solemnly called as its minister. If Old Goshenhoppen should desire to sever her connection with us, we will, nevertheless, pay you the full amount promised. We fear greatly that our flock may be scattered, and on this account the more urgently request you to show your love toward us, by accepting our call. The Lord will in future be with us and bless His word to the salvation of our souls.

Undersigned by our hands as elders and deacons of the joint congregations, and given by us on the 31st day of March, A.D. 1819

JOHN GERY		JOHN HILLEGASS	
ADAM EVERHART	*Elders*	ADAM HILLEGAS	*Deacons.*
HENRY OTT		MICH. ROUDENBUSH	
JACOB DUBBS			

The expectations of New Goshenhoppen and Great Swamp that Old Goshenhoppen would acquiesce in the choice of the majority were not fulfilled. The opposition to Mr. Faber was so serious that they refused to reconsider their action, but appealed to Synod for help.

At the meeting of the Synod held on September 5 and following days of the year 1819, at Lancaster,

a letter from the Old Goshenhoppen congregation was read, in which the Reverend Synod was requested to permit them to secure services on Sunday afternoon through a minister of Synod. A committee, consisting of Messrs. Wack, Sen., Hinsch and Elder Graff was appointed to take this letter under consideration.

On the following day the committee handed in the following report:

The committee appointed to consider the conditions in the Old and New Goshenhoppen and Great Swamp congregations, report: "That they had found that Rev Mr Faber has been elected pastor by a very large majority in the New Goshenhoppen and Swamp congregations, the Old Goshenhoppen congregation, however, does not seem to be inclined to Mr. Faber." It is the judgment of the committee that it would be advisable for Synod to give the Old Goshenhoppen congregation the friendly advice, to unite with the other two congregations rather than sever a bond of eighty-two years standing, for the committee cannot imagine how the Old Goshenhoppen congregation will gain anything by withdrawing from the union with New Goshenhoppen and Great Swamp.[234]

At the same meeting of Synod, in 1819, John T. Faber reported as his congregations Old Goshenhoppen, New Goshenhoppen, Great Swamp and Trappe in Montgomery County. He had baptized 90, confirmed 35, buried 34, and 202 members had communed. He also reported one school. The inclusion of Old Goshenhoppen was probably due to the fact that the final decision as to the attitude of the congregation had not yet been rendered. When it was rendered it was adverse to accepting Mr. Faber as its pastor, in spite of the friendly advice of Synod.

At the meeting of the Classis of Philadelphia, held at Philadelphia on April 30 to May 1, 1820,

a letter was read from the congregation of the Rev. J. Faber, in which they expressed their satisfaction with his ministry. A letter from Mr. Faber was also read in which he excused his absence because of sickness. The excuse was unanimously accepted.

The minutes of Synod of 1820 show also what had become of Old Goshenhoppen. Jacob William Dechant is reported as pastor of Pikeland, Chester County, Old Goshenhoppen in Montgomery County and Hilltown. His baptisms at Old Goshenhoppen begin on December 25, 1819. On December 30, 1820, he signed a receipt in the Old Goshenhoppen account book for 170 dollars salary.

The separation of the Old Goshenhoppen congregation, which occurred in 1819, was final. It never returned to

[234] Minutes of the Synod of 1819, p 19, § 15, p 21, § 9

THE PENNSYLVANIA-GERMAN SOCIETY.

REV. CLEMENT Z. WEISER.

THE NEW YORK
PUBLIC LIBRARY

ASTOR, LENOX
TILDEN FOUNDATIONS

Faber's Death

the former charge. The congregation of Upper Milford took its place and remained under Faber's care to the end of his life.

There is only one later event in the pastorate of the younger Faber which deserves some notice. It is the remarkable manner of his death, almost an exact reproduction of that of his father. We quote fittingly the description of Dr. C. Z. Weiser, who has done so much to preserve the history of the congregation:[235]

> Pastor Faber's history, like that of his sainted father, came suddenly and solemnly to a close. At the funeral services of Mrs. Peter Maurer he was taken ill in the middle of his discourse, and sank away. The excitement of the congregation cannot well be described. It was on the first day of February, just forty-five years later than the time his father had received his final call to the eternal world. Several helping hands bore the sick pastor away to the school-house and subsequently to the parsonage. Here he lingered ten days. His death occurred on the 10th of February, 1833, at an age of 61 years, 4 months and 11 days. His remains were laid alongside of those of his father, beneath the chancel of the church. Over the elder Faber's tomb were placed the words: "Approach lightly." Over that of the son: "Depart softly."

With the division of the charge and the second pastorate of John T. Faber the first part of its history came to a close. In 1827 the first century of congregational life was ended. Having reached this point, our task is accomplished and we lay down our pen, leaving the later history to some future historian.

[235] Weiser, *Monograph*, p. 106.

Church Records
of the
Goshenhoppen Reformed Church
1731=1830

TRANSLATED AND EDITED BY
PROF. WILLIAM J. HINKE, Ph.D., D.D.

Church Records

CHURCH RECORDS OF THE NEW GOSHENHOPPEN REFORMED CONGREGATION, UPPER HANOVER TOWNSHIP, MONTGOMERY COUNTY, PA.

VOLUME I, 1731–1761.
VOLUME II, 1762–1832.

Translated and Edited by
William J. Hinke, Ph.D., D.D.

The church record herewith published has the unique distinction of being the oldest known record book of the Reformed Church in the United States. It is the property of the New Goshenhoppen Reformed congregation, which worships in the New Goshenhoppen Reformed Church, a building standing about one mile west of East Greenville, Montgomery County, Pa., close to the east bank of the Perkiomen Creek.

The book measures $7\frac{1}{2}$ inches in width and $12\frac{3}{8}$ inches in length. It is bound in heavy, leather-bound, oak covers. The leather was at one time tastefully tooled, but it is now torn and shows the signs of age. It was also provided with iron clasps, but they have mostly disappeared, and only parts of them have survived. The number of leaves still in the book is eighty-one. They are water-stained and yellow with age.

The publication of this record is justified by both historical as well as genealogical considerations. It is on the one hand an important source of family history for the Goshenhoppen region, making us acquainted with some of the most prominent families in the Perkiomen Valley. But it is also important as a source for church history, because it contains the record of the ministerial labors of some of the earliest Reformed ministers in Pennsylvania.

The title page is especially interesting and important. It was written by John Henry Goetschius (or Goetschy). Being undated it was formerly thought to have been written as early as 1731, when the first baptismal entries were made. But this is now known to be an error, because documents both in Switzerland and Pennsylvania prove that Mr. Goetschy did not come to Pennsylvania till 1735. As the title page of the Great Swamp record was written in 1736, so it is most likely the case with this record. At least we cannot be far from right when we say that it was entered about the year 1736.

The title page reads verbatim et literatim:

      Das Buch Kost 5 schiling
           Tauf Buch
   der Gemeind von Coschenhope
  In welchem verzeichnet sind die Namen
         der Kinderen
welche durch die H. Tauf nach dem Befehl Jesu
  under die Gemeine Gottes als Glieder an-
genomen worden, im beyseyn Christlicher Tauf
Zeugen, der(en) Namen samt der Getauften Kinder(en)
  Eltern von den(en) rechtmesigen Lehrern hier
        eingezeichlet worden

      Gott wolle Ihre Namen
      mit dem Blut Jesu aus
      dem Sunden Buch auslosch(en)
      und in das Lebens Buch
      ein Schreiben. Amen
                Joh Henricus Goetschius, V. D. M
        Helvetiae Tigurinae
        et   cet.
     Pronuncia[n]s veritatem in
Schippach, Alt Coschenhopen, Neu Coschenhopen, Schwam, Sacen, Aegipten, Macedonia, Missillem, Oli, Bern, Dolpenhacen

This means:

> This Book costs 5 shillings.
> Baptismal Book
> of the Congregation of Goshenhoppen,
> in which are recorded the names
> of the children,
> who, through H. Baptism, according to the command of Jesus
> were received into the congregation as
> members, in the presence of Christian wit-
> nesses, whose names together with those of the
> parents of the baptized children have been here
> recorded by the regular ministers
>
> May God erase their names
> with the blood of Jesus from
> the book of sin
> and enroll them
> in the book of life   Amen
>
> John Henry Goetschius, V D M,
> of Zurich, Switzerland, etc,
> preaching the truth at
> Skippack, Old Goshenhoppen, New Goshenhoppen,
> [Great] Swamp, Saucon, Egypt, Maxatawny,
> Moselem, Oley, Berne and Tulpehocken

LIST OF THE HEADS OF FAMILIES BELONGING TO THE CONGREGATION OF NEW GOSHENHOPPEN, REFORMED MEMBERS

[1] Johan Steinmann
[2] Henrich Galman
[3] Johanes Bingeman
[4] Joh. Georg Welker
[5] Benedict Strohm
[6] Philip Emmert
[7] Johanes Hut
[8] Abraham Transu
[9] Andreas Greber
[10] Philip Ried
[11] Georg Mess
[12] Joh. Georg Pfalzgraff
[13] Jacob Fischer
[14] Paul Staab
[15] Wendel Wiand
[16] Herman Fischer
[17] Conrad Colb
[18] Joh. Michael Moll
[19] Fridrich Hilligas
[20] Michael Reder
[21] Joh Bartholomeus Kuker
[22] Michael Lutz
[23] Andreas Lohr
[24] Georg Mertz
[25] Michael Fabion
[26] Henrich Jung
[27] Philip Jacob Schellhammer
[28] Leonhardt Knopf
[29] Jacob Knopf
[30] Caspar Kamm

[31] Caspar Holzhauser
[32] Michael Zimmerman
[33] Baltasar Hut
[34] Niclaus Ensly
[35] Jacob Maurer
[36] Fridrich Maurer
[37] Christian Knopf
[38] Fridrich Pfanenbeker
[39] Benedict Raderly
[40] Valentin Griesemer
[41] Lorentz Hartman'
[42] Georg Philip Dotder
[43] Jacob Meyer
[44] Daniel Lawar
[45] Peter Walper[t].

[This list of 45 members is in the handwriting of Mr. Goetschius and was therefore made sometime between 1736-1739.]

LIST OF THE HEADS OF FAMILIES WHO IN NEW GOSHENHOPPEN BELONG TO THE CONGREGATION OF THE REV. GEORGE MICHAEL WEISS.

[1] Peter Beissel
[2] Philip Ried
[3] Berenh[ard] Gucker
[4] Adam Bosserdt
[5] Andres Ohl
[6] Conrad Zimmerman
[7] Jacob Ridi
[8] J Adam Hillikas
[9] Georg Peter Hillikas
[10] Fridrich Hillikas
[11] Henerich Gallman
[12] J. Gallman
[13] Andres Greber
[14] Ullrich Greber
[15] Wilhelm Griesemer
[16] Peter Lauer
[17] Michael Roeder
[18] Jost Schlicher
[19] David Schmidt
[20] Jacob Gery
[21] Valadin Griesemer
[22] Caspar Holtzhauser
[23] Leonhardt Griesemer
[24] J. Georg Steinman
[25] Benedict Strohm
[26] Henrich Jung
[27] Michael Moll
[28] J. Georg Welcker
[29] Conrad Wannenmacher
[30] Melchior Kolb
[31] Michael Ried
[32] Andres Mauerer
[33] Abraham Segler
[34] Weygandt Pannenbeek
[35] J Schell
[36] Georg Zimmerman
[37] Wilhelm Geiger
[38] J Nicolaus Jung
[39] Georg Michael Kolb
[40] Samuel Somani
[41] J Mack
[42] Herman Fischer
[43] Wendel Wigand
[44] Jacob Mauerer
[45] Friderich Mauerer
[46] J. Huth, Senior
[47] J Huth, Junior
[48] Philip Huth
[49] J. Nicolaus Ohl
[50] Henerich Gebel
[51] Michael Schell, Junior
[52] Jacob Fischer

LIST OF THE HEADS OF FAMILIES WHO IN OLD GOSHENHOPPEN BELONG TO THE CONGREGATION OF THE REV. GEORGE MICHAEL WEISS

[1] Johannes Jost
[2] Jacob Hauk
[3] Jacob Weitman
[4] Samuel Schuler
[5] Benedict Schwob
[6] Daniel Hister
[7] Jost Keller
[8] Hennerich Buhl
[9] Felix Lee
[10] Jacob Grub
[11] J Hollenbusch
[12] H. Hollenbusch
[13] J Werman
[14] Jacob Isset
[15] J Gantz
[16] J. Muck
[17] H Bamberger
[18] J. Brunner
[19] Andres Muller
[20] Philip Wentz
[21] Johannes Faust
[22] Kilian Zimmerman
[23] Ullerich Herzel
[24] J Denig
[25] Hoffel Dickenschitt
[26] Jacob Hoffman
[27] Gabriel Schuler
[28] J. Gotz
[29] Simon Mag
[30] J. Lee, Junior
[31] J Denig, Junior
[32] Baltasar Lamper
[33] Philip Ried
[34] H Bamberger, Junior
[35] N— Dickenschitt, Junior
[36] J Gotz, Junior
[37] N —* Hildenbeidel

LIST OF THE HEADS OF FAMILIES WHO IN GREAT SWAMP BELONG TO THE CONGREGATION OF THE REV GEORGE MICHAEL WEISS

[1] Franz Rus
[2] Ullerich Rieser
[3] Ludwig Bitting
[4] Alexander Diefendorfer
[5] Peter Linn
[6] J. Schmidt
[7] Christian Muller
[8] N.— Muller
[9] Jacob Dubs
[10] Jacob Wetzel, Junior
[11] N — Kehler
[12] Jacob Wetzel, Junior
[13] Felix Brunner
[14] J. Reiswick
[15] Joseph Eberhardt
[16] Michael Eberhardt
[17] Michael Eberhardt, Junior
[18] Uly Spinner
[19] J. Bleiler
[20] Hennerich Bleyler
[21] Peter Bleyler
[22] Philip Heger
[23] N — Hitz
[24] J. Huber
[25] Abraham Faust
[26] Hennerich Huber
[27] Jacob Huber
[28] Rudy Huber, the wagoner
[29] N — Huber, the tailor
[30] Son-in-law of Mr. Hitz [cf. No. 23]
[31] Rudy Frick

* N — means that the name was unknown to the writer.

[32] Abraham Ditloh
[33] N. — Ditloh, Junior
[34] J Nicolaus Mombauer
[35] Paul Samsel
[36] N — Villauer [Christian Willauer]
[37] Johannes Huber
[38] J Huber, Junior
[39] Philip Boehm, the locksmith
[40] Valadin Kaiser
[41] Daniel Hucken
[42] N —* Huber, bro of Huber, the tailor
[43] A weaver living at Ditloh's
[44] G. — Weiss
[45] N — Kunius
[46] David Streib
[47] Andres Greber

[These three lists were entered by Rev. George Michael Weiss, probably in the year 1758, when the record book came into his hands, according to a note entered on p. 37 of the original]

[I. BAPTISMS BY THE REV. JOHN PETER MILLER, 1731-1734]

In August, 1731
    Elisabetha, parents, Philip LABAAR and wife Witnesses, Fridrich Hillegas and wife.
    Anna Maria and Jacob, parents, Fridrich MAURER and wife Witnesses, Anna Maria Segler and Jacob Maurer.
    Maria Susanna, parents, Johan Georg WELCKER and wife. Witnesses, Maria Susanna Zimmermann.
    Anna Catharina, parents, Herman FISCHER and wife Witness, Anna Catharina, wife of Joh. Mack.
    Johann Wilhelm, parents, Andreas HAG and wife Witnesses, Joh Wilhelm Schmidt and wife
    Johann Adam, parents, Henrich RETHER and wife Witnesses, Michael Rether and Susanna Zimmermann.
    Elisabetha Barbara, parents, Joh Michael LUTZ Witnesses, Friddich Hilligas and wife.

June 6, 1731
    Anna, parents, Herman DECKER and wife Witness, Anna, wife of Georg Best
    Johann Adam, parents, Michael HEYDER. Witness, Johann Adam Blanck.
    Johanna Elisabetha, parents, Joh Wilhelm LABAAR and wife Witness, Johanna Elisabetha, Frantz Stupp's daughter
    Johann Abraham, parents, Abraham TRANSOU and wife. Witness, Michael Schell

August 22.
    Johann Adam, parents, Johann Jost KOB and wife. Witnesses, Johann Adam Beuscher and wife.

* N — means that the name was unknown to the writer.

Johannes, parents, Jacob DANCKEL and wife Witnesses, Johannes Bingeman and wife

Anna Maria Elisabetha, parents, Jost HENCKEL and wife, Witnesses, Valentin Griesemer and his wife and Marie Elisabetha Henckel.

September 21.

Maria Margaretha, parents, Georg RAUTENBUSCH and wife Witnesses, Jacob Danckel and wife

Johann Philip, parents, Johannes HUTH and wife Witnesses, Johann Philip Emmerth and wife.

October 31

Johann Jacob, parents, Wilhelm SCHMITT and wife Witnesses, Jacob Keller and wife

1732, April 9

Maria Magdalena, parents, Elias LANG and wife Witnesses, Maria Magdalena, wife of Ludwig Schlosser, Anna Maria, wife of Georg Philip Schuman

Anna Elisabetha, parents, Johannes BLEULER and wife Witnesses, Peter Diethert and wife

Johann Jost, parents, Joh. Jost SELER and wife. Witnesses, Jost Henckel and wife

April 11.

Wilhelm and Abraham, parents, Jacob SCHMIT and wife Witnesses, Wilhelm Schmit, Abraham Saler

April 15

Johannes, parents, Johan Philip EMMERT and Maria Catharina, his wife Witnesses, Johan Hut and wife.

April 16

Andreas, parents, Burckhard HOFFMAN and wife. Witnesses, Andreas Maurer and Anna Maria Zimmermann.

Johann Peter, parents, Jacob WETZEL and wife Witness, Johann Peter Muller

June 4

Johann Wilhelm, parents, Hans Adams BLANCK and wife Witnesses, Wilhelm Labaar and wife

Elisabetha Barabara, parents, Fridrich HILLIGAS and wife Witness Anna Barbara, daughter of Kaspar Kamm.

Anna Maria, parents, Thomas HAMMAN and wife Witness, Anna Maria, wife of Christian Lehman.

Anna Clara, parents, Henrich BISSBING and wife Witnesses, Henrich Bissbing and wife.

Christophorus, parents, Philip Jacob SCHELLHAMMER and wife Witness, Christophorus Schmitt

June 11
  Johan Leonhard, parents, Valentin GRIESHEIMER and wife Witness, Johann Leonhard Hochgenuch
  Johann Michael, parents, Joseph EBERHARD and wife. Witnesses, Johan Michael Eberhard
  Elisabetha, parents, Johannes RENNBERG and wife Witness, Adam Wanner
  Anna Margaretha, parents, Joseph EBERHARD and wife. Witness, Margaretha, wife of Michael Eberhard
July 30.
  Johann Georg, parents, Johan Peter LAUER and wife Witness, Johann Georg Zimmerman
  Andreas, parents, Jacob MAURER and wife Witness, Andreas Maurer.
November 24.
  Leonhard, parents, Johann Adam EUCHELING and wife Witnesses, Leonhard Schmid and Anna Maria Herbig, both single
  Susanna, parents, Bartholomeus GUCKER and wife Witnesses, Christopher Schmit and wife
  Christophorus, parents, Peter WALBERT and wife Witnesses, Christopher Schmit and wife
1733. January 21
  Susanna Catharina, parents, Johan Adam STADLER and wife Witnesses, Philip Emmert and wife
  Johann Fridrich, parents, Johann Fridrich MAURER and wife Witnesses and wife, Fridrich Hilligas and wife
March 25
  Johannes, parents, Paul STAP and wife. Witnesses, Johannes Hut and wife
  Maria Margaretha, parents, Michael DOTTERER and wife Witnesses, Hermann Fischer and wife
April 22
  Johann Conrad, parents, Balthasar HUTH and wife Witness, Conrad Kolb
May 20
  Johann Jacob, parents, Jacob FISCHER and wife Witnesses, Jacob Hoffman and wife
  Maria Catharina, parents, Johann Philip EMMERT and wife Witnesses, Adam Stadler and wife
  Johann Georg, parents, Ulrich HERTZEL and wife Witness, Peter Moll
  Catharina, parents, Christopher MOLL and wife Witnesses, Jacob Fischer and wife

Henrich, parents, Johann BINGEMAN and wife. Witnesses, Henrich Rether and wife

Peter, parents, Georg RAUTENBUSCH and wife. Witness, Peter Rautenbusch

Joh. Michael, parents, Michael ZIMMERMAN and wife Witnesses, Michael Rether and Susanna Zimmermàn

June 17.

Johannes, parents, Casparus HOLTZHAUSER and wife. Witness, Johannes Bingeman

Anna Margaretha, parents, Adam WANNER and wife. Witnesses, Martin Budding and wife

July 15.

Maria Barbara, parents, Herman FISCHER and wife Witnesses, Andreas Eccert, single, and Maria Barbara Mack, single.

August 12.

Johann Henrich, parents, Peter HESS and wife Witnesses, Henrich Rether and wife

Anna Maria, parents, Wilhelm LABAR and wife Witnesses, Adam Blanck and wife

September 16

Anna Maria, parents, Peter DIETERTH and wife Witness, Anna Maria, wife of Joh. Bleuler.

October 17.

Feronica, parents, Andreas LOHER and wife. Witnesses, Johannes Zechler and wife

Anna, parents, Jacob DANCKEL and wife Witnesses, Georg Heilig and wife

November 11.

Anna Barbara, parents, Joh. Georg STEINMAN and wife. Witnesses, Anna Barbara Steinman

1734 January 1

Johann Adam, parents, Christian WILLAUER and wife Witness, Johann Adam Beuscher.

Maria Margaretha, parents, Peter MATERN and wife Witnesses, Henrich Buskerk and Margaretha, his wife.

July 28

Johann Jacob, parents, Abraham TRANDSU and Anna Margaretha, his wife Witnesses, Jacob Keller and Anna Maria, his wife

Anna Maria, parents, Michael HEITER and wife Catharina. Witness, Anna Maria Heck.

Johan Adam, parents, Hans Michael BUTZ [Lutz] and Maria Margaretha, his wife Witness, Johann Adam Beuscher

Margaretha, parents, Joh Georg KRONER and Anna Elisabetha, his wife Witnesses, Johannes Geiger and Anna Margaretha, his wife
Johannes, parents, Joh HUT and Anna Maria, his wife Witness, Joh Philip Emmerth
Anna Maria, parents, Joh Philip EMMERTH and Maria Catharina, his wife Witnesses, Joh Hut and Anna Maria, his wife.

[These 69 baptisms were entered during the ministry of John Peter Miller. The chirography is that of a well educated man and the natural inference is that Mr Miller himself made these entries His ministry at Goshenhoppen is placed beyond doubt by the letters of Mr. Boehm, quoted above (see p. 79) His statements are supported by the fact that in the 26th baptism, on April 16, 1732, Johann Peter Muller acted as sponsor (see p 278), a role which the pastor frequently filled in early times. Cf the 56th baptism of Mr. Goetschy (see p. 284), and the 8th baptism of Frederick Casimir Muller (see p 286).]

[II BAPTISMS BY JOHN HENRY GOETSCHY, 1736-1740]

LIST OF THE CHILDREN WHOM I, J. HENRICUS GOETSCHIUS, HAVE BAPTIZED IN THE CONGREGATION OF GOSHENHOPPEN, A 1736

April 25, Hans Martin, father Henrich SCHMID, mother Anna Margaretha, witnesses, Hans Hut and Eva Maria, wife of Michel Sebastian
Same, Hans Petter, parents, Hans Adam STADLER and Susanna Caterina Witnesses, Johannes Schellenberger, Anna Schellenberger
May 9, Georg Peter, parents, Fridrich HILLIGAS and wife Lisabarbara Witnesses, John Jorg Gut and wife
Same, Philip Henrich, parents, Andreas LOHR and Christina Witnesses, John Philip Emmert and wife
Same, Jorg Antonius, parents, Peter BEISEL and wife Susanna. Witnesses, Jorg Mertz and wife.
Same, Eva Lisabeth, parents, Bartlmaus GUGER and wife Catharina Witnesses, Fridrich Hilledagas[¹] and daughter Eva Lisabeth
Same, Fronegg [Veronica], parents, Michael ZIMMERMAN and wife Anna Witnesses, Philip Doder and wife
Same, Catrina, parents, Michael HEIDER and wife Catrina Witness, Catrina Herweg
Same, Susan, parents, Tomas HAMMAN and wife Susan Witnesses, Christian Leeman and daughter Anna Mary.
Same, Margreth, parents, Hans WOLET and wife Margreth. Witnesses, Herman Fischer and wife.

May 23, Margret, parent, Philip RID
June 6, Maria Lisabeth, parents, Feltin [Valentin] GRISEMER and Anna Mary Witnesses, Jacob Dihl and wife Maria Lisabeth
June 20, Sophia, parents, Wendel WIAND and Anna Margreth Witnesses, Jacob Fischer and wife Sophia
Same, Anna Catharina, parents, Michael FABION and Dorothea. Witnesses, Fridrich Nuz and wife Catharina
Same, Elisabetha, parents, Abraham TRANSO and Anna Margretha. Witness, Elisabeth Schunk.
Aug. 1, Johannes, parents, Herman FISCHER and Margaretha Witnesses, Johannes Magg and Margaretha Zimmerman
Same, Johan Christophel, parents, Michael MOLL and Rosina Witnesses, Christophel Moll and wife Anna Catharina
Sept 5, Johannes, parents, Johan Jost OLLWEIN and Anna Eva Witnesses, Johannes Magg and Maria Marg Zimmerman
Oct 10, Anna Catrina, parents, Hans SCHELLENBERGER and Anna Witnesses, Anna Catrina Kem and husband Kaspar.
Oct. 31, Johan Jorg, parents, Johan Philip EBERD and Maria Catrina Witnesses, Johan Jorg Pfalzgraf and wife Anna Barbara
Dec. 5, Anna Maria, parents, Daniel SCHWARZ and Eva Gretha. Witnesses, Niclaus Ensli and wife Anna.

1737.

March 27, Anna Margreth, parents, Michael REDER and Susanna Witnesses, Georg Welcker and wife Anna Margretha
April 11, Jacob Fridrich, parents, Conrad KOLB and Maria Barbara Witnesses, Jacob Muller and Eva Elisabeth Hillgas
Same, Johannes, parents, Jacob SCHMIDT and Apolonia Witnesses, Johannes Schuck and wife Anna Maria
Same, Anna Margreth, parents, Caspar HOLZHAUSER and Margaretha Witnesses, Wendel Wiand and wife, Margaretha
Same, Hans Leonhardt, parents, Georg Peter KNECHT and Christina. Witnesses, Hans Leonhardt Herzel and Anna Maria Galmann
Same, Johan Andreas, parents, Andreas MAURER and Anna Maria. Witnesses, Andreas Sechler and Anna Maria Sechler
Same, Maria Lisabeth, parents George SCHUTZ and Anna Christina Witnesses, Leonhardt Bock and wife Maria Lisabeth
May 8, Anna Margaretha, parents, Herman FISCHER and Margretha Witnesses, Wendel Wiand and wife Margaretha.
Same, Johannes, parents, Conrad WANNENMACHER and Barbara Witnesses, Johannes Bess and wife Susanna.

Same, Anna Maria, parents, Niklaus ENSLI and wife Anna. Witnesses, Anna Maria Wagenseiler, daughter of Christina and Christopher Wagenseiler
Same, Maria Barbara, Anna Maria, parents, Ludwig DETRER and Anna Barbara Witnesses, Anna Barbara Heriger, daughter of Gottlieb Heriger, Hans Adam Hilligas, Anna Maria Steger, wife of Hans Steger.
June 19, Elisabeth Barbara, parents, Jacob MAURER and Sophia Lisabeth Witnesses, Fridrich Hilligas and wife Elizabeth Barbara
Same, Anna Margreth, parents, Henrich REDER and Anna Witnesses, Hans Jorg Welker and wife Anna Margareth.
July 14, Eva Barbara, parents, Leonhardt UX [Ochs] and Catrina Witness, Eva Barbara Kunius.
Same, Maria Susanna, parents, Philip Jacob SCHELLHAMMER and wife Anna Margreth. Witnesses, Maria Lang and Susanna Schmidt
Same, Anna Catrina, parents, Ulrich ARNER and Ferena. Witness, Anna Catrina Strom, wife of Benedict Strom
Aug. 21, Johan Caspar, parents, Michael FABION and Dorothea Witnesses, Johan Caspar Grisemer and his mother
Nov 20, Elisabeth, parents, Hanes MAGG and Margreth. Witness, Elisabetha Zimmermann

1738.

Febr 1, Anna Christina, parents. Johann Philip EMMERT and Mary Catrina Witnesses, Johannes Hut and wife Anna Maria
Febr 5, Johan Michael and Jacob, parents, Michael DODDER and Anna Maria Witnesses, Wendel Wiand and Anna Margreth, Jacob Fischer and Sophia Lisabeth
Same Philipina, parents, Wendel WIAND and Anna Margreth. Witnesses, Daniel Schoner and Maria Catrina.
Dec 3, Eva Margretha, parents, Joh Jorg BREY and Maria Catrina Witnesses, Conrad Tettrer and Eva Margretha Hut
Dec. 31 Joh Adam, parents, Conrad KOLB and Anna Barbara Witnesses, Johan Adam Hilligas and Eva Hilligas, his sister

1739

Aug 19, Johan Georg, parents, Herman FISCHER and Margaretha Witness, Johann Georg Mack
Same, Joh Valentin, parents, Leonhart HARTMAN and Maria Catrina Witnesses Valentin Grisemer and Anna Mary, his wife
Sept. 2, Jacob, parents, Jacob LINGEL and Anna Ursula Witnesses, Jacob Fischer and wife Sophia
Same, Anna Lisabeth, parents, Conrad WANNENMACHER and Maria Barbara Witnesses, Georg Jagi (?) and Helena Elisabeth.

Oct. 24, Georg Ulrich, parents, Michael LUTZ and Anna Margretha. Witnesses, Georg Ulrich Engler and Anna Margareth.

Same, Michael, parents, Georg Michael KOLB and Anna Elisabeth Witnesses, Michael Reder and Susanna.

1740.

Sept 24, Johan Niclaus, parents, Jacob BISEKER and Anna Maria Witnesses, Joh. Niclaus Mumbauer and Susanna Schmid

Same, Georg, parents, Michael ZIMMERMAN and Anna Witness, Georg Zimmerman

Same, Jacob, parents, Johannes ZECHLER and Anna Maria. Witnesses, Jacob Maurer and wife Susana Lisabeth.

Same, Isaac, parents, Conrad FREY and Ester Witness, Henrich Gotschy

Same, Jacob, parents, Wendel WIAND and Anna Margreth. Witnesses, Jacob Selzer and wife Elisabeth

Same, Lisabeth, parents, Michael REDER and Susanna Witness, Lisabeth Zimmerman.

Same, Lisabeth Margreth, parents, Michael MOLL and Rosina. Witnesses, Melchior Sussholz and Lisabeth

Same, Anna Margreth, present, Michael FABION and Anna Dorothea Witness, Anna Margaretha Dankels.

[III BAPTISMS BY REV PETER HENRY DORSIUS, 1741-1744]
Anno 1741, August 30.

Johan Andreas, parents, Andreas LOHR and Cadarina [Christina] Witnesses, Philip Emmert and wife

Andreas, parents, Caspar HOLTZHAUSER and Margretha, his wife Witness, Andreas Greber

Johan Conrad, parents, Peter MUELLER and wife Maria Witnesses, Conrad Kolb and wife.

Johannes, parents, Georg WELCKER and Anna Margreth Witnesses, Johannes Mack and wife.

Anna Margretha, parents, Johannes MACK and Margreth Witnesses, Georg Welcker and wife.

Eva Elisabeth, parents, Philip RIET and Veronica Witness, Elisabetha Hilligas

Anna Maria, parents, Jacob MAURER and Sophia Witness, Anna Maria Segler.

Catharina, parents, Jacob LINGEL and Ursula Anna. Witnesses, Johannes Bingeman and wife.

Elisabetha, parents, Johann Georg FRITLE (?) and Anna Catrina Witness, Elisabetha Ris

Abraham, parents, Philip LABAHR and Sara   Witness, Caspar Holtzhauser
Sara, parents, Philip LABAHR and Sara   Witness, the mother.
Eva Elisabetha, parents Philip LABAHR and Sara   Witness, Eva Elisabetha Hillegas.
Elisabetha, parents, Conrad WANNENMACHER and Barbara   Witness, Gôrg Jorg and wife
    1742, September 4
Johan Michel, parents, Adam HILLIGAS and Margaretha   Witnesses, Michel Reder and his wife
Anna Maria, parents, Wendel WEIGAND and Anna Margaretha   Witnesses Johannes Segler and wife
Elisabeta, parents, Bernhard DOTTER and Gertraut   Witness, the mother herself
Andreas, parents, Johannes SEGLER and Anna Mary   Witnesses, Wendel Wigand and his wife
Elisabeta, parents, Niklaus ROTENBURGER and Margareta Anna   Witness, Elisabeth Hatai (?)
Joseph, parents, Georg Michel KOLB and Elisabeth.   Witness, Joseph Fabion.
    These children were baptized the fifth of May, Anno 1744
Anna Maria, parents, Hans Rudolph ECK and Anna Cathrina   Witness, Anna Maria ——
Johann Georg, parents, Molger [Melchior] SUESSHOLTZ and Elisabeth   Witness, Catarina Zimmerman
Johann Friederich, parents, Adam BOSSERT and wife Jacobe   Witness, Friedrich Gotz
Maigreda, parents, Andreas MAURER and Anna Maria   Witness, Anna Margreda Lauer
Michel, parents, Michel MOL and Rosina   Witness, Michel Reitenbach
Th Friedrich, parents, Jos. SEGLER and Anna Maria.   Witness, the father himself

[These 25 children were baptized by the Rev. Peter Henry Dorsius, of Nehaminy, Bucks County   The entries were not made by him, but are in a wretched scrawl, made perhaps by one of the elders. The letters of Mr. Boehm, quoted above (see p. 137), make it evident that Mr. Dorsius was in Goshenhoppen, both before as well as after his journey to Holland, which took place from May, 1743, to January, 1744   The presence of Mr Dorsius at Goshenhoppen on May 6, 1744, is also vouched for by Mr. Boehm (see (p 142).   On the previous day he baptized the last six children]

[IV BAPTISMS BY FREDERICK CASIMIR MUELLER, 1745-1750.]

1745.

July 7, Daughter, parents, Peter MAY and wife   Witness, Michel Hubert and Anna Maria Maurer

Aug. 11, Son, born July 21, parents, Andres GERBER and wife. Witness, Philip Ried and wife

Sept 1, Son, parents, Jorg Michel KOLB and Anna Elisabeth   Witness, Philip Emert and Maria Catarina

Aug. 25, Daughter, parents, Jacob SCHEL and wife. Witness, Anna Gertrant Griesemer.

Sept. 8, Son, born Jan. 23, 1745, parents, Christian STROM and wife Anna Margretha   Witness, Benedict Strom

Oct 27, Son, parents, Bernhart WANNEMACHER and wife   Witness, Jacob Wannemacher.

Sept 3, Son, parents, Wilhelm MACK and wife   Witness, John Mack.

Sept 27, Son, parents, Johan Adam MENGEL and wife   Witness, Friedrich C. Muller.

1746.

March 23, Son, parents, Friederich Casimir MUELLER and wife   Witnesses, Joh. Hoffmann, Friedrich Helwig

April 7, Son, parents, Casper GRIESEMER and Elisabetha. Witness, Abraham Eckmann.

April 6, Johann Michel, parents, Georg FREY and Christina   Witness Michel Huber and Anna Maria Fischer

April 6, Johann Jacob, parents, Jorg WELCKER and Anna Gretha   Witnesses, Benedict Strom and Catharina

June 15, Johannes, parents, Jacob LINGEL and Ursula   Witness, Johannes Mack and Margaretha

Aug 23, Johannes, parents, Philip RAFFSCHNEIDER and Susanna. Witness, Johannes Hoffmann

Oct. 17, Michel, Jeremias, David, Daniel, Catarina, Johanna, parents, Jorg RAUTENBUSCH and wife *   Witnesses, Michel Roder, Valentin Griesemer, Andreas Graber Weygand Pfannebecker

Nov 1, Jorg Michel, parents, Jorg Michel KOLB and wife. Witnesses, Michel Kurtz and wife

Oct 25, Anna Maria, parents, Jacob GORY and wife   Witness, Valentin Griesemer and wife.

1747.

Jan 26, Johannes, parents, Paul ANTONI and wife. Witness, Johannes Sechler.

* Baptisms on Oct 17th, entered by the same hand as those on May 4, 1744

Jan. 31, Johanna Maria, parents, Lehnhart LOOTZ [Lutz] and wife. Witnesses, Johannes Otto and wife

✓ March 15, Johannes, parents, Michel ROEDER and wife. Witnesses, Johannes Mack and wife

March 24, Anna Maria, parents, [Wendel] WIEGAND and wife. Witnesses, Johannes Sechler and wife.

July 26, Rutolph, parents, Johannes SECHLER and wife Witnesses, Rutolph Maurer and wife

March 27, Paul, parents, Jacob LINGEL and wife Witness, Paul Lingel.

1748.

Sept. 25, Lisa Barbara, parents, Peter MAY and wife. Witnesses, Barbara Hoffmann, Lisa Moll.

1749.

Jan. 21, Susanna, parents, Joh MACK and wife. Witnesses, Michel Roder and wife

Febr 12, Christina, parents, Hermann FISCHER and wife Witness, Christina Moser

March 5, Henrich, parents, Wegand PFANNEBECKER and wife Witness, Michel Roder and wife

March 25, Cattarina, parents, Jacob GERY and wife. Witnesses, Valentin Grisemer and wife

July 30, Joseph, parents, Johannes SECHLER and wife Witness, Joh Sechler himself

1750

April 28, Joh Philip, parents, Jacob LINGEL and wife Witnesses, Casper Burger and wife

[These 35 entries (except one or two) are in the wretched, but well-known handwriting of Frederick Casimir Miller. His presence is also vouched for by the eighth and ninth baptisms, which contain his name As the entries of Rev. Weiss began in 1747 (see p. 301), the ministry of Miller seems to have extended from 1745 to 1747 But the later entries prove that he made occasional visits to Goshenhoppen and baptized children there as late as April 28, 1750. As the record remained in the hands of his followers, he was able to make these later entries. Cf the following note of Weiss on p 37.]

Before the church record made its appearance [in 1757], the

names of the baptized children were generally taken care of and recorded by the parents themselves.

[Note in the handwriting of G. M. Weiss.]

[V BAPTISMS BY THE REV GEORGE MICHAEL WEISS, 1748-1761]

From 1748 till the year 1758 the following adult persons were baptized, upon the profession of their faith, by me, George Michael Weiss.

> Anna Maria Neiss, Georg Neiss,
> Stedler, the blacksmith and his bro. the wheelwright,
> Wife of Wilhelm Schuler,
> Wife of Samuel Schuler,
> Mr. Schambach's second wife,
> Philip Wentz, Peter Wentz,
> H. Pannebeck, N Meyer,
> The two oldest daughters of Conrad Dotterer,
> J Schell, Michael Schell,
> Elisabeth Sell, Peter Sell,
> J Muller, Joseph Muller,
> The three daughters of Mr Hucken and a son,
> Paul Neiss, Benjamin Sommer,
> Samuel Somani, Anna Maria Hildebeidel

Parents	Children Date of Baptism	Witnesses
1757		
Michael Ried and Anna Maria	Anna Maria Dec 2	Daniel Hamm and wife
Michael Roeder and Catharina	Anna Maria Dec 2	A Margaretha Knauss
Carl Dorr and Christina	Ullrich Dec 4	Ullrich Greber and Anna Margaretha
Matthys Brickerdt and Maria Elisabetha	J Jacob Dec. 7	J Nicol Jung and wife
Andreas Ohl and Eva	Wilhelm Nov. 3	Wilhelm Horst, Susanna Horlacher
Jacob Meyer and Anna Meyer	Conrad Dec. 18	Conrad Hillikas and Creth Muller
Jacob Klotz and Sophia	Wendel Dec 24	Wendel Wigandt and his wife

New Goshenhoppen—Vol. I Baptisms

Parents	Children Date of Baptism	Witnesses
1758.		
Peter Bleyler and N*	Anna Maria Jan 1	J Bleyler and wife
Daniel Hucken and Magdalena	Maria Catharina Jan. 1	J Hucken
J. Adam Eckman and Christina	Maria Margaretha June 7	Friedrich Muller and wife
Jacob Isset and Anna Maria	Maria Catharina Jan 8	J Lee and wife
Philip Ried and Maria Elisabeth	Balthasar Jan 8	Balthasar Fritz and Maria B Fischer
J. Schmidt and Maria Elisa	J. Jacob Jan. 13	Jacob Wannenmacher and wife
Johannes Huth and Barbara	Johannes Jan 19	J. Huth and wife
J Adam Heckman and Anna Elisabetha	Christina Jan 20	Daniel Neidich and wife Anna Margaretha
Christian Setzman and Susanna	George Daniel Jan. 20	Georg Daniel Peiffer and Eva Muller
Daniel Muller and Anna Margaretha	J Daniel Jan 20	J Gallman and wife Catharina
Wendel Kuhner and Rosina Dorothea	Johannes Jan 20	J. Rood [Roth] and wife Anna Barbara
Abraham Driess and ———	Johannes Febr 4	J. Neidish and wife Elisabetha
J Scherer and Anna Margaretha	Maria Catharina Febr 14	J Gallman and wife Catharina
✓ Philip Boehm and ✓ Catharina	J Georg Febr. 23	J Georg Reider and wife Elisabetha
Walter Muller and Anna Maria	Anna Maria Febr. 23	Jacob Becker and wife Anna Maria
Caspar Hoffman and Dorothea	Samuel Febr 26	Samuel Lieser and Barbara Lieser
Andres Maurer and Anna Maria	Jacob and Anna Maria March 8	Jacob Mauerer
Friederick Wigerdt and Maria Eva	Anna Maria March 8	Andreas Mauerer
Peter Edelman and Maria Elisabetha	Maria Elisabetha March 11	J Georg Edelman and wife Maria Cath

*The letter N is used in German to indicate an unknown name

Parents	Children Date of Baptism	Witnesses
Bernhard Wannenmacher and wife Catharina	J. Casper March 11	J Caspar Brendt and wife
Jacob Morheadt and wife Anna	J Michel March 12	J. Michel Gressler and Elizabetha Lee
J Peter Nikum and Anna Maria	Anna Catharina March 17	Georg Zimmerman and Anna Catharine Zimmerman
Simon Hirsch and Anna Maria	Anna Margaretha March 24	Conrad Zimmerman and Anna Margaretha, his wife
Philip Gressler and Anna Margaretha	Maria Margaretha April 2	Michel Bastian and wife Philip Lee and wife
Christoffel Schuhmann and Maria Elisabetha	J Wilhelm April 10	J Wilhelm Geiger and wife Anna Maria
Philip Wendel and Maria Christina	Johannes April 23	J. Lee, Maria Catharine ——
Adam Bossert and Jacobina	J. Adam April 23	J. Adam Lautenschlager and wife
Michel Jo and ——	Veronica April 23	——
Peter Stadler and Catharina	Anna Margaretha April 30	J. Heil and wife
Rudy Huber and wife	J Huber May 6	Henrich Huber and wife
Hennerich Huber and wife Anna	Jacob May 6	Jacob Huber and wife
Christian Hagel and Susanna	Mathys May 14	Mathys and wife Elisabeth Barbara
✓ J Adam Hillikas and Catharina	Anna Margaretha May 15	Anna Margaretha Bitting
Jacob Weidknecht and Anna Margaretha	Jacob May 20	Jacob Funk and wife Anna
J Schmidt and Gertrudt	Wilhelm May 21	Wilhelm Schneider
Ullrich Spinner and Ursula	David May 28	David Streib and wife Susanna
Georg Schmidt and wife	Anna May 28	Henrich Huber and wife Anna

Parents	Children Date of Baptism	Witnesses
Henrich Huber and Susanna	Abraham May 28	Henrich Huber and wife Anna
Valadin Huber and Barbara	J Peter May 28	Peter Kuster and wife Dorothea
Andreas Mauerer and Barbara	J Jacob June 29	J Jacob Mauerer
Christian Rincker and Catharina	Maria Elisabeth July 3	Samuel Susseidt and Elisabetha Riess
Philip Schmidt and Anna Catharina	Maria Catharina July 3	J. Martin Derr, Anna Catharina Semm
Wilhelm ——(?)	Maria Sept 3	Elisabeth Liser
J Caspar Berendt and Elisa Lena	Johannes Sept 9	Joh. Schmidt and wife Maria Elisabetha
Weigandt Pannebeck and Nelche	—— Sept 3	Weigandt Panneback and wife
Jacob Hamm and Maria Barbara	Maria Catharina Sept 30	——
Michael Eberhardt and Anna	Barbara Oct 7	Felix Brunner and wife Barbara
Roland Jung and Catharina	J. Henrich Oct 13	Henrich Jung and Margaretha Fischer
Baltasar Stiel and Christina	Maria Elisabetha Nov. 12	Jacob Spinner and Maria Elisabeth Ziegenfuss
Jacob Ridy and Susunna	Susanna Nov 25	J Martin Reyer and Susanna Horlacher
J Leonhardt and wife	Elisabetha Nov 26	Andres Heisser and his sister
Jacob Schuster and wife	Andres Dec 4	——
Jost Schlicher and Catharina	Maria Margaretha Dec 4	Maria Gertraudt Neukerch
Adam Hocker and wife	Eva Margaretha Dec 10	Peter Beissel and wife
Georg Klein and Maria	Anna Sibilla Dec. 17	J Jerger and wife
Daniel Hamm and wife	Elisabeth Dec 25	Elisabeth Moll
Peter Lauer and wife	Peter Dec 25	Peter Reiff and wife

Parents	Children Date of Baptism	Witnesses
Isaak Somani with all his children	Anna Barbara Abraham Elisabetha Christian Catherina Dec 26	Susanna, wife of Christian Brobst (?)

1759.

Parents	Children Date of Baptism	Witnesses
Philip Heger and Anna Barbara	J. Philip Jan 1	Peter Christ and wife Catharina
Philip Huth and Anna Eva	J Jacob Jan. 12	Jacob Christman and wife Anna Eva
Feb. 3, was baptized	David Brunner's wife, Anna Maria	Her husband, David Brunner and J Brunner
Nicolaus Mombauer and wife	J Henrich Febr. 4	J Henrich Heiss and wife
Philip Jacob Egi and Catharina	J Georg Febr 18	Georg Heilig and wife Elisa Barbara
Johannes Huth and Anna Barbara	Anna Catharina Febr 24	Michael Roeder and wife Catharina
Leonhardt Fggelin and wife	Anna Margaretha March 4	J. Jost Keller and wife
Jacob Meyer and Anna	Eva Elisabeth March 4	Eva Eberhardt Lavar
Johannes Gotz and Anna Maria	Anna Margaretha March 4	——
Abraham Dauber and Anna Christina	Maria Catharina March 19	Peter Haas and wife Catharina
Peter Wetzel and Anna Margaretha	Johannes March 19	J. Wetzel
Martin Werffel and Ann Maria	Maria Barbara March 19	Maria Barb Rieser
March 22, were baptized by me, G. M. Weiss, upon their confession of faith,	Eva Meyer, Anna Meyer	
Henrich Van Sluys and Catharina	Daniel March 25	Daniel Hiester and wife Catharina
Johannes Schell and Veronica	J Jacob April 13	Jacob Mauerer and wife
Georg Zimmermann and Anna Catharina	J. Nicolaus April 16	Nicolaus Seibel and wife

Parents	Children Date of Baptism	Witnesses
Johannes Cunius and Catharina	J. Nicolaus April 16	Jacob Geri and wife
Johannes Frey and Elisa Barbara	Elisa Barbara April 16	Fridrich Hillikas and wife Elisa Barbara
Jacob Trolinger and Anna Maria	Anna Maria Catharina April 22	Peter Stroh and wife
Michael Lieser and Maria Elisabetha	Veronica Dorothea April 22	Caspar Hoffman and wife
April 20, David Levi went over from Judaism to Christianity, upon the profession of his faith in Jesus Christ and was baptized by me, G M Weiss	David Levi	
✓ Georg Peter Hillikas and Elisa Barbara	Friderich April 26	Fridrich Hillikas and wife Elisa Barbara
Johannes Derr and Anna Maria	J Georg April 29	—
Philip Lehmann and Anna Maria	Elisabetha May 6	—
Zacharias Ditterer and wife	Christina May 9	Jacob Wannenmacher and wife, also the parents of Zacharias Detterer
J. Jacob Reiniger and Anna Margaretha	J Jacob May 10	Jacob Wittmer and Maria Cath. May
Johannes Stab and Catharina	Anna Maria May 10	Benedict Strohm and wife Anna Maria
Hennerich Bleyler and Susanna	Abraham May 20	Peter Bleyler and wife Hanna
Johannes Martin and Anna Barbara	Samuel Christian Johannes May 25	Andreas Greber and wife Gertrudt Georg Peter Hillikas and wife Barbara Joh Gallman and wife Catharina
Philip Stein and Barbara	Johann Henrich May 27	Jacob Hoffman and wife Barbara

Parents	Children Date of Baptism	Witnesses
Johannes Neiss and Anna Maria	J. Georg May 27	J. Georg Weickerdt and wife Magdalena
Jacob Geri and Gertraudt	Johannes June 3	Fridrich Helwig and wife Magdalena
Jacob Klein and Anna Maria	Anna Barbara June 17	Anna Barbara Sieber
Gabriel Klein and Elisabeth Dorothea	Ludwig June 24	Ludwig Bitting and Anna Sabina
Matthys Bruckerdt and Maria Elisa	J. Henrich June 24	J Nicolaus Jung and wife Anna Gertraudt
J. Georg and Maria Catharina	Elisabetha June 24	Melchior Sussholtz and wife Elisabetha
Jost Keller and Margaretha	Jacob July 8	—
Henrich Buhl and Susanna	Henrich July 8	—
Michael Schmidt and Anna Maria	J. Jacob July 29	Jacob Isset and wife Magdalena
Henrich Keppel and Margaretha Elisa	J Henrich July 29	J. Jacob Werner and wife Catharina
J Carl Derr and Christina	J. Martin July 29	J. Martin Derr and Anna Clara Hinterleiter
Jacob Weidknecht and Anna Margaretha	Johannes Martin Aug 5	—
Jost Weigardt and Barbara	Johannes August 5	Johannes Derr and wife Anna Maria
Jacob Pfannenbecker and Christina	Jacob Aug 19	Conrad Seeler and Anna Susanna Dotter
Jacob Hildenbeitel and wife	Johannes Aug 19	Johannes Klein and wife
Ulrich Greber and Anna Margaretha	Anna Maria Aug. 26	Andreas Greber and wife Anna Maria
Michael Schell and Catharina	Anna Catharina Aug. 26	Jacob Griesemer and wife Anna Catharina
Nicolaus Ohl and Anna Margaretha	J Henrich Sept 16	Henrich Muller and wife Anna Gertraudt
Johannes Sperri and Maria Margaretha	Johannes Sept. 23	—

Parents	Children Date of Baptism	Witnesses
Johannes Diebendorfer and wife	Johannes Sept. 23	Henrich Muller and Anna Gertraudt
Abraham Segler and wife	Johannes Oct 7	Johannes Segler
Peter Linn and Anna Margaretha	Theobald Oct. 14	Theobald Meglin and wife Elisabeth
Henrich Grub and Adelheid	Anna Catharina Oct 14	Henrich Huber and wife Catharina
J Lee and Margaretha	Elisabeth Oct 21	Alexander Negeley and Elisaoeth Rieder
Samuel Schuler and wife	——— Oct 21	Kilian Gaukler and wife Margaretha
Melchior Kolb and Catharina	Anna Catharina Oct 26	Anna Catharina Weber
Peter Nicum and Anna Maria	Philip Oct 27	J Philip Boehm and wife Catharina J Nicol. Nicum and Anna Marg. Wingerd
Abraham Herp and Gertrudt	Abraham Oct 28	Jacob Walter and wife Rosina
Jacob Walter and Rosina	Jacob Oct 28	Abraham Herp and wife Gertrudt
Peter Stro[h] and Anna Maria	Catharina Oct 28	Catharina Moll
Jacob Fischer and Hanna	Johannes Oct. 28	Johannes Fischer and wife Catharina
Johann Michel Hartman and Anna Margaretha	Dillo Jacob Nov 4	J. Jacob Holtzhauser and Anna Marg Redmann
Samuel Hirsch and wife Anna Maria	J Henrich Nov 4	J Henrich Hirsch and Maria Marg Scholl
Peter Stadler and Catharine	Eva Catharina Nov 5	Melchior Kolb and wife Eva Catharina
Andreas Ohl and Anna Eva	Andreas Nov 12	J Wilhelm and Eva Ried
J. Adam Hillikas and Catharina	J Peter Nov 28	Georg Peter Hillikas and wife Barbara
Andreas Greber and Anna Maria	Anna Margaretha Dec 16	Ulrich Greber and Anna Margaretha
J Martin and Anna Barbara	J Michel and Eva Catharina Dec. 24	Michael Roeder and wife Catharina

Parents.	Children Date of Baptism	Witnesses
1760.		
J Kunerdt and Agnes Barbara	Fridrich Jan. 5	Fridrich Schmilin (?)
Michael Bischoff and Maria Eva	Barbara Jan. 6	Michel Eberhardt and wife
Joseph Eberhardt and Catharina	Anna Margaretha Febr 17	Peter Wetzel and wife Margaretha
Bastian Ruf and Susanna	Anna Maria Febr. 17	Georg Adam Sangmeister and wife
Johannes Muck and Elisabetha	Catharina March 1	Nicolaus Wohlfaht and wife Catharina
Adam Darms (?) and Anna Margaretha	J Peter March 2	J. Peter Wetzel and wife Anna Margaretha
Peter Hollenbusch and Anna Maria	Maria Catharina Febr 24	Henrich Beyer and wife Mary Magdalena
Wilhelm Geyer and Anna Maria	Johan Michel March 23	J. Michael Reiffschneider and wife Juliana
Jacob Berger and Barbara	Andreas March 25	Andreas Beyer and wife Gertrudt
J. Gotz and Anna Maria	Georg Fridrich April 6	Fridrich Wambold and wife Catharina
Benedict Swob and Susanna	—— April 7	J Georg Welcker and wife
Philip Boehm and Catharina	J Jacob May 11	Conrad Zimmermann and wife Anna Margaretha
Thomas Gant and Margaretha	Maria Eva May 11	J Adam Willauer and wife Anna Maria
Henrich Huber and wife	Catharina May 30	Henrich Huber and wife
Peter Lahb and Creth [Margaret]	—— May 4	——
Conrad Biehn (?) and Sophia Magdalena	Nicolaus May 4	Nicolaus Finck and wife Maria Elisabetha
Michael Roeder and Catharina	——	Johann Arend Weiss and wife
Jacob Isset and Magdalena	Elisabetha June 8	Daniel Hister and wife Catharina

New Goshenhoppen—Vol. I. Baptisms

Parents	Children Date of Baptism	Witnesses
Christoffel Peirmann and Catharina	Jacob June 8	Jacob Muller and wife Catharina
Michael Jo and Veronica	—— June 8	Peter Jo and Maria Hoffmann
Johann Jacob Mohrhed and Anna	—— June 8	Adam Hollenbusch and Maria Marg Hoost
Peter Sell and Catharina	Johannes June 15	Johannes Fischer and wife Catharina
Rutolf Frick and Veronica	Matheis June 22	Mathys Scheiffeli and wife Gretha
Stephan Schoner and Christina	Ulrich July 4	Ulrich Hertzel and wife
✓ Conrad Hillikas and Maria Margaretha	Johannes July 13	Johannes Schellenberger and wife
J Nicolaus Walber and Elisabeth	Susanna July 10	David Streib and wife Elisabetha
J Nicolaus Walber and Elisabeth	Elisabetha July 10	David Gissi and wife Elisabetha
Salomo Sell and Sophia	Anna Margaretha and Elisabetha July 27	Anna Marg Bitting
Benjamin Sommer and Catharina	J Ludwig Aug 3	J Ludwig Lang and wife Elisabetha
Henrich Muller and Gertraudt	Anna Elisabetha Aug 3	Jacob Danckel and wife Elisabeth
Georg Lauer and Barbara	Anna Barbara Aug 3	Christian Muller and wife Anna Barbara
Johannes Freyer and Babara	Georg Jacob Aug 10	Georg Peter Hillikas and wife Barbara
Michael Ried and Anna Maria	Elisabeth Aug 17	Jacob Maurer and Elisabeth Ried
Johannes Schmidt and Anna Gertraudt	Johann Henrich Aug 17	J Henrich Mincker and Eva Meyer
Jacob Wetzel and wife	Jacob Aug 24	Jacob Wetzel, Sr, and wife
J. Henrich Ott and Catharina	Anna Margaretha Aug 24	J. Georg Ziegenfuss and wife, Anna Margaretha
Conrad Ludwig and Anna Appollonia	Elisabeth Sept 7	Henrich Moll and wife Elisabeth
Peter Mauerer and Maria Margaretha	Anna Sept. 7	Mattheus Mauerer and wife Anna Berends

Parents	Children Date of Baptism	Witnesses.
Michael Hettenbach and Catharina	Wilhelm and Peter Oct. 2	Wilhelm Geiger and wife Anna Maria Peter Michael Schlonecker and wife Anna Maria
Wilhelm Dickenschitt and Catharina	Margaretha Oct 12	Christoffel Dickenschitt and Maria Margaretha
Johannes Fischer and wife	—— Oct 19	——
Jacob Huber and Catharina Elisabetha	J Jacob Oct 26	Paul Samsel and wife Margaretha
Ullrich Greber and Margaretha	Sara Oct. 26	Sara Lawar
Johannes Danckel and Lenche [Nelly]	Johann Jacob Dec. 21	Jacob Dankel and wife Elisabeth
Johannes Zeller and Anna Maria	Catharina Dec 21	J. Gallman and wife Catharina
Johannes Wien and Appollonia	Margaretha Dec 25	Margaretha Moll

1761.

Parents	Children Date of Baptism	Witnesses.
Georg Peter Hillikas and Barbara	A. Catharina Jan 29	J Adam Hillikas and wife Catharina
Philip Jacob Egi and Gertraudt	Elisa Barbara Febr. 1	Georg Heilig and wife Barbara
Abraham Friess and Anna Margaretha	J Leonhardt Febr 9	J. Leonhardt Neudig
Adam Neudig and Anna Barbara	Anna Barbara Febr 9	Daniel Neudig and wife Anna Margaretha
Wendel Renninger and Anna Margaretha	Anna Margaretha Febr 22	Peter May and wife Juliana
Mathys Brickerdt and Maria Gertraudt	Andreas Febr. 22	Andreas Jung and Elisa Barb Wannemacher
Jacob Weidknecht and Susanna Margaretha	Anna Maria Febr 22	Jacob Ratzel and wife Maria
Georg Reinheimer and Maria Catharina	Maria Margaretha Elisa March 21	Lorentz Sussholtz and Anna Marg. Elisa Reiffschneider
Joseph Eberhardt and wife	Johann Benjamin March 22	Michael Eberhardt and wife

New Goshenhoppen—Vol. I. Baptisms 299

Parents	Children Date of Baptism	Witnesses
Michel Eberhardt and wife	Johannes March 22	Michael Bischoff and wife
Michael Scheib and Anna Barbara	Anna Maria March 29	Johannes Gotz and wife Maria
Christian Scheid and Maria Elisa	Johann Georg March 29	Joh Georg Loness and wife Catharina Elisa
Jacob Daub and Elisabetha	Jacob April 5	Jacob Wigandt and Susanna Roder
Jost Schlicher and Catharina	J Georg April 5	J Georg Schlicher
J. Jacob Dankel and Elisabetha	J Henrich April 5	J. Henrich [Dankel] and wife Gertraudt
Jacob Ridi and Susanna	Anna Margaretha April 9	Jacob Lang and wife Anna Margaretha
Joh Philip Schmidt and Catharine	Johann Philip April 19	Johann Martin Derr and wife Maria Gertraudt
Johann Huth and Maria Barbara	Eva Margaretha April 24	Jacob Christmann and wife Eva Margaretha
Simon Hirs and Anna Maria	Simon April 25	Henrich Mathys and Veronica
Ludwig Hirs and Catharina	Anna Maria April 25	Peter Scholl and wife Anna Maria
Michael Roder and Catharina	Peter April 26	Peter Hillikas and √ wife Barbara
Caspar Hoffmann and Dorothea	Anna Eva April 26	J Ulrich Kuhl and Eva Lieser
Theobald Breuchler and Maria	Barbara Elisa May 3	——
Felix Linn and Jacobina	Peter May 3	Peter Wetzel and wife Catharina
Adam Bosserdt and Jacobina	Anna Elisabetha May 10	Andreas Ohl and wife Anna Elisabetha
✓ J Adam Hillikas and Catharina	Anna Christina May 10	Henrich Funck and wife Anna Christina
Henrich Laba[r] and Elisabetha	Leonhardt May 10	Leonhardt Beyer and Elisabeth Fux
Philip Ried and Anna Elisabetha	J. Philip May 10	J Philip Fischer and wife Philipina
Michael Raudenbusch and Anna Maria	Henrich June 7	Henrich Hoffman and Cath Raudenbusch

Parents	Children Date of Baptism	Witnesses
Georg Zimmermann and Anna Catharina	Maria Elisabetha June 7	Maria Elisabetha ——
Michael Lieser and wife	Johannes June 7	Johannes Keck and wife
Jost Keller and Margaretha	Maria June 21	J Nicolaus Schneider and Maria Gerkess
Peter Sell and Catharina	Anna Margaretha June 28	Anna Marg Welcker
Peter Lauer and Sara	Catharina June 28	Johannes Cunius and wife Catharina
Philip Heist and Susanna	Anna Elisabetha July 4	J. Nicolaus Heist and wife Elisabetha
Henrich Bleyler and Susanna	Anna Maria July 6	Anna Maria Bleyler
Michael Resch and Anna	—— July 6	J Sparri and wife Anna Margaretha
Jacob Meyer and Anna	Anna Barbara July 12	J Martin and wife Anna Barbara
Gerhardt Stricker and Catharina	Catharina July 12	Valentin Neugisser and wife Catharina
Isaac Somani and Magdalena	Eva Elizabetha July 12	Andreas Ohl and wife
Paul Schwenger and Barbara	Nicolaus July 12	J Bisecker and wife Christina
Philip Huth and Eva	J Stoffel July 19	J Stoffel Weiss and wife
J Stab and Catharina	Maria Margaretha July 19	Jacob Wittmer and wife
Christoffel Heisser and Barbara	Barbara July 26	J. Georg Lauer
Philip Becker and Maria	Maria Magdalena July 26	J. Michael Bastian and wife Magdalena
Weigandt Pannenbecker and Nelche [Nelly]	Elisabeth Aug 9	Melchior Süssholtz and wife Elisabeth
Peter Stro[h] and Maria	Henrich Aug 9	Henrich Schwalbach
J Cunius and Catharina Elisa	Anna Margaretha Aug 9	J Adam Dillo and wife Anna Margaretha
Caspar Bucher and Catharina	Maria Elisa Aug 9	J Schmidt and wife Maria Elisabetha

New Goshenhoppen—Vol. I. Marriages

[The foregoing 240 baptisms were entered by Rev. G. M Weiss. He died in August, 1761 See the history above, p 171 It is not known who officiated at the two following baptisms]

Andreas Graber and Anna Maria	Henrich Sept 16	Henrich Bitting
Jost Wiandt and Barbara	Anna Maria Oct 7	Anna Maria Wiand

[VI MARRIAGES BY REV GEORGE MICHAEL WEISS, 1747-1761.]

THOSE PERSONS WHO FROM THE YEAR 1747 TO THE YEAR 1758 HAVE BEEN MARRIED BY ME, GEORGE MICHAEL WEISS, V.D M.

[1] John Neiss and Catharina Hahn
[2] George Neiss and Anna Dotter
[3] Jacob Arend and Anna Elizabeth Geiger
[4] Abraham Arend and Catharina Ried
[5] J. George Leidich and Catharina Arend
[6] John Schicher and Catharina N——
[7] John Gressman and widow Hauk
[8] John Gressman's son and ——
[9-10] John Gressman's two daughters and ——
[11] Jacob Ried and Magdalena Leidich
[12] J Zirkel and N——
[13] Benedict Schwob and Susanna Welcker
[14] Dietrich Welcker and Sara de Haven
[15] Philip Wentz and daughter of Ulrich Hartman of Schipbach
[16] Stoffel Wagner and second daughter of Bastian Schmid of Schipbach
[17] J Breneman and N——
[18] Benjamin Sommer and Anna Maria Scholl
[19] J Denig and Elizabeth Eichel
[20] Jacob Riedi and Susanna Gucker
[21] Andreas Ohl and Eva Gucker
[22] Peter Beissel and Maria Schwenk
[23] N Ohl and Elisa Barbara Gucker
[24] Michel Welcker and Anna Maria Ried
[25] Theobald Wink and Cretha Ried
[26] J. Adam N and Maria Magdalena Beissel
[27] Michel Ried and Anna Maria Mauer
[28] Michel Schell and Catharina Lauer
[29] John Schell and Veronica Mauer
[30] David Haag and Elisa Catharina Wagenseil
[31] Melchior Schultz and Catharina Kahlbach
[32] Adam Hillikas and Catharina Bitting

[33] Peter Hillikas and Barbara Hornberger
[34] Philip Huth and Eva Weiss
[35] John Huth and Barbara Zimmerman
[36] J. Arendt Weiss and Susanna Huth
[37] Georg Schley and Catharina N——
[38] Caspar Berend and Elisa Lena Wannenmacher
[39] Hennerich Berendt and Anna Maria Luer
[40] Harmon Luer and Katharina Kieffer
[41] J Luer and Barbara Weber
[42] Jacob Fischer and Hannah Dankler
[43] Roland Jung and Catharina Fischer
[44] Henrich Haas and N Jung
[45] J Huebner and Anna Dotter
[46] Jacob Zimmerman and Sophia Wigand
[47] Abraham Segler and Barbara Moll
[48] Henrich, a blacksmith, and Elizabeth Moll
[49] Daniel Hamm and Anna Maria Segler
[50] Wendel Lemli and Scharl M Wigand
[51] Jacob Weidknecht and Creth [Margaret] Boehm
[52] Antoni Hamser and Anna Marg. Raudenbusch
[53] Benedict Strohm and Anna Maria N——
[54] Andreas Mauerer and Maria Barbara Steinman
[55] Paulus Rothaermel and Maria Cretha Mauer
[56] J Schmidt and Gentrude N——
[57] Leonhardt Griesemer and N. Leveber
[58] Georg Lauer and Maria Barbara N——
[59] Michel Roeder and Catharina Erb
[60] Henrich Lobach and Margaretha Roeder
[61] Michel Stab and Catharina N——
[62] Mathys Reicherdt and Creth Hillikas
[63] Nicolaus Jeger and Anna Hillikas
[64] J Kiefer and Barbara Hillikas
[65] Wilhelm Gedman and Susanna Jekel
[66] Andres Greber and Anna Maria Bitting
[67] Ulrich Greber and Creth Labar
[68] Peter Laub and Creth Muss
[69] Carl Doerr and Christina Muss
[70] John Dankel and N——
[71] Hennerich Mueller and Gertrudt Diefendoerffer
[72] Nicolaus Ohl and Anna Marg Diefendoerffer
[73] Gabriel Klein and Elisabetha Dorothea Bitting
[74] Alexander Dieffendoerffer and Gertrude N. [Leidig]
[75] Fridrich Lang and N Scholl
[76] Christian Mueller and Elisabeth Wetzler
[77] Jacob N—— and Veronica Wetzler
[78] J. Haag and Anna Marg. Wetzler

[79] Peter Wetzel and Creth Eberhard
[80] J Mecklin and Creth Kehler
[81] N. Weitzel and Barbara Kehler
[82] Andreas Muehlschlagel and Anna Maria Emet
[83] Henrich Kumpf and Catharina Emet
[84] Michel Eberhardt and Catharina Bleyler
[85] Peter Bleyler and Hannah N——
[86] Philip Vackenthal and Elisabeth Bleyler
[87] Ulrich Hornecker and Barbara Eberhard
[88] Ulrich Hornecker and Creth Eberhard
[89] Valentin Keiser and Barbara Huber
[90] H Heger and Eva Huber
[91] N—— and Creth Huber
[92] Nicolaus Mombauer and Magdalena N——
[93] J Adam N—— and Creth Hitz
[94] Jacob Huber and Elisabetha Samsel
[95] Henrich Huber and Barbara N
[96] Philip Schmidt and Creth Doerr
[97] J. Goetz and Catharina N.
[98] N Zimmermann and Jacob Hoffman's daughter
[99] N Zimmermann and Jacob Hoffman's daughter
[100] Of the Henerichs in Schipbach several have intermarried
[101] J. Oftengraff (Op ten Graf) and N Oftengraf
[102] Abraham, a tailor, and N Hamman
[103] Henrich Bartholome and Elisa Barbara Erb
[104] J Reiswick and Creth Erb
[105] N Dickenschitt and N——
[106] Henrich Frey and N——
[107] J Schmidt and N——
[108] Conrad Moll and Elisa Barbara Hill
[109] Georg Weidner and Catharina Moll
[110] N—— and Anna Marg Moll
[111] Diel Neiss and N Hahn
[112] Salomon Rockenstuhl and widow of Grossjockel
[113] J Adam Schneider and N. Levan
[114] J. Brobst and Jacob Levan's oldest daughter
[115] Ludwig Workman and Catharina Braun
[116] Richardt Klein and Elisabeth Horneck
[117] Georg Hertzel and Catharina Neiss
[118] Andreas Workman and Catharina Frey
[119] Mathys Brickerdt and Maria Elisabetha N
[120] Andres Niet and Catharina N
[121] Georg Edelman and N——
[122] J. Mueller and N——
[123] Marcus Wannenmacher and N——
[124] J. Schmidt and Anna Margaretha N——
[125] Lorentz Bamberger and Scharlotta N——
[126] J Kugeler and Catharina Bamberger

[127] Jacob Hildenbeitel and Anna Maria N——
[128] J. Button and N Klein
[129] Widow Fried and her servant
[130] Simon Hirsch and Maria Elisabeth Lawar
√ [131] Philip Boehm and Elisabeth Cath Mombauer
[132] Philip Jans and Barbara Detweiler
[133] Jost Keller and Hannah N
[134] Johannes Schneider and Catharina Dieringer
√ [135] Johannes Jost and Creth Schneider
[136] J Koster and John Johnson's daughter
[137] N—— and Bastian Schmidt's daughter of Schipbach
[138] N—— and Brenneman's daughter of Schipbach
[139] Georg Meyer and Weideman's oldest daughter
[140] Philip Henrich's second son and N. Johnson
[141] J Georg Linckheimer and N——
√ [142] Jacob Schaefer and Catharina, widow of Henrich Bitting
[143] Abraham Schreiner and Anna Maria Schmid
[144] Samuel Somani and N Greff.
[145] N Henrichs and N. Gottschalk
[146] N—— and a daughter of the young Gottschalk
[147] N—— and a daughter of the young Gottschalk
[148] 1 Son of Leonhardt Hennerichs and daughter of Paul Hennerichs

[149] 2 Son of Leonhardt Hennerichs and daughter of Paul Hennerichs
[150] 3 Son of Leonhardt Hennerichs and N——
[151] Son of Paul Hennerichs and daughter of John Frey
[152] N—— and daughter of Christian Weber of Madetschi
[153] Son of Kaiser of Madetschi and N——
[154] N—— and daughter of Jost Becker
[155] Son of John Frey and daughter of Paul Hennerichs
[156] Son of Felix Lee and N——
[157] Servant of Uly Stauffer and his maid servant
[158] N—— and daughter of W Keiber
[159] N—— and oldest daughter of Mathys Ochs
[160] N. Obenbeck of Cockscreek and N
[161] J Weitzel and daughter of John Gressman
[162] John, son of Philip Zimmer and daughter of Kilian Zimmerman
[163] Son of Lorentz Hennerichs and N Gottschalck
[164] Third son of Lorentz Hennerichs and N—— of Madetschi
[165] W Weitzel and N—— of Dinikum
[166] Henrich Gremmeling and Catharina, stepdaughter of Georg Heilig
[167] N—— and Catharina, daughter of Philip Zimmer

New Goshenhoppen—Vol. I. Marriages 305

[168] N—— and daughter of Kilian Zimmerman
[169] J. Weiss and N——
[170] Jacob N—— and Anna Weiss
[171] N—— and N. Weiss
[172] Henrich N—— and Anna Maria Gemehli
[173] Henrich Huber and Christina N——
[174] Caspar Huber and Anna N——
[175] N. Weiss and N——, widow living at Hosensack
[176] J Schlosser and N——
[177] Thomas Koch and N——
[178] Abraham Lucken and Margareth Frey
[179] J. Hoffman and Catharina Zimmerman
[180] Caspar Hoffman and Dorothea Lieser
[181] Henrich Schmidt and Rachel Denny
[182] J. Seller and Nany Johnson
[183] Baltasar Rabanus and Elisabetha Kremer
[184] Christian Buhler and Sarah Huntzberger
[185] Melchior Schultz and Catharina Kohlbeck

1758.

[186] Jan 7, J. Adam Eckman and Christina N——
[187] Jan 26, Balthasar Stiel and Christina Wickerd
[188] Jan 26, Johann Jacob Mueller and Margaretha Eckerd
[189] Febr 7, Johann Schwenck and Anna Cath. Christ Huber
[190] March 6, J. Martin Mueller and Catharina Gruen
[191] March 30, Matthys Rittenhausen and Catharina Von Vasen
[192] March 28, Georg Schill and Eva Merg Kraessler
[193] March 4, Philip Heiss and Susana Schmid
[194] March —, J. Jacob Huber and Anna Cath. Kehler
[195] March 26, Wilhelm Mueller and Catharina Schultz
[196] April 20, Joseph Schmidt and Catharina Frey
[197] April 18, Johan Adam Willauer and Anna Maria Linn
[198] April 11, Johan Peter Seib and Anna Maria Erb
[199] May 2, Georg Reinheimer and Maria Cath Suessholtz
[200] May 30, David Brunner and Maria Landess
[201] June 6, Paul Schwanger and Barbara Biseker
[202] June 27, David Schultz and Elisabetha Lar
[203] July 15, Henrich Fritz and Maria Anders (?)
[204] Sept. 26, Mathys Kern and Veronica Weidman
[205] Oct 19, Georg Gargwehr and Maria Melchior
[206] Nov. 14, Andres Beyer and Philippina Wigand

1759.

[207] Jan 4, Wendel Reiniger and Anna Marg. Mey
[208] Jan 9, Joh Christ Kahlbach and Anna Cath Fabian
[209] Jan 18, Jacob Griesemer and Catharina Hahlmann

[210] Jan 27, Valladin [Valentin] Schillig and Maria Elis Moll
[211] April 3, Joseph Eberhardt and Catharina Siegel
[212] April 5, Henrich Huber and Anna Cath. Huber
[213] April 17, Jacob Beyer and Anna Maria Worth
[214] April 15, J Zeller and Anna Barbara Jeckels
[215] April 20, Sylvanus Mabury and Le Miatta de Blema (?)
[216] June 26, Andreas Haag and Christina Hinderleiter
[217] Aug. —, Peter Sell and N—— Allwein
[218] Sept. 27, Peter Mauerer and C. Berst
[219] Oct 9, Peter Kumpf and Eva Elisabetha Kiefer
[220] Oct 8, Johan Fischer and Catharina Gabel
[221] Oct 26, Jacob Wetzel and Anna Maria Hag
[222] Oct. 23, Peter Weber and Anna Marg. Kayser
[223] Nov. 13, Johannes Wiehn and Appolonia Moll
[224] Nov 18, Daniel Gicherdt and Barbara Mosser (?)
[225] Nov 20, Peter Samsel and Maria Catharina Sem
[226] Dec 18, Henrich Jacob Rauch and Magdalena Kierner
1760
[227] Jan 8, Ludwig Bieder (?) and Margaretha Fischer
[228] Feb 5, Johannes Meyer and Esther Contir
[229] Febr 26, Michael Roeder and Barbara Meyer
[230] Febr 28, Wilhelm Rittenhaus and Margaretha Umstett
[231] March 25, Hartman Leibenguth and Anna Barbara Hornberger
[232] April 15, Johann Michel Seib and Anna Barbara Eidel
[233] April 17, Jacob Kuester and Elisabeth von Vossen
[234] (?), J Georg Lahr and Catharina Fink
[236] Oct 28, J Christian Scheitt and Maria Elis. May
[237] Nov 25, Philip Lahi and Elisabeth Mack
[238] Nov 25, J Henrich Stedler and Anna Catharina Mack
[239] Nov 26, Johann Fridrich Reiss, Lutheran minister at New Goshenhoppen, and N——
[240] June 17, Johann Jacob Dankel and Elisabeth Roeder
[241] June 19, Simon Conrad Grineus and Anna Marg Rab
[242] Oct 14, Casper Bucher and Catharina Wannenmacher
[243] Dec 14, Johann Michael Hettenbach and Anna Maria Dahl
[244] Nov 25, Johannes Mauerer and Anna Marg Ohl
1761
[245] May 12, Johann Philip Dosch and Veronica Eberhard
[246] May 12, Georg Fischer and Anna Barbara Eberhard
[247] May 19, Johannes Wetzel and Eva Meyer
[248] May 13, Philip Hahn and Anna Marg Hiester
[249] June 16, Johannes Eberhardt and Cath Elisabetha Ried

[VII CATECHUMENS OF THE REV. GEO. M WEISS, 1748-1761]

From the year 1748 to the year 1758 the following persons have been admitted to the Holy Communion for the first time by me, George Michael Weiss, V D M [Verbi Divini Minister]

Jacob Ried
Catharina Ried
Jacob Schneider
Sara Schneider
Veronica Schneider
Creth Schneider ✓
Susanna Schneider
Anna Maria Moy
J Moy
Anna Maria Hiester
Anna Maria Wegelin
Elisabetha Wegelin
Sara Gerkess
Elisabetha Gerkess
Hoffman's five oldest daughters
Philip Zimmer's sons
David and a daughter
Elisabetha Ried
Anna Maria Ried
Eva Ried
Sophia Mauer[er]
Veronica Mauer[er]
Barbara Mauer[er]
Jacob Mauerer
Andreas Mauerer
Jacob Mauerer
Mathys Mauerer
Peter Mauerer
Rudolf Mauerer
John Mauerer
Maria Eva Mauerer
John Mauerer
Elisabetha Mack
Catharina Mack
Creth Mack
Creth Fischer
John Fischer

J. Georg Fischer
Sophia Wigandt
Philipina Wigandt
Daniel Schwartz's two oldest daughters
Cath Holtzhacker
Barbara Moll
Elisabetha Moll
Cretha Moll
C. Moll
Stoffel Moll
Michel Moll
Andreas Jung
J Wannenmacher
Anna Lena Wannenmacher
Elisa Barbara Wannenmacher
Philip Berendt
Michael Kolb
Joseph Kolb
Andres Holtzhauser
Jacob Holtzhauser
Creth Holtzhauser
Michel Roeder
Maria Creth Roeder
Catharina Roeder
Elisabetha Roeder
J Wendel
Georg Peter Hillikas
Conrad Hillikas
Barbara Hillikas
Philip Huth
John Huth
Elisabetha Schmid
Henrich Rauch
Elis Christman
Susanna Christman
Maria Barbara Steinmann

Creth Welcker
John Welcker
Catharina Stapp
Creth Fink
Elisabetha Fink
Catharina Berendt
Anna Maria Lur
Barbara Lur
The three oldest daughters of the old Steinman
Barbara Steinman
Elisabetha Steinman
Catharina Steinman
N Jung, daughter of H Jung
Catharina Wannenmacher
J. Wilhelm Beissel
Maria Magdalena Beissel
J. Ried
Elisa Barbara Gucker
Eva Gucker
Susanna Gucker
Philip Boehm
Creth Boehm
Ludwig Hersch
Henrich Hersch
Creth, maid servant of Reider's
J. Leonhardt N——
Creth Mueller
Christina Muss
Ludwig Bitting
Henrich Bitting
Anton Bitting
Anna Maria Bitting
Elisabetha Bitting
Anna Marg Dieffendoerffer
Gertrudt Dieffendoerffer
Godfried Dieffendoerffer
J. Dieffendoerffer
Elisabetha Rieser
Maria Elisa Rieser
Valentin Kaiser
Anna Maria Kaiser
Barbara Kaiser

Anna Maria Linn
Catharina Eib
Elis. Barbara Erb
Creth Erb
Eva Erb
Lorentz Erb
Caspar Erb
Ludwig Erb
Joseph Eberhard's five sons
Joseph Eberhard's five daughters
Michel Eberhard's daughter
Hennerich Bleiler
Michel Bleiler
Peter Bleiler
Elisabetha Bleiler
Catharina Bleiler
Hanna, Peter Bleiler's wife
Susanna, H Bleiler's wife
J Siegel
Ullerich Spinner's son
Creth Huber
Susanna Cath Huber
J Huber
Michel Huber
J. Jacob Dandel
J Dandel
Hanna Dandler
Anna Marg Dandler
Michel Raudenbusch
Peter Raudenbusch
Georg M Raudenbusch
David Raudenbusch
Jacob Wetzel's three daughters
Jacob Wetzel's two sons
M. Kehler's two daughters
M. Kehler's son
Scharlotta Heid
Eva Herd
Grossjockel's son
Grossjockel's daughter
Creth Willauer
Anna Maria Willauer
J. Adam Willauer

Anna Maria, maid servant of Conrad Zimmermann
Johannes Dubs
Peter Lauer
Georg Lauer
Elisabeth Zimmermann
Veronica Zimmermann
Catharina Zimmermann
Michel Zimmermann
J. Zimmermann
Peter Scholl's two oldest daughters
Kilian Russ
Georg Russ
Elisabetha Russ
Balthasar Lamper's sister's daughters, Elisabetha, Barbara
Sebastian Schmid's son
Sebastian Schmid's three daughters
Jacob Bruner
David Bruner
J. Bruner
Andres Beyer's son
Andres Beyer's daughter
The old Dreher's two sons
The old Dreher's daughter
Creth May
Catharina May
J Faust
N Faust
Ulrich Herzel's six sons
Kilian Zimmerman's three daughters
Cath. Huber
Maria Barbara Huber
Elisabeth Brand
Catharina Brand
Maria Cath. Suessholtz
Cath Schroemling
J Goetz and his wife
J Georg Steinman
Stoffel Walberdt
Catharina Moll
Conrad Moll

Henrich Bingeman
Gertraudt Bingeman
Elisabeth Lawar
Margaretha Lawar
J. Kunius
Abraham Ditloh and wife
Henrich Mombauer
Elisa Cath Mombauer
Abraham Faust's son
Hitz's second daughter
Samsel's two sons
Samsel's daughter
Catharina Mack
J Stab
Leonhard Griesemer's wife
J Denich
C Lutz
Philip Henrich N——'s three sons
Jost Keller
Barbara Sem
Henrich Arndt
Sophia Dotter
Anna Dotter
Catharina Hahn
Nany Dotter
Christian Lehmann's three sons
Christian Lehmann's daughter
Andres Weiss's two daughters
N. Herp and wife
Jacob Gruben's daughter
Anna Maria Emet
Christiana Emet
Catharina Emet
Georg Emet
Jacob Danner's four sons
J Danner's daughter
Michael Stepp's wife
Catharina Lauer
Henrich Mueller
Conrad Huth
Conrad Huth's two sisters
Peter Stedler
Susanna Stedler

Anna Marg Stedler
Michael Burkardt
J Adam Burkardt
Christian Lawer
Abraham Schellhammer
Catharina Schellhammer
Mr Haack of Maxatani, three daughters and son
Jacob Hildenbeitel and wife
Handwerk's wife
Henrich Eckman
Elisabetha Lichter
J Herp
Andres Herp and wife
Catharina Hilli
Adam Hilli
Catharina Dieringer
Manenschmidt's wife of Maxatani
Son of Mr Kutz of Maxatani
Eva Lehmann
Jacob Weidman's sister
Peter Beissel's servant Jacob
Ulrich Hartman's of Schipbach two daughters
Catharina Bitting and her sister
Maria Schmid
W Keiber's two daughters
1758
Alexander Diebendoerffer
Philip Bitting
Felix Linn
Susanna Cath Roeder
Anna Maria Schambach
J Georg Fischer
Anna Marg. Fischer
Johannes Fischer
Barbara Moll
Elisabetha Moll
Catharina Moll
Apollonia Moll
Stoffel Moll
Henrich Moll
Peter Moll

Elisabetha Mack
Catharina Mack
Anna Maig Mack
Anna Marg Welcker
John Welcker
Maria Cath Suessholtz
1759
Andres Ried
Michel Hillikas
Johannes Hillikas
Elisabetha Bankens
Joh. Steinman
Cath Schmid
Anna Maria Rieser
John Peter Eberhardt
Anna Cath. Siegel
Maria Elisa Fink
Catharina May
Eva Meyer
J. Georg Mack
Anna Maria Mack
Elisabetha Kolb
Elisabeth Mauerer
Anna Marg. Mauerer
Anna Maria Mauerer
Catharina Mauerer
Jacob Segler
Johannes Segler
1761
Jacob Becker
Jacob Wigandt
Peter Pannebeck
Georg Kolb
Michael Kolb
Jacob Welcker
Nicholaus Nickum
Anna Maria Pannebeck
Marg Suessholtz
Anna Maria Geri
Anna Sophia Ludwig
Sophia Fischer
Barbara Lawar
Anna Maria Weber

Anna Marg. Aleigod (?)
J. Lee
Johannes Huester
Daniel Huester
Benjamin Schueler
Catharina Zimmerman
Conrad Leydich
Susanna Mack
Jacob Becker
Anna Maria Mombauer

Elisabetha Fink
C Faust
Jacob Bischoff
Susanna Bischoff
N Bischoff
J Peter Bitting
J. Weiss
J Reiswick
Catharina Mucker
Anna Eva Hillikas

[VIII MISCELLANEOUS ENTRIES OF JOHN HENRY GOETSCHY, 1735-38]

[1] List of members who have died during my ministry
MDCCXXXVII—
18, December, Jacob Knopf died. His age, 75 years
MDCCXXVIII—
2, March, John Georg Pfalzgraff died, son of Georg Pfalzgraff, his age 2 years, 5 months

[2] List of couples who have been married in New Goshenhoppen.
1735, Dec. 21. Daniel Schwartz and Eva Marg Raderli.
1736, June 22 Georg Peter Knecht, shoemaker, and Christine Herzel, daughter of Mr Herzel of Schipbach.
1736, June 22 Georg Meyer and Maria Gerwegen, daughter of Hans Gerwegen of Goshenhoppen, both single

[3] List of the new communicants, who have been instructed by me, Henrico Goetschio, and admitted to the holy communion for the first time and thus have entered into the Christian congregation, October 10, 1736.

Hans Adam Hilligas, son of Fred Hilligas.
Anna Maria Galman, daughter of Henr Gallman
Anna Marg Raehder, daughter of the late Adam Reder
Anna Maria Knopf, wife of Leonhard Knopf, who came over from the Schwenkfelder faith into our most holy Reformed faith.
Eva Marg. Hut, daughter of John Hut

[4] List of the men who have served under me, J Henrico Goetschio, V D M, as elders of the congregation
A°. 1736, April 25, were elected as elders
Johannes Steinmann.
Johannes Bingemann
J Georg Welcker
Heinrich Galmann
A°. 1738, January 1, were honorably released from the duties of their office
Johannes Steinmann.
Heinrich Gallmann.
In their places were elected·
Benedict Strom
Philip Emert

CHURCH RECORD OF THE NEW GOSHENHOPPEN REFORMED CONGREGATION, MONTGOMERY COUNTY, PA.

SECOND VOLUME, 1762-1832.

Church Record for the Congregation of New Goshenhoppen, from the year in which Rev. Weiss died [1761], [containing the names of] all the children, who from that year to the year 1766 were baptized by me, Jacob Riess, Leyte [Leydich] and Michel and also those of later years.

JOHANN EHRHART WEISS,	JACOB RIESS, *Pastor.*
Elder.	MICHAEL MOLL, *Elder.*
ULRICH GREBER, *Deacon,*	PETER HILLEGASS, *Deacon.*

[I. BAPTISMAL RECORDS.]

[1. ENTRIES BY THE REV. JACOB RIESS, 1762-1766.]

CUNIUS, WILHELM, s. of Johannes Cunius, born 1755, Jan. 24; sp. Wilhelm Griesemer and his wife.

CUNIUS, JOHANNES, s. of Johannes Cunius, b. 1756, Dec. 15; sp. Jacob Kriesemer and Catharina Roder.

CUNIUS, ANNA MARIA, d. of Johannes Cunius, b. 1759, March 14; sp. Jacob Goery and wife.

CUNIUS, ANNA MARGARETHA, d. of Johannes Cunius, b. 1761, July 20; sp. Michel Hartmann Dillo and wife.

CUNIUS, CATHARINA, d. of Johannes Cunius, b. 1763, Sept. 27; sp. Peter Lauer and wife.

CUNIUS, JOHANNES, s of Johannes Cunius, b 1765, Oct 7, sp. Johannes Kriesemer and Anna Marya Gohrisen.

FISCHLR, JOHANNLS, s of Joerg Fischer, b 1762, March 15, sp Johannes Fischer and wife

FISCHER, JOSEPH, s of Joerg Fischer, b 1763, Aug 3; sp. Joseph Eberhart and wife.

FISCHER, ANNA MARGARETHA, d. of Joerg Fischer, b. 1765, Febr 13; sp. Anna Margaretha Fischer

GRAEBER, LUDWIG, s of Andres Graeber, b 1752, Nov 29, sp Ludwig Bitting and wife

GRAEBER, ANDREAS, s of Andreas Graeber, b 1755, Jan 6, sp grandfather and grandmother

GRAEBER, MARIA ELISABETH, d of Andreas Graeber, b 1757, July 6, sp. Dorothea Lisbeth Bitting

GRAEBER, HENRICH, s of Andreas Graeber, b 1761, Aug 6, sp Henrich Bitting and wife

GRAEBER, ANNA MARGARETHA, d of Andreas Graeber, b 1763, Sept 30, sp. Ulrich Graeber and wife

GRAEBER, CHRISTINA, d of Andreas Graeber, b 1765, Nov. 5, sp. Philip Graeber and Christina Bitting

GRAEBER, CHRISTINA, d of Ulrich Graeber, b 1756, Sept. 26; sp. Carl Deri and wife Christina

GRAEBER, ANNA MARIA, d of Ulrich Graeber, b. 1759, Aug 5, sp Andreas Graeber and wife Anna Maria

GRAEBER, EVA, d of Ulrich Graeber, b 1763, Aug 3, sp. Philip Graeber and Eva Lawar

HILLEGAS, PETER, s of Peter Hillegas, b 1756, Jan 19, sp wife of John Martin Abbel

HILLEGAS, CATHARINE, d of Peter Hillegas, b 1761, Jan 23, sp Adam Hillegas and wife

HILLEGAS, ELISABETHA BARBARA, d of Peter Hillegas, b. 1763, Oct. 17, sp. Johannes Frey and wife Rev. Leyte (Leydich) baptized (child)

HILLEGAS, JOHANNES, s. of Peter Hillegas, b. 1766, June 15; sp Johannes Hillegas and Christina Reichert, d of Mathes Reichert

MAUER, ANNA MARYA, d of Peter Mauer(er), b 1762, June 28, sp Johannes Mauer and wife

MAUER, JOHANNES, s of Peter Mauer, b 1764, Aug 8, sp Michel Rieth and wife

DANCKEL, HENRICH, s of Jacob Danckel, b 1761, March 21, sp. Henrich Muller and wife

DANCKEL, JOHANN JACOB, s. of Jacob Danckel, b 1763, Jan 6, sp grandfather and grandmother

DANCKEL, CATHARINA, d of Jacob Danckel, b 1765, July 15, sp grandfather and grandmother

STROH, MARIA, d of Petter Stroh, b 1763, May 8; sp father and mother

STROH, ELISABETHA, d of Petter Stroh, b 1765, Sept 1, sp Johannes Stab and wife

FISCHER, MARIA MARGRETA, d of Johannes Fischer and Catarina Elisabeta Fischer, b 1760, Aug 29, sp Georg Fischer and Maria Margareta Fischer

FISCHER, JOHANNES, s. of Johannes Fischer and wife Catarina Elisabeta, b 1763, Sept 17, sp Georg Fischer and Barbara Fischer.

FISCHER, JOHANN PHILIP, s of Johannes Fischer and wife Catarina Elisabeta, b 1765, March 17· sp Johann Philip Gabell and Elisabeta Catarina Gabell

LEYENDECKER, CONRAD, s of Philip Leyendecker, b. 1766, Jan. 29; sp. Conrad Ludwig and his wife Anna Abell

HAUSWIRTH, JOHANN JACOB, s of Jacob Hauswirth, b. 1766, Apr. 11, sp Abraham Gerhart and wife

1766, Jan. 26, Thomas Mabry brought two negroes to Holy Baptism The father was baptized Mathias, sp Mathias Barthel, the son baptized Bernhart, sp Bernhart Eyl

[2. ENTRIES BY THE REV JOHN THEOBALD FABER, 1766–1779.]

Children which were baptized by me, Johann Theobald Faber and are herein recorded.

FATEL, PETRUS, s of Peter Fatel, born 1767, Jan. 18, sp Peter Heiss and wife.

FISCHER, CATARINA ELISABETHA, d of Georg Fischer, b ——; sp Johannes Fischer and wife

HELLICAS, ELISA BARBARA, d of Conrad Hellicas, b 1767, Jan. 8, sp Georg Petrus Hellicas and wife

MAURER, PETRUS, s. of Petrus Maurer, b 1767, Jan. 31, sp Petrus Pannenbecker and Anna Maria Maurer

WALDER, JOHANNES MATHEUS, s of Henrich Walder, b 1767, Febr 12, sp Matheus Walder and wife

COLB, ELISABETHA, d of Joseph Colb, b 1767, Febr. 19, sp. Georg Michael Colb and wife

WETZEL, JOHANNES JACOB, s of Johannes Wetzel, b. 1767, Apr 18, sp Jacob Wetzel.

CONRAD, ELISABETHA, d of Christian Conrad, b 1767, Apr 12; sp Georg Mack and wife

DANCKEL, JOHANN JACOB, s of Johannes Jacob Danckel, b 1767, Apr 27; sp Jacob Danckel and wife

SELL, ELISABETHA, d. of Henrich Sell, b. 1767, Febr. 18; sp Weiant Pannebecker and wife

BAUER, MAGDALENA, d of Abraham Bauer, b 1766, Dec 18, sp Isaac Somni and wife

MAURER, JOHANNES FRIEDRICH, s of Andreas Maurer, b 1766, ———, sp Friedrich Maurer and Anna Maria Risser

GRISMER, JOHANNES GEORG, s of Leonhart Grismer, b. 1767, ———; sp Johann Georg Besbing

RATZ, DANIEL, s of Johannes Ratz, b 1767, July 14, sp Michael Stepp and wife

PAULUS, CATHARINA, d of Philip Paulus, b 1767, June 28, sp the mother

SEGLER, ANNA ROSINA, d of Abraham Segler, b 1767, May 31, sp Michael Moll and wife

GRAEBER, EVA BARBARA and ANNA CHRISTINA, daughters of Andreas Graeber, born 1767, July 10, sp Henrich Bitting and wife

MAURER, FRONICA, d of Rudolph Maurer, b 1767, Aug 11, sp Fronica Frick and Rudi Frick

RITH, ELISABETHA, d of Michael Rith, b 1767, Aug 28, sp Peter Hellicas and wife.

LEVI, JOHANNES ADAM, s of David Levi, b 1767, Sept 18; sp Joh Adam Hellicas and wife

GRAEBER, ANDREAS, s of Ulrch Graeber, b 1767, Dec 28; sp. Andreas Graeber and wife

HARN, ABRAHAM, s. of Adam Harn, b 1767, Nov 12, sp Abraham Segler and wife

JORG, ANNA BARBARA, d of Andreas Jorg, b 1767, Nov. 28, sp Matheus Brickert and wife

ENGLET, ELISABETHA, d of Caspar Englet, b 1768, Jan 16; sp Ulrich Graeber and wife

HELLICAS, MARIA MARGRETA, d of Joh Helicas, b 1768, Febr 26, sp Jacob Geri and wife

HOLSHAUSEN, JOH NICOLAUS, s of Andreas Holshausen, b 1768, March 11, sp Michael Holshausen and Catarina Wiant

HELLICAS, EVA, d of Peter Hellicas, b 1768, March 20; sp Georg Horlacher and wife

SCHLIEGER, ANNA MARIA, d of Jost Schlieger, b 1768, Febr 1; sp Stoffel Schlieger and wife.

STAUT, JOH, s of Joh Staut, b 1768, June 1; sp Wendel Reiniger and wife.

FISCHER, STINA, d of Wendel Fischer, b 1768, May 12, sp Joh Segler and Stina Fischer

LISER, BARBARA, d of Michael Liser, b 1768, ———, sp Casper Hoffman and wife.

HOFFMANN, MARIA ELISABETHA, d of Casper Hoffmann, b 1768, Jan 1; sp Michael Liser and wife
SEGLER, JACOB, s. of Abraham Segler, b 1768, Sept. 15; sp. Jacob Segler and Margaretha Moll
WILLAUER, ELISABETHA, d of Joh Willauer, b 1768, Sept 12, sp Henrich Maurer and Elisabetha Willauer
MOLL, MICHAEL, s. of Stoffel Moll, b 1768, June 12, sp Michael Moll.
DRALINGER, JOHANNES PETRUS, s of Jacob Dralinger, b 1767, ——, sp. Petrus Stroh, living in Erfort township
SCHELLE, MARIA SUSANNA, d of Joh Schelle, b 1768, Oct 16, sp Anna Maria Maurer
WETZEL, PETRUS, s. of Joh. Wetzel, b 1768, Sept 23, sp Petrus Wetzel and wife.
COLB, GEORG MICHAEL, s. of Josephus Colb, b 1768, Sept 1, sp. Georg Michael and Eva Stellwagen, Jr
WIANT, JOSEPHUS, s of Jacob Wiant, b. 1768. Oct 19, sp Josephus Wiant and Anna Margretha Zimmermann, d of Conrad Zimmermann
RIEDT, JACOB, s. of Andreas Riedt, b 1768, Dec. 6, sp Jacob Leydy and wife
FISCHER, CHRISTIANUS, s. of Joh Fischer, b 1768, Oct. 19; sp. Christianus Fischer and wife
FISCHER, JOHANNES GEORG, s. of Georg Fischer, b. 1768, Nov. 3; sp Johannes Georgus Mack and wife
GERI, JOH PETRUS, s of Jacob Geri, b. 1769, Jan. 25, sp Peter Hellicas and wife.
SELL, MARGARETA, d. of Henrich Sell, b 1769, Jan. 14, sp. Margreta Welcker.
MAURER, ANNA MARGRETHA, d. of Peter Maurer, b. 1769, Febr. 15; sp. Than Maurer and wife.
RAUCH, JOH. GEORGUS, s. of Philip Rauch, b 1768, Nov. 5; sp Georg Steinmann and wife.
SUESSHOLTZ, ELISABETHA, d. of Philip Suessholtz, b 1769, March 3, sp. Benedict Moll and Elisabetha Reffschneider
BRENNESHOLTZ, JOHANNES, s of Georg Brennesholtz, b 1769, March 7; sp Johannes Jung and Catharina Weiss.
SUESSHOLTZ, HENRICUS, s. of Lorentz Suessholtz, b 1769, Febr. 21, sp. Henrich Dass and Elisabetha Suessholtz
SCHINLIN, STINA, d of Friedrich Schinlin, b. 1769, Febr 1, sp Melchior Kolb and wife
HORNE, JOH ERHARTUS, s of Benedict Horne, b 1769, May 16, sp Joh Erhartus Weis and wife
DANCKEL, JOH MICHAELUS, s of Jacobus Danckel, b. 1769, May 31, sp Joh Michaelus Rheder and wife.

WIEGERT, HENRICUS, s. of Friederich Wiegert, b 1769, Apr 22, sp Henrich Maurer and Elisabetha Suessholtz

HORLACHER, JOHANNES GEORGUS, s of Peter Horlacher, b 1769, June 10, sp Georg Horlacher and wife.

BAUER, SUSANNA, d of Abrahamus Bauer, b 1769, May 28, sp Valendin Finck and Susanna Hupper

WEIS, MICHAELUS, s of Erhard Weis, b 1769, June 12; sp Michael Rhoeder and wife

GRAEBER, JOHANNES, s of Andreas Graeber, b 1769, June 22, sp. Henricus Bitting and wife

HELLICAS, MARIA MARGRETHA, d of Conrad Hellicas, b 1769, Aug 3, sp Joh Schelleberger and wife

HERRSCH, ELIAS, s of Henrich Herrsch, b 1769 July 24; sp. Elias Lang and wife

SPIELMANN, JACOBUS, s of Michael Spielmann, b 1769, July 30, sp Jacobus Bossert and Maigretha Wertz

GRAEBER, JOHANNES, s of Philip Graeber, b. 1769, July 13; sp Joh. Rhoeder and Stina Bitting

MAENNER, CATHARINA, d of Joh Petrus Maenner, b 1769, Aug 26; sp Joh. Jung and Catharina Weis

WIANT, DAVID, s of Elias Wiant, b 1769, Aug 17, sp David Levi and wife

STEINMANN, ANNA MARIA, d of Joh Steinmann, b 1769, Nov 29, sp Agnes Steinmann, widow.

FISCHER, JOHANNES, s of Wendel Fischer, b 1769, Oct 8, sp Joh Fischer and wife

HAUSWIRTH, JOHANNES, s of Jacob Hauswirth, b 1769, Nov 1, sp. Joh Fischer and wife

REINHEIMER, ELISABETHA, d of Georg Reinheimer, b 1769, Nov 2, sp Henrich Mauier and Elisabetha Suessholtz

KOLB, ANNA CATH , d. of Joseph Kolb, b 1769, Nov 20, sp Georg Wagner and wife

LEVI, HANNA, d of David Levi, b 1769, Dec 4, sp Abraham Dillo and wife

LOESER, MARIA ROSINA, d of Michael Loeser, b 1769, Apr. 26, sp Philip Leidecker and wife

LEIDECKER, MARIA ELISABETHA, d of Philip Leidecker, b 1769, July 11, sp Michael Loeser and wife

KOLB, MARIA MAGDALENA, d of Joh Georg Kolb, b. 1769, Dec 17, sp. Melchior Kolb and wife

ROEDER, HENRICUS, s. of Michael Roeder, b. 1769, Dec. 18; sp. Johannes Henrich Mueller and wife

KRISEMER, MARGARETHA, d of Leonhart Krisemer, b. 1770, Jan 17; sp the mother

RUDOLPH, CATHARINA, d. of Peter Rudolph, b. 1770, Jan. 5, sp Wendel Wiant, Jr, and wife.

LAUER, ANNA MARGARETHA, d. of Peter Lauer, b 1770, Jan. 24, sp Anna Margaretha Reiss, living on the Oley mountains

JORG, JOH. GEORGUS, s of Andreas Jorg, b 1770, March 12; sp. Georg Welcker

WETKNECHT, BARBARA, d of Jacob Wetknecht, b. 1770, Jan. 15; sp Jost Wiant, Jr., and Anna Barbara Reder.

MOLL, JOHANNES GEORGUS, s. of Stoffel Moll, b. 1770, March 1, sp. Georg Moll and wife

MOTZ, SUSANNA, d. of Johannes Motz, b 1770, March 4, sp Matheus Motz and wife.

RAUDENBUSCH, JOHANNES GEORGUS, s of Jeremias Raudenbusch, b 1770, Apr 24; sp Bernhart Gilbert and wife

NUS, CATHARINA, d. of Conrad Nus, b. 1770, May 3; sp Michael Raeder and wife.

√ JOST, JOHANNES, an adult, bapt. Apr. 9, 1770, also instructed in the faith.

SEGLER, ANNA MARIA, d of Abraham Segler, b 1770, June 2, sp. Johannes Segler and wife.

FISCHER, ANNA MARIA, d of Georg Fischer, b. 1770, June 11, sp Joh Jost Wiant and Anna Maria Mack.

MAURER, JOHANNES, s of Joh. Maurer, b 1770, June 9, sp. Johannes Cunius and wife.

SEGLER, SOPHIA, d. of Joh Segler, b 1770, June 13; sp Petrus Eberhart and wife

TRUMP, ELISABETHA, d of Adam Trump, b 1770, Oct. 4; sp. Leonhart Krisemer and wife

SCHMIDT, JOSEPHUS, s of Lorentz Schmidt, b 1770, Oct 23, sp Joseph Colb and wife.

WIANT, SUSANNA, d of Wendel Wiant, b. 1770, Oct 16; sp Erhart Weiss and wife

SCHUETZ, JOHANNES JACOBUS, s of Philip Schuetz, b 1770, Aug 18; sp. Jacob Schmidt and Elisabetha Erdmann.

PANNEBECKER, ANNA MARIA, d of Petrus Pannebecker, b 1770, Dec. 4; sp. Anna Maria Kern

REITENAUER, JOHANNES, s of Stoffel Reitenauer, b 1769 (or 1770), June 15, sp. Johannes Klein and wife

REITENAUER, JOHANNES HENRICUS, s of Stoffel Reitenauer, b. 1770, Oct 9; sp. the father himself

CUNIUS, JOH PHILIP, s of Joh Cunius, b 1770, Dec 6; sp Philip Heiss and wife.

HEILIG, ELISABETHA BARBARA, d of Georg Heilig, b 1771, Febr. 3; sp Georg Michael Renter and wife Elisabetha

RIEDT, PHILIP, s of Andreas Riedt, b 1771, Jan 26, sp Philip Riedt and wife.

TRALINGER, PETRUS, s. of Peter Tralinger, b 1770, Dec 20, sp Andreas Riedt and wife

GERHART, ELISABETHA, d. of Abraham Gerhart, b. 1771, Jan 2; sp Daniel Neier and wife

STAUT, JOHANNES GEORGUS, s. of Joh Staut, b 1771, March 17; sp Georg Rosemann and Juliana May

HELLICAS, SUSANNA, d. of Conrad Hellicas, b. 1771, May 3; sp Jacob Danckel and wife.

MEYER, ANDREAS, s of Jacob Meyer, b 1771, Febr 9, sp Andreas Maurer and wife.

SPILLMANN, ANNA MARIA, d of Michael Spielmann, b. 1771, Apr. 13, sp Anna Maria Wertz

MACK, CATHARINA, d of George Mack, b 1771, March 1, sp. Henrich Stettler and wife

WELCKER, GEORGUS, s of Jacob Welcker, b. 1771, May 9, sp. Georg Welcker.

FRACK, JOH, s of Daniel Frack, b 1771, Apr. 13; sp Conrad Grob and wife.

MAYER, FRIEDERICUS, s of Jacob Mayer, b 1771, May 12, sp. Friedericus Pannebecker

HORNE, JOH. FRIEARTUS, s of Benedict Horne, b 1771, Apr 5, sp Rehartus Weiss and wife.

HELLICAS, JOH GEORG, s of Georg Hellicas, b. 1771, Aug 15; sp. Georg Horlacher and wife

LEVI, ANNA MARGRETHA, d of David Levi, b 1771, July 7, sp Abraham Dittlo and wife

DANCKEL, HENRICH, s of Jacob Danckel, b 1771, June 30, sp Henrich Muellei and wife

GERI, JOH MICHAELUS, s of Jacob Geri, b 1771, July 13, sp Joh Cunius and wife

GUCKER, HANNA, d of Peter Gucker, b 1771, July 5, sp Maria Cath. Geiger.

WILLAUER, JOHANNES, s of Joh Willauer, b 1771, Aug 30, sp Christian Wannemacher.

REINHEIMER, JOHANNES PHILIPUS, s of Georg Reinheimer, b 1771, Sept. 8, sp. Joh Philip Suessholtz

NUS, JACOBUS, s of Conrad Nus, b 1771, Sept 22; sp Jacob Danckel and wife.

KOLB, JOH GEORGUS, s of Joseph Kolb, b 1771, Aug 10, sp Georg Kolb and wife.
RUDOLPH, ELISABETHA, d. of Peter Rudolph, b 1771, Sept. 4; sp Joh Jacob Schneider and wife.
BAUER, MARIA, d of Abraham Bauer, b 1771, Aug 24, sp. Benedict Strom and wife
FABER, JOHANNES THEOBALT, s of Rev Faber, b 1771, Sept 24, sp Daniel Gros, minister in Saucon and Springfield
DORWORTH, JOH PHILIP, s of Jacob Dorworth, b 1771, Nov 5, sp Philip Schutz and wife
SELL, HENRICH, s. of Henrich Sell, b 1771, Sept 19; sp Henrich Pannebecker
STEINMANN, MARIA MARGARETHA, d of Joh. Steinmann, b. 1771, Sept 17; sp Sophia Maurer
BRENNESHOLTZ, CHRISTIAN, s of Georg Brennesholtz, b 1771, Oct 8, sp Mueller and wife.
FISCHER, HERMANN, s of Georg Fischer, b 1771, Nov 15, sp Joh Fischer and wife.
LAUER, JOH PHILIP, s of Peter Lauer, b 1771, Dec 1, sp Philip Heiss and wife
SEGLER, MARIA BARBARA, d of Abraham Segler, b. 1771, Dec 7; sp Maria Barb Suessholtz.
HORLACHER, ELISABETHA, d of Georg Horlacher, b 1772, Jan 11, sp. Georg Hellicas and wife.
MOLL, MARGARETHA, d of Stoffel Moll, b 1772, Febr 5, sp Margretha Moll
SUESSHOLLSS, EVA CATHARINA, b 1772, Jan 7; sp Abraham Bauer and wife, d of Lorens Suessholss.
WIANT, ANNA MARIA ELISABETHA, d of Elias Wiant, b. 1772, March 13; sp. Rudolph Dresch and wife
✓ HELLICAS, JOH., s of Peter Hellicas, b 1772, Febr 27; sp Reichert Klein and wife
RAEDER, ELISABETHA, d of Michael Raeder, b 1772, Febr 18, sp Philip Laar and wife
SEGLER, JOH RUDOLPHUS, s of Joh Segler, b 1772, Febr 21, sp. Rudolph Segler
ECKERT, WILHELM, s of Justus Eckert, b 1771, Aug 14, sp Conrad Hellicas, instead of Wilhelm Boos
LEIDECKER, JOH. JACOBUS, s of Philip Leidecker, b 1771, Sept 30, sp Joh. Jacob Meisenheimer and Susanna Hupper.
WIANT, SUSANNA, d of Jost Wiant, b. 1772, May 23, sp Jacob Danckel and wife.

WALTER, JOH GEORG, s of Henrich Walter, b 1772, June 1, sp Joh. Georg Ziegenfuss and wife

V HELLICAS, JOH JACOB, s of Joh Adam Hellicas, b 1772, Apr. 26; sp. David Levi and wife

BERRET, JACOBUS, s of Casper Berret, b 1772, June 15, sp Jacobus Wanemacher and wife

WIANT, WENDEL, s of Wendel Wiant, b 1772, Aug 8, sp Wendel Wiant and wife.

RAUTENBUSCH, ANNA MARIA, d of Jeremias Rautenbusch, b 1772, July 31, sp. Michael Rautenbusch and wife.

LIESER, MARIA ELISABETHA, d of Michael Lieser, b. 1772, June 28, sp Anna Elisabetha Leidecker

SCHENLIN, ANNA MARIA, d of Friedr Schenlin, b 1772, July 3; sp Henrich Walter and wife.

WETKNECHT, ANDREAS, s. of Jacob Wetknecht, b 1772, July 20, sp. And Riedt and wife

FRACK, JOHANNES JACOBUS, s of Dan Frack, b 1772, Sept 4, sp Jacobus Frack and wife.

CUNIUS, ELISABETHA, d of Johannes Cunius, b 1772, Nov 6, sp Leonhart Grisemer and wife

MAURER, ANDREAS, s. of Andreas Maurer, b. 1772, Jan 17; sp the parents

FINCK, JOHANNES, s of Valet Finck, b 1772, Oct 5, sp Joh Nicol Finck

MAURER, ANNA BARBARA, d of Peter Maurer, b 1773, Febr 7; sp Margretha Fisher.

HELLICAS, JOHANNES, s of Joh. Georg Hellicas, b. 1773, Febr. 11, sp. Joh Hellicas and wife

KRISEMER, SUSANNA, d of Leonhhart Krisemer, b 1773, Jan 14, sp Philip Laar and wife

KRISEMER, JOH FRIEDRICH, s of Joh Krisemer, b 1773, March 5, sp Fried. Hellicas and Catharina Krisemer

WILLAUER, JOHANN GEORG, s of Joh. Willauer, b 1773, March 25, sp Stoffel Reitenauer and wife

SEGLER, FERENA, d of Abraham Segler, b 1773, May 13; sp Andreas Maurer and wife

RAUCH, DANIEL, s of Philip Rauch, b 1772, Nov 10; sp the father

STAUT, PETRUS, s of Joh Staut, b 1773, Apr 12, sp Peter Finck and Barbara May.

DANCKEL, JOHANNES, s of Jacob Danckel, b. 1773, May 25, sp. Joh. Raeder and Christina Graeber

KOLB, SUSANNA, d of Georg Kolb, b 1773, May 16, sp. Peter Gucker and wife.

RIED, ANNA MARGARETHA, d. of Andreas Ried, b. 1773, June 22; sp. Conrad Hellicas and wife

MERTZ, ELISABETHA, d. of Nicolas Mertz, b. 1773, June 2, sp. Martin Kleber and wife

FABER, DANIEL, s of Rev. Faber, b. 1773, Aug. 3, sp. the parents.

RAUTEBUSCH, MICHAEL, s of Michael Rautebusch, b 1773, Sept. 21; sp the father.

PANNEBECKER, ANNA MARGRETHA, d of Peter Pannebecker, b. 1773, Aug 20, sp Georg Welcker and wife

WIANT, CATHARINA, d of Jost Wiant, b 1773, Aug 8, sp Michael Raeder and wife

LEVI, JACOBUS, s. of David Levi, b 1773, Aug 22, sp Jacob Lang and wife

ECKART, JOH, s of Justus Eckart, b 1773, Sept 18, sp Joh Keuper and Maria Elis. Bernhart.

KOHL, CATHARINA, d of Jacob Kohl, b 1773, Sept 22; sp Cath Wiant.

FISCHER, PHILIP, s of Georg Fischer, b 1773, Sept 9; sp Philip Laai and wife

SEGLER, JACOBUS, s of Rudolph Segler, b 1773, May 11, sp Jacob Segler

STOFFLET, ANNA MARIA, d. of Michael Stofflet, living at Falckner Swamp, b 1771, May 9, sp. Elis Kiesler

NUS, SUSANNA, d of Coniath Nus, b 1773, Nov 3; sp Jacob Danckel and wife

HORNE, ELISABETHA, d. of Benedict Horne, b 1773, Nov 17, sp Henrich Schmidt and wife.

KOLBEIN, SUSANNA, d of Joseph Kolbein, b 1773, Oct 20, sp. And Jung and wife.

RAUBER, ELISABETHA, d. of Jacob Rauber, b 1773, Oct. 13, sp the parents

STEINMANN, JOHANNES, s of Joh. Steinmann, b 1773, Sept 8; sp Joh Schell

KUCKER, CATHARINA, d of Peter Kucker, b 1773, Oct 29; sp Henr Stettler and wife

SELL, JOHANNES, s of Henr Sell, b. 1773, Nov 27; sp the father

HELLIGAS, FRIEDERICUS, s of Conr Helligas, b 1774, Jan 13, sp Andreas Riedt and wife

FINCK, JACOBUS, s of Valentin Finck, b. 1773, Dec. 6, sp Jacobus Wittmer and wife

RENINGER, JOH. FRIEDERICUS, s. of Fried Reninger, b. 1774, Jan 3, sp. Peter Helligas and Juliana May

MOLL, CHRISTOPHORUS, s of Stoffel Moll, b 1774, Febr , sp Christoph. Schlieger and wife

WALTER, ELISABETHA, d of Henrich Walter, b. 1774, March 16, sp Fried Scheneling and wife

STELLWAGEN, MARGARETHA, d. of Hen Stellwagen, b 1774, May 19; sp Con Helligas and wife
FISCHER, HERMANN, s. of Wendel Fischer, b 1774, Jan. 5, sp. Georg Fischer and wife
JUNG, ANDREAS, s of Andreas Jung, b. 1774, Apr 26, sp Erhart Weis and wife
SULSHOIS, BARBARA, d of Phil Sueshols, b 1774, May 8, sp Het Helligas and Barbara Sueshols
BAUER, MARIA CATHARINA, d of Abr. Bauer, b 1774, Apr 2, sp Hen Walter and wife.
RAUCH, PETRUS, s of Phil Rauch, b 1774, March 7, sp Peter Stroh and wife
NEITELINGER, MARIA ELISABETHA, d of Bened. Neitelinger, b 1773, Nov. 8, sp. Michael Hinerleiter and Elis Beyer
GILLEM, ANDREAS, s of Con Gillem, b 1774, Jan 19, sp Andreas Graeber and Cathar Gillem
HOLTZEHAUSLN, ANNA MARIA, d of Jacob Holtzehausen, b 1774, March 25, sp Henrich Muller and wife
LIESER, MARIA, d of Michael Lieser (who was buried the same day that the child was baptized), b 1773, Dec. 10, sp the mother
SEGLER, JOH., s of Joh Segler, b 1774, May 4; sp Joh. Steinmann and wife.
LEIEDECKER, MARIA ROSINA, d of Philip Leiedecker, b. 1774, June 1, sp the parents
DIMIG, JOH. MICHAEL, s. of Peter Dimig, b. 1774, June 25; sp Michael Rauter and wife
WAGNER, GEORG FRIED, s of Zacharias Wagner, b 1774, Aug 17; sp Georg Heisst and Maria Heilig
WEILER, JOHANNES, s of Andreas Weiler, b 1774, Oct 6, sp Joh Mack.
MUELLER, ANNA ELISABETHA, d of Jacob Mueller, b. 1774 Sept 30, sp Jacob Koerwer and wife.
LAR, ELISABETHA, d of Philip Lar, b 1774, Oct 18, sp Froni Mack
STROH, PETER, s of Peter Stroh, b 1774, Oct 30, sp the parents
WETKNECHT, MICHAEL, s of Jacob Wetknecht, b 1774, July 13, sp Michael Huper and Magd Zimmermann
MOLL, JOHANNES, s of Georg Moll, b 1774, Nov. 10, sp Stoffel Moll
RAEDER, MAGDALENA, d. of Michael Raeder, b 1774, Oct. 19, sp Casper Erb and wife
GRISEMER, JACOBUS, s of Leonhart Grisemer, b 1774, Nov 28, sp Joh Jacob Geri and Marg. Cunius
KOLB, MAGDALENA, d of Joseph Kolb, b 1775, Jan 27, sp Georg Kolb and wife

DOERL, RETSCHEL (RACHEL), d of Andreas Doerl, b 1775, Febr 24; sp. the parents, living in Hertfort township, Berks County.

EMERICH, LUDWIG, s of Ludwig Emerich, b 1775, Jan 27, sp Ludw Graeber and Margaret Mumbauer

FRACK, HENRICH, s. of Daniel Frack, b Febr 19; sp. Henrich Hertzel and wife

HECKMAN, SUSANNA, d. of Joh Heckman, b 1774, Dec 8, sp. Georg Heilig and wife

ESPESCHID, EVA BARBARA, d of Jacob Espeschid, b 1773, March 24; sp Joh Neukomer and wife

ESPESCHID, HENRICH, s of Jacob Espeschid, b 1775, Jan 18, sp Hen Hapel

WIANT, ELISABETHA, d of Wendel Wiant, b. 1775, Jan 20; sp Elis Weiss and Peter Helligas.

SEGLER, JOHANNES, s. of Rudolph Segler, b 1775, Febr. 27, sp. Nicol. Wolfart and wife

HELLIGAS, EVA, d of Georg Helligas, b 1775, May 25, sp Georg Horlacher and wife.

WINCKES, HENRICH, s of Peter Winckes, b 1775, May 13, sp Hen. Stettler and wife.

NUS, ANNA MARIA, d of Conrad Nus, b 1775, May 4, sp Hen Walter and wife

ECKEL, JOHANNES, s of Philip Eckel, b. 1775, March 6; sp Joh. Wilh Cunius and Elis. Geri.

STEINMAN, JOH. GEORG and PETRUS, sons of Joh Georg Steinman, b 1775, Jan 26, sp. for the first the parents, for the 2nd Philip Rauch and wife

FISCHER, SUSANNA, d of Georg Fischer, b 1775, June 14; sp. Jacob Segler and Susanna Mack

LEVI, SARA, d. of David Levi, b. 1775, June 29, sp Adam Schneider and wife

MAYER, ABRAHAM, s of Jacob Mayer, b 1775, June 6, sp. Abraham Maurer

HELLIGAS, ANNA MARIA MARGARETHA, b 1775, June 14; sp Adam Helligas and Magreta Hornecker

RAUDEBUSCH, PETRUS, s of Michael Raudebusch, b 1775, Aug 18; sp. the parents

FABER, EVA, d of Rev Faber, b 1775, Aug 28, sp my sister Eva

HELLIGAS, ANNA MARIA, d of Conrad Helligas, b 1775, Aug 18, sp. Andreas Ried and wife

FINCK, ANNA MARIA, d of Valentin Finck, b. 1775, June 22, sp. David Sissholtz and wife

WOLB, CATHARINA, d. of Andreas Wolb, b. 1775, July 27, sp Jost Schlieger and wife
RIED, ANDREAS, s of Andreas Ried, b 1775, Oct. 20, sp. Philip Neis and wife
HECKMANN, JOH ADAM, s. of Adam Heckmann, b 1775, Oct 10, sp Adam Ziegenfuss and Marg Bobermayer.
TAND, DANIEL, s. of Joh Tand, b. 1775, Oct 19; sp Daniel Moyer and wife.
KOLB, PETRUS, s of Georg Kolb, b 1775, Dec 20; sp Peter Gucker and wife.
PANNEBECKER, JOHANNES, s of Fried Pannebecker, b. 1775, Nov 4; sp Joh Neukomer.
HOFFMANN, ELISA BARBARA, d of Andreas Hoffmann, b. 1775, Aug 21, sp Georg Heilig and wife.
MAURER, ANNA MARIA, d. of Peter Maurer, b. 1775, Dec 29, sp. Joh. Mack and Anna Maria Schell.
WEILLLER, ANDREAS, s. of Andreas Weiller, b 1776, March 5, sp And Weiller and wife.
BLUM, JOH MARTIN, s of David Blum, b 1776, Febr 1, sp Martin Lang and Christina Hering
KUCKER, MARIA BARBARA, d of Peter Kucker, b 1776, Apr 16; sp Joseph Kolb and wife
KOLB, PETRUS, s. of Joseph Kolb, b 1776, Apr. 18, sp. Petrus Kucker and wife
STEINMAN, MARIA CATHARINA, d of Joh. Steinman, b 1776, Jan 13, sp Catharina Schell
HITTEL, ANNA MARIA, d of Adam Hittel, b 1776, March 7, sp Ben. Sell and wife
JUNG, ANNA MARIA, d of Andreas Jung, b 1776, May 1; sp Joseph Kolb and wife
SEGLER, JULIANA, d of Joh Segler, b 1776, May 4, sp Juliana Fischer
WILLAUER, JOH JACOBUS, s of Johannes Willauer, b 1775, Oct 26, sp. Jacob Wannemacher and wife.
HOLSHAUSEN, ANNA MARIA, d of Jacob Holshausen, b 1776, May 19, sp Andreas Graeber and wife.
MOLL, HENRICUS, s of Stoffel Moll, b 1776, June 17; sp Hen Segler.
WIANT, JOHANNES, s. of Jost Wiant, b. 1774, Nov 15; sp. Joh Raeder and Christiana Wiant.
FISCHER, ANNA MARIA, d. of Wendel Fischer, b 1776, Apr 10; sp Joh. Mack and wife
WIANT, JOHANNES HENRICUS, s. of Wendel Wiant, b. 1776, Aug 4, sp Hen. Mueller and wife

SCHLIEGER, ANNA MARIA, d of Hen Schlieger, b 1776, July 31, sp Andreas Miller and wife

RUDOLPH, ANNA MARIA, d of Peter Rudolph, b 1776, Aug 17, sp Maria Huper and Peter Lauer.

ECKART, JOHANNES, s of Justus Eckart, b 1776, Aug 28, sp the parents

HOFMANN, JOH. MICHAEL, s of Casper Hofmann, b 1776, May 18, sp. Michael Keck and Eva Liser

HECKMANN, JOH PHILIPPUS, s of Adam Heckmann, b. 1776, Nov 22; sp. Gabriel Bobenmayer.

MACK, JOHANNES, s of Joh Mack, b 1776, Dec 19; sp. Joh Mack

HORNE, SUSANNA, d of Benedict Horne, b 1776, Nov 10, sp Erhart Weis and wife

ESPESCHIED, JOH. JACOBUS, s of Jacob Espeschied, b. 1776, Oct 21; sp Jacob Nus and Christina Wiant

SELL, ANNA MARIA, d. of Hen. Sell, b. 1776, Oct 7; sp. Peter Helligas and wife.

RAEDER, DANIEL, s of Joh Raeder, b 1776, Dec. 16, sp Michael Raeder and wife

SCHMIDT, ——, d of Lorentz Schmidt, b 1776, Aug 26, sp Georg Reinheimer and wife

MESSIN, JOHANNES, s of Thomas Messin, b. 1776, May 24, sp. Mich. Raeder and wife.

KILLER, JOH MICHAEL, s of Martin Killer, b. 1774, Febr 17; sp Michael Raeder and wife.

KILLER, SUSANNA, d of Martin Killer, b. 1775, Dec. 1, sp. Con. Nus and wife

MAURER, ANNA MARGARETA, d. of Andreas Maurer, b 1776, March 25, sp. parents.

MOLL, JOH. GEORG, s of Georg Moll, b. 1777, Apr. 3, sp Daniel Neier and wife.

FRICK, SUSANNA, d of Hen Frick, b 1777, March 23, sp Wendel Wiant and wife

LOCH, JACOBUS, s of Peter Loch, b 1777, May 12, sp Maria Dorothea Wannemacher

GRISEMER, ABRAHAM, s. of Leonhart Grisemer, b 1777, Apr 16, sp. Abraham Grisemer and Elis Geri

SEIB, FRIEDERICUS, s of Bernhart Seib, b. 1777, Aug 31, sp Fried. Wartin and Margretha Dresch

WINCKES, MAGDALENA, d of Peter Winckes, b 1777, July 29; sp Georg Kolb and wife

BREY, EVA CATHARINA, d of Wendel Brey, b 1777, July 29, sp Georg Reyer and Eva Catharina Brey.

MUELLER, JOH. GEORG, s of Georg Mueller, b 1777, Nov 5, sp. Joh Nicol Schupert

SALOMON, MARIA ELISABETHA, d. of Gabriel Salomon, b 1777, Nov. 20, sp. Maria Elis. Etgae(?)

SCHLIEGER, JOST, s of Hen Schlieger, b 1777, Oct 17, sp Jost Schlieger and wife.

SCHMIDT, JOH JACOB, s of Jacob Schmidt, b 1777, Oct 15, sp Jacob Strauss and wife

FISCHER, CHRISTINA, d. of Georg Fischer, b. 1777, Oct 28; sp. Joh. Segler and wife

HELLIGAS, JOH JACOB, s of Peter Helligas, b 1777, Nov 2, sp David Hottenstein and wife.

WEILER, JOH JOST, s of Andreas Weiller, b 1777, Sept 28, sp. Joh Weiller and Fronica Mack

RIEDT, JOHANNES, s of Andreas Riedt, b 1778, Febr. 17, sp Jacob Riedt and wife.

KOLB, SAMUEL, s of Georg Kolb, b 1777, Oct 4, sp Samuel Kolb

CUNIUS, JOHANNES, s of Wilh Cunius, b 1777, Dec 5, sp Joh. Cunius and wife.

REINHEIMER, MARIA BARBARA, d of Georg Reinheimer, b 1778, Febr 20, sp. Michael Dille and wife

HELLIGAS, MAGDALENA, d. of Conrad Helligas, b 1778, March 8, sp. Conrad Schelleberger and wife

MAYER, ISAAK, s of Jacob Mayer, b 1777, Oct —; sp. Andreas Maurer and Maria Maurer.

FABER, GEORGUS, s. of Rev Faber, b 1778, Febr 1; sp my bro-in-law Daniel Roos and wife

RUDOLPH, DANIEL, s of Peter Rudolph, b. 1778, Apr 1; sp Joh. Mack and wife

PANEBECKER, MARIA MARGARETHA, d of Fred Panebecker, b 1777, Apr 9, sp Hen Alles and wife

SEGLER, GEORGUS, s. of Joh. Segler, b 1778, Febr 8, sp George Steinman and wife.

STEINMAN, JOHANNES, s. of Georg Steinman, b 1778, Jan 29; sp Joh Segler and wife

LEVI, ANDREAS, s of David Levi, b 1778, Apr. 28, sp Andreas Ried and wife

SCHMIDT, GEORG PETRUS, s of Philip Jacobus Schmidt, b 1778, June 2; sp Christian Zoller and wife

MUELLER, JOH HENRICUS, s of Hen. Mueller, b 1778, June 29, sp. Hen. Bitting and wife

DIEL, ELISABETHA, d of Michael Diel, b. 1778, July 2; sp. Valentin Frick and wife.

JUNG, SUSANNA, d of Andreas Jung, b 1778, May 22; sp Nicolaus Jung and wife.

STAUT, JACOBUS, s of Joh Staut, b 1778, Aug 7; sp Jacob Mayer and Sara May

KIESLER, MARTIN, s of Martin Kiesler, b 1778, July 18, sp Jost Wiant and wife

KLEIN, CATHARINA, d of Gabriel Klein, b 1778, Nov 5, sp Joh. Cunius and wife

CHRISTMAN, JOH PHILIPPUS, s. of Philip Christman, b 1779, Febr 1, sp. Antoni Steller and wife

PANEBECKER, ELISABETHA, d of Fried Panebecker, b 1779, Febr 11, sp. Weiant Panebecker and wife

FRICK, MAGDALENA, d. of Henrich Frick, b 1779, March 2, sp Wendel Wiant, Sr, and wife

SCHMIDT, HENRICUS, s of Jacob Schmidt, b 1779, Apr. 19, sp Hen Schmidt and wife

EISENHAUER, CATHARINA, d of Martin Eisenhauer, b 1779, May 1, sp Nicolaus Mertz and wife

RAEDER, SAMUEL, s. of Joh. Raeder, b 1779, May 8, sp. Conrad Nus and wife.

WIANT, JOH. HENRICUS, s of Jost Wiant, b 1779, May 31, sp. Henr. Mueller and wife

FRITZINGER, MARIA ELISABETHA, d of Ernst Fritzinger, b 1779, May 24, sp Joh. Braun and wife

STEINMAN, JOH GEORGUS, s of Joh. Steinman, b 1779, March 13, sp the parents

SELL, CATHARINA, d of Henr Sell, b 1779, June 18, sp. Antoni Sell and wife

FISCHER, JACOBUS, s of George Fischer, b 1779, June 24, sp Jacob Eberhart and wife.

FISCHER, MARGARETHA, d of Wendel Fischer, b 1779, June 27; sp Petrus Lauer and wife Margretha.

KOLB, ANNA MARIA, d of Georg Kolb, b 1779, Sept 18; sp Samuel Stettler and wife

ECKART, GEORGUS, s. of Justus Eckart, b 1779, Oct 6, sp Joh Theob. Faber and wife

[Rev John Theobald Faber left Goshenhoppen in October, 1779, having accepted a call to Lancaster, Pa]

[3 ENTRIES MADE BY SUPPLIES, 1780-1781]

1780

Children	Parents	Witnesses
Jacob, born May 7, baptized June 18	Leonhard Hartranf, wife Christina	Joh Jacob Mayer, Creth May, single
Catharina Elisabetha, b July 9, bap July 27	Peter Lauer and wf. Margaretha	Johannes Fischer, Catharina Elisa, wf.
Andreas, b July 2, bap Sept 3	Ludwig Graeber and wf. Elisabetha	Andreas Graeber and wf Anna Maria
Christina, b July 31, bap Sept 3	Henrich Buedding and wf Eva	Franciscus Leydich, wf Christina
Margaretha, b Apr. 20, bap Sept 3	Johannes Segler and wf Christina	Margaretha Fischer, widow
Wendel, b Aug 30, bap Sept 17	Jacob Weiss and wf. Elisabetha	Wendel Wiand and wf. Catharina
Andreas, b Sept 18, bap. Oct 20	Johannes Weyler and wf Margaretha	Andreas Weyler and wf Anna Maria
Johannes, b Sept 4, bap Oct. 20	Conrad Hess and wf wf Margaretha	Johannes Roeder and wf. Anna Maria
Henrich, b. Oct 1, bap Nov. 8	Abraham Maurer and wf Barbara	Henrich Maurer and wf. Margaretha
Henrich, b. Apr. 27, bap May 11	Andreas Jung and wf Susanna	the parents
Anna Maria, b Sept 16, bap Oct 8	Christophel Moll and wf Elisabetha	Johannes Mack and wf Anna Maria
Michael, b Apr 22, bap May 13	Jacob Nuss and wf Anna Maria	Michael Roeder and wf Catharina
Joh Jacob, b Apr 18, bap. May 13	Philip Christmann and wf Margaretha	Jacob Hahn and wf Regina
Michael, b July 6, bap. ——	Andreas Ried and wf Anna Maria	Michael Kolb and wf Magdalena
Hans Adam, b Nov 12, bap Dec	Georg Hillegas and wf Elisabeth	Hans Adam Hillegas and wf. Anna
John Adam, b Nov 12	George Hillegas	Adam Hillegas and wife
Jacob, b Mar. 12	Daniel Cooper	Jacob Gery and wife

[Most of these entries are in the handwriting of Rev John H Helffrich]

[4 ENTRIES OF REV. FREDERIC DELLIKER, 1782-1784]

List of the children who received Holy Baptism through me, Frederick Delliker, in this congregation of New Goshenhoppen, Anno 1782.

Children	Parents	Witnesses
Abraham, b. Nov 20, '81, bap. Mar. 3	Benedict Horning and wf. Elisabeth	Abraham Gerhard and wf Margreth
Samuel, b Sept. 27, '81, bap. Mar. 3	Jost Wyand and wf. Barbara	Conrad Nuss and Margreth
Isaac, b. Feb. 9, bap. Mar. 3	Peter Heinrich and wf Catharina	Andreas Gieber and wf. Anna Maria
Susanna, b. Nov. 27, '81, bap. Mar. 3	Ludwig Greber and wf Elisabeth	Dietrich Reier and wf. Elisabeth
Michel, b Nov. 30, '81, bap Mar 11	Georg Hillegas and wf Elisabeth	Michel Hillegas and wf Catharina
George, b Oct. 13, '81, bap Mar. 24	Hans Georg Kolb and wf Magdalena	Georg Gugger and Christina Huber
Peter, b Dec. 3, '81, bap Mar 24	Peter Lauer, Jr, and wf Margreth	Peter Lauer, Sr, and wf. Susanna
Peter, b Oct 16, '81, bap Mar 27	Peter Schell and wf. Barbara	Peter May and Juliana
Elisabeth, b. Oct. 24, '81, bap. Mar 29	Heinrich Pfannenbeker and wf Susanna	Michel Huber and wf. Elisabeth
Eva, b Nov 25, '81, bap Apr. 14	Jacob Boshard and wf Eva	Heinrich Schmid and and wf. Elisabeth
Hannes, b. Sep 25, '81, bap. May 5	Andreas Greber, Jr, and wf Anna	Andreas Gieber, Sr, and wf Anna Maria
Andreas, b Mar 3, bap May 5	Abraham Maurer and wf Elisabeth	Phil. Jacob Schmid and wf Margreth
Andreas, b. Mar. 17, bap May 9	Ernst Fritzinger and wf. Elisabeth	Andreas Ohl, Sr, and wf Eva
Elisabeth, b. Aug 30, '81, bap. May 11	Christian Wannenmacher and wf Elisabeth	Heinrich Sechler and Elisabeth Baeret
Barbara, b Nov. 4, '81, bap May 12	Heinrich Sell and wf Anna Maria	the parents
Wendel, b. May 6, bap. July 16	Georg Fischer and wf. Barbara	Wendel Wyand, Jr., and wf. Catharina
Elisabeth, b Mar 6, bap July 16	Hannes Zaerby and wf Anna	Abraham Gerhard and wf. Margreth

On May 26th was baptized by me, after preceding instruction, Barbara Benkes, wife of Peter Benkes, also confirmed and admitted to the Holy Communion, her age 24 years

New Goshenhoppen—Vol. II. Baptisms 331

Children	Parents	Witnesses
Jacob, b. May 31, bap. July 7	Jacob Gery, Jr, and Elisabeth	Jacob Gery, Sr, and wf Gertraud
Heinrich, b. July 10, bap July 28	Adam Boshard and wf. Margreth	Heinrich Schmid and wf Elisabeth
Joh. Friedrich, b Aug 21, bap. Sept 8	Justus Ekarth and wf Elisabeth	J Fridric Delliker and wf Barbara
Anna Maria, b. Aug 23, bap Sept 8	Joh Reder and wf Maria	Maria Catharina Neukirch
Anna Maria, b. Aug 6, bap Sept.	Dietrich Reier and wf. Maria Elisabeth	Andreas Greber and wf. Anna Maria
Wilhelm, b May 28, bap July 28	Michel Geier and wf. Catharina	Wilhelm Geier and wf. Anna Maria
Maria, b. Oct 12, '81, bap. Dec. 2	Georg Steinemann and and wf. Catharina	the parents
Daniel, b Oct 26, bap Dec. 6	Johannes Staut and wf. Juliana	Peter May and wf. Juliana
Wilhelm, b Oct 28, bap. Dec. 6	Johannes Mack and wf. Maria	Philip Laar and wf Elisabeth
Johannes, b Oct. 30, bap. Dec. 7	Johannes Schell and wf Elisabeth	Johannes Maurer and Catharina Maurer
Catharina, b Mar 13, 81, bap ——	Friderich Hillegas and wf. Anna	Anna M. Hillegas
Friderich, b Oct. 30, bap. Dec 14	Friderich Hillegas and wf. Anna	Heinrich Huber, Sr, and Catharina Hillegas

1783

Children	Parents	Witnesses
Catharina b Dec. 15, '82, bap. Jan. 5	Philip Weiss and wf. Anna Maria	Wendel Wyand, Sr, and wf. Catharina
Joh Adam, b Jan 2, bap Jan 9	Andreas Ried and wf. Maria	Jacob Boshard and wf. Eva
Joh Friderich, b Dec. 5, '82, bap Febr 2	Peter Hillegas and wf. Elis Barbara	Wendel Wyand, Jr, and wf Catharina
Peter, b. Dec 9, bap. Febr 2	Peter Finck and wf Catharina	Conrad Finck and wf. Catharina
Jacob, b. Dec. 14, bap. Febr 2	Martin Eisenhauer and wf Maria	Joh Cunius and wf. Catharina
Elisabeth, b Dec 25, bap Febr. 2	Conrad Nuss and wf. Anna Margreth	Jost Wyand and wf. Barbara
Maria Catharina, b. Jan 27, bap Febr 7	Conrad Hillegas and wf. Maria	the parents
Magdalena, b. Dec. 2, '82, bap Febr. 23	Johannes Segler and wf Christina	Georg Kolb and wf. Magdalena

Children	Parents	Witnesses
Catharina, b Dec. 1, '82, bap Febr. 23	Peter Schell and wf Barbara	Jacob Schell and wf Catharina
Georg Peter, b Mar 2, bap Apr 5	Johannes Maurer and wf Catharina	Peter Hillegas, Sr , and wf Elisa. Barbara
Anna Maria, b June 31, '82, bap Apr 21	Joseph Kolb and wf. Anna Maria	Casper Baiet and wf Magdalena
Elisabeth, b Nov 16, '82, bap Apr 21	Michel Huber and wf Elisabeth	Catharina Hillegas, the widow
Catharina, b Jan 28, bap Apr. 21	Christopher Moll and wf. Elisabeth	Elisabeth Witman, Sr

On May 24th were baptized, after preceding instruction, the following·
Johannes Ris, single, aged 23 years,
Elisabeth Greber, wife of Ludwig Greber, aged 27 years,
Susanna Reder, wife of Adam Reder, aged 25 years,
Susanna Wigner, single, aged 20 years
The same were also confirmed this day for the Holy Communion

Children	Parents	Witnesses
Henrich, b Febr 21, bap June 8	Peter Rudolph and wf. ———	Andreas Hofman and wf Eva
Johannes, b. May 18, bap June 8	Jacob Schell and wf. Catharina	Joh. Weyer and Maigreth Schell
Johannes, b Febr 1, bap June 8	Peter Schmid and wf Christina	Abr Geihard and wf. Margreth
Peter, b Mar 1, bap June 29	Friderich Pfannebecker and wf Elisabeth	Peter Gugger and wf Susanna
Catharina, b. Dec. 11, '81, bap ———	Friderich Pfannebecker and wf Elisabeth	Catharina Croppen
Johannes, b July 1, bap. July 20	Philip Christmann and wf Margreth	Franz Wesco and wf Eva
Anna Maria, b July 10, bap. July 20	David Sussholz and wf Maria Elisabeth	Wilhelm Geyer and wf Anna Maria
Andreas, b. ———, bap July 29	Heinrich Maurer and wf Philipina	Andreas Maurer and wf. Anna Maria
Elisabeth, b June 29, bap. Aug 31	Ludwig Greber and wf Elisabeth	Christopher Moll and wf Elisabeth
Anna Margreth, b Mar 25, '81, bap Sept 15	Andreas Weiss and wf. Margreth	Abraham Gerhard and wf. Margreth
Georg, b. Jan 13, bap Sept 15	Andreas Weiss and wf Margreth	the parents
Maria Magdalena, b. May 26, bap Sept 21	Heinrich Strohman and wf Elisabeth	Andreas Rid and wf Maria Magdalena

New Goshenhoppen—Vol. II. Baptisms 333

Children	Parents	Witnesses
Peter, b Aug. 18, bap. Sept 21	Adam Raeder and wf. Susanna	Peter Trump and Eva Reder
Maria Elisab., b. Oct. 1, bap. Nov 2	Friderich Reifener and wf. Margreth	Georg Zumpero and Maria Elis. Resch
Philip, b. Oct. 10, bap. Nov. 9	Casper Baret and wf Helena	Joseph Kolb and wf Anna Maria
Magdalena, b Dec 7, '82, bap Nov. 9	Christian Wannemacher and wf. Elisabeth	Casper Baret and wf Helena
Margreth, b. Sept 19, bap. Nov. 16	Jacob Berteau and wf Veronica	Christoph Schlicher and wf Margreth
Catharina, b Sept 7, bap. Nov 23	Jacob Nuss and wf. Maria	Heinrich Jund and Catharina Reder
Anna Maria, b Nov. 23, bap. Dec. 26	Michel Geyer and wf Catharina	Wilhelm Geyer and wf Anna Maria

1784

Children	Parents	Witnesses
Joh Georg, b Dec 1, '83, bap Jan 11	Georg Lang and wf. Anna Maria	Joh. Georg Roth and wf Catharina
Maria Catharina, b Dec 24, '83, bap Jan 11	Jacob Lang and wf Sara	Maria Catharina Lang, widow
Catharina, b. Jan 25, bap Febr 3	Andreas Rid and wf. Maria Magdalena	David Levi and wf. Margreth
Jacob, b. Jan 11, bap. Febr 8	Heinrich Hirsch and wf. Catharina	Andreas Boshard and Maria Hirsch
Peter, b. Nov. 23, '83, bap. Febr 15	Jacob Gery and wf. Elisabeth	Peter Lauer and wf Susanna
Peter, b Febr 6, bap Febr. 15	Samuel Kolb and wf Anna	Peter Maurer
Magdalena, b. Nov. 22, bap Febr 15	Georg Fischer and wf Barbara	Wendel Wyand, Sr., and wf Magdalena
Elisabeth, b. Dec 7, '83, bap Mar. 7	Hannes Crisemer and wf Catharina	Georg Hillegas and wf Elisabeth
Anna Maria, b. Dec. 8, '83, bap Mar 7	Michel Doerr and wf Margreth	Heinrich Schlicher and wf Christina
Elisabeth, b Jan. 17, bap. Mar 21	George Kolb and wf wf. Magdalena	Friderich Schenling and wf Elisabeth
Heinrich, b Aug 20, bap. ——	Georg Hillegas and wf. Elisabeth	Andreas Young and wife

[5 ENTRIES MADE BY REV. FREDERICK WM VON DER SLOOT, 1784]

List of the children who received Holy Baptism from me, Fridrich Wilhelm Von der Sloot, in this congregation of New Goshenhoppen, 1784.

Children	Parents	Witnesses
Joh Adam, b. Mar 14, bap Apr 25	Abraham Maurer	Adam Hillegas, Anna Hillegas
Anna Maria, b Mar 25, bap Apr 25	Jacob Boshard	Joh. Reder and wife
Joh Georg, b. Febr. 17, bap Apr 25	Joh Weigard	Joh Staud and wife
Joh. Georg, b. Mar 2, bap May 4	Isaac Wides	Joh. Rheder and wife
——, b. Mar. 9, bap. May 16	Lorenz Schmidt and wf Susanna	Maria Reinheimer
George, b ——, bap. May 31	Michael Kolb and wf Maria Magdalena	George Kolb and wife
Anna Margareta, b May 10, bap June 6	Henrich Schlicher and wf Christina	Adam Geri and wife
Elisabet, b. Nov —, '83, bap. June 6	Georg Grob and wf Margareta	Philip Lauer and wife
Anna Maria, b Nov. 3, '83, bap June 27	Peter Benker and wf Barbara	Joseph Kolb and wf. Anna Maria
Anna Maria, b May 1, bap July 3	Joh Nicol. Muth and wf. Anna Margareta	Andreas Graeber and wf Anna Maria
Andreas, b. Sept 2, bap Sept. 19	Justus Eckard and wf Elisabeth	Ulrich Graeber and wife
Elisabet, b. July 14, bap. Oct 10	Jost Wigand and wf. Barbara	Wendel Wigand and wf Catharina
Anna Maria, b July 27, bap Oct. 10	Henrich Maurer and wf Philipina	Joh Dotter and wf. Anna Maria
Fridrich, b July 9, bap. Oct 22	Jacob Ried and wf Anna Maria	V d Sloot and wf Anna Margareta
Maria Catarina, b July 6, bap Oct 27	Conrad Gillam and wf. Maria Catarina	Susanna Hozhauser
——, b ——, bap. Oct 31	Joh Georg Hillegas	Andreas Jung and wife
Johannes, b. Sept 4, bap. Nov 15	Michael Hofman and wf Catarina	Andreas Hofman and wife
Mar Lena, b. Sept. 19, bap Nov. 21	Henrich Segler and wf. Elisabeth	Michael Segler and Mar. Lena Kuker

Children	Parents	Witnesses
Elisabet, b Sept 1, bap. Nov 21	Peter Lauer and wf Margareta	Jacob Geri and wf. Elisabet
Joseph, b Mar 7, bap Nov 21	Joseph Kolb and wf Anna Maria	George Derr and wife
Sella, b Aug —, bap Nov 21	David Mi (May) and wf. Elisabet	Rosina ——
Michel, b Aug 13, bap Sept 25, 1785	Adam Reder and wf Susanna	Michel Reder and wf Catharina
Jacob, b June 25, bap Sept 25	Ludwig Greber and wf Elisabeth	Andreas Greber and wf Anna

[The last two baptisms were entered by Mr. Delliker.]

Elisabetha, b Aug 16, bap. Oct 9 (1785)	Joh Nicolaus Muth and wf, Anna Margaretha	Ludwig Graeber and wf Elisabetha

[This baptism was entered by the Rev John H Helffrich]

[6. ENTRIES MADE BY REV. JOHN THEOBALD FABER, SR, 1786-1788]

Children who were baptized by me, Joh. Theobald Faber, in the year 1786

Joh Georg, b Mar. 6, bap June 4	Carl Walter and wife	Peter Timich and wife
Henrich, b Febr 27, bap June 4	Henrich Maurer and wife	Moses Kel and wife
Henrich, b. Dec 2, '85, bap June 4	Joh Georg Kolb and wife	Henrich Segler and wife
Isaac, b. Febr. 22, '84, bap June 16	Cath Schliecher	Jost Schlieger and wife
Georg Adam, b June 1, bap June 25	Georg Adam Helligas and wife	George Maurer and Cath. Schultz
Barbara, b Apr 14, bap June 25	Lorenz Schmidt and wife	Joseph Kolb and wife
Henrich, b June 4, bap June 25	Alexander Oehl and wife	Henr Mueller and wife
Johannes, b. July 23, bap. July 27	Val Brobst and wife	Abraham Levi
——, b ——, bap Aug. 6	Peter Helligas and wife	——
——, b May 24, bap. Aug. 6	George Huber and wife	Wendel Wiand and wife
Wilhelm, b Nov. 3, bap. Aug 6	Joh Liester and wife	Ludwig Graeber and wife

Children	Parents	Witnesses
Catharina, b. July 15, bap Aug 27	Georg Schener and wife	David Spinner and wife
Margreta, b June 30, bap Aug. 27	David Blum and wife	Margreta Ried
Michael, b. May 20, bap. Aug. 27	Jost Wiant and wife	Michael Raeder and wife
Elisabetha, b Apr 14, bap Sep. 9	Joh Bim (Boehm) and wife	Joh Mueller and wife
Johannes, b. Sept. 27, bap. Sept 29	Joh Doerr and wife	Georg Kolb and wife
Barbara, b Oct 7, bap. Oct. 22	Joh Daniel Jung and wife	Adam Hollebusch and wife
Catharina, b. Sept 18, bap. Nov. 16	Wendel Wiand and wife	parents
Joh Georg, b Sept 19, bap. Nov 19	Andreas Benkes and wife	Joh George Grisemer, Elisabeth Kolb
Michael, b Dec 16, bap Nov. 19	Jacob Huber and wife	Michael Huber and wife
Martin, b. Sept 25, bap Nov 19	Martin Eisenhauer and wife	Martin Kleber and wife
Barbara, b Oct 11, bap Dec 2	Joseph Kolb and wife	Peter Benkes and wife
Maria Elisabet, b Nov. 13, bap. Dec 3	Daniel Jost and wife	Conrad Helligas and wife
Wilhelm, b Febr 9, '79, bap ——	—— Knippell	parents
Conrad, b Nov 30, '80, bap ——	—— Knippell	parents
Johannes, b Sept 3, '85, bap ——	—— Knippell	Joh Raeder and wife
Johannes, b Oct. 29, bap Dec 27	—— Knippell	Jost Schlieger and wife
	1787	
Johannes, b Dec 25, '86, bap Jan 1	Joh Schmidt and wife	Joh. Schwenck and wife
Henrich, b. Nov 29, '86, bap. Jan 21	Joh Diter and wife	Henrich Graeber, Anna Maria Hillegas
Joh Jacobus, b Oct. 30, '86, bap Jan 21	Joh. Mueller and wife	Joh. Fischer and wife
Johannes, b June 2, bap Jan. 21	Isaac Wittes and wife	Stoffel Schlieger and Elisabeta Strom

Children	Parents	Witnesses
Anna Maria, b Dec. 15, '86, bap Febr 25	Daniel Schwenck and wife	Michael Rautebusch and wife
Joh Peter, b Oct. 29, '86, bap. Mar 4	Joh Heckman and wife	Conrad Nuss and wife
Abraham, b. Febr 23, bap Mar. 25	Joh. Schell and wife	Abraham Schell, Eva Horlacher
Joh Georg, b Febr. 11, bap. Mar. 25	Joh. Adam Geri and wife	Henrich Schlieger and wife
Catharina, b Febr 23, bap. Mar 25	Christian Mueller and wife	Joh Cunius and wife
Jacobus, b. Nov. 5, '86, bap Mar 25	Peter Finck and wife	Jacob Zoern and Rosina Jung
Georg Petrus, b Jan 6, bap. Apr. 1	Georg Heist and wife	Georg Roth and wife
Catharina, b Jan 15, bap. Apr 9	Joh Geri and wife	Joh Raeder and wife
Sara, b Dec. 5, '86, bap. Apr. 9	Fried, Panebecker and wife	Henr Panebecker and wife
Henrich, b Nov. 4, '85, bap. ——	Fried Panebecker and wife	parents
Catharina, b. Febr. 19, bap Apr 15	Peter Trumb and wife	Michael Raeder, Sr, and wife
George Adam, b Dec. 10, '86, bap May 5	Conrad Netz and wife	Georg Adam Zoern and wife
Jacobus, b. Jan. 14, bap May 6	Jacob Ried and wife	Jacob Cronrad and wife
Jacobus, b Mar. 15, bap May 6	Jacob Bossert and wife	Stoffel Schlieger and Catharina Raeder
Adam, b. May 10, bap. May 27	Adam Bossert and wife	Andreas Bossert and and wife
Elisabetha, b. Apr 29, bap May 27	Andreas Bossert and wife	Henr. Schmidt and wife
Elisabetha, b. Apr 23, bap June 3	Joh Georg Helligas and wife	Joh Nicol Jung and wife
Joh. Jacobus, b. May 14, bap. June 17	Casper Bambes and wife	Jacob Brobst and wife
Joh Jacobus, b May 14, bap June 17	Adam Trump and wife	Jacob Frey and Cath Schultz
Henrich, b. June 19, bap July 8	Joh. Raeder and wife	Henr Schlieger and wife
Johannes, b. Apr 12, bap July 29	Joh Fischer and wife	Philip Fischer and Magdalena Kucker

Children	Parents	Witnesses
Michael, b June 16, bap. July 29	Conrad Nuss and wife	Michael Raeder and wife
Georgus, b. June 3, bap. July 29	Peter Helligas and wife	Georg Maurer and Eva Helligas
Carolus, b June 22, bap July 4	Joseph Bitting and wife	Carolus Sieg and wife
Elisabetha, b Sept 15, bap July 5	Henr Segler and wife	Anna Maria Segler
Anna, b. July 6, bap. Aug 8	Joh. Faber and wife	parents
Joh Jacobus, b July 18, bap Aug. 19	Joh. Grisemer and wife	Jacob Geri and wife
Johannes, b June 30, bap Aug 19	Jacob Geri and wife	Joh Cunius and wife
Christophel, b June 29, bap Aug 19	Conrad Knoeple and wife	Christophel Schlieger, Elis Grisemer
Susanna, b May 16, bap Aug 19	George Mich Kolb and wife	Peter Helligas and wife
Daniel, b June 4, bap Aug 19	Jacob Schell and wife	Fried. Helligas and wife
Anna Margreta, b Mar 16 bap. Sept. 9	Georg Mueller and wife	Widow Anna Margreta
Johannes, b June 10, bap Sept. 9	Ludwig Greber and wife	Jacob Stahl and wife
Johannes, b Aug 19, bap. Oct 21	Nicol Muth and wife	Joh Graeber and Anna Maria Bitting
Catharina, b Aug 12, bap Oct. 21	Henrich Maurer and wife	Michael Doderer and wife
Petrus, b Sept 17, bap Nov 12	Jacob Zimmerman and wife	Nicol Zimmerman, Anna Maria Sell
Elisabetha, b Sept 28, bap Nov. 11	Matheus Hinerleiter and wife	Abraham Gerhard and wife
Joh Henrich, b Oct. 5, bap Nov 11	Jacob Mayer and wife	Joh Wiltzen and Eva Stofelsen
Friedrich, b Sept 17, bap Nov 17	Fried, Schaefer and Elis Berret	Joh. Barret and Elis Willauer
Michael, b Oct 12, bap Dec 2	Georg Doerr and wife	Georg Michael Kolb and Elisabetha Doerr

1788.

Children	Parents	Witnesses
Johannes, b. Oct 15, '85, bap Jan. 5	Christian Wanemacher and wife	Joh Berret and Christina Roscho

New Goshenhoppen—Vol II. Baptisms

Children	Parents	Witnesses
Petrus, b Mar 10, bap. Jan. 5	Christian Wanemacher and wife	Peter Roscho and wife
Henrich, b Jan 5, '80, bap Febr 13	Jacob Mayer and wife	Moses Kehl and wife
Margreta, b June 28, bap. Febr. 13	Jacob Mayer and wife	Andreas Maurer and wife
Maria Magdalena, b Nov 27, '87, bap Febr. 24	Abraham Hartranft and wife	Leonhart Hartranft and wife
Margreta, b Dec. 26, bep Mar 21	Lorenz Suessholtz and wife	Christoffel Schlieger and wife
Joh. Georg, b Mar 29, bap. Apr. 6	Peter Helligas and wife	Joh. Georg Horlacher and wife
Jacobus, b Febr 23, bap May 11	Fried. Panebecker and wife	Jacob Welcker and wife
Johannes, b Jan 30, bap May 18	Joseph Kolb and wife	Christian Stettler and wife
Isaac, b. Febr 3, bap. June 8	Jacob Stahl and wife	Ludwig Graeber and wife
Elisabetha, b Apr. 22, bap. June 9	Peter Finck and wife	Valentin Finck and wife
Barbara, b Febr. 27, bap July 20	Valentin Meckelin and wife	Peter Helligas and wife
Johannes, b. May 4, bap July 20	Alexander Oehl and wife	Joh. Bleiler and wife

Children	Parents	Witnesses
Elisabetha, b July 7, bap. Aug 10	Philip Christman and and wife	Joh Moll and Elis Christman
Philip, b Apr. 2, bap Aug 24	Henrich Sell and wife	Benjamin ———
Georg, b Aug 31, bap Oct 12	Michael Doerr and wife	Georg Schlieger and Elis. Doerr
Anna Catharina, b Mar 8, bap Oct 29	Peter Benckes and wife	parents
Anna Maria, b Sept. 14, bap. Oct. 12	Daniel Jost and wf Barbara	Johannes Jost and wife
Catharina, b Sept 2, '86, bap June 13	David Suessholz and wf Maria	———
Jacob, b May 27, bap. ———	Georg Hillegas and wife	David Spiner and wife

[The last three baptisms are entered by other hands.]

[7. ENTRIES MADE BY REV NICOLAS POMP, 1789-1790.]

After the Rev J. Theobald Faber had died unexpectedly on November 2, 1788, and the congregation had been without a pastor for more than a year, I, N. Pomp, was called to serve in his place, and commenced my ministry here, in the name of God, in these congregations, in the beginning of the month of December, 1789, and baptized the following children·

1789

Children	Parents	Witnesses
Elisabeth, b Nov. 12, bap Nov 26	Adam Bossert and wf. Margareth	Andreas Bossert and wife
Susanna, b. Oct. 15, bap Nov 29	Henrich Schlicher and wf Christina	Georg Wiegener and wife
Magdalena, b. Oct. 31, bap Nov. 29	Johannes Staut and wf. Juliana	Johannes Fischer and wife
Henrich, b. Sept. 24, bap. Nov 29	Ludwig Graeber and wf Elisabeth	———
Magdalena, b. Sept 5, bap. Nov. 29	Joh Nicol Muth and wf. Anna Margareth	Dieder Rayer and wife

1790.

Children	Parents	Witnesses
Georg Adam, b Dec. 10, '89, bap. Jan. 2	Joh. Adam Klein and wf. Elisabeth	Christian Schneider and wife
Hanna, b. Dec 20, '89, bap. Jan 14	Joseph Kolb and wf Anna Maria	Jacob Fink and wife
Petrus, b Dec. 8, bap Jan 17	Jacob Stahl and wf. Hanna	———
Georg, b Dec 29, '89, bap Jan. 17	Johannes Stahl and wf Elisabeth	Georg Wiesener and wife
John, b ———, bap. Jan 17	Abr. Witman and wf Elisabeth	John Faber and wife
Joh Georg, b Sept 23, bap. Jan. 22	Johannes Griesinger and wf. Anna Barbara	Georg Leonh. Griesemer and wife
Elisabeth, b. Dec 12, '89, bap Febr 25	Jacob Zimmerman and wf. Catharina	Margareth Zimmerman
Johannes, b Jan. 10, bap Febr 28	Jacob Brauer and wf Magdalena	Joh. Moll and Cathrina Eckly
William, b. Jan. 9, bap Mar 14	Friedrich Pannebecker and wf, Elisabeth	Wigand Pannebecker
Peter, b. Dec. 24, bap. Mar. 21	Peter Gucker and wf. Elisa	Peter Gucker and wife
Andreas, b. Mar 11, bap Mar 22	Jacob Bossert and wf Eva	Andreas Bossert

Children	Parents	Witnesses
Jacob, b Jan 5, '87, bap. Mar. 22	Jacob Erb and wf Maria	———
Catharina, b. Oct 25, '89, bap Mar. 22	Jacob Erb and wf Maria	———
Eva, b. Mar 10, bap. Mar. 28	Georg Heisst and wf. Elisa	Friedrich Heisst and wife
Catrina, b Nov 5, '89, bap. Apr. 2	Gottfried Wieseler and wf Eva	Wendel Wiegand and wife
Georg, b Jan 16, bap. Apr 11	Peter Tinck and wf Cathrina	———
Elisabeth, b Febr 12, bap. Apr. 11	Jacob Doerr and wf Anna Maria	Ludwig Graeber and wife
Jacob, b Febr 5, bap Apr 11	Abraham Hartranft and wf Cathrin	Jacob Hirsch
Maria Margreth, b Apr 26, bap May 29	*Adam Jost and wf Susanna	Conrad Hillegas and wife
David, b Nov 29, '89, bap. May 23	David May and wf. Elisabeth	———
Joseph, b Apr. 22, bap. June 13	George Michael Kolb and wf. Elisabeth	Joseph Kolb
Peter, b May 22, bap. June 13	David Suessholz and wf. Maria	Casper Berry
Daniel, b May 22, bap June 27	Henrich Raudenbusch and wf Catharina	Daniel Schwenck and wf Catharina
Henrich, b June 13, bap July 25	Michael Doerr and wf Margareth	Henrich Raeder and Maria Schlicher
1791		
Anna, b Mar 26, bap. May 22 ['91]	Jacob Huber and wf Christina	George Huber and wf. Elisa
Michael, b. Nov. 30, '90, bap. May 22	Johannes Fischer and wf Christina	Michael Huber and wf. Elisabeth

[The last two entries were made by Rev John Wm Hendel]

[8. ENTRIES MADE BY THE REV. JOHN THEOBALD FABER, JR., 1792-1795]

Those children are here recorded whom I, John Faber, baptized in the congregation New Goshenhoppen Anno Domini 1792

John Peter, b Dec. 7, 1791	Peter Hillegas	John Hillegas, Barbara Maurer
Maria Catharina, b. May 31, '92	Philip Mukenhaupt	Adam Zoern and wife

Children	Parents	Witnesses
Henrich, b. Mar. 29, '92	John Staud	Henrich ——
John Jacob, b Mar 13	William Schmith	John Braun and wife
Elisabeth, b Febr 13, '91	Jacob Erb	Elis Rheinerts
Eva, b Mar. 1, '92	George Miller	parents
George, b Mar 1, '92	George Miller	George Engel and wife
Adam, b. June 28, '92	Diederich Miller	Adam Miller and wife
Jacob, b May 4	Peter Hillegas	Jacob Hillegas, Anna Maria Hillegas
Michael, b June 25	Michael Doerr	Conrad Nuss and wife
——, b. Aug 8	Andreas Bossert	George Mumbauer, Catharina Leydich
Georg Michael, b. Nov 26, '91	John Schell	Peter Hillegas, Sr, and wife
Magdalena, b Jan. 19, '75, bap. ——, '92	John Raeder's stepdaughter	
Tobias, b Febr. 4, '91	Fried Panebecker	John Shell and wife
Jacobus, b June 10, '91	Heinr. Segler	Jacob Segler and Elisa Segler
Margretha, b Sept 6, '92	Will. Schaefer	Conrad Hillegas and wife
Caty, b. Nov. 11	John Doerr	Casper Rieser and wife
Anna Maria Caty, b July 9, '91	Casper Reeser	Peter Schuler and wife
John, b Dec 26, '92	George Welker	parents
John, b June 19, '92	John Berret	John Staud and Elis Berret
Courtis, b Febr 6, '92	Edward Larkin	Samuel Cooper and wife
Gorsuaway (!), b. Febr 6. '92	Edward Larkin	Jiesbinon (!) Lange and wife
Jonathan, b Nov 13, '92	John Griesemer	Peter Horlacher and wife
Friedrich, b. Aug 14, '92	Fried Zoern	Adam Zoein and wife
Anna, b July 31	Jacob Goeri	John Goeri and wife
John, b. Sept. 9, '92	Jacob Goeri	Michael Goeri and Magdalena Wigner

New Goshenhoppen—Vol II. Baptisms

Children	Parents	Witnesses
	1793	
George, b Oct 19, '92, bap Jan 3, '93	John Walter	George Kolb and wife
Daniel, b Mar. 1, '92, bap Mar 24	Daniel Jost ✓	John Jost and wife ✓
John, adult, b Oct 8, —, bap. Mar. 27, '93	George Walter	——
Susanna, adult, b Jan 20, —, bap Mar 27	Michael Shell	John Shell and wife
Michael, b June 26, '92, bap May 26	John Raudenbush	Michael Raudenbush
Jacob, b. May 8, 1790	George Kolb	Jacob Gilbert and wife
Susanna, b Nov. 8, '93	Nic Sechler	Philip Christman
Catharina, b. Nov. 29, '93	Adam Bossert	Widow Bossert
Anna Maria, b. Nov 17, '93	George Roth	John Heist and wife
John, b Nov. 18, '93	Heinr Heist	John Heist and wife
	1794	
John, b Nov 11, '93	Daniel Sperr	wife
——, b. Oct 24	Heinrich Graeber	Andreas Graeber
John, b Nov 30, '91	—— Geiger	J W. Geiger and wife
Margretha, b. Dec. 3, '93, bap Dec 25	Charles Henzey	George Rhod [Roth],, Margretha Reed
Susanna, b Nov 8,'93	Philip Christman	H Nicol. Sechler
Christina, b Dec. 31	Jacob Hauswirth	parents
Wilhelm, b Jan 15, bap. Mar 8	Lorentz Smith	Wilhelm Stelwagen and wife
Elisabeth, b Aug 26, bap Nov. 1	John Fisher	Philip Fisher and wife
Elisabeth, b. Mar 1, bap. ——	John Hauswirth	Georg Heilig, Sr, and wife
	1795	
Margretha, b Nov. 22, '94, bap Jan 21	John Berret	Michael Raudenbush and Maria Sell
Elisabeth, b Oct 25, '94, bap. Jan 22	Jacob Braisch	Jost Wiant and wife
George, b Oct 21,'93, bap Jan 22	Jacob Braisch	Adam Braisch and wife
Conrad, b Dec 27,'94, bap Febr 12	Adam Jost	Conrad Hillegas and ✓ wife

Children	Parents	Witnesses
Maricha (!) b. Dec 2, '93	Peter Hillegas	Maria Hillegas
John, b Febr. 24, '95, bap. Apr. 5	Andreas Graeber	Ulrich Graeber and wife
Maria Catharina, b Apr. 2, '95, bap. Apr. 6	Leonh. Miller	Catharina Detweiler
Salome, b. May 2, '94, bap. Apr 21	Joseph Kolb	Elisabetha Schmitt
Friedrich, b Dec 24, '94, bap Apr 19	Jacob Maurer	Friedrich Maurer and Eva Faber
Petrus, b Mar. 19, '95, bap Apr. 19	Abraham Levy	Peter Hillegas, Sr., and wife
Michael, b. Nov. 5, '94, bap May 10	Henrich Raudenbush	Michael Raudenbush and wife
Jacobus, b. Febr. 1, '93, bap May 23	John Frey	Jacob Frey and wife
Sarah, b. May 3, bap. ——	Margreth Copelberger	Henrich Copelberger and wife
Margretha, b Sept. 12, '95	Ludwig Ache	John Pohlig
Daniel, b Dec. 13, 1807, bap. ——	Samuel Rader and wife Elisa	Johannes Rader
Sara, b. June 17, 1804	David Schultz and wf. Barbara	Anna Barb. Kohl
Abraham, b Apr 24,	David Schulz and wife	Abr. Levi and wf Eva

1806

Anna Catharina, b July 14, 1808	David Schulz and wife	Joh Hillegas and wf. Anna Catharina
Anna Maria Magdalena, b Oct. 28, 1809	David Schulz and wife	Samuel Keppler and wf Maria Magdalena
Sus Elisab Barbara, b. Sept. 9, 1811	David Schulz and wife	Salome Fries and wf. Susanna

[Baptisms entered by various hands]

New Goshenhoppen—Vol. II. Baptisms

[9 ENTRIES BY THE REV ALBERT HELFFENSTEIN, 1808-1811.]

List of those who were baptized here since my presence here, June, 1808

Children	Parents	Witnesses
		A. HELFFENSTEIN.
Elisabeth, b. Apr 21, 1808	Georg Ewald and wife Magdalena	Adam Ewald, Susanna Ewald
Henrich, b. Jan 16, 1808	Johann Hillegas and wife Catharina	Henrich Schlicher, Christina Schlicher
Johann, b. Mar 6, 1808	Johann and Catharina Hillegas	Abr Levy and Eva
Esther, b June 4, 1808	Samuel and Anna Wiant	——
Anna Catharina, b July 14, 1808	David and Barbara Schultz	Johann and Catharina Hilligas
Jonas, b July 10, 1808	Georg Huber and wife Elisabeth	Henrich Rauch and ✓ Rosina
Hans Adam, b. July 13, 1808	Hans Adam Hillegas and Elisabeth	Ludwig Graber and wife Elisabeth
Susanna, b June 27, 1808	Georg Wenner and wife Elisabeth	Johan Moll and Catharina
Henrich, b Aug 5, 1808	Johan Leser and wife Hanna	Abr. Marsteller and Elisabeth
Johan, b Aug 5, 1808	Johan Leser and wife Hanna	Wilhelm Will and Elisabeth
Daniel, b Sept. 16, 1808	Georg Wigner and wife	Daniel Heil and wife
Michael, b May 15, 1808	Michael Hoffman and wife	Johann Rauch and wife
Maria, b June 30, 1808	Jacob Griesemer and wife	Philip Herzog and wife
Elisabeth, b Dec 31, 1808	Christian Dorwart and wife	Johan Kucker and Marg. Lang
Margaretha, b Aug 19, 1808	Johan Schneider and Elisabeth	Georg Kehl and Margareth
Samuel, b Jan 10, 1808	Georg Kehl and Margareth	Samuel Kohler and Magdalena
Georg, b Oct 14, 1808	Jacob Fischer and wife	Barbara Fischer
Polly, b Sept 24, 1808	Johan More and Catharina	Wendel Wiant and Catharina

Children	Parents	Witnesses
	1809.	
Samuel, b Aug 12, 1808, bap Jan 1,	Samuel Kolb and wife	Johann Sussholz
	1809	
Jacob, b Apr 16, 1808, bap. Febr 6	Henrich Rauch and wife	Jacob Berent and Cath Rauch
Jacob, b June 1, 1809, bap July 22	Johan Sussholz and ——	Johan Geiger, Cath Sussholz
Susanna, b June 24, 1809, bap. Sept. 17	Andreas Jung	Susanna Jung
Elisabeth, b. March 24, bap ——	Andreas Gräber and Sibella	Georg Wohnsidler and Barbara
Peter, b. Aug 13, bap Sept. 17	Jacob Schell and Maria	Andreas Graber and Sibella
Samuel, b April 17, bap. ——	Johann Pfannenbecker and wife	Johann Schneider and wife
Maria, b Aug 7, bap Dec. 10	Jacob Hartranft and wife	Johan Georg Hilligas and wife
Elisabeth, b Oct 23, bap. Dec 10	Daniel Staut and wife	Johan Staut and wife
Johannes, b Sept 29, bap Dec 10	Johannes Dimmig	——
Jacob, b Aug. 11, bap. Dec. 15	Jacob Fischer and wife	——
Alexander Copeland, b Sept. 17, bap Dec. 15	Jacob Peck and wife	——
Maria, b Nov 9, bap ——	Daniel Kepler and wife	——
Polly, b Febr 14, bap ——	Antony Kehl and Barbara	Henrich Bernt and Nancy
	1810.	
Elisabeth and Rebecca, b Mar 6, bap Apr 2	Antony Kehl	——
Sarah, b Febr 15, bap Apr 15	Samuel Rother and Elisabeth	Philip Christman and Margareth
David, b. Febr 22, bap. May 10	Jacob Griesemer and wife	——
Maria, b Febr 2, bap May 7	Johannes Huttel and Maria	——
Christian, b Dec 25, bap. May 7	Johannes Sasseman and Barbara	Christian Sasseman and Sophia

New Goshenhoppen—Vol. II. Baptisms 347

Children	Parents	Witnesses
Elisabeth, b Febr 11, bap. ——	Georg Wenn and Elisabeth	Carl Huber and Susanna
Hanna, b Jan. 6, bap. ——	Jacob Sussholz and Magdalena	Johan Sussholz and Barbara
Adam, b June 18, bap July 22	Jacob Hillegas and Rosina	Henrich Keck and Maria
Sophia, b Sept 28, bap ——	Jacob Bock and wife	Johannes Bolig and Margareth
Sally, b Aug 10, bap Sept. 30	Johann Sell and Barbara	Jacob Loch and Molly
Juda, b. Febr 23, bap Sept 30	Michael Hoffman and Maria	Wilhelm Will and Nancy Miller
Michael, b. Apr 8, bap Sept 30	Georg Querry and Anna	Johannes Aerny and Salome
Samuel, b. Apr 17, bap Sept 30	Conrad Heyl and Maria	Samuel McNoldy and wife
Salomon, b Jan 18, bap. Sept 30	Philip Brey and Nancy	Hans Adam Hilligas and Elisabet
Carl, b. Apr. 27, bap. Sept 30	Philip Reed and Margaretha	the parents

1811.

Georg, b Sept 28, bap Jan. 1	Georg Steinman and Elis.	Georg Steinman, Sr
Salome, b Jan 4, bap May 19	Johan Fischer and Anna	Georg Moll and Eva
Magdalena, b Febr 11, bap. May 19	Samuel McNoldy and Magdalena	Andreas Grabers and Sibylla

[10 ENTRIES MADE BY THE REV. FREDERICK WM. VON DER SLOOT, JR, 1813-1818]

1813.

Sara, b. Dec 16, '12, bap Jan 24, '13	Johann Roth and Catharina	Abrah Levi and Eva
Magdalena, b Aug 24, bap Febr 11, '13	Dan. Hittel and wife Magdalena	Cath Willauer
Johan Adam, b Dec 17, '12, bap Mar. 7, '13	David Schulz and Barbara	John Maurer, Cath Hillegas, both single
Daniel, b. Febr 1, bap Mar 7, '13	Daniel Rieser and Maria	Jacob Schell and wife Maria

Children	Parents	Witnesses
Maria, b Jan. 16, bap. Mar. 26, '13	Jacob Wenner and Maria	Johann Schlicher and wife Maria
Elisabeth, b. Oct 15, '12, bap. Apr. 16, '13	Ludwig Bernd and Elisabeth	Andreas Grabers and Sybilla
Salomon, b Mar 15, bap Apr 9	John Röder and Magdalena	John Roder
Maria, b Apr 24, bap June 30, '13	John Hallman and Catharina	Peter Schell and Maria

1814

Children	Parents	Witnesses
Maria, b Dec 2, '13, bap. May 1, '14	Fred (?) Kohl and Barbara	George Kolb and Anna
——, b. Apr 17, bap. June 12, 1814	George Wiegner and Susanna	Peter Steinman and wife Magdalena
Elisabeth, b May 18, bap Aug 21, '14	John Sussholz and wife Barbara	George Welker and Elis Sell
Mathaus, b. Jan. 2, '15, bap Mar, '15	Michel Huber and wife Elisabeth	Jacob Huber and wife Elisabeth
Abraham, b Dec 8, '14, bap May 15, '15	Abraham Geier and wife Sophia	John Sassaman and wife Barbara
Henrich, b. June 22, '16, bap. Sept. 8	Jacob Huber and wife Elisabeth	Henrich Mumbauer and wife Catharina
Henriette, b July 21, '16, bap Sept 8	George Walter and wife Regina	Magdalena Hummel
Daniel, b Nov. 26, '16, bap Apr 6, '17	John Sasseman and wife Barbara	Daniel Sasseman and Susanna Geier
Catharine, b. May 6, '17, bap July 20, '17	Georg Jacob and wife Elisabetha	Catharine Staud
Jesse, b May 5, '17, bap. July 20, '17	Jacob Mecklin and wife Catharina	Johannes Hoffman and wife Elisabetha
Samuel, b Oct 21, '17 bap. Dec 14	Peter Heilig and wife Magdalena	Georg Welker and wife Catharina
Sara, b Jan 12, '18, bap. May 31	Heinrich Scherr and Margareth	John Sussholz and wife Barbara
John, b. July 14, '18, bap Aug 23	George Walter and wife Regina	John Hartman and wife Maria

[11 ENTRIES MADE BY JOHN FABER, Jr., 1819-1833]

Children	Parents	Witnesses
Jacob, b Sept 13, '19, bap Dec 1, '19	Johannes Hittel and wife Maria	the parents
Salomon, b Oct 16, '19, bap Jan 2, '20	Jacob Steier and wife Catharina	Gottfried Wissler and wife Eva

New Goshenhoppen—Vol. II   Baptisms   349

Children	Parents	Witnesses
Johann Friedrich, b Nov 2, bap. Apr 12, '19	Joh Stephan Diehl and wife Elisabetha	the parents
Uria, b Jan 8, '20, bap. Febr 13	Andreas Weiss and wife Maria	Johannes Ritz, Catharina Christman
Jesse, b. Aug 28, '19, bap. Mar. 26, '20	Philip Rith and wife Margareth	Adam Hillegas and wife Elisabetha
Rufina, b Oct 11, '19, bap. Apr 9, '20	Georg Kolb and wife Anna Catharine	Samuel Kepler and wife Magdalena
Tobias, b Febr. 5, '20, bap. Apr 3, '20	John Grenn and wife Sara	Jacob Kammery and wife Louisa
Maria, b. Jan. 10, '20, bap Mar 27	John Roder and wife Magdalena	Catharina Marsteller, widow
William, b Febr 18, '20, bap Apr. 3	John Graber and wife Christina	Andreas Graber and wife Sibilla
Edward, b. May 7, '20, bap May 18	John Moll and wife Eva	Andreas Gräber and wife Sibilla
Carolina, b Jan. 7, bap June 4	Jacob Beck and wife Eleonora	the parents
Eleonora, b Jan 11, bap. June 18	Johannes Jacob and wife Catharina	Carl Hillegas, Elisabeth Willauer
Johan Georg, b. July 1, bap. Aug. 27	Johannes Sasseman and wife Susanna	Jonas Borgen and wife Catharina
Abraham, b June 24, '20, bap Sept 10	Georg Mack and wife Magdalena	the parents
Henrich, b Nov 23, '20, bap. Mar. 11, '21	Valentin Ache and wife Christina	Heinrich Ache, Fronica Walter
Karl, b Mar. 18, '21, bap May 13	Georg Walter and wife Regina	Karl Walter and wife Margaretha
Susanna, b Oct 29, '20, bap May 13, '21	David Zimmerman and wife Magdalena	Susanna Zimmerman
Jacob, b Febr. 24, '21, bap May 6, '21	Philip Sell and wife Elisabetha	Abraham Sechler and wife Margaretha
——, b Mar. 19, bap Apr 22	Daniel Christman and wife Elisabetha	Philip Christman and wife Margaretha
Georg, b. Apr 11, bap May 7	Philip Schmidt and wife Sara	Catharina Reichart
Anna Magdalena, b Mar 9, '21, bap Aug. 30, 1821	Jacob Sechler and wife Elisabetha	Mrs Magdalena Detweiler
Samuel, b. Nov. 3, '21, bap Dec 30, '21	Jacob Hilffiker and wife Maria	Samuel Roeder and wife Elisabeth

Children	Parents	Witnesses
David and Elias, b. Nov. 9, '21, bap. Dec 30	Andreas Weiss and wife Maria	John Weidner, Lydia Smeyer, Henry Shell, Barbar Trumb
Liwayne [Lavina], b Nov 8, '21, bap. Jan 27, '22	John Graber and wife Christina	Henrich Wickert and wife Lydia
John Jacob and Karl, b. Jan 19, '21, bap Mar. 13, '21	John Stephanus Diehl and wife Elisabetha	Jacob Wilhelm Dechant
George, b. Febr 5, '22, bap. June 15, '22	Valentin Ache and wife	George Walter and wife
Isaac, b. Apr. 25, '22, bap. June 15	John Willauer and wife	Isaac Reifschneider and wife
Eliza, b. June 13, '18, bap ——	John Dixon and wife Maria	——
Mary Ann, b Febr. 1, '20	ditto	——
William, b. Apr 1, '22	ditto	——
——, b Febr. 26, '22, bap. Aug. 18	John Kolb and wife Susanna	Christian Kolb, Nancy Zigler
Elisabeth, b July 18, '22, bap Sept. 8	Wendel Wiant and wife	Samuel Roeder and wife Elisabeth
Maria, b May 26, bap. Sept. 8	Peter Gery and wife	John Gery and wife Catharina

1823.

Children	Parents	Witnesses
Jonas, b June 4, bap. June 25	John Wiand and wife Maria	Wendel Wiand and wife Catharina
Charles, b. Aug. 13, bap. Nov 2	Henry Graber and wife Susanna	John Gery and wife
William, b Sept. 14, bap Nov. 2	Jacob McNoldy and wife Sara	Daniel Heil and wife Catharina
Johannes, b Sept 10, '23, bap. Nov. 23, '23	George Carl and wife Catharina	John Gery and wife
Anna Maria, b Jan 2, '24, bap. Mar. 7, '24	George Marsteller and wife Salome	John Roeder and wife
Jacob, b. Oct. 27, '23, bap Febr 28, '24	Jacob Kemmerer and wife	the parents
Catharina, b Febr. 7, '24, bap Mar. 25	John Hersch and wife	parents
Maria, b Oct. 19, '23, bap. ——	John Hofman and wife Maria	Daniel Christman and wife Elisabeth

Children	Parents	Witnesses
Daniel, b. Dec 14. '19, bap —, '24	David Shultz and wife	parents
Joseph, b. May 30, '24, bap July 11, '24	Peter Gery and wife Elisabeth	John Gery and wife
Allen, b. May 17, bap July 11	Jacob Bender and wife Susanna	Anthony Freyer and wife Susanna
Amlina, b. Sept 2, bap Oct. 24	Philip Sell and wife Elisabeth	Jacob Sechler and wife Elisabeth
Maria Anna, b Sept. 5, bap. Oct. —	Johannes Greber and wife Christina	Adam Wonsetler and wife Susanna
Rebecca, b Dec 6, '24, bap Jan 16, '25	Philip Rufner and wife Peggy	Samuel Kepler and wife
John William, b Nov 2, '24, bap. Dec. 26, '24	Jacob Hillegas and Hannah	Samuel Kepler and wife

1825

Children	Parents	Witnesses
Jacob, b Mar 7, '24, bap. ——	Jacob Steier and wife Catharina	Henrich Barent and Elis Steier
Edward, b Apr 30, '24, bap. Aug. 1	Jacob Steier and wife Catharina	Peter Gery and Lydia
Lydia, b Jan 31, '25, bap. May 1, '25	Herry Graeber and Susanna	John Gery and wife
Ruben, b Mar 26, '25, bap. [May] 23, '25	Heinrich Moll and wife	Jacob Heisch and wife
Levi, b. Mar 24, bap June 12, '25	Abr. Meyer and Catharina	Jacob Huber and wife
Samuel, b May 3, '25, bap. July 3, '25	George Carl and wife Catharina	John Gery and Mary Ann Schaffer
Christian, b Apr 23, '25, bap Sept 11	Henry Gaugler and Catharina	John Gery, Sr , and wife
William, b. Mar. 30, '25, bap Nov. 6	Daniel Fitzcharles and wife Elisabeth	John Jacob and Catharina
George, b Dec 12, '25, bap Jan. 29, '26	Peter Gery and wife Elisabeth	Henry Halman and wife Catharina
Jacob Samuel, b Mar. 13, '26, bap May 14, '26	Jacob Hillegas and wife Hanna	Samuel Kepler and wife Maria
Catharina, b July 8, '26, bap. Aug. 7, '26	Peter Deisher and wife Maria	John Gery, Sr , and wife Catharina
Rhein, b June 9, '26, bap. Sept. 17, '26	Philip Berret and wife Elis	John Erb and wife Elis

Children	Parents	Witnesses
Johannes, b. Aug. 6, '26, bap Oct 29, '26	John Ritz and wife Sophia	Joseph Gery, Lydia Ritz
Rebecca, b. Oct. 1, '26, bap. Dec. 10, '26	George Carl and wife Catharina	John Heilig and wife Anna
Rebecca, b Dec. 31, '26, bap. Mar. 25, '27	John Graeber and wife	John Blanck and wife
Rachel, b Sept. 27, '27, bap. Nov 10, '27	Jacob Huber and wife Margaret	Henry Hofman and wife Catharina
Carl, b Jan 22, '27, bap Mar 25	Johan Graeber and wife Christiana	Salmon Wicker and wife Elisabeth
Nathanael, b Apr 19, '28, bap June 29, '28	Henry Steier and wife Elisabeth	John Ruekstiche and wife Christina
Anna Elisabeth, b. June 3, '29, bap Aug 23, '29	Jonas Nyce and wife Rachel	Jacob Hillegas and wife Anna
Carl, b. Nov. 7, '29, bap. Apr. 9, '30	Amos Antrim and wife Lydia	Henry Craeber and wife Susanna
Carolina, b Febr. 5, '30, bap. Apr 11, '30	Jacob Huber and wife Peggy	Peter Fegly and wife Elis.
Isaac, b. Aug. 14, '32, bap Oct 21, '32	Jacob Huber and wife Maria	George Huber and wife Elis.
Johannes, b June 2, '28	James Tagert and wife	the parents
Maria Anna, b Jan 20, '31	James Tagert and wife	the parents
Jacobus, b. Dec. 21, '32	James Tagert and wife	the parents

[12. ENTRIES MADE BY LATER HANDS.]

Thomas, b. Oct. 27, '35	Johannes Gerhard and wife Lea	Georg Gerhard and wife Susanna
Mahlon Jacob, b May 8, '40	Johannes Gerhard and wife Lea	Nathan Levy and wife Maria
Luisa Susanna, b Aug. 2, '50	Johannes Gerhard and wife Lea	Louisa Kemmerer, maternal grandmother
Elisabeth, bap. May 4, '34	Daniel Schneider and wife Sara	Joseph Gery and wife Anna
Johannes, bap. May 4, '34	Joh. Steier and wife Rebecca	the parents
Robert, bap. May 24, '34	James Taggert and wife	Jacob Taggert and wife

Children	Parents	Witnesses
Israel, bap June 15, '34	Franz Weth and Maria Weth	David Staut and Cath Jacob
Esther, bap. July 27, '34	Heinr. Edelman and wife	the parents
Judith, b Oct 10, '34, bap. Nov 30	Jonas Kolp and Ester Kolp	Georg Kolp and wife
Carl, bap Feb 21, '36	Daniel Schneider and wife Sara	Daniel Nuss and wife
Jonathan, b Nov 18, '46	Johannes Roeder, Jr, and wife Christina	Johannes Roeder, Sr, and wife Christina
Lewis, b Apr 2, '48	Johannes Roeder, Jr, and wife Christina	Lewis Schuler and wife Anna
——, b Sept 20, '50	Johannes Roeder, Jr, and wife Christina	the parents

[II BURIAL RECORDS]

Persons buried by me, John Th. Faber, who were also recorded by me, as follows:

1766, Oct 21. Abraham Segler's little daughter was buried

1766, Dec 8 Andreas Graber's little daughter was buried

1766, Dec. 26 Jacob Meyer was buried.

1767, Jan 3 Bernd Lent's little daughter was buried

1767, Febr. 20. The old Mr. Layendecker was buried.

1767, June 4 A little son of Peter Hellicas was buried, named Johannes, aged 1 year less 14 days.

1767, June 23. A son of Georg Reinheimer was buried, named Johannes, aged 2 years, 2 months, 4 days, of New Goshenhoppen.

1767, July 20 A daughter of Johannes Staut was buried named Anna Maria, aged 1 year, 3 months, less several days.

1767, Aug 17 A daughter of Michael Raeder was buried, aged 2 years, 8 months, 4 weeks

1767, Nov 24 Peter Mack, brother of Peter Mayer's wife of New Goshenhoppen, was buried, born 1707, aged 55 years

1767, Nov 14 The wife of Mathias Walder was buried, named Anna Maria, born 1714, Nov 4, aged 53 years, less several days.

1768, June 7 A daughter of Peter Hellicas was buried, named Eva, born 1768, March 20; aged 11 weeks and 1 day

1768. An old woman was buried, born in the year (I don't know), aged about 60 years

1769, March 7 A daughter of Mr Lauer was buried, named Sara, born 1769, Jan 23; aged 6 weeks and 3 days

1769, March 18. A daughter of Henrich Barleman was buried, named Anna Margaretha, born 1766, June 4; aged 4 years, 9 months and 5 days

1769, May 28 David Mayn was buried, born in 1738, aged 38 years, 8 months and 15 days.

1770 Febr 14 A son of —— was buried, named John Erhart, born 1769, May 15, aged 8 months, 3 weeks, 4 days.

1770, Jan. 21 Anna Margareta Faabin was buried; born 1749, Oct 9, aged 20 years, 4 months, 9 days

1770, Febr 14 Michael Moll was buried; born 1700; aged 70 years

1770, Apr 10 Michael Huper's son was buried, named Johannes, born 1769, Dec 16, aged 17 weeks and several days

1770, Apr 23 A son of John Jacob Danckel was buried, named Henrich, born 1761, March 21; aged 9 years, 1 month

1770, Dec. 14 A daughter of Peter Panebecker was buried, named Anna Maria, born 1770, Dec 4, aged 9 days and 1 night

1771, March 25 Elisabeth Panebecker was buried, born 1750, June 8, aged 20 years, 9 months, 3 weeks

1771, Apr 18 Anna Margaretha Danckel was buried; born 1696, Febr. 10; aged 75 years, 2 months, 5 days

1771, July 27. Margaretha Getto Morin (a negress), daughter of Getto Mor, was buried; born 1756; aged 15 years.

1771, Aug 27 Robert Bel was buried, born 1735, aged 36 years, 20 weeks and several days

1772, Febr. 7 The old Mr Conrad was buried, born 1699, aged a little above 73 years

1772, Apr 1. Conrad Wannenmacher was buried, born 1701, aged 70 years, 3 months and 20 days

1772, May 30 Magdalena Schuler was buried, born 1715, June 17, aged 57 years less 16 days

1772, June 3 Catharina Gucker was buried; born 1696, aged about 76 years.

1771, Aug 4 Georg Reinheimer's son was buried, named Joh Philippus, born 1771, Sept 8; aged 1 year less 5 weeks

1772, Sept 6. Michael Raeder's daughter was buried, named Elisabetha, born 1772, Febr 18, aged half a year less 4 weeks

1771, Nov. 21 Peter Gesell was buried, born 1726, Sept 7, aged 46 years, 2 months, 1 week and 5 days

1773, Jan 24 Sarah Laur was buried, born 1737, Oct 24; aged 35 years, 3 months

1773, Jan 29 Michael Raeder's child was buried, born 1772, Jan 16; aged 1 year, 2 weeks

1773, Febr. 12. Michael Raeder's child was buried, born 1770, Apr. 11, aged 3 years less 8 weeks and 3 days

1773, Febr. 21 A child of Michael Raeder; born 1762, March 5; aged 11 years less 2 weeks

1773, Apr 8 A negro child of John Adam Hellicas; born about 1771, aged about 2 years and several months.

1773, Apr. 10 A daughter of Wilh Geiger was buried; born 1756, Nov. 29; aged 16 years, 4 months, 10 days.

1773, March 17. The wife of young Mr. Mack was buried; born 1743, April 3, aged 27 years, 11 months, 13 days.

1773, May 18 A son of Andreas Jung was buried; born 1770, March 12; aged 3 years, 2 months, 5 days

1773, June 3 Joh. Valentin Grisemer was buried, born 1688, Jan 4, aged 85 years, 5 months less 4 days

1773, June 22 A daughter of Rudolph Dresch was buried, born 1772, Aug 7; aged 1 year less 8 weeks

1773, Aug 13. Peter Lauer's daughter was buried, born 1770, Jan 24, aged 3 years, 5 months, 13 weeks and several days

1773, Oct 11 A daughter of Michael Schell was buried; born 1758, March 10, aged 14 years, 7 months

1773, Nov 12 A daughter of Leonhart Kriesemer was buried, born 1773, Jan 14, aged 10 months, 4 days

1774, Jan 5 A son of Henr. Rauch was buried, born 1773, Dec 24; aged 11 days

1774, Febr 23 Anna Maria Gillwein (a negress) was buried, born 1750, aged 23 years and about 6 months

1774, Febr 2 Joh Engel was buried, born 1706; aged 68 years

1774, March 25 Adam Bosseit was buried; born 1714, aged 62 years

1774, June 3 A son of Conrad Helligas was buried; born 1774, Jan 13, aged 4 months, 2 weeks, 5 days

1774, June 13 Michael Lieser was buried, born 1720, aged about 54 years

1774, Sept 18. A daughter of Joh Georg Kolb was buried; born 1773, May 16, aged 1 year, 4 months

1774, Dec 15 A daughter of Abr Gerhart was buried; born 1771, Jan 2, aged 3 years, 11 months, 12 days.

1775, Jan 15 A daughter of Philip Leidecker was buried; born 1774, June 1, aged 7 months, 13 days

1775, Febr 14 A daughter of Conrad Nuss was buried, born 1773, Nov 4, aged 1 year, 3 months, 1 week.

1775, Jan 17 A daughter of the late Michael Lieser was buried, born 1774, Dec. 9, aged 1 year, 5 months, several days.

1775, Apr. 19 The old Mrs Steinmann was buried; born 1708, March 18; aged 68 years, 6 weeks, 1 day.

1775, Apr. 19. A daughter of Joseph Kolb was buried, born 1775, Jan 25; aged 11 weeks, 3 days

1775, Apr 11 A son of Justus Eckhart was buried, born 1773, Sept. 18, aged 1 year, 6 months, 3 weeks.

1775, March 6. A son of Georg Schutz was buried; born 1768, March 25, aged 7 years less 3 weeks.

1775, March 8. A son of Henr Schneider was buried; born 1775, Jan. 24, aged 6 weeks, 5 days.

1775, March 14. A son of Jacob Kugler was buried, born 1774, Sept, 7; aged 6 months, 6 days.

1775, Apr. 27. Jacob Frack was buried, born 1690, Aug. 16; aged 84 years, 8 months

1775, Apr 27 A son of Conrad Gillam was buried; born 1774, Jan 19; aged 1 year, 3 months, 6 days.

1775, May 23. Anna Maria Reninger was buried, born 1745, May 6, aged 30 years.

1775, Aug 15 Elis. Barbara Staut was buried, born 1748, July 24, aged 27 years, 21 days.

1775, Aug 9. A son of Peter Heisst was buried, born 1773, July 22; aged 2 years, 18 days.

1775, Aug 17. A son of Jacob Lang was buried, born 1774, Febr 7, aged 3 years, 6 months, 8 days.

1775, Aug 23 A daughter of Peter Maurer was buried; born 1762, June 28, aged 13 years, 7 weeks, 6 days.

1775, Sept 13 A daughter of Joh Cunius was buried; born 1772, Nov. 6; aged 2 years, 10 months, 6 days.

1775, Dec 20 A son of Henr Bachmann was buried; born 1773, Febr 2; aged 2 years, 11 months, 14 days

1775, Dec 23 A daughter of Daniel Lambrecht was buried; born 1774, Aug 9, aged 1 year, 4 months, 3 weeks, 3 days.

1775, Dec 26 A daughter of Daniel Lambrecht was buried, born 1773, March 4; aged 2 years, 9 months, 20 days

1775, Dec 27 Ludwig Bitting was buried, born 1703; aged about 73 years.

1776, Jan 6 A daughter of Joh Schell was buried; born 1773, July 29; aged 2 years, 5 months, 8 days

1776, Jan 22 A daughter of Jacob Holzhausen was buried; born 1774, March 25; aged 1 year, 9 months, 26 days.

1776, Febr 22 The wife of Phil Wischang was buried, born 1702, about 74 years of age

1776, Apr. 25   John George Hering was buried, born 1753, Nov. 13; aged 22 years, 6 months

1776, May 1   A daughter of Henr Mueller was buried; born 1770, Nov. 13; aged 5 years, 5 months, 13 days.

1776, May 17   Catharine Weber was buried, born 1709, April 6, aged 67 years, 1 month, 9 days

1776, July 5.   Anna Maria Geitruta Reiter was buried; born 1709, Apr 26, aged 67 years, 2 months, 7 days.

1776, Sept. 24   Rudolph Segler was buried; born 1747, May 4; aged 29 years, 4 months, 3 weeks, several days.

1776, Nov 24   Margaretha Raudebusch was buried; born 1702, aged 74 years and 8 weeks.

1776, Dec 26   A son of Wendel Wiant was buried, born 1776, Aug 4, aged 20 weeks and some days.

1777, Jan 7.   A son of Caspar Bastian was buried, born 1777, Jan 18, aged 2 weeks and 4 days.

1777, Jan. 7   A son of Joseph Leopold was buried; born 1775, March 26, aged 1 year, 10 months, 1 week

1777, Febr 5.   A son of Jacob Wetknecht was buried, born 1757, March 11, aged 19 years, 10 months, 12 days.

1776, Oct 20   A son was born (!) to Fried. Schell named Magdalena, witnesses Georg Kolb and wife.

1777, Jan 5   The old Mrs. Segler was buried, born 1709, Dec 25; aged 68 years, 8 days

1777, March 3   Michael Huper was buried; born 1715, July 29, aged 61 years, 7 months

1777, March 14.   Johannes Gillam was buried, born 1761, Nov. 22; aged 15 years, 3 months, 3 weeks.

1777, March 19   Anna Maria Berret was buried, born 1699; about 78 years old

1777, Apr 12   Anna Maria Holshaus was buried, born 1740, March 19; aged 37 years, 12 days.

1777, Apr 14.   Peter Maurer's wife was buried, born 1740, Febr. 15; aged 36 years, 2 months, less a few days.

1777, Apr 18   Benedict Moll was buried, born 1742, about November; aged about 35 years.

1777, May 4   Joh Schell was buried; born 1729, Jan 22, aged 48 years and 3 months.

1777, May 6.   A daughter of Adam Hilligas was buried; aged 9 days

1777, May 25.   A child of Peter Loch was buried, aged 12 days.

1777, May 23.   A son of Fried Muller was buried, aged 12 years, 2 months and 6 days.

1777, Aug. 12. Three children of Andreas Weiller were buried, namely, two daughters and one son, the oldest daughter was born 1758, Ap 16, aged 19 years, 4 months, less some days, the second daughter was born 1759, Aug 25, she was 18 years less a week and some days, the son was born 1766, June 9, aged 11 years, 2 months, 2 days

1777, Aug 7 A daughter of Peter Maurer was buried; born 1773, Febr 7, aged 4 years and 6 months

1777, Aug. 4 A son of Herman Fischer was buried; born 1774, Jan 5, aged 3 years and 7 months.

1777, Aug. 25. A son of Andreas Weiller was buried; born 1763, Oct 6, aged 14 years, 1 month, 5 days Eight days later another son was buried.

1777, Aug 26. The old Mrs. Haas was buried; born 1702; aged 75 years

1777, Aug 16 Joh Staut was buried, born 1776, July 27; aged 1 year, 3 weeks.

1777, Aug. 30 A child of Jacob Espenschiedt was buried, born 1775, Jan. 18, aged 2 years, 7 months, 8 days

1777, Sept 21. A child of Benedict Horne was buried, born 1771, Apr 5, aged 6 years, 5 months, 14 days

1777, Sept. 30 A child of Peter Timich was buried, born 1776, Dec 3, aged 10 months less 4 or 5 days

1777, Oct. 22 A son of Jacob Muller was buried, born 1766, Jan. 7, aged 11 years, 9 months, 2 weeks.

1777, Dec 1. The wife of the Schoolmaster Schubart was buried; born ———, aged 68 years, less 3 months and 4 days.

1777, Nov. 20. Margaretha Geiger was buried; born 1762, Aug 4, aged 15 years, 3 months, 12 days

1778, May 1. A child of Martin Eisenhauer was buried, born Jan 5; aged 4 months less 4 days

1778, May 17. A daughter of Eberh. Christoffel Schart was buried; born 1762, Dec 20, aged 15 years, 22 weeks and 3 days

1778, May 21 A child of Lorens Schmidt was buried; born 1776, Sept. 2, aged 1 year, 9 months, 17 days

1778, Dec 10 Georg Reinheimer was buried, born 1727, Febr 21; aged 51 years, 10 months, several weeks.

1779, Jan 2 A daughter of Peter Gucker was buried; born 1771, July 5, aged 7 years, 6 months, less 5 days

1779, Jan 12 A daughter of Peter Gucker was buried, born 1773, Oct 23, aged 5 years, 3 months, less 9 days

1779, March 13 The old Adam Hilligas was buried, born 1717, Jan. 5; aged 62 years, 3 months, 8 days

1779, May 2. A child of Joh Sanger was buried, born 1775, May 31, aged 4 years, 2 months

1779, June 7 A son of Henry Schlieger was buried, born 1777, Oct 17; aged 1 year, 7 months, 3 weeks
1779, June 15 A child of Conrad Nus was buried, born 1778, Aug 17, aged 10 months, less 3 days.
1779, June 18 A child of Georg Hilligas was buried, born 1778, Oct 5; aged 1 year, 9 months, 12 days
1779, Aug. 5 A daughter of the late Michael Moll was buried, born 1739, about March, aged about 40 years

Record of those who died and were buried during the ministry of Friedrich Delliker, V.D M, in this congregation of New Goshenhoppen

1783

January 5 Abraham, 1 year, 1 month, 14 days old; parents are Benedict Hoining and his wife Elisabeth.
January 11 Joh Adam, 8 days, 8 hours old, parents are Andreas Rid and wife Maria
May 23. Johannes Steinmann, his age 39 years, 4 months
June 25 Maria, 1 year, 8 months, 11 days old, parents Georg Steineman and Catharine, his wife
June 30 Samuel Kolb, his age 29 years, several days
August 12 Georg Raudenbusch, his age 84 years.
Sept 5 Joh Philip Rid, born 1698, Jan 26; his age 85 years, 7 months, 8 days.
Oct 15 Johannes Mack, his age 32 years, 9 months, 4 days He died by an accidental fall from a wagon within 17 days
Dec 4 Elisabeth, 14 years, 7 months, 6 days old; parents Daniel Ekbrett and Elisabeth his wife.
December 5 Abraham Segler, his age 54 years, 2 months. He fell from his horse near his house and was found dead in the water

A° 1784

Feb 8 Catharine, 14 days, 6 hours old, parents Andreas Rid and his wife Maria.
March 11 David Levi, his age not quite 56 years

Buried during the ministry of Fried Wilh V. d Sloot

1784.

Apr 25 Peter May, his age 70 years, 2 months, a Lutheran
June 12 Maria Nuss, née Reder, aged 27 years.
Oct 16 Anna Margaretha, her father Georg Fischer; her age 19 years, 8 months

Those persons who were buried by me, Joh Theob Faber, in the year 1786. Date of birth.
1785, May 4, Sus. Cath. Nus, aged 1 year, several weeks.
1783, May 24, Petrus Huper, aged 3 years less 5 weeks.
1786, Apr 27, Johannes Huper, aged 1 month, 2 weeks
1786, May 4, child of young Grisemer, aged 4 months, 2 days
1786, July 27, child of Val. Brobst, aged 11 days.
1786, July 18, child of Peter Hilligas, aged 7 weeks, 2 days.
1751, Jos. Leobold, aged 35 years.
1786, Sept 27, child of Georg Dorr, aged 13 days
1720, old Mrs Benkes, aged 66 years
1718, Nov. 6, Adam Geri, aged 68 years
1786, Nov 27, child of Jacob Geri, aged 2 years, 3 weeks
1716, Oct 16, Conrad Zimmerman, aged 70 years, 1 month, 3 weeks
1761, Dec 19, Peter Zimmerman, aged 25 years.

1787.

1764, Mar 13, Henr Herger, aged 22 years, 11 months, 11 days.
1775, Aug. 18, Peter Rautebusch, aged 11 years, 8 months, less 10 days.
1784, Sept 29, Johannes Heisst, aged 2 years, 6 months, 2 weeks
1786, Oct 5, Johannes, Trumb, aged 6 months, 11 weeks
1730, Jacob Holshauser, aged 57 years
1767, Mar 25, daughter of Phil Jacob Schmid, aged 20 years, 2 months.
1709, July 14, old Mr Wendel Wiant, aged 78 years
1787, Febr 23, child of Mr Dimig, aged 3 months, 12 days.
1787, Aug 10, child of Andr. Ried, aged 8 days
1783, Nov 22, child of Georg Fischer, aged 3 years, 10 months, 11 days.
1784, Mar. 25 child of Joh Bidling, aged 3 years, 6 months, 17 days.
1735, Apr. 3, Joh Fischer, aged 52 years, 6 months, 10 days.
1784, Febr 6, child of Joh. Muller, aged 3 years, 9 months
1787, Oct 9, child of Peter Trumb, aged 2 years, 1 month, 3 days
1785, Aug 13, child of Adam Roeder, aged 2 years, 3 months
1783, Aug 18, child of Adam Roeder, aged 4 years, 3 months
1787, Oct 12, child of Joh Fischer, aged 7 months, 18 days.
1717, old Mrs. Jung, aged 71 years
1713, old Wm Grisemer, aged 75 years, several months.

1788

1784, Febr 1, child of Jacob Stahl, aged 4 years less a month
1787, Apr 27, child of young Adam Schneider, aged 8 months, 14 days.
1786, Febr. 8, child of Georg Lang, aged 1 year, 11 months, 11 days
1787, Aug —, child of Mr Schwartz.

1786, Nov 29, child of Joh Lambrecht, aged 13 months, 21 days
1786, May 12, child of Zach Wagner, aged 1 year, 8 months, 12 days.
1726, Cath. Schlieger, aged 62 years.
1783, Jan 27, Maria Cath Hillegas, aged 5 years, 1 week, 4 days.
1782, July 28, son of Ludwig Bitting, aged 5 years, 7 months
1784, Mar. 5, child of Georg Dorr, aged 4 years less 4 days.
1784, Oct. 26, child of Henr Panebecker, aged 3 years, 4 months, 5 days
1788, Sept 19, Joh. Georg, aged 1 year, 6 months.
1746, Henrich Maurer, aged 42 years.
1781, Febr. 9, Catharina, aged 7 years, 6 months, 4 weeks.

1789

Members at New Goshenhoppen who died and were buried by N. Pomp.
Date of birth.
1768, Dec 6, Jacob Rieth, aged 20 years 11 months, 28 days
1718, Dec. 25, Peter Miller, aged 70 years, 11 months, 19 days
Buried Febr 16, George Michael Kolb, aged 81 years, 25 days.
Buried Febr. 16, Anna Maria Stroh, aged 59 years, 7 months, 2 days
Buried Mar, 25, Dorothea Hollebusch, aged 68 years.
Buried June 16, Elisabeth Gehry, aged 25 years, 10 months, 21 days

Those persons who were buried by me, Joh Theob Faber, Jr.

1791.

Date of birth.
1787, June 3, child of Peter Hilligas, aged 4 years, 6 months, 8 days

1792

1790, July 24, Susan, child of George Wigner, aged 1 year, 8 months
1707, Sept. 29, Maria Kemp, widow, aged 82 years, 6 months, 2 weeks
1716, July 27, Fried Miller, aged 75 years, 8 months, 3 weeks, 2 days
——— child of Joseph Kolb, aged 12 years, 2 months, 13 days
——— Andr. Weiler, aged 68 years, 5 months, 3 weeks, 4 days
——— wife of Stev. Shoner.
——— wife of Georg Horlacher, aged 33 years, 2 months, 3 week, 2 days.
May 6, Georg Orffer (?).
May 12 (buried), Wife of Heinr. Miller, aged 56 years, 1 month, 1 day.
March 1, Elisabeth

1795.

1746, July 31, Anna Marg Borleman, aged 48 years, 5 months, 2 weeks, 4 days
1717, Dec , Weyand Panebecker, aged 79 years, 2 months, 2 days.

1785, Dec 25, Susana, child of Godf. Wissler, aged 9 years, 2 months
1785, Apr 16, Jacob, child of Adam Hittel, aged 9 years less 3 days.
1787, Febr 9, Catharine, daughter of Peter Trumb, aged 8 years, 3 weeks, 5 days
1794, Apr 23, Maria Cath., daughter of Henry Geiger, aged 11 months, 4 days

Names of those who were buried in New Goshenhoppen in 1808 A Helffenstein [pastor]
Hanna Hering, died June 21, 1808, aged 38 years, 8 months, 14 days
Salina Wannemacher, died July 19, 1808, aged 4 years, 4 months, 11 days.
Johan Kehl, aged 5 months, 5 days.
Henrich Liser
Conrad Nuss, died March 18, 1808, aged 64 years, 5 months, 4 days
Conrad Heyl, a Lutheran, died Sept 24, 1808, aged 59 years, 7 weeks, 4 days.
Jacob Kehl, died Sept 30, 1808, aged 4 years, 7 months, 11 days
Lorenz Sussholz, died Oct 16, 1808, aged 69 years, 11 months, 5 days

1809.

1805, July 17, Joel ———, aged 3 years, 6 months, 13 days
1737 (about), Susanna Gucker, aged about 72

Those who were buried since the beginning of my ministry. On Nov. 12, 1812, I entered upon my ministry, but funerals did not occur till 1813
[V D Sloot, Jr.]
Date of birth.
1813, Jan. 24, Magdalena Hittel, aged 2 months, 5 days
1809, Dec 25, Sophia Wigand, aged 3 years, 4 months, 24 days.
1773, Oct. 7, Marg Gery, née Steinmann, aged 39 years, 4 months, 13 days
1743, Magdalena Sell, died 1813, Febr 27, buried March 2, aged 70 years
1812, Dec 10, Israel, buried March 26, 1813, in the Schwenkfelder Cemeetery, aged 3 months, 14 days

[III MARRIAGE RECORDS.]

Those persons who were joined in marriage by me, Joh. Theob Faber.
1767, March 3, Johannes Hellicas, son of Adam Hellicas, of New Goshenhoppen, and Anna Maria Geri, daughter of Jacob Geri, also of New Goshenhoppen.
1767, May 26, Wendel Fischer, son of the late Herman Fischer, of Upper Hanover, and Juliana Schneider, daughter of Adam Schneider, of Douglas township

1767, May 26, Michael Moll, son of Michael Moll, of Upper Hanover, and Margaretha Schmeck, daughter of the late Johannes Schmeck, of Elsass township.

1767, June 16, Johannes Steinmann, son of the late Georg Steinmann, of Herford township, and Anna Catharina Maurer, daughter of the late Jacob Maurer, of New Goshenhoppen

1767, June 23, Christoph Schliger, son of the late Johannes Otto Schliger, of New Goshenhoppen, and Margaretha Mack, daughter of Johannes Mack, of New Goshenhoppen

1767, June 23, Friedrich Maurer, son of the old Friedrich Maurer, of New Goshenhoppen, and Catharina Beyer, daughter of the late Henrich Beyer, of Herford township.

1767, Nov 10, Michael Hellicas, son of Adam Hellicas, of New Goshenhoppen, and Catharina Geri, daughter of Jacob Geri, of New Goshenhoppen.

1768, Febr. 4, Andreas Riedt, son of Philip Riedt, of New Goshenhoppen, and Anna Maria Leidi, daughter of Jacob Leidi, of Franconia township.

1768, June 28, Jacob Segler, son of the late Joh. Segler, of New Goshenhoppen, and Christina Fischer, daughter of the late Herman Fischer, of Upper Hanover township

1768, Sept 6, Jacob Frack's son, Daniel Frack, of New Goshenhoppen, and Catharina, daughter of the late Jost Wiand of New Goshenhoppen

1768, Nov 22, Jacob Kammerer, son of Friedrich Kammerer, of Upper Milford, and Andreas Maurer's daughter, Elisabetha Maria, of New Goshenhoppen

1769, Jan 10, Jacob, son of the late Joh Taub, of New Goshenhoppen, and Anna Margaretha, daughter of Conrad Zimmerman, of New Goshenhoppen.

1769, Apr 25, Georg Michael, son of Georg Michael Kolb, of New Goshenhoppen, and Eva Maria, daughter of Friedr. Stellwagen, of Marion township

1769, Aug 22, Conrad, son of the late Jacob Nus, of Upper Hanover township, and Maria Margaretha Roeder, daughter of Michael Roeder, of Upper Hanover township

1769, Aug 15, Lorentz, son of David Schmid, of Plumstet township, and Susanna Kolb, daughter of Georg Michael Kolb, of Hanover township

1769, Oct 12, Jacob, son of Jacob Schlosser, of Old Goshenhoppen, and Anna Cath. Schwartz, daughter of Weiland Schwartz, of Old Goshenhoppen

1769, Oct 17, Jacob, son of the late Jacob Lutz, of Maxatawny, and Anna Christina Bossert, daughter of Adam Bossert, of New Goshenhoppen.

1770, April 17, Jacobus, son of the late Jost Wiant, of New Goshenhoppen, and Catharina Schlichter, daughter of John Schlichter, of New Goshenhoppen.

1770, Sept 30, Joh. Georg, son of Adam Hellicas, of New Goshenhoppen, and Elisabeth Jung, daughter of Joh Nicolaus Jung, of New Goshenhoppen

1770, Oct. 2, Melchior Kolb, widower, of New Goshenhoppen, and Anna Maria Stettler, widow, of Falkner Swamp.

1771, Jan 4, Jost, son of Wendel Wiant, of Upper Hanover township, and Anna Barbara Roder, daughter of Michael Roder, of Upper Hanover.

1772, Jan. 14, Valentin, son of Joh Nicolas Finck, of Herford township, and Elisabetha, daughter of Melchoir Süssholz, of New Goshenhoppen

1772, May 5, Johannes, son of Joh. Krisemer, of Leter (¹) Creek, and daughter of Joh Adam Hellicas, of New Goshenhoppen

1772, Oct. 13, Marty, son of Marty Hiller, of Limerick township, and Anna Roeder, daughter of Michael Raeder, of New Goshenhoppen.

1772, Oct 13 Jacob, son of the late Jacob Hohl, of New Goshenhoppen, and Magdalena, daughter of Jacob Datismon, of New Goshenhoppen

1773, Sept 23, Christian, son of Joh. Henr. Schmid, of Upper Milford township, and Maria Geri, daughter of Thomas Geri, of Rockhill township.

1773, Nov. 2, Peter, son of Engel Binkes, of New Goshenhoppen, and Barbara, daughter of the late Henrich Stettler, of New Goshenhoppen

1773, Oct 25, Adam, son of Zach Haller, of Lynn township, and Catharina, daughter of Wilh. Geier, of New Goshenhoppen

1773, Dec 7, Andreas, son of Andreas Weiller, of New Goshenhoppen, and Anna Maria, daughter of Joh Mack, of New Goshenhoppen.

1774, June 14, Albertus Spring, son of the late Andreas Spring, of New Goshenhoppen, and Barbara, daughter of Peter Gettel, of New Goshenhoppen.

1774, Aug 14, Carl Schelleberger, son of Joh Schelleberger, of Hatfield township, and Margaret Hellicas, daughter of Adam Helligas, of New Goshenhoppen.

1774, Nov 20, Friedrich Panebecker, son of the late Weiant Panebecker, of New Goshenhoppen, and Elis Neukomer, daughter of Joh Neukomer, of Lower Saucon.

1774, Dec. 27, Joh Taudt, son of Michael Taudt, of New Goshenhoppen, and Susanna Benvil, daughter of the late Thomas Benvil, of Berks County.

1775, March 21, Joh Klein, son of Joh Klein, of Nentmil [Nantmill] township, and Cath Bitting, daughter of Ludwig Bitting, of Great Swamp

New Goshenhoppen—Vol II. Marriages

1775, July 4, Wendel Wiant, widower, of New Goshenhoppen, and Magdalena Datismann, wife of the late Mr Datismann, but now widow, of New Goshenhoppen

1775, July 2, Jost Wiant, son of Jost Wiant, of Upper Milford township, and Margareta Long, daughter of Peter Long, of Upper Milford township.

1775, Aug. 15, Jacob Bossert, son of the late Adam Bossert, of Lower Salford, and Eva Schlieger, daughter of Jost Schlieger, of New Goshenhoppen

1775, Dec. 12, Henr Schlieger, son of Jost Schlieger, of New Goshenhoppen, and Christina Weiller, daughter of Andreas Weiller, also of New Goshenhoppen

1776, Febr 20, Joh. Mack, son of Joh Mack, of New Goshenhoppen, and Anna Maria Schell, daughter of Joh. Schell, also of New Goshenhoppen

1776, May 7, Joh Roeder, son of Michael Roeder, of New Goshenhoppen, and Maria Cath. Wiegner, of New Goshenhoppen

1776, May 5, Valentin Schneider, son of the late Georg Schneider, of New Goshenhoppen, and Maria Wagner, daughter of Michael Wagner, of Old Goshenhoppen

1776, June 11, Henr Panebecker, son of Weyant Panebecker, of New Goshenhoppen, and Susana Huper, daughter of Michael Huper, of Douglas township.

1776, June 11, Joh. Adam Geri, son of Jacob Geri, of New Goshenhoppen, and Barbara Weiller, daughter of Andreas Weiller, of New Goshenhoppen.

1776, June 9, Philip Vorschong, of New Goshenhoppen, and Anna Benges, of New Goshenhoppen.

1776, July 2, Adam Helligas, son of Joh Adam Helligas, of New Goshenhoppen, and Anna Schultz, daughter of Melchior Schultz, of New Goshenhoppen.

1777, Sept 30, Michael Diel, son of the late Jacob Diel, of Upper Milford township, and Barbara Sussholtz, daughter of Melchior Sussholtz, of New Goshenhoppen.

1777, Dec 2, Georg Faust, son of Georg Faust, of Tulpehocken, and Christina Maurer, daughter of Andreas Maurer, of New Goshenhoppen

1778, Jan 13, Jacob Dorr, son of Joh Dorr, of Great Swamp, and Margaretha Muller, daughter of Henr. Muller, of New Goshenhoppen

1778, Dec 22, Dietrich Reiher, son of Martin Reiher, of Malbrick [Marlborough] township, and Elisabeth Graeber, daughter of Andreas Graeber, of New Goshenhoppen

1779, Febr 23, Jacob Nus, son of the late Jacob Nus, of New Goshenhoppen, and Anna Maria Roeder, daughter of Michael Roeder, of New Goshenhoppen.

1779, March 9, Andreas Graeber, son of Andreas Graeber, of New Goshenhoppen, and Anna Weiss, son of Georg Weiss, of Upper Milford township

1779, March 16, Joh Petrus Helligas, son of Georg Petrus Helligas, of New Goshenhoppen, and Anna Maria Maurer, daughter of Andreas Maurer, of New Goshenhoppen.

1779, June 22, Jacob Brendel, son of the late Andreas Brendel, of Colebrookdale township, and Elis Ritschert, daughter of James Ritschert, of Daumensich [Toamensing] township

1779, Sept 17, Georg Long, son of the late Elis Long, of New Goshenhoppen, and Anna Maria Graeber, daughter of Ulrich Graeber, of New Goshenhoppen.

1779, July 21, Ludwig Graeber, son of Andreas Graeber, of New Goshenhoppen, and Elis Joter, daughter of Jacob Joter, of Rocklin [Rockland] township

1779, Sept 30, Peter Lauer, son of Peter Lauer, of New Goshenhoppen, and Margaretha Fischer, daughter of Joh Fischer, of New Goshenhoppen.

List of those persons who were joined in marriage by me, Friedrich Delliker

1782

March 24, Georg Zerby and Maria Klein

June 25, Georg Grob, son of Jacob Grob, of New Hanover township, and Margaretha Lar, daughter of Philip Lar.

Sept 3, David Sussholtz, widower, of New Hanover township, and Elisabeth Muller, daughter of Peter Muller, of Rockhill township.

1783

May 20, Samuel Kolb, son of Melchior Kolb, and Anna Maurer, daughter of Peter Maurer.

1784.

Febr. 3, Heinrich Segler, son of Abraham Segler, and Elisabeth Gugger, daughter of Peter Gugger, of Upper Hanover township.

Febr. 15, Philip Pauly and Elisabeth Mosch, daughter of Joh Mosch, of Eastown

March 16, Hans Niclas Mud, Jacob Mud's son and Anna Margaret Greber, daughter of Andreas Greber, both of this congregation

List of the Persons who were united in marriage by me, Fridrich Wilhelm Von der Sloot

1784

May 11, Johannes Keri [Geri], son of Jacob Keri, of New Goshenhoppen, and Susanna Wigner, daughter of the late George Wigner

May 25, Peter Jost, son of Johannes Jost, of Fredrick township, and Eva Hillegas, daughter of Conrad Hillegas, of New Goshenhoppen

June 27, Johannes Bergman, of Germany, and Anna Stromann

June 29, Rev Dalikei married me, Friedrich Wilhelm Von der Sloot, only son of Friedrich Heinrich Von der Sloot, late minister in Anhalt-Zeibst, Germany, to Añna Margaretha Riedt, oldest daughter of Jacob Ried, of Hatfield township, Philadelphia County.

July 13, Conrad Wolf, son of Conrad Wolf, of Upper Milford township, and Catharina Jakels, daughter of Jeremias Jakel, of Upper Milford township.

Sept 28, Peter Trump, son of Adam Trump, of Milford township, and Eva Rheder, daughter of Michael Reder, of Upper Hanover township.

Those persons who were united in marriage by me, John Theobald Faber

1786

Aug 6, Joh Stephan Linck, of Malburi [Marlborough] township, and Margaret Maurer, of New Hanover

Dec 19, Math Hinerleiter, of Maxatawny, and Catharina Gerhard, of Douglas township

1787.

March 6, Jacob Maurer, of New Goshenhoppen, and Eva Horneckei, of the same place

March 13, Henr Graeber and Christina Haas, both of Lower Saucon

March 13, Martin Wetknecht, of New Goshenhoppen, and Maria Pertroin, of Old Goshenhoppen

Apr 22, Pettus Stehler, of Upper Milford, and Christina Graeber, of New Goshenhoppen

Apr. 24, Jeremias Schiefer, of Upper Milford, and Catharina Schlieger, of New Goshenhoppen

Apr. 24, Jacob Bierman and Christina Fischer, both of Berks County

May 3, —— Weitner, of ——, and —— Wagner

May 15, Wendel Wiant, of New Goshenhoppen, and Margaretha Sell, of New Goshenhoppen

June 12, Johannes Finck, of New Goshenhoppen, and Elisabetha Neudorf, in New Goshenhoppen

June 24, Peter Lang and Cath Hageberg, both of Upper Milford township

June 26, Joh Faust, of Frederick township, and Susanna Walber, of the same township
July 7, Georg Reinheimer, of New Goshenhoppen, and Margareth Cogg.
Oct 23, Georg Frey, of Limerick township, and Margaretha Griesemer, of New Goshenhoppen.
Dec 18, Peter Willauer, of New Goshenhoppen, and Rebecka Geri, also of New Goshenhoppen.

1788

Jan. 8, Joh. Martin Schmidt, of Malbork [Marlborough] township, and Barbara Wetknecht, of the same township.
April 22, Georgus Maurer and Catharina Schultz, both of New Goshenhoppen.
May 6, Johannes Wittner, of Oly, and Anna Margareta Cunius, of New Goshenhoppen.
May 13, Fried Hering and Anna Levi, both of New Goshenhoppen

N. Pomp, minister of the three united congregations, has duly married the following persons, beginning with December 1, 1789
Dec. 22, Philip Schmayer, of Macungie, and Catharina Miller, daughter of Peter Miller, of New Goshenhoppen
Dec 26, Philip Hubner, of Frederick township, Montgomery County, and Elisabeth Neiss, of Old Goshenhoppen.

1790

Jan 17, Henrich Raudenbusch and Catharina Schneider, both of New Goshenhoppen.
March 23, Johannes Dorr and Gertraut Schliecher.
March 30, Johannes Raudenbusch and Salome Hildebeutel
June 1, Christophel Schlicher and Gertraut Schneider, married at Upper Milford
Aug. 10, Michael Dotter and Maria Margareth Hillegas   ✓

Those persons who were duly united in marriage by me, John Faber, in New Goshenhoppen.

1793

Andreas Graeber and Sibilla Wolzetler.
Samuel Brode and Barbara Berckstroser
Jacob Geri and Elisabeth Dreisler
Joseph Fischer and Barbara Miller
Jan 22, John Christman and Catharina Wiant, both of New Goshenhoppen.
Febr. 26, Michael Moll and Elizabetha Sell
Apr 2, Heinrich Rhoeder and Maragaretha Kowern

May 7, Michael Diederle and Barbara Borlemann
June 2, John Hauswirth and Elisabeth Miller.
Aug. 20, Jacob Roth, of Lower Saucon, and Margaretha Barkstroser
Michael Brauchler, of Berks County, and Elisabetha Kittelmann.

1794

Apr 15 John Maurer and Maria Stahl, both of New Goshenhoppen
Apr 15, Abraham Joder and Elisabeth Maurer, both of New Goshenhoppen
May 11, Abraham Levi and Eva Hillegas, daughter of Peter Hillegas ✓
Nov, 1794, John Kuhler, son of John Kuhler, and Eva Sussholtz, daughter of Lorenz Sussholtz

1795.

Jan 4, Johannes Loch and Caty Neudig
April 7, Daniel Zimmerman and Catharina Weiss
May 10, Henrich Boyer and Madlena Wissler
May 31, Jacob Ache and Maricha Hillegas ✓
June 7, William Lick and Catharina Wiand
June 7, John George Hillegas and Maria Hillegas ✓
June 25, Peter Gerhard and Elisabetha Himmels
June 28, Johannes Young and Barbara English
August, Johannes Hillegas and Catharina Hillegas ✓
December, Henrich Sell and Margaretha Schmitt
November, 1796, George Staud and Hanna Sell
1797, April, Michael Rhaudenbusch and Maria Sell
1797, May, George Renninger and Mary Hein
1797, June 1, David Zerby and Maria Magdalena Jung

List of those persons who were united in marriage by me, Albert Helffenstein

June 12, 1808

Peter Lepold and Cath Richard, Aug 14
Georg Reiter and Polly Freyer, Aug 14.
Mr. Ball and Miss Eberhard, ——
Mr Klein and Miss Mumbauer, Oct. 10.
Mr Gering and Miss Marsteller.
Mr Handschu and Miss Schelly

1810

Febr 9, Philip Freyer and Elisabeth Brey
Febr 11, Abraham Reifschneider and Christina Schmidt.
Hanrich Steuer and Elis Freyer
Henrich Hauch and Elis Schutler.
Wilhelm Koch and Bewey Waidermeyer

[IV. LISTS OF CATECHUMENS]

Children of the congregation of New Goshenhoppen who were confirmed by me, Joh. Th Faber, in the year 1767, on April 17th, as follows:

Boys
1. Friedrich Segler, aged 23 years
2. Joseph Segler, aged 18 years
3. Christian Wanemacher, aged 14 years

Girls
1. Fronica Rid, confirmed by herself because of sickness, aged 16 years
2. Elisabeth Grob, aged 15 years

In the year 1768, April 1st

1. Johannes Mack, aged 18 years
2. Erhard Hudt, aged 15 years
3. Johannes Hudt, aged 14 years
4. Erhard Weis, aged 14 years

1. Anna Maria Wiant, aged 15 years
2. Barbara Reder, aged 15 years

In the year 1769, March 24th.

1. Joh. Adam Geri, aged 17 years
2. Conrad Finck, aged 16½ years
3. Ludwig Graeber, aged 15 years
4. Benedict Finck, aged 15 years
5. Wilh Pannebecker, aged 15 years
6. Stephen Schlieger, aged 19 years
7. Jacob Geri, aged 14 years
8. Henr Schlieger, aged 16½ years
9. Abr Zimmermann, aged 14 years
10. Petrus Binckes, aged 16½ years
11. Jost Wiant, aged 16 years

---

1. Susanna Huper, aged 15½ years
2. Eva Schlieger, aged 15½ years
3. Cath Kleber, aged 14½ years
4. Sib. Cath. Wiant, aged 13½ years

In the year 1770, May 13th.

1. Michael Huper, aged 14½ years
2. Joh Schell, aged 16½ years
3. Joseph Kleport, aged 18½ years
4. Wilh. Kunius, aged 15½ years
5. Phil Jacob Kolb, aged 18 years

Adult persons who were instructed and baptized:
1. Phil Lar, aged 28 years
2. Hen Sell, aged 30 years
3. Susanna Gucker, aged 28 years
4. Anna Maria Kolb, aged 27 years
5. Magdalena, wife of Georg Kolb

1. Fereni Mack, aged 15 years
2. Barbara May, aged 15 years
3. Sara May, aged 15½ years
4. Marg Panebecker, aged 14½ years
5. Barbara Susshols, aged 15 years
6. Marg Schmitt, aged 14 years
7. Elis. Marg Rosenauer, aged 15 years
8. Anna Reder, aged 15½ years
9. Anna Christina Kraeber, aged 14 years
10. Fereni Schell, aged 15 years
11. Christina Maurer, aged 15 years

In the year 1771, March 29th.

1 Georg Adam Hellicas, aged 15 years
) 2. Friedr. Hellicas, aged 13 years
3 Peter Hellicas, aged 15 years
4. Joh. Wetknecht, aged 15 years

1 Gertr Schlieger, aged 15 years
2 Anna Marg. Geiger, aged 15 years
3 Barbara Weitner, aged 16 years
4 Marg Weitner, aged 15 years

In the year 1772, April 17th

1 Andreas Graeber, aged 17 years
2 Andr Benkes, aged 16 years
3 Wendel Wiant, aged 16 years
4 Jacob Kunsert, aged 16 years

1 Marg Elis Graeber, aged 14 years
2 Anna Maria Moor, aged 20 years
3 Marg Hupper, aged 14 years
4 Marg. Hellicas, aged 15 years

In the year 1773, April 25th

1. Joh. Adam Bossert, aged 15 years
2 Phil Wetknecht, aged 16 years
3 Peter Lauer, aged 14 years

1. Mar. Cath Schell, aged 15 years
2 Marg Schlieger, aged 15 years
3 Elis Geri, aged 16 years
4 Anna Marg Graeber, aged 14 years
5 Anna Mar Roeder, aged 15 years
6. Magdalena Zimmerman, aged 14 years
7 Cath Kolb, aged 14 years
8. Elisabeth ——, aged 14 years
9 Anna Mar Mauer, aged 15 vears

In the year 1774, April 1st

1 Phil Eckel, aged 16 years
2 Wenert Knop, aged 16 years
3 Georg Finck, aged 18 years
4 Mich Geiger, aged 14 years
5 Christian Muller, aged 17 years
6 Henrich Oehl, aged 15 years

1 Mar. Cunius, aged 15 years
2 Mar Kleber, aged 15 years
3 Anna Marg Muller, aged 15 years
4 Christian Wiant, aged 15 years

In the year 1775, April 14th.

1 Joh. Maurer, aged 18 years
2 Henr Segler, aged 16 years
3 Joh. Geri, aged 16 years
4 Joh Weiller, aged 14 years
5 Jacob Schell, aged 18 years

1 Elis. Zerny, aged 15 years
2 Magd Zerney, aged 15 years
3. Emma Mauer, aged 14 years
4 Anna Maria Maurer, aged 14 years

6 Jacob Zörli, aged 17 years
7 Ludw. Zorli, aged 15 years

5 Anna Mar Maurer, aged 16 years
6 Elis Grisemer, aged 17 years
7. Anna Mar Grisemer, aged 15 years
8 Cath Lauer, aged 14 years
9 Anna Mar. Wiant, aged 14 years
10 Mar. Weiller, aged 15 years
11. Barb Geier, aged 18 years
12 Christina Wiant, aged 18 years

In the year 1776, April 13th

1 Adam Roeder, aged 15 years
2 David Schultz, aged 16 years
3 Joh Fischer, aged 14 years
4 Nicol Muth, aged 16 years
5 Jacob Schell, aged 16 years
6 Michael Frack, aged 17 years
7 Jacob Frack, aged 14 years
8. Joh Berret, aged 17 years
9 Hen Berret, aged 15 years
10 Georg Kucker, aged 15 years
11 Peter Helligas, aged 15 years
12 Joh Doerr, aged 15 years
13. —— Schliger, aged 15 years

1 Marg Fischer, aged 15 years
2. Christina Fischer, aged 14 years
3. Cath Helligas, aged 15 years
4 Anna Mar. Geier, aged 14 years
5 Anna Schultz, aged 18 years
6 Elis. Helligas, aged 14 years
7 Anna Marg Cunius, aged 14 years
8 Eva Elis Helligas, aged 14 years
9 Cath. Holhauser, aged 14 years

In the year 1777, April 12th

Peter Zimmerman, aged 15 years
Henr Heineman, aged 15 years

Eva Graeber, aged 14 years
Cath Levi, aged 14 years
Cath Müller, aged 14 years
Elis Muller, aged 16 years
Cath Muller, aged 15 years
Anna Maria Lauer, aged 14 years
Anna Maria Reinheimer, aged 14 years
Cath Schultz, aged 15 years
Anna Barb Mayer, aged 15 years
Christina Mayer, aged 14 years

In the year 1779, April 2nd

1 Jacob Halshausen
2 Henr. Geier
3. Peter Gerhart

1 Marg. Wiegert, aged 15 years
2 Marg Stroh, aged 16 years
3 Susanna Mess, aged 15 years

New Goshenhoppen—Vol. II. Catechumens 373

4 Michael Jung
5 Joh Griesemer
6 Henr. Stroh
7 Henr. Stroh
8 Henr Graeber
9 Weiant Panebecker
10 Jacob Huper
11 Elias Ritz
12. Jacob Geri
13 Leonhart Hartranft
14 Phil Rauch
15 Georg Rauch

4 Anna Maria Helligas, aged 15 years
5 Christina Huper, aged 15 years
6 Eva Trolinger, aged 16 years
7. Eva Helligas, aged 15 years
8. Cath. Cunius, aged 16 years
9 Eva Roeder, aged 15 years
10 Cath Schleiger, aged 15 years
11 Marg Lar, aged 15 years
12 Elis. Gucker, aged 15 years
13. Elis. Barret, aged 15 years
14 Elis Lauer, aged 15 years
15 Cath Roeder, aged 17 years
16 Elis. Helligas, aged 15 years
17 Maria Hartranf, aged 17 years

On May 26th, 1782, the following children were confirmed by me, Friedrich Delliker.

Married persons.

Peter Schell   Barbara Benkes

Single persons

Philip Fischer   Catharina Ekhard
Johannes Maurer   Margaret Weitknecht
Abraham Sechler   Elisabeth Stromann
Johannes Moll   Anna Stromann
Johannes Raudenbusch   Elisabeth Barbara Hillegas
Heinrich Ringer   Anna Maria Schlicher
                       Rebecca Geri
                       Elisabeth Kolb
                       Elisabeth Jung
                       Magdalena Gugger
                       Catharina Christman
                       Barbara Baret
                       Elisabeth Moll
                       Elisabeth Barbara Horning
                       Margareth Horning
                       Catharina Horning

Confirmed May 24, 1783
Married persons.
Elisabeth Greber
Susanna Reder

Single persons

Johannes Ris
Daniel Weissel
Jacob Rid
Johannes Fischer
Andreas Greber
Abraham Zarn
Andreas Weyand
Peter Weyand

Susanna Wigner
Christina Greber
Anna Maria Zeller
Catharina Zeller
Rosina Segler
Margareth Schell

The following persons were confirmed by me, Friedrich Wilhelm Von der Sloot, in the year 1784:

1 George Huber, who was also baptized this day, aged 17 years
2 Wilhelm Geier, aged 15 years
3. Jacob Reps, aged 18 years
4 Jacob Kunius, aged 15 years
5 Christian Neukammer, aged 21 years
6. Barbara Jung, aged 16 years
7 Elisabeth Stroh, aged 18 years
8. Elisabeth Holzhausen, aged 15 years
9. Susanna Holzhausen, aged 16 years

Married persons:

10 Christina Sell, 20 years.
11 Anna Marg Schoener, 22 years

Children of the two congregations, New Goshenhoppen and Great Swamp, who were confirmed by me, Joh Theob Faber, in the year 1787, April 9th.

Boys
1 Joh Faber, aged 15 years
2. Phil. Cunius, aged 16 years
3 Peter Roeder, aged 19 years
4 Phil Lauer, aged 15 years
5 Joh Staut, aged 18 years
6 Joh. Graeber, aged 17 years
7 Wendel Wiant, aged 21 years
8 Georg Stahl, aged 16 years
9 Joh Stahl, aged 18 years
10 Wendel Wiant, aged 14 years
11 Adam Levi, aged 18 years
12 Michael Moll, aged 19 years

Girls
1. Eva Maurer, aged 18 years
2 Cath Stahl, aged 14 years
3 Maria Neukirch, aged 16 years
4. Marg. Helligas, aged 17 years
5. Susanna Helligas, aged 16 years
6 Maria Stahl, aged 15 years
7 Susanna Wiant, aged 16 years
8 Margareta Levi, aged 15 years
9. Anna Levi, aged 16 years
10. Anna Maria Fischer, aged 17 years
11 Eva Helligas, aged 17 years

New Goshenhoppen—Vol. II Catechumens

13 Jacob Helligas, aged 15 years
14 Georg Staut, aged 16 years
15. Joh Georg Fischer, aged 19 years
16 Georg Reninger, aged 16 years
17 Joh Helligas, aged 15 years
18 Jacob Hauswirt, aged 20 years
19 Johannes Hauswirt, aged 18 years
20 Peter Geri, aged 18 years
21 Michael Geri, aged 16 years
22 Wendel Reninger, aged 17 years
23 Friedr Maurer, aged 15 years
24 Jacob Mayer, aged 21 years
25 Peter Maurer, aged 17 years
26 Michael Kolb, aged 18 years
27 Georg Reinheimer, aged 19 years
28. Georg Welcker, aged 16 years
29 Georg Hustner, aged 25 years
30 Herman Bingeman, aged 20 years
31. Henr Roeder, aged 17 years
32 Jacob Linck, aged 17 years
33 Phil Riedt, aged 16 years
34 Joh Fischer, aged 17 years

12 Elis Maurer, aged 18 years
13 Anna Margr. Maurer, aged 18 years
14 Marg. Eckart, aged 16 years
15 Susanna Gucker, aged 18 years
16 Cath Nuss, aged 16 years
17 Bebi Maurer, aged 18 years
18. Anna Maria Welcker, aged 18 years
19 Elis Sell, aged 18 years
20 Marg Sell, aged 17 years
21. Margr Rid
22. Margr Griesemer
23 Magd Kolb
24. Elis. Dimig
25 Betti Reinheimer
26 Cath. Kolb
27. Sophia Derr

From the Swamp Congregation the following children were confirmed together with those of the New Goshenhoppen congregation

1. Abr Eberhart, aged 14 years
2. Georg Helligas, aged 16 years
3 Bastian Buchert, aged 17 years
4 Antoni Willauer, aged 16 years
5 Henr Bitting, aged 19 years
6 Joh Helligas, aged 15 years
7 Adam Willauer, aged 17 years

1 Hanna Huper, aged 16 years
2 Christina Hagenberg, aged 16 years
3 Eva Bitting, aged 19 years
4 Gert. Linn, aged 17 years
5 Cath Samsel, aged 15 years
6. Eva Samsel, aged 14 years

Children who in the year 1788, on April 12th, were confirmed by me, Joh. Theob Faber from the New Goshenhoppen congregation in the Swamp congregation:

1. Christian Willauer, aged 23 years

1 Elis. Frack, aged 30 years
2 Elis. Willauer, aged 20 years

2 Jacob Berret, aged 15 years
3 Joh Willauer, aged 15 years
4. Joh Georg Moll, aged 18 years
5 Joh Georg Helligas, aged 16 years
6 Joh. Helligas, aged 15 years
7 Jacob Nus, aged 16 years
8 Martin Wetknecht, aged 26 years
9 Peter Trolinger, aged 19 years

3. Elis Werner, aged 17 years
4. Mrs Margaretha Frack, aged 24 years
5 Marg Moll, aged 16 years
6 Marg. Jung, aged 16 years
7. Susanna Wiant, aged 15 years
8. Maria Steinmann, aged 18 years
9 Marg Steinman, aged 16 years
10 Barb Roeder, aged 14 years
11 Elis Mengel, aged 15 years
12. Salome Christman, aged 16 years
13 Catharina Christman, aged 15 years
14 Susanna Trolinger, aged 17 years

1790

This year fifty-two children were confirmed and admitted to the Lord's Supper at Pentecost, of whom the following belong to the New Goshenhoppen congregation

Boys

Herman Fischer, aged 18; father, Georg Fischer
Jacob Welcker, aged 17; father, Jacob Welcker
Michael Raudenbusch, aged 16, father, Michael Raudenbusch
Heinrich Sell, aged 17; father, Henrich Sell
Philip Fischer, aged 16; father, George Fischer
Johannes Sell, aged 15, father, Henrich Sell
Carl Geyger, aged 18, father, Benjamin Geyger
Jacob Reinheimer, aged 16; father, late Georg Reinheimer
Friedrich Reninger, aged 16, father, Friedrich Reninger
Jacob Neiss, aged 16, father, late Georg Neiss (received Holy Baptism at the same time)
Georg Kolb, aged 19, father, Joseph Kolb
Peter Kolb, aged 18; father, Michael Kolb
Johannes Kunius, aged 21, father, Johan Kunius

Girls

Catharina Bostert, aged 14; father, Jacob Bostert
Susanna Fischer, aged 15; father, Georg Fischer
Mary Maurer, aged 15; father, Peter Maurer
Maria Hillegas, aged 15, father, Peter Hillegas
Margaret Steinman, aged 16; father, Georg Steinman

Eva Hillegas, aged 15, father, George Hillegas
Maria Hillegas, aged 15, father, Conrad Hillegas
Elisabeth Wieand, aged 15, father, Wendel Wieand
Barbara Holshauser, aged 17, father, Jacob Holshauser
Elisabeth Laar, aged 16, father, Philip Laar
Susanna Zeller, aged 19, father, John Zeller
Fronica Segler, aged 17; father, Abraham Segler
Catharina Wiand, aged 16, father, Jost Wiand ✓
Sarah Levi, aged 15, father, late David Levi

These children of the New Goshenhoppen congregation were confirmed on Pentecost of the year 1792 in the Swamp congregation by me, Johannes Faber, Jr.

Boys
1 Andreas Reed, aged 17 years
2 Andreas Young, aged 17 years
3 Jacob Levi, aged 18 years
4. John Panebecker, aged 17 years
5. Joseph Schmith, aged 21 years
6 Michael Hillegas, aged 16 years
7 Jacob Stahl, aged 18 years
8 Georg Steinman, aged 16 years
9 Peter Steinman, aged 16 years
10. Friedrich Griesemer, aged 19 years
11 John Panebecker, aged 14 years
12 Joseph Fischer, aged 27 years

Girls
1. Elisabeth Schmit, aged 19 years
2 Magdalena Wiegner, aged 27 years
3 Anmaria Schlichter, aged 17 years
4 Polly Young, aged 19 years
5 Anmaria Young, aged 16 years
6 Margretha Panebeker, aged 16 years
7 Susanna Stahl, aged 16 years
8. Eva Mack, aged 17 years
9 Anmaria Nuss, aged 16 years
10 Barbara Guker, aged 18 years
11 Anmaria Griesemer, aged 18 years
12 Magdalena Hillegas, aged 15 years
13 Maricha Sell, aged 17 years
14 Susana Kolb, aged 17 years

The children of the New Goshenhoppen congregation who on March 29, 1793, were confirmed in the Old Goshenhoppen Church by me, Johannes Faber, Jr.

Boys
1. Peter Staud, aged 18 years
2. Philip Christman, aged 17 years
3 Peter Kolp, aged 17 years

Girls
1 Eva Miller, aged 15 years
2. Susanna Schell, aged 18 years
3 Barbara English, aged 17 years

4 John Walter, aged 23 years (who received baptism at the same time)
5. Antony Kehl, aged 17 years
6. Charles Huber, aged 22 years
7. John Moll, aged 18 years
8 Heinrich Moll, aged 16 years
9 Stophel Moll, aged 18 years
10 Georg Moll, aged 15 years
11. John Wiant, aged 18 years
12 Wendel Wiant, aged 16 years

4 Mary Sofia Weis, aged 16 years
5. Elisabeth Hillegas, aged 20 years

Those children of the New Goshenhoppen congregation who on Easter of the year 1794 were confirmed by me, Joh Faber, Jr., in this New Goshenhoppen Church

Boys·
1 Jacob Fischer, aged 15 years
2 Heinrich Christman, aged 15 years
3. Philip Christman, aged 15 years
4 John Griesemer, aged 17 years
5 Jacob Griesemer, aged 19 years
6 John Steinman, aged 21 years
7. John Reed, aged 16 years
8 Jeremias Reimer, aged 18 years
9 Jacob Deis, aged 17 years
10. Heinrich Fritz, aged 21 years
11. Joseph Fritz, aged 17 years
12 Heinrich Miller, aged 16 years
13. John Mack, aged 18 years

Girls:
1 Christina Fischer, aged 17 years
2 Anna Marg Maurer, aged 18 years
3 Eva Griesemer, aged 15 years
4 Elisabeth Schuler, aged 17 years
5. Catharina Steinman, aged 18 years
6 Maria Hein, aged 17 years

Those children of this congregation who on Easter of the year 1795 were confirmed in the Swamp congregation by me, John Faber, Jr

Boys:
1 Samuel Roeter, aged 16 years
2 Samuel Kolb, aged 16 years
3 David Christman, aged 16 years
4. Jacob Hillegas, aged 17 years
5 Heinrich Panebeker, aged 17 years
6 Heinrich Derr, aged 17 years
7 Andreas Levi, aged 16 years

Girls
1 Elisabetha Panebeker, aged 14 years
2 Susanna Young, aged 17 years

1808

Names and number of those who were confirmed this year and admitted to the Lord's Supper from the three congregations

Boys.
24 Isaac ——
1 Jonathan Griesemer, aged 16 years
2 Johan Geiger, aged 18 years
3. Jacob Geiger, aged 16 years
4 Georg Welcker, aged 17 years
5. Johan Welcker, aged 16 years
6 Johan Willauer, aged 16 years
7 Johan Beret, aged 16 years
8 Jacob Wenner, aged 22 years
9 Heinrich Mumbauer, aged 16 years
10 Jacob Kolb, aged 18 years
11 Johan Bussert, aged 18 years
12. Georg Nice, aged 17 years
13. Daniel Schissly, aged 18 years
14 Jacob Scheid, aged 16 years
15 Daniel Pfannebeker, aged 18 years
16 Heinrich Huber, aged 22 years
17 Georg Reed, aged 17 years
18 Peter Hilligas, aged 18 years
19 Henrich Kehler, aged 22 years
20 Henrich ——
21 Wilhelm Schuler
22 Jacob Ried
23 Samuel Schuler

Girls
1. Margareth Finck, aged 16 years
2 Hetty Wittis, aged 17 years
3 Polly Hillegas, aged 16 years
4 Cathr Maurer, aged 16 years
5 Sally Hering, aged 16 years
6 Elis Willauer, aged 15 years
7. Magr. Bleiler, aged 17 years
8 Cath Bossert, aged 16 years
9. Sophia Neis, aged 17 years
10 Elisabeth Mumbauer, aged 18 years
11 Nancy Graber, aged 16 years
12 Susanna Bikhart, aged 17 years
13 Marg Nusting, aged 15 years
14 Cath. Acker, aged 16 years
15 Hanna Waidemayer, aged 17 years
16 Maria Wiant, aged 17 years
17 Maricha Graber, aged 18 years
18 Margareth Houck, aged 17 years
19 Cath Baumer, aged 17 years
20 Cath Faust, aged 16 years
21. Christian Faust, aged 19 years
22. Nancy Pack, aged 29 years
23 Esther Fischer, aged 24 years

[V. LISTS OF COMMUNICANTS.]

Names and number of those persons who partook of the Lord's Supper in the fall of 1808.

Men
1 Jacob Huber
2 Michael Jung
3 Philip Christman
4 Johan Goring
5 Godfried Wisler

Women
1 Margaret Christman
2 Susanna Goring
3 Maria Goring
4 Eva Wisler
5 Juliana Staut

6 Johannes Staut
7 Friedrich Hilligas, Sr.
8 Friedrich Hilligas, Jr
9. Peter Finck
10 Harry Wiegener
11. Michael Goring
12 Georg Steinman
13. Antony Kehl
14. Samuel Roter
15. Daniel Oehl
16 James Pockly
17 Jacob Sechler

6 Anna Hilligas
7 Elis Finck
8 Cath Finck
9. Susanna Wiegner
10 Susanna Weiss
11. Anna Maria Goring
12 Elisabeth Steinman
13. Catharina Steinman
14 Barbara Kehl
15 Elisabeth Rother
16 Sarah Rother
17. Magdalena Oehl
18 Christina Huber
19. Cath. Huber
20 Susanna Schmidt
21 Cath. Zern
22 Sally Troxel ✓
23. Margaret Miller
24 Catharina Hilligas
25. Elisabeth Maurer
26. Cath Schmidt
27. Cath. Berdo
28 Cath Schnell
29 Christina Berdo
30 Cath Lutz
31. Mary Glory

Names of those who on Oct. 24, 1813, after previous preparation, communed.

1 Heinrich Traxel
2 Sarah, his wife
3 Andreas Graber
4 Anna, his wife
5 Andreas, his son
6 Maria, his daughter
7 Anna Blank
8 Michel Rautebusch
9 Anna Maria, his wife
10 Conrad Hillegas, Sr ✓
11 Maria Margaretha, his wife
12 Samuel Roder
13 Elisabeth, his wife

14 Susanna Welker
15. Margaretha, her sister
16 Johannes Mack
17 Conrad McNolty
18 Daniel Christman
19 Joseph Wiegner
20 Michel Gery
21 Jacob McNolty
22 Heinrich Moll
23 Heinrich Muller
24 George Muller
25. Abraham Levi
26 Eva, his wife

New Goshenhoppen—Vol. II. Communicants

27 Susanna Schmidt
28 Maria Gilbert
29 Elisabeth Reifschneider
30 Cath Althaus
31 Marg. Hillegas
32. Barbara Longenecker
33. Elis. Willauer
34 Margr Wiegner
35. Sara Kremer
36. Susanna Geri
37 Christina Sechler
38. Elisabeth Walter
39 Sara Mack
40 Mar. Walter
41. Margareta Maurer
42. Elisabeth Oel
43. Ego [V. D. Sloot]
44. Sara Sell

Names of those who on April 9, 1814, attended preparatory services and on the 10th, on Easter Day, the Lord's Supper

1 Jacob Welker
2 Andreas Graber
3. John, his son
4. Philip Christman
5 Margareta, his wife
6 Daniel, his son
7 Heinrich Traxel
8. Sara, his wife
9. Peter Fink
10 Magdalena, his daughter
11. Elisabeth, his daughter
12 Michael Jung
13. Catharina, his wife
14 Johann Geier
15 Georg Maurer
16. Catharina, his wife
17 Heinrich Pannebecker
18 Susanna, his wife
19 Michel Moll
20. Adam Muller
21 Adam, his son
22 Heinrich, his son
23 Georg, his son
24 John Roder
25 Magdalena, his wife
26 Jacob Hillegas
27 Rosina, his wife
28 Anna, his sister
29 Friedrich Hillegas, Sr
30 Anna, his wife
31. Alexander Oel
32 Wilhelm, his son
33. Elias Hirsch
34. Elias, his son
35 Jacob Gery
36 Elisabeth, his wife
37 Elisabeth, his daughter
38 Jacob Huber
39. Christina, his wife
40 Jacob, his son
41 Catharina, his daughter
42 Andreas Jung
43. Elisabeth, his wife
44 Michel Huber
45. Jacob Huber
46 Elisabeth, his wife
47 Daniel Roder
48. Catharina, his sister
49 Heinrich Roder
50 Peter Hillegas
51 Johann Georg Hillegas ✓
52 Maria, his wife
53. John Gery
54 Lorenz Kern
55. Michel Moll
56. Nathan Moll
57 Jacob Moll
58 Jacob Sechler
59. Georg Walter
60 Johann Walter

61 Samuel Fried
62. George Gery
63 Heinrich Schneider
64 Isaac Hergel (?)
65 Maria Hillegas
66 Maria Ried
67 Hanna Dottre (?)
68 Sus. McNolty
69 Maria Keppler
70 Salome Nuss
71. Sus Dimig
72 Magd. McNolty
73. Maria Lang
74 Eva Kern
75. Christina Graber
76. Elisabeth Schneider
77. Ego [V. d. Sloot]
78. Elisabeth Meng
79 John Hillegas
80. Heinr. Sperr

On September 25, 1814, the following persons communed:

1 Marg Christman
2 Catharina Christman
3. Elisabeth Traxel ✓
4. John Gery
5. Susanna, his wife
6. Karl, his son
7 Anna, his daughter
8 Alex Oel
9. Magdalena, his daughter
10. Georg Wiegner
11. Susanna, his wife
12. John Wiegner
13 Elisabeth, his daughter
14. Susanna Weiss
15. John Gery
16. Catharina, his wife
17 Daniel Staut
18 Michel, his brother
19 Catharina, his sister
20. John Hillegas
21 Catharina, his wife
22 Heinrich Freyer
23 Magdalena, his wife
24 Michel Hillegas
25 Anna Margaretha, his wife (?)
26 Georg Hillegas
27. Adam Bossert
28. Johannes Schlicher
29 Maria, his wife
30 Jacob Hillegas
31 Peter Levi
32. Sara Levi
33. Andreas Fink
34 Michel Frey
35 John Barret
36 Magd. Steinman
37 Maria Willauer
38. Maria Klein
39. Catharina Lutz
40 Margaretha Fink
41 Elisabeth Lutz
42 Elisabeth Barret
43. Ego, Von der Sloot
44. Catharina Van der Sloot
45 Elisabetha Gotz
46 Susanna Schmidt
47. Maria Reiter
48. Elis Klein
49. Maria Adam
50. Judith Grosskopf
51. Heinrich Hirsch
52. Margaretha Levi
53 Cathar Raut

On the first of April, 1815, the following persons attended the preparatory services and on the second the Lord's Supper:

1 Philip Christman
2. Margareta, his wife
3 Daniel, his own
4 Andreas Graber
5 John, his son
6. Jacob Barret
7. Rachel, his wife
8 Heinrich Pannebecker
9. Susanna, his wife
10. Jacob Huber
11. Christina, his wife
12 Jacob, his son
13 Heinrich Rochoe
14 Catharina, his daughter
15 John Hillegas
16 Heinrich Schlicher
17 Christina, his wife
18 John Roder
19 Georg Graber
20 Michel Jung
21 Catharina, his daughter
22 Elisabeth, his daughter
23. Susanna, his daughter
24 Andreas Graber
25. Anna, his wife
26 Elisabeth, his daughter
27. George Hillegas
28 Maria, his wife
29. Jacob Hillegas
30 Rosina, his wife
31 Anna, his daughter
32 Jacob Frey
33 John Roder
34 Magdalena, his wife
35 Cath. Roth
36 Isaac Reifschneider
37 Elisabeth, his wife
38 Samuel Roder
39 Elisabeth, his wife
40 Andreas Jung
41 Elisabeth, his wife
42 Jacob Griesemer
43 Susanna, his wife
44. Mattheus Rummel
45 Elisabeth, his wife
46 Samuel Gery
47 Susanna, his wife
48 Michel Wiegand
49 Peter Hillegas
50 Mar Hillegas
51 Friedr Hillegas
52 Jonathan Griesemer
53. Peter Kolb
54 Daniel Sasseman
55. Jacob Fink
56. Michel Raut
57 Catharina, his sister
58 Philip Renner
59 Daniel Christman
60 John Gery
61 Samuel McNoldy
62 Jacob, his brother
63. John Welker
64 Margaret, his sister
65. Henrich Schneider
66 Michel Geri
67. Henrich Roder
68 Georg Hillegas
69 Gottfried Coisler
70 Eva, his wife
71 Henrich Hirsch
72. John Sussholz
73 Magdalena Dettweiler
74 Magdalena Walter
75 Christian Graber
76 Anna Maria Lang
77 Elisabeth Graber
78 Barabara Sell
79 Salome, his daughter
80. Elisabeth, his daughter

81. Magdalena Heilig
82. Christina Schad
83. Magdalena Schmidt
84. Elisabeth Gerjel
85. Salome Graber
86. Maria Christman
87. Salome Levi
88. Margaretha Hillegas
89. Catharina Thiel
90. Margaretha Maurer
91. Elisabetha Schneider
92. Marg Wannemacher
93. Christina, her sister
94. Susanna Geri
95. Salome Nuss
96. Elisab Geri
97. Philip Ried, Esq.
98. Ego [V D Sloot]
99. Marg Ried
100. Marg Bossert
101. Henrich Ruh (?)
102. Marg. Levi

The following were confirmed.

Boys:
1 Carl Levi, aged 16¼ years
2 Samuel Dorwarth, aged 18 years
3 Carl Foster, aged 15 years
4 Jesse McNoldy, aged 15½ years
5 Jacob Schneider, aged 17 years
6. Philip Bossert, aged 17 years
7 Carl Hillegas, aged 16 years
8. Daniel Durr, aged 16 years
9. Samuel Durr, aged 18 years
10 David Eberhard, aged 17 years
11. Joseph Rotburger, aged 15½ years
12 John Sell, aged 18½ years
13 Heinrich Sell, aged 16 years
14 Edw, E W. Francis, aged 16 years
15 John Rochon, aged 16½ years
16 Will. Rochon, aged 15½ years
17. John Moll, aged 17 years
18 Joseph Diez, aged 17 years
19 Henrich Rudolph, aged 16 years
20 George Ott, aged 20 years
21 Jerem Rochon, aged 17 years
22 George Mumbauer, aged 16 years

Girls:
1 Catharina Schneider, aged 16 years
2 Eva Graber, aged 18 years
3 Mar Graber, aged 16 years
4 Mar. Hillegas, aged 14¼ years
5 Christina Graber, aged 16 years
6. Maria Zeress, aged 16 years
7. Maria Jackson, aged 15 years
8. Sara Wisler, aged 15½ years
9 Lydia Heering, aged 18 years
10. Susanna Stahler, aged 15½ years
11. Maria Huber, aged 17 years
12 Cath. Schwenk, aged 15¼ years
13. Sara Huber, aged 16 years
14 Maria Steinman, aged 15½ years
15 Marg Jung, aged 15 years
16. Cath. Freyer, aged 15½ years
17 Mar Seyfert, aged 16 years
18 Veronica Walter, aged 16 years
19 Elis. Wiant, aged 15¼ years
20. Elis. Espich, aged 17 years
21 Marg Ache, aged 15 years
22. Elis. Kirschner, aged 15 years
23 Cath Scholl, aged 16 years
24 Elis. Sechler, aged 19 years
25 Christian Neiss, aged 16 years

Total, 149

CHURCH RECORD OF THE OLD GOSHENHOPPEN REFORMED CONGREGATION, UPPER SALFORD TOWNSHIP, MONTGOMERY COUNTY, PA., 1764–1833.

Translated and Edited by
Prof. William J. Hinke, Ph.D., D.D.

Church Record for the Reformed Congregation in Old Goshenhoppen,

in which are recorded the names of the children who were reported, as was announced by me, Jacob Riess, pastor, and were baptized by me during my ministry up to the year 1766. In this book other necessary church matters may be entered. Elders at this time: Jacob Hauck, Johannes Götz; deacons: Isaac Sumne, Andreas Ohl.

Members of the congregation as follows:

Gabriel Schuler	Henrich Bamberger
Peter Hollebusch	Henrich Hüster
Johannes Faust	Jacob Iset
Johannes Kraus	Samuel Schuler
Nicklas Wolfahrt	Wilhelm Schuler
Fridrig Götz	Johannes Muck
Christoffel Dickeschit	Christian Hollebusch

[I. BAPTISMS ENTERED BY JACOB RIESS, 1762–1766.]

1765, Jan. 22, a son was born to Johannes Muck, named Johannes in Holy Baptism. Witnesses, Martin Reyer and his wife.

1765, July 6, a daughter was born to Georg Kugler, named Mary Gretha in Holy Baptism. Witnesses, Henrich Bamberger and his wife.

1764, June 5, a daughter was born to Isaac Sumne and his wife, named Magdalena in Holy Baptism. Witnesses, Conrad Bien and his wife.

1757, July 25, a daughter was born to Jonhannes Goetz, named Elizabeth in baptism. Witnesses, Bernhart Goetz and Elisabeth Goetz

1758, December 4, a daughter was born to Johannes Goetz, named Margaretha in baptism. Witnesses, Johann Goerg Ziegenfuss and his wife.

1760, January 24, a son was born to Johannes Goetz, named Georg Fridrich in baptism. Witnesses, Friedrich Wambold and his wife.

1762, July 7, a daughter was born to Johannes Goetz, named Anna Maria in baptism. Witnesses, Matthias Walter and his wife.

1764, June 19, a daughter was born to Johannes Goetz, named Christina in baptism. Witnesses, Fridrich Goetz and his wife

1766, March 15, a daughter was born to Johannes Goetz, named Elisa Barbara in baptism Witnesses, Volatin Hag and Elisa Barbara Bossert.

[II. BAPTISMS ENTERED BY REV JOHN THEOBALD FABER, 1766–1779]

Reformed Church Record for the members of the congregation in Old Goshenhoppen, in which were recorded by me, John Theobald Faber, in the year 1766, not only the names of those who were baptized, but also those who died and those who were married by me

Children who were baptized by me in the year 1766.

1766, Nov. 26, born Eva Elisabetha, daughter of Michael Alt. Witnesses, Andreas Ohl and his wife

1766, Oct 20, born Andreas, son of Peter Weyand Witness, Andreas Ohl

1766, Dec 12, born Johannes Petrus, son of Georg Mayer Witnesses, Peter Gavel [Gabel] and wife

1766, Sept 16, born Maria Magdalena, daughter of Jacob Schmidt Witnesses, Henrich Bayer and his wife

1766, Nov. 28, born Elisabetha, daughter of Ulrich Streib Witnesses, Conrad Boyer and Miss Swenck.

1767, Jan 21, born son of Jacob Iset. Witnesses, Henrich Bayer and wife.

1767, Jan. 21, born Andreas, son of Henrich Werner Witnesses, Andreas Werner and wife.

1766, Nov. 6, born Susanna, daughter of Gerhard Stricker Witnesses, Jacob Hartenstein and Catarina Klein

1766, Dec. 5, born Hanna, daughter of Georg Hertzel. Witnesses, Philip Hahn and wife.

1767, Febr. 11, born Susanna, daughter of Friedrich Dueckenschueth Witness, Susanna Dueckenschueth

1767, March 6, born Maria, daughter of Johann Martin Wer. Witnesses, Christian Hollenbusch and wife

1767, March 6, born Johannes Georgus, son of Lenert Grisinger Witnesses, Johann Georg Gauckler and Margaretha Schmid

Old Goshenhoppen—Baptisms 387

1767, March 7, born Eva Elisabetha, daughter of Daniel Kaiser Witnesses, Bernt Goetz and wife

1767, April 17, a negro was baptized named Wilhelm Witness, Mr Hollenbusch.

1767, April 18, Mrs Kan was baptized. Witnesses Daniel Hiester and wife. The name Maria was given to her

1767, Jan. 17, born Conradus, son of Johannes Hudt. Witnesses, Comradus Zimmermann and wife

1767, April 24, born Henrich, son of Henrich Hertzel. Witnesses, Peter Bater and his wife.

1767, April 9, born Catharina, daughter of Andreas Ohl Witnesses, Daniel Hister and wife

1767, April 30, born Johannes, daughter of Peter Loch Witnesses, Johannes Loch and wife

1767, April 4, born Jost Friedrich, son of Friedrich Andreas Witnesses, Jost Friedrich and his wife

1767, June 12, born Jacob, son of Henrich Borlemann. Witnesses, Jacob Detweiler and wife

1767, ——, born Johannes, son of Johannes Nais [Nice] Witnesses, ——

1767, June 8, born Johannes, son of Johannes Miller Witnesses, ——

1767, July 12, born Johann Jacob, son of Ulrich Hertzel Witnesses, Ulrich Hertzel and wife

1767, July 15, born Salome, daughter of Christian Hildebeutel Witnesses, Salome Gerges and Adam Hildebeutel

1767, Oct 18, born Conrad, son of Peter Miner Witnesses, Conrad Geise and wife.

1767, Dec 2, born Margaretha, daughter of Michael Spielmann Witnesses, Margaretha Wertz and son of Adam Bossert

1768, Jan 14, born Philip, son of Christian Reiff. Witnesses, Philip Gabel and wife.

1767, Nov 27, born Johannes Georg, son of Peter Becker Witnesses, Georg Lenert Krisinger and wife

1767, Dec 6, born Joh. Henrich, son of Joh Leh Witnesses, Joh Ried and wife

1768, Febr 19, born Maria, daughter of Henrich Huhl. Witness, Mrs. Norbeck.

1768, March 8, born Maria Christina, daughter of Henrich Werner Witnesses, Wilhelm Bayer and wife.

1768, Jan 1, born Henrich, son of Johannes Frey Witnesses, Caspar Gann and wife.

1768, Dec 16, born Elisabetha, daughter of Michael Groll Witness, Elisabetha Wentz

1768, April 9, born Elisabetha, daughter of Joh Muck   Witnesses, Adam Bossert and wife.

1767, July 30, born Elisabetha, daughter of Joh Mainer   Witnesses, Joh Muck and wife.

1768, April 16, born Maria, daughter of David Geri   Witnesses, Johann Georg Brey and wife

1768, March 11, born Anna Sara, daughter of Adam Scheffer   Witnesses, Joh. Clein and Sara Dan

1768, March 7, born Catharina, daughter of Joh Goetz   Witnesses, father and mother.

1768, May 22, born Christina, daughter of Lenert Loss (a negro)   Witnesses, Lenert Schneider and wife

1768, Febr 28, born Joseph, son of Batin (a negro)   Witness, Bastian Niel and Elisabetha Naiss

1767, Nov 8, born Georg, son of Georg Lortz   Witnesses, Georg Hertzel and wife.

1768, Febr. 7, born Catharina, daughter of Joh Georg Lortz   Witness, Catharina Wambolt

1768, March 12, born Elisabetha, daughter of Conrad Cantzlert   Witnesses, Jost Keller and wife.

1768, July 30, born Maria Christiana, daughter of Georg Mayer.   Witnesses, Wilhelm Bayer and wife

1768, July 24, born Johannes, son of Nicolaus Wolfart   Witnesses, Joh Jost and wife from Falkner Swamp

1768, Aug 7, born Jacob, son of Ludwig Hersch   Witnesses, Jacob Taub and Anna Margretha Zimmermann

1768, Sept 14, born Joh Adam, son of Conrad Rickhart.   Witnesses, Joh. Adam Hollenbush and wife

1768, ——, born ——, daughter of —— Wormen.   Witness, —— Warmke, a widow

1768, Nov 5, born Susanna, daughter of Hister Damm.   Witness, Susanna Walter.

1768, Dec. 14, born Philip, son of Philip Bayer.   Witness, Peter Haust (?)

1768, Nov. 30, born Margreta, daughter of Henrich Schneider   Witnesses, Isaac Sommi and wife.

1769, Jan 24, born Elisabetha, daughter of Bernhard Goetz.   Witness, wife of Johannes Muck.

1769, Jan 23, born Joh Philip and Johannes Georg, sons of Georg Bub   Witnesses, ——

1769, Jan. 12, born Johannes, son of Jacobus Liethel.   Witness, Antoni Liethel.

1769, Jan 5, born Elisabetha, daughter of Antoni Lichtel   Witnesses, Joh. Muck and wife.

Old Goshenhoppen—Baptisms 389

1769, Febr 2, born Johannes, son of Fried Dickenschied Witnesses, Christopfer Dickenschied and wife.

1769, Jan. 27, born Magdalena, daughter of Henrich Hertzel Witnesses, Philip Mais and Margretha Hertzel

1769, Jan 19, born Elisabetha, daughter of Adam Stall Witnesses, Marx Hertzel and wife.

1769, Febr 14, born Anna Christina, daughter of Carl Doerr Witnesses, Henrich Loppel and wife.

1769, April 19, born Elisabeth, daughter of Valentin Haack Witnesses, Bernhard Goetz and wife

1769, May 2, born Maria Susanna, daughter of Henrich von Huhl Witnesses, Abraham Wolfart and Maria Schwartz

1769, May 8, born Joh, son of Joh Hudt Witnesses, Killian Zimmermann and wife

1769, May 12, born Elisabetha, daughter of Peter Loch Witnesses, Jacob Unterkafler and Elisabeth Merkels

1769, April 13, born Sara, daughter of Michael Groll Witnesses, Jacob Wentz and wife Elisabetha

1769, May 26, born Bastian, son of Bastian Haupt Witnesses father and mother.

1769, March 13, born Johannes, son of Salomon Gromly. Witnesses, Joh. Herrger and wife

1768, May 2, born Elisabetha, daughter of Ludwig Reimer. Witnesses, Salomon Gromly and wife. Father and mother live in Falkner Swamp

1769, June 28, born Jacobus, son of Conrad Minig Witnesses, father and mother

1769, July 9, born Benjamin, son of Jost Keller Witnesses, the father himself

1769, June 12, born Joh Georgus, son of Georg Hertzel. Witnesses, Ulrich Hertzel and wife

1769, June 30, born Anna Maria, daughter of Jacob Graff Witness, Anna Maria Lichtel

1769, July 16, born Wilhelm, son of Henrich Werner Witnesses, Wilhelm Bayer and wife

1769, Aug 7, born Daniel, son of Joh Mueller Witnesses, Daniel Hiester and Elisabeth Schneider

1769, June 20, born Catharina, daughter of Fried. Andreas. Witness, Ludwig Hering's wife, a widow

1769, Oct 1, born Susanna, daughter of Andreas Ohl. Witnesses, Erhard Weis and wife

1769, Sept. 3, born Joh Philip, son of Marx Hertzel Witnesses, Philip Nais and Margaretha Hertzel.

1769, Aug 30, born Catharina, daughter of Martin Liethel. Witnesses, Martin Bauer and wife

1769, Sept. 7, born Magdalena, daughter of Henrich Hollebusch Witnesses, Jost Hollebusch and Magdalena Schillig

1769, Oct. 29, born Johannes, son of Wilhelm Bayer Witnesses, Valentin Bayer and wife

1769, Nov 20, born Sophia, daughter of Henrich Kuppelberger. Witnesses, Joh. Hiester and Sophia Jung

1769, Nov. 13, born Johannes, son of Joh Hildebeutel. Witnesses, Georg Derr and wife

1770, Jan. 31, born Joh Georg Michael, son of Georg Michael Schwartz. Witnesses, Joh Hudt and wife.

1770, Jan. 6, born Susanna Barbara, daughter of Georg Mayer. Witnesses, Joh Petrus Gabel and wife.

1770, March 18, born Maria Catharina, daughter of Andreas Werner. Witnesses, Joh Jung and Maria Cath Menger.

1770, Febr 4, born Anna Catharina, daughter of Andreas Weitman Witnesses, Martin Lichtel and wife.

1770, March 20, born Johannes, son of Abraham Koebler Witnesses, Johannes Koebler and wife

1770, Dec. 28, born Johannes, son of Georg Draxel. Witnesses, Johannes Koebler and wife

1770, March 13, born Margaretha, daughter of Ulrich Hertzel Witnesses, Margaretha Hertzel and Philip Fischer

1770, April 13, born Jacobus, son of Conrad Worman. Witness, the father himself.

1770, April 9, born Maria Elisabetha, daughter of Peter Becker. Witnesses Georg Dill and wife.

1770, July 31, born Johannes, son of Valedin Hog Witnesses, Johannes Goetz and wife

1770, Aug 16, born Maria Magdalena, daughter of Conrad Steiner. Witnesses, Zacharias Nais and wife

1770, Aug 24, born Catharina, daughter of Michael Groll. Witness, Catharina Wentz

1770, Oct. 17, born Henricus, son of Conrad Rickart Witnesses, Henrich Hollebusch and wife

1770, Nov 14, born Joh Georgus, son of Petrus Loch Witnesses, Georg Weickart and wife

1771, Jan 27, born Joh. Georgus, son of Marx Hertzel Witness, Joh Georg Hertzel

1770, Dec 14, born Johannes, son of Henrich Hollebusch. Witnesses, Joh Hartenstein and Magdalena Hollebusch.

Old Goshenhoppen—Baptisms

1770, Nov 20, born Elisabetha, daughter of Christian Reiff Witnesses, Johannes Namgesser and Elisabetha Gauckler

1770, Dec 31, born Johann Philippus, son of Paul Hoffmann Witnesses, Philip Fischer and Elisabetha Soger

1770, Dec 21, born Henricus, son of Henrich Dietz Witness, the father himself.

1771, March 19, born David, son of Friederich Dickenschiedt Witnesses, David Scheib and wife

1770, Sept 7, born Friedericus, son of Joseph Mueller Witnesses, Friedrich Dickenschiedt and wife.

1771, Febr. 11, born Joh Georgus, son of Ludwig Mayer Witnesses, Joh Georg Weitmann and wife.

1771, Febr 18, born Christina Elisabetha, daughter of Leonhart Koff. Witnesses, Joh. Nicolaus Eitel Mueller and wife.

1771, April 24, born Maria Barbara, daughter of Antoni Lichtel. Witnesses, Dieterich Reier and Barbara Muck

1771, March 24, born Johannes, son of Hermann Ache Witness, the father himself.

1771, June 9, born Susanna, daughter of Wilhelm Panebecker. Witnesses, father and mother

1771, July 13, born Catharina, daughter of Henrich Daub Witnesses, Nicolaus Wolfart and wife

1771, May 2, born two children to Salomon Grimli, the one named Salomon, his witnesses, Jacob Klein and wife; the other named Maria Magdalena, her witnesses, Georg Worman and Maria Wagner

1770, Sept 29, born Elisabetha, daughter of Conrad Minig Witness, the mother herself

1771, June 9, born Abraham, son of Conrad Worman Witness, the father himself

1771, Aug. 18, born Magdalena, daughter of Georg Weitman Witness, Jacob Unerkofler and wife

1771, Aug 2, born Joh Jacobus, son of Martin Lichtel Witnesses, Matheus Kern and wife.

1771, Aug 22, born Maria Barbara, daughter of Peter Faust. Witnesses, Johann Hut and wife

1771, Aug. 12, born Elisabetha, daughter of Andreas Werner Witnesses, Ben Schuler and Catharina Minger

1771, Nov. 3, born Johannes, son of Georg Henrich Schneider. Witnesses, Joh Numgasser and Margaretha Sommi

1771, Aug. 21, born Anna Maria, daughter of Joh. Hiltebeutel. Witness, Anna Maria Hiltebeutel

1771, Nov. 29, born Anna Maria, daughter of Joh Hudt. Witnesses, Andreas Riedt and wife

1771, Nov. 12, born Michael, son of a negro, named Thomas. Witnesses, Michael Eiten Muller, Jr., and Margareta Somni

1771, Nov 17, born Johannes, son of Daniel Kreiter Witnesses, Henrich Sander and wife

1772, Jan 20, born Maria Barbara, daughter of Adam Faust Witness, Maria Barbara Hut

1772, March 5, born Joh Georgus, son of Georg Mayer Witnesses, Henrich Werner and wife.

1772, March 13, born Joh Nicolaus, son of Andreas Ohl Witnesses, Andreas Werck and wife

1772, Febr 17, born Joh Petrus, son of Peter Maenner Witnesses, Erhart Weiss and wife

1771, Dec. 27, born Elisabetha, daughter of Jacob Mayer. Witnesses, Bernt Eitel and wife

1772, Jan 14, born Anna, daughter of Michael Groll. Witnesses, Maria Elisabetha Wentz

1772, July 6, born Magdalena, daughter of Joh Reinert. Witnesses, Georg Weickart and wife.

1772, Oct 4, born Joh Petrus, son of Isaac Horneker. Witnesses, Peter Mathias and Catarina Nes

1772, Oct 4, born Joh Petrus, son of Henrich Hollebusch Witnesses, Peter Hollebusch and Margareta Hollebusch

1772, Sept. 29, born Michael, son of Peter Stroh Witness, the father himself.

1772, Oct 15, born Susanna, daughter of Peter Loch. Witnesses, Elisabeth Unterkofler and Jacob Weitman.

1772, Oct 19, born Anna Maria, daughter of Conrad Rickart. Witnesses, Philippina Hollebusch and Henrich Ziegler.

1772, Nov. 8, born Anna Maria, daughter of Adam Faust. Witness, Anna Maria Faust.

1772, Sept 6, born Daniel, son of Joh Faust. Witnesses, David Hiester and wife.

1772, Sept 6, born Joh Petrus, son of Philip Jacob Eckel Witnesses, Joh. Petrus Stroh and wife.

1772, July 28, born Catharina, daughter of Valentin Haack. Witnesses, Henrich Rorich and Catharina Lemer.

1772, Nov 25, born Catharina, daughter of Benjamin Schuler Witnesses, Gabriel Schuler and Sophia Werner

1772, Dec 13, born Johannes, son of Bernhart Goetz. Witnesses, Joh. Muck and wife.

1773, Jan 22, born Catharina, daughter of Joseph Eckli Witnesses, Joh Zep and wife

Old Goshenhoppen—Baptisms

1773, Jan 22, born Johann Wilhelm, son of Stoffel Brickert. Witnesses, Wilh Brickert and Marg Somni

1773, Jan 2, born Comradus, son of Conrad Worman Witness, the father himself

1773, March 20, born Jacobus, son of Fried. Dickenschiedt Witnesses, Jacob Scheib and Elisabetha Sieh

1773, April 3, born Catharina, daughter of Christian Reif Witnesses, Joh Braun and wife

1773, Febr 2, born Johannes, son of Fried Rudi Witnesses, the parents

1773, June 17, born Anna Marg, daughter of Georg Moyer Witnesses, Anton Hamscher and wife

1773, March 24, born Joh Philippus, son of Peter Maenner Witnesses, Philip Weis and Marg Panebecker

1773, June 9, born Elisabetha, daughter of Henrich Werner Witnesses, Johann Jost and wife

1773, June 29, born Philip Jacobus, son of Georg Reinheimer Witnesses, Philip Jacob Schmidt and wife

1773, May 21, born two children to Adam Hiltebeutel, the one named Johannes, the other Daniel Witnesses were Johannes Hiltebeutel and wife, for the other the father himself.

1773, July 11, born Abraham, son of Johann Hiltebeutel Witnesses, Abraham Gerkes and Cath Beyer

1773, Aug 3, born Cath. Elisabetha, daughter of Henrich Hemsing Witnesses, Joh Zep and wife

1773, Nov 9, born Anna Magdalena, daughter of Ludwig Mayer Witnesses, Abraham Gerhart and wife

1773, Sept 29, born Jacobus, son of Michael Groll Witnesses, Jacob Wentz and wife

1773, Dec 2, born Johannes, son of Benjamin Schuler. Witnesses, Johannes Schuler and Catharina Gaukler

1773, Dec 2, born Elisabetha, daughter of Joh Hudt Witnesses, Erhart Weis and wife

1774, Jan 25, born Paulus, son of Paul Hoffmann Witnesses, the parents themselves.

1774, Jan 30, born Johannes, son of Andreas Werner. Witnesses, Johannes Schuler and Sophia Werner

1774, April 15, born Elisabetha, daughter of Andreas Ohl Witnesses, Michael Ohl and wife

1774, Febr 24, born Cath Elisabetha, daughter of Martin Lichtel Witnesses, Jacob Wettman and Catharina Hud.

1774, March 7, born Anna, daughter of Simon Contzler (negro of Mr. Hister). Witnesses, Jost Martin and wife

1774, March 11, born Christina, daughter of Christian Scheid. Witnesses, Henrich Schneider and wife

1774, July 18, two children born to Henrich Ludwig Dop, named Cath. Magdalena and Maria Scharlotta. Witnesses Jacob Dartsch and wife, and Christian Scheid and wife.

1774, May 14, born Maria Elisabetha, daughter of Johann Hartenstein Witness, Maria Hollebusch.

1774, March 17, born Anna, daughter of Salomon Grimli Witnesses, Samuel Panebecker and wife

1774, June 9, born Catharina, daughter of Georg Henrich Schneider. Witnesses, Valentin Schneider and Catharina Somni.

1774, July 14, born Johannes, son of Adam Hollebusch Witnesses, Joh. Henrich Hollebusch and wife.

1774, Sept 25, born Jacobus, son of Henrich Hollebusch. Witnesses, Ludwig Hartenstein and wife

1773, Dec 9, born Eva, daughter of Johann Jost Hollebusch. Witnesses, Jacob Schmidt and wife

1774, Dec 7, born Jacobus, son of Johann Jost Hollebusch. Witnesses, Jacobus Boyer and Anna Maria Hollebusch

1774, Sept 3, born Johannes, son of Christoffel Brickert Witnesses, Valentin Kugler and Elis Kebler

1774, Oct 30, born Christina, daughter of Ludwig Hersch Witnesses, Herrich Taub and wife

1774, Dec. 30, born Johann Fridericus, son of Christian May Witnesses, Friedrich May and wife

1774, Oct. 10, born Christina, daughter of Henrich Strohman Witnesses, the parents

1774, Dec. 31, born Catharina, daughter of Wilhelm Antig Witnesses, Catharina Hud and Johann Philip Wentz

1774, Nov. 24, born Catharina, daughter of Abraham Schaeffer. Witnesses, Philip Bayer and wife

1774, Dec 17, born Anna Maria, daughter of Adam Hiltebeutel Witness, Anna Maria Hiltebeutel

1775, Febr 3, born Fronica [Veronica], daughter of Johann Roerig Witnesses, Friedrich Dickenschid and wife

1775, Jan. 28, born Anna Maria, daughter of Christian Reif Witnesses, Johann Benner and wife

1775, Jan. 24, born Johannes, son of Conrad Bickart Witnesses, Joh. Hiltebeutel and wife

1775, May 26, born Henrich, son of Henrich Kopelberger. Witnesses, Henrich Ohl and Catharina Jung

1775, April 9, born Philippus, son of Friedrich Rudi Witnesses, Philip Gabel and wife.

Old Goshenhoppen—Baptisms

1775, July 6, born Catharina, daughter of Abraham Wolfart Witnesses, Nicolaus Wolfart and wife

1775, May 24, born Johannes, son of Jacob Mayer Witnesses, Joh Buch and Sophia Werner.

1775, April 18, born Rebeka, daughter of Michael Groll Witness, Elizabeth Wentz.

1775, June 28, born Margaretha, daughter of Adam Faust Witnesses, Peter Schreiner and wife

1775, Aug 11, born Ludwig, son of Henrich Hersch Witnesses, Ludwig Lang and wife

1775, Aug. 22, born Catharina, daughter of Andreas Ries Witnesses, Henrich Schneider and wife

1775, Oct 7, born Johannes, son of Johann Jacob Schwesfort Witnesses, Joh Nais and wife.

1775, Sept 4, born Elisabetha, daughter of Friedrich Dickenschied. Witnesses, Henrich Killi and wife.

1775, Sept 9, born Johannes, son of Georg Mayer Witnesses, Joh Nais and wife

1775, Sept 6, born Johannes, son of Henrich Haas Witnesses, Michael Jung and wife.

1775, Oct 20, born Elisabetha, daughter of Johannes Hiltebeutel Witnesses, Adam Hiltebeutel and wife.

1776, Feb. 28, born Georg, son of Christoffel Brickert Witnesses, Georg Kessler and Cath. Martin

1776, Jan. 23, born Johannes, son of Paul Hoffman Witnesses, Joh Braun and wife

1776, March 13, born Albertina Philipina, daughter of Andreas Ohl Witnesses, Nicolaus Handwerck and wife

1776, March 29, born Johannes, son of Johann Eckli. Witnesses, Joh Henemann and Barbara Nais.

1776, Febr 16, born Elisabetha, daughter of Benjamin Schuler. Witness, Elisabetha Schuler

1776, April 4, born Johann Henrich, son of Johann Hartenstein. Witnesses, Henrich Hollebusch and wife

1776, May 18, born Elisabetha, daughter of Henrich Hemsing Witnesses, the parents themselves

1776, April 25, born Magdalena, daughter of Martin Lichtel Witnesses, Jacob Wagner and wife

1776, May 1, born Magdalena, daughter of Henrich Taub Witnesses, Abraham Wolfart and wife

1776, June 30, born Regina, daughter of Georg Weitman Witnesses, David Unterkofler and Bina (¹) Pflaltzgraf

1776, June 8, born Margaretha, daughter of Christian May Witnesses, Margareta Hister.

1776, June 8, born Johann Carolus, son of Simon (a negro of Daniel Hister). Witnesses, Carolus Krieg and wife

1776, July 23, born Anna Catharina, daughter of Henrich Stellwagen Witness, Anna Cath. Koller

1776, July 28, born Margaretha, daughter of Ludwig Mayer Witnesses, Abraham Gerhart and wife

1776, Aug. 25, born Cathairna, daughter of Jacob Bosert. Witnesses, Jost Schlieger and wife

1776, Aug. 12, born Jacobus, son of Valentin Haack Witnesses, Jacobus Bosert and wife

1776, Sept 25, born Joh Georgus, son of Georg Hoerner Witnesses, Georg Mack and wife

1776, Sept 22, born Johann Jacobus, son of Georg Henrich Schneider Witnesses, Jacob Westman and Cath. Somni

1776, Sept 25, born Anna Catharina, daughter of Paul Knoeper. Witness, Anna Cath. Knoeper

1776, June 29, born Catharina, daughter of Henrich Strohmann. Witnesses, Johann Zep and wife

1776, Sept 5, born Georgus, son of Georg Rueckstahl. Witnesses, Georg Bilger and Christina Hartenstein.

1776, Oct 9, born Maria Magdalena, daughter of Andreas Werner Witness, Anna Mar. Werner

1776, Dec 1, born Johann Matheus, son of Joh Matheus Scheiflin Witnesses, Joh. Math Kern and wife.

1776, Oct 18, born Anna Margareta, daughter of Abraham Wolfart. Witnesses, Hen. Wilh Panebecker and Anna Margareta Gauckler.

1776, Nov 9, born Eva Elisabetha, daughter of Henrich Ohl Witnesses, Andreas Ohl and wife

1776, Dec 31, born Samuel, son of Debit (!) Gehann Witnesses, the parents themselves

1777, Jan. 18, born Friedrich, son of Salomon Grimli Witness, Friedrich Rudi

1776, Sept 27, born Petrus, son of Jost Hollebusch Witnesses, Petrus Hollebusch and Margareta Keller.

1777, Jan 23, born Magdalena, daughter of Adam Henrich. Witnesses, Catharina Hollebusch and David Unerkofler

1777, March 5, born Maria Margareta, daughter of Friedrich Rudi. Witnesses, Friedrich Rudi and wife.

1776, Dec 26, born Susanna, daughter of Michael Groll Witness, Maria Elis. Wentz

Old Goshenhoppen—Baptisms

1777, Jan 23, born Maria Barbara, daughter of Adam Faust Witnesses, Johannes Hut and wife

1777, Febr 14, a daughter born to the late Rudolph Segler, named Maria Christina. Witnesses, Johannes Segler and wife

1777, Jan 5, born Henrich, son of Georg Roerig Witnesses, Henrich Roerig and wife

1777, Febr 25, born Elisabetha, daughter of Henrich Roerig Witness, Anna Maria Roerig

1777, Febr. 14, born Elisabetha, daughter of Jacob Wagner Witnesses, Maria Wagner and Valentin Schneider

1777, April 2, born Comradus, son of Conrad Bickart Witnesses, Christian Hollebusch and wife

1777, Nov. 10, born Johannes, son of Friedrich Loesch. Witnesses, Michael Doerr and Maria Schneider.

1777, April 24, born Johannes, son of Daniel Krauter Witnesses, Joh Krauter and wife

1777, March 25, born Johannes, son of Carl Doerr Witnesses, Wilhelm Antig and wife.

1777, May 25, born Elisabetha, daughter of Johann Huepner Witnesses, Philip Bayer and wife

1777, June 19, born Berret, son of Berret Goetz Witnesses, Jacob Bossert and wife

1777, May 29, born Anna Margareta, daughter of Gabriel Klein Witnesses, Anna Margaretha Cunius and Georg Klein

1777, July 26, born Henrich, son of Philip Weis. Witnesses, Henrich Ohl and wife.

1777, September 11, born Elisabetha, daughter of Johannes Schuler Witnesses, Jacob Schuler and wife

1777, Aug 12, born Wilhelm, son of Johannes Heinemann. Witnesses, Joh Nais and wife

1777, Nov 26, born Catharina, daughter of Joh. Jacob Schweisforth. Witnesses, Daniel Krauter and wife.

1777, Dec. 13, born Johannes, son of Abraham Nais. Witnesses, Joh. Gerhart and Magdalena Hertzel

1777, Dec. 11, born Elisabeth, daughter of Georg Mayer. Witnesses, Henrich Werner and wife

1778, Febr. 21, born Samuel, son of Benjamin Schuler. Witnesses, Jacob Schuler and wife

1777, Nov 28, born Margareta, daughter of Andreas Werner Witnesses, Henrich Woerner and wife

1778, Febr 16, born Michael, son of Jacob Wagner. Witnesses, Valentin Schneider and wife.

1778, March 2, born Johannes, son of Johannes Hartenstein. Witnesses, Georg Gauckler and Christina Hartenstein

1778, March 3, born Jacobus, son of Henrich Hersch. Witnesses, Jacob Taub and wife.

1778, March 25, born Georgus, son of Christian May Witnesses, Georg Walbert and wife.

1778, March 31, born Catharina, daughter of Georg Weitemayer Witnesses, Catharina Faust and Philip Wentz

1778, March 11, born Jacobus, son of Adam Hiltebeutel. Witnesses, Jacob Klein and wife

1778, April 17, born Johannes, son of Henrich Kobelberger. Witnesses, Henrich Nibel and Elisabetha Jung.

1778, April 10, born Johann Jacobus, son of Johannes Nais Witnesses, Georg Buechler and Margaretha Huth

1778, March 16, born Catharina, daughter of Paul Hofman. Witnesses, Georg Hertzel and wife

1778, April 3, born Jacobus, son of Johannes Hiltebeutel. Witnesses, the parents themselves

1778, July 16, born Eva, daughter of Jost Schatz Witnesses, Eva Ohl and Baltzer Ried

1778, June 27, born Leonhart, son of Henrich Huhl Witnesses, Jacob Schuler and wife.

1778, June 14, born Johann Henricus, son of Henrich Strohman Witnesses, Joh Hess and wife

1778, Sept. 20, born Georgus, son of Henrich Ohl Witnesses, Georg Engel and Eva Ohl

1778, Oct 18, born Elisabetha, daughter of Henrich Mueller Witnesses, Johannes Schweisfort and wife

1778, Oct. 9, born Susanna, daughter of Jacob Weiss. Witness, Susanna Weis

1778, Dec 5, born Elisabetha, daughter of Paul Knoepper Witnesses, Henrich Ziegler and wife

1779, Febr 1, born Jacobus, son of Philip Weiss. Witnesses, Jacob Straus and wife.

1779, March 23, born Petrus, son of Abraham Wolfart. Witnesses, Petrus Taub and Catharina Segler.

1779, March 1, born Henricus, son of Benedict Horne. Witnesses, Henrich Schmidt and wife.

1779, Jan 30, born Jacobus, son of Peter Maener. Witnesses, Jacob Weiss and wife

1779, April 10, born Johannes, son of Math Schenfli. Witness, Johannes Exel.

1779, April 31, born Susanna, daughter of Andreas Werner Witness, Sophia Werner.
1779, May 2, born Catharina, daughter of Joh. Jost Hollebusch Witnesses, Catharina Hollebusch and Elias Hartenstein
1779, April 9, born Anna Maria, daughter of Peter Loch Witnesses, Georg Wettman and wife.
1779, April 16, born Georgus, son of Daniel Krauter Witnesses, Georg Dorscht and Maria Langbein
1779, April 15, born Maria Fronica, daughter of Johann Heineman. Witnesses, Joh. Nais and Fronica Heineman
1779, March 31, born Johannes, son of Michael Groll Witnesses, the parents themselves
1779, June 1, born Andreas, son of Georg Hen Schneider Witnesses, Andreas Ried and wife
1779, May 20, born Christina, daughter of Friedrich Rudi Witnesses, Hen. Bernt and Christina Gaukler
1779, June 7, born Adam, son of Jacob Bossert Witnesses, Adam Bossert and Gertraut.
1779, June 28, born Daniel, son of Andreas Gamel. Witnesses, the parents themselves
1779, June 11, born Catharina, daughter of Conrad Bickart. Witness, Dorethea Hollebusch
1779, Dec. 3, born Abraham, son of Abraham Nais Witnesses, Georg Hertzel and wife
1779, Sept 12, born Daniel, son of Henrich Hemsing. Witness, Daniel Faber.
1779, Febr 8, a child was born to a negro, named Seimen [Simon], name name of child, Sele Witness, Barbara Hass
1779, Sept 28, born Wilhelmus, son of Jacob Schuler. Witnesses, Johannes Schuler and wife.
1779, Sept 24, born Susanna Maria, daughter of Henrich Hollebusch Witnesses, Adam Henrich and wife.

The following children were baptized by me, Johann Wilhelm Ingold, pastor loci

Children	Parents	Witnesses
Heinrich, born 1780, Sept. 2	Georg Weidemeyer	Henrich Bernt, Catharina Rukshel
Leonhard, b 1780, Nov 10	Henrich Hirsch	Leonhard Schneider and wife
Eva Elisabetha, b. 1779, Febr 20, bap Apr. 11, 1779	Johannes Ohl and wife Barbara	David Schulz and Eva Ohl

Children	Parents	Witnesses
Johann Jacob, b 1780, Aug. 30	Henrich Strohman	Jacob Zoepp, Elisabetha Ohl
Anna Maria, b 1780, Nov 14	Jacob Straus	Philip Weiss and wife Anna Maria
Catharina, b. Nov. 18, 1781, Febr 13	Henrich Frick and wife Philippina	Wendel Wiant and wife Catharina
Peter, b. 1781, May 3, bap 1781, June 24	Conrad Bikhard and wife Catharina	Peter Baumann and wife Sophia
Andreas, b. 1781, July 21, bap 1781, Aug. 3	Andreas Gemmel and wife Fronica	the parents
Elisabetha, b 1781, June 27, bap. 1781, Aug 5	Wilhelm Ohl and wife Elisabetha	Georg Schedler and wife, Catharina Elisabetha, the grandparents
Jacob, b 1781, Aug 1, bap. 1781, Aug. 26	Joseph Eckli and wife Dorothea	Jacob Zoepp and Anna Maria Schneider
Maria Magdalena, b 1781, July 15, bap 1781, Aug 26	Jacob Scheib and wife Catharina	Martin Scheib and wife Magdalena
Catharina, b 1781, Febr 20, bap 1781, Aug 5	Balthasar Ried and wife Maria Elisabetha	Philip Ried, Catharina Ried, both single
Magdalena, b 1781, July 1, bap 1781, Aug. 5	Valentin Kuchler and wife Elisabetha	Michael Kuchler and Sophia Becker
Joseph, b 1781, July 29, bap 1781, Aug 26	Henrich Faust and wife Catharina Margaretha	Joseph Beringer and wife Anna Margaretha
Catharina, b 1781, July 12, bap 1781, July 30	Jacob Schuler and wife Elisabetha	Benjamin Schuler and wife Catharina

Record of the children who received Holy Baptism through me, Friedrich Dalliker, in this congregation of Old Goshenhoppen. 1782

Children	Parents	Witnesses
Daniel, b 1781, Dec 31, bap 1782, Mar. 17	Georg Scheid and wife Anna Maria	Daniel Creider and wife Catharina
Maria Elis, b. Febr 3, 1782, bap Mar. 17	Michael Guderman and wife Maria	Georg Scheid and wife Anna Maria
Elisabeth, b. Febr 21, 7182, bap. Mar 17	Jost Schaz and wife✓ Catharina	Philip Rid and wife Elisabeth

Children	Parents	Witnesses
Andreas, b Mar. 8, 1782, bap. Mar 29	Hannes Weiss and wife Eva	Andreas Ohl, Sr, and wife Eva
Eva, b. Febr. 11, 1782, bap. Apr 29	Peter Loch and wife Eva	Jacob Untercoveler and wife Magdalena
Catharina, b Apr 6, bap May 9	Peter Daub and wife Catharina	Jacob Daub and wife Catharina
Sophia, b Apr 24, bap June 30	Johann Schuler and wife Catharina	Georg Schneider and wife Sophia Becker
Anna, b. Nov. 1, 1781, bap July 21	Thomas Sens and wife Anna Maria	Henrich Schmid and wife Barbara
Maria, b Aug 28, bap Nov, 3	Jacob Wagner and wife Barbara	Valentin Schneider and wife Maria
Joh. Adam, b. Oct 9, bap Nov. 3	Peter Miner and wife Elis Barbara	Joh Adam Neidich and wife Anna Barbara
Elisabeth, b. Oct 9, bap. Nov 3	Peter Miner and wife Elis Barbara	Peter Hochstatt and wife Barbara
Philip, b. Oct 28, bap. Nov. 24	Balsar Rid and wife Maria Elisab	Philip Rid and wife Maria Elisab.

1783.

Children	Parents	Witnesses
Catharina, b Nov 4, '79, bap. Jan 1, '83	Charles Landes and wife Catharina	Georg Hertzel and wife Catharina
Margreth, b Dec 1, '81, bap Jan 1	Charles Landes and wife Catharina	Georg Hertzel and wife Catharina
Johann Georg, b Dec 13, '82, bap. Jan. 26	Benjamin Schuler and wife Catharina	Philip Mud and wife Barbara
Heinrich, b Dec. 20, '82, bap. Febr 16	Velten Kugler and wife Elisabeth	Jost Keller and wife Catharina
Johann Jacob, b Dec 23, '82, bap Febr 16	Matheis Scheufely and wife Margareth	Jacob Kugler and wife Catharina
Maria Magdalena, b Jan 23, '83, bap. Mar 9	Heinrich Schmid and wife Barbara	Sebastian Goetz and wife Maria Magdalena
Jacob, b Febr 22, bap. Apr. 6	Jacob Weiss and wife Elisabeth	Philip Weiss and wife Anna Maria
Philip, b Jan 31, bap Apr 20	J Heinrich Muller and wife Anna Elis.	J. Philip Zep and Catharina Henner
Georg, b Mar. 15, bap Apr 20	Johann Heineman and wife Barbara	Georg Schneider and Elisabeth Neiss
Daniel, b Febr 17, bap May 11	Christian Scheid and wife Maria Elisabeth	Daniel Creider and wife Catharina

On May 24 was baptized by me, after preceding instruction, Anna Margareth Weiss, wife of Johannes Weiss, aged 24 years, and on the same day admitted to the Lord's Supper.

Children	Parents	Witnesses
Eva Elisabeth, b. Apr 27, bap June 1	Wilhelm Ohl and wife Elisabeth	Andreas Ohl, Sr., and wife Eva
Hanna, b Apr 14, bap June 22	George Meyer and wife Hanna	Heinrich Beyer and Charlotte Raudebusch
Magdalena, b Apr 29, bap. June 22	Jacob Hauch and wife Margareth	Philip Gabel and wife Margareth
A. Catharina, b. Nov 18, bap Dec 7	Johannes Neiss and wife Anna Margreth	George Heitzel and wife Catharina
Hans Georg, b Dec 8, bap Dec 28	Peter Dinges and wife Anna Maria	H Georg Dast, Elisabeth Has

1784.

Joh. Jacob, b Dec. 1, '83, bap Jan 18	Joh Jacob Scheib and wife Catharina	Peter Scheib and wife Christina
Regina, b. Nov. 17, '83, bap. Jan. 18	Andreas Gemel and wife Veronica	the parents

Record of the children who were baptized by me, Friedrich Wilhelm Von der Sloot

Joh Heinrich, b Dec. 11, '83, bap. May 2, '84	Baltasar Ried	Maria Diasch and Philip Ried
Joseph, b May 24, bap. June 13	Simon Scentschler and wife	Joseph Keller and wife
Peter, b. May 3, bap May 23	Peter Daub and wife Catharina	Nicolaus Caupler and wife Maria
Regina, b July 25, bap ——	Martin Lichtel, Catarina	Joh Neis and wife Margaretha
Joseph, b Sept 29, bap Nov 7	Joseph Ekli and wife Dorothea	Jost Keller and wife Catarina
Johannes, b Sept 22, bap Oct 14	Johannes Buch and wife Catharina	Philip Gabel and wife Margaretha

Those children who were baptized by me, Johan Theobald Faber, 1786

Johannes, b May 4, bap. June 5	Jacob Weiant and wife	Georg Weiant and Elis. Rener
Isaac, b Apr 10, bap June 5	Jacob Schmidt and wife	Isaac Schmidt and Susanna Walbert

Children	Parents	Witnesses
Joh. Henrich, b Apr 27, bap June 18	Michael Gaukler and wife	Jacob Filman and wife
Joh Georg, b. May 8, bap July 30	Jacob Salate and wife	Joh Salate and wife
Barbara, b Oct 7, bap Oct 22	Joh Daniel Jung and wife	Adam Hollebusch and and wife
Johannes, b Sept 22, bap. Nov. 12	Wilhelm Gerges and wife	Joh Hiltebeutel and wife
Joh Jacobus, b ——, bap Nov 12	Joh Salate and wife	——

1787

Children	Parents	Witnesses
Jacobus, b Dec 31, '86, bap Mar 18	Georg Scheid and wife	Jacob Schaefer and wife
Margareta, b. Dec. 31, '86, bap Mar. 18	Henrich Bossert and wife	Adam Bossert and wife
Joh Georg, b Febr. 17, bap Mar. 18	Peter Dimig and wife	Isaac Hilligas and wife
Elisabetha, b Jan. 15, '87, bap Apr. 29	Ludwig Ache and wife	Herman Ache and wife
Johannes, b. Febr 27, bap Apr. 29	Peter Kuntz and wife	Joh Salate and wife
Johannes, b. July 16, '86, bap Apr 29	Martin Lichtel and wife	Henr Schmidt and wife
Anna, b. July 16, '86, bap Apr 29	Henrich Schmidt and wife	Martin Lichtel and wife
Michael (illegitimate child), b Nov. 22, '76, bap. ——	——	Martin Lichtel and wife
Cath Appollonia, b June 29, bap July 21	Michael Oesterlin and wife	Peter Faust and wife
Susanna, b. Sept 2, '86, bap July 21	Isaac Oschek and wife	Joh. Roscher and wife
Joseph, b Apr 17, '87, bap Aug 12	Henrich Stroman and wife	Jos. Eckle and wife
Scharlotta, b Aug 15, '87, bap Oct 14	Friedr. Rudi and wife	parents
Abraham, b Aug 2, '87, bap Nov 25	Joh Schneider and wife	Abraham Weber and Elis Schneider
Maria, b Aug. 25, '87, bap Nov 25	Adam Hamscher and wife	Peter Hamscher and Maria Weber
Anna Barbara, b Sept. 26, bap Nov. 25	Georg Weitemayer and wife	Joh Ruckstahl and Anna Barbara Diter

Children	Parents	Witnesses
Wilhelm, b. Oct. 5, bap. Dec. 26	Adam Hieltebeutel and wife	the parents

1788.

Children	Parents	Witnesses
Georg, b. Nov. 18, '87, bap Jan. 27, '88	Jacob Hauk and wife	Philip Gabel and wife
Sara, b. Oct 17, '87, bap. Jan 27, '88	Nicolaus Gauckler and wife	Philip Gabel and wife
Elisabeth, b. Febr 12, '88, bap. Mar. 30	Wilh. Entersen and wife	Salomon Grimli and wife
Johannes, b Dec. 28, '87, bap Mar. 30	Henrich Mueller and wife	Henrich Schmidt and wife
Daniel, b ——, bap. June 1	Joh. Georg Wuttlin and wife	Daniel Herz and Cath Lambein
Johannes, b. Mar 29, bap. June 22	Jacob Schmid and wife	Joh Schmid and wife
Johan Henrich, b. May 7, bap. July 13	Michael Gukerman and wife	Christian Scheid
Johannes, b May 29, bap. July 13	Joh Faust and wife	Peter Faust and wife
Magdalena, b. Febr. 21, bap. July 13	Philip Schillig and wife	——
Anna Margareta, b June 21, bap. July 13	Joh Daniel Jung and wife	Philip Gabel and wife
Susanna, b June 19, bap Aug. 3	Daniel Schwenck and wife	Georg Schwenck and wife
Samuel, b Apr. 9, bap Aug. 3	Gabriel Schuler and wife	Conrad Grimm and wife
Jacobus, b. May 23, bap Aug 3	Ludwig Age [Ache] and wife	Jacob Age and Marg. Hertzel
Catharina, b. June 21, bap. Oct 5	Jacob Schneider and wife	Elisabeth Wentz

After the death of the sainted Mr. Faber, when the congregation was without a minister, the following children were baptized, some by Mr. Roeler, some by the ministers who visited this congregation, and at the request of the parents their names were entered by Johann Daniel Jung, schoolmaster.

Children	Parents	Witnesses
Johannes, b. ——, bap. Febr 14, '89	Peter Hollebusch and wife Susanna	Joh Adam Hollebusch and wife Barbara
Johannes, b. May 7, 1789, bap May 31	Samuel Schuler and wife Magdalena	Johannes Schuler and Susanna Meyer

Old Goshenhoppen—Baptisms

Children	Parents	Witnesses
Magdalena, b. Apr. 6, '87, bap May 20, '87	Johannes Buch and wife	Philip Fischer and wife
Catharina, b Oct. 13, '89, bap Nov 29	Georg Herzel and wife Margretha	Ulrich Herzel and wife

After I, N[icholas] Pomp, in the beginning of the month of December of the year 1789, entered upon my ministry in the congregation of Old Goshenhoppen, the following children were baptized by me, beginning at the above mentioned time:

1790

Children	Parents	Witnesses
Catharina, b Nov. 14, '89, bap Jan 10, '90	Jacob Schmid and wife Magdalena	Peter Deschler and Christina Faust
Johannes, b. Oct. 16, '89, bap Jan 10, '90	Johannes Schichler and wife Catharina	Johannes Saladi
Maria Elisabeth, b Dec. 28, '89, bap. Jan 10, '90	Johann Daniel Jung and wife Ann Margreath	William Penno and wife
Andreas, b. July 5, '89, bap Mar 13, '90	Johannes Merckel and wife Elisabeth	Andreas Hauser
Elisabeth, b Dec 25, '89, bap Mar 14, '90	Jacob Hauch and wife Margareth	John Kohlhon
Andreas, b. Jan 23, '90, bap Mar 14	Friedrich Nebel and wife Catharina	Andreas Bage
Jacob, b Dec 12, '89, bap Apr 26	Georg Weidenmayer and wife Elisabeth	Jacob Ruckstahl and Cath. Lichtel
Wilhelm, b Jan. 11, '90, bap. Apr. 26	Gabriel Schuler and wife Catharina	Peter Deschler
Henrich, b Jan 7, bap Apr. 26	Martin Lichtel and wife Catharina	Peter Deschler
Elisabeth, b —, bap Apr. 26 (7 years, 9 months)	Christoph Bickel and wife Susanna	Johannes Roschon and Elisabeth Scheffeli
Georg, B —, bap Apr. 26 (8 months)	Christoph Bickel and wife Susanna	Johannes Roschon and Elisabeth Scheffeli
Elisabeth, b Apr 3, bap May 16	Johannes Faust and wife Susanna	Peter Hamscher and Christina Faust
Johann Henrich, b May 23, bap. June 6	Peter Hollebusch and wife Susanna	Henrich Hollebusch, Anna Maria Hollebusch
Susanna, b. Febr 20, bap June 27	Ludwich Ache and wife Maria	Friedrich Brod and Barbara Schneider

Children	Parents	Witnesses
Daniel, b Apr. 19, bap July 18	Friedrich Huebner and wife Christina	Henrich Roschon and wife
Joseph, b. June 1, bap. July 18	John Tallaty and wife Elisabeth	Jacob Sieber and wife
Elisabeth, b. June 11, bap Aug. 15	Valentin Lichty and wife Maria	Henrich Lichly and wife
Maria Magdalena, b. Aug 5, bap. Sept.26	William Anderson	Georg Mald, Maria Crimle
Maria, b —, bap Oct 17	Philip Huebner and wife Elisabeth	David Deschler, Maria ?
Margareth, b. Oct 19, bap. Nov. 28	Samuel Schichler and wife Magdalena	Georg Dash, Barbara Schneider
Christina, b. Nov 27, bap. Dec. 19	Peter Faust and wife Elisabeth	Paul Hoffman and wife
Henrich, b Nov. 29, bap Dec. 19	Henrich Faust and wife Catharina	Henrich Roschon and wife

1791.

Children	Parents	Witnesses
Maria Magdalena, b. Dec. 22, '90, bap. Jan. 30	Jacob Hedrich and wife Christina	Johannes Hedrich and wife
Magdalena, b Dec.20, '90, bap Apr 3	Jacob Schneider and wife Elisabeth	Henrich Schneider and wife
Catharina, b. Febr. 12, bap. Apr 3	Daniel Jost and wife Barbara	Jacob Jost and Anna Maria Hillegas
Elisabeth, b. Dec. 14, bap. Febr. 4	Johann Mickel Faust and wife Elisabeth	Henrich Faust and Elisabeth Bayer
Catharina, b. Dec. 14, bap. Febr. 4	Johann Nickel Faust and wife Elisabeth	Michael Oesterlein and wife
Thomas, b. Febr. 13, bap Febr 4	John Jost and wife Benigna	N Pomp and wife
Elisabeth, b. Febr. 11, bap Apr 24	Johannes Buch and wife Catharina	Jacob Schmidt and Elisabeth Bayer
Philip, b. Jan 2, bap. May 15	Philip Schillig and wife Salome	John Grimle and Elisabeth Peters
Magdalena, b. Oct. 25, '90, bap. May 15	Joh Georg Wutte and wife Anna	the parents
Rachel, b. Dec 27, '90, bap. May 15	Samuel Cooper and wife Susanna	Lorenz Jacobi and wife
Margareth, b June 5, bap. June 30	Georg Doerr and wife Sophia	Johannes Bernth and Margareth Sell

Children	Parents	Witnesses
Georg, b May 19, bap July 17	Michael Guterman and wife Maria	Georg Bayer and wife
Magdalena, b Oct 20, '90, bap. July 29	Matheis Geist and wife Elisabeth	the parents
Johannes, b Dec 5, '90, bap. July 29	Emmanel Karner and wife Catharina	the parents
Magdalena, b. July 31, '90, bap July 29	Philip Kohl and wife Magdalena	the parents ✓
Peter, b May 8, bap Aug 28	Martin Lichtel and wife Catharina	Peter Deschler
Catherina, b. Aug. 30, bap. Sept 18	Johann Daniel Jung and wife Anna Margaretha	Friedrich Rudy and wife
Michael, b Sept 28, bap Oct 30	Georg Hertzel and wife Margareth	Michael Hartmann

1792

Children	Parents	Witnesses
Jacob, b. Jan. 7, bap Mar 25	Jacob Schmid and wife Magdalena	Jacob Klein and wife
Jacob, b. Jan. 12, bap Mar. 25	Jacob Rudy and wife Catharina	—— Sieber and wife
Samuel, b Febr 26, bap. May 28	Johannes Schuler and wife Catharina	Samuel Schuler and wife Magdalena

The children who were baptized by me, John Faber, in this congregation, are recorded here.

Children	Parents	Witnesses
Abraham, b Jan. 3, '92	Johannes Rieh	Conrad Gerkes and wife
Jacob, b May 11	Johannes Faust	Jacob Schmit and wife
Joseph, b Sept 18, '91	Friedrich Huebner	Peter Roshang and wife
Johann Georg, b. May 17, '92	Johannes Salety and wife Elisabeth	Philip Zepp and wife Maria
Maria Margaretha, b July 15, '93	John Stroman	Jacob Zepp and wife Maria
Margaretha, b. Aug. 6, '92	Jacob Hauk	Nicolaus Gaukler and wife
Henrich, b Nov. 6, '92	Peter Renninger	Henrich Leh, Molly Roschong
Peter, b. Sept 20, '92	Peter Faust	Philip Hoffman, Madlena Ruhdi

Children	Parents	Witnesses
Antonius, b Nov. 17, '92	David Dickenschied	Antonius Sell and wife
Georg and ——, b Jan 13, '93	John Nice	Georg Hertzel and wife, John Reichard
George, b. Jan. 16, '93	Jacob Schmith	George Weiss and wife
Henrich, b Febr. 6, '93	Joseph Schmit	Heinrich Schmith and wife
John, b May 2, '93	Ludwig Ache	John Ache and Margaretha Schmit
Maria Margaretha, b. July 15	John Stroman	Jacob Zepp and wife
Elisabeth, b Jan 25, 1787	Jacob Wagner	——
Barbara, b. Jan. 6, 1793	Jacob Wagner	——
Abraham, b. Aug 20, 1788	Jacob Wagner	——
Anna Maria, b. Oct. 10, 1793	Francis McLaw	Abraham Salmon and wife
Heinrich, b. Nov 25, 1793	Philip Jones	Heinrich Schmit and wife
Sophia, b May 15, 1793	Catharina Werner	George Derr and wife

Those children who were baptized by me, Johannes Faber, in this congregation, from the first day of the new year to the first day of the next year

Anno 1795

Children	Parents	Witnesses
Heinrich, b Nov 18, 1794, bap Jan. 22, 1795	George Derr	Heinrich Schaefer and wife
Jacob, b. Febr. 3, 1795, bap Apr 12	Balser Reed	Jacob Rudy and wife
Josua, b. Febr 22, 1795, bap Apr 12	Joseph Young	John Neis and wife

The number of those children who were baptized by me, A [lbert] Helffenstein.

1808

Children	Parents	Witnesses
Philip, b July 9, 1808	Henrich Sell	Christian Martin and Catharina

Children	Parents	Witnesses
Johannes, b Aug 4, 1808	Abraham Hiltebeutel and wife Margaret	Johann Hiltebeutel and wife Maria
Sarah, b. Nov. 10, 1808	Johann Reisinger and wife Deborah	——
Elisabeth, b Aug. 2, 1808	John and Margaretha Lind	Daniel and Elisabeth Rismiller
Barbara, b. Febr 2, 1806	Abr and Elisabeth Merkel	George and Elis Waidemayer
Sarah, b Nov. 17, 1807	Johan and Catharina Scheiwley	Jacob and Elisabeth Scheiwley
Wilhelm, b Aug 3, 1808	Jacob Scheid and Elisabeth	Johan Jost and Bina (!)
Nathaniel, b July 27, 1808	Tobias Sell and Elisabeth	Christian Scheid
Margareth, b Aug. 19, 1808	Johann Schneider and Elisabeth	Georg Stahl and Margareth
Maricha, b. Aug 11, 1808	Conrad Geyer and wife	——
Wilhelm, b. Jan 6, 1809	Wilhelm Schmidt and Sally	Peter Acker and Elis Esterlein

In the year 1813 the following were baptized by me, Friedrich Wilhelm Van der Sloot

Children	Parents	Witnesses
Maria Magdalena, b. Dec 4, 1812, bap. Febr 28, 1813	Johann Friedrich	Johann Scheid and wife
Johannes, b. Jan 12, bap Apr. 10, 1813	Johannes Johns and wife Catharina	the parents
Heinrich, b Nov 10, 1812, bap. Apr. 10, 1813	Heinrich Zink and wife Elisabeth	the parents
Hermann, b. June 21, 1813, bap. Aug 15	Valentin Achi and wife Catharina	Adam Neidig and wife Maria
Christina, b Dec. 13, 1812, bap. Aug 15, 1813	Daniel Fries and wife Barbara	Philippina Ganz
Heinrich, b. Dec 16, 1791, bap. Apr 16, 1814	Johannes Gerber and wife Hanna	the parents
Daniel, b Jan. 18, 1814, bap May 15	Daniel Hiltebeutel and Elisabeth	the parents

Children	Parents	Witnesses
Johannes, b. Jan. 23, 1814, bap Apr 3	Heinrich Gerber and wife Catharina	Joh Achi and Barbara
Henrietta, b Apr. 28, 1814, bap June 26	Ludwig Hummel and wife Margareta	Heinrich Schueck and Catharina
Johannes, b Apr 11, 1814, bap. Aug. 11	Jan (!) Kieler and wife Barbara	the parents
Tobias, b Aug 9, 1814, bap. Sept. 18	Abraham Kuppelberger and wife Elisabeth	Michael Kuppelberger and Maria Schaz
Friedrich, b Mar 14, 1801	Jacob Schmidt and wife Catharina	Jacob Klein, Sr., and Gertraut
Jacob, b Jan 8, 1803	[same parents]	Jacob Klein and Gertraut
Johannes, b. Febr. 26, 1805	[same parents]	Jacob Klein and Gertraud
Valentin, b Sept 13, 1807	[same parents]	Jacob Schmidt and Catharina
Georg, b July 27, 1810	[same parents]	Peter Reichert and Sara
Samuel, b Mar 23, 1813	[same parents]	Jacob Klein, Sr, and Gertraud
Jonas, b Jan. 22, 1815, bap Oct 8	Heinrich Pikhart and wife Susanna	Peter Schweisfort and Maria
Sophia, b Sept 28, 1816, bap. Nov. 3	Jan Schuler and wife Maria	Georg Walter, Bally [Polly] Schaz
Nathaniel, b Nov. 9, 1817, bap Dec 28	John Miller and Magdalena	the parents

[Entries made during the ministry of Rev. Jacob W. Dechant]

Henrich, b Nov 1, 1819, bap Dec 25, 1819	Jacob Reed and wife Maria	Philip Reed and wife Elisabetha
Nathan, b Nov 15, 1818, bap. Jan. 30, 1819	—— Hertzel	Georg Herzel and wife Catharina
Maria, b Nov 21, 1819, bap May 4, 1820	John Weil and wife Sara	Maria Schmidt
Johann Jeremias, b. Jan. 22, 1820, bap. Mar 5, 1820	Georg Nice and wife Maria	John Ruckstuhl and Christina Nice

Old Goshenhoppen—Baptisms

Children	Parents	Witnesses
Heinrich, b Febr 10, 1820, bap May 14	Jacob Schneider and wife Magdalena	Heinrich Grob and Magdalena
Sara, b Nov 17, 1819, bap. Apr 23, 1820	Georg Randzell and wife Catharina	the parents
Georg, b Febr 9, 1820, bap June 4	Johan Tengler and wife Susanna	Georg Pikhardt and Cath Graff
Peter, b Apr 15, 1820, bap. June 25	Michael Miller and wife Maria	Jacob Ruckstuhl and wife Barbara
Henrich, b Febr. 27, 1818, bap June 14	Jacob Klein and wife Susanna	Heinrich Grob and wife Anna Maria
Jacob, b. July 25, 1820, bap Aug 28	Jacob May and wife Elisabeth	Georg May and Cath. Fillmann
Urias, b June 25, 1820, bap Sept 19	Heinrich Grob and wife Susanna	Heinrich Grob and wife Anna M
Matilda, b July 13, 1820, bap Oct. 8	Wm Cooper and wife Baby (¹)	Jacob Hauser, Maria Hilligas
Anna, b July 8, 1820, bap. Nov. 19	Conrad Keeler and wife Catharina	Reinhard Reeler and wife Philippina
William, b Sept 7, 1820, bap Nov 19	Jacob Rees and wife Maria	Wm Antes, Rebecka Hefelfanger
Anna, b Sept 19, 1820, bap. Nov. 19	Abraham Rees and wife Rachel	Abr Phul, Maria Rees
Seth, b May 18, 1816, bap June 20	Jacob Schmidt and wife Catharina	Johannes Klein and wife Susanna
Francis William, b Oct. 15, 1820	Silas Himmelreich	Samuel Schuler and wife Sarah
Elisabetha, b Dec. 10, 1820, bap. Mar. 4, 1821	John Hauk and wife Elisabetha	John Dietr Schmidt and wife Elisabetha
Jesse, b Nov. 13, 1820, bap Mar 1, 1821	Math Hertzell and wife Catharina	Sam Geisinger, Maria Hertzell
Anna, b Febr 7, 1821, bap Mar 25	Mathias Slemmer	Heinrich Zink and wife Elisabetha
Daniel Walter, b. Mar 6, 1821, bap Mar. 25	Jacob Slemmer	Heinrich Kerr and wife Anna
Jesse, b Jan. 22, 1821, bap Apr 20	Daniel Hiltebeutel and wife Elisabetha	the parents
Heinrich, b Mar 10, 1821, bap Apr. 6	John Ruckstuhl and wife Christina	Lorenz Jacoby and wife Sara
Jesaias, b Febr. 16, 1821, bap Apr 6	Benj Weil and wife Elisabetha	Wm Weil and Maria Sell
Ester, b Mar 6, 1821, bap July 8	Conrad Dotterre and wife Ester	Georg Heffelfanger, Johanna Pannebecker

Children	Parents	Witnesses
Johannes, b. Dec 31, 1820, bap July 8, 1821	Fr. Wagner and wife Hanna	Henry Rudy, Elisabetha Dommenick
Charles, b May 24, 1821, bap. July 29	Abraham Schleifer and wife Elisabeth	Heinr Schleifer and wife Dorothea
Jefferson, b. Mar 16, 1821, bap July 29	Jacob Mueller and wife Catharina	Heinr Keeler, Maria Dalleker
Anna Catharina, b May 6, 1821, bap Sept. 9	David Zeis and wife Sara	Georg Emmert, Catharina Graff
Maria Magdalena, b —, bap Oct. 3, 1821	H Long and wife Margaretha	Magdalena Schuler
Peter, b Nov. 4, 1821, bap. Dec 25	Georg Neis and wife Maria	Abraham Linsenbiegler and wife Christina
Elias, b. Dec. 6, 1821, bap. Apr. 3, 1822	Isaac Gerhard and wife Magdalena	the parents
Georg, b Oct 13, 1821, bap. Apr. 7, 1822	Georg Mayer and wife Maria	Georg Keeler, Elisabeth Kraus
Benjamin, b. Dec. 7, 1821, bap Apr 7, 1822	Jacob Schneider and wife Magdalena	the parents
Elisabetha b. Febr. 8, 1822, bap May 12	Charles Bayer and wife Sara	Philip Christmann and wife Elisabetha
Elisabetha, b. Mar. 29, 1822, bap. June 9	Jacob May and wife Elisabetha	Peter Nais and wife Elisabetha
Henriette, b Febr 14, 1822, bap June 20	Heinrich Hauk and wife Elisabetha	Georg More and wife Barbara
Johan Philip, b ——, bap. Nov 2, 1822	Philip Hubner and wife Catharina	the parents
Levina, b Jan. 29, 1819, bap June 30, 1822	Heinrich Ziegler and wife Catharina	John Hein and Lus. Schneider
Catharina, b Jan. 14, 1821, bap June 30, 1822	Heinrich Ziegler and wife Catharina	Catharina Mayer
Isaac, b Jan. 8, 1822, bap. May 19, 1822	Jacob Schneider and wife Hanna	Valentin Keely and wife Maria
Johannes, b. Aug 18, 1822, bap Dec 24	Johan Dengler and wife Susan	Joh Schnayfort, Christina Groff
Reinhardt, b. Sept 30, 1822, bap Febr 16, 1823	Conrad Keeler and wife Catharina	Joseph Keeler and wife Maria
Peter, b Nov. 12, 1822, bap. Febr. 16, 1823	John Hauck and wife Elisabetha	Tobias Albrecht and wife Catharina

Children	Parents	Witnesses
Johannes, b. June 23, 1819, bap. Aug. 8	Jacob Hilficker and wife Maria	Johannes Bayer and wife

Baptized by the Rev Samuel Helffenstein.

Children	Parents	Witnesses
Adelaide, b Nov. 26, 1822, bap Jan 26, 1823	Mathias Slemmer and wife Margaretha	Jacob Slemmer and Hanna Hiltebeutel
Sara, b Jan 31, 1823, bap June 1	Abraham Rees and wife Rachel	Conrad Neuman, Elis Pannebecker
Friedrich, b Febr 25, 1823, bap June 1	Georg Hefelfanger and wife Hanna	Fried. Hildebrand and wife Catharina
Saliane (¹) [Sally Anna], b. Apr. 18, 1823, bap July 13	Heinr. Grob and wife Susanna	Jacob Hetler, Sara Kraus
Lydia, b. July 9, 1823, bap. Oct 5	Benjamin Weil and wife Elisabeth	John Groff, Lydia Unterkobler
Jacob, b. Nov. 10, 1814, bap Febr 29, 1824	John Schuler and wife Maria	Jacob Reed and wife Magdalena
Mente (?), b. May 24, 1819, bap Feb 29, 1824	John Kelly and wife Sara	Fried Grimly and wife Elisabetha
Matilda, b. Nov 24, 1822, bap. Febr 29	John Kelly and wife Sara	——
Elisabetha, b June 9, 1824, bap. July 25	Georg Nice and wife Maria	the parents
Peter, b ——, bap July 25	John Weil and wife Sara	Peter Weil and wife Catharina
Jacob, b Febr 19, 1824, bap. July 25	Jacob Pannebeker and wife —— Christmann	Philip Christmann and wife Elisabeth
Elisabetha, b —, bap. Aug 15, 1824	John Heffelfinger	Sam Unterkobeler, N Scholl
Sara, b. May 4, 1824, bap Nov. 7	Abraham Schmidt and wife Sara	Jacob Faust, Sara Hauk
Anna Catharina, b May 10, 1824, bap Nov 7	Samuel Taub and wife Catharina	Philip Ruthy and wife Elisabetha
Ester, b Sept 16, 1824, bap Dec 19	Charles Bayer and wife Sara	Jos Graff and wife Elisabetha
Jacob, b Sept 26, 1824, bap Jan 30, 1825	Joh Bedmann and wife Catharina	Georg Emert, Sara Wagner
Josua, b. Dec 19, 1824, bap June 26, 1825	Heinrich Klein and wife Susanna	Jacob Schneider and wife Maria

Children	Parents	Witnesses
Edward, b Sept 30, 1824, bap July 17, 1825	John Keely and wife Dorothea	Salomon Grimly and wife
Catharina, b June 12, 1825, bap Sept. 18	Jacob Faust and wife Barbara	Friedrich Wald and wife Magdalena
Franz, b ——, bap Sept 18	Salomon Andreas and wife Magdalena	the parents
Josua, b Aug 9, 1825, bap Oct 30	John Hauck and wife Elisabetha	Heinr Jost and Elisa Bayer ✓
Albert, b Sept 16, 1825, bap Oct 30	Friedrich Grimly and wife Elisabeth	Wm. Dechant and wife Rebeka Maria
Heinrich, b July 12, 1825, bap. Oct. 25	Jacob Hilfiker and wife Maria	Dan. Hiltebeutel and wife Elisabetha
Kidiane (¹) [Kitty Anna], b. Aug. 20, 1825, bap Oct 25	Michael Hartzell and wife Catharina	Jonas Hartzell, Sara Klein
Isaac, b Sept 24, 1825, bap Oct 26	Tillmann Kolb and wife Elisabetha	Jacob Hilfiker and wife Maria
Franciscus, b Sept. 29, 1825, bap. Nov 20	Jos Keeler and wife Maria	Conrad Keeler and wife Catharina
Adelheit, b. Sept 18, 1825, bap Nov. 20	Wm. Nice and wife Catharina	Jacob Reifschneider and wife Catharina
Samuel, b. Nov 7, 1825, bap Jan. 22, 1826	Jacob Faust and wife Sara	Peter Faust, Becki Nice
Sariane (¹) b Feb 5, 1826, bap. May 28	John Grimly and wife Mariane (¹)	the parents
Anna, b Dec. 14, 1825, bap. May 28, 1826	Michael Deker and wife Magdalena	Conrad Keeler and wife Catharina
Georg, b May 2, 1826, bap June 18	Jacob Wunderlich and wife Christina	Jacob Scheid and wife Elisabeth
Jacob, b. ——, bap. Sept 10, 1826	Jacob Zepp and wife Sara	Jacob Zepp and wife Catharina
Johannes, b July 30, 1826, bap. ——	Fr. Canner and wife Elisabeth	Jonas Hartzell and Catharina Reimer
Georg, b Aug 30, 1826, bap. Oct. 1	Georg Nice and wife Maria	Sam Scholl and wife Maria
Catharina, b Oct 28, 1826, bap. Apr. 12, 1827	John Weill and wife Sara	Joseph Schmidt and wife Maria
Catharina, b. Dec. 1, 1826, bap. May 20, 1827	Conrad Keeler and wife Catharina	Sam Unerkofeler and wife Susanna

Old Goshenhoppen—Burials

Children	Parents	Witnesses
Johannes, b. Mar 30, 1827, bap June 10	Ben Weil and wife Catharina	Jacob Wambold and wife Catharina
Sara, b Febr. 11, 1827, bap June 10	Jacob Faust and wife Barbara	Jacob Wagener and Sara Wald
Elisabetha, b Jan 29, 1827, bap June 10	Sam. Weil and wife Ester	Wm Eisenberg and Sara Weil
Anna, b Jan 13, 1827	Jacob Fischer and wife Esther	Conrad Geiger and wife Maria
Cammilla, b Apr 27, 1827, bap. Sept 2	Jacob Bok and wife Anna	Jacob Quilmann and wife Margaretha
Johan, b Sept 17, 1827, bap. Oct. 13	Jacob Wunderlich and wife Christina	Heinr. Grob and wife Esther
William, b Oct 8, 1827, bap Nov 25	Jacob Schmidt and wife Maria	John Hiltebeutel and wife Sara
Wilhelm, b June 16, 1827, bap. Nov. 25	Wilhelm Nice and wife Catharina	Georg Nice and wife Maria
Joseph, b Apr. 11, 1828, bap June 22	Michael Deker and wife Magdalena	the parents
Nancy, b Apr 18, 1828, bap Aug 3	Benjamin Weil and wife Catharina	Peter Weil and wife Catharina
Jesse, b Mar 5, 1828, bap Aug. 3	Georg Zink and wife Lydia	John Dreisbach and wife Elisabetha
Jonas, b. June 23, 1828, bap. Aug 24	Jacob Reed and wife Maria	Jonas Hamberger and wife Dina
Maria, b Dec 13, 1825, bap Aug 24, 1828	Robert Yost and wife Elisabetha	the parents
Mersers (¹), b Mar 11, 1828, bap Aug 24	Robert Yost and wife Elisabetha	Alexander Yost, Maria Pannebeker
Rebecca, b July 19, 1828, bap. Sept 14	Thomas Yost and wife Christina	Jacob —— and wife Elisabetha
Hanna, b Apr 17, 1828, bap. Sept 14	Salomon Enderson and wife Maria	——
Matilda, b June 27, 1828, bap Oct 5	Sam Weil and wife Esther	the parents
Jonas, b Sept —, bap Oct 26	Jacob Hauk and wife Susanna	Georg Borger and wife Margaretha
Sophia, b. July 19, 1828, bap. Dec 7	Sam. Slifer and wife Ester	Heinr Moll and wife Elisa
Isabella, b ——, bap June 14, 1829	Wm. Nice and wife Catharina	M Ziegler and wife Nancy

Children	Parents	Witnesses
Michael, b June 11, 1828, bap. June 14, 1829	Michael Hartzell and wife Catharina	the parents
Joseph, b Mar. 2, 1829, bap. July 26	Johannes Weil and wife Sara	Daniel Weil, Catharina Schmidt
Jacob, b. June 25, 1829, bap. July 26	Friedrich Schmidt and wife Maria	Jacob Klein and wife Susanna
Sara, b. June 28, 1829, bap. Aug. 29	Peter Acker and wife Ester	Jacob Ruckstuhl and wife Sara Aker
Heinrich, b Sept. 13, 1829, bap. Nov 8	Georg Schmidt and wife Maria	Heinr. Hauk and wife Elisabetha
Jesaias, b Jan. 16, 1830, bap. June 6	Jacob May and wife Elisabetha	Hr. Franz and wife Sophia
Philip Heinrich, b. May 3, 1830, bap June 27	Heinrich Grobb and wife Ester	Philip Christmann and wife Elisabeth
Catharina, b Apr. 13, 1830, bap July 18	Sam. Weil and wife Ester	Jonas Hiltebeutel and wife Elisabeth
Luisa, b. Febr 12, 1830, bap. Aug 8	Sam Schlifer and wife Ester	Wm Wohr and Sara Scholl
Samuel, b Sept —, 1830, bap. Nov. 5	Joseph Gompher and wife Maria	Jacob Mak and Sarah Geiger
Heinrich, b. Sept 9, 1830, bap Nov 5	Jacob Hartzell and wife Catharina	Jacob Hartzell and wife Maria
Kidijane (!) [Kitty Jane], b ——, bap Dec. 12, 1830	Samuel Christmann and wife	——
Catharina, b Jan 25, 1831	John Hartzell and wife Hanna	——
Melan, b Dec 12, 1830, bap. Mar. 27, 1831	Jacob Schmidt and wife Margaretha	Conrad Keeler and wife Catharina
Elomine (¹), b Jan 30, 1831, bap Apr 17	Sam Leydy and wife Sophia	Daniel Kaiser, Margaretha Kaiser
Debora, b. Febr 15, 1831, bap May 21	Jonathan Scholl and wife Sara	John Nice and wife Debora
Heinrich, b Jan 22, 1831, bap May 22	Jacob Grobb and wife Catharina	Heinrich Grobb and wife Ester
Hanna, b Febr. 28, 1831, bap May 22	Jacob Huebner and wife Barbara	Georg Hartzell and wife Catharina
Elisabetha, b Oct 21, 1830, bap May 22, 1831	M Hartzell and wife Catharina	Philip Rudy and wife Elisabetha

Old Goshenhoppen—Burials

Children	Parents	Witnesses
Heinrich, b Jan. 3, 1831, bap May 22	Enoch Roscho and wife Sara	Heinrich Faust and wife Margaret
Jacob, b. May 11, 1831, bap May 22	Georg Erb and wife Maria	Jacob Erb and wife Magdalena
Heinrich, b May 4, 1831, bap May 22	Jesse Ziegler and wife Catharina	Michael Ziegler and wife Hanna
Johannes, b. Nov 26, 1830, bap May 29, 1831	Michael Gaukeler and wife Ester	Leoy Leidy and Sara Geiger
Sara, b. Aug. 7, 1831, bap Sept 10	Joh. Rukstuhl and wife Christina	Daniel Grimm and wife Sara
Sophia, b. Oct. 1, 1831, bap. Dec 25	Johan Achy and wife Catharina	Heinrich Franz and wife Sophia
Sariane (¹), b. Febr. 15, 1832, bap Apr 8	John Andree and wife Catharina	Jonas Hilt and wife Catharina
Rebecka, b. Oct. 9, 1831, bap June 2, 1832	David Zeis and wife Sara	Elisabeth Friedrich
Johannes, b Febr. 12, 1832, bap June 3	Georg Pikhard and wife Maria	John Schmidt and Maria Pickhardt
Ester, b Dec 26, 1831, bap June 3, 1832	Sam Weil and wife Ester	the parents
Johannes, b Oct 20, 1831, bap July 1, 1832	Joh. Weil and wife Sara	Sam Weil and wife Ester
Christina, b Sept 29, 1831, bap July 1, 1832	Friedrich Focht (?) and wife Juliane	the parents
James, b. Dec 12, 1831, bap July 1, 1832	'Jacob Bok and wife Anna	John Scheid and wife Maria
Francis, b Nov 8, 1831, bap. July 22, 1832	John Huth and wife Elisabetha	Georg Hartzell and wife Catharina
Mariane [Mary Anne], b. June 10, 1832, bap. July 22	Jacob Herzell and wife Catharina	Jacob Quilmann and wife Margareta
Maria Anna, b Apr 26, 1832, bap Aug 7	Georg Mayer and wife Catharina	Abel Kahr and Marie
Daniel, b. Apr 30, 1832, bap July 22	Henry Grobb and wife Ester	Daniel Grobb and wife Hanna
Johannes, b. May 30, 1832, bap Sept 2	Jacob Schneider and wife Magdalena	John Grobb and wife Maria
Sophia, b Mar. 8, bap. May 18, 1833	John Ruckstuhl and wife Christina	Georg Poly

Elders and Deacons who were installed by me, Friedrich Delliker, on June 30, 1782

Elders George Herzel, Andreas Ohl, Sr.

Deacons Benjamin Schuler, Heinrich Hohlenbusch, Heinrich Ohl, Martin Lichty.

[BURIAL RECORDS]

The persons who were buried by me, J. T. Faber, in the year 1766, as follows

1766, Dec 26, was buried Jacob Mayer, of Old Goshenhoppen

Persons who were buried by me, John T. Faber, in he year 1767, as follows:

1767, Jan 3, Bernd Eitel's little daughter, living at Old Goshenhoppen, was buried

1767, Jan 7, Johannes, son of Antoni Lichti, was buried, of the congregation of Rittschwell.

1767, April 6, Henrich Bamberger was buried, of the congregation of Old Goshenhoppen

1767, May 8, Johannes, son of Johannes Maurer, was buried, of New Goshenhoppen.

1767, May 20, Andreas, son of Hermann Gerlach, was buried, of Old Goshenhoppen

1767, May 29, Albertina, daughter of Andreas Ohl, was buried, aged 2 years, 9 months and several weeks, of Old Goshenhoppen.

1767, March 6, Anna Maria, daughter of Johann Merden [Martin] Wer, was buried, aged half a year, several weeks, of Old Goshnehoppen.

1767, Sept 8, a son of Jacob Wentz was buried, named ——; aged 2 years, 9 months, 5 days

1767, Sept 8, Johannes Alsentz, son of Johann Georg Alsentz, was buried, aged 4 years, 5 months, less 2 days, of Germantown

1768, Jan 31, Alleda, daughter of Sem (!) Schuler, was buried, aged 19 years, 3 weeks less 2 days

1768, April 14, Peter Hollenbusch was buried, aged 59 years.

1769, Febr. 27, a woman, named Regula, of Old Goshenhoppen was buried, aged 70 years

1769, July 10, Margaretha, wife of Jost Keller, of Old Goshenhoppen, was buried, aged about 40 years.

1769, Aug 24, Margaretha, daughter of Georgus Kuchler, of Old Goshenhoppen, buried, aged 2 years and several months.

1769, Aug. 26, Elisabetha, daughter of Joh Mainer, of Old Goshenhoppen, was buried, aged 2 years and several months.

1769, Oct 16, Elisabetha, daughter of Adam Schmidt, was buried, of Old Goshenhoppen, aged 1 year and 1 day

Old Goshenhoppen—Burials 419

1769, Nov 8, Johannes, son of Wilhelm Bayer, of Old Goshenhoppen, was buried, aged 1 year, 7 months and about 8 days.

1770, March 6, Johann Petrus, son of George Mayer, of Old Goshenhoppen, was buried; aged 3 years, 4 months and 20 days.

1770, April 19, Anna Catharina Eckert, of Old Goshenhoppen, was buried, born in the year 1740, about April, aged 30 years, 4 months and several days.

1770, June 30, the old Mr. Panebecker, of Old Goshenhoppen, was buried, aged 59 years, 4 months and 8 days; he was born March 10, 1710

1771, Jan 4, a widow, named Barbara, of Old Goshenhoppen, was buried; aged 61 years less 9 weeks

1771, Febr. 12, Ulrich Herzel, of Old Goshenhoppen, was buried; born 1705, Aug 20, aged 65 and a half years less 9 days

1771, Febr 12, Johann Marx Hertzel, of Old Goshenhoppen, was buried He was born 1746, date unknown, aged 24 years, 3 months, etc

1771, March 16, Johannes, a son of Henrich Raess, of Indianfield, was buried. He was born 1754, March 26, aged 17 years less 10 days

1771, March 18, Georg Wagner was buried He was born 1702, Febr 2, aged 69 years, 1 month, 16 days.

1771, May 8, Cornelius, son of Ernst Harr, of Indianfield, was buried He was born 1749, Febr 1, aged 21 years, 3 months, 16 days

1772, April 5, Eva ——, of Old Goshenhoppen, buried Born in the year 1699, date unknown, aged about 73 years

1772, June 13, Henrich Mieker, of Old Goshenhoppen, was buried He was born 1715, date unknown, aged about 57 years.

1772, May 23, a son of Peter Maener, was buried. Born 1772, Febr. 17, aged 13 weeks and 3 days.

1772, July 12, Johann Cantz was buried Born 1718, date unknown, aged about 53 years

1772, July 12, a daughter of Wilhelm Demflin was buried Born 1771, August 15, aged 10 months, 3 weeks, 5 days.

1772, July 16, Johann Petrus, son of Johann Leh, was buried Born 1771, Nov. 14, aged 8 months less a few days

1772, June 28, a child, named Jacobus was buried Born 1771, March 10, aged 1 year, 3 months 2 weeks and 1 day

1772, Aug 25, a child of Johann Mabri was buried Born 1769, Nov. 13, aged 3 years, 9 months, 9 days

1772, Sept. 28, Johann Mieker was buried Born 1753, date unknown, aged 20 years, etc

1772, Oct. 14, Henrich, a son of Henrich Hohl, was buried. Born 1759, May 6, aged 13 years and perhaps 5 months

1773, Febr 1, Catharina Schuler was buried Born May 4, 1695, aged 77 years, 3 months and several days.

1773, Jan. 14, a child of Benjamin Schuler was buried. Born 1772, Nov. 25, aged 7 weeks

1773, Febr. 5, a child of Johannes Hudt was buried. Born 1771, Nov. 29, aged 1 year, 2 months, 4 days.

1773, March 30, a son of Friedrich Mueller was buried. Born 1767, March 1, aged 6 years, 4 weeks

1773, Aug 12, a son of Henrich Hemsig was buried Born 1771, Jan 30, aged 2 years and a half, 11 days.

1773, Aug 30, a son of Ludwig Hersch was buried Born 1773, July 21, aged 5 weeks, 4 days.

1774, Jan 29, a son of Georg Michael Schwartz was buried Born 1768, June 8, aged 5 years, 7 months, 2 weeks, 5 days.

1774, Jan 31, son of Andreas Werner was buried. Born 1773, Nov. 6, aged 14 months, 3 weeks, 2 days

1774, May 21, a woman, named —— was buried. Born 1730, Aug —, aged 43 years, 9 months.

1775, Jan. 1, Samuel Schuler was buried Born 1717, beginning of February, aged 58 years.

1775, March 20, the wife of Johann Faust was buried Born 1720, June 25, aged about 55 years

1775, April 3, a son of Simon May was buried Born 1752, day unknown, aged 23 years, 6 months.

1775, May 31, a daughter of Johannes Hud was buried. Born 1765, Sept. 26, aged 9 years, 9 months, 2 weeks, 4 days

1775, Oct 7, Mr. Roerig was buried Born 1698, day unknown, aged about 77 years.

1775, Dec 13, the wife of Philip Gerig was buried Born 1696, day unknown, aged about 79 years.

1776, Febr 24, the old Jacob Hauk was buried Born 1690, day unknown, aged about 87 years.

1776, April 9, the old Mrs. Hud was buried. Born 1707, day unknown, aged about 76 years

1776, June 23, the old Mrs Mebri was buried. Born 1699, beginning of November, aged 76 years and 7 months and several weeks.

1776, Nov. 30, a son of Andreas Werner was buried. Born 1774, Febr. 1, aged 2 years, 10 months, 3 weeks, 4 days

1777, Febr 21, a daughter of Henrich Hemstich was buried Born 1776, May 18, aged 9 months, 1 day

1777, March 21, Joh Simon May was buried. Born 1701, beginning of April, aged 77 years.

1777, July 12, a son of Joh Jacobus Schweissfort was buried. Born 1775, Oct 5, aged 2 years less 3 months

Old Goshenhoppen—Burials

1777, Aug 11, Erhart Weis, an elder, was buried   Born 1723, Jan 6, aged 54 years, 7 months and some days.

1777, Sept. 4, a son of Jacob Wagner was buried.   Born 1777, Febr. 14, aged 6 months, 3 weeks.

1777, Sept 6, a child of Philip Bayer was buried   Born 1777, Jan. 1, aged 8 months, 9 days

1777, Sept 6, a child of Peter Hofstatt was buried.   Born 1774, June 25, aged 3 years, 2 months and some days

1777, Sept 6, a daughter of Henrich Werner was buried   Born 1768, March 25, aged 9 years, 5 months, 3 weeks

1777, Sept. 20, a child of Peter Maener was buried   Born 1776, March 10, aged 1 year, 4 months, 8 days.

1777, Sept 24, a child of Ludwig Moyer was buried.   Born 1776, July 28, aged 1 year, 2 months, 3 weeks, 2 days.

1777, Sept 29, a son of Peter Maener was buried.   Born 1761, Febr. 10, aged 16 years, 7 months, 2 weeks, 4 days.

1777, Sept 21, a daughter of Henrich Hut was buried   Born 1769, May 2, aged 8 years, 4 months, 3 weeks

1777, Oct 17, a son of Friedrich Rudi was buried   Born 1775, April 9, aged 2 years, 6 months, 8 days.

1777, Oct 19, a child of Adam Hildebeutel was buried   Born 1773, May 21, aged 4 years, 5 months less 3 days

1777, Dec 13, the wife of Martin Lichtel was buried   Born 1750, Jan 12, aged 27 years,, 11 months

1777, Nov. 15, a daughter of the old Mr Goetz was buried   Born 1722, Oct. 28, aged 55 years, 2 weeks, 1 day.

1777, Dec 12, Antoni Lichtel was buried   Born 1702, day unknown, aged 75 years and a half.

1777, Dec 23, the old Mr Goetz was buried   Born 1696, day unknown, aged 81 years

1778, Jan 27, the wife of Johann Huepner was buried   Born 1727, Dec. 5, aged 50 years, 1 month, 3 weeks

1778, Febr 24, Catharina Kraeber was buried   Born 1709, day unknown, aged about 68 years.

1778, June 5, a son of Joh Nais was buried   Born 1778, April 10, aged 7 weeks, 5 days

1778, July 23, a son of Adam Hollebusch was buried   Born 1774, July 14, aged 4 years, 9 days.

1778, July 28, the wife of Christian Hollebusch was buried   Born 1709, day unknown, aged 69 years

1778, Aug. 3, a son of Conrad Rickard was buried, born 1775, Jan. 25, aged 3 years, 7 months

1778, Aug 27, Christian Hollebusch was buried   Born 1718, March 1, aged 60 years, 6 months, less 6 days

1778, Nov 18, a child of Andreas Ohl was buried   Born 1776, ——, aged 2 years, 8 months, 3 days.

List of the dead and buried during the ministry of Friedrich Daelliker, pastor of this congregation of Old Goshenhoppen

Anno 1783.

Febr. 12, Wilhelm, son of Samuel Schuler and wife Elisabeth; aged two weeks and 5 days.

May 3, Johann Adam, son of Peter Minner and Barbara, his wife, aged 7 months less 7 days

July 13, Anna Maria Magdalena Wenz, wife of the late Philip Wenz, aged 61 years, 5 months, 11 days

1784

Jan. 15, Georg, son of Heinrich Faust and Catharina, his wife; aged 3 weeks, 3 days.

Under the ministry of Frid Wilh v. d Sloot.

July 10, Catarina Weigant, aged 82 years, 5 months.

Those persons who were buried by me, Joh Theob Faber, in the year 1787.

Febr 27, Elisabetha Huepner was buried; aged 33 years less 1 month.

April 8, the wife of Peter Hauk was buried, aged 62 years, 9 months

May 12, a negro of George Hertzel was buried; aged 19 years less a quarter.

Nov 15, a child of Jacob Gerhart was buried, aged 3 years, 3 months, 11 days.

Dec 4, the young Henrich Bok was buried; aged 21 years, 4 months, 3 days.

1788

April 17, a son of our schoolmaster, Johann Daniel Jung, was buried, named Johann Friedrich, aged 4 years, 1 month, 12 days

April 20, Elisabeth Bittel was buried; aged 85 years, 3 months, 1 day

April 21, the old Mr Dickenschied was buried, aged about 90 years

April 29, the old Mrs Boyer was buried; aged 78 years, 8 months, 17 days

Oct. 6, a daughter of Johann Salate was buried, aged 3 years, 11 months less 3 days.

Those persons who were buried by me, John Theo Faber, Jr, in this congregation

1792

June 22, a daughter of Henrich Faust was buried, aged 4 months, 14 days
A daughter of Johannes Buek was buried, aged 5 years, 8 months, 27 days

1793.

Daniel Hofman, aged 66 years.
Mrs Gemmel, aged 43 years, 8 months, 2 weeks
Old Mrs Moy, aged 90 years
John Neise's child, aged 9 years, 7 months, 19 days
Christian Scheid's wife, aged 54 years.
John Scheid's child, aged 3 years, 6 months, 3 days
John Saladay's child, aged 6 years, 10 months, 3 weeks, 3 days
John Saladay's child, aged 3 years, 2 months, 2 weeks, 2 days
Jacob Weyand's child, aged 9 years, 6 months, 2 weeks, 2 days
Balser Reed's child, aged 9 years, 8 months, 3 days
Ludwig Mayer, aged 69 years.
Ludwig Ache's child (born 1788, May 23), aged 5 years, 4 months, 3 weeks.
Ludwig Ache's child (born 1790, Febr 20), aged 3 years, 8 months.
William Anderson's child (born 1788, Febr 12), aged 5 years, 8 months, 1 week, 1 day.
William Anderson's child (born 1790, Aug. 5), aged 3 years, 2 months, 3 weeks, 3 days
John Leets (born 1731, Aug.), aged 64 years.
—— Vaust, a small child, a few days old
George Hertzel's child, Johannes, born 1794, Febr 27, aged 1 year, 11 days
Jacob Smith, born 1757, April 1, aged 38 years, 1 month less 2 days.

List of those persons who were buried by me in the year 1808, June 12
Magdalena Ache, died July 11, 1808, aged 3 years, 2 months, 14 days
Johann Bidding, aged about 28 years, 10 months
Scharlotte Faust, aged 41 years, 6 months, 4 days
Jacock Zinck, died Dec 14, aged 5 months, 8 weeks

1809

Jacob Schuler, buried Febr 27, aged 8 years, 7 months, 3 weeks

MARRIAGES

Those persons who were united in marriage by me, John Th Faber, in the year 1767

1767, Jan 20, Bernd, son of Friedr Goetz, of Old Goshenhoppen, married Eva Elisabetha, daughter of Johannes Mack, of New Goshenhoppen

1767, May 7, Georg, son of Johannes Mack, of New Goshenhoppen, married Elisabetha, daughter of David Martin, of the Oley Mountains.

1767, Sept. 24, Georg, son of the late Mr Brenneholtz, of New Goshenhoppen, married Anna Maria, daughter of Samuel Mils, of Heidelberg township

1768, April 14, Georg Henrich, son of the late George Schneider, of Philadelphia, married Elisabetha, daughter of Isaac Somni, of Old Goshenhoppen.

1768, May 30, Henrich, son of Henrich Diets, of Upper Salford, married Catharina, daughter of the late Mr Gerhart, of Franconia township.

1768, Sept 15, Valentin, son of Valentin Haak, of Lower Salford township, married Maria Elisabetha, daughter of Petrus Edinger, of Lower Salford.

1768, Sept 25, Martinus, son of Anton Lichtel, of Upper Salford, married Catharina, daughter of the late Jacob Weidmann, of Upper Salford.

1769, March 28, Wilhelmus, son of Henrich Frey, of Lower Salford, married Christina, daughter of Mr. Heineman, of Lower Salford (the father is still in Germany).

1769, May 23, Joh Schmidt, son of the late Wilhelm Schmidt, of Falckner Swamp, married Catharine Nungasser, widow of the late Mr Nungasser, of Old Goshenhoppen

1769, Aug 22, Christoph, son of Jacob Bruckert, of Old Goshenhoppen, married Magdalena, daughter of Georg Kuchler, of Old Goshenhoppen

1769, Nov 21, Simon Crineus, widower, of Old Goshenhoppen, married Margaretha Klapper, widow, of Old Goshenhoppen.

1770, Jan. 9, Wendel, son of Wendel Wiand, of New Goshenhoppen, married Catharina, daughter of Erhart Weis, of Old Goshenhoppen.

1770, June 21, Johannes Jung (the father is still in Germany), of New Goshenhoppen, married Susanna Walder, daughter of the late Jacob Walder, of Old Goshenhoppen.

1771, April 2, Johannes, son of Friedr. Kern, married Maria Magdalena Rudi, daughter of Dietrich Rudi, of Ridgewell

1771, June 11, Philippus, son of the Georg Schambach, of Lower Salford, married Margaretha Henrich, daughter of Henrich Henrich, of Hatfield township

Old Goshenhoppen—Marriages

1771, Oct. 27, Jacob Elinger, widower, of Old Goshenhoppen, married Barbara Schenck, widow, of Old Goshenhoppen.

1772, April 28, Philip Nais, son of the late Joh Nais, of Old Goshenhoppen, married Elisabetha Leidig, daughter of Jacob Leidig, of Franconia township.

1772, May 12, Adam Hiltebeutel, son of the late Martin Hiltebeutel, of Old Goshenhoppen, married Salome Klein, daughter of Johannes Klein, of Old Goshenhoppen

1772, May 19, Jacob Gerhart, son of the late Peter Gerhart, of Franconia township, married Elisabetha Detter, daughter of Conrad Detter, of Franconia township

1772, June 2, Conrad Gerhart, son of the late Peter Gerhart, of Franconia township, married Anna Maria Nais, daughter of Johan Nais, of Falckner Swamp

1772, Sept 15, Benjamin Schuler, son of Samuel Schuler, of Old Goshenhoppen, married Catharina Mincker, daughter of the late Henr Minker, of Old Goshenhoppen.

1772, Nov 17, Rudolph Segler, son of the late Joh Segler, of Old Goshenhoppen, married Catharina Wolfart, daughter of Nicolaus Wolfart, of Old Goshenhoppen

1773, May 27, Joh Hartenstein, son of Ludwig Hartenstein, of Old Goshenhoppen, married Magdalena Hollebusch, son of the late Peter Hollebusch, of Old Goshenhoppen

1774, Jan. 4, Christian May, son of Friedrich May, of Old Goshenhoppen, married Maria Elis Krein, daughter of the late Joh Jacob Kien (¹), of Old Goshenhoppen.

1774, Jan 6, Andreas Ries, son of the late Henrich Ries, of Old Goshenhoppen, married Margaretha Somni, daughter of Isaac Somni, of Old Goshenhoppen

1774, March 1, Joseph Werner, son of Joh. Werner, of Old Goshenhoppen, married Barbara Graf, daughter of Jacob Graf, of Old Goshenhoppen

1774, March 8, Joh Roerich, son of Nicolas Roerich, of Old Goshenhoppen, married Regina Kaemmer, daughter of the late Jacob Kaemmer, of Old Goshenhoppen

1774, Aug 21, Abraham Wolfart, son of Nicolaus Wolfart, of Old Goshenhoppen, married Anna Margr Panebecker, daughter of Weyand Panebecker, of New Goshenhoppen

1775, April 4, Jacob Weiant, son of Georg Weiant, of Old Goshenhoppen, married Salome Renn, daughter of the late Michael Renn, of Old Goshenhoppen

1775, Nov 2, Paul Knoepper, son of the late Conrad Knoepper, of Lower Salford, married Margaretha Hollebusch, daughter of Christian Hollebusch, of Old Goshenhoppen.

1775, Oct. 29, Hartman Keil, son of the late Adam Keil, of Franconia township, married Catharina Herschberger, daughter of Abraham Herschberger, of Franconia township

1776, Jan 16, Henrich Ohl, son of Andreas Ohl, of Old Goshenhoppen, married Margaretha Sitzman, daughter of Christian Sitzman, of Lower Milford township.

1776, May 7, Jacob Wagner, son of the late Michael Wagner, of Old Goshenhoppen, married Barbara Deis, daughter of the late Peter Deis, of Lower Salford

1776 May 14, Philip Weiss, son of Erhart Weiss, of Old Goshenhoppen, married Anna Marg Schmid, daughter of the late Henrich Schmid, of New Goshenhoppen

1776, May 26, Abraham Graf, son of Jacob Graf, of Old Goshenhoppen, married Magd Wagner, daughter of the late Michael Wagner, of Old Goshenhoppen

1776, July 2, Jacob Schmidt, son of the late Henrich Schmid, of New Goshenhoppen, married Elisabetha Weis, daughter of Erhart Weis, of New Goshenhoppen

1776, July 2, Jacob Schuler, of Macungie, married Elisabetha Schneider, daughter of Leonhart Schneider, of Old Goshenhoppen

1776, Aug 20, Joh Hiebner, son of Joh Hiebner, of Old Goshenhoppen, married Maria Naiman, daughter of Marcus Naiman, of Limerick township

1776 Sept. 3, Adam Henrich, son of Joh Henrich, of Limerick township, married Anna Maria Hollebusch, daughter of the late Peter Hollebusch, of Old Goshenhoppen.

1776, Aug 28, Abraham Berge, son of the late Joh. Ulrich Berge, of Lower Salford, married Salome Gerges, daughter of the late Wilhelm Gerges, of Lower Salford township

1776, Oct. 22, Joh. Nais, son of the late Joh Nais, of Old Goshenhoppen, married Catharina Hud, daughter of Joh Hudt, of Old Goshenhoppen

1776, Oct. 31, Joh. Heinemann, son of the late Henrich Heinemann, of Old Goshenhoppen, married Barbara Nais, daughter of Joh Nais, of Old Goshenhoppen.

1777, Febr 11, Joh Schuler, son of the late Samuel Schuler, of Old Goshenhoppen, married Catharina Eitemueller, daughter of Joh Eitemueller, of Old Goshenhoppen.

1777, Febr. 4, Jonas Schatz, son of the late Philip Schatz, of Old Goshenhoppen, married Catharina Ried, daughter of Phil Ried, of Old Goshenhoppen.

1777, May 25, Abraham Nais, son of the late Joh. Nais, of Old Goshenhoppen, married Magdalena Cantes, daughter of the late Mr Cantes, of Old Goshenhoppen

1777, Aug 26, Gerhart Bingeman, son of Fried Bingeman, of Limerick township, married Elis. Kentel, daughter of Joseph Kentel, of Limerick township.

1777, Nov 25, Jacob Weiss, son of the late Erhart Weiss, of Old Goshenhoppen, married Elisabetha Schmidt, daughter of the late Henrich Schmidt, of Old Goshenhoppen

1778, March 10, Johann Gerhart, son of the late Peter Gerhart, of Franconia township, married Magdalena Hertzel, daughter of Georg Hertzel, of Old Goshenhoppen.

1778, June 9, Philip Leydich, son of the Rev Leydich, of Frederick township, married Rosina Bucher, daughter of Dietrich Bucher, of Falckner Swamp

1779, April 11, Martin Lichtel, son of the late Antoni Lichtel, of Old Goshenhoppen, married Catharina Graf, daughter of Joh Graf, of Upper Salford

1779, June 13, David Graf, widower, married Anna Maria Henwin, widow, both of Old Goshenhoppen

1779, October 5, Felix Leh, son of Joh Leh, of Old Goshenhoppen, married Margaretha Tresman, daughter of the late Joh Georg Tresman, of Providence township.

List of those persons who were united in marriage by me, Friedrich Dellicker.

1782.

Aug 6, Jacob Seibel, son of the late Conrad Seibel, married Anna Magdalena Zern, daughter of Hans Adam Zern, of Malbruk (¹) township, Philadelphia County

September 19, Richard Herrison, son of John Herrison, of Union township, Berks County, married Catharina Zug, daughter of Abraham Zug, of Old Goshenhoppen

September 22, Godfrid Wiseler, son of Jacob Wiseler, and Eva Catharina Weiss, daughter of the late Hans Edward Weiss, both of Frederick township.

1783

Febr. 20, Peter Dinges married Maria Haas, both of Malbrouk township

May 20, Johannes Buch, son of the late Jacob Buch, married Catharina Schlotter, daughter of Wilhelm Schlotter, of Upper Salford

List of the persons who were united in marriage by me, F W v. d Sloot

1784

Nov 25, Jacob Schoet, son of Henrich Schoet, of Whitpain township, married Elisabetha Bock, daughter of the late Peter Bock, of Marlebrucht (¹) township

1794

Aug. 23, Solomon Grimly, son of Solomon Grimly, of Old Goshenhoppen, married Hannah Druckenmiller, also of Old Goshenhoppen

Persons who were united in marriage by me, Joh. Theob. Faber.

1787

Febr 27, Joh. Gipsen married Nensi [Nancy] Mils, both of Old Goshenhoppen

Aug 14, Valentin Kili, of Montgomery township, married Maria Grimli, of Old Goshenhoppen

Dec 2, Philip Schillig, of Skippack township, married Salome Grimli, both of Old Goshenhoppen.

March 11, Gabriel Schuler married Catharina Ren, both of Old Goshenhoppen.

1788

April 15, Peter Hollebusch, of Old Goshenhoppen, married Susanna Schell, of Falkner Swamp.

List of the persons who were united in marriage by me [Albert Helffenstein], in the year 1808, beginning July 12th.
Philip Rudi and Elisabeth Taub, Oct 17th

LIST OF CATECHUMENS.

List of those persons who were confirmed by me on April 17, 1767, in Great Swamp, they being from the Old Goshenhoppen congregation.

Boys:
1 Jacob Weiant, aged 21 years
2. Henrich Faust, aged 16 years
3. Philip Nais, aged 16 years
4 Johan Nais, aged 13 years
5 Conrad Ferdinand, aged 17 years
6 Wilhelm Antig, aged 16 years
7. Hardman, aged 17 years
8 A negro, named Coff, aged 30 years

Girls:
1. Maria Gan, aged 20 years
2. Sophia Jung, aged 15 years
3. Catharina Jung, aged 14 years
4. Elisabetha Kuchler, aged 16 years
5. Anna Marg. Hollebusch, aged 13 years
6. Anna Maria Faust, aged 14 years
7. Catharina Licht, aged 14 years
8. Christina Stricker, aged 13 years

Old Goshenhoppen—Catechumens

April 10, 1768

1. Daniel Schambach, aged 15 years
2. Peter Hollenbusch, aged 15 years
3. Peter Schuck, aged 15 years

1. Margaretha Somni, aged 14 years
2. Catharina Wolfart, aged 15 years
3. Maria Elis Kaub, aged 14 years
4. Anna Christina Laub, aged 15 years

March 24, 1769

1. Christian May, aged 13½ years
2. Joh Sem, aged 15 years
3. Joseph Keller, aged 16½ years
4. Wilh. Keller, aged 17½ years
5. Alexander Ohl, aged 15½ years
6. Joh Adam Mueller, aged 13 years
7. Joh. Ohl, aged 13½ years

1. Magd Hollebusch, aged 14½ years
2. Barbara Keiter, aged 14½ years
3. Magdalena Bruckert, aged 15½ years
4. Anna Mar. Hollebusch, aged 13½ years
5. Barbara Muck, aged 14 years

May 13, 1770.

1. Jacob Weitman, aged 15 years
2. Friedr Stall, aged 15 years
3. An adult named Jacob Schwartz, aged 27 years

1. Elisabetha Weis, aged 14 years
2. Maria Wolfart, aged 14 years
3. Maria Hollebusch, aged 19 years
4. Magdalena Keller, aged 15 years
5. Magd Ruckstuhl, aged 15 years
6. Hanna Sibilla Muller, aged 17 years

March 29, 1771

1. Valentin Schneider, aged 17½ years
2. Ludwig Schambach, aged 15 years
3. Wilhelm Hiester, aged 14 years

1. Anna Maria Schneider, aged 19½ years
2. Elisabetha Jung, aged 15 years
3. Elis Barbara Faust, aged 15 years

April 17, 1772

1. Ludwig Volckert, aged 17½ years
2. Wilhelm Daniel Bruckert, aged 16 years
3. George Adam Derr, aged 19 years
    Besides these three men

April 24, 1773.

1. Henrich Hersch, aged 14 years
2. Friedr. Mueller, aged 14 years
3. Jacob Muck, aged 14 years
4. Abraham Nais, aged 17 years

1. Eva Weis, aged 14 years
2. Catharina Hud, 14 years
3. Catharina Somni, aged 14 years
4. Marg Hertzel, aged 16 years
5. Barbara Nais, aged 15 years
6. Anna Mar. Mueller, aged 16 years

April 1, 1774

Boys
1. Felix Leh, aged 18 years
2. Philip Riedt, aged 13 years
3. Baltzer Riedt, aged 16 years
4. Wilhelm Ohl, aged 16 years
5. Johann Weitman, aged 16 years

1. Catharina Lueck, aged 15 years
2. Catharina Hollebusch, aged 14 years

April 14, 1775.

1. Joh. Weis, aged 14 years
2. Samuel Schuler, aged 15½ years
3. Georg Nais, aged 16 years

1. Anna Maria Hersch, aged 15 years
2. Eva Marg Hud, aged 14 years
3. Magdalena Jung, aged 15 years
4. Magdalena Hertzel, aged 15 years

April 13, 1776.

1. Nicolaus Maenner, aged 16 years
2. —— Ohl, aged 16 years
3. —— Bossert, aged 16 years

1. Eva Somni, aged 15 years
2. Cath Hertzel, aged 16 years
3. Elis. Ohl, aged 14 years

April 12, 1777

1. Georg Kerschner, aged 16 years
2. Jacob Schreiner, aged 14 years
3. Jacob Lehe, aged 16 years

1. Barbara Hersch, aged 15 years

April 2, 1779

1. Margaretha Wolfart, aged 14 years
2. Anna Trolinger, aged 17 years
3. Margaretha Manner, aged 15 years

Old Goshenhoppen—Catechumens

The following children were confirmed at Old Goshenhoppen by me, Joh. Wilh Ingold, of this congregation, from Old Goshenhoppen.

April 21, 1781.

Boys:
1. Jacob Rudi, aged 17 years
2. Philip Neumann, aged 15 years
3. Samuel Schuler, aged 14 years
4. Ludwig Ache, aged 18 years
5. Jacob Schuler, aged 17 years
6. Jacob Ache, aged 14 years
7. Ulrich Rukstul, aged 17 years
8. Henrich Schuler, aged 17 years
   From Great Swamp·
9. Henrich Huber, aged 17 years
10. Valentin Huber, aged 18 years
11. Conrad Nunnbauer, aged 16 years
12. Peter Willauer, aged 16 years
13. Peter Samsel, aged 17 years
14. Emanuel Hecher, aged 17 years
15. Georg Dittlo, aged 17 years
    From New Goshenhoppen
16. Jacob Maurer, aged 19 years
17. Joh Nicol Zimmermann, aged 16 years
18. Georg Maurer, aged 16 years
    From Kestenberg:
19. Jacob Huber, aged 14 years
20. Joh Berkenstok, aged 15 years
21. Henrich Huber, aged 19 years

1. Catharina Rudi, aged 16 years
2. Elisabetha Neus, aged 18 years
3. Susanna Dikenschid, aged 15 years
4. Maria Neus, aged 16 years
5. Charlotta Mayer, aged 15 years
6. Catharina Ohl, aged 14 years
7. Margaretha Doerr, aged 18 years
8. Margaretha Walliser, aged 18 years
9. Susanna Hirsch, aged 15 years
10. Anna Elisa Wund, aged 15 years
    From Great Swamp·
11. Catharina Huber, aged 14 years
12. Barbara Eberhard, aged 14 years
13. Catharina Eberhard, aged 15 years
14. Anna Maria Eberhard, aged 14 years
15. Margaretha Dittlo, aged 17 years
    From Kestenberg
16. Magdalena Menxel, aged 17 years
17. Barbara Stahlneker, aged 15 years
18. Maria Gock, aged 16 years
19. Fronica Huber, aged 16 years

On May 26, 1782, the following were confirmed by me, Friedrich Dellicker.

Christian Bidhard
Heinrich Ebrecht
Conrad Hut
Georg Weiss

Sara Ebrecht
Sophia Leen
Veronica Heinemann
Dorothea Holdenbusch

On May 24, 1783, the following were confirmed.

Conrad Misnner
Heinrich Bock
Daniel Freymeier
Johannes Schuler
Abraham Zaerckel

Anna Margareth Neiss, married
Magdalena Schuler
Catharina Zaerkel

Those persons who were confirmed by me, Joh Theob Faber, on April 6, 1787, here in Old Goshenhoppen:

Boys:
1. Henrich Hersch, aged 14 years
2. Peter Hersch, aged 15 years
3. Adam Bickart, aged 18 years
4. Peter Bock, aged 15 years
5. Bil Schuler, aged 15 years
6. Johann Ache, aged 15 years
7. Daniel Berto, aged 20 years
8. Antoni Berto, aged 15 years
9. Joh Grimli, aged 16 years

Girls:
1. Sela Grol, aged 17 years
2. Balle Rudi, aged 17 years
3. Catharina Werner, aged 17 years
4. Marg Hertzel, aged 17 years
5. Salome Grimli, aged 18 years
6. Maria Berto, aged 17 years
7. Catharina Lichtel, aged 17 years
8. Anna Maria Zanckmeister, aged 18 years
9. Elisabetha Scholl, aged 17 years
10. Susanna Scholl, aged 17 years

Those children from Old Goshenhoppen who on April 12, 1788, were confirmed by me, Joh Theob Faber, in the church at Great Swamp

1. Andreas Wetknecht, aged 15 years
2. Johann Stroman, aged 17 years
3. Joh. Georg Moyer, aged 15 years
4. Martin Schmidt, aged 22 years
5. Johann Keller, aged 23 years
6. Johann Weittemayer, aged 17 years
7. David Dickenschied, aged 16 years
8. Abraham Mayer, aged 17 years
9. Solomon Grimli, aged 16 years

1. Magdalena Moyer, aged 14 years
2. Anna Maria Stroman, aged 15 years
3. Anna Marg Coppelberger, aged 16 years
4. Margaretha Wentz, aged 15 years
5. Magdalena Eckli, aged 15 years
6. Christina Mayer, aged 17 years
7. Catharina Eckli, aged 15 years
8. Catharina Groll, aged 16 years
9. Magdalena Grimli, aged 16 years

Old Goshenhoppen—Catechumens 433

10 Abr Bingeman, aged 18 years

10 Elisabeth Reimer, aged 19 years
11 Anna Maria Lein, aged 15 years
12. Elis. Zaerkel, aged 18 years
13 Marg Zaerkel, aged 16 years

Those persons who on March 29, 1793, were confirmed by me, Joh Faber, in Old Goshenhoppen

No boys

Girls
Catharina Strohman, aged 17 years
Catharina Weyer, aged 16 years
Catharina Schweifort, aged 16 years
Catharina Lichti, aged 16 years
Magdalena Brickert, aged 16 years
Magdalena Sassaman, aged 17 years

Those children of this congregation who on Easter Sunday, 1794, were confirmed in New Goshenhoppen by me, Joh. Faber

Boys:
1. Jacob Maenner, aged 15 years
2 Christian Reifinger, aged 15 years
3. John Copelberger, aged 16 years

Girls
1 Catharina Reifinger, aged 17 years
2. Sophia Schmit, aged 18 years
3 Elisabetha Galester, aged 19 years

Those children of this congregation who on Easter Sunday of 1795 were confirmed in Great Swamp by me, Joh Faber·

Boys
1 Philip Bauman, aged 17 years
2 Conrad Bickhard, aged 16 years
3. John Hildebeutel, aged 22 years
4 Abraham Hildebeutel, aged 20 years
5 Michael Wagner, aged 17 years
6 Daniel Hildebeutel, aged 21 years
7 Conrad Geist, aged 21 years
8. Philip Fries, aged 21 years

Girls.
1 Mary Hildebeutel, aged 19 years
2 Elisabetha Hildebeutel, aged 17 years
3. Mary Hildebeutel, aged 17 years
4. Susanna Kiehler, aged 19 years
5. Margaretha Geist, aged 18 years
6 Elisabetha Geist, aged 17 years
7. Catharina Geist, aged 15 years
8 Catharina Bruch, aged 16 years

LIST OF COMMUNICANTS

Names of those who after preceding preparation partook of the Lord's Supper, administered by me, Fr. v. d. Sloot, on June 7, 1813.

1. Johann Hildebeutel
2. Georg Herzel
3. Balthasar Ried
4. Elisabeth, his wife
5. Johann Keller
6. Ulrich Herzel
7. Heinrich Reifinger
8. Philip Ried
9. Wilhelm Endersen
10. Friedrich Rudy
11. Heinrich Keller
12. Margareth, his wife
13. Salome Grimli
14. Hanna, his wife
15. Johann Kuppelberger
16. Johann Hederich
17. Jesse Schmidt
18. Elisabeth, his wife
19. Peter Faust
20. Elisabeth, his wife
21. Heinrich Pickhart
22. Abraham Kuppelberger
23. Henrich Hauk
24. Conrad Koler
25. Isaac Herzel
26. Jacob Ried
27. Catharina Graff
28. Johann Berns
29. Elisabeth Grimli
30. Hanna Grimli
31. Elis Fillmann
32. Maria Hering
33. Christina Leistern
34. Elisabeth Weidmann
35. Barbara Scheid
36. Anna Hol
37. Sarah Jacoby
38. Elisabeth Scheid
39. Nathan Schue
40. Christina Fridemann
41. Catharina Schrifli
42. Gertraud Klein
43. Sarah Reichart
44. Maria Schwenk
45. Magd Pannbecker
46. Nathan Schwenk
47. Magdalena Wambold
48. Salome Bains
49. Elisabeth Schmidt
50. Elisabeth Zink
51. Nathan Baumann
52. Susanna Neiss

Names of those who commenced on October 16, 1813, after preceding preparation·

1. Ulrich Herzel
2. Philip Ried
3. Heinrich Pickhard
4. John Schuler
5. George Pickhard
6. Andreas Achi
7. Sophia Achi
8. Margareta Kraus
9. Anna Pickhard
10. Catarina Klein
11. Susanna Klein
12. Barbara Meier
13. Margareta Hummel
14. Sophia Groll
15. Maria Herzel
16. Maria Schuler
17. Margaretha Faust
18. Margareta Scholl
19. Ego [I, Fr. v d Sloot]

Old Goshenhoppen—Communicants

On April 23, 1814, the following appeared at the preparatory services.

1 Johann Neiss
2 Georg Herzel
3 Jacob Neiss
4 Johann Keller
5 Ulrich Herzel
6 Johann Achi
7 Wilh Enderson
8. Heinrich Hauk
9. Balthasar Ried
10 Heinrich Strohmann
11 Michael Ziegler
12. Johann Christmann
13. George Wunderlich
14 Henrich Hutter
15 Margaretha, mother
16. Fridrich Rudi
17 Fridrich Scholl
18. Jacob Ried
19 Andreas Achi
20 Daniel Hauk
21 Konrad Kichler
22 Joseph Kichler
23 Henrich Hauk
24 Hanna, his wife
25 Philip Christmann
26 Elisabeth, his wife
27 Jesse Schmidt
28 Elisabeth, his wife
29 Nathan Klein
30 Johann Neiss
31 Debora, his wife
32 Margareth Neiss
33 Maria Miller
34. Elisabeth Ried
35 Jacob Ruckstuhl
36 Elis Weidemeier
37 Barbara Achi
38. Sophia, the daughter
39 Catharina Wunderlich
40 Michael Herzel
41 Salome Krimli
42. Hanna, his wife
43 Elisabeth, the mother
44. Christian Oister
45 Barbara Scheid
46 Sara Reichert
47 Sara Jacobi
48. Elisabeth Schmidt
49 Sara Hauk
50 Nathan Nieler
51 Catharina Baumann
52 Maria Schuler
53 Nathan Gatter
54. Magdalena Wambold
55. Elisabeth Neiss
56. Magd. Koppelberger
57 Marg Faust
58 Salome Banz
59 Ego, Fr W v. d Sloot
60 Will Neiss

Names of the communicants of Sept 18, 1814.

1. Christian Pickhard
2. Friedrich Rudi
3. John Salledy
4 Christian May
5 George, his son
6. Caspar, his son
7. John Hauk
8 Elisabeth, his wife
9 George Kolb
10 Catharina, his wife
11 George Herzel
12 Samuel Scholl
13 Georg Neiss
14 Catharina Taub
15 Catharina Groll
16 Margareth Nees

17. Katharina Kob
18. Maria Heering
19. Elis. Schmidt
20. Sophia Groll
21. Ego, v der Sloot

Names of those who appeared at the preparatory services, April 15, 1815:

1 Susanna Neiss
2. Johan Keller
3 Balthasar Ried
4. Elisabeth, his wife
5 Jacob Schmidt
6 Gertrud Klein
7 Ulrich Herzel
8 Wilhelm Schuler
9 Samuel Schuler
10. Catharina, his daughter
11 Margareth Lang
12 Johann Schuler
13 Samuel Schuler
14. Georg Neiss
15. Henrich Pickhard
16 Philip Ried
17. John Christman
18. Samuel Geissinger
19. John Endres
20. Michel Scholl
21. Michel Heffelinger
22. Isaac Grimli
23 John Grimli
24 Michel Koppelberger
25 Magdalena Koppelberger
26 Elisabeth Koppelberger
27 Henrich Hukker
28 David Salady
29. John Ruckstuhl
30 Jesse Schmidt
31 Elis Salady
32. Jonas Wollfahrt
33 Johannes Schmidt
34. Andreas Achi
35 Sophia Achi
36 Elisabeth Wollfahrt
37. Elisabeth Ganz
38. Margareth Neiss
39. Sara Borns
40. Barbara Scheid
41. Elisabeth Sellers
42. Maria Zepp
43. Sara Reicher
44. Susanna Klein
45. Katharina Herzel
46. Elisabeth Kraus
47 Elisabeth Kraus
48 Maria Pannebecker ˅
49. Susanna Ried
50 Elisabeth Zink
51. Kathar. Schwenk
52 Maria Herzel
53 Peter Weil
54 Katharina Weil
55 Elisabeth Scheidt
56. Maria Enderson
57. Susanna Baumann
58 Margaretha Scholl
59. Catharina Baumann
60 Catharina Geier
61 Christina Baumann
62 Rachel Scheitel
63 Ego [v. der Sloot]
64 Marg. Hukker
65. George Herzel, Esq.
66 Jesse Schillich

Names of the communicants on Oct 12, 1815˙

1. John Ried
2 John Hukker
3. John Barns
4 Katharina Acker
5. Katharina Meier
6. Maria Heering
7 Elisabeth Schmidt
8. Margareth Keppel
9 Elisabeth Fried

CHURCH RECORD OF THE GREAT SWAMP REFORMED CONGREGATION, LOWER MILFORD TOWNSHIP, LEHIGH CO., PA., 1736–1833.

TRANSLATED BY PROF. WM. J. HINKE, PH.D.

Church Record
of the Christian Congregation at
Great Swamp,

In which are recorded: First, the articles of the Christian Church Order, which this Congregation (together with others in this land) has adopted. Secondly, the names of the children that have been baptized, their parents and their sponsors.

The beginning was made in the year of our Lord Jesus Christ, 1736,
the 24th of April.
Joh. Henricus Goetschius,
V. D. M. Helvetico-Tigurinus.

Memorandum of the Articles of the Church Order.

1. Four elders, honorable men, who have a good report among their neighbors, shall be named by the minister and be elected by the majority of the voters. Each shall remain in office for two years.

The Duty of the Elders shall be:

a. To exercise good oversight over the members of the congregation and to make known everything disorderly, (1) to the minister alone; (2) to the minister and the other elders; (3) to the whole congregation, if the first and second admonition had no effect, in order that those who give public offense may not be tolerated in the congregation of God.

b The youngest of them shall take up the collection for one year, the next to the youngest the following year, at every divine service One of them shall collect the amount and keep it faithfully until the time of accounting, which shall take place every half year before the whole congregation.

Expenditure of the Alms

The collections or alms shall be expended as follows:

a They shall be applied to needy persons who may be in or outside of the congregation.

b To the church or schoolhouse, if there is anything to improve or to build

c For bread and wine at the communion service,

Or whatever else may be found to be a necessary expenditure in the judgment of the Christian congregation.

The Second Article, regarding the Congregation

1 Every one who confesses the Evangelical Reformed religion and wishes to belong to this congregation shall make a solemn vow before God and men, and faithfully promise by the signature of his own name, that he and his household will be obedient to every divine ordinance Otherwise he shall not be regarded as a Christian member, but shall be excluded from all gifts and privileges which the members of this congregation enjoy

2 Each one shall contribute every year, according to his pleasure and ability, whatever will be necessary for the maintenance of the divine worship

3 Should any member or those of his family lead offensive lives and will not show amendment of life through the preaching of God's Word or private admonition, he can expect exclusion from the Lord's Supper and even from the congregation.

EBERHART, ELISABETHA, da of Joseph Eberhart and Catherine, his wife, born June 2, 1742, bapt July 18, sponsors, Joseph Zimmerman and wife Maria Elisabetha

RIDY, CONRAD, son of Jacob Ridy and Maria Elisabetha, his wife, b Oct 19, 1747, sponsors, Conrad Zimmerman, Dieter Mombauer, Anna Maria Schwenck, Margaretha Zimmerman

BRAUN, EVA CATHERINE, da. of Michael (!) Braun and Agnes, his wife, born Febr 2, 1739; sp, Catharine Heist

BRAUN, J. GEORG, son of Jacob Braun and Agnes, his wife, b Jan 30, 1742, sp, Georg Heist

BRAUN, MATHYS, son of Jacob Braun and Agnes, his wife, b July 10, 1744, sp, Mathys Nuss (?) and Catharine, his wife (?)

Names of the parents, children and sponsors. A. 1736 [baptized by John H Goetschy].

Children	Parents	Sponsors
April 24		
Joseph	Joseph Eberhard, Catharina, his wife	Joseph Zimmerman
Abraham	Christian Willauer, Catrina, his wife	Abraham Penny
Anna Margreth	Peter Titer, Anna Margreth	the mother herself, Anna Marg Titer
Anna Margreth	Valentin Keiser, Agnes	Lorentz Erb, Anna Margreth
Anna Margreth	Jacob Wezel, Anna Barbara	Michael Eberhart and wife
Anna Sibilla	Michael Kohler, Sibilla	Peter Walper, Sibilla
October 31.		
Anna Maria	Georg German, Barbara	Mathias Ox, Anna Maria, his wife
Eva Catrina	Georg Kunz, Anna Catrina	Leonhardt Ox, Anna Catrina
April 11.	A. 1737.	
Fridrich	Joh Georg Margstaler, Anna Margretha	Fridrich Margstaler, Anna Barbara
Eva Margreth	Christian Willauer, Eva Catrina	Michael Eberhardt and Margreth
October 3		
Joh. Jacob	Michael Kehler, Sibilla	Jacob Wezel, Eva Barbara
Febr. 28	A. 1738	
Felix	Jacob Dups, Froneka [Veronica]	Felix Brunner, Barbara
Anna Margreth	Michael Eberhardt, Anna Margreth	Anna Margreth Brunner, daughter of Felix Brunner
Anna Maria	William Eich, Magdalena	Mathias Ox, Anna Maria

[Entries by the Rev. George Michael Weiss, 1748-1751]

Ludwig Rippel, Sybilla Maria	J. Erhardt	J Erhardt Roos, Maria Eva

Parents	Children	Sponsors
February 12, 1749.		
Georg ——(?)	J. Michel	J Michel Eberhardt, Anna Maria Wetzel
March 5th [1749].		
David Streib, Susanna	Veronica	Ullrich Spinner, Ussula
Caspar Ritter, Anna Maria	J. Martin	Martin Ritter, Maria Gretha
November 24, 1748.		
Georg Klein, Maria Catharina	J Henrich	Jost Henrich Sassemanshausen, Anna Sybilla, Catharina Walwerd
March 26th [1749].		
Georg Hercker (?), Magdalena	Anna Rosina	Franz Roos, Anna Rosina Roos
J Schaut, Sybilla Catharina	Lena Catharina	Peter Wetzel, Lena Catharina Keiber
April 16th [1749].		
Georg Bernhardt Rim, Anna Maria	J. Adam	J Adam Schneider and wife Anna Elisa
May 7th [1749]		
Joseph Zimmerman, Elisabetha	Baltzer	Baltzer Gering, Catharina Eberhardt
Franz Michel Bischoff, Maria Eva	Catharina	Joseph Eberhardt, Catharina
June 16th [1749].		
J Henerich Matzinger, Anna Clara	Susanna Else	J Jost Ohlwil, Anna Eva
July 30th [1749]		
J. Grisemer, Anna Maria	Felix	Felix Brunner, Anna Barbara
J. Bernhardt Roos, Maria Eva	J. Daniel	J Daniel Kober, Maria Eva
August 18th [1749].		
Ullrich Rieser, Anna Barbara	Andres	Andres Grebei, Gretha Greber
August 20th [1749].		
Wilhelm Mack, Maria Lisa	David, Anna Lisa	Anna Lisa Zimmermann, David Streib, Susanna

Great Swamp—Baptisms

Parents	Children	Sponsors
Jacob Schmidt, Elisabetha	Jacob	Mathys Ochs, Anna Maria
September 8th [1749]		
Michel Keiber, Magdalena	Maria Elisa	Daniel Heller, Maria Elisabetha Keiber
November 13th [1749]		
J Daniel Kober, Maria Eva	J. Erhardt	J Erhardt Gros, Maria Eva
Michel Jung, Maria Adelheidt	J Jacob	J Jacob Guckerdt, Margretha
December 24th [1749].		
Valentin Roth, Maria Margaretha	Abraham	Abraham Kreider, Anna Margaretha
March 18th [1750]		
Jacob Mathys, Susanna	Barbara	Jacob Wetzel, Barbara Wetzel
Nicolaus Mombauer, Magdalena	J Philip	J. Philip Vackendael, Maria Catharina Mombauer
Theobald Breuchler, Anna Maria	J. Michel	Leonhardt Bock, Christina Bock, Michel Schwenck, Elisa Samsel
1744, April 5th		
Jacob Dubs, Veronica	Barbara	Jacob Wetzel, Barbara Wetzel
1746		
Jacob Dubs, Veronica	Margaretha	Anna Maria Wetzler
1748, October 28th		
Jacob Dubs, Veronica	Daniel	Daniel Christmann, Margaretha
1750, October 16th		
Jacob Dubs, Veronica	Elisabetha	Elisabetha Huber
1750, Nov 4th.		
Jacob Buss, Catharina	Christina	Melchior Wecher, Christina Wecher
1751, June 2nd.		
Ullrich Rieser, Barbara	Casper	Caspar Holzhausen, Margaretha Holzhausen
Adam Drumpf (?), Anna Maria	J. Jacob	Jacob Wetzel, Anna Barbara

Children who were baptized by me, J T. Faber

Parents	Children	Sponsors
Christofel Reiter	Anna Maria, 1766, Nov. 19	Johannes Klein and wife
Jacob Peiffer	Maria Elisabetha, 1767, Jan. 2	Georg Stallenecker and wife
Michael Eberhard	Anna Maria, 1766, Dec. 29	Anna Maria Bleiler
Simon Walder	Johannes Jacob, 1767, Febr 8	Johann Jacob Keller and wife
Johannes Jacob Stahl	Johan Georg, 1766, Dec. 6	Joh. Georg Stahl and wife
Nicolaus Schubing	Jacob, 1767, May 14	—— Holshauser and wife
Jacob Bischof	Catharina, 1767, Sept. 3	Daniel Hister and wife
Martin Sax	Johannes Stofel, 1767, Oct. 31	Stofel Sax, Margaretha Huber, da of Henrich Huber
Christian Willauer	Anna Catharina, 1767, Nov. 1	Christian Willauer and wife
Joh. Nicolaus Faust	Anna Margaretha, 1767, Nov 1	Susanna Mathes
Benjamin Somer	Maria Margaretha, 1767, Nov 18	Henrich Hersch and wife
Henrich Bitting	Henrich, Eva, 1767, Nov. 15	Andrew Greber and wife
Philip Seller	Abraham, 1767, Aug. 30	the father
Rudolf Frick	Anna, 1768, Jan 26	Rudolph Hupper and wife
Jacob Keller	Anna Barbara, 1768, Febr 5	Simon Walter and wife
Peter Wetzel	Anna Barbara, 1768, Febr. 9	Christian Mueller and wife
Bernhart Kaufman	Leonhart, 1768, Jan. 4	Lenert Ochs and wife
Georg Schütz	Georg Ludwig, 1768, March 25	Georg Ziegenfuss and wife
Peter Eberhard	Conrad, 1768, March 4	Conrad Reiswig, Anna Maria Luni
Georg Meyer	Magdalena, 1760, Jan. 11	Nicolaus Mumbauer and wife

Great Swamp—Baptisms

Parents	Children	Sponsors
Jacob Reiber	Christophorus, 1768, March 12	Stoffel Ott, Elisabetha Bayer
Peter Weber	Maria Catharina, 1768, Apr 15	Velten [Valentin] Lieser and wife
Jacob Holshauser	Susanna, 1768, May 4	Jacob Danckel and wife
Henrich Betz	Henrich, 1767, Nov. 8	Henrich Haas, Elisabetha Reinhart
Joh. Maurer	Anna Maria, 1768, June 5	Michael —— and wife
Valendin Hupper	Anna Barbara, 1768, Aug 23	Philip Heger and wife
Peter Strein	Anna Margaretha, 1768, July 21	Joh Georg Ziegenfuss and wife
a foundling was baptized	Anna Elisabetha, 1768, ——	Henrich Hupper and wife
Valendin Dickenschidt	Anna Maria, 1768, Nov. 6	Michael Ried and wife Anna Maria
Georg Ziegenfus	Joh Jacob, 1768, Dec 4	Georg Schutz and wife
Philip Heger	Elisabetha, 1769, March 1	Jacob Zimmerman, Elisabeta Wagner
Joseph Eberhardt	Elisabetha, 1769, Jan. 22	Jacob Keller and wife
Simon Walder	Abraham, 1769, Jan. 15	Jacob Stollenecker, Anna Elis Reinnold
Christian Willauer	Adam, 1769, Jan 15	Adam Willauer and wife
Felix Lien	Petrus, 1769, Febr. 17	Petrus Lien and wife
Henrich Bleiler	Daniel, 1769, March 1	Petrus Bleiler and wife
Joh. Umstaet	Elisabetha, 1769, Febr 7	Georg Philip Dill and wife
Abraham Dittlo	Abraham, 1769, March 12	David Levi and wife
Petrus Schuler	Catharina Barbara, 1769, March 30	Fried Delb and wife
Jacob Mayer	Catharina, 1769, March 30	Joh. Steinman
Daniel Frick	Anna Maria, 1769, May 30	Johannes Hellicas and wife

Parents	Children	Sponsors
Christoph Henrich	Joh Jacobus, 1769, June 3	Joh Jacob Erdman, Margretha Bischof
Jacob Weil	Joh Jacobus, 1769, July 8	Jacobus Hupper and wife
Jacobus Hupper	Anna Eva, 1769, July 16	Nicolaus Samsel, Anna Eva Stallenecker ✓
Henrich Bitting	Ludwig, 1769, Sept. 28	Ludwig Bitting and wife
Henrich Ott	Susanna, 1769, Nov. 28	Joh. Georg Ziegenfuss and wife
Joh Nicolaus Diets	Maria Eva, 1769, Dec. 22	Franz Michael Bischof and wife
Jacob Kehler	Anna Elisabetha, 1769, Dec 15	Christoph Ott, Anna Elis. Dups
Georg Schütz	Joh Georg ——, 1770, March 1	Georg Ziegenfuss and wife
Georg Steiner	Susanna, 1769, Oct 25	Susanna Reiswig and Jonas Petri
Fried Diell	Jacobus, 1770, Jan 7	Jacob Spiner and wife
Petrus Linn	Gertrude, 1770, March 23	Carolus Fred Sili, Gertrude Cok
Joh Cock	Elisabeth, 1770, Febr 6	Joh Schmidt and wife
Peter Eberhart	Christina, 1770, Apr. 30	Johannes Segler and wife
Michael Hellicas	Rebecca, 1770, Apr. 3	Jacob Geri and wife
Rudi Huper	Joh. Petrus, 1770, June 2	Henrich Huper and wife
Peter Wetzel	Anna Catharina, 1770, June 13	Joseph Eberhard and wife
Mathias Sax	Michael, 1770, Aug 13	Michael Breuchler, Catharina Sax
Reinhart Kaufmann	Joh. Jacobus, 1770, Aug. 11	Jacob Eberhart and wife
Simon Walter	Anna Eva, 1770, Sept 24	Eva Olewein
Georg Stiehl	Joh. Jacobus, 1770, Dec. 4	Jacob Holtzhauser and wife
Jacobus Reiber	Anna Margretha, 1770, Nov. 8	Fried Mueller, Eva Margaretha
Andreas Walb	Anna Maria, 1770, Oct 24	Peter Eberhart and wife

Great Swamp—Baptisms

Parents	Children	Sponsors
Henrich Mueller	Susanna, 1770, Nov 13	Jacob Danckel and wife
Peter Strein	Elisabeth, 1771, Jan 26	Peter Wetzel and wife
Peter Samsel	Abraham, 1771, Febr. 26	Abraham Dittlo and wife
Joh Hellicas	Joh. Georg, 1771, Febr. 28	Georg Horlacher and wife
Georg Mack	Elisabetha, 1771, Febr 7	Philip Mumbauer, Elisabeth Neukomer
Joh. Nicolaus Faust	Elisabetha ——, 1771, Febr. 15	Caspar Berret and wife
Nicolaus Samsel	Catharina, 1771, June 18	Elisabetha Samuel
Christoffel Sax	Elis Margretha, 1771, Aug 15	Martin Sax and wife
Henrich Bleiler	Johannes, 1771, Aug. 25	Petrus Bleiler
Philip Heger	Joh Petrus, 1771, Nov 5	Valentin Huper and wife
Michael Hellicas	Johannes, 1772, Jan 16	Johannes Hellicas and wife
Balzer Stiehl	Joh Abraham, 1771, Nov 29	Abraham Stahl and wife
Joseph Eberhart	Susanna, 1772, March 5	Peter Eberhart and wife
Jacob Maxel	Johannes, 1772, May 4	Jacob Eberhart and wife
Jacob Holtzhausen	Maria Barbara, 1772, March 23	Georg Stahl and wife
Henrich Bitting	Johannes, 1771, June 24	Joh Jost and wife
Adam Romich	Jacobus, 1772, March 12	Michael Helligas
Jacob Kehler	Joh. Jacobus, 1772, Oct 26	Jacob Stohlenecker, Magdalena Weis
Peter Wetzel	Joh Georgus, 1772, Nov 9	Joh Georg Ziegenfuss and wife
Henrich Alles	Maria Elisabetha, 1772, Sept. 6	Elisabeth Neukomer, David Gangewer
Joh Neukomer	Joh Georgus, 1772, Oct. 24	Georg Blanck and wife

Parents	Children	Sponsors
Abraham Bachman	Elisabetha, 1772, Oct. 21	Peter Gottel and wife
Abraham Dittlo	Elisabetha, 1773, Febr. 7	David Levi and wife
Peter Eberhart	Abraham, 1773, March 24	Joseph Eberhart and wife
Andreas Walp	Joh Jacobus, 1773, March 31	Jacob Walp, Eva Schlieger
Georg Hoerner	Anna Maria, 1773, Apr. 8	Jacob Weis, Maria Roeder
Peter Hogerberg	Joh Petrus, 1773, June 22	Peter Wetzel and wife
Georg Stiel	Elisabetha, 1773, June 3	Theob Franck, Elisabeta Berger
Jost Leobald	Anna Maria, Margaretha, 1773, June 12	Philip Mumbauer, Anna Maria Dittlo, Joh Maurer and wife
Joh Stoer	Joh. Rosina, 1773, Febr. 7	Leonhart Beutelman and wife
Jacob Dorwart	Eva Barbara, 1773, Sept. 9	Barbara Spiner
Henrich Ott	Anna Eva, 1773, Aug. 11	Jacob Kehler and wife
Mich Helligas	Elisabetha, 1773, Nov. 1	Adam Geri, Elisabetha Neukomer
Christoffel Ott	Anna Catharina, 1774, Jan. 16	Henr. Huper, Catharina Ott
Baltzer Stiehl	Johannes, 1773, Dec. 31	Joh Helligas and wife
Conr. Worman	Johannes, 1774, Febr. 8	Catharina Funk
Nicolaus Faust	Henricus, 1774, Jan. 24	Hen. Matheus and wife
Adam Willauer	Eva Jacobina, 1774, Jan. 13	Felix Linn and wife
Adam Rauch	Catharina, 1774, March 19	Melchior Knople and wife
Joh Ohlinger	Johannes, 1774, March 20	Henr Ott and wife
Peter Hagenberg	Johannes, 1774, Aug 27	Valentin Huper and wife

Great Swamp—Baptisms

Parents	Children	Sponsors
Felix Linn	Johannes, 1774, June 20	Joh Linn and wife
Henr Bleiler	Anna, 1774, July 30	Anna Mad Bleiler
Abraham Bachman	Johannes, 1774, June 30	Joh Halteman, Margaretha Schmid
Jacob Dorwort	Elisabetha, 1775, Apr 12	Daniel Dups and wife
✓ Jost Leopold	Joh Daniel, 1775, March 26	Daniel Lambrecht and wife
Georg Stiel	Anna Maria, 1775, June 21	Maria Christina Dallman
⟵ Joh. Helligas	Catharina, 1775, June 3	Michael Helligas and wife
Heni Bitting	Anna Margaretha, 1775, May 15	Anna Marg. Mumbauer
Joh Nicol Samsel	Johannes, 1775, Sept 11	Michael Ott, Elisabeth Huper
Daniel Dups	Johannes, 1775, Sept 7	Martin Schwarz
Mich Helligas	Michael, 1775, Nov 15	Joh. Cunius and wife
Jacob Kehler	Eva Sibilla, 1775, Sept 27	Eva Stollenecker
Adam Romich	Joh. Adam, 1776, Febr. 10	Christian Mueller and wife
Fried. Delp	Anna Margreta, 1776, March 19	Wilhelm Rieser and Anna Margaretha Doerr
Jacob Rauber	child, 1776, May 18	Jacob Koehler and wife
Conr Worman	Maria, 1775, Aug 4	the parents
Georg Mack	Susanna, 1776, June 3	Georg Hoerner and wife
Joh Jacobi	Daniel, 1776, Aug 2	Peter Eberhart and wife
Joh Kocken	Anna Maria, 1776, Aug. 5	Georg Rumfeld, Anna Maria Muellei
Doctor Lin	Jonathan, 1776, Aug 21	Adam Willauer and wife
Conr Worman	Andreas, 1776, Dec 22	the father
Philip Mumbauer	Johannes, 1777, Jan 11	Valentin Huper and wife

Parents	Children	Sponsors
Adam Willauer	Maria Elis , 1777, Apr 25	Joh Lin and wife
Henr Bleiler	Lazarus, 1777, Jan. 21	Peter Bleiler
Georg Dill	Henrich, 1776, Nov 7	Henr. Wenig and wife
Henrich Ott	Johannes, 1777, Apr 7	Jacob Kehler and wife
Joh Halteman	Elisabeta, 1776, Sept 5	Johannes Neukomer and wife
Georg Worman	Magdalena, 1777, June 14	Magdalena Worman
Ludwig Nuspickel	Ludwig, 1774, Nov. 1	the parents
Daniel Dups	Anna Maria, 1777, June 17	Anna Maria Schwenk
Joh Olinger	Joh Jacobus, 1777, May 4	Christoffel Ott and wife
Jacobus Wolff	Anna Maria, 1777, June 17	Joh Hauser and wife
Peter Weber	Anna Barbara, 1777, July 1	Valentin Huper and wife
Christofel Reitenauer	Joh Adam, 1777, Apr 13	Adam Willauer and wife
Peter Schmidt	Catharina, 1770, July 25	Peter Linn and wife
✓ Georg Helligas	Anna Margaretha, 1777, Oct 5	Nicol. Goery and wife
Georg Mack	Maria Eva, 1777, Oct. 3	Cathar Willauer
Joh Linn	Johannes, 1772, Febr 17	Joh Schmidt and wife
Joh Linn	Elisabetha, 1777, Nov 29	Joh. Stahl and wife
Georg Math Kolb	Elisabetha, 1777, Dec. 7	Elis Weickert, Henr Schmidt
Joseph Eberhart	Daniel, 1778, Jan 17	Michael Eberhart and wife
ˇ Mich Helligas	Eva, 1777, Dec 20	Georg Horlacher and wife
Joh. Adam Geri	Barbara, 1778, Jan. 12	Jacob Geri and wife
Adam Romich	Barbara, 1778, March 25	Joh Theob Faber and wife

Great Swamp—Baptisms

Parents	Children	Sponsors
Henr Bitting	Andreas, 1778, Apr 23	Andreas Greber and wife
Joh Jacobi	Elisabetha, 1778, Aug. 30	Elis. Jacobi
Christofel Ott	Johannes, 1778, Sept. 7	Rudi Huper and wife
Georg Schutz	Catharina, 1778, Nov. 15	Georg Lang and wife
Jacob Doerr	Michael, 1778, Oct 20	Michael Doerr and Elis Mueller
Jacob Duecker	Cath Dorothea, 1778, Aug. 31	Margretha Bayer
Jacob Dorwart	Daniel, 1778, Dec 31	Daniel Doerr and wife
Philip Mumbauer	Elisabetha, 1778, Jan 9	Ursula Spinner
Andreas Walb	Johannes, 1778, Dec 11	Joh Helligas and wife
Conr Worman	Joh Henricus, 1779, Jan. 30	Michael Worman
Petrus Eberhart	Johannes, David, 1779, Jan. 15	Jacob Kehler and wife, the parents
Georg Worman	Maria, 1779, May 12	Henr Ott and wife
Valentin Beutelman	Johannes, 1779, Jan 31	Joh. Jacobi and wife
Fried. Diel	David, 1779, Apr. 10	David Spiner, Cath Gaeri
Daniel Dups	Joh. Jacobus, 1779, June 21	Jacob Dillinger and wife
Jacob Wolf	Jacobus, 1779, July 7	Henr Huper and wife
Georg Hoerner	Petrus, 1779, July 1	Peter Eberhart and wife
Jacob Wittmer	Elisabetha, 1779, July 30	Philip Lar and wife
Fried. Weitman	Johannes, 1779, Sept 9	Henr Bitting and wife
Joh Linn	Jacobus, 1779, Sept. 1	Adam Willauer and wife
Ludwig Nuspickel	Susanna, 1777, July 30	Barbara Faber
Jacob Rauber	Catharina, 1779, Oct 27	Dorothea Bayer, widow

[Baptisms entered by various hands following the removal of the Rev. John Theobald Faber, September, 1780, to August, 1781.]

Parents	Children	Sponsors
Simon Walter	Elisabetha, 1780, Sept. 18	Jacob Keller and wife
Henrich Bleyler and wife Susana	Thomas, b 1780, Dec 22, bap 1782, March 15	Valentin Huber and wife Barbara
Theobald Samuel and wife Maria	Joh Jacob, b. 1780, Oct 8, bap 1781, Febr. 6	Joh. Jacob Lang, Anna Marg Lang, single
Adam Rotenberger	Joh Adam, 1780, Oct 8	Peter Theis and wife Elisabeth
Peter Smith and wife Maria	Anna Elisabetha, b 1780, Oct 13, bap 1781, Jan 14	Christian Deily and wife Anna Maria
Elias Kuter	Johannes, 1780, Nov 25	Joh Cunius and wife Catarina
Christoph Reitenaur and wife Anna Maria	Susanna, b 1780, Aug. 9, bap 1781, March 18	Christian Sneider and wife Susanna
Friedrich Weidman and wife Margareth	Joh Henrich, b 1781, Febr. 3, bap 1781, March 18	Henrich Bitting and wife Eva
Valentin Beidelman and wife Elisabeth	Daniel, b. 1781, Apr. 6, bap 1781, Aug 12	Joh. Jacobi and wife Anna
Philip Mumbauer and wife Barbara	Magdalena, b 1781, May 19, bap 1781, July 22	Nicolaus Mumbauer and wife Magdalena, grandparents
Friedrich Diel and wife Susanna	Abraham, b 1781, Febr 29, bap 1781, July 22	David Spinner, single

Record of the children who received Holy Baptism from me, Friedrich Delliker, in this congregation of Great Swamp, 1782

Peter, b Oct 16, 1781, bap. March 10, '82	Hannes Crisemer, Catharine, his wife	Peter Eberhard, Sophia, his wife
Anna Maria, b Oct. 16, 1781, bap. March 10	Michael Hillegas, Catharine, his wife	George Hillegas, Elisbeth, his wife
Margreth, b Jan 7, 1781, bap March 10	Johannes Dickert, Elisabeth, his wife	Dorothea Beyer

Great Swamp—Baptisms

Children	Parents	Sponsors
Sophia, b. Oct. 25, 1781, bap March 10	Peter Hackenburger and wife Elisabeth	Peter Eberhard and wife Sophia
Peter, b Febr 9, '82, bap. March 30	Hannes Linn and wife Anna Maria	Peter Eberhard and wife Sophia
Adam, b. Febr 27, bap. March 30	Joseph Eberhard and wife Catharina	Adam Geri and wife Barbara
Elisabeth, b Febr 17, bap. March 30	Jacob Huber and wife Anna Maria	Jacob Eberhard and wife Elisabeth
Jacob, b Febr 3, bap. Apr. 21	Georg Reichenbach and wife Catharina	Jacob Gery and wife Gertraud
Catharina, b. Febr. 28, bap. Apr 21	Michel Doerr and wife Maria Margareth	Joh Doerr, Jr, Gertraud Schlicher
M Barbara, b Febr 12, bap. Apr 21	Sebastian Wendly and wife Barbara	Daniel Doerr and wife Barbara
Peter, b. Jan 5, bap May 12	H Nikel Ditz and wife Elisabeth	Heinrich Huber, Catharine Linn
M Elisabeth, b March 28, bap. May 12	Georg Mack and wife Barbara	Jacob Koehler and wife Elisabeth
Anna Maria, b. May 23, bap. June 23	Hans Becker and wife Elisabeth	Barbara Berger
Magdalena, b Aug 20, bap Oct 27	Jacob Durr and wife Anna Margreth	Hannes Durr, Sr., and wife Magdalena
A. Margreth, b. Oct. 23, bap. Dec 8	Adam Gery and wife Barbara	Hannes Hillegas and wife Anna Maria
Jacob, b. Aug 2, bap. Dec 29	Valentin Beutelman and wife Elisabeth	Peter Eberhard and wife Sophia

1783

Children	Parents	Sponsors
Daniel, b Dec 24, 1781, bap Jan 19, '83	Elias Cuder and wife Catharina	Daniel Clein and wife Magdalena
Cath Elisabeth, b Dec. 14, 1781, bap. Jan 17	Matheis Sax and wife Elisabeth	Heinr Mambauer, Catharina Didlo
Elisabeth, b. Dec. 15, 1781, bap. Jan 17	Friedrich Weidman and wife Margreth	Georg Horner and wife Susanna
Conrad, b. Dec. 18, 1782, bap March 2	Jacob Wolf and wife Margreth	J. Conrad Wolf and wife Maria Elisabeth
Elisabeth, b Jan 27, bap. Apr 13	Georg Doerr and wife Sophia	Johannes Fischer, Elis Gugger
M Barbara, b. Mar 31, bap. Apr 13	Georg Schuez and wife Catharine	Valentin Cuder and wife Margreth

Children	Parents	Sponsors
Hannes, b. Apr. 25, bap. May 25	Georg Horner and wife Susanna	Hannes Hillegas and wife Anna Maria
M. Elisabeth, b June 11, bap. July 6	Hannes Riser and wife Eva	Georg Stallnecker and wife Elisabeth
Hannes, b May 15, bap. July 27	Simon Walter and wife Barbara	Hannes Riser and wife Eva
Catharina, b Mar. 15, bap. Sept. 7	Jacob Fux and wife Anna Maria	Heinrich Mumbauer and wife Catharine
Elisabeth, b. July 18, bap. Sept. 7	Dewalt Samsel and wife Anna Maria	Jacob Huber and wife Elisabeth
Wilhelm, b Sept 8, bap Oct. 19	Hannes Linn and wife Anna Maria	Christian Willauer, Susanna Schmid
Anna Maria, b. Aug. 14, bap Oct. 19	Peter Deis and wife Elisabeth	Hannes Riser and wife Eva
Christina, b Sept. 26, bap. Nov 30	Peter Schmid and wife Maria	Valentin Huber, Sr., and wife Barbara
H. Wilhelm, b Oct. 8, bap. Dec. 21	Heinrich Biding [and wife] Eva Barbara	Andres Greber and wife A. Maria
Catharina, b Sept. 29, bap Dec. 27	David Spinner and wife Catharina	Georg Horlacher and wife Eva

1784

Catharina, b. Nov 11, bap Jan. 11	Daniel Kupper and wife Elisabeth	Johannes Gery, Catharina Kupper
A Catharina, b. Nov. 29, bap. March 18	Joh. Huber and wife Anna	Anna Huber

Baptized by me, Frid. Wilh. Von der Sloot

Catarina, b. Dec. 5, 1783, bap Apr 18, 1784	Daniel Dups and wife Elisabet	Jacob Dillinger and wife
Joh George, b Mar 5, bap Apr 18	George Doerr and wife Sophia	George Kulp and wife
Maria Barbara, b Apr. 20, bap May 30	George Klein and wife Barbara	George Klein and wife Maria
Elias, b. Apr 27, bap. July 11	Fried Tiele and wife Susanna	David Spinner and wife Catharina
Peter, b. March 5, bap July 11	George Mack	Peter Eberhard and wife
Catarina, b. Apr 5, bap July 11	Philip Mombauer	Heinrich Mombauer and wife Catarina

Great Swamp—Baptisms 453

Children	Parents	Sponsors
Anna Catarina, b March 18, bap. Sept. 13	George Reichenbach and wife Catarina	Anna Marg Hillegas, Philip Eberhard
Anna Maria, b Apr 18, bap. Sept 13	Valentin Kuter and Margareta	Maria Fuchs, Georg Mueller

1785

Children	Parents	Sponsors
Joh George, b. Aug 2, bap Aug 21	Elias Kuter and wife Catarina	J George Horlacher and wife Eva
Johan Jacob, b. Mar. 6, bap Nov 3	Thomas Beyer and wife Christina	Johannes Dickert
Anna Barbara, b Aug 3, bap. Nov. 3	Joh Dickert and wife Elisabet	Thomas Beier and wife
Joh David, b Oct 30, bap. Dec 6	Joh. Mombauer	Nicolaus Mombaur
Joh. Daniel, b. Oct 20, bap. Dec. 11	Michael Brauchler and wife Anna Maria	Daniel Klein and wife
Joh Catarina, b Nov. 28, bap Dec 25	Philip Eberhard and wife Margareta	Catarina Eberhard

1786

Children	Parents	Sponsors
Joh Abraham, b. Mar. 4, 1785, bap. Mar. 5	Valentin Beutelman and wife Elisabeth	Peter Eberhard and wife
Johanna Eva, b. Nov. 6, 1785, bap Mar 5	Joh. Rieser and wife Eva	Barbara Stalnecker
Joh Michael, b Jan. 18, bap Mar. 22	Georg Reichenbach and wife Catarina	Michael Kuhner, Elisabeth Ochs
Joh Catarina, b Mar. 10, bap Apr 9	Heinr Mombauer and wife Catarina	Joh. Mombauer and wife
Johan Daniel, b Apr 7, bap May 14	Daniel Dups and wife Elisabeth	Heinr. Bergheimer and wife Rosina

Children who have been baptized by me, John Theobald Faber, 1786.

Children	Parents	Sponsors
Joh. Peter, b. Apr. 12, bap July 23	Georg Mueller and wife	Peter Eberhart and wife
Anna Margreth, b. May 17, bap. July 23	Jacob Huper and wife	Margaret Heger
Johannes, b June 19, bap Aug 13	Joh Huper and wife	Christofel Ott and wife
Joh Martin, b. July 28, bap Sept 3	Henr Kopelberger and wife	Martin Yung, Charlota Mayer

Children	Parents	Sponsors
Elisabeth, b Oct 15, bap Nov 5	Joh Keler and wife	Jacob Keler and wife
Maria Dorothea, b. July 10, bap Sept 24	Georg Mack and wife	Dorothea Baier
Joh. Jacobus, b Nov 10, bap Nov. 25	Wendel Reninger and wife	Wendel Renninger and wife
Johannes, b Nov. 4, bap Nov 26	Joh. Huper and wife	Joh Dittlo and Catharine Huper
David, b Febr. 17, bap. Apr 1	Elias Kuther and wife	David Spinner and wife

1787

Children	Parents	Sponsors
David, b Mar 30, 187, bap. June 3	Christian Huper and wife	David Spiner and wife
Maria Magdalena, b. Oct 19, 1786, bap July 15	Valentin Beutelman and wife	Abr Kehler, Maria Cerfink
Friedrich, b. Jan 20, bap July 15	Fried. Diel and wife	David Spinner and wife
Johannes, b May 21, bap July 15	Philip Eberhart and wife	Joh Helligas and wife
Johannes, b Oct 22, 1786, bap July 15	Joh Georg Krug and wife	Joh Georg Funk and wife
Elisabetha, b. July 5, bap Aug. 5	Casper Riser and wife	the parents
Magdalena, b May 26, bap Aug 26	Felix Brunner and wife	Henr Huper and wife
Jacob, b Febr 28, bap Aug 26	Ludwig Reichert and wife	Jacob Berret and wife
Joh. Henrich, b Aug 15, bap. Sept. 15	Henr. Grob and wife	Andreas Schutz, Susanna Schutz
Johannes, b. May 13, bap Sept 16	Henr. Zeislef and wife	Joh Zeusler and wife
Jacobus, b Aug. 15, 1786, bap Oct 6	Jacob Wittmer and wife	parents
Jacobus, b. Aug. 5, bap Oct 28	Georg Dittlo and wife	Philip Mumbauer and wife
Catharina, b. Sept. 16, bap. Oct 28	Michel Breuchler and wife	Christofel Ott and wife
Catharina, b Sept 7, bap Nov. 18	Joh Georg Ott and wife	Jacob Bischof and wife
Elisabetha, b. Oct 20, bap Dec 9	Emanuel Heger and wife	Philip Heger, Elis Schneider

Great Swamp—Baptisms

Children	Parents	Sponsors
David, b Dec 1, bap Dec. 25	Henr Mumbauer and wife	Joh Dittlo
Maria Barbara, b Dec 4, bap Dec 31	Anton Stehler and wife	Philip Stehler and wife

1788

Children	Parents	Sponsors
Johannes, b Nov 4, 1787, bap Febr 8, 1788	Daniel Kupper and wife	Joh. Helligas and wife
Joh Georg, b. Jan 31, bap. March 2	Ditter [Dietrich] Mueller and wife	Georg Hoerner and wife
Jacobus, b. Oct 26, '87, bap. Mar 2,'88	Jacob Huper and wife	Jacob Mekahl and Cath Scholl
Catharina, b Dec 22, '87, bap. Mar 2	Henr Huper and wife	Jacob Mekahl and Cath Scholl
Jacob, Christian, b. Febr 25, bap Mar 2	Joh Georg Muller	Jacob Kehler, Georg Muller and wife
Jacobus, b Febr 7, bap Mar. 23	Michael Ott and wife	——
Catharina, b. Nov. 13, '87, bap Mar 23	Georg Ruh and wife	Elisabeth Kehler
Margreta, b. Jan. 15, bap. Apr 13	Philip Mumbauer and wife	Ad Bossert and wife
Johannes, b Mar 21, bap Apr 13	Georg Schoener and wife	Abraham Levi, Eva Horlacher
Elisabetha, b July 16, 1775, bap Apr 13	Georg Dill and wife	the parents
Joh Henrich, b Nov. 7, 1776, bap Apr. 13, 1788	Georg Dill and wife	the parents
Magdalena, b Oct 4, 1778, bap. Apr 13	Georg Dill and wife	the parents
Catharina, b Aug 14, 1780, bap Apr. 13	Georg Dill and wife	the parents
Margaretha, b Dec 5, 1782, bap. Apr 13	Georg Dill and wife	the parents
Joh Jacob, b. Mar 25, 1785, bap Apr. 13	Georg Dill and wife	the parents
Georg, b Sept 7, 1787, bap Apr 13	Georg Dill and wife	the parents
Jacob, b Mar 19, bap. May 12	Fried Weittman and wife	Jacob Burhart and wife

Children	Parents	Sponsors
Barbara, b Mar. 1, bap. May 12	Joh. Huper and wife	Valentin Huper and wife
Elisabetha, b. Febr. 25, bap. Mar. 12	Peter Lang and wife	Peter Hagenberg and wife
Philip, b. Apr 25, bap Aug. 6	Joh. Zeislef and wife	the parents
Daniel, b July 8, bap. Aug 17	Christofel Ott and wife	Georg Worman and wife
Jacob, b. July 8, bap Aug. 17	Peter Busch and wife	Jacob Huper and wife
Henrich, b. Aug. 1, bap Sept. 7	Jost Reling and wife	Henr Huper and Susanna Klein
Andreas, b. May 30, bap. Sept 28	Widow Stahl	Andreas Rieser and wife
Johannes, b Sept 7, bap. Oct. 19	Daniel Dups and wife	Joh Dillinger, Elisabeth Ott
Jacob, b. Aug 31, bap Oct 19	Peter Willauer and wife	Jacob Geri and wife
Catharina, b. Aug 3, bap Oct. 22	Fried. Diel and wife	Ursula Spinner
Elisabeth, b. Apr. 1, bap ——	Abraham Bleiler and wife	Ludwig Bender
George, b Aug 17, bap. ——	Isaac Klein and wife	Georg Klein and wife

[The last two entries were made by another hand]

Children baptized by me, N[icholas] Pomp

1790.

Children	Parents	Sponsors
David, b. Oct. 5, 1789, bap. Jan 3, '90	John Huber and wife Margareth	David Ditlo, Maria Horn
Henrich, b. Dec 12, '89, bap. Jan 3	Jacob Krebs and wife Susanna	Gottfried Wiesemer and wife
Joseph, b. July 2, '89, bap Jan 3	William Lickenbotten and wife	Daniel Heller, Maria Eberhard
Susanna, b Sept 18, bap Febr 14	Georg Hoerner and wife Susanna	Peter Schmid and wife
Johanna, b Febr —, bap Mar. 28	Jacob Dillinger and wife Catharina	Johannes Kehler and wife
Maria, b Oct 3, '89, bap Mar 28	Georg Urman and wife Catarina	Jacob Eugelmann
Joh. Ludwig, b Mar 16, bap. Apr 1	Abraham Bleiler and wife Margareth	Ludwig Bender and wife

Great Swamp—Baptisms

Children	Parents	Sponsors
Georg Valentin, b Oct 1, '89, bap May 9	Michael Rudolph and wife Margareth	Valentin Paul and wife
Anna Maria, b. June 14, '86, bap May 30	Jacob Berend and wife	——
Magdalena, b June 3, bap June 18	Peter Willauer	John Willauer, Margareth Hillegas

1792

Anna Maria, b Apr 5, bap June 2	Philip Eberhard and wife Anna Margareth	Henrich Eberhard, Catharina Hillegas

Children who were baptized by me, John Faber, A D 1792.

Daughter, b Febr. 8	Conrad Eberhart	——
Elisabetha, b. Dec. 19	Peter Busch	——
Anna Maria, b Febr. 10	Abraham Bleiler	Jacob Weiss and wife

Children who were baptized by me, John Faber, in 1793

Heinrich, b. Dec. 19, '92, bap Febr 9	Henrich Mumbauer and wife	Abr Ditlo and wife
Elisabeth, b. Jan 4, bap Mar. 10	Jacob Weis and wife	Georg Herner and wife
Susanna, b Oct. 18, '92, bap Mar 31	John Young and wife	John Adam Rhodeberger and wife
Hanna, b. Sept. 7, '92, bap. Mar 31	Heinr. Huber and wife	John Huber, Hanna Weigert
Samuel, b July 31, bap Mar 31	Peter Dorder and wife	Godfrid Wiesemer and wife
John, b. Nov 10, '92, bap Mar. 3	Emanuel Huber and wife	John Huber and wife
Heinrich, b Febr 12, bap. Apr 21	Michael Weber and wife	Catarina Mattinger, Heinr Huber
Anna Margreth, b Jan. 29, bap. Apr 21	John Zeislef	Casper Riser and wife
Maria Elisabetha, b Febr 29, bap. Apr. 21	Jacob Rodenburger	Maria Elis Stahleker, widow
Maria, b. Aug. 1	Christian Huber	Ulrich Shitz and wife
John George, b. June 24	Jacob Sneider	Fried. Wagner, Cath Herings
Daniel, b July 25	Adam Brauchler	Daniel Klein and wife

Children	Parents	Sponsors
Joseph, b. May 14	Ulrich Shitz	Velt Huber, Eva Willauer
Susanna, b. May 4	Peter Kuter	Conrad Eberhard and wife
Heinrich, b. Febr. 12	Michael Weber	Heinr. Huber, Cath. Madinger
Anna Marg, b Jan. 29	John Zeislef	Caspar Riser and wife
Maria Elis, b. Febr. 27	Jacob Rodenburger	Maria Elis Stahlecker
Susanna, b. Oct. 18, 1792	John Young	John Rodenburger
Hanna, b. Sept 7, 1792	Heinr Huber	John Huber, Nancy Weigert
John George, b. July 14, 1793	Jacob Sneider	Fried. Wagner, Caty Horinger
Daniel, b. July 25	Adam Brauchler	Daniel Klein and wife
Samuel, b. Apr 5	Peter Kifer	Valentin Paul and wife
	1795	
George, b. Dec 15, 1794, bap. Mar 2	Henr. Ott	Jacob Eberhardt and wife
Maria, bap. Mar 2	John Welker	Georg Ruch and wife
John Adam, b Jan 8, 1795, bap. Apr. 5	Adam Schutze	George Busch and wife
Elisabetha, b. May 6, 1792, bap. Apr 5	Sally Scheiffly	Jacob Eberhard and wife
Jacob, b Jan. 11, bap Apr 5	Henry Mumbauer	Daniel Miller and wife
Joseph, b Febr 28, bap. Apr. 5	Nath Wetknecht	George Hillegas, Barb. Bertoin
Anna Maria, b Nov. 18, 1794, bap. Apr 26	Peter Bush	Jacob Zerfinger
	1796.	
Michael, b Sept. 20	Heinrich Eberhard	Daniel Dups
Anna Maria, b Sept 9	John Dillinger	Jacob Dillinger and wife

Record of the children who were baptized by me, Albert Helffenstein

Johan (?), b Aug 22, 1808	Johann Schitz and wife Eva	Ulrich Schitz and Mat Schitz

Great Swamp—Baptisms 459

Children	Parents	Sponsors
Johann, b July 4, 1808	Jacob Wenig and wife Elisabet	Johannes Boogter, Frena Boogter
Hanna, b Aug 9, 1808	Henrich Stehler and wife Elisabet	Henrich Romich and wife Magdalena
Samuel, b. Sept 7, 1808	Adam Schneider and wife Elisabet	Jacob Willauer, Susanna Miller
Maria Magdalena, b. Sept. 17, 1808	Abraham Henrichs and wife	Jacob Schwenk and wife
Michael, b Nov. 28, 1808	Georg Dubs and wife	Henrich Eberhard and wife

1809

Children	Parents	Sponsors
Lydia, b. Oct. 23, bap. Dec. 3	Jacob Schwenk and wife Molly	Johan Dillinger and wife Maricha
Jacob, b. July 27, bap. Oct 1	Michael Scholl and wife	Johan Sechler and wife Elisabeth
Sarah, b. Oct. 10, bap ———	Jacob Schneider and wife	Johan Schultz and wife Eva

[Irregular entries made by various hands]

Children	Parents	Sponsors
Lydia, b Dec 17, 1800	Johannes Rodenburger and wife Anna Margaret	Adam Rodenburger and wife
Samuel, b Febr. 20, 1803	Johannes Rodenburger and wife Anna Margaret	Adam Stahlecker
Johannes, b. Febr 14, 1806	Johannes Rodenburger and wife Anna Margaret	Peter Rodenburger and wife
Catharina, b Nov. 27, 1809	Johannes Rodenburger and wife Anna Margaret	Jacob Deis and wife
David, b Sept. 30, 1812	Johannes Rodenburger and wife Anna Margaret	Jacob Schwenk and wife
Daniel, b. May 26, 1816, bap Aug 9, 1816	Johannes Rodenburger and wife Anna Margaret	Wilhelm Dillinger and Anna Schwenk
Reuben, b June 17, 1816, bap. Aug. 4, 1816	Daniel Dubs and wife Elisabeth	Jacob Dubs and wife Maria
Elias, b May 21, 1816, bap. Aug. 25	Abraham Hendricks and wife Charlotta	Samuel Ruecker and wife Catharina

Children	Parents	Sponsors
Anna Maria, b. Aug 28, 1819, bap Oct. 2	Johannes Rothenburger and wife Margreta	Joseph Dubs, Anna Rothenburger
Elisabeth, b Nov 8, 1822	Johan Rothenburger and wife Margreta	Cathrina Rothenburger
Marianne, b Aug 8, 1816, bap. Aug 15	John Oel and wife Elisabeth	Samuel Roeder and Elisabeth

[Baptisms by Rev Fr. Wm. Von der Sloot, Jr, 1814-1818 *]

Parents	Children	Witnesses
Jacob Stauffer, Margareth, his wife	Jacob, b. Oct 21, 1813, bap May 22, 1814	George Mumbauer, Catharine, his wife
Henrich Dubs, Maria, his wife	Salome, b. April 19, 1815, bap. June 4, 1815	Daniel Dubs, Elisabetha, his wife
David Eberhard, Margareta, his wife	Margreta, b Mar 21, 1815, bap Jan 28, '16	Peter Diez, Susanna, his wife
Daniel Eberhard, Maria, his wife	George, b March 9, '16, bap. April 21, '16	Johan Erdmann, Anna his wife
John Handschuh, Magdalena, his wife	Johann, b. March 1, '16, bap April 21, '16	Valent. Huber, Magdalena, his wife
John Rudolph, Sara, his wife	Karl, b. March 8, '16, bap. April 21	George Rudolph, Elisabeth Muller
Wilh Schutz, Sara, his wife	Katharina, b. Dec. 20, '16, bap Oct. 19, 1817	Johannes Buskirk, Katharina, his wife
George Nees, Maria, his wife	John Elias, b. May 22, 1817, bap. Oct. 18, 1817	John Schaab, Hanne, his wife
John Nees, Elisabeth, his wife	Joseph, b July 7, 1817, bap. Oct 19, 1817	Joseph Kob, Cathar, his wife
Henrich Durr, Elisabeth, his wife	Maria, b Sept. 12, 1817, bap Nov 9, 1817	David Durr, Elis Birkenstock
Henrich Dubs, Margaretha, his wife	Hanna, b May 6, 1818, bap June 6, 1818	Salome Dubs, Elisa Sarburger (?)
Jacob Schwenck, Magdalena	Thomas, b May 6, 1818, bap June 28, 1818	Jacob Theiss, Eva, his wife

* These baptisms are entered in the account book.

Great Swamp—Baptisms

Parents	Children	Witnesses
Jacob Diel, Marg, his wife	Susanne, b. May 24, 1818, bap. Aug. 30, 1818	Cathar Engelman, widow
Abraham Hendriks, Charlotte, his wife	Hanna, b July 10, '18, bap Aug 30, '18	Abrah Dorsch, Maria, his wife
Jacob Dubs, Anna Maria	Jacob, b July 18, '18, bap Aug 30, '18	Michel Schneider, Margaretha, his wife
Henrich Huber, Katharina	Sophie, b July 8, '18, bap Aug 30, '18	Jacob Hedrich, Sara, his wife
Christian Doll, Maria his wife	Washington, b Aug 19, 1818, bap. Sept. 20, 1818	John Klein, Veronica, his wife
Jacob Knecht, Katharina, his wife	Johannes, b Sept. 20, 1818, bap Nov 22, 1818	Henrich Durr, Elisab, his wife
John Rudolph, Sara, his wife	Elisa Mathilda, b Sept 11, 1818, bap Nov 22, 1818	Jacob Erdmann, Hanna, his wife

May 2, 1819, David Etwein, aged 17 days. Witn, David Spinner and his wife.*

[Baptisms by John Theobald Faber, Jr, 1819–1831]

Parents	Children	Witnesses
William Shitz, Sarah, his wife	Elias, b. Sept 24, 1819, bap Nov 13, 1819	Ulrich Shitz and wife
Peter Engelman, Maria, his wife	Salome, b Sept 23, 1819, bap Nov. 13, 1819	Cath Engelman
John Shaeffer, Susanna	Henrich, b. Nov 14, 1819, bap. Dec 12, 1819	Christian Scherer and wife
Henry Engelman and Elisabeth	Marcus Luis, b. April 25, 1819, bap. Febr 6, 1820	Paul Heller and wife
George Miller and Catharina	William, b. Nov. 24, 1819, bap April 16, 1820	John Mechlin and wife
John Miller and Elisabeth	Joel, b Jan 20, 1820, bap. April 16, 1820	Jesse Stahl, Cath Miller
Henry Derr and Elisabeth	Elias, b April 29, 1820, bap June 25	Jacob Mohn and wife

* Entered by another hand.

Parents	Children	Witnesses
Daniel Eberhard and Maria	Elisabeth, b June 13, bap Aug 6	Samuel Derr, Elis. Erny
Adam Wieder, Christina, his wife	Maria Anna, b June 27, bap Aug 6	Philip Weickel and wife
Jacob Erdman, Hanna, his wife	Charles, b. June 14, 1820, bap Aug 20	Conrad Rinker, Elis. Huber
Heinrich Bauman, Sarah, his wife	Sarah, b Nov 29, 1820, bap. Febr. 11, 1821	John Kline and wife Maria
Peter Dietz, Susanna, his wife	Peter, b. Jan 4, 1821, bap. March 4, 1821	Abr. Dietz, Sophia Eberhard
Peter Engelman, Maria, his wife	——, b. Jan 11, 1821, bap March 25, 1821	David Derr, Magd. Horlacher
John Berkestock, Cath., his wife	——, b Nov. 1, 1820, bap. March 25, 1821	And. Engelman and wife
Jacob Derr, Magdalena, his wife	——, b Febr 22, 1821, bap. April 23, 1821	John Felman and wife
George Gerhart, Susanna, his wife	Thomas, b. March 20, 1821, bap May 6	Jacob Fassbenner and wife
Abraham Ditlow, Catharine, his wife	——, b. ——, bap. May 6, 1821	David Kuns, Mary Mumbauer
Heinrich Huber, Catharina, his wife	Elisabeth, b April 1, 1821, bap Jan 17, 1822	David Huber and wife
Peter Rau, Rahel, his wife	George, b Dec 18, 1821, bap. Febr. 24, 1822	Geo. Wener and wife
Michael Eberhard, Elisabeth, his wife	Maria Esther, b Febr. 6, 1822, bap. March 17, 1822	Catharina Kneppley, widow
Daniel Rader, Eva	Caroline, b Febr 18, 1822, bap. Febr 27, 1822	the parents themselves
John Berkenstock, Catharina	Levina, b. May 26, 1822, bap July 22, 1822	Anton Emig and Hanna
Daniel Eberhard, Maria	Lydia, b. June 25, 1822, bap July 22, 1822	Valentin Huber and wife
Jacob Derr, Magdalena	Thomas, b July 30, 1823	George Miller, Maria Derr
David Eberhard [and wife]	Wilhelm, b ——, bap. Oct. 26	Georg Ditz and wife

Great Swamp—Baptisms

Parents	Children	Witnesses
George Gerhart, Susanna, his wife	Enos, b Aug 17, 1823, bap. Oct. 26, 1823	Adam Eberhard and wife
John Kline, Elisabeth, his wife	Johannes, b Dec 15, 1823, bap March 21, 1823[24]	Margreth Diehl
David Eberhart, Maria, his wife	Maria Anna, b Dec. 3, 1823, bap March 21, 1823[24]	Conrad Eberhart and wife
John Rudolf, Sarah	Carolina, b May 28, 1825, bap Aug 6, 1825	Daniel Eberhard and Maricha
Jacob Derr, Magdalena	William, b. Nov. 5, 1825, bap Jan 22, 1826	George Derr, Elisa Helman
George Gerhart, Susanna, his wife	George, b Dec 15, 1826, bap March 18, 1827	Philip Gerhart and wife Sara
David Huber, Susanna	Susanna, b Febr 1, 1827, bap April 29, 1827	Daniel Eberhard and Anna Maria
George Kline, Susanna, his wife	Salomon, b Febr 12, 1827, bap April 29, 1827	Isaac Kline and wife Barbara
John Funk and wife	John, bap July 5, 1829	John Dubs, Elisabeth, his wife
Jonathan Ditlow, Anna, his wife	Allen David, b —— 19, 1825, bap Dec 2, 1827	David Ditlow and wife Anna Maria
Jonathan Ditlow, Anna, his wife	Henrietta, b. Dec. 30, 1826, bap. Sept 2, 1827	David Huber, Susanna, his wife
Jacob Dover, Lidia, his wife	Jacob, b Febr 1, 1824, bap Sept. 2, 1827	David Ditlow and Anna Mary, his wife
Jacob Dover, Lidia, his wife	Solomon, b Oct 24, 1825, bap Sept 2, 1827	Jacob Dover and Lidia, the parents
George Kline, Susanna, his wife	Anna Maria, b March 18, 1828, bap June 1, 1828	Enoch Erdman, Rebecca, his wife
George Gerhart, Susanna, his wife	Susanna, b April 8, 1829, bap July 5, 1829	Daniel Roder, Eve, his wife

Parents	Children	Witnesses
Jacob Rudolf, Elisabeth, his wife	Daniel, b. April 26, 1829, bap July 26, 1829	Michael Rudolf, Elisabeth, his wife
Conrad Reinhardt, Lydia, his wife	Elisabeth, b ——, bap Aug. 16, 1829	John Ruch, Elisabeth, his wife
Jacob Dover, Lydia, his wife	Maria Ann, b July 9, 1829, bap. Sept. 6, 1829	Jacob Dubbs and wife
John Rudolf and Sarah	Sarah Anna, b. Oct. 23, 1829, bap Dec. 20	Samuel Rinker, Catharina, his wife
George Kline and Susanna	Johann Isaac, b May 3, 1829, bap. ——	Jacob Shell, Maria, his wife
Jacob Deiss and Elisabeth	Levi, b Aug 30, 1830, bap. Nov. 21, 1830	Michael Reichenbach, Maria, his wife
Jacob Derr, Magdalena	Sophia, b Oct 12, 1830, bap. Dec. 12, 1830	Joseph Miller, Sophia Everhart
Samuel Derr, Catharina	Sophia, b Sept. 28, 1830, bap. Dec 12, 1830	Michael Reichenbach, Maria, his wife
John Rudolf, wife Sarah	Levina, b. Oct. 3, 1830, bap. June 18, 1831	John Ruch, Elisabeth, his wife
Jacob Dover, wife Lydia	Elisabeth, b. June 14, 1831, bap. July 31, 1831	John Gerhard, Sophia Eberhard

[This concludes the baptismal entries by Mr. Faber]

Jacob Derr, Magdalena	Jacob, b. April 4, 1833	Peter Engelman and Magd
George Gerhart and Susanna	David, b June 13, 1833, bap Sept 8	David Kemmerer, Margareta Eberhard

[These baptisms were performed by Rev Andrew Strasburger. They are followed by 81 baptisms entered by the Rev Daniel Weiser, from September 3, 1833, to January 25, 1863]

[BURIAL RECORDS.]

Those persons who were buried by me, John Theobald Faber They are as follows:

1767, April 21, the young Eberhard was buried, who lived in the congregation of Great Swamp

1767, May 14, a son of Joseph Eberhard was buried, named Benshamer, from the Swamp

1768, May 24, John Phil Fackenthal was buried, living in the congregation at Springfield.

1768, Oct 3, Henry Grob was buried His aged 57 years, of the Swamp congregation

1768, Nov 19, Franz Russ was buried His aged 31 years, of the Swamp congregation.

1769, Sept 6, Ulrich Spinner was buried His age 52 years, 3 months, 3 days, of the Swamp congregation

1770, June 22, Valentin Dickenschied was buried His age 36 years, 7 months and 3 weeks less one day

1771, Jan 29, Peter Bleiler's daughter was buried, named Anna Catharine, of the Swamp congregation; aged 10 years, 11 months and some days.

1771, June 22, Christian Willauer was buried, born 1706, Jan 20 His age: 64 years, 5 months

1771, Nov 18, Joh Zoeller was buried, born 1728, Nov 16; his age 43 years, 2 days.

1772, January 16 (or 23), Mr. Thowahrt's little son was buried His name George Jacob, his aged 2 years, 6 weeks and some days

1772, Oct 21, Jacob Kehler's daughter was buried, her name Anna Barbara, was born 1768, Febr 5; her age 4 years, 10 months, 16 days

1772, Nov. 3, Michael Eberhart was buried, born 1698, March 4th His age 74 years and a half and 9 weeks

1773, Jan 6, Agnes Kaiser was buried, born 1702, the date is unknown, her age about 72 years

1773, Apr. 2, George Mecklin's daughter was buried, born 1771, Febr 7 Her age 2 years, 2 months and 6 days

1773, June 6, the wife of Mr Zeiner died, born 1738, Dec 3 Her age 37 years and some months

1773, July 15, Baltzer Stiel's child was buried, born 1772, Nov. 27 Age 1 year, 8 months and some days

1774, Apr 1, Peter Linn's daughter was buried, born 1771, August 23 Her aged 2 years, 7 months, 7 days

1774, Apr. 27, son of Ludwig Nusspickel was buried, aged 2 years, 2 days

1774, May 5, daughter of Ludwig Nusspickel was buried; aged 6 years, 3 months, 1 day

1774, June 15, daughter of Christophel Ott buried; aged 4 months, 28 days.

1775, Jan. 15, Valentin Huper's daughter was buried Her age 6 years, 5 months, 10 days

1775, Febr 22, Theobald Bräuchler's daughter was buried, aged 11 years, 3 weeks, some days

1775, June 24, Anna Margaretha Weis was buried; born April 7, 1706. Her age 69 years, 2 months and 2 weeks

1775, Sept 15, Jacob Rauber's daughter was buried, born 1773, Oct 13. Her age 1 year, 11 months, 2 days

1775, Oct 15, Adam Rauchert's daughter was buried; born 1774, Oct. 9, aged 1 year less 17 days.

1775, Nov. 3, John Neukomer's wife was buried; born Febr 28, 1735 Her age 40 years, 8 months.

1776, Aug 15, Michael Bischoff's wife was buried, born 1722, March 17th, her age 54 years, 5 months less 2 days

1776, Nov 4, Jacob Wittmer's wife was buried; born 1742, about the middle of Sept Her age 34 years and about 6 weeks

1777, May 12, John George Schonsebach was buried, born 1746, day unknown. His age, about 51 years

1777, Aug 3, Jacob Rauber's daughter was buried; born 1760, Febr. 6. Her age 17 years, 6 months less 5 days.

1777, July 25, two children of Daniel Dubs were buried at the same time, namely a son and a daughter. The son was born 1775, Sept 7, the daughter 1774, Jan. 20 The age of the boy was 1 year, 10 months and 2 weeks, the girl 3 years, 7 months and 4 days

1777, Aug. 16, Joseph Eberhart's child was buried; born 1769, Jan 22; aged 8 years, 7 months less 6 days

1777, Aug 24, Baltzer Stiehl's daughter was buried, born 1759, on Wednesday after ———?, her age 17 years, 4 months, 8 days

1777, Aug. 27, Mrs. Schansebach was buried; born 1723, May 8th, her age 54 years, 4 months, 3 weeks

1777, Aug. 26, Jacob Wittmer's daughter was buried, born 1765, Aug 4 Her age 12 years and about 3 weeks

1777, Aug 31, John Jacobi's child was buried; born 1776, Aug 2, aged 1 year and 4 weeks Soon afterwards another one of his children was buried.

1777, Aug. 30, Michael Eberhart's wife was buried, born 1725, April 15th, aged 52 years, 4 months, 2 weeks

1777, Aug 30, Joseph Eberhart's child was buried, born 1772, March 5th, aged 5 years and 5 months less 6 days

1777, Aug 30, Rudi Huper's son was buried, born 1770, Jan 2, aged 7 years, 8 months less one day

1777, Sept 7, Peter Weber's daughter was buried, born 1768, Apr. 15th; aged 9 years, 5 months

1777, Sept. 22, Felix Bruner's child was buried; born 1772, July 14, aged 5 years, 2 months, 7 days

1777, Oct 14, John Lohe's child was buried; born 1770, July 10, aged 7 years, 3 months, 2 days

1777, Oct. 3, George Mack's daughter was buried, born 1776, June 23, aged 1 year, 3 months, 1 week, 3 days

1777, Oct 5, Henr Ott's child was buried; born 1777, April 4th; aged half a year

1777, Oct. 6, Georg Kern's son was buried, born 1772, Apr 23; aged 5 years, 5 months, 10 days

1778, Jan. 8, Henry Huper was buried; born 1715, Apr 15th, aged 62 years, 9 months less 7 days.

1778, March 6, Felix Bruner's daughter was buried, born 1774, Nov 19, aged 3 years, 3 months, 5 days.

1779, Febr 9, the old Mrs Schutz was buried, born 1698, Aug 20, aged 80 years, 5 months, 3 weeks

1779, Febr. 10, the old Mrs. Willauer was buried, born 1710, about November, aged about 68 years, 3 months

1779, March 29, Rudolph Huper was buried; born 1722, May 1st, aged 56 years, 10 months, 4 weeks

1779, Apr. 16, Nicolaus Biber's daughter was buried, born 1776, Nov 27, aged 2 years, 4 months, 2 weeks, 4 days.

1779, June 11, Heter (¹) Bock's child, named Susanna, was buried, born 1778, Sept 18th, aged 8 months, 3 weeks and one day

List of those who died and were buried under the ministry of Fr Delliker, in this congregation

1783.

April 17, Michael Eberhard, aged 51 years, 2 weeks

April 18, Anna Maria Scholl, widow of the late Peter Scholl. Her age 65 years, 1 month, second weeks

April 27, Verena Rudolph, widow of the late Heinrich Rudolph, her age 64 years, 10 months

May 4, Margreth Holzhauser, wife of Caspar Holzhauser, aged 79 years

✓ Oct. 24, Anna Huber, widow of the late Heinrich Huber, aged 67 years

1784

Buried by me, Frederick William Von der Sloot

Sept 6, Ulrich Rieser, born 1709, April 8, aged 75 years, 4 months, 20 days

1785

Febr 25, Daniel Hitz was buried, aged 85 years, 7 months

Sept 7, Valentin Kaiser, aged 76 years, 11 months

1786

March 26, Anna Maria Bleiler was buried, aged 82 years, 10 months.

April 3, John Mombauer's child, John David

Those persons who were buried by me, John Theobald Faber

1786.

Aug. 17, a daughter of Daniel Dubs was buried, named Catharine, aged 2 years, 8 months, 10 days

Nov 20, Peter Eberhart, a deacon, was buried, aged 42 years and a half year.

Dec. 1, Peter Eberhart's wife was buried, aged 40 years, 4 months, 8 days.

1787.

Jan 6, daughter of Henry Huper, named Anna, was buried, aged 11 months, 1 day

Apr. 5, the old Mrs Hitz was buried; aged 76 year, 2 weeks, 1 day

Oct. 11, the old Mr Reiswig was buried; aged 77 years, 5 months, 18 days.

1788.

Febr. 28, Felix Bruner's daughter, Magdalene, was buried; aged 8 months, 2 days.

Apr. 8, Anna Maria Sax was buried; aged 35 years, 2 months, 3 weeks and one day.

May 31, Anna Rosina Bergheimer was buried; aged 37 years.

Sept 28, John Georg Muller's child was buried; aged 7 months

Oct. 22, David Spinner's daughter, named Maria, was buried, aged 3 years, 2 months, 2 days.

N Pomp, pastor.

1790

Apr. 4, Anna Margaretha Reisswig, a widow, 77 years old

Those persons who were buried by me, John Theobald Faber [Jr.]

1790

John Swenk, a child, 3 years, 7 months, 2 days

1792.

—— Breuchler, a child.

1793

Jacob Huber's child, 7 years, 2 weeks, 6 days.

Jacob Mory, 66 years, 4 months less 2 days.

Henr. Huber's child.

1794

Jonathan Klein, born Dec 24, 1794, aged 1 year, 2 weeks, 6 days

Anna Barbara, his wife, born April 4. 1732, aged 62 years, 10 months, 6 days

Anna Maria Hillegas, born 1746, Oct. 25, aged 48 years, 5 months, 3 days. √

Those persons who were buried by me, Albert Helffenstein, in the year 1808.

Barbara Huber, died July 11, 1808, aged 72 years, 2 months, 7 days.
Catarina Dillinger, died Aug. 2, 1808, aged 1 year, 5 months, 5 days
Andreas Engelman, —— 86 years, 4 months
Abraham Didlo, aged about 77 years.
Joseph Eberhard, died Oct 14, aged 72 years.

1809.

Anna Huber, born Dec. 8; aged 83 years less 3 days
Valentin Huber, born May 7, aged 78 years, 2 weeks, 2 days

[MARRIAGE RECORD]

Those persons who were joined in marriage by me, John Theobald Faber

1767, March 5, Georg Sem, son of Georg Sem, of Lower Milford, and Elisabeth Reiswig, daughter of John Reiswig, of Upper Milford, were married

1768, March 8, David Mehn, son of Adam Mehn, of Great Swamp, and Elisabetha Redelmeyer, daughter of the late Martin Redelmeyer, of New Goshenhoppen

1768, April 4, Peter Linn, son of the late Peter Linn, of Upper Saucon, and Catharina Cock, daughter of the late John Cock, of Upper Saucon.

1768, May 26, Peter Schuller, son of Adam Schuller, of Upper Milford, and Maria Catharina Riser, daughter of Ulrich Riser, of Upper Milford.

1768, Nov. 17, Friedr. Dill, son of the late Simon Dill, of Pikeland township, Bucks County, and Susanna Spinner, daughter of Ulrich Spinner, of Great Swamp.

1768, Dec 4, Jacob Mack, son of Wilhelm Mack, of Rockhill township, Bucks County, and Catharine Drumbauer, daughter of Andreas Drumbauer, of Franconia township, Phila County

1769, Jan 3, Joh Nicolaus Diets, son of Adam Diets, of Upper Saucon, and Catharine Bischoff, daughter of Michael Bischoff, of Swamp

1770, Aug. 26, Joh Nicolaus Sanfels, son of the late Carl Sanfels, of Lower Milford, and Anna Elis Ott, daughter of Henr. Ott, of Upper Milford

1771, May 14, Henr. Ott, widower, of Great Swamp, and Margretha Ziegenfuss, widow, of Tohickon.

1771, Nov 17, Joh Olinger, son of the late Carl Olinger, of Great Swamp, and Anna Maria Ott, daughter of Henr. Ott, of Great Swamp

1771, Nov 26, Joh Petrus Reiswig, son of Joh. Reiswig, of Great Swamp, and Maria Eva Engelman, daughter of Andreas Engelmann, of Great Swamp.

1772, May 5, Joh Hermer, son of Joh Georg Hermer, of Springfield, and Susanna Reiswich, daughter of John Reiswig, of Upper Milford

1772, Nov. 22, Joh Hauser, son of Jacob Hauser, of Macungie township, and Anna Maria Barb. Wolf, daughter of Wm Wolf, of Macungie township

1772, Nov. 30, Christoffel Ott, son of Henr Ott, of Great Swamp, and Attli Hupper, daughter of Rudi Hupper, at Great Swamp

1773, Jan. 17, Joh. Jacobi, son of the late Peter Jacobi, of Hekok (!) township, and Anna Eberhart, daughter of the late Michael Eberhart, of Great Swamp

1774 Aug 16, Philip Hederig, son of Peter Hederig, of Richland township, and Cath Scheib, daughter of Martin Scheib, of Hekok township.

1775, Nov. 14, Georg Adam Dorr, son of the late Georg Dorr, of Old Goshenhoppen, and Christina Heger, daughter of Philip Heger, of Great Swamp

1775, Nov. 28, Henr Weis, widower, of Great Swamp, and Margreta Burger, widow, of Great Swamp

1776, Febr 13, Philip Mombauer, son of Nicolas Mombauer, of Great Swamp, and Barbara Spinner, daughter of the late Ulrich Spinner, of Great Swamp

1776, Aug 11, Joseph Hornecker, son of the late Ulrich Hornecker, of Upper Saucon, and Hanna Weber, daughter of Henr. Weber, of Upper Saucon

1777, Febr 4, Henr Weber, son of Henr Weber, of Upper Saucon, and Margareta Hornecker, daughter of Ulrich Hornecker, of Rockhill township

1778, Febr. 8, Michael Ott, son of Henr Ott, of Great Swamp, and Hanna Braun, daughter of Daniel Braun, of Upper Saucon.

1778, Apr. 21, Jacob Huper, son of Rudolph Huper, of Great Swamp, and Anna Maria Heres, widow of the late Mr Heres, of Lower Milford

1778, June 4, Jacob Klemer and Elisabetha Andres, both of Lower Milford

1778, Sept 15, Jacob Wittmer and Susanna Mack, daughter of John Mack, of New Goshenhoppen.

1778, Sept 29, Joh Becker, of Upper Milford, and Elisabetha Berger, of Upper Milford.

1779, Apr 11, Daniel Klein, son of Michael Klein, of Great Swamp, and Magdalena Brauchler, daughter of Theobald Brauchler, of Great Swamp

1779, May 23, Michael Rudolph, son of Henr Rudolph, and Margareta Ott, daughter of Henr. Ott, both of Upper Milford.

1779, Aug 9, Georg Michael Trumbauer, son of Andres Trumbauer, and Cath Bock, daughter of Peter Bock, of Lower Milford township

List of persons married by Friedrich Delliker

1782

April 23, Georg Doerr, son of Hannes Doerr, of this congregation, and Sophia Stetler, daughter of the late Henrich Stetler, of New Goshenhoppen

October 29, Peter Kufer, son of Johan Kufer, of Tinicum township, and Cath. Elisab. Engelmann, daughter of Andres Engelman, of Upper Milford

Nov 26, David Spinner, son of the late Urich Spinner, and Catharine Herlacher, daughter of Georg Herlacher, of Lower Milford

1783

Apr. 1, Heinrich Mumbauer, son of Niclas Mumbauer, and Catharina Didlo, daughter of Abraham Didlo, both of Lower Milford, Bucks County

Persons married by me, Friedrich Wilh Von der Sloot

June 20th, Caspar Mumfeld, son of Henrich Mumfeld, and Catharina Schanzenbach, daughter of George Schanzenbach.

Aug 10, Jacob Tracksel, son of Peter Tracksel, and Margaretha Eberhart, daughter of Joseph Eberhard

Dec 2, Philip Eberhard, son of the late Michael Eberhard, of Upper Milford township, and Margaretha Hillegas, oldest daughter of Johannes Hillegas, of Upper Milford township

1785.

Aug 23, Georg Ditlo, son of Abraham Ditlo, and Maria Magdalena Meier, oldest daughter of Wendel Meier

Sept 6, Peter Weber, son of Peter Weber and Maria Reichenbach

Persons who were married by me, John Theob Faber, in the year 1786

Nov. 21, Henr. Grob, of Lower Milford township, and Margareta Schutz, of —— township

1787.

May 15, John George Ott, of Upper Milford, and Catharina Bishof, of Lower Milford.

1788.

Apr. 13, Philip Bitting and Elis. Derrscham, both of Great Swamp.

These persons were married by me, John Faber, Jr, in the year 1792 —— Brauchler and —— Mack.

1793

Nov. 28, Christian Heger and Caty Long, of Great Swamp.

[CATECHUMEN RECORD]

Children who were admitted by me, John T. Faber, on April 17, 1767, in the congregation of Great Swamp, to the Lord's Supper:

Boys:
1 Jacob Mack, aged 21 years
2. Jonas Peters, aged 14 years
3 Jacob Huber, aged 16 years

Girls:
1 Catharina Mack, aged 15 years
2 Margaretha Bischoff, aged 14 years
3 Anna Maria Buchner, aged 14 years
4. Catarina Huber, aged 16 years
5 Anna Maria Winder, aged 14 years

Confirmed at Pentecost, from Saucon

1 Catharina Cock, aged 16 years
2 Elisabetha Cock, aged 22 years
3 A woman, Maria, Cock, aged 22 years
4. Henrich Faust, aged 21 years, from Upper Soucon

In the year 1768, April 1 were confirmed

1. Peter Reiswig, aged 20 years
2 Henrich Frick, aged 17 years
3. Henrich Hupper, aged 17 years
4 Jacob Hupper, aged 16 years
5 Johannes Grob, aged 14 years
6. Valentin Heger, aged 14 years
7. Michael Ott, aged 14 years

1 Anna Maria Ott, aged 16 years
2. Gertrude Cock, aged 15 years

In the year 1769, March 24th
John Linn, 15 years

Great Swamp—Catechumens

In the year 1770, March 13th, were confirmed

1. Caspar Rieser, aged 17 years
2. Henrich Hupper, aged 15 years
3. Petrus Cock, aged 15 years

1. Christina Bachman, aged 20 years
2. Anna Maria Derr, aged 15 years
3. Anna Marg Derr, aged 14 years
4. Cath. Mumbauer, aged 13 years
5. Elisabeth Gronert, aged 17 years

In the year 1771, March 29th, were confirmed

1. Joh Hupper, aged 16 years
2. Peter Frickel

1. Anna Maria Hupper, aged 14 years
2. Anna Hupper, aged 15 years
3. Christina Heger, aged 15 years
4. Barbara Spinner, aged 15 years
5. Cath Ott, aged 15 years
6. Anna Mar. Grob, aged 14 years
7. Elis Hell. Linn, aged 14 years
8. Sara Faust, aged 14 years
9. Elis. Neukomer, aged 15 years

In the year 1772, April 17th, were confirmed

1. Joh Wilh Rieser, aged 15 years
2. Michael Eberhard, aged 16 years
3. Philip Eberhard, aged 15 years
4. Peter Bleiler, aged 15 years
5. Jonas Wetzel, aged 15 years

1. Elis. Berger, aged 15 years
2. Anna Maria Ditlo, aged 15 years

In the year 1773, April 29, were confirmed.

1. Joh Huper, aged 14 years
2. Georg Mohr, aged 15 years
3. Joh Peter Huper, aged 15 years
4. Christian Huper, aged 17 years
5. David Spinner, aged 15 years
6. Henr Mumbauer, aged 14 years
7. Joh Wetzel, aged 14 years

1. Christina Doerr, aged 15 years
2. Marg Dits, aged 14 years
3. Anna Maria Schmid, aged 17 years
4. Anna Mar Bleiler, aged 15 years

In the year 1774, April 1st, were confirmed·

1. Cath Grob, aged 15 years
2. Susanna Faust, aged 14 years

In the year 1775, April 14th, were confirmed

1 Henr Ott, aged 17 years
2 Phil Heger, aged 16 years

1. Anna Marg. Eberhart, aged 15 years
2 Cath Rauber, aged 15 years
3. Marg Ott, aged 14 years
4 Elis Still, aged 15 years
5 Marg. Heger, aged 14 years

In the year 1776, April 13, were confirmed

1. Georg Eckel, aged 15 years
2 Georg Doerr, aged 17 years
3 Christian Willauer, aged 15 years
4 Joh Huper, aged 15 years
5 Wilh Mueller, aged 16 years

1. Barbara Ecklin, aged 14 years
2. Elis. Doerr, aged 15 years

In the year 1777, April 12th, were confirmed

1 John Eberhart, aged 16 years
2 Heinr. Grob, aged 15 years

1 Hanna Hornecker, aged 24 years
2. Anna Huper, aged 15 years

In the year 1779, April 2nd, were confirmed:

1 Henr. Stetler, aged 16 years
2. Joh Rauber, aged 16 years
3 Joh Kehler, aged 17 years
4 Abr Kehler, aged 15 years
5 Joh Georg Ott, aged 16 years
6 Joh. Georg Eberhart, aged 15 years
7. Heni. Eberhart, aged 15 years
8 Jacob Engelman, aged 15 years

1 Marg. Stob, aged 18 years

1782

May 26th, the following were admitted to the Holy Communion by me, Friedrich Delliker·

Philip Biding   Anna Maria, his sister

May 24, 1783.

Georg Felix Linn   Heinr Bleuler
Jacob Meixel   Peter Delp
Conrad Eberhard   Adam Brauchler
Henr Georg Mumbauer   Johannes Samsel

Henr Nikel Samsel
Matheis Welter
Jacob Rothenburger
Christian Heger
Catharina Spinn
Janette Samsel
Elisabeth Funk
Anna Marg Hillegas
Anna Christina Eberhard

Anna Margaret Hillegas
Catharina Hachenburger
Catharina Samsel
Elisabeth Meixel
Margreth Doerr
Anna Maria Koppenberger
Elisabeth Heger
Maria Servin
Eva Servin

On June 12, 1784, the following persons were admitted to the Holy Communion by me, Fridrich Wilhelm Von der Sloot

Johann Willauer, aged 17 years
David Ditlow, aged 15 years

Elisabeth Hachenberg, aged 17 years

Children who were confirmed by me, Joh Theob Faber, on April 12, 1788

1 Ludwig Bitting, aged 17 years
2 Jacob Kehler, aged 15 years
3 Nicol Stehler, aged 16 years
4 Michael Wolder, aged 15 years
5 David Seller, aged 18 years
6 Joh. Romich, aged 19 years
7 Peter Romich, aged 17 years
8 Jacob Seller, aged 15 years
9 Phil Dorwart, aged 16 years

1. Cath. Mack, aged 16 years
2 Anna Maria Horner, aged 15 years
3 Anna Maria Ox, aged 15 years
4 Cath Romich, aged 14 years

Children who were admitted to the Holy Communion on Pentecost, 1790, in the Great Swamp congregation

Johannes Biding, aged 18 years, son of Henrich Biding.
Georg Neukomer, aged 18 years, son of Johannes Neukomer.
Jacob Daudy, aged 20 years, son of the late Wilh. Daudy.
Anna Marg. Biding, aged 15 years, daughter of Henr Biding.
Elisabeth Horner, aged 15 years, daughter of Georg Horner.
Catharine Hillegas, aged 15 years, daughter of Johannes Hillegas
Eva Willauer, aged 16 years, daughter of Adam Willauer
Elisabeth Fretz, aged 18 years, daughter of Henrich Fretz
Elisabeth Ditlo, aged 16 years, daughter of Abraham Ditlo
Barbara Dorwart, aged 16 years, daughter of Jacob Dorwarth
Magdalena Diel, aged 18 years, daughter of Fridrich Diel

The children who were confirmed by me, John Faber, in the year 1792, on Pentecost:

                      Anna Bleiler, aged 17 years
                      Elisabeth Willauer, aged 15 years

Children who were confirmed on March 29, 1793.

Leonhard Gebhard, aged 19 years
Christian Dorward, aged 17 years

Children of this congregation who were confirmed on Easter, 1794, in New Goshenhoppen by me, John Faber:

Lazarus Bleiler, aged 17 years	Elisabetha Mumbauer, aged 17 years
John Mumbauer, aged 18 years	Anna Maria Dubs, aged 15 years
John Eberhart, aged 15 years	Barbara Berto, aged 17 years
Daniel Eberhart, aged 16 years	Eva Hillegas, aged 17 years
Jacob Dups, aged 15 years	
George Herner, aged 16 years	

The children who were confirmed on Easter, 1795, from this congregation by me, John Faber

Michael Derr, aged 17 years	Catharina Hillegas, aged 16 years
Jacob Derr, aged 15 years	Madlena Willauer, aged 15 years
Henrich Ott, aged 16 years	Catharina Huber, aged 17 years
John Ott, aged 15 years	Barbara Huber, aged 18 years
John Ott, aged 17 years	
Andreas Bitting, aged 16 years	
Daniel Dorwart, aged 16 years	

                      1790

On January 24, 1790, the following elders and deacons, after having been elected for three years were installed into their offices

David Spinner	Philip Eberhard
John Huber	Jacob Schmid

Elders and deacons who were installed by me, Friederich Delliker, in the congregation of Great Swamp, on May 12, 1782·

Elders.	Deacons.
Johannes Doerr	Daniel Dubs
Joseph Eberhard	Christoph Ott

[Communicant Lists of Rev Fr Wm Von der Sloot]

Names of those who on March 16th went to the preparatory service and on the 17th [1814] to the communion·

1. Daniel Eberhard
2. Georg Scholl
3. Henrich, son
4. Cathar, daughter
5. Michel Ott
6. Johann Huber
7. Christian Doll
8. Christian, son
9. Nicolaus Ley
10. Daniel Dubs
11. Elisabeth, wife
12. Adam Rotenburger
13. Jacob Dubs
14. Adam Eberhard
15. Johann Oel
16. David Huber
17. Elisabeth Furer (?)
18. Johann Handschuh
19. Magdal, wife
20. Michel Scholl
21. Maria, wife
22. Jacob Schwenk
23. Magdalena, wife
24. Wilhelm Mumbauer
25. Ester Mumbauer
26. Jacob Frener
27. David Spinner
28. John Rudolph
29. George Rudolph
30. David Mumbauer
31. Jacob Mumbauer
32. Michel Brauchler
33. Elisabeth Roteburger
34. Anna Maria Dillinger
35. Elisabeth Berthold
36. Eva Horlacher
37. Cathar. Spinner
38. Adam Dorwarth
39. Margaret Schafer
40. Susanna Eberhard
41. Magdal. Brauchler
42. Margar. Rieser
43. Sophia Levi
44. Ego, Von der Sloot
45. Maria Rieser

Names of the catechumens·

1. Heinrich Gerber, aged 23 years
2. Valentin Huber, aged 22 years
3. Mattheas Rummel, aged 25 years
4. Philip Wannemacher, aged 18 years
5. Michel Frei, aged 19 years
6. Michel Staut, aged 19 years
7. Samuel Geisinger, aged 19 years
8. Andreas Fink, aged 17 years
9. Heinrich Hirsch, aged 15½ years
5. Margareta Wannemacher, aged 15 years
6. Katharina Staut, aged 16 years
7. Elisabeth Barret, aged 15 years
8. Sus. Bauman, aged 15 years
9. Kathar. Geier, aged 16 years
10. Salome Levi, aged 15 years
11. Lydia Kerr, aged 16 years
12. Anna Geri, aged 16 years
13. Margaretha Christman, aged 15 years
14. Susanna Brauchler, aged 16 years

10 Daniel Salade, aged 17 years
11. George Herzel, aged 15 years
12 Jacob Hillegas, aged 15¼ years
13 Karl Gery, aged 16 years
14 John Ruckstuhl, aged 16 years
15 John Barret, aged 18 years
16 Alex Mumbauer, aged 16 years
17. Jacob Rudolf, aged 17 years
18 Henrich Stahler, aged 17 years
19 Georg Neiss, aged 17 years
20. Joseph Kolb, aged 17 years

1 Elis Traxel, aged 16 years
2. Elis Lutz, aged 17 years
3 Elis. Gotz, aged 17½ years
4 Christian Wannemacher, aged   years

15 Christian Bauman, aged 16 years
16 Catharina Geier, aged 17½ years
17 Elis. Wiegner, aged 15 years
18. Elisab. Salledi, aged 15 years
19. Kathar Schuler, aged 16 years

Married Women·
1. Margareta Eberhard, aged 27 years
2. Elisabeth Hunsberger, aged 22 years
3 Elisabeth Hummel, aged 25 years
4 Catharina Huber, aged 23 years
Total 43

[This first list is followed by other lists, on September 10, 1814, April 29, 1815, October 14, 1815, April 21, 1816, November 17, 1816, April 13, 1817, October 19, 1817, April 26, 1818, October 11, 1818]

Names of those who on April 13, 1818, were admitted to the Lord's Supper

1 Jacob Schwenk
2 Magdalena, wife
3 George Diez
4 Elisabeth, wife
5. Valentin Huber
6. Adam Levi
7 John Ried
8. Hanna, wife
9 Adam Roteburger
10. Daniel Dubs
11. Michel Breuchler
12. Michel, his son
13 Susanna, his daughter
14. David Spinner
15 Katharina, wife
16. Henrich Dubs
17. Philip Dorwarth
18. Henrich Dorr
19 Elisabeth, wife
20 Michel Rudolph
21 George Ott
22. Samuel Derr
23. Jacob Derr
24. Ludwig Rudolph
25 Abrah Mumbauer
26 George Schmeier
27. Elisabeth Schmeier
28. Henrich Mumbauer
29 Georg Rudolph
30. John Derr
31 Daniel Derr
32. Samuel Dietz
33. Jacob Rudolph
34. George Mumbauer
35 David Derr
36 Samuel Dorwarth
37 Jacob Schmeier
38 Eva Horlacher

39 Eva Levi
40 Kathar Spinner
41 Margareta Derr
42 Elisabeth Roteburger
43 Hanna Erdmann
44 Kathar Funk
45 Kathar Schutz
46 Elisab Oel
47 Anna Sax
48. Sophia Levi
49 Maria (?) Rieser
50 Elisabeth Huber
51. Margaretha Rieser
52 Maria Derr
53 Maria Derr
54 Esther Stahl
55 Hanna Rotheburger
56 Susanna Widemer
57 Kathar Schwenk
58 Elisabeth Espich
59 Margaretha Schuster
60 Maria Brauchler
61. Maria Huber
62 Elisab Wiener
63. Ego [Von der Sloot]
64 Anna Dorwarth
65. Elisab. Dubs

Names of the catechumens.

1 John Schwenk, aged 15½ years
2. Henrich Durr, aged 17 years
3. David Dorwarth, aged 17 years
4. Abr. Leidi, aged 18 years
5 John Mumbauer, aged 17 years
6. George Huber, aged 16½ years
7. Dan Knolety (?), aged 15 years
8 John Schmeier, aged 20 years
9 Jacob Kroh, aged 17 years
10 Joseph Geri, aged 16 years
11 John Scott, aged 19 years
12 John Rautenbusch, aged 17 years
13 Henrich Brauchler, aged 17 years
14 George Mumbauer, aged 17 years
15. Karl Rachon (?), aged 21 years
16 John Ritz, aged 18 years
17. John Huber, aged 17 years
18. Jonathan Dorwarth, aged 15 years
19 George Mack aged 27 years
1. Kathar Dorwarth, aged 16 years
2. Sally Grenn, aged 16 years
3. Kathar Sell, aged 17 years
4 Magdal Sell, aged 15 years
5 Hanna Maurer, aged 17 years
6 Barbara Kolb, aged 16½ years
7 Kath. Schutz, aged 16 years
8 Sophia Traxel, aged 16 years
9 Marg. Faster, aged 18 years
10 Mar Rautenbusch, aged ——
11 Maria Neiss, aged 17 years
12 Kathar Brauchler, aged 17 years
13. Susan Dorwarth, aged 16 years
14 Magd. Ditlo, aged 16 years
15 Kathar Ott, aged 21 years

INDEX.

ABBOTSTOWN, 265
Aberli, Hans Rudolf, 107
Ache, A M , 227
Acrelius, *History of New Sweden,* 89
Albert, Michel, 81
Albrecht, Joseph, 25, 26
Alexandria, N J , 232
Allemaengel, 138
Allen, Andrew, Esq , 189-191
Allen, Wm , 31
Allentown, 240
Alsentz, Rev. John George, 216, 217
Amen, Valentin Hans, 58
American Ancestry, 115
American Weekly Mercury, 44 115
Amman, Hans Ulrich, 106
Amsterdam Classis, 7, 19, 38, 39, 41, 43, 50, 56, 57, 58, 61, 74, 75, 85, 119, 120, 122, 125, 126, 128, 135, 137, 148, 196
Amwell, N. J , 232
Andreae, Rev J C , 145, 163
Andrews, Rev Jedidiah, 36, 37, 77, 90, 110, 111, 112
Anspacher, Hans J , 24, 26
Arnd, Bernhard, 144
Arndt, Jacob, 183
Arndt, Johan Jacob, 58
Arner, Hans Ulrich, 107
Aweeg, Gertrude, 9
Aweeg, Jan, 9

BACH, Henrich, 172
Bach, Nickel, 172
Baerents, Anna, 9
Baltimore, Md , 234, 246, 256

Bartells, Henry, 10
Bartels, Sebastian, 9, 10
Barth, Johannes, 24, 26
Bartholomie, Rev D , 195
Baumann, Hans Jerg, 58
Bausel, Jacob, 24, 26
Bechtold, Rev , 83, 84 ,
Becker, Rev Christian L., 256
Beissel, Conrad, 89, 95
Bensalem, 8
Berger, Rev F. J , 83
Berigt, 28, 65, 66, 67, 68, 122
Berlin, 265
Bermudian, 265
Berne, 117, 119, 154
Best, Georg, 127
Bertschinger, Jacob, 107
Beyer, Abraham, 164
Bingemann, John, 117
Biographisch Wordenbock, 29
Bischof, Mattheis, 172
Bitting, Ludwig, 172
Blatt, Johann Georg, 173
Bleiler, Henrich, 173
Bleiler, Peter, 173
Bleyler, Johannes, 172
Bloemers, Mary, 9
Blum, Frantz, 127
Blumer, Rev. A , 240, 250
Bock, Leonhard, 14
Boehm, Rev Chas L., 219
Boehm, John Philip, 12, 19, 30, 31, 35, 36, 39, 40, 50, 51, 57, 60, 62, 64, 66, 68, 74, 80, 83, 84, 87, 88, 90, 94, 114, 116, 120, 125, 135, 137, 138, 160, 161
Boehm's *Life and Letters,* 8, 10, 13,

19, 31, 35, 36, 39, 40, 50, 60, 66, 69, 71, 74, 76, 82, 85, 96, 116, 121, 125, 126, 127, 128, 129, 135, 137, 140, 195
Boehm, *Warnungsbrief,* 90
Bohn, Peter, 6, 9, 10
Boltzius, Rev. John Martin, 86
Bon, Margaret, 9
Borger, Peter, 58
Bossart, Baltasar, 106
Bottle, Michel, 24, 26
Bower, George, 205
Bowman, Hans Georg, 24, 35
Bradford, Andrew, 42, 44
Brauchler, Dewalt, 172, 173
Braun, Michel, 172
Broenck, Anna, 158
Brownback s Church, 155, 195
Brunner, Heinrich, 106
Brunner, Philip, 172
Bucher, Jacob, 106
Buck, *Hist. of Montg Co.,* 115
Bucks Co Hist. Soc., *Papers,* 10, 56, 132, 148
Budingische Sammlung, 31
Burnetsfield, N. Y, 43, 158

CARLISLE, 258
Catskill, N Y, 32, 69, 158
Chambers, *Early Germans,* 232
Charity schools, 169, 170
Christian Intelligencer, 20
Circular Schreiben, 166, 167
Classical Archives, Amsterdam, 56, 64, 69, 111, 121, 126, 128, 129, 137, 194
Cocalico, 82, 84, 155, 169
Coleman, John, 175
Colonial Records of Pa , 22, 26, 165
Conestoga, 35, 40, 79, 81, 84, 88, 119, 161
Congressional Library, 41

Corwin, *Manual,* 19, 32, 66, 96, 130, 136, 147, 156
Coventry, 155, 195
Cremmer, Hans Jorg, see Kremer
Crob, Henrich, 173
Cuntz, Johan Jacob, 24, 26

DECHANT, Rev Jacob Wm , 270
Decker, John Henry, 83
Deer, John Martin, 15
Delliker, Rev. Frederick, 230-234, 237, 250
Delliker, Mrs Maria, 234
De Long's Ch , 200
Demme, Rev Karl R., 262
Dentzler, Jacob, 106
Dewees, Cornelius, 9, 10
Dewees, G H , 10
Dewees, Wm , 9, 10, 12
Diel, Hans Jacob, 73
Diel, Hans Michel, 24, 26, 34
Dilbeck, Isaac, 9, 10, 13
Dilbeck, Jacob, 9, 10
Diemer, Dr John J , 44, 52, 55, 70, 78
Ditlo, Abraham, 172, 173
Dodder, George Philip, 55, 59
Dorsius, Peter H., 93, 121, 127, 128, 129, 131-148
Dotterer, *Hist. Notes,* 7, 9, 13, 35, 59, 60, 96, 97, 194, 196
Dotterer, *Perkiomen Region,* 5, 6, 7, 94
Dotterer, *Rev J P Boehm,* 31
Dreisbach, Simon, 197
Dryland, 226
Dubbs, *Manual,* 71
Dubbs, *Ref. Ch. in Pa.,* 19, 71, 72, 91, 96, 166, 234, 243
Dubs, Jacob, 172, 269
Dubendorfer, Alexander, 24, 27, 35, 172
Dubendorfer, Heinrich, 106

Dubendorfer, Jacob, 106
Dubendorfer, Kilian, 106
Dunkers, Seventh Day, 85, 87, 88, 91, 93
Dutch Reformed, 8, 38, 50, 56, 130

EASTERN Salisbury, 210
Easton, 225
Ebenezer, Ch, 200
Eberhardt, Barbara, 106
Eberhard, Joseph, 172, 212
Eberhart, Michel, 14, 113, 212
Eberhardt, Philip, 253
Eccl Records of N Y, 7, 39, 43, 49, 50, 112, 136, 148
Eckmann, Johannes, 24, 26
Egg, Rudolf, 106
Egypt, 117, 118, 119, 254
Elizabethtown, 258
Emmert, John Philip, 14
Endross, Mr, 172
Enschockhoppa, 6, 17
Ephrata Chronicle, 20, 78, 84, 88, 89, 93
Erb, Caspar, 172
Euchelen, Hans Adam, 14
Everhart, Adam, 269
Everhart, Joseph, 113

FABER, John Theobald, Jr., 249-255, 257, 267-271
Faber, John Theobald, Sr, 215-223, 237, 238-240, 241, 242
Faber, Mrs. Barbara, 216, 246
Fabion, George Michel, 15
Falkner Swamp, 5, 7, 12, 38, 39, 142, 194, 195, 231, 234, 242, 245, 246
Faust, Abraham, 172
Faust, Nicholas, 173
Ferer, Jost, 58
Fetter, Richard, 48
Fidler, Gottfried, 91

Forks of Delaware, 120
Foxhill, N J, 230, 232, 233
Frelinghausen, Rev. Mr, 128, 129
Fresenius, *Nachrichten*, 91
Frey, Jacob, 106
Frey, Tobias, 24, 26
Frick, Rudi, 172, 173
Friedrich, Mr, 156
Frohlich, Hans Michael, 48, 55
Fry, *Luth Ch in Reading*, 91

GABEL, Philip, 144
Gabel, Rightyers, 9
Gallman, Henry, 117
Gallman, Johannes, 176
Gauckler, Kilian, 15
Geiger, Johannes, 15
Gerlach, Balsar, 144
Germantown, 8, 30, 32, 39, 74, 78, 116, 261
German Valley, N J, 230, 232, 233
Gernan, Jerg, 58
Gery, John, 269
Geweiler, Conrad, 101, 106
Gobrecht, Rev John Christopher, 83, 220
Goetschy family, 96
Goetschy, John Henry, 13, 96-130, 131
Goetschy, Rev. Maurice, 97, 101, 102, 104, 133
Gohr, Johannes, 81
Good, *History*, 19, 38, 66, 71, 96, 147, 156, 157, 196, 229, 257
Good, Prof. James I, 11, 28, 67
Gordon, *Gazetteer*, 94
Gordon, Patrick, Governor, 11, 22
Goshenhoppen, 19
    first occurrence, 5
    forms of name, 6
    location, 5
    legend, 16-18
Gotz, Johannes, 207

Gräff, Sebastian, 24, 26
Great Swamp, 86, 87, 94, 113, 117, 126, 139, 161, 171, 193, 208, 211, 212-214, 218, 226, 227, 232, 233, 236, 237, 246, 251, 252, 258, 261, 269, 270
Greber, Ulrich, 207
Greenwich, 226
Griesemer, Valentine, 14, 73, 172
Gross, Rev. Daniel, 249
Gucker, John B., 14
Guldin, Samuel, 40
Guntz, Caspar, 107
Guth, Felix, 58

HABERACKER, Johannes, 24, 27
Hack, Andreas, 59
Hague Archives, 44, 52, 62, 78, 79, 80, 135, 153, 161, 166, 167
Hain's Ch., 155
Hallesche Nachrichten, 28, 31, 91, 210
Halsbrun, Andreas, 81
Hamilton, Andrew, 31
Hamman, Thomas, 14, 73
Hanf, Jacob, 58
Harbaugh, *Fathers,* 19, 71, 96, 147, 194, 196, 229, 231, 266
Harbaugh, *Life of Schlatter,* 152, 159, 194
Harbaugh Manuscripts, 11
Harrisburg, State Library, 23
Hartman, Joh. Henrich, 25, 27
Hartman, Lorentz, 14
Hartwick, N. J., 233
Hauck, Jacob, 207
Hautz, Rev. Anthony, 83
Hazard's *Register,* 37, 38, 77, 92
Hebron Diary, 151, 155, 156
Heger, Philip, 172
Heid, Johannes, 106
Heidschuh, Hans Ph., 58
Heidelberg, Lehigh Co., 199, 228

Heidelberg University, 20, 44, 71, 215, 224
Heisler, *Fathers,* 258
Helffenstein, Rev. Albert, 256-258
Helffenstein, Rev. J. C., 221
Helffrich, Rev. John H., 228, 250, 257, 261
Helffrich, *Geschichte,* 198, 199, 200, 202, 209
Heller, Rudolf, 81
Heller's Ch., 82, 84
Helwig, Friedrich, 149, 155, 199
Hemsing, Henrich, 221, 252
Hendel, Rev. Wm., 219, 250, 253, 260
Hendricks, Arent, 9
Hendricks, Mary, 9
Henkel, Rev. Anthony, 85
Herr, Willem, 24, 26
Hersch, Ludwig, 174
Hertzel, Heinrich, 202
Hertzel, Ulrich, 14, 221
Hertzel, Hans Georg, 24, 27
Herzel, Hans Lönhart, 14
Hess, John Peter, 14
Heuver, Henrich, 58
Hiester, Daniel, 161, 217
Hilligass, Adam, 14, 175, 221, 269
Hilligass, George Peter, 55, 183, 207
Hilligass, John, 269
Hilligass, John F., 14, 24, 26, 35
Hilligass, Michael, 55
Hilltown, 270
Hiltebeutel, Martin, 58
Hitz, Henrich, 172, 173
Hochgenug, Lenhart, 14, 73
Hochreutner, Rev. John J., 195
Hock, John Jacob, 81, 83
Hoffman, Burckhard, 14
Hoffman, Henry, 205
Hoffman, Johan, 149
Hoffmeier, Rev. John H., 257, 261

Index. 485

Holland Donations, 169
Hollebusch, Peter, 252
Holtzhauser, Caspar, 14, 126
Holsbacher, Andreas, 24, 26
Holtzschwam, 265, 266
Hornberger, Michel, 172
Hottinger, Mr, 52
Hotz, Rudolf, 106
Huber, Heinrich, 106, 172, 173
Huber, Jacob, 174
Huber, Johannes, 172
Huber, John, 161
Huber, Rudi, 172, 173
Huber, Valentin, 173
Hug, Heinrich, 106
Huth, Johannes, 14, 24, 26, 35
Huth, John, 161

IN DE HAVEN (Im Hoffe), Evert, 10
In de Haven, Herman, 10
In de Haven, Gerhart, 10, 12, 55, 58, 70
In de Haven, Peter, 10
Indian Creek, 197, 206, 227, 228, 237, 238, 239, 247, 254
Indian Field, see Indian Creek
Indians, 5, 40, 41, 43, 211
Ingold, Mrs. Catherine B, 228
Ingold, Rev John W., 224-228

JACOBS Church, Lehigh Co, 199
Jaeger, John H, 119
Janssen, *Catalogus*, 44
Jordan, 254
Jost, Jacob, 24, 26
Journal of Presb Hist Soc, 6, 7, 8, 12, 13, 19, 35, 36, 40, 50, 74, 76, 85, 149, 150, 151, 159, 160, 162
Jung, Daniel, 241, 252, 254, 261
Jung, Dewalt, 55, 58
Jung, Johannes, 253
Jung, John Henrich, 14

KEIBER (Keupper), Wendel, 55, 58
Keipper, Carl Ludwig, 59
Kelker, Luther R, 23, 26
Keller, Conrad, 107
Keller, Jacob, 113, 146, 147
Keller's Church, 83
Kern, Verena, 106
Keyser, *Hist. of Germantown*, 10
Kidenweiler, see Kittweiler
Kittweiler, Rev Rudolph, 208-211
Klopp, *Hist. of Tabor Ch*, 157
Knecht, George Peter, 14
Knibbe, Rev David, 56, 131
Kohler, Michel, 171, 173
Kreither, Abraham, 172
Kremer, Hans Georg, 25, 26, 34
Kreutz Creek, 138
Kubler, Hans, 107

LANCASTER, 82, 84, 163, 195, 219, 221, 238
Lancaster Co. Hist. Soc, Proceedings, 82
Lange, Rev Carolus, 216
Lebanon Ref Church, 155, 157
Lebo, Johannes, 58
Lecohe, Pieter, 55, 70
Lefeber, Johannes, 58
Lehigh Co Hist Soc *Proceedings*, 210
Lehman, Christian, 73, 144, 147
Leib, Johannes, 25, 27
Leibecker, Caspar, 89
Leidy, Jacob, 59
Lein, Gorg, 172
Leman, Johannes, 58
Leydich, Rev John Philip, 166, 193, 194-196
Liebenstein, Hans Martin, 24, 27
Lienhardt, Ludwig, 107
Lischy, Rev Jacob, 82, 138, 141, 166, 168

Lohr, Andreas, 14
Longswamp, 155, 199, 202, 210
Loscher, 83
Loscher Nicklas, 58
Lowhill, 202
Luckenbach, John Adam, 138
Lutherans, 15, 28, 31, 38, 68, 82, 85, 86, 90, 91, 113, 115, 142, 143, 162, 170, 200, 211

MABRY, Thomas, 207
Macungie, 94
Masius, 132
Matern, Peter, 14
Maurer, Hans Adam, 58, 146, 147
Maxatawny, 94, 117, 200, 228
Mayer, Jacob, 25, 27
Mayer, John, 6
Meels, Catrina, 9
Meels, Hans Hendricks, 8, 10
Meier, Jacob, 174
Mengel, John Adam, 149
Mennonites, 38, 68, 111, 115, 119
Mercersburg Review, 7, 39
Merck, Heinrich, 107
Mertz, Georg, 14
Mettler, Jacob, 106
Mey, Simon, 73
Meyer, Conrad, 106
Meyer, Elias, 24, 27
Meyer, Hans, 106
Meyer, Henrich, 24, 27
Meyer, Jacob, 14, 107
Michael, Mrs Sara, 203, 204
Michael, Rev. Philip Jacob, 194, 197–205, 210
Michael's Church, 202
Mill, Hans Martin, 26
Miller, Daniel, *Ref. Ch. in Reading*, 91, 200, 229
Miller, Frederick Casimir, see Mueller
Miller, Hans Adam, 26

Miller (Mueller), Rev John Peter, 20, 71–95
Miller, Michel, 91
Minisink, 138
Minutes of Coetus of Pa, 12, 30, 129, 131, 140, 154, 170, 171, 193, 197, 200, 201, 217, 219, 220, 222, 225, 234, 237, 238, 239, 250
Minutes of Presb. of Phila, 112
Minutes of Synod, 257, 260, 261
Moll, Christopher, 14
Moll, Johann Michel, 14
Moll, Johan Peter, 14 48
Moll, Michael, 207
Montandon, David, 48, 58
Montbauer, Nicholas, 161, 172, 173, 174
Moor, Gideon, 176, 182
Moravians, 85, 90, 138, 141, 156
Moselem, 117
Muddy Creek, 82, 155
Muehlenberg, 28, 31
Muehlenberg, *Selbstbiographie*, 31, 86
Mueller, Frederick Casimir, 83, 149–157, 159, 160, 168
Mueller, Hans, 107
Mueller, Jacob, 107
Mumbauer, Philip, 253

NAFF, Conrad, 101, 107
Naff, Jacob, 107
Neshaminy, 8, 56, 131, 132, 147
Neuschwanger, Christian, 6
New Born, 40, 41
New Brunswick Archives, 56, 132, 136
New Goshenhoppen, 7, 13, 19, 39, 87, 94, 110, 114, 116, 117, 126, 138, 139, 142, 143, 149, 150, 151, 152, 154, 159, 160, 161, 165, 193, 197, 206, 208, 217, 218, 220, 221, 226, 228, 232, 233, 236, 237, 238,

241, 246, 249, 250, 251, 257, 261, 269, 270
New Holland, 255
Newton, N J, 233
Nolton, N. J., 233
Norristown Register, 165
North Holland Synod, 49, 50, 52, 60
Northampton, 254
Notzh, Caspar, 106
Nussbach, Michel, 172

OHL, Andreas, 207
Ohlwein, John Jost, 15
Old Goshenhoppen, 7, 15, 19, 85, 110, 113, 126, 142, 143, 144 (Cornerstone), 145, 149, 159, 160, 161, 162, 162, 193, 197, 207, 208, 217, 221, 224, 226, 227, 232, 233, 236, 237, 241, 246, 247, 250, 251, 252, 261, 269, 270
Oley, 40, 41, 116, 129, 150
Op de Graef, Jacob, 9
Organ, Church, 200
Ott, Hans, 106
Ott, Henry, 269
Otterbein, Rev Wm, 193
Oxford, 265

PALATINATE, Consistory, 29, 31, 32, 34, 36, 37, 49, 60
Pannebacker, Hendricks, 9, 10, 114
Pannebecker, Weygand, 221
Pastorius, 9
Pauli, Rev Philip R, 261
Penn Germania, 41, 165
Pennsylvania Archives, 5, 22, 23, 73, 96, 118, 136, 202, 234, 256
Pennsylvania-German, 71, 163, 202
Pennsylvanische Berichte, 165
Pennypacker, *Hendrick Pannebacker,* 114
Pennypacker, *Germantown,* 9, 114
Petter, Jeorg, 25, 26

Pfalzgraff, Georg, 14
Pfautz, Hans Michel, 24, 27
Philadelphia, 30, 31, 39, 44, 45, 46, 47, 49, 53, 54, 55, 62, 69, 74, 76, 78, 110, 161, 169, 262
Philadelphia, Salem Ch, 263-265
Pieterse, Jacob, 9
Pigeon Hill, 265
Pikeland, 270
Pomp, Rev Nicholas, 234, 241-248, 250, 253, 261
Pomp, Mrs Elizabeth, 245
Pomp, *Ewiges Evangelium,* 247, 248
Pomp, Rev Thomas, 245
Possart (Bossart), Jacob, 106
Pottstown, 195
Presbyterians, 74, 77, 79, 110, 111, 120, 129
Presbytery of Phila, 10, 77, 112
Providence, 194

QUAKERS, 8, 28, 30, 38, 68, 111

RADNER, Michael, 141
Ranck, Johan Philip, 48
Raudenbusch, Peter, 14
Reading, 200
Records of Presb. Ch, 10, 77, 111
Ref Church Messenger, 20, 41, 82, 84, 85, 155
Ref Church Review, 198
Ref. Church Record, 84, 85
Ref Quarterly Review, 10, 46, 53, 54, 60
Reiff, Conrad, 70
Reiff, George, 55, 58
Reiff, Jacob, 32, 44, 46-65, 121, 129, 132, 161
Reiff, Johannes, 48
Reiher, Michael, 113, 144, 146, 147
Reincke, *Register,* 138
Rembergh, Dirk, 9, 10
Rembergh, Gertrude, 9

Rembergh, Michael, 10
Rembergh, William, 9, 10
Rebenstock, Johannes, 9, 10, 13
Revenstock (Rebenstock), Sebille, 9
Reyer's Church, 82
Rheinlender, Ph Jacob, 25, 26
Rhinebeck, N. Y., 158, 160
Richards, Prof Geo W, 216, 254
Ried, Jacob, 237
Ried, Johan Philip, 14, 58
Rieger, Rev. John B., 30, 44, 52, 78, 83, 116, 160
Riess, John Jacob, 151, 194, 205-208
Riser, Ulrich, 172
Rite, Jacob, 172
Rockaway, N. J., 120, 230, 232, 233
Rohrig, Hans W, 54, 55, 70
Roeller, Rev Conrad, 241
Ross, George, 89
Rosstown, 265
Roth, Daniel, 118
Roth, *Falkner Swamp* Ch 231
Roudenbusch, Michael, 269
Rubel, Rev. John, 168
Rudi, Hans Ernst, 25, 27
Rudi, Johan Diedrich, 25, 27
Rundle, Daniel, 165, 171, 184-189, 207
Rupp, *Hist of Lanc. Co.*, 38
Rupp, *Immigrants*, 13, 136, 151, 208
Rutschly, Philip, 27

SACHSE, *Sectarians*, 41, 71, 72, 82
Sahler, Abraham, 14
Sailer, Hans Ulrich, 164, 165
Salem Ch, Phila, 263-265
Salzburg, Lehigh Co, 195, 228
Samsel, Paul, 173
Samsel, Peter, 173
Saucon, 94, 117, 119, 127, 138, 249
Saur, Christopher, 165, 247

Saur, *Pennsylv Berichte*, 156, 163, 165
Schaeffer, Wm. J., 222
Schefer, Ludwig, 59
Schellenberg, Jacob, 106
Schellenberg, Martin, 106
Scherer, Johannes, 73
Schertlein, Rev Jacob Fred, 210
Scheuchzer, Heinrich, 107
Scheuler, Jost, 58
Schipbower, Elizabeth, 9
Schlatter, Rev Michael, 119, 149, 150, 151, 152, 161, 166, 168
Schlatter's *Bibles*, 168
Schlatter's *Journal*, 149, 150, 152, 159, 160, 194
Schmauk, *Hist of Luth. Ch.*, 85
Schmid, Jacob, 253
Schmidt, Bastian, 58
Schmidt, Christopher, 6, 55, 58
Schmidt, Jacob, 106
Schmidt, John H., 73
Schmidt, Wilhelm, 59
Schneider, Christian, 144, 147, 161, 174, 177, 178, 191
Schneider, Conrad, 144
Schol, Else, 9
Scholl, Frederick, 59
Scholl, Johannes, 58
Scholl, Peter, 172
Schoolmasters, 119, 138, 167, 168, 169, 227, 241, 252
Schools, 171
Schreiber, Heinrich, 106
Schumacher, Rev Daniel, 210
Schumacher, Jerich, 24, 26
Schultze, Mrs Anna Rosina, 164, 165
Schultze, David, 115, 163, 171, 178, 183, 184-192, 207, 217
Schultze, *Guide*, 138
Schuyler, Gabriel, 9, 12, 162
Schwab, Hans Georg, 24, 26, 35, 81

Index. 489

Schweikhardt, Hans Philip, 24, 27
Schweitzer, Lorentz, 58
Seitz, Johan Peter, 24, 26
Selle, Maria, 9
Seltenreich, Leonhart, 24, 35
Selzer, Jacob, 48
Senn, Rev Jacob, 254, 257
Shakahoppa, 6, 17
Sheidt, Christian, 240
Siegvolck, Paul, 247
Sigmund, Bernhard, 73
Sippen, Henry, 27
Skippack, 6, 7, 12, 28, 30, 38, 39, 46, 47, 50, 53, 54, 56, 57, 59, 60, 64, 68, 74, 76, 87, 110, 116
Smith, *Mennonites*, 38
Smith, Sebastian, 24, 35
Soller, Philip H, 58
South Holland Synod, 27, 29, 49, 50, 59, 60, 65
Spengler, Hans Caspar, 24, 26
Spinner, David, 253
Spinner, Ulrich, 173, 211
Sprague, *Annals*, 130
Springfield, 119, 206, 249
Sproegel, John Henry, 114, 115
Sprogel, Ludwig Christian, 115
Sprogel, widow, 45, 115
Stadler, John Adam, 14
Staels, Caspar, 9, 10
Steger, Hans Jerg, 14
Steiner, Rev John Conrad, 168
Steinmann, Hans, 14, 117
Stephan, Ulrich, 25, 35, 58
Stoever, Rev Caspar, 86
Stoudt, Rev John B, 15, 198
Straher's Church, 265
Streib, David, 172
Strohm, Benedict, 14, 24, 35
Stupp, Frantz, 14
Summe, Isaac, 207
Swatara, 156
Synodical Deputies, 29, 44, 52, 60, 62, 93, 128, 135, 139, 151, 159, 160, 224, 231

TANNENHAUSER, 221
Taylor, *Annals*, 130
Tempelman, Conrad, 35, 79, 80, 81, 82, 83, 156
Ten Heuven, Evert, 8, 9, 10
Ten Heuven, Gerhart, 9, 10
Ten Heuven, Herman, 9, 10
Ten Heuven, Peter, 9, 10
Tennent, Rev. Gilbert, 128, 129
Thomas, Leonhard, 186
Tibben, Henry, 9, 10
Tohickon, 206, 207, 227, 238, 239, 254
Transu, Abraham, 14, 73
Trappe, 261, 270
Traxel, Peter, 118
Trexler, *Skizzen*, 198
Trumbauer's Ch, 220, 228, 239
Tulpehocken, 80, 84, 85, 88, 93, 117, 129, 161, 195

UPPER Milford, 195, 228, 271
Union Church, 254

VAN BASTEN, John H, 135, 136
Van der Sloot, Rev. F W., Sr, 235-237
Van der Sloot, F W., Jr, 258-266
Vandersloot, Lewis, *History*, 236, 259
Van Vlecq, Rev Paulus, 8, 10, 12
Vincent, Chester Co, 194, 195, 234, 245
Vock, Lewis Ferdinand, 83
Vogelle, Hans Jerg, 25, 26
Von Thierem, Bernhard, 85

WACK, Rev Caspar, 227, 238, 257, 260
Wackerli, Abraham, 107

Wagner, *Geschichte*, 156
Walbert, Peter, 172
Waldschmidt, Rev John, 83, 168
Walder, Rudolf, 106
Walter, Christoph, 25, 27
Weber, Johannes, 58
Weber, Ludwig, 99, 105, 107
Weber, Peter, 174
Weber, *Hinckende Bot*, 99
Weicker, George, 15
Weidman, Abraham, 106
Weidman, Rudolf, 106
Weimer, Jacob, 155, 199
Weinel, Nicholas, 252, 257
Weisenburg, Church, 200, 209
Weiser, Conrad, 89, 91
Weiser, Dr. C. Z, 15, 271
Weiser, *Monograph*, 5, 6, 38, 114, 118, 211, 215, 221, 239, 240, 242, 250, 258, 262, 267, 271
Weiss, Mrs. Anna, 158, 174, 180, 181–183, 186, 191, 207
Weiss, Rev George M, 19–70, 76, 79, 84, 121, 154, 158–192, 193, 207
Weiss, *Traveling Preacher*, 41, 42
Weiss, *On Indians*, 43
Weiss, Johann Ehrhardt, 207
Weiss, John Michael, 21
Weiss, Nicolas, 20
Welcker, Hans George, 14, 24, 27, 35, 117
Wellecker, Rudolf, 25, 26, 34
Weller, Hans Heinrich, 35, 55, 70
Weller, Hans Martin, 25, 26
Wentz, Peter, 7, 58
Wentz's Church, 7
Werns, Conrad, 48, 81
Wetzel, Jacob, 172
Weyberg, Rev C D, 217
Whitemarsh, 7, 8, 9, 12, 13, 38, 39

Wiant, Jost, 253
Wiant, Wendel, 14, 48
Wieser, Mr, 83
Wigand, John Wm, 167
Wilhelmius, Dr. Johannes, 29, 32, 46, 47, 48, 52, 56, 59, 68, 78, 103, 105, 109, 120, 121, 122, 128, 129, 131–133
Willauer, Adam, 174
Willauer, Christian, 172, 173
Willhe, Johannes, 58
Wirtz (Wuertz), Rev. Conrad, 96, 100, 101, 103, 119, 120
Wissler, 168
Wittner, Rev John George, 82, 83, 216
Witpen (Boehm's), 225, 247
Wolff, Hans Jerg, 24, 26
Worcester (Wentz's Ch), 225
Wust, Jacob, 107
Wuertz, see Wirtz
Wynckhaus, Rev John H, 235

YERCKES, Anthoni, 9, 10
Yodder, Johannes, 9
York, 120

ZELLER, Rev Daniel, 268
Zeltenreich (Seltenreich), 82
Zenger, Peter, 40
Ziegel Church, 199
Ziegler, Hans Georg, 24, 27
Ziewer, Johann, 144
Zigler, Filib, 25, 26
Zimmermann, Conrad, 172
Zimmermann, Hans Michel, 14, 27, 35
Zurich Library, 97, 99, 104, 105, 107, 230

Printed in the USA
CPSIA information can be obtained
at www.ICGtesting.com
LVHW021619210624
783663LV00010B/461